Literary Functions

Fiction, Poetry, & Drama

2015 Edition

Michael S. Kelly, Editor

ASSISTANT PROFESSOR OF ENGLISH,
ARKANSAS STATE UNIVERSITY-BEEBE

Literary Functions

Fiction, Poetry, & Drama

2015 Edition

Michael S. Kelly, Editor

ASSISTANT PROFESSOR OF ENGLISH,
ARKANSAS STATE UNIVERSITY-BEEBE

ISBN-13: 978-1508661771
ISBN-10: 1508661774

Beebe, Arkansas

Cover Photo
Petit Jean Mountain, Arkansas by Stacy Hudson, 2013

for

Stacy Hudson

my inspiration

In Appreciation

The editor would like to thank the following for their support and important feedback. Such an endeavor as this is hardly achieved by a single person but involves many hours of discussion, materials contributed, and endless amounts of encouragement.

- *Dr. Dennis Humphrey,* Associate Professor of English and Chair of the English and Fine Arts Division, Arkansas State University-Beebe

- *Suzanne Lindsey,* Assistant Professor of English, Arkansas State University-Beebe

- *Dr. David Jones,* Associate Professor of English, Arkansas State University-Beebe

TABLE OF CONTENTS

Poetry—1800-1850

Poetry—1850-1922

Literary Studies

Editor's Note

This text was born out of a love for learning, a respect for students, and a curiosity for the enormous breadth of literature freely available by law. The public domain texts collected here are but a small fraction of what is available.

In recent years, I have seen the cost of textbooks increase as the wallets of my students decrease. New editions of textbooks have appeared more frequently than I can ever remember, and due to the questionable absence of the used textbook editions, students have had to pay full-price, a higher price, every two years for a textbook. This is unacceptable. I do not believe that the changes in these texts assist my students to read or learn.

Some may make an argument for access to recent literature (since 1923); after all, such texts are typically more accessible to younger students, and the idea for these students is to read, read, read. Or, is it? Not only do I ask my students to read, I ask them to learn.

So, whether or not a text is easy to read does not seem to be an effective criteria for determining its suitability. Students are likely to speed-read through an accessible text, but does that mean they are learning? It seems as if many aspects of contemporary society are based upon speed: fast food, fast commutes, and a fast track to the end of a class. Yet, learning is not fast, and it is certainly not a race. Learning means slowing down, reading and comprehending content, and asking the deeper questions that can lead to a fulfilling life. To read is fine, to learn is the future.

For, learning is a transformative behavior in which students develop from an uninformed state to a condition better equipped to reason effectively, to determine their destiny, and to declare their inner most feelings. In sum, learning is self-empowerment. So, must I have literature written in 2014 to achieve this? No. Emphatically no.

I also want to share some of the history of literature with my students, so they can experience the beauty, the wonder, and the awe of a people they never knew. I want my students to understand that real people lived and died long before themselves. I want my students to enjoy the elegance of the wording from long ago because we simply do not talk like that anymore. You would not see such writing in a text message, and you certainly would not hear it in a television commercial. These stories, poems and dramas express so much of the human condition—not merely for their era but for all time.

Michael S. Kelly

About the Text

Organization. The literature has been grouped into the traditional genres of Fiction, Poetry, and Drama simply because it is the most common method for an introduction to literature.

Footnotes. With the intention of providing an easily readable copy for my students, footnotes have been added to explain the text (with the help of dictionaries and credible sources). The end result, hopefully, encourages students to read in a meaningful manner.

Headings. To improve memory retention and essay writing, headings have been added— these are not part of the original text.

Line Numbers. Because we have powerful word processors on desktop computers, literature can be formatted in ways that authors and publishers did not foresee. As a result, it is virtually impossible to reproduce line numbers that agree with all of the translations and/or texts available.

Public Domain and Copyright

U.S. Copyright Office

The public domain is not a place. A work of authorship is in the "public domain" if it is no longer under copyright protection or if it failed to meet the requirements for copyright protection. Works in the public domain may be used freely without the permission of the former copyright owner.

§ 107 · Limitations on exclusive rights: Fair use

Notwithstanding the provisions of sections 106 and 106a, the fair use of a copyrighted work, including such use by reproduction in copies or phonorecords or by any other means specified by that section, for purposes such as criticism, comment, news reporting, teaching (including multiple copies for classroom use), scholarship, or research, is not an infringement of copyright.

Duration of Copyright by the United States Copyright Office

According to the United States Copyright Office, on their *Information Circulars and Factsheets* page, Number 15a, under "Effect of 1976 Act on Length of Subsisting Copyrights," ". . . all works published in the United States before January 1, 1923, are in the public domain."

FICTION

Allegory of the Cave

Plato
380 BCE

The *Allegory of the Cave* is Book VII in *The Republic*, a Socratic dialogue, written by Plato around 380 BCE, concerning the definition of justice, the order and character of the just city-state and the just man. The passage often called *The Allegory of the Cave* is written as a dialogue between Plato's brother Glaucon and his mentor Socrates, narrated by the latter. The allegory is include in Book 2 of Plato's *Republic*. From *The Republic*. Translated by Benjamin Jowett New York, C. Scribner's sons, 1871.

Imprisonment in the Cave

And now, I said, let me show in a figure how far our nature is enlightened or unenlightened:—Behold! human beings living in a underground den, which has a mouth open towards the light and reaching all along the den; here they have been from their childhood, and have their legs and necks chained so that they cannot move, and can only see before them, being prevented by the chains from turning round their heads. Above and behind them a fire is blazing at a distance, and between the fire and the prisoners there is a raised way; and you will see, if you look, a low wall built along the way, like the screen which marionette players have in front of them, over which they show the puppets.

I see.

And do you see, I said, men passing along the wall carrying all sorts of vessels, and statues and figures of animals made of wood and stone and various materials, which appear over the wall? Some of them are talking, others silent.

You have shown me a strange image, and they are strange prisoners.

Like ourselves, I replied; and they see only their own shadows, or the shadows of one another, which the fire throws on the opposite wall of the cave?

True, he said; how could they see anything but the shadows if they were never allowed to move their heads?

And of the objects which are being carried in like manner they would only see the shadows?

Yes, he said.

And if they were able to converse with one another, would they not suppose that they were naming what was actually before them?

Very true.

And suppose further that the prison had an echo which came from the other side, would they not be sure to fancy when one of the passers-by spoke that the voice which they heard came from the passing shadow?

No question, he replied.

To them, I said, the truth would be literally nothing but the shadows of the images.

That is certain.

Departure from the Cave

And now look again, and see what will naturally follow if the prisoners are released and disabused of their error. At first, when any of them is liberated and compelled suddenly to stand up and turn his neck round and walk and look towards the light, he will suffer sharp pains; the glare will distress him, and he will be unable to see the realities of which in his former state he had seen the shadows; and then conceive some one saying to him, that what he saw before was an illusion, but that now, when he is approaching nearer to being and his eye is turned towards more real existence, he has a clearer vision,—what will be his reply? And you may further imagine that his instructor is pointing to the objects as they pass and requiring him to name them,—will he not be perplexed? Will he not fancy that the shadows which he formerly saw are truer than the objects which are now shown to him?

Far truer.

And if he is compelled to look straight at the light, will he not have a pain in his eyes which will make him turn away to take refuge in the objects of vision which he can see, and which he will conceive to be in reality clearer than the things which are now being shown to him?

True, he said.

And suppose once more, that he is reluctantly dragged up a steep and rugged ascent, and held fast until he is forced into the presence of the sun himself, is he not likely to be pained and irritated? When he approaches the light his eyes will be dazzled, and he will not be able to see anything at all of what are now called realities.

Not all in a moment, he said.

He will require to grow accustomed to the sight of the upper world. And first he will see the shadows best, next the reflections of men and other objects in the water, and then the objects themselves; then he will gaze upon the light of the moon and the stars and the spangled heaven; and he will see the sky and the stars by night better than the sun or the light of the sun by day?

Certainly.

Last of all he will be able to see the sun, and not mere reflections of him in the water, but he will see him in his own proper place, and not in another; and he will contemplate him as he is.

Certainly.

He will then proceed to argue that this is he who gives the season and the years, and is the guardian of all that is in the visible world, and in a certain way the cause of all things which he and his fellows have been accustomed to behold?

Clearly, he said, he would first see the sun and then reason about him.

Return to the Cave

And when he remembered his old habitation, and the wisdom of the den and his fellow-prisoners, do you not suppose that he would felicitate himself on the change, and pity them?

Certainly, he would.

And if they were in the habit of conferring honours among themselves on those who were quickest to observe the passing shadows and to remark which of them went before, and which followed after, and which were together; and who were therefore best able to draw conclusions as to the future, do you think that he would care for such honours and glories, or envy the possessors of them? Would he not say with Homer, 'Better to be the poor servant of a poor master,' and to endure anything, rather than think as they do and live after their manner?

Yes, he said, I think that he would rather suffer anything than entertain these false notions and live in this miserable manner.

Imagine once more, I said, such an one coming suddenly out of the sun to be replaced in his old situation; would he not be certain to have his eyes full of darkness?

To be sure, he said.

And if there were a contest, and he had to compete in measuring the shadows with the prisoners who had never moved out of the den, while his sight was still weak, and before his eyes had become steady (and the time which would be needed to acquire this new habit of sight might be very considerable), would he not be ridiculous? Men would say of him that up he went and down he came without his eyes; and that it was better not even to think of ascending; and if any one tried to loose another and lead him up to the light, let them only catch the offender, and they would put him to death.

No question, he said.

Remarks on the Allegory

This entire allegory, I said, you may now append, dear Glaucon, to the previous argument; the prison-house is the world of sight, the light of the fire is the sun, and you will not misapprehend me if you interpret the journey upwards to be the ascent of the soul into the intellectual world according to my poor belief, which, at your desire, I have expressed—whether rightly or wrongly God knows. But, whether true or false, my opinion is that in the world of knowledge the idea of good appears last of all, and is seen only with an effort; and, when seen, is also inferred to be the universal author of all things beautiful and right, parent of light and of the lord of light in this visible world, and the immediate source of reason and truth in the intellectual; and that this is the power upon which he who would act rationally either in public or private life must have his eye fixed.

I agree, he said, as far as I am able to understand you.

Moreover, I said, you must not wonder that those who attain to this beatific vision are unwilling to descend to human affairs; for their souls are ever hastening into the upper world where they desire to dwell; which desire of theirs is very natural, if our allegory may be trusted.

Yes, very natural.

And is there anything surprising in one who passes from divine contemplations to the evil state of man, misbehaving himself in a ridiculous manner; if, while his eyes are blinking and before he has become accustomed to the surrounding darkness, he is compelled to fight in courts of law, or in other places, about the images or the shadows of images of justice, and is endeavouring to meet the conceptions of those who have never yet seen absolute justice?

Anything but surprising, he replied.

Any one who has common sense will remember that the bewilderments of the eyes are of two kinds, and arise from two causes, either from coming out of the light or from going into the light, which is true of the mind's eye, quite as much as of the bodily eye; and he who remembers this when he sees any one whose vision is perplexed and weak, will not be too ready to laugh; he will first ask whether that soul of man has come out of the brighter life, and is unable to see because unaccustomed to the dark, or having turned from darkness to the day is dazzled by excess of light. And he will count the one happy in his condition and state of being, and he will pity the other; or, if he have a mind to laugh at the soul which comes from below into the light, there will be more reason in this than in the laugh which greets him who returns from above out of the light into the den.

That, he said, is a very just distinction.

Education

But then, if I am right, certain professors of education must be wrong when they say that they can put a knowledge into the soul which was not there before, like sight into blind eyes.

They undoubtedly say this, he replied.

Whereas, our argument shows that the power and capacity of learning exists in the soul already; and that just as the eye was unable to turn from darkness to light without the whole body, so too the instrument of knowledge can only by the movement of the whole soul be turned from the world of becoming into that of being, and learn by degrees to endure the sight of being, and of the brightest and best of being, or in other words, of the good.

Very true.

And must there not be some art which will effect conversion in the easiest and quickest manner; not implanting the faculty of sight, for that exists already, but has been turned in the wrong direction, and is looking away from the truth?

Yes, he said, such an art may be presumed.

And whereas the other so-called virtues of the soul seem to be akin to bodily qualities, for even when they are not originally innate they can be implanted later by habit and exercise, the virtue of wisdom more than anything else contains a divine element which always remains, and by this conversion is rendered useful and profitable; or, on the other hand, hurtful and useless. Did you never observe the narrow intelligence flashing from the keen eye of a clever rogue—how eager he is, how clearly his paltry soul sees the way to his end; he is the reverse of blind, but his keen eye-sight is forced into the service of evil, and he is mischievous in proportion to his cleverness?

Very true, he said.

But what if there had been a circumcision of such natures in the days of their youth; and they had been severed from those sensual pleasures, such as eating and drinking, which, like leaden weights, were attached to them at their birth, and which drag them down and turn the vision of their souls upon the things that are below—if, I say, they had been released from these impediments and turned in the opposite direction, the very same faculty in them would have seen the truth as keenly as they see what their eyes are turned to now.

Very likely.

Yes, I said; and there is another thing which is likely, or rather a necessary inference from what has preceded, that neither the uneducated and uninformed of the truth, nor yet those who never make an end of their education, will be able ministers of State; not the former, because they have no single aim of duty which is the rule of all their actions, private as well as public; nor the latter, because they will not act at all except upon compulsion, fancying that they are already dwelling apart in the islands of the blest.

Very true, he replied.

Adventure of the German Student

Washington Irving
1824

Collected in *Tales of a Traveller* (1824) under the section of "Part I: Strange Stories by a Nervous Gentleman."

On a stormy night, in the tempestuous times of the French Revolution, a young German was returning to his lodgings, at a late hour, across the old part of Paris. The lightning gleamed, and the loud claps of thunder rattled through the lofty narrow streets—but I should first tell you something about this young German.

Gottfried Wolfgang was a young man of good family. He had studied for some time at Gottingen,[1] but being of a visionary and enthusiastic character, he had wandered into those wild and speculative doctrines which have so often bewildered German students. His secluded life, his intense application, and the singular nature of his studies, had an effect on both mind and body. His health was impaired; his imagination diseased. He had been indulging in

---

[1] A university town in Germany

fanciful speculations on spiritual essences, until, like Swedenborg, he had an ideal world of his own around him.[2] He took up a notion, I do not know from what cause, that there was an evil influence hanging over him; an evil genius or spirit seeking to ensnare him and ensure his perdition. Such an idea working on his melancholy temperament produced the most gloomy effects. He became haggard and desponding. His friends discovered the mental malady preying upon him, and determined that the best cure was a change of scene; he was sent, therefore, to finish his studies amidst the splendors and gayeties of Paris.

Wolfgang arrived at Paris at the breaking out of the revolution. The popular delirium at first caught his enthusiastic mind, and he was captivated by the political and philosophical theories of the day: but the scenes of blood which followed shocked his sensitive nature, disgusted him with society and the world, and made him more than ever a recluse. He shut himself up in a solitary apartment in the Pays Latin, the quarter of students.[3] There, in a gloomy street not far from the monastic walls of the Sorbonne, he pursued his favorite speculations. Sometimes he spend hours together in the great libraries of Paris, those catacombs of departed authors, rummaging among their hoards of dusty and obsolete works in quest of food for his unhealthy appetite. He was, in a manner, a literary ghoul, feeding in the charnel-house of decayed literature.

Wolfgang, thought solitary and recluse, was of an ardent temperament, but for a time it operated merely upon his imagination. He was too shy and ignorant of the world to make any advances to the fair, but he was a passionate admirer of female beauty, and in his lonely chamber would often lose himself in reveries on forms and faces which he had seen, and his fancy would deck out images of loveliness far surpassing the reality.

While his mind was in this excited and sublimated state, a dream produced an extraordinary effect upon him. It was of a female face of transcendent beauty. So strong was the impression made, that he dreamt of it again and again. It haunted his thoughts by day, his slumbers by night; in fine, he became passionately enamored of this shadow of a dream. This lasted so long that it became one of those fixed ideas which haunt the minds of melancholy men, and are at times mistaken for madness.

Such was Gottfried Wolfgang, and such his situation at the time I mentioned. He was returning home late on stormy night, through some of the old and gloomy streets of the Marais, the ancient part of Paris.[4] The loud claps of thunder rattled among the high houses of the narrow streets. He came to the Place de Greve, the square, where public executions are performed. The lightning quivered about the pinnacles of the ancient Hotel de Ville,[5] and shed flickering gleams over the open space in front. As Wolfgang was crossing the square, he shrank back with horror at finding himself close by the guillotine. It was the height of the reign of terror, when this dreadful instrument of death stood ever ready, and its scaffold was continually running with the blood of the virtuous and the brave. It had that very day been actively employed in the work of carnage, and there it stood in grim array, amidst a silent and sleeping city, waiting for fresh victims.

Wolfgang's heart sickened within him, and he was turning shuddering from the horrible engine, when he beheld a shadowy form, cowering as it were at the foot of the steps which led up to the scaffold. A succession of vivid flashes of lightning revealed it more distinctly. It was a female figure,

---

[2] Emanuel Swedenborg (1688-1772), Swedish scientist, philosopher, and mystic. Swedenborg devoted the latter part of his life to psychical and spiritual inquiry.

[3] The Latin Quarter, on the left (south) bank of the Seine, is adjacent to the Sorbonne, France's most famous university.

[4] The Marais, a district of old streets and ancient houses, lies to the north of the Seine. The rue des Marais was the home of the famous public executioner, Sanson, and his descendants.

[5] The Hôtel de Ville (town hall) faces the Pace de l'Hôtel de Ville, formerly the Place de Grève.

dressed in black. She was seated on one of the lower steps of the scaffold, leaning forward, her face hid in her lap; and her long dishevelled tresses hanging to the ground, streaming with the rain which fell in torrents. Wolfgang paused. There was something awful in this solitary monument of woe. The female had the appearance of being above the common order. He knew the times to be full of vicissitude, and that many a fair head, which had once been pillowed on down, now wandered houseless. Perhaps this was some poor mourner whom the dreadful axe had rendered desolate, and who sat here heart-broken on the strand of existence, from which all that was dear to her had been launched into eternity.

He approached, and addressed her in the accents of sympathy. She raised her head and gazed wildly at him. What was his astonishment at beholding, by the bright glare of the lighting, the very face which had haunted him in his dreams. It was pale and disconsolate, but ravishingly beautiful.

Trembling with violent and conflicting emotions, Wolfgang again accosted her. He spoke something of her being exposed at such an hour of the night, and to the fury of such a storm, and offered to conduct her to her friends. She pointed to the guillotine with a gesture of dreadful signification.

"I have no friend on earth!" said she.

"but you have a home," said Wolfgang.

"Yes—in the grave!"

The heart of the student melted at the words.

"If a stranger dare make an offer," said he, "without danger of being misunderstood, I would offer my humble dwelling as a shelter; myself as a devoted friend. I am friendless myself in Paris, and a stranger in the land; but if my life could be of service, it is at your disposal, and should be sacrificed before harm or indignity should come to you."

There was an honest earnestness in the young man's manner that had its effect. His foreign accent, too, was in his favor; it showed him not to be a hackneyed inhabitant of Paris. Indeed, there is an eloquence in true enthusiasm that is not to be doubted. The homeless stranger confided herself implicitly to the protection of the student.

He supported her faltering steps across the Pont Neuf,[6] and by the place where the statue of Henry the Fourth had been overthrown by the populace. The storm had abated, and the thunder rumbled at a distance. All Paris was quiet; that great volcano of human passion slumbered for a while, to gather fresh strength for the next day's eruption. The student conducted his charge through the ancient streets of the Pays Latin, and by the dusky walls of the Sorbonne, to the great dingy hotel which he inhabited. The old portress who admitted them stared with surprise at the unusual sight of the melancholy Wolfgang, with a female companion.

On entering his apartment, the student, for the first time, blushed at the scantiness and indifference of his dwelling. He had but one chamber—an old-fashioned saloon—heavily carved, and fantastically furnished with the remains of former magnificence, for it was one of those hotels in the quarter nobility. It was lumbered with books and papers, and all the usual apparatus of a student, and his bed stood in a recess at one end.

When lights were brought, and Wolfgang had a better opportunity of contemplating the stranger, he was more than ever intoxicated by her beauty. Her face was pale, but of a dazzling fairness, set off by a profusion of raven hair that hung clustering about it. Her eyes were large and brilliant, with a singular expression approaching almost to wildness. As far as her black dress permitted her shape to be seen, it was of perfect symmetry. Her whole appearance was highly striking, though she was dressed in the

---

[6] The Point Neuf (New Bridge), now the oldest bridge in Paris, links the Latin Quarter with the right bank of the Seine.

simplest style. The only thing approaching to an ornament which she wore, was a broad black band round her neck, clasped by diamonds.

The perplexity now commenced with the student how to dispose of the helpless being thus thrown upon his protection. He thought of abandoning his chamber to her, and seeking shelter for himself elsewhere. Still he was so fascinate by her charms, there seemed to be such a spell upon his thoughts and senses, that he could not tear himself from her presence. Her manner, too, was singular and unaccountable. She spoke no more of the guillotine. Her grief had abated. The attentions of the student had first won her confidence, and then, apparently, her heart. She was evidently an enthusiast like himself, and enthusiasts soon understand each other.

In the infatuation of the moment, Wolfgang avowed his passion for her. He told her the story of his mysterious dream, and how she had possessed his heart before he had even seen her. She was strangely affected by his recital, and acknowledge to have felt an impulse towards him equally unaccountable. It was the time for wild theory and wild actions. Old prejudices and superstitions were done away; everything was under the sway of the "Goddess of Reason." Among other rubbish of the old times, the forms and ceremonies of marriage began to be considered superfluous bonds for honorable minds. Social compact were the vogue. Wolfgang was too much of theorist not to be tainted by the liberal doctrines of the day.

"Why should we separate?" said he: "our heart are united; in the eye of reason and honor we are as one. What need is there of sordid forms to bind high soul together?"

The stranger listened with emotion: she had evidently received illumination at the same school.

"You have no home nor family," continued he: "Let me be everything to you, or rather let us be everything to one another. if form is necessary, form shall be observed — there is my hand. I pledge myself to you forever."

"Forever?" said the stranger, solemnly.

"Forever!" repeated Wolfgang.

The stranger clasped the hand extended to her: "Then I am yours," murmured she, and sank upon his bosom.

The next morning the student left his bride sleeping, and sallied forth at an early hour to seek more spacious apartments suitable to the change in his situation. When he returned, he found the stranger lying with her head hanging over the bed, and one arm thrown over it. He spoke to her, but received no reply. He advanced to awaken her from her uneasy posture. On taking her hand, it was cold—there was no pulsation—her face was pallid and ghastly. In a word, she was a corpse.

Horrified and frantic, he alarmed the house. A scene of confusion ensued. The police was summoned. As the officer of police entered the room, he started back on beholding the corpse.

"Great heaven!" cried he, "how did this woman come here?"

"Do you know anything about her?" said Wolfgang eagerly.

"Do I?" exclaimed the officer: "she was guillotined yesterday."

He stepped forward; undid the black collar round the neck of the corpse, and the head rolled on the floor!

The student burst into a frenzy. "The fiend! the fiend has gained possession of me!" shrieked he; "I am lost forever."

They tried to soothe him, but in vain. He was possessed with the frightful belief that an evil spirit had reanimated the dead body to ensnare him. He went distracted, and died in a mad-house.

Here the old gentleman with the haunted head finished his narrative.

"And is this really a fact?" said the inquisitive gentleman.

"A fact not to be doubted," replied the other. "I had it from the best authority. The student told it me himself. I saw him in a mad-house in Paris."

The Birthmark

Nathaniel Hawthorne
1843

The story was first published in the March 1843 edition of *The Pioneer*.
Lator, it was collected in Hawthorne's 1846 *Mosses from an Old Manse.*

In the latter part of the last century there lived a man of science, an eminent proficient in every branch of natural philosophy, who not long before our story opens had made experience of a spiritual affinity more attractive than any chemical one. He had left his laboratory to the care of an assistant, cleared his fine countenance from the furnace smoke, washed the stain of acids from his fingers, and persuaded a beautiful woman to become his wife. In those days when the comparatively recent discovery of electricity and other kindred mysteries of Nature seemed to open paths into the region of miracle, it was not unusual for the love of science to rival the love of woman in its depth and absorbing energy. The higher intellect, the imagination, the spirit, and even the heart might all find their congenial aliment in pursuits which, as some of their ardent votaries believed, would ascend from one step of powerful intelligence to another, until the philosopher should lay his hand on the secret of creative force and perhaps make new worlds for himself. We know not whether Aylmer possessed this degree of faith in man's ultimate control over Nature. He had devoted himself, however, too unreservedly to scientific studies ever to be weaned from them by any second passion. His love for his young wife might prove the stronger of the two; but it could only be by intertwining itself with his love of science, and uniting the strength of the latter to his own.

Such a union accordingly took place, and was attended with truly remarkable consequences and a deeply impressive moral. One day, very soon after their marriage, Aylmer sat gazing at his wife with a trouble in his countenance that grew stronger until he spoke.

"Georgiana," said he, "has it never occurred to you that the mark upon your cheek might be removed?"

"No, indeed," said she, smiling; but perceiving the seriousness of his manner, she blushed deeply. "To tell you the truth it has been so often called a charm that I was simple enough to imagine it might be so."

"Ah, upon another face perhaps it might," replied her husband; "but never on yours. No, dearest Georgiana, you came so nearly perfect from the hand of Nature that this slightest possible defect, which we hesitate whether to term a defect or a beauty, shocks me, as being the visible mark of earthly imperfection."

"Shocks you, my husband!" cried Georgiana, deeply hurt; at first reddening with momentary anger, but then bursting into tears. "Then why did you take me from my mother's side? You cannot love what shocks you!"

To explain this conversation it must be mentioned that in the centre of Georgiana's left cheek there was a singular mark, deeply Interwoven, as it were, with the texture and substance of her face. In the usual state of her complexion—a healthy though delicate bloom—the mark wore a tint of deeper crimson, which imperfectly defined its shape amid the surrounding rosiness. When she blushed it gradually became more indistinct, and finally vanished amid the triumphant rush of blood that bathed the whole cheek with its brilliant glow. But if any shifting motion caused her to turn pale there was the mark again, a crimson stain upon the snow, in what Aylmer sometimes deemed an almost fearful distinctness. Its shape bore not a little similarity to the human hand, though of the smallest pygmy size. Georgiana's lovers were wont to say that some fairy at her birth hour had laid her tiny hand upon the infant's cheek, and left this impress there in token of the magic endowments that were to give her such sway over all hearts. Many a desperate swain would have risked life for the privilege of pressing his lips to the mysterious hand. It must not be concealed, however, that the impression wrought by this fairy sign manual varied exceedingly, according to the difference of temperament in the beholders. Some fastidious persons—but they were exclusively of her own sex—affirmed that the bloody hand, as they chose to call it, quite destroyed the effect of Georgiana's beauty, and rendered her countenance even hideous. But it would be as reasonable to say that one of those small blue stains which sometimes occur in the purest statuary marble would convert the Eve of Powers to a monster. Masculine observers, if the birthmark did not heighten their admiration, contented themselves with wishing it away, that the world might possess one living specimen of ideal loveliness without the semblance of a flaw. After his marriage,—for he thought little or nothing of the matter before,—Aylmer discovered that this was the case with himself.

Had she been less beautiful,—if Envy's self could have found aught else to sneer at,—he might have felt his affection heightened by the prettiness of this mimic hand, now vaguely portrayed, now lost, now stealing forth again and glimmering to and fro with every pulse of emotion that throbbed within her heart; but seeing her otherwise so perfect, he found this one defect grow more and more intolerable with every moment of their united lives. It was the fatal flaw of humanity which Nature, in one shape or another, stamps ineffaceably on all her productions, either to imply that they are temporary and finite, or that their perfection must be wrought by toil and pain. The crimson hand expressed the ineludible gripe in which mortality clutches the highest and purest of earthly mould, degrading them into kindred with the lowest, and even with the very brutes, like whom their visible frames return to dust. In this manner, selecting it as the symbol of his wife's liability to sin, sorrow, decay, and death, Aylmer's sombre imagination was not long in rendering the birthmark a frightful object, causing him more trouble and horror than ever Georgiana's beauty, whether of soul or sense, had given him delight.

At all the seasons which should have been their happiest, he invariably and without intending it, nay, in spite of a purpose to the contrary, reverted to this one disastrous topic. Trifling as it at first appeared, it so connected itself with innumerable trains of thought and modes of feeling that it became the central point of all. With the morning twilight Aylmer opened his eyes upon his wife's face and recognized the symbol of imperfection; and when they sat together at the evening hearth his eyes wandered stealthily to her cheek, and beheld, flickering with the blaze of the wood fire, the spectral hand that wrote mortality where he would fain have worshipped. Georgiana soon learned to shudder at his gaze. It needed but a glance with the peculiar expression that his face often wore to change the roses of her cheek into a deathlike paleness, amid which the crimson hand was brought strongly out, like a bass-relief of ruby on the whitest marble.

Late one night when the lights were growing dim, so as hardly to betray the stain on the poor wife's cheek, she herself, for the first time, voluntarily took up the subject.

"Do you remember, my dear Aylmer," said she, with a feeble attempt at a smile, "have you any recollection of a dream last night about this odious hand?"

"None! none whatever!" replied Aylmer, starting; but then he added, in a dry, cold tone, affected for the sake of concealing the real depth of his emotion, "I might well dream of it; for before I fell asleep it had taken a pretty firm hold of my fancy."

"And you did dream of it?" continued Georgiana, hastily; for she dreaded lest a gush of tears should interrupt what she had to say. "A terrible dream! I wonder that you can forget it. Is it possible to forget this one expression?—

'It is in her heart now; we must have it out!' Reflect, my husband; for by all means I would have you recall that dream."

The mind is in a sad state when Sleep, the all-involving, cannot confine her spectres within the dim region of her sway, but suffers them to break forth, affrighting this actual life with secrets that perchance belong to a deeper one. Aylmer now remembered his dream. He had fancied himself with his servant Aminadab, attempting an operation for the removal of the birthmark; but the deeper went the knife, the deeper sank the hand, until at length its tiny grasp appeared to have caught hold of Georgiana's heart; whence, however, her husband was inexorably resolved to cut or wrench it away.

When the dream had shaped itself perfectly in his memory, Aylmer sat in his wife's presence with a guilty feeling. Truth often finds its way to the mind close muffled in robes of sleep, and then speaks with uncompromising directness of matters in regard to which we practise an unconscious self-deception during our waking moments. Until now he had not been aware of the tyrannizing influence acquired by one idea over his mind, and of the lengths which he might find in his heart to go for the sake of giving himself peace.

"Aylmer," resumed Georgiana, solemnly, "I know not what may be the cost to both of us to rid me of this fatal birthmark. Perhaps its removal may cause cureless deformity; or it may be the stain goes as deep as life itself. Again: do we know that there is a possibility, on any terms, of unclasping the firm gripe of this little hand which was laid upon me before I came into the world?"

"Dearest Georgiana, I have spent much thought upon the subject," hastily interrupted Aylmer. "I am convinced of the perfect practicability of its removal."

"If there be the remotest possibility of it," continued Georgiana, "let the attempt be made at whatever risk. Danger is nothing to me; for life, while this hateful mark makes me the object of your horror and disgust,—life is a burden which I would fling down with joy. Either remove this dreadful hand, or take my wretched life! You have deep science. All the world bears witness of it. You have achieved great wonders. Cannot you remove this little, little mark, which I cover with the tips of two small fingers? Is this beyond your power, for the sake of your own peace, and to save your poor wife from madness?"

"Noblest, dearest, tenderest wife," cried Aylmer, rapturously, "doubt not my power. I have already given this matter the deepest thought—thought which might almost have enlightened me to create a being less perfect than yourself. Georgiana, you have led me deeper than ever into the heart of science. I feel myself fully competent to render this dear cheek as faultless as its fellow; and then, most beloved, what will be my triumph when I shall have corrected what Nature left imperfect in her fairest work! Even Pygmalion, when his sculptured woman assumed life, felt not greater ecstasy than mine will be."

"It is resolved, then," said Georgiana, faintly smiling. "And, Aylmer, spare me not, though you should find the birthmark take refuge in my heart at last."

Her husband tenderly kissed her cheek—her right cheek—not that which bore the impress of the crimson hand.

The next day Aylmer apprised his wife of a plan that he had formed whereby he might have opportunity for the intense thought and constant watchfulness which the proposed operation would require; while Georgiana, likewise, would enjoy the perfect repose essential to its success. They were to seclude themselves in the extensive apartments occupied by Aylmer as a laboratory, and where, during his toilsome youth, he had made discoveries in the elemental powers of Nature that had roused the admiration of all the learned societies in Europe. Seated calmly in this laboratory, the pale philosopher had investigated the secrets of the highest cloud region and of the profoundest mines; he had satisfied himself of the causes that kindled and kept alive the fires of the volcano; and had explained the mystery of fountains, and how it is that they gush forth, some so bright and pure, and others with such rich medicinal virtues, from the dark bosom of the earth. Here, too, at an earlier period, he had studied the wonders of the human frame, and attempted to fathom the very process by which Nature assimilates all her precious influences from earth and air, and from the spiritual world, to create and foster man, her masterpiece. The latter pursuit, however, Aylmer had long laid aside in unwilling recognition of the truth—against which all seekers sooner or later stumble—that our great creative Mother, while she amuses us with apparently working in the broadest sunshine, is yet severely careful to keep her own secrets, and, in spite of her pretended openness, shows us nothing but results. She permits us, indeed, to mar, but seldom to mend, and, like a jealous patentee, on no account to make. Now, however, Aylmer resumed these half-forgotten investigations; not, of course, with such hopes or wishes as first suggested them; but because they involved much physiological truth and lay in the path of his proposed scheme for the treatment of Georgiana.

As he led her over the threshold of the laboratory, Georgiana was cold and tremulous. Aylmer looked cheerfully into her face, with intent to reassure her, but was so startled with the intense glow of the birthmark upon the whiteness of her cheek that he could not restrain a strong convulsive shudder. His wife fainted.

"Aminadab! Aminadab!" shouted Aylmer, stamping violently on the floor.

Forthwith there issued from an inner apartment a man of low stature, but bulky frame, with shaggy hair hanging about his visage, which was grimed with the vapors of the furnace. This personage had been Aylmer's underworker during his whole scientific career, and was admirably fitted for that office by his great mechanical readiness, and the skill with which, while incapable of comprehending a single principle, he executed all the details of his master's experiments. With his vast strength, his shaggy hair, his smoky aspect, and the indescribable earthiness that incrusted him, he seemed to represent man's physical nature; while Aylmer's slender figure, and pale, intellectual face, were no less apt a type of the spiritual element.

"Throw open the door of the boudoir, Aminadab," said Aylmer, "and burn a pastil."

"Yes, master," answered Aminadab, looking intently at the lifeless form of Georgiana; and then he muttered to himself, "If she were my wife, I'd never part with that birthmark."

When Georgiana recovered consciousness she found herself breathing an atmosphere of penetrating fragrance, the gentle potency of which had recalled her from her deathlike faintness. The scene around her looked like enchantment. Aylmer had converted those smoky, dingy, sombre rooms, where he had spent his brightest years in recondite pursuits, into a series of beautiful apartments not unfit to be the secluded abode of a lovely woman. The walls were hung with gorgeous curtains, which imparted the combination of grandeur and grace that no other species of adornment can achieve; and as they fell from the ceiling to the floor, their rich and ponderous folds, concealing all angles and straight lines, appeared to shut in the scene from infinite space. For aught Georgiana knew, it might be a pavilion among the clouds. And Aylmer, excluding the sunshine, which would have interfered with his chemical processes, had supplied its place with perfumed lamps, emitting flames of various hue, but all uniting in a soft, impurpled radiance. He now knelt by his wife's side, watching her earnestly, but without alarm; for he was confident in his science, and felt that he could draw a magic circle round her within which no evil might intrude.

"Where am I? Ah, I remember," said Georgiana, faintly; and she placed her hand over her cheek to hide the terrible mark from her husband's eyes.

"Fear not, dearest!" exclaimed he. "Do not shrink from me! Believe me, Georgiana, I even rejoice in this single imperfection, since it will be such a rapture to remove it."

"Oh, spare me!" sadly replied his wife. "Pray do not look at it again. I never can forget that convulsive shudder."

In order to soothe Georgiana, and, as it were, to release her mind from the burden of actual things, Aylmer now put in practice some of the light and playful secrets which science had taught him among its profounder lore. Airy figures, absolutely bodiless ideas, and forms of unsubstantial beauty came and danced before her, imprinting their momentary footsteps on beams of light. Though she had some indistinct idea of the method of these optical phenomena, still the illusion was almost perfect enough to warrant the belief that her husband possessed sway over the spiritual world. Then again, when she felt a wish to look forth from her seclusion, immediately, as if her thoughts were answered, the procession of external existence flitted across a screen. The scenery and the figures of actual life were perfectly represented, but with that bewitching, yet indescribable difference which always makes a picture, an image, or a shadow so much more attractive than the original. When wearied of this, Aylmer bade her cast her eyes upon a vessel containing a quantity of earth. She did so, with little interest at first; but was soon startled to perceive the germ of a plant shooting upward from the soil. Then came the slender stalk; the leaves gradually unfolded themselves; and amid them was a perfect and lovely flower.

"It is magical!" cried Georgiana. "I dare not touch it."

"Nay, pluck it," answered Aylmer,—"pluck it, and inhale its brief perfume while you may. The flower will wither in a few moments and leave nothing save its brown seed vessels; but thence may be perpetuated a race as ephemeral as itself."

But Georgiana had no sooner touched the flower than the whole plant suffered a blight, its leaves turning coal-black as if by the agency of fire.

"There was too powerful a stimulus," said Aylmer, thoughtfully.

To make up for this abortive experiment, he proposed to take her portrait by a scientific process of his own invention. It was to be effected by rays of light striking upon a polished plate of metal. Georgiana assented; but, on looking at the result, was affrighted to find the features of the portrait blurred and indefinable; while the minute figure of a hand appeared where the cheek should have been. Aylmer snatched the metallic plate and threw it into a jar of corrosive acid.

Soon, however, he forgot these mortifying failures. In the intervals of study and chemical experiment he came to her flushed and exhausted, but seemed invigorated by her presence, and spoke in glowing language of the resources of his art. He gave a history of the long dynasty of the alchemists, who spent so many ages in quest of the universal solvent by which the golden principle might be elicited from all things vile and base. Aylmer appeared to believe that, by the plainest scientific logic, it was altogether within the limits of possibility to discover this long-sought medium; "but," he added, "a philosopher who should go deep enough to acquire the power would attain too lofty a wisdom to stoop to the exercise of it." Not less singular were his opinions in regard to the elixir vitae. He more than intimated that it was at his option to concoct a liquid that should prolong life for years, perhaps interminably; but that it would produce a discord in Nature which all the world, and chiefly the quaffer of the immortal nostrum, would find cause to curse.

"Aylmer, are you in earnest?" asked Georgiana, looking at him with amazement and fear. "It is terrible to possess such power, or even to dream of possessing it."

"Oh, do not tremble, my love," said her husband. "I would not wrong either you or myself by working such inharmonious effects upon our lives;

but I would have you consider how trifling, in comparison, is the skill requisite to remove this little hand."

At the mention of the birthmark, Georgiana, as usual, shrank as if a redhot iron had touched her cheek.

Again Aylmer applied himself to his labors. She could hear his voice in the distant furnace room giving directions to Aminadab, whose harsh, uncouth, misshapen tones were audible in response, more like the grunt or growl of a brute than human speech. After hours of absence, Aylmer reappeared and proposed that she should now examine his cabinet of chemical products and natural treasures of the earth. Among the former he showed her a small vial, in which, he remarked, was contained a gentle yet most powerful fragrance, capable of impregnating all the breezes that blow across a kingdom. They were of inestimable value, the contents of that little vial; and, as he said so, he threw some of the perfume into the air and filled the room with piercing and invigorating delight.

"And what is this?" asked Georgiana, pointing to a small crystal globe containing a gold-colored liquid. "It is so beautiful to the eye that I could imagine it the elixir of life."

"In one sense it is," replied Aylmer; "or, rather, the elixir of immortality. It is the most precious poison that ever was concocted in this world. By its aid I could apportion the lifetime of any mortal at whom you might point your finger. The strength of the dose would determine whether he were to linger out years, or drop dead in the midst of a breath. No king on his guarded throne could keep his life if I, in my private station, should deem that the welfare of millions justified me in depriving him of it."

"Why do you keep such a terrific drug?" inquired Georgiana in horror.

"Do not mistrust me, dearest," said her husband, smiling; "its virtuous potency is yet greater than its harmful one. But see! here is a powerful cosmetic. With a few drops of this in a vase of water, freckles may be washed away as easily as the hands are cleansed. A stronger infusion would take the blood out of the cheek, and leave the rosiest beauty a pale ghost."

"Is it with this lotion that you intend to bathe my cheek?" asked Georgiana, anxiously.

"Oh, no," hastily replied her husband; "this is merely superficial. Your case demands a remedy that shall go deeper."

In his interviews with Georgiana, Aylmer generally made minute inquiries as to her sensations and whether the confinement of the rooms and the temperature of the atmosphere agreed with her. These questions had such a particular drift that Georgiana began to conjecture that she was already subjected to certain physical influences, either breathed in with the fragrant air or taken with her food. She fancied likewise, but it might be altogether fancy, that there was a stirring up of her system—a strange, indefinite sensation creeping through her veins, and tingling, half painfully, half pleasurably, at her heart. Still, whenever she dared to look into the mirror, there she beheld herself pale as a white rose and with the crimson birthmark stamped upon her cheek. Not even Aylmer now hated it so much as she.

To dispel the tedium of the hours which her husband found it necessary to devote to the processes of combination and analysis, Georgiana turned over the volumes of his scientific library. In many dark old tomes she met with chapters full of romance and poetry. They were the works of philosophers of the middle ages, such as Albertus Magnus, Cornelius Agrippa, Paracelsus, and the famous friar who created the prophetic Brazen Head. All these antique naturalists stood in advance of their centuries, yet were imbued with some of their credulity, and therefore were believed, and perhaps imagined themselves to have acquired from the investigation of Nature a power above Nature, and from physics a sway over the spiritual world. Hardly less curious and imaginative were the early volumes of the Transactions of the Royal Society, in which the members, knowing little of the limits of natural possibility, were continually recording wonders or proposing methods whereby wonders might be wrought.

But to Georgiana the most engrossing volume was a large folio from her husband's own hand, in which he had recorded every experiment of his scientific career, its original aim, the methods adopted for its development, and its final success or failure, with the circumstances to which either event was attributable. The book, in truth, was both the history and emblem of his ardent, ambitious, imaginative, yet practical and laborious life. He handled physical details as if there were nothing beyond them; yet spiritualized them all, and redeemed himself from materialism by his strong and eager aspiration towards the infinite. In his grasp the veriest clod of earth assumed a soul. Georgiana, as she read, reverenced Aylmer and loved him more profoundly than ever, but with a less entire dependence on his judgment than heretofore. Much as he had accomplished, she could not but observe that his most splendid successes were almost invariably failures, if compared with the ideal at which he aimed. His brightest diamonds were the merest pebbles, and felt to be so by himself, in comparison with the inestimable gems which lay hidden beyond his reach. The volume, rich with achievements that had won renown for its author, was yet as melancholy a record as ever mortal hand had penned. It was the sad confession and continual exemplification of the shortcomings of the composite man, the spirit burdened with clay and working in matter, and of the despair that assails the higher nature at finding itself so miserably thwarted by the earthly part. Perhaps every man of genius in whatever sphere might recognize the image of his own experience in Aylmer's journal.

So deeply did these reflections affect Georgiana that she laid her face upon the open volume and burst into tears. In this situation she was found by her husband.

"It is dangerous to read in a sorcerer's books," said he with a smile, though his countenance was uneasy and displeased. "Georgiana, there are pages in that volume which I can scarcely glance over and keep my senses. Take heed lest it prove as detrimental to you."

"It has made me worship you more than ever," said she.

"Ah, wait for this one success," rejoined he, "then worship me if you will. I shall deem myself hardly unworthy of it. But come, I have sought you for the luxury of your voice. Sing to me, dearest."

So she poured out the liquid music of her voice to quench the thirst of his spirit. He then took his leave with a boyish exuberance of gayety, assuring her that her seclusion would endure but a little longer, and that the result was already certain. Scarcely had he departed when Georgiana felt irresistibly impelled to follow him. She had forgotten to inform Aylmer of a symptom which for two or three hours past had begun to excite her attention. It was a sensation in the fatal birthmark, not painful, but which induced a restlessness throughout her system. Hastening after her husband, she intruded for the first time into the laboratory.

The first thing that struck her eye was the furnace, that hot and feverish worker, with the intense glow of its fire, which by the quantities of soot clustered above it seemed to have been burning for ages. There was a distilling apparatus in full operation. Around the room were retorts, tubes, cylinders, crucibles, and other apparatus of chemical research. An electrical machine stood ready for immediate use. The atmosphere felt oppressively close, and was tainted with gaseous odors which had been tormented forth by the processes of science. The severe and homely simplicity of the apartment, with its naked walls and brick pavement, looked strange, accustomed as Georgiana had become to the fantastic elegance of her boudoir. But what chiefly, indeed almost solely, drew her attention, was the aspect of Aylmer himself.

He was pale as death, anxious and absorbed, and hung over the furnace as if it depended upon his utmost watchfulness whether the liquid which it was distilling should be the draught of immortal happiness or misery. How different from the sanguine and joyous mien that he had assumed for Georgiana's encouragement!

"Carefully now, Aminadab; carefully, thou human machine; carefully, thou man of clay!" muttered Aylmer, more to himself than his assistant. "Now, if there be a thought too much or too little, it is all over."

"Ho! ho!" mumbled Aminadab. "Look, master! look!"

Aylmer raised his eyes hastily, and at first reddened, then grew paler than ever, on beholding Georgiana. He rushed towards her and seized her arm with a gripe that left the print of his fingers upon it.

"Why do you come hither? Have you no trust in your husband?" cried he, impetuously. "Would you throw the blight of that fatal birthmark over my labors? It is not well done. Go, prying woman, go!"

"Nay, Aylmer," said Georgiana with the firmness of which she possessed no stinted endowment, "it is not you that have a right to complain. You mistrust your wife; you have concealed the anxiety with which you watch the development of this experiment. Think not so unworthily of me, my husband. Tell me all the risk we run, and fear not that I shall shrink; for my share in it is far less than your own."

"No, no, Georgiana!" said Aylmer, impatiently; "it must not be."

"I submit," replied she calmly. "And, Aylmer, I shall quaff whatever draught you bring me; but it will be on the same principle that would induce me to take a dose of poison if offered by your hand."

"My noble wife," said Aylmer, deeply moved, "I knew not the height and depth of your nature until now. Nothing shall be concealed. Know, then, that this crimson hand, superficial as it seems, has clutched its grasp into your being with a strength of which I had no previous conception. I have already administered agents powerful enough to do aught except to change your entire physical system. Only one thing remains to be tried. If that fail us we are ruined."

"Why did you hesitate to tell me this?" asked she.

"Because, Georgiana," said Aylmer, in a low voice, "there is danger."

"Danger? There is but one danger—that this horrible stigma shall be left upon my cheek!" cried Georgiana. "Remove it, remove it, whatever be the cost, or we shall both go mad!"

"Heaven knows your words are too true," said Aylmer, sadly. "And now, dearest, return to your boudoir. In a little while all will be tested."

He conducted her back and took leave of her with a solemn tenderness which spoke far more than his words how much was now at stake. After his departure Georgiana became rapt in musings. She considered the character of Aylmer, and did it completer justice than at any previous moment. Her heart exulted, while it trembled, at his honorable love—so pure and lofty that it would accept nothing less than perfection nor miserably make itself contented with an earthlier nature than he had dreamed of. She felt how much more precious was such a sentiment than that meaner kind which would have borne with the imperfection for her sake, and have been guilty of treason to holy love by degrading its perfect idea to the level of the actual; and with her whole spirit she prayed that, for a single moment, she might satisfy his highest and deepest conception. Longer than one moment she well knew it could not be; for his spirit was ever on the march, ever ascending, and each instant required something that was beyond the scope of the instant before.

The sound of her husband's footsteps aroused her. He bore a crystal goblet containing a liquor colorless as water, but bright enough to be the draught of immortality. Aylmer was pale; but it seemed rather the consequence of a highly-wrought state of mind and tension of spirit than of fear or doubt.

"The concoction of the draught has been perfect," said he, in answer to Georgiana's look. "Unless all my science have deceived me, it cannot fail."

"Save on your account, my dearest Aylmer," observed his wife, "I might wish to put off this birthmark of mortality by relinquishing mortality itself in preference to any other mode. Life is but a sad possession to those who have attained precisely the degree of moral advancement at which I stand. Were I weaker and blinder it might be happiness. Were I stronger, it might be endured hopefully. But, being what I find myself, methinks I am of all mortals the most fit to die."

"You are fit for heaven without tasting death!" replied her husband "But why do we speak of dying? The draught cannot fail. Behold its effect upon this plant."

On the window seat there stood a geranium diseased with yellow blotches, which had overspread all its leaves. Aylmer poured a small quantity of the liquid upon the soil in which it grew. In a little time, when the roots of the plant had taken up the moisture, the unsightly blotches began to be extinguished in a living verdure.

"There needed no proof," said Georgiana, quietly. "Give me the goblet I joyfully stake all upon your word."

"Drink, then, thou lofty creature!" exclaimed Aylmer, with fervid admiration. "There is no taint of imperfection on thy spirit. Thy sensible frame, too, shall soon be all perfect."

She quaffed the liquid and returned the goblet to his hand.

"It is grateful," said she with a placid smile. "Methinks it is like water from a heavenly fountain; for it contains I know not what of unobtrusive fragrance and deliciousness. It allays a feverish thirst that had parched me for many days. Now, dearest, let me sleep. My earthly senses are closing over my spirit like the leaves around the heart of a rose at sunset."

She spoke the last words with a gentle reluctance, as if it required almost more energy than she could command to pronounce the faint and lingering syllables. Scarcely had they loitered through her lips ere she was lost in slumber. Aylmer sat by her side, watching her aspect with the emotions proper to a man the whole value of whose existence was involved in the process now to be tested. Mingled with this mood, however, was the philosophic investigation characteristic of the man of science. Not the minutest symptom escaped him. A heightened flush of the cheek, a slight irregularity of breath, a quiver of the eyelid, a hardly perceptible tremor through the frame,—such were the details which, as the moments passed, he wrote down in his folio volume. Intense thought had set its stamp upon every previous page of that volume, but the thoughts of years were all concentrated upon the last.

While thus employed, he failed not to gaze often at the fatal hand, and not without a shudder. Yet once, by a strange and unaccountable impulse he pressed it with his lips. His spirit recoiled, however, in the very act, and Georgiana, out of the midst of her deep sleep, moved uneasily and murmured as if in remonstrance. Again Aylmer resumed his watch. Nor was it without avail. The crimson hand, which at first had been strongly visible upon the marble paleness of Georgiana's cheek, now grew more faintly outlined. She remained not less pale than ever; but the birthmark with every breath that came and went, lost somewhat of its former distinctness. Its presence had been awful; its departure was more awful still. Watch the stain of the rainbow fading out the sky, and you will know how that mysterious symbol passed away.

"By Heaven! it is well-nigh gone!" said Aylmer to himself, in almost irrepressible ecstasy. "I can scarcely trace it now. Success! success! And now it is like the faintest rose color. The lightest flush of blood across her cheek would overcome it. But she is so pale!"

He drew aside the window curtain and suffered the light of natural day to fall into the room and rest upon her cheek. At the same time he heard a gross, hoarse chuckle, which he had long known as his servant Aminadab's expression of delight.

"Ah, clod! ah, earthly mass!" cried Aylmer, laughing in a sort of frenzy, "you have served me well! Matter and spirit—earth and heaven —have both done their part in this! Laugh, thing of the senses! You have earned the right to laugh."

These exclamations broke Georgiana's sleep. She slowly unclosed her eyes and gazed into the mirror which her husband had arranged for that purpose. A faint smile flitted over her lips when she recognized how barely perceptible was now that crimson hand which had once blazed forth with such disastrous brilliancy as to scare away all their happiness. But then her eyes sought Aylmer's face with a trouble and anxiety that he could by no means account for.

"My poor Aylmer!" murmured she.

"Poor? Nay, richest, happiest, most favored!" exclaimed he. "My peerless bride, it is successful! You are perfect!"

"My poor Aylmer," she repeated, with a more than human tenderness, "you have aimed loftily; you have done nobly. Do not repent that with so high and pure a feeling, you have rejected the best the earth could offer. Aylmer, dearest Aylmer, I am dying!"

Alas! it was too true! The fatal hand had grappled with the mystery of life, and was the bond by which an angelic spirit kept itself in union with a mortal frame. As the last crimson tint of the birthmark—that sole token of human imperfection—faded from her cheek, the parting breath of the now perfect woman passed into the atmosphere, and her soul, lingering a moment near her husband, took its heavenward flight. Then a hoarse, chuckling laugh was heard again! Thus ever does the gross fatality of earth exult in its invariable triumph over the immortal essence which, in this dim sphere of half development, demands the completeness of a higher state. Yet, had Alymer reached a profounder wisdom, he need not thus have flung away the happiness which would have woven his mortal life of the selfsame texture with the celestial. The momentary circumstance was too strong for him; he failed to look beyond the shadowy scope of time, and, living once for all in eternity, to find the perfect future in the present.

The Cask of Amontillado

Edgar Allan Poe
1846

The story was first published in the November 1846 issue of *Godey's Lady's Book*.

The thousand injuries of Fortunato I had borne as I best could, but when he ventured upon insult, I vowed revenge. You, who so well know the nature of my soul, will not suppose, however, that I gave utterance to a threat. At length I would be avenged; this was a point definitively settled—but the very definitiveness with which it was resolved precluded the idea of risk. I must not only punish, but punish with impunity. A wrong is unredressed when retribution overtakes its redresser.[1] It is equally unredressed when the avenger fails to make himself felt as such to him who has done the wrong.

It must be understood that neither by word nor deed had I given Fortunato cause to doubt my good will. I continued as was my wont, to

---

[1] This sentence presents an archaic manner in which to say: Revenge does not work if you are caught. Using words such as "redresser" suggests that Montresor is making this a moral issue of right and wrong.

smile in his face, and he did not perceive that my smile now was at the thought of his immolation.[1]

He had a weak point—this Fortunato—although in other regards he was a man to be respected and even feared. He prided himself on his connoisseurship in wine.

Few Italians have the true virtuoso spirit. For the most part their enthusiasm is adopted to suit the time and opportunity to practise imposture upon the British and Austrian millionaires. In painting and gemmary, Fortunato, like his countrymen, was a quack, but in the matter of old wines he was sincere. In this respect I did not differ from him materially; I was skilful in the Italian vintages myself, and bought largely whenever I could.

It was about dusk, one evening during the supreme madness of the carnival season,[2] that I encountered my friend. He accosted me with excessive warmth, for he had been drinking much. The man wore motley.[3] He had on a tight-fitting parti-striped dress and his head was surmounted by the conical cap and bells.[4] I was so pleased to see him, that I thought I should never have done wringing his hand.

I said to him—"My dear Fortunato, you are luckily met. How remarkably well you are looking to-day! But I have received a pipe of what passes for Amontillado,[5] and I have my doubts."

"How?" said he, "Amontillado? A pipe? Impossible ? And in the middle of the carnival?"

"I have my doubts," I replied; "and I was silly enough to pay the full Amontillado price without consulting you in the matter. You were not to be found, and I was fearful of losing a bargain."

"Amontillado!"

"I have my doubts."

"Amontillado!"

"And I must satisfy them."

"Amontillado!"

"As you are engaged, I am on my way to Luchesi. If any one has a critical turn, it is he. He will tell me"—

"Luchesi cannot tell Amontillado from Sherry."

"And yet some fools will have it that his taste is a match for your own."

"Come let us go."

"Whither?"

"To your vaults."[6]

"My friend, no; I will not impose upon your good nature. I perceive you have an engagement Luchesi"—[7]

"I have no engagement; come."

---

[1] immolation: The word is derived from Latin when it was used in conjunction with an ancient Roman ritual. Here, however, the immolation suggests the pleasure Montresor feels at imagining Fortuanto on fire.

[2] carnival season: in areas that are predominantly Catholic, the "party" is marked by people dressing up in masquerade typically in February—the American version *Mardi Gras* occurs in Louisiana.

[3] motley: multi-colored, a party-like outfit

[4] conical cap and bells: suggests the proverbial "dunce" cap; "dunce cap" appears first in the 1840 novel *The Old Curiosity Shop* by Charles Dickens (6 years prior to the publication of Poe's story).

[5] Amontillado is a variety of Sherry wine. It is named for the Montilla region of Spain, where the style originated in the 18th century. Amontillado is typically fortified to approximately 17.5 percent alcohol.

[6] vaults: these are the wine vaults, typically located underground where it was dark and cool—appropriate for keeping wine fresh.

[7] Luchesi: probably the name of another wine connosieur

"My friend, no. It is not the engagement, but the severe cold with which I perceive you are afflicted . The vaults are insufferably damp. They are encrusted with nitre."[8]

"Let us go, nevertheless. The cold is merely nothing. Amontillado! You have been imposed upon; and as for Luchesi, he cannot distinguish Sherry from Amontillado."

Thus speaking, Fortunato possessed himself of my arm. Putting on a mask of black silk and drawing a roquelaire closely about my person, I suffered him to hurry me to my palazzo.[9]

There were no attendants at home; they had absconded[10] to make merry in honour of the time. I had told them that I should not return until the morning and had given them explicit orders not to stir from the house. These orders were sufficient, I well knew, to insure their immediate disappearance, one and all, as soon as my back was turned.

I took from their sconces two flambeaux,[11] and giving one to Fortunato bowed him through several suites of rooms to the archway that led into the vaults. I passed down a long and winding staircase, requesting him to be cautious as he followed. We came at length to the foot of the descent, and stood together on the damp ground of the catacombs of the Montresors.[12]

The gait of my friend was unsteady, and the bells upon his cap jingled as he strode.

"The pipe," said he.

"It is farther on," said I; "but observe the white webwork which gleams from these cavern walls."

He turned towards me and looked into my eyes with two filmy orbs that distilled the rheum of intoxication.

"Nitre?" he asked, at length

"Nitre," I replied. "How long have you had that cough!"

"Ugh! ugh! ugh!—ugh! ugh! ugh!—ugh! ugh! ugh!—ugh! ugh! ugh!—ugh! ugh! ugh!

My poor friend found it impossible to reply for many minutes.

"It is nothing," he said, at last.

"Come," I said, with decision, we will go back; your health is precious. You are rich, respected, admired, beloved; you are happy as once I was. You are a man to be missed. For me it is no matter. We will go back; you will be ill and I cannot be responsible. Besides, there is Luchesi"—

"Enough," he said; "the cough is a mere nothing; it will not kill me. I shall not die of a cough."

"True—true," I replied; "and, indeed, I had no intention of alarming you unnecessarily—but you should use all proper caution. A draught of this Medoc[13] will defend us from the damps."

Here I knocked off the neck of a bottle[14] which I drew from a long row of its fellows that lay upon the mould.

"Drink," I said, presenting him the wine.

---

[8] nitre: Niter (American English) or nitre (most English-speaking countries) is the mineral form of potassium nitrate, KNO_3, also known as saltpeter in America or saltpetre in other English speaking countries. Potassium and other nitrates are of great importance for use in fertilizers and, historically, gunpowder.

[9] palazzo: A palace is a grand residence, especially a royal residence, the wealthy or the home of a head of state or some other high-ranking dignitary, such as a bishop or archbishop.

[10] absconded: departed

[11] flambeaux: torches

[12] catacombs of the Montresors: these were the underground burial chambers of the family

[13] Medoc: a region of France, well known as a wine growing region

[14] knocked off the neck of a bottle: while cork was already in use since Roman times, here knocking off the bottle's neck may mean that a cork screw was not available.

He raised it to his lips with a leer. He paused and nodded to me familiarly, while his bells jingled.

"I drink," he said, "to the buried that repose around us."

"And I to your long life."

He again took my arm and we proceeded.

"These vaults," he said, are extensive."

"The Montresors," I replied, "were a great numerous family."

"I forget your arms."

"A huge human foot d'or, in a field azure; the foot crushes a serpent rampant whose fangs are imbedded in the heel."[15]

"And the motto?"

"*Nemo me impune lacessit.*"[16]

"Good!" he said.

The wine sparkled in his eyes and the bells jingled. My own fancy grew warm with the Medoc. We had passed through walls of piled bones, with casks and puncheons[17] intermingling, into the inmost recesses of the catacombs. I paused again, and this time I made bold to seize Fortunato by an arm above the elbow.

"The nitre!" I said: see it increases. It hangs like moss upon the vaults. We are below the river's bed. The drops of moisture trickle among the bones. Come, we will go back ere it is too late. Your cough"—

"It is nothing" he said; "let us go on. But first, another draught of the Medoc."

I broke and reached him a flagon of De Grave.[18] He emptied it at a breath. His eyes flashed with a fierce light. He laughed and threw the bottle upwards with a gesticulation I did not understand.

I looked at him in surprise. He repeated the movement—a grotesque one.

"You do not comprehend?" he said.

"Not I," I replied.

"Then you are not of the brotherhood."

"How?"

"You are not of the masons."[19]

"Yes, yes," I said "yes! yes."

"You? Impossible! A mason?"

"A mason," I replied.

"A sign," he said.

"It is this," I answered, producing a trowel from beneath the folds of my roquelaire.[20]

---

[15] foot crushes a serpent: A biblical allusion to The Bible's Genesis in which the Serpent is portrayed as a deceptive creature or trickster (usually identified as Satan), promoting as good what God had directly forbidden, and particularly cunning in its deception. (Gen. 3:4–5 and 3:22). God curses the serpent in Genesis 3:15: *And I will put enmity between thee and the woman, and between thy seed and her seed; it shall bruise thy head, and thou shalt bruise his heel.*

[16] *Nemo me impune lacessit* is the Latin motto of the Order of the Thistle and of three Scottish regiments of the British Army. It means *No one attacks me with impunity*. It is also alternatively translated into English as *No one can harm me unpunished*.

[17] puncheons: a container for wine and/or spirits

[18] De Grave: meaning of the Grave, a Bordeaux wine estate located in the Pessac-Léognan region of the Graves

[19] masons: Fortunato might mean a reference to Freemasonry, an organization initially based upon stonemasons, possibly dating back to the fourteenth century. However, Montresor plays on the word, probably meaning he is a bricklayer or mason—a craftsman who lays bricks to construct brickwork.

[20] roquelaire: probably a reference to a cloak but with a twist in its word origin. Roquelaure is a Catholic commune in the Gers department in southwestern France.

"You jest," he exclaimed, recoiling a few paces. "But let us proceed to the Amontillado."

"Be it so," I said, replacing the tool beneath the cloak, and again offering him my arm. He leaned upon it heavily. We continued our route in search of the Amontillado. We passed through a range of low arches, descended, passed on, and descending again, arrived at a deep crypt, in which the foulness of the air caused our flambeaux[21] rather to glow than flame.

At the most remote end of the crypt there appeared another less spacious. Its walls had been lined with human remains piled to the vault overhead, in the fashion of the great catacombs of Paris.[22] Three sides of this interior crypt were still ornamented in this manner. From the fourth the bones had been thrown down, and lay promiscuously upon the earth, forming at one point a mound of some size. Within the wall thus exposed by the displacing of the bones, we perceived a still interior recess, in depth about four feet, in width three, in height six or seven. It seemed to have been constructed for no especial use in itself, but formed merely the interval between two of the colossal supports of the roof of the catacombs, and was backed by one of their circumscribing walls of solid granite.

It was in vain that Fortunato, uplifting his dull torch, endeavoured to pry into the depths of the recess. Its termination the feeble light did not enable us to see.

"Proceed," I said; "herein is the Amontillado. As for Luchesi"—

"He is an ignoramus," interrupted my friend, as he stepped unsteadily forward, while I followed immediately at his heels. In an instant he had reached the extremity of the niche, and finding his progress arrested by the rock, stood stupidly bewildered. A moment more and I had fettered him to the granite. In its surface were two iron staples, distant from each other about two feet, horizontally. From one of these depended a short chain. from the other a padlock. Throwing the links about his waist, it was but the work of a few seconds to secure it. He was too much astounded to resist. Withdrawing the key I stepped back from the recess.

"Pass your hand," I said, "over the wall; you cannot help feeling the nitre. Indeed it is very damp. Once more let me implore you to return. No? Then I must positively leave you. But I must first render you all the little attentions in my power."

"The Amontillado!" ejaculated my friend, not yet recovered from his astonishment.

"True," I replied; "the Amontillado."

As I said these words I busied myself among the pile of bones of which I have before spoken. Throwing them aside, I soon uncovered a quantity of building stone and mortar. With these materials and with the aid of my trowel, I began vigorously to wall up the entrance of the niche.

I had scarcely laid the first tier of my masonry when I discovered that the intoxication of Fortunato had in a great measure worn off. The earliest indication I had of this was a low moaning cry from the depth of the recess. It was NOT the cry of a drunken man. There was then a long and obstinate silence. I laid the second tier, and the third, and the fourth; and then I heard the furious vibrations of the chain. The noise lasted for several minutes, during which, that I might hearken to it with the more satisfaction, I ceased my labours and sat down upon the bones. When at last the clanking subsided, I resumed the trowel, and finished without interruption the fifth, the sixth, and the seventh tier. The wall was now nearly upon a level with my breast. I again paused, and holding the flambeaux over the mason-work, threw a few feeble rays upon the figure within.

---

[21] a torch

[22] Ironically, the city of Paris has been associated with the city of love, or a haven for relaxation and rehabilitation.

A succession of loud and shrill screams, bursting suddenly from the throat of the chained form, seemed to thrust me violently back. For a brief moment I hesitated—I trembled. Unsheathing my rapier,[23] I began to grope with it about the recess; but the thought of an instant reassured me. I placed my hand upon the solid fabric of the catacombs, and felt satisfied. I reapproached the wall. I replied to the yells of him who clamoured. I re-echoed—I aided—I surpassed them in volume and in strength. I did this, and the clamourer grew still.[24]

It was now midnight, and my task was drawing to a close. I had completed the eighth, the ninth, and the tenth tier. I had finished a portion of the last and the eleventh; there remained but a single stone to be fitted and plastered in. I struggled with its weight; I placed it partially in its destined position. But now there came from out the niche a low laugh that erected the hairs upon my head. It was succeeded by a sad voice, which I had difficulty in recognising as that of the noble Fortunato. The voice said—

"Ha! ha! ha!—he! he!—a very good joke indeed—an excellent jest. We will have many a rich laugh about it at the palazzo—he! he! he!—over our wine—he! he! he!"

"The Amontillado!" I said.

"He! he! he!—he! he! he!—yes, the Amontillado . But is it not getting late? Will not they be awaiting us at the palazzo, the Lady Fortunato and the rest? Let us be gone."

"Yes," I said "let us be gone."

"For the love of God, Montresor!"

"Yes," I said, "for the love of God!"

But to these words I hearkened in vain for a reply. I grew impatient. I called aloud—

"Fortunato!"

No answer. I called again—

"Fortunato!"

No answer still. I thrust a torch through the remaining aperture and let it fall within. There came forth in return only a jingling of the bells. My heart grew sick—on account of the dampness of the catacombs. I hastened to make an end of my labour. I forced the last stone into its position; I plastered it up.

Against the new masonry I reerected the old rampart of bones. For the half of a century no mortal has disturbed them.

In pace requiescat! [25]

---

[23] rapier: a slender, sharply pointed sword, ideally used for thrusting attacks, used mainly in Early Modern Europe during the 16th and 17th centuries.

[24] clamourer: loud noise

[25] *In pace requiescat!:* Latin for "Rest in Peace," often on tombstones as "R.I.P." Similar forms of the phrase and initials are said to have been used on tombs of early Christians. The phrase or initials became common on the tombs of Catholics in the 18th century and was used in the Catholic Tridentine Mass as early as 1570.

The Celebrated Jumping Frog of Calaveras County

Mark Twain
1865

The story was first published in *The Saturday Press*, where it appeared in the November 18, 1865 edition as "Jim Smiley and His Jumping Frog."

In compliance with the request of a friend of mine, who wrote me from the East, I called on a good-natured, garrulous old Simon Wheeler, and inquired after my friend's friend, Leonidas W. Smiley, as requested to do, and I hereunto append the result. I have a lurking suspicion that Leonidas W. Smiley is a myth; that my friend never knew such a personage; and that he only conjectured that, if I asked old Wheeler about him, it would remind him of his infamous Jim Smiley, and he would go to work and bore me nearly to death with some infernal reminiscence of him as long and tedious as it should be useless to me. If that was the design, it certainly succeeded.

I found Simon Wheeler dozing comfortably by the barroom stove of the old, dilapidated tavern in the ancient mining camp of Angel's, and I noticed that he was fat and bald-headed, and had an expression of winning gentleness and simplicity upon his tranquil countenance. He roused up and gave me good-day. I told him a friend of mine had commissioned me to make some inquiries about a cherished companion of his boyhood named Leonidas W. Smiley—Rev. Leonidas W. Smiley—a young minister of the Gospel, who he had heard was at one time a resident of Angel's Camp. I added, that, if Mr. Wheeler, could tell me anything about this Rev. Leonidas W. Smiley, I would feel under many obligations to him.

Simon Wheeler backed me into a corner and blockaded me there with his chair, and then sat me down and reeled off the monotonous narrative which follows this paragraph. He never smiled, never frowned, he never changed his voice from the gentle-flowing key to which he turned the initial sentence, he never betrayed the slightest suspicion of enthusiasm; but all through the interminable narrative there ran a vein of impressive earnestness and sincerity, which showed me plainly that, so far from his imagining that there was anything ridiculous or funny about his story, he regarded it as a really important matter, and admitted its two heroes as men of transcendent genius in finesse. To me, the spectacle of a man drifting serenely along through such a queer yarn without ever smiling, was exquisitely absurd. As I said before, I asked him to tell me what he knew of Rev. Leonidas W. Smiley, and he replied as follows. I let him go on in his own way, and never interrupted him once:

There was a feller here once by the name of Jim Smiley, in the winter of '49—or maybe it was the spring of '50—I don't recollect exactly, somehow, though what makes me think it was one or the other is because I remember the big flume wasn't finished when he first came to the camp; but anyway, he was the curiousest man about always betting on anything that turned up you ever see, if he could get anybody to bet on the other side; and if he couldn't, he'd change sides. Any way that suited the other man would suit him—any way just so's he got a bet, he was satisfied. But still he was lucky, uncommon lucky—he most always come out winner. He was always ready and laying for a chance; there couldn't be no solit'ry thing mentioned but that feller'd offer to bet on it, and take any side you please, as I was just telling you. If there was a horse-race, you'd find him flush, or you'd find him busted at the end of it; if there was a dog-fight, he'd bet on it; if there was a cat-fight, he'd bet on it; if there was a chicken-fight, he'd bet on it; why, if there was two birds setting on a fence, he would bet you which one would fly first; or if there was a camp-meeting, he would be there reg'lar, to bet on

Parson Walker, which he judged to be the best exhorter about here, and so he was, too, and a good man. If he even seen a straddle-bug start to go anywheres, he would bet you how long it would take him to get wherever he was going to, and if you took him up, he would foller that straddle-bug to Mexico but what he would find out where he was bound for and how long he was on the road. Lots of the boys here has seen that Smiley, and can tell you about him. Why, it never made no difference to him—he would bet on anything—the dangdest feller. Parson Walker's wife laid very sick once, for a good while, and it seemed as if they warn't going to save her; but one morning he came in, and Smiley asked how she was, and he said she was consid'able better—thank the Lord for his inf'nit' mercy—and coming on so smart that, with the blessing of Prov'dence, she'd get well yet; and Smiley, before he thought, says, "Well, I'll risk two-and-a-half that she don't anyway."

Thish-yer Smiley had a mare—the boys called her the fifteen-minute nag, but that was only in fun, you know, because, of course, she was faster than that—and he used to win money on that horse, for all she was so slow and always had the asthma, or the distemper, or the consumption, or something of that kind. They used to give her two or three hundred yards start, and then pass her under way; but always at the fag-end of the race she'd get excited and desperate-like, and come cavorting and straddling up, and scattering her legs around limber, sometimes in the air, and sometimes out to one side amongst the fences, and kicking up m-o-r-e dust, and raising m-o-r-e racket with her coughing and sneezing and blowing her nose—and always fetch up at the stand just about a neck ahead, as near as you could cipher it down.

And he had a little small bull pup, that to look at him you'd think he warn't worth a cent but to set around and look ornery and lay for a chance to steal something. But as soon as money was up on him, he was a different dog; his under-jaw'd begin to stick out like the fo'castle of a steamboat, and his teeth would uncover, and shine savage like the furnaces. And a dog might tackle him, and bully-rag him, and bite him, and throw him over his shoulder two or three times, and Andrew Jackson—which was the name of the pup—Andrew Jackson would never let on but what he was satisfied, and hadn't expected nothing else—and the bets being doubled on the other side all the time, till the money was all up; and then all of a sudden he would grab that other dog jest by the j'int of his hind leg and freeze to it—not claw, you understand, but only jest grip and hang on till they throwed up the sponge, if it was a year. Smiley always come out winner on that pup, till he harnessed a dog once that didn't have no hind legs, because they'd been sawed off by a circular saw, and when the thing had gone along far enough, and the money was all up, and he come to make a snatch for his pet holt, he saw in a minute how he'd been imposed on, and how the other dog had him in the door, so to speak, and he 'peared surprised, and then he looked sorter discouraged-like, and didn't try no more to win the fight, and so he got shucked out bad. He give Smiley a look, as much to say his heart was broke and it was his fault for putting up a dog that hadn't no hind legs for him to take holt of, which was his main dependence in a fight, and then he limped off a piece and laid down and died. It was a good pup, was that Andrew Jackson, and would have made a name for hisself if he'd lived, for the stuff was in him, and he had genius—I know it, because he hadn't no opportunities to speak of, and it don't stand to reason that a dog could make such a fight as he could under them circumstances, if he hadn't no talent. It always makes me feel sorry when I think of that last fight of his'n, and the way it turned out.

Well, thish-yer Smiley had rat-tarriers, and chicken-cocks, and tom-cats, and all them kind of things, till you couldn't rest, and you couldn't fetch nothing for him to bet on but he'd match you. He ketched a frog one day, and took him home, and said he cal'lated to educate him; and so he never done nothing for these three months but set in his back yard and learn that frog to jump. And you bet you he did learn him, too. He'd give him a little punch behind, and the next minute you'd see that frog whirling in the air like a doughnut—see him turn one summerset, or maybe a couple, if he got a good start, and come down flat-footed and all right, like a cat. He got him up so in the matter of catching flies, and kept him in practice so constant, that he'd nail a fly every time as far as he could see him. Smiley said all a frog wanted was education, and he could do most any thing—and I believe him. Why, I've seen him set Dan'l Webster down here on this floor—Dan'l Webster was the name of the frog—and sing out, "Flies, Dan'l, flies!" and quicker'n you could wink, he'd spring straight up, and snake a fly off'n the counter there, and flop down on the floor again as solid as a gob of mud, and fall to scratching the side of his head with his hind foot as indifferent as if he hadn't no idea he'd been doin' any more'n any frog might do. You never see a frog so modest and straight-for'ard as he was, for all he was so gifted. And when it come to fair and square jumping on the dead level, he could get over more ground at one straddle than any animal of his breed you ever see. Jumping on a dead level was his strong suit, youn understand; and when it come to that, Smiley would ante up money on him as long as he had a red. Smiley was monstrous proud of his frog, and well he might be, for fellers that had traveled and been everywhere all said he laid over any frog that ever they see.

Well, Smiley kept the beast in a little lattice box, and he used to fetch him downtown sometimes and lay for a bet. One day a feller—a stranger in the camp, he was—come across him with his box, and says:

"What might it be that you've got in the box?"

And Smiley says, sorter indifferent like, "It might be a parrot, or it might be a canary, maybe, but it ain't—it's only just a frog."

An' the feller took it, and looked at it careful, and turned it round this way and that, and says, "H'm—so 'tis. Well, what's he good for?"

"Well," Smiley says, easy and careless, "He's good enough for one thing, I should judge—he can outjump any frog in Calaveras county."

The feller took the box again, and took another long, particular look, and give it back to Smiley, and says, very deliberate, "Well, I don't see no p'ints about that frog that's any better'n any other frog."

"Maybe you don't," Smiley says. "Maybe you understand frogs, and maybe you don't understand 'em; maybe you've had experience, and maybe you ain't only a amature, as it were. Anyways, I've got my opinion, and I'll risk forty dollars that he can outjump any frog in Calaveras county."

And the feller studied a minute, and then says, kinder sad like, "Well, I'm only a stranger here, and I ain't got no frog; but if I had a frog, I'd bet you."

And then Smiley says, "That's all right—that's all right—if you'll hold my box a minute, I'll go and get you a frog." And so the feller took the box, and put up his forty dollars along with Smiley's, and set down to wait.

So he set there a good while thinking and thinking to hisself, and then he got the frog out and prizes his mouth open and took a teaspoon and filled him full of quail shot—filled him pretty near up to his chin—and set him on the floor. Smiley he went to the swamp and slopped around in the mud for a long time, and finally he ketched a frog, and fetched him in, and give him to this feller, and says:

"Now, if you're ready, set him alongside of Dan'l, with his fore-paws just even with Dan'l, and I'll give the word." Then he says, "One—two—three—jump!" and him and the feller touched up the frogs from behind, and the frog hopped off, but Dan'l give a heave, and hysted up his shoulders—so—like a Frenchman, but it wasn't no use—he couldn't budge; he was planted as solid as an anvil, and he couldn't no more stir than if he was anchored out. Smiley was a good deal surprised, and he was disgusted, too, but he didn't have no idea what the matter was, of course.

The feller took the money and started away; and when he was going out the door, he sorter jerked his thumb over his shoulder—this way—at Dan'l, and says again, very deliberate, "Well, I don't see no p'ints about that frog that's any better'n any other frog."

Smiley he stood scratching his head and looking down at Dan'l a long time, and at last he says, "I do wonder what in the nation that frog throw'd off for—I wonder if there ain't something the matter with him—he 'pears to look mighty baggy, somehow." And he ketched Dan'l by the nap of the neck, and lifted him up and says, "Why, blame my cats, if he don't weigh five pound!" and turned him upside down, and he belched out a double handful of shot. And then he see how it was, and he was the maddest man—he set the frog down and took out after that feller, but he never ketched him. And—

(Here Simon Wheeler heard his name called from the front yard, and he got up to see what was wanted.) And turning to me as he moved away, he said: "Just set where you are, stranger, and rest easy—I ain't going to be gone a second."

But, by your leave, I did not think that a continuation of the history of the enterprising vagabond Jim Smiley would be likely to afford me much information concerning the Rev. Leonidas W. Smiley, and so I started away.

At the door I met the sociable Wheeler returning, and he buttonholed me and recommended:

"Well, thish-yer Smiley had a yeller one-eyed cow that didn't have no tail, only jest a short stump like a bannanner, and—"

"Oh, hang Smiley and his afflicted cow!" I muttered, good-naturedly, and bidding the old gentleman good-day, I departed.

The Luck of Roaring Camp

Bret Harte
1868

The story was first published in the *August Overland Monthly*, 1886.

There was commotion in Roaring Camp. It could not have been a fight, for in 1850 that was not novel enough to have called together the entire settlement. The ditches and claims were not only deserted, but "Tuttle's grocery" had contributed its gamblers, who, it will be remembered, calmly continued their game the day that French Pete and Kanaka Joe shot each other to death over the bar in the front room. The whole camp was collected before a rude cabin on the outer edge of the clearing. Conversation was carried on in a low tone, but the name of a woman was frequently repeated. It was a name familiar enough in the camp—"Cherokee Sal."

Perhaps the less said of her the better. She was a coarse and, it is to be feared, a very sinful woman. But at that time she was the only woman in Roaring Camp, and was just then lying in sore extremity, when she most needed the ministration of her own sex. Dissolute, abandoned, and irreclaimable, she was yet suffering a martyrdom hard enough to bear even when veiled by sympathizing womanhood, but now terrible in her loneliness. The primal curse had come to her in that original isolation which must have made the punishment of the first transgression so dreadful. It was, perhaps, part of the expiation of her sin that, at a moment when she most lacked her sex's intuitive tenderness and care, she met only the half-contemptuous faces of her masculine associates. Yet a few of the spectators were, I think, touched by her sufferings. Sandy Tipton thought it was "rough on Sal," and, in the contemplation of her condition, for a moment rose superior to the fact that he had an ace and two Bowers in his sleeve.

It will be seen also that the situation was novel. Deaths were by no means uncommon in Roaring Camp, but a birth was a new thing. People had been dismissed from the camp effectively, finally, and with no possibility of return; but this was the first time that anybody had been introduced ab initio. Hence the excitement.

"You go in there, Stumpy," said a prominent citizen known as "Kentuck," addressing one of the loungers. "Go in there, and see what you kin do. You've had experience in them things."

Perhaps there was a fitness in the selection. Stumpy, in other climes, had been the putative head of two families; in fact, it was owing to some legal informality in these proceedings that Roaring Camp—a city of refuge—was indebted to his company. The crowd approved the choice, and Stumpy was wise enough to bow to the majority. The door closed on the extempore surgeon and midwife, and Roaring Camp sat down outside, smoked its pipe, and awaited the issue.

The assemblage numbered about a hundred men. One or two of these were actual fugitives from justice, some were criminal, and all were reckless. Physically they exhibited no indication of their past lives and character. The greatest scamp had a Raphael face, with a profusion of blonde hair; Oakhurst, a gambler, had the melancholy air and intellectual abstraction of a Hamlet; the coolest and most courageous man was scarcely over five feet in height, with a soft voice and an embarrassed, timid manner. The term "roughs" applied to them was a distinction rather than a definition. Perhaps in the minor details of fingers, toes, ears, etc., the camp may have been deficient, but these slight omissions did not detract from their aggregate force. The strongest man had but three fingers on his right hand; the best shot had but one eye.

Such was the physical aspect of the men that were dispersed around the cabin. The camp lay in a triangular valley between two hills and a river. The only outlet was a steep trail over the summit of a hill that faced the cabin, now illuminated by the rising moon. The suffering woman might have seen it from the rude bunk whereon she lay, seen it winding like a silver thread until it was lost in the stars above.

A fire of withered pine boughs added sociability to the gathering. By degrees the natural levity of Roaring Camp returned. Bets were freely offered and taken regarding the result. Three to five that "Sal would get through with it;" even that the child would survive; side bets as to the sex and complexion of the coming stranger. In the midst of an excited discussion an exclamation came from those nearest the door, and the camp stopped to listen. Above the swaying and moaning of the pines, the swift rush of the river, and the crackling of the fire rose a sharp, querulous cry—a cry unlike anything heard before in the camp. The pines stopped moaning, the river ceased to rush, and the fire to crackle. It seemed as if Nature had stopped to listen too.

The camp rose to its feet as one man! It was proposed to explode a barrel of gunpowder; but in consideration of the situation of the mother, better counsels prevailed, and only a few revolvers were discharged; for whether owing to the rude surgery of the camp, or some other reason, Cherokee Sal was sinking fast. Within an hour she had climbed, as it were, that rugged road that led to the stars, and so passed out of Roaring Camp, its sin and shame, forever. I do not think that the announcement disturbed them much, except in speculation as to the fate of the child. "Can he live now?" was asked of Stumpy. The answer was doubtful. The only other being of Cherokee Sal's sex and maternal condition in the settlement was an ass. There was some conjecture as to fitness, but the experiment was tried. It was less problematical than the ancient treatment of Romulus and Remus, and apparently as successful.

When these details were completed, which exhausted another hour, the door was opened, and the anxious crowd of men, who had already formed themselves into a queue, entered in single file. Beside the low bunk or shelf, on which the figure of the mother was starkly outlined below the blankets, stood a pine table. On this a candle-box was placed, and within it, swathed in staring red flannel, lay the last arrival at Roaring Camp. Beside the candle-box was placed a hat. Its use was soon indicated.

"Gentlemen," said Stumpy, with a singular mixture of authority and ex officio complacency, "gentlemen will please pass in at the front door, round the table, and out at the back door. Them as wishes to contribute anything toward the orphan will find a hat handy."

The first man entered with his hat on; he uncovered, however, as he looked about him, and so unconsciously set an example to the next. In such communities good and bad actions are catching. As the procession filed in comments were audible—criticisms addressed perhaps rather to Stumpy in the character of showmen: "Is that him?" "Mighty small specimen;" "Hasn't more'n got the color;" "Ain't bigger nor a derringer." The contributions were as characteristic: A silver tobacco box; a doubloon; a navy revolver, silver mounted; a gold specimen; a very beautifully embroidered lady's handkerchief (from Oakhurst the gambler); a diamond breastpin; a diamond ring (suggested by the pin, with the remark from the giver that he "saw that pin and went two diamonds better"); a slung-shot; a Bible (contributor not detected); a golden spur; a silver teaspoon (the initials, I regret to say, were not the giver's); a pair of surgeon's shears; a lancet; a Bank of England note for £5; and about $200 in loose gold and silver coin. During these proceedings Stumpy maintained a silence as impassive as the dead on his left, a gravity as inscrutable as that of the newly born on his right. Only one incident occurred to break the monotony of the curious procession. As Kentuck bent over the candle-box half curiously, the child turned, and, in a spasm of pain, caught at his groping finger, and held it fast for a moment. Kentuck looked foolish and embarrassed. Something like a blush tried to assert itself in his weather-beaten cheek.

"The d-d little cuss!" he said, as he extricated his finger, with perhaps more tenderness and care than he might have been deemed capable of showing. He held that finger a little apart from its fellows as he went out, and examined it curiously. The examination provoked the same original remark in regard to the child. In fact, he seemed to enjoy repeating it. "He rastled with my finger," he remarked to Tipton, holding up the member, "the d-d little cuss!"

It was four o'clock before the camp sought repose. A light burnt in the cabin where the watchers sat, for Stumpy did not go to bed that night. Nor did Kentuck. He drank quite freely, and related with great gusto his experience, invariably ending with his characteristic condemnation of the newcomer. It seemed to relieve him of any unjust implication of sentiment, and Kentuck had the weaknesses of the nobler sex. When everybody else had gone to bed, he walked down to the river and whistled reflectingly. Then he walked up the gulch past the cabin, still whistling with demonstrative unconcern. At a large redwood-tree he paused and retraced his steps, and again passed the cabin. Halfway down to the river's bank he again paused, and then returned and knocked at the door. It was opened by Stumpy.

"How goes it?" said Kentuck, looking past Stumpy toward the candle-box.

"All serene!" replied Stumpy. "Anything up?"

"Nothing." There was a pause—an embarrassing one -Stumpy still holding the door. Then Kentuck had recourse to his finger, which he held up to Stumpy. "Rastled with it—the d-d little cuss," he said, and retired.

The next day Cherokee Sal had such rude sepulture as Roaring Camp afforded. After her body had been committed to the hillside, there was a formal meeting of the camp to discuss what should be done with her infant. A resolution to adopt it was unanimous and enthusiastic. But an animated discussion in regard to the manner and feasibility of providing for its wants at once sprang up. It was remarkable that the argument partook of none of those fierce personalities with which discussions were usually conducted at Roaring Camp. Tipton proposed that they should send the child to Red Dog—a distance of forty miles—where female attention could be procured. But the unlucky suggestion met with fierce and unanimous opposition. It was evident that no plan which entailed parting from their new acquisition would for a moment be entertained. "Besides," said Tom Ryder, "them fellows at Red Dog would swap it, and ring in somebody else on us." A disbelief in the honesty of other camps prevailed at Roaring Camp, as in other places.

The introduction of a female nurse in the camp also met with objection. It was argued that no decent woman could be prevailed to accept Roaring Camp as her home, and the speaker urged that "they didn't want any more of the other kind."

This unkind allusion to the defunct mother, harsh as it may seem, was the first spasm of propriety—the first symptom of the camp's regeneration. Stumpy advanced nothing. Perhaps he felt a certain delicacy in interfering with the selection of a possible successor in office. But when questioned, he averred stoutly that he and "Jinny"—the mammal before alluded to—could manage to rear the child. There was something original, independent, and heroic about the plan that pleased the camp. Stumpy was retained. Certain articles were sent for to Sacramento. "Mind," said the treasurer, as he pressed a bag of gold-dust into the expressman's hand, "the best that can be got, lace, you know, and filigree-work and frills—d—n the cost!"

Strange to say, the child thrived. Perhaps the invigorating climate of the mountain camp was compensation for material deficiencies. Nature took the foundling to her broader breast. In that rare atmosphere of the Sierra foothills—that air pungent with balsamic odor, that ethereal cordial at once bracing and exhilarating—he may have found food and nourishment, or a subtle chemistry that transmuted ass's milk to lime and phosphorus. Stumpy inclined to the belief that it was the latter and good nursing. "Me and that ass," he would say, "has been father and mother to him! Don't you," he would add, apostrophizing the helpless bundle before him, "never go back on us."

By the time he was a month old the necessity of giving him a name became apparent. He had generally been known as "The Kid," "Stumpy's Boy," "The Coyote" (an allusion to his vocal powers), and even by Kentuck's endearing diminutive of "The d-d little cuss." But these were felt to be vague and unsatisfactory, and were at last dismissed under another influence. Gamblers and adventurers are generally superstitious, and Oakhurst one day declared that the baby had brought "the luck" to Roaring Camp. It was certain that of late they had been successful. "Luck" was the name agreed upon, with the prefix of Tommy for greater convenience. No allusion was made to the mother, and the father was unknown. "It's better," said the philosophical Oakhurst, "to take a fresh deal all round. Call him Luck, and start him fair." A day was accordingly set apart for the christening.

What was meant by this ceremony the reader may imagine who has already gathered some idea of the reckless irreverence of Roaring Camp. The master of ceremonies was one "Boston," a noted wag, and the occasion seemed to promise the greatest facetiousness. This ingenious satirist had spent two days in preparing a burlesque of the Church service, with pointed local allusions. The choir was properly trained, and Sandy Tipton was to stand godfather. But after the procession had marched to the grove with music and banners, and the child had been deposited before a mock altar, Stumpy stepped before the expectant crowd. "It ain't my style to spoil fun, boys," said the little man, stoutly eyeing the faces around him, "but it strikes me that this thing ain't exactly on the squar. It's playing it pretty low down on this yer baby to ring in fun on him that he ain't goin' to understand. And ef there's goin' to be any godfathers round, I'd like to see who's got any better rights than me."

A silence followed Stumpy's speech. To the credit of all humorists be it said that the first man to acknowledge its justice was the satirist thus stopped of his fun. "But," said Stumpy, quickly following up his advantage, "we're here for a christening, and we'll have it. I proclaim you Thomas Luck, according to the laws of the United States and the State of California, so help me God."

It was the first time that the name of the Deity had been otherwise uttered than profanely in the camp. The form of christening was perhaps even more ludicrous than the satirist had conceived; but strangely enough, nobody saw it and nobody lalghed. "Tommy" was christened as seriously as he would have been under a Christian roof, and cried and was comforted in as orthodox fashion.

And so the work of regeneration began in Roaring Camp. Almost imperceptibly a change came over the settlement. The cabin assigned to "Tommy Luck"—or "The Luck," as he was more frequently called—first showed signs of improvement. It was kept scrupulously clean and whitewashed. Then it was boarded, clothed, and papered. The rosewood cradle, packed eighty miles by mule, had, in Stumpy's way of putting it, "sorter killed the rest of the furniture." So the rehabilitation of the cabin became a necessity. The men who were in the habit of lounging in at Stumpy's to see "how 'The Luck' got on" seemed to appreciate the change, and in self-defense the rival establishment of "Tuttle's grocery " bestirred itself and imported a carpet and mirrors. The reflections of the latter on the appearance of Roaring Camp tended to produce stricter habits of personal cleanliness. Again Stumpy imposed a kind of quarantine upon those who aspired to the honor and privilege of holding The Luck. It was a cruel mortification to Kentuck—who, in the carelessness of a large nature and the habits of frontier life, had begun to regard all garments as a second cuticle, which, like a snake's, only sloughed off through decay—to be debarred this privilege from certain prudential reasons. Yet such was the subtle influence of innovation that he thereafter appeared regularly every afternoon in a clean shirt and face still shining from his ablutions.

Nor were moral and social sanitary laws neglected. "Tommy," who was supposed to spend his whole existence in a persistent attempt to repose, must not be disturbed by noise. The shouting and yelling, which had gained the camp its infelicitous title, were not permitted within hearing distance of Stumpy's. The men conversed in whispers or smoked with Indian gravity. Profanity was tacitly given up in these sacred precincts, and throughout the camp a popular form of expletive, known as " D—n the luck!" and "Curse the luck! " was abandoned, as having a new personal bearing.

Vocal music was not interdicted, being supposed to have a soothing, tranquilizing quality; and one song, sung by " Man-o'War Jack," an English sailor from her Majesty's Australian colonies, was quite popular as a lullaby. It was a lugubrious recital of the exploits of "the Arethusa, Seventy-four," in a muffled minor, ending with a prolonged dying fall at the burden of each verse, " On b-oo-o-ard of the Arethusa." It was a fine sight to see Jack holding The Luck, rocking from side to side as if with the motion of a ship, and crooning forth this naval ditty. Either through the peculiar rocking of Jack or the length of his song -it contained ninety stanzas, and was continued with conscientious deliberation to the bitter end—the lullaby generally had the desired effect. At such times the men would lie at full length under the trees in the soft summer twilight, smoking their pipes and drinking in the melodious utterances. An indistinct idea that this was pastoral happiness pervaded the camp. "This'ere kind o' think," said the Cockney Simmons, meditatively reclining on his elbow, "is 'evingly." It reminded him of Greenwich.

On the long summrer days The Luck was usually carried to the gulch from whence the golden store of Roaring Camp was taken. There, on a blanket spread over pine boughs, he would lie while the men were working in the ditches below. Latterly there was a rude attempt to decorate this bower with flowers and sweet-smelling shrubs, and generally someone would bring him a cluster of wild honeysuckles, azaleas, or the painted blossoms of Las Mariposas. The men had suddenly awakened to the fact that there were beauty and significance in these trifles, which they had so long trodden carelessly beneath their feet. A flake of glittering mica, a fragment of variegated quartz, a bright pebble from the bed of the creek, became beautiful to eyes thus cleared and strengthened, and were invariably put aside for The Luck. It was wonderful how many treasures the woods and hillsides yielded that "would do for Tommy."

Surrounded by playthings such as never child out of fairyland had before, it is to be hoped that Tommy was content. He appeared to be serenely happy, albeit there was an infantine gravity about him, a contemplative light in his round gray eyes, that sometimes worried Stumpy. He was always tractable and quiet, and it is recorded that once, having crept beyond his "corral,"—a hedge of tessellated pine boughs, which surrounded his bed—he dropped over the bank on his head in the soft earth, and remained with his mottled legs in the air in that position for at least five minutes with unflinching gravity. He was extricated without a murmur. I hesitate to record the many other instances of his sagacity, which rest, unfortunately, upon the statements of prejudiced friends. Some of them were not without a tinge of superstition.

"I crep' up the bank just now," said Kentuck one day, in a breathless state of excitement, "and dern me kin—if he wasn't a-talking to a jaybird as was a-sittin' on his lap. There they was, just as free and sociable as anything you please, a-jawin' at each other just like two cherrybums." Howbeit, whether creeping over the pine boughs or lying lazily on his back blinking at the leaves above him, to him the birds sang, the squirrels chattered, and the flowers bloomed. Nature was his nurse and playfellow. For him she would let slip between the leaves golden shafts of sunlight that fell just within his grasp; she would send wandering breezes to visit him with the balm of bay and resinous gum; to him the tall redwoods nodded familiarly and sleepily, the bumblebees buzzed, and the rooks cawed a slumbrous accompaniment.

Such was the golden summer of Roaring Camp. They were "flush times," and the luck was with them. The claims had yielded enormously. The camp was jealous of its privileges and looked suspiciously on strangers. No encouragement was given to immigration, and, to make their seclusion more perfect, the land on either side of the mountain wall that surrounded the camp they duly preempted. This, and a reputation for singular proficiency with the revolver, kept the reserve of Roaring Camp inviolate. The expressman—their only connecting link with the surrounding world— sometimes told wonderful stories of the camp. He would say, "They've a street up there in 'Roaring' that would lay over any street in Red Dog. They've got vines and flowers round their houses, and they wash themselves twice a day. But they're mighty rough on strangers, and they worship an Ingin baby."

With the prosperity of the camp came a desire for further improvement. It was proposed to build a hotel in the following spring, and to invite one or two decent families to reside there for the sake of The Luck, who might perhaps profit by female companionship. The sacrifice that this concession to the sex cost these men, who were fiercely skeptical in regard to its general virtue and usefulness, can only be accounted for by their affection for Tommy. A few still held out. But the resolve could not be carried into effect for three months, and the minority meekly yielded in the hope that something might turn up to prevent it. And it did.

The winter of 1851 will long be remembered in the foothills. The snow lay deep on the Sierras, and every mountain creek became a river, and every river a lake. Each gorge and gulch was transformed into a tumultuous watercourse that descended the hillsides, tearing down giant trees and scattering its drift and dedbris along the plain. Red Dog had been twice under water, and Roaring Camp had been forewarned. "Water put the gold into them gulches," said Stumpy. "It's been here once and will be here again!" And that night the North Fork suddenly leaped over its banks and swept up the triangular valley of Roaring Camp.

In the confusion of rushing water, crashing trees, and crackling timber, and the darkness which seemed to flow with the water and blot out the fair valley, but little could be done to collect the scattered camp. When the morning broke, the cabin of Stumpy, nearest the river-bank, was gone. Higher up the gulch they found the body of its unlucky owner; but the pride, the hope, the joy, The Luck, of Roaring Camp had disappeared. They were returning with sad hearts when a shout from the bank recalled them.

It was a relief-boat from down the river. They had picked up, they said, a man and an infant, nearly exhausted, about two miles below. Did anybody know them, and did they belong here?

It needed but a glance to show them Kentuck lying there, cruelly crushed and bruised, but still holding The Luck of Roaring Camp in his arms. As they bent over the strangely assorted pair, they saw that the child was cold and pulseless. "He is dead!" said one. Kentuck opened his eyes. "Dead?" he repeated feebly. "Yes, my man, and you are dying too." A smile lit the eyes of the expiring Kentucky "Dying!" he repeated; "he's a-taking me with him. Tell the boys I've got The Luck with me now;" and the strong man, clinging to the frail babe as a drowning man is said to cling to a straw, drifted away into the shadowy river that flows forever to the unknown sea.

Markheim

Robert Louis Stevenson
1884

Originally prepared for the *Pall Mall Gazette* in 1884, but published in 1885 in *The Broken Shaft: Tales of Mid-Ocean* as part of *Unwin's Christmas Annual*.[1] The story was later published in Stevenson's collection *The Merry Men and Other Tales and Fables* (1887).

"Yes," said the dealer, "our windfalls are of various kinds. Some customers are ignorant, and then I touch a dividend on my superior knowledge. Some are dishonest," and here he held up the candle, so that the light fell strongly on his visitor, "and in that case," he continued, "I profit by my virtue."

Markheim had but just entered from the daylight streets, and his eyes had not yet grown familiar with the mingled shine and darkness in the shop. At these pointed words, and before the near presence of the flame, he blinked painfully and looked aside.

The dealer chuckled. "You come to me on Christmas Day," he resumed, "when you know that I am alone in my house, put up my shutters, and make a point of refusing business. Well, you will have to pay for that; you will have to pay for my loss of time, when I should be balancing my books; you will have to pay, besides, for a kind of manner that I remark in you to-day very strongly. I am the essence of discretion, and ask no awkward questions; but when a customer cannot look me in the eye, he has to pay for it." The dealer once more chuckled; and then, changing to his usual business voice, though still with a note of irony, "You can give, as usual, a clear account of how you came into the possession of the object?" he continued. "Still your uncle's cabinet? A remarkable collector, sir!"

[1] *The Broken Shaft: Tales of Mid-Ocean* (ed. H. Norman), *Unwin's Christmas Annual*, London: T. Fisher Unwin, December 1885.

And the little pale, round-shouldered dealer stood almost on tiptoe, looking over the top of his gold spectacles, and nodding his head with every mark of disbelief. Markheim returned his gaze with one of infinite pity, and a touch of horror.

"This time," said he, "you are in error. I have not come to sell, but to buy. I have no curios to dispose of; my uncle's cabinet is bare to the wainscot; even were it still intact, I have done well on the Stock Exchange, and should more likely add to it than otherwise, and my errand to-day is simplicity itself. I seek a Christmas present for a lady," he continued, waxing more fluent as he struck into the speech he had prepared; "and certainly I owe you every excuse for thus disturbing you upon so small a matter. But the thing was neglected yesterday; I must produce my little compliment at dinner; and, as you very well know, a rich marriage is not a thing to be neglected."

There followed a pause, during which the dealer seemed to weigh this statement incredulously. The ticking of many clocks among the curious lumber of the shop, and the faint rushing of the cabs in a near thoroughfare, filled up the interval of silence.

"Well, sir," said the dealer, "be it so. You are an old customer after all; and if, as you say, you have the chance of a good marriage, far be it from me to be an obstacle. Here is a nice thing for a lady, now," he went on, "this hand glass—fifteenth century, warranted; comes from a good collection, too; but I reserve the name, in the interests of my customer, who was just like yourself, my dear sir, the nephew and sole heir of a remarkable collector."

The dealer, while he thus ran on in his dry and biting voice, had stooped to take the object from its place; and, as he had done so, a shock had passed through Markheim, a start both of hand and foot, a sudden leap of many tumultuous passions to the face. It passed as swiftly as it came, and left no trace beyond a certain trembling of the hand that now received the glass.

"A glass," he said hoarsely, and then paused, and repeated it more clearly. "A glass? For Christmas? Surely not?"

"And why not?" cried the dealer. "Why not a glass?"

Markheim was looking upon him with an indefinable expression. "You ask me why not?" he said. "Why, look here—look in it—look at yourself! Do you like to see it? No! nor I—nor any man."

The little man had jumped back when Markheim had so suddenly confronted him with the mirror; but now, perceiving there was nothing worse on hand, he chuckled. "Your future lady, sir, must be pretty hard favored," said he.

"I ask you," said Markheim, "for a Christmas present, and you give me this—this damned reminder of years and sins and follies—this hand-conscience! Did you mean it? Had you a thought in your mind? Tell me. It will be better for you if you do. Come, tell me about yourself. I hazard a guess now, that you are in secret a very charitable man?"

The dealer looked closely at his companion. It was very odd, Markheim did not appear to be laughing; there was something in his face like an eager sparkle of hope, but nothing of mirth.

"What are you driving at?" the dealer asked.

"Not charitable?" returned the other, gloomily. "Not charitable; not pious; not scrupulous; unloving, unbeloved; a hand to get money, a safe to keep it. Is that all? Dear God, man, is that all?"

"I will tell you what it is," began the dealer, with some sharpness, and then broke off again into a chuckle. "But I see this is a love match of yours, and you have been drinking the lady's health."

"Ah!" cried Markheim, with a strange curiosity. "Ah, have you been in love? Tell me about that."

"I!" cried the dealer. "I in love! I never had the time, nor have I the time to-day for all this nonsense. Will you take the glass?"

"Where is the hurry?" returned Markheim. "It is very pleasant to stand here talking; and life is so short and insecure that I would not hurry away from any pleasure—no, not even from so mild a one as this. We should rather cling, cling to what little we can get, like a man at a cliff's edge. Every second is a cliff, if you think upon it—a cliff a mile high—high enough, if we fall, to dash us out of every feature of humanity. Hence it is best to talk pleasantly. Let us talk of each other; why should we wear this mask? Let us be confidential. Who knows, we might become friends?"

"I have just one word to say to you," said the dealer. "Either make your purchase, or walk out of my shop."

"True, true," said Markheim. "Enough fooling. To business. Show me something else."

The dealer stooped once more, this time to replace the glass upon the shelf, his thin blond hair falling over his eyes as he did so. Markheim moved a little nearer, with one hand in the pocket of his greatcoat; he drew himself up and filled his lungs; at the same time many different emotions were depicted together on his face—terror, horror, and resolve, fascination, and a physical repulsion; and through a haggard lift of his upper lip, his teeth looked out.

"This, perhaps, may suit," observed the dealer; and then, as he began to re-arise, Markheim bounded from behind upon his victim. The long, skewer-like dagger flashed and fell. The dealer struggled like a hen, striking his temple on the shelf, and then tumbled on the floor in a heap.

Time had some score of small voices in that shop, some stately and slow as was becoming to their great age, others garrulous and hurried. All these told out the seconds in an intricate chorus of tickings. Then the passage of a lad's feet, heavily running on the pavement, broke in upon these smaller voices and startled Markheim into the consciousness of his surroundings. He looked about him awfully. The candle stood on the counter, its flame solemnly wagging in a draught; and by that inconsiderable movement, the whole room was filled with noiseless bustle and kept heaving like a sea: the tall shadows nodding, the gross blots of darkness swelling and dwindling as with respiration, the faces of the portraits and the china gods changing and wavering like images in water. The inner door stood ajar, and peered into that leaguer of shadows with a long slit of daylight like a pointing finger.

From these fear-stricken rovings, Markheim's eyes returned to the body of his victim, where it lay both humped and sprawling, incredibly small and strangely meaner than in life. In these poor, miserly clothes, in that ungainly attitude, the dealer lay like so much sawdust. Markheim had feared to see it, and, lo! it was nothing And yet, as he gazed, this bundle of old clothes and pool of blood began to find eloquent voices. There it must lie; there was none to work the cunning hinges or direct the miracle of locomotion—there it must lie till it was found. Found! aye, and then? Then would this dead flesh lift up a cry that would ring over England, and fill the world with the echoes of pursuit. Aye, dead or not, this was still the enemy. "Time was that when the brains were out," he thought; and the first word struck into his mind. Time, now that the deed was accomplished—time, which had closed for the victim, had become instant and momentous for the slayer.

The thought was yet in his mind, when, first one and then another, with every variety of pace and voice—one deep as the bell from a cathedral turret, another ringing on its treble notes the prelude of a waltz—the clocks began to strike the hour of three in the afternoon.

The sudden outbreak of so many tongues in that dumb chamber staggered him. He began to bestir himself, going to and fro with the candle, beleaguered by moving shadows, and startled to the soul by chance reflections. In many rich mirrors, some of home designs, some from Venice or Amsterdam, he saw his face repeated and repeated, as it were an army of spies; his own eyes met and detected him; and the sound of his own steps, lightly as they fell, vexed the surrounding quiet. And still as he continued to fill his pockets, his mind accused him, with a sickening iteration, of the thousand faults of his design. He should have chosen a more quiet hour; he should have prepared an alibi; he should not have used a knife; he should have been more cautious, and only bound and gagged the dealer, and not killed him; he should have been more bold, and killed the servant also; he should have done all things otherwise; poignant regrets, weary, incessant toiling of the mind to change what was unchangeable, to plan what was now useless, to be the architect of the irrevocable past. Meanwhile, and behind all this activity, brute terrors, like the scurrying of rats in a deserted attic, filled the more remote chambers of his brain with riot; the hand of the constable would fall heavy on his shoulder, and his nerves would jerk like a hooked fish; or he beheld, in galloping defile, the dock, the prison, the gallows, and the black coffin.

Terror of the people in the street sat down before his mind like a besieging army. It was impossible, he thought, but that some rumor of the struggle must have reached their ears and set on edge their curiosity; and now, in all the neighboring houses, he divined them sitting motionless and with uplifted ear—solitary people, condemned to spend Christmas dwelling alone on memories of the past, and now startlingly recalled from that tender exercise; happy family parties, struck into silence round the table, the mother still with raised finger: every degree and age and humor, but all, by their own hearths, prying and hearkening and weaving the rope that was to hang him. Sometimes it seemed to him he could not move too softly; the clink of the tall Bohemian goblets rang out loudly like a bell; and alarmed by the bigness of the ticking, he was tempted to stop the clocks. And then, again, with a swift transition of his terrors, the very silence of the place appeared a source of peril, and a thing to strike and freeze the passer-by; and he would step more boldly, and bustle aloud among the contents of the shop, and imitate, with elaborate bravado, the movements of a busy man at ease in his own house.

But he was now so pulled about by different alarms that, while one portion of his mind was still alert and cunning, another trembled on the brink of lunacy. One hallucination in particular took a strong hold on his credulity. The neighbor hearkening with white face beside his window, the passer-by arrested by a horrible surmise on the pavement—these could at worst suspect, they could not know; through the brick walls and shuttered windows only sounds could penetrate. But here, within the house, was he alone? He knew he was; he had watched the servant set forth sweethearting, in her poor best, "out for the day" written in every ribbon and smile. Yes, he was alone, of course; and yet, in the bulk of empty house about him, he could surely hear a stir of delicate footing—he was surely conscious, inexplicably conscious of some presence. Aye, surely; to every room and corner of the house his imagination followed it; and now it was a faceless thing, and yet had eyes to see with; and again it was a shadow of himself; and yet again behold the image of the dead dealer, reinspired with cunning and hatred.

At times, with a strong effort, he would glance at the open door which still seemed to repel his eyes. The house was tall, the skylight small and dirty, the day blind with fog; and the light that filtered down to the ground story was exceedingly faint, and showed dimly on the threshold of the shop. And yet, in that strip of doubtful brightness, did there not hang wavering a shadow?

Suddenly, from the street outside, a very jovial gentleman began to beat with a staff on the shop door, accompanying his blows with shouts and railleries in which the dealer was continually called upon by name. Markheim, smitten into ice, glanced at the dead man. But no! he lay quite still; he was fled away far beyond ear-shot of these blows and shoutings; he was sunk beneath seas of silence; and his name, which would once have caught his notice above the howling of a storm, had become an empty sound. And presently the jovial gentleman desisted from his knocking and departed.

Here was a broad hint to hurry what remained to be done, to get forth from this accusing neighborhood, to plunge into a bath of London multitudes, and to reach, on the other side of day, that haven of safety and apparent innocence—his bed. One visitor had come: at any moment another might follow and be more obstinate. To have done the deed, and yet not to reap the profit, would be too abhorrent a failure. The money, that was now Markheim's concern; and as a means to that, the keys.

He glanced over his shoulder at the open door, where the shadow was still lingering and shivering; and with no conscious repugnance of the mind, yet with a tremor of the belly, he drew near the body of his victim. The human character had quite departed. Like a suit half-stuffed with bran, the limbs lay scattered, the trunk doubled, on the floor; and yet the thing repelled him. Although so dingy and inconsiderable to the eye, he feared it might have more significance to the touch. He took the body by the shoulders, and turned it on its back. It was strangely light and supple, and the limbs, as if they had been broken, fell into the oddest postures. The face was robbed of all expression; but it was as pale as wax, and shockingly smeared with blood about one temple. That was, for Markheim, the one displeasing circumstance. It carried him back, upon the instant, to a certain fair day in a fishers' village: a gray day, a piping wind, a crowd upon the street, the blare of brasses, the booming of drums, the nasal voice of a ballad singer; and a boy going to and fro, buried over head in the crowd and divided between interest and fear, until, coming out upon the chief place of concourse, he beheld a booth and a great screen with pictures, dismally designed, garishly colored: Brownrigg with her apprentice; the Mannings with their murdered guest; Weare in the death grip of Thurtell; and a score besides of famous crimes. The thing was as clear as an illusion; he was once again that little boy; he was looking once again, and with the same sense of physical revolt, at these vile pictures; he was still stunned by the thumping of the drums. A bar of that day's music returned upon his memory; and at that, for the first time, a qualm came over him, a breath of nausea, a sudden weakness of the joints, which he must instantly resist and conquer.

He judged it more prudent to confront than to flee from these considerations; looking the more hardily in the dead face, bending his mind to realize the nature and greatness of his crime. So little a while ago that face had moved with every change of sentiment, that pale mouth had spoken, that body had been all on fire with governable energies; and now, and by his act, that piece of life had been arrested, as the horologist, with interjected finger, arrests the beating of the clock. So he reasoned in vain; he could rise to no more remorseful consciousness; the same heart which had shuddered before the painted effigies of crime, looked on its reality unmoved. At best, he felt a gleam of pity for one who had been endowed in vain with all those faculties that can make the world a garden of enchantment, one who had never lived and who was now dead. But of penitence, no, not a tremor.

With that, shaking himself clear of these considerations, he found the keys and advanced toward the open door of the shop. Outside, it had begun to rain smartly; and the sound of the shower upon the roof had banished silence. Like some dripping cavern, the chambers of the house were haunted by an incessant echoing, which filled the ear and mingled with the ticking of the clocks. And, as Markheim approached the door, he seemed to hear, in answer to his own cautious tread, the steps of another foot withdrawing up the stair. The shadow still palpitated loosely on the threshold. He threw a ton's weight of resolve upon his muscles, and drew back the door.

The faint, foggy daylight glimmered dimly on the bare floor and stairs; on the bright suit of armor posted, halbert in hand, upon the landing; and on the dark wood carvings and framed pictures that hung against the yellow panels of the wainscot. So loud was the beating of the rain through all the house that, in Markheim's ears, it began to be distinguished into many different sounds. Footsteps and sighs, the tread of regiments marching in the distance, the chink of money in the counting, and the creaking of doors held stealthily ajar, appeared to mingle with the patter of the drops upon the cupola and the gushing of the water in the pipes. The sense that he was not alone grew upon him to the verge of madness. On every side he was haunted and begirt by presences. He heard them moving in the upper chambers; from the shop, he heard the dead man getting to his legs; and as he began with a great effort to mount the stairs, feet fled quietly before him and followed stealthily behind. If he were but deaf, he thought, how tranquilly he would possess his soul! And then again, and hearkening with ever fresh attention, he blessed himself for that unresting sense which held the outposts and stood a trusty sentinel upon his life. His head turned continually on his neck; his eyes, which seemed starting from their orbits, scouted on every side, and on every side were half rewarded as with the tail of something nameless vanishing. The four-and-twenty steps to the first floor were four-and-twenty agonies.

On that first story the doors stood ajar, three of them like three ambushes, shaking his nerves like the throats of cannon. He could never again, he felt, be sufficiently immured and fortified from men's observing eyes; he longed to be home, girt in by walls, buried among bedclothes, and invisible to all but God. And at that thought he wondered a little, recollecting tales of other murderers and the fear they were said to entertain of heavenly avengers. It was not so, at least, with him. He feared the laws of nature, lest, in their callous and immutable procedure, they should preserve some damning evidence of his crime. He feared tenfold more, with a slavish, superstitious terror, some scission in the continuity of man's experience, some willful illegality of nature. He played a game of skill, depending on the rules, calculating consequence from cause; and what if nature, as the defeated tyrant overthrew the chessboard, should break the mold of their succession? The like had befallen Napoleon (so writers said) when the winter changed the time of its appearance. The like might befall Markheim: the solid walls might become transparent and reveal his doings like those of bees in a glass hive; the stout planks might yield under his foot like quicksands and detain him in their clutch; aye, and there were soberer accidents that might destroy him: if, for instance, the house should fall and imprison him beside the body of his victim; or the house next door should fly on fire, and the firemen invade him from all sides. These things he feared; and, in a sense, these things might be called the hands of God reached forth against sin. But about God himself he was at ease; his act was doubtless exceptional, but so were his excuses, which God knew; it was there, and not among men, that he felt sure of justice.

When he got safe into the drawing-room, and shut the door behind him, he was aware of a respite from alarms. The room was quite dismantled, uncarpeted besides, and strewn with packing cases and incongruous furniture; several great pier glasses, in which he beheld himself at various angles, like an actor on a stage; many pictures, framed and unframed, standing, with their faces to the wall; a fine Sheraton sideboard, a cabinet of marquetry, and a great old bed, with tapestry hangings. The windows opened to the floor; but by great good fortune the lower part of the shutters had been closed, and this concealed him from the neighbors. Here, then, Markheim drew in a packing case before the cabinet, and began to search among the keys. It was a long business, for there were many; and it was irksome, besides; for, after all, there might be nothing in the cabinet, and time was on the wing. But the closeness of the occupation sobered him. With the tail of his eye he saw the door—even glanced at it from time to time directly, like a besieged commander pleased to verify the good estate of his defenses. But in truth he was at peace. The rain falling in the street sounded natural and pleasant. Presently, on the other side, the notes of a piano were wakened to the music of a hymn, and the voices of many children took up the air and words. How stately, how comfortable was the melody! How fresh the youthful voices! Markheim gave ear to it smilingly, as he sorted out the keys; and his mind was thronged with answerable ideas and images; church-going children and the pealing of the high organ; children afield, bathers by the brookside, ramblers on the brambly common, kite-flyers in the windy and cloud-navigated sky; and then, at another cadence of the hymn, back again to church, and the somnolence of summer Sundays, and the high, genteel voice of the parson (which he smiled a little to recall), and the painted Jacobean tombs, and the dim lettering of the Ten Commandments in the chancel.

And as he sat thus, at once busy and absent, he was startled to his feet. A flash of ice, a flash of fire, a bursting gush of blood, went over him, and then he stood transfixed and thrilling. A step mounted the stair slowly and steadily, and presently a hand was laid upon the knob, and the lock clicked, and the door opened.

Fear held Markheim in a vise. What to expect he knew not, whether the dead man walking, or the official ministers of human justice, or some chance witness blindly stumbling in to consign him to the gallows. But when a face was thrust into the aperture, glanced round the room, looked at him, nodded and smiled as if in friendly recognition, and then withdrew again, and the door closed behind it, his fear broke loose from his control in a hoarse cry. At the sound of this the visitant returned.

"Did you call me?" he asked pleasantly, and with that he entered the room and closed the door behind him.

Markheim stood and gazed at him with all his eyes. Perhaps there was a film upon his sight, but the outlines of the newcomer seemed to change and waver like those of the idols in the wavering candlelight of the shop: and at times he thought he knew him; and at times he thought he bore a likeness to himself; and always, like a lump of living terror, there lay in his bosom the conviction that this thing was not of the earth and not of God.

And yet the creature had a strange air of the common-place, as he stood looking on Markheim with a smile; and when he added: "You are looking for the money, I believe?" it was in the tones of every-day politeness.

Markheim made no answer.

"I should warn you," resumed the other, "that the maid has left her sweetheart earlier than usual and will soon be here. If Mr. Markheim be found in this house, I need not describe to him the consequences."

"You know me?" cried the murderer.

The visitor smiled. "You have long been a favorite of mine," he said; "and I have long observed and often sought to help you."

"What are you?" cried Markheim: "the devil?"

"What I may be," returned the other, "cannot affect the service I propose to render you."

"It can," cried Markheim; "it does! Be helped by you? No, never; not by you! You do not know me yet; thank God, you do not know me!"

"I know you," replied the visitant, with a sort of kind severity or rather firmness. "I know you to the soul."

"Know me!" cried Markheim. "Who can do so? My life is but a travesty and slander on myself. I have lived to belie my nature. All men do; all men are better than this disguise that grows about and stifles them. You see each dragged away by life, like one whom bravos have seized and muffled in a cloak. If they had their own control—if you could see their faces, they would be altogether different, they would shine out for heroes and saints! I am worse than most; myself is more overlaid; my excuse is known to me and God. But, had I the time, I could disclose myself."

"To me?" inquired the visitant.

"To you before all," returned the murderer. "I supposed you were intelligent. I thought—since you exist—you would prove a reader of the heart. And yet you would propose to judge me by my acts! Think of it; my acts! I was born and I have lived in a land of giants; giants have dragged me by the wrists since I was born out of my mother—the giants of circumstance. And you would judge me by my acts! But can you not look within? Can you not understand that evil is hateful to me? Can you not see within me the clear writing of conscience, never blurred by any willful sophistry, although too often disregarded? Can you not read me for a thing that surely must be common as humanity—the unwilling sinner?"

"All this is very feelingly expressed," was the reply, "but it regards me not. These points of consistency are beyond my province, and I care not in the least by what compulsion you may have been dragged away, so as you are but carried in the right direction. But time flies; the servant delays, looking in the faces of the crowd and at the pictures on the hoardings, but still she keeps moving nearer; and remember, it is as if the gallows itself were striding toward you through the Christmas streets! Shall I help you—I, who know all? Shall I tell you where to find the money?"

"For what price?" asked Markheim.

"I offer you the service for a Christmas gift," returned the other.

Markheim could not refrain from smiling with a kind of bitter triumph. "No," said he, "I will take nothing at your hands; if I were dying of thirst, and it was your hand that put the pitcher to my lips, I should find the courage to refuse. It may be credulous, but I will do nothing to commit myself to evil."

"I have no objection to a death-bed repentance," observed the visitant.

"Because you disbelieve their efficacy!" Markheim cried.

"I do not say so," returned the other; "but I look on these things from a different side, and when the life is done my interest falls. The man has lived to serve me, to spread black looks under color of religion, or to sow tares in the wheat field, as you do, in a course of weak compliance with desire. Now that he draws so near to his deliverance, he can add but one act of service— to repent, to die smiling, and thus to build up in confidence and hope the more timorous of my surviving followers. I am not so hard a master. Try me. Accept my help. Please yourself in life as you have done hitherto; please yourself more amply, spread your elbows at the board; and when the night begins to fall and the curtains to be drawn, I tell you, for your greater comfort, that you will find it even easy to compound your quarrel with your conscience, and to make a truckling peace with God. I came but now from such a death-bed, and the room was full of sincere mourners, listening to the man's last words; and when I looked into that face, which had been set as a flint against mercy, I found it smiling with hope."

"And do you, then, suppose me such a creature?" asked Markheim. "Do you think I have no more generous aspirations than to sin, and sin, and sin, and, at last, sneak into heaven? My heart rises at the thought. Is this, then, your experience of mankind? or is it because you find me with red hands that you presume such baseness? and is this crime of murder indeed so impious as to dry up the very springs of good?"

"Murder is to me no special category," replied the other. "All sins are murder, even as all life is war. I behold your race, like starving mariners on a raft, plucking crusts out of the hands of famine and feeding on each other's lives. I follow sins beyond the moment of their acting; I find in all that the last consequence is death; and to my eyes, the pretty maid who thwarts her mother with such taking graces on a question of a ball, drips no less visibly with human gore than such a murderer as yourself. Do I say that I follow sins? I follow virtues also; they differ not by the thickness of a nail, they are both scythes for the reaping angel of Death. Evil, for which I live, consists not in action but in character. The bad man is dear to me; not the bad act, whose fruits, if we could follow them far enough down the hurtling cataract of the ages, might yet be found more blessed than those of the rarest virtues. And it is not because you have killed a dealer, but because you are Markheim, that I offered to forward your escape."

"I will lay my heart open to you," answered Markheim. "This crime on which you find me is my last. On my way to it I have learned many lessons; itself is a lesson, a momentous lesson. Hitherto I have been driven with revolt to what I would not; I was a bondslave to poverty, driven and scourged. There are robust virtues that can stand in these temptations; mine was not so: I had a thirst of pleasure. But to-day, and out of this deed, I pluck both warning and riches—both the power and a fresh resolve to be myself. I become in all things a free actor in the world; I begin to see myself all changed, these hands the agents of good, this heart at peace. Something comes over me out of the past; something of what I have dreamed on Sabbath evenings to the sound of the church organ, of what I forecast when I shed tears over noble books, or talked, an innocent child, with my mother. There lies my life; I have wandered a few years, but now I see once more my city of destination."

"You are to use this money on the Stock Exchange, I think?" remarked the visitor; "and there, if I mistake not, you have already lost some thousands?"

"Ah," said Markheim, "but this time I have a sure thing."

"This time, again, you will lose," replied the visitor, quietly.

"Ah, but I keep back the half!" cried Markheim.

"That also you will lose," said the other.

The sweat started upon Markheim's brow. "Well, then, what matter?" he exclaimed. "Say it be lost, say I am plunged again in poverty, shall one part of me, and that the worse, continue until the end to override the better? Evil and good run strong in me, hailing me both ways. I do not love the one thing, I love all. I can conceive great deeds, renunciations, martyrdoms; and though I be fallen to such a crime as murder, pity is no stranger to my thoughts. I pity the poor; who knows their trials better than myself? I pity and help them; I prize love, I love honest laughter; there is no good thing nor true thing on earth but I love it from my heart. And are my vices only to direct my life, and my virtues to lie without effect, like some passive lumber of the mind? Not so; good, also, is a spring of acts."

But the visitant raised his finger. "For six-and thirty years that you have been in this world," said he, "through many changes of fortune and varieties of humor, I have watched you steadily fall. Fifteen years ago you would have started at a theft. Three years back you would have blenched at the name of murder. Is there any crime, is there any cruelty or meanness, from which you still recoil?—five years from now I shall detect you in the fact! Downward, downward lies your way; nor can anything but death avail to stop you."

"It is true," Markheim said huskily, "I have in some degree complied with evil. But it is so with all: the very saints, in the mere exercise of living, grow less dainty, and take on the tone of their surroundings."

"I will propound to you one simple question," said the other; "and as you answer, I shall read to you your moral horoscope. You have grown in many things more lax; possibly you do right to be so; and at any account, it is the same with all men. But granting that, are you in any one particular, however trifling, more difficult to please with your own conduct, or do you go in all things with a looser rein?"

"In any one?" repeated Markheim, with an anguish of consideration. "No," he added, with despair, "in none! I have gone down in all."

"Then," said the visitor, "content yourself with what you are, for you will never change; and the words of your part on this stage are irrevocably written down."

Markheim stood for a long while silent, and indeed it was the visitor who first broke the silence. "That being so," he said, "shall I show you the money?"

"And grace?" cried Markheim.

"Have you not tried it?" returned the other. "Two or three years ago, did I not see you on the platform of revival meetings, and was not your voice the loudest in the hymn?"

"It is true," said Markheim; "and I see clearly what remains for me by way of duty. I thank you for these lessons from my soul; my eyes are opened, and I behold myself at last for what I am."

At this moment, the sharp note of the door bell rang through the house; and the visitant, as though this were some concerted signal for which he had been waiting, changed at once in his demeanor.

"The maid!" he cried. "She has returned, as I forewarned you, and there is now before you one more difficult passage. Her master, you must say, is ill; you must let her in, with an assured but rather serious countenance—no smiles, no overacting, and I promise you success! Once the girl within, and the door closed, the same dexterity that has already rid you of the dealer will relieve you of this last danger in your path. Thence-forward you have the whole evening—the whole night, if needful—to ransack the treasures of the house and to make good your safety. This is help that comes to you with the mask of danger. Up!" he cried: "up, friend; your life hangs trembling in the scales: up, and act!"

Markheim steadily regarded his counselor. "If I be condemned to evil acts," he said, "there is still one door of freedom open—I can cease from action. If my life be an ill thing, I can lay it down. Though I be, as you say truly, at the beck of every small

temptation, I can yet, by one decisive gesture, place myself beyond the reach of all. My love of good is damned to

barrenness; it may, and let it be! But I have still my hatred of evil; and from that, to your galling disappointment, you shall see that I can draw both energy and courage."

The features of the visitor began to undergo a wonderful and lovely change: they brightened and softened with a tender triumph; and, even as they brightened, faded and dislimned. But Markheim did not pause to watch or understand the transformation. He opened the door and went downstairs very slowly, thinking to himself. His past went soberly before him; he beheld it as it was, ugly and strenuous like a dream, random as chance-medley—a scene of defeat. Life, as he thus reviewed it, tempted him no longer; but on the farther side he perceived a quiet haven for his bark. He paused in the passage, and looked into the shop, where the candle still burned by the dead body. It was strangely silent. Thoughts of the dealer swarmed into his mind, as he stood gazing. And then the bell once more broke out into impatient clamor.

He confronted the maid upon the threshold with something like a smile.

"You had better go for the police," said he: "I have killed your master."

A White Heron

Sarah Orne Jewett
1886

The story was originally published in *A White Heron & Other Stories* (1886), then reprinted in *Tales of New England* (1890). This text is from a reprinting of the 1914 edition of *A White Heron & Other Stories*.

I

The woods were already filled with shadows one June evening, just before eight o'clock, though a bright sunset still glimmered faintly among the trunks of the trees. A little girl was driving home her cow, a plodding, dilatory, provoking creature in her behavior, but a valued companion for all that. They were going away from whatever light there was, and striking deep into the woods, but their feet were familiar with the path, and it was no matter whether their eyes could see it or not.

There was hardly a night the summer through when the old cow could be found waiting at the pasture bars; on the contrary, it was her greatest pleasure to hide herself away among the huckleberry bushes, and though she wore a loud bell she had made the discovery that if one stood perfectly still it would not ring. So Sylvia had to hunt for her until she found her, and call Co'! Co'! with never an answering Moo, until her childish patience was quite spent. If the creature had not given good milk and plenty of it, the case would have seemed very different to her owners. Besides, Sylvia had all the time there was, and very little use to make of it. Sometimes in pleasant weather it was a consolation to look upon the cow's pranks as an intelligent attempt to play hide and seek, and as the child had no playmates she lent herself to this amusement with a good deal of zest. Though this chase had been so long that the wary animal herself had given an unusual signal of her whereabouts, Sylvia had only laughed when she came upon Mistress Moolly at the swamp-side, and urged her affectionately homeward with a twig of birch leaves. The old cow was not inclined to wander farther, she even turned in the right direction for once as they left the pasture, and stepped along the road at a good pace. She was quite ready to be milked now, and seldom stopped to browse. Sylvia wondered what her grandmother would say because they were so late. It was a great while since she had left home at half-past five o'clock, but everybody knew the difficulty of making this errand a short one. Mrs. Tilley had chased the hornéd torment too many summer evenings herself to blame any one else for lingering, and was only thankful as she waited that she had Sylvia, nowadays, to give such valuable assistance. The good woman suspected that Sylvia loitered occasionally on her own account; there never was such a child for straying about out-of-doors since the world was made! Everybody said that it was a good change for a little maid who had tried to grow for eight years in a crowded manufacturing town, but, as for Sylvia herself, it seemed as if she never had been alive at all before she came to live at the farm. She thought often with wistful compassion of a wretched geranium that belonged to a town neighbor.

"'Afraid of folks,'" old Mrs. Tilley said to herself, with a smile, after she had made the unlikely choice of Sylvia from her daughter's houseful of children, and was returning to the farm. "'Afraid of folks,' they said! I guess she won't be troubled no great with 'em up to the old place!" When they reached the door of the lonely house and stopped to unlock it, and the cat came to purr loudly, and rub against them, a deserted pussy, indeed, but fat with young robins, Sylvia whispered that this was a beautiful place to live in, and she never should wish to go home.

The companions followed the shady wood-road, the cow taking slow steps and the child very fast ones. The cow stopped long at the brook to drink, as if the pasture were not half a swamp, and Sylvia stood still and waited, letting her bare feet cool themselves in the shoal water, while the great twilight moths struck softly against her. She waded on through the brook as the cow moved away, and listened to the thrushes with a heart that beat fast with pleasure. There was a stirring in the great boughs overhead. They were full of little birds and beasts that seemed to be wide awake, and going about their world, or else saying good-night to each other in sleepy twitters. Sylvia herself felt sleepy as she walked along. However, it was not much farther to the house, and the air was soft and sweet. She was not often in the woods so late as this, and it made her feel as if she were a part of the gray shadows and the moving leaves. She was just thinking how long it seemed since she first came to the farm a year ago, and wondering if everything went on in the noisy town just the same as when she was there, the thought of the great red-faced boy who used to chase and frighten her made her hurry along the path to escape from the shadow of the trees.

Suddenly this little woods-girl is horror-stricken to hear a clear whistle not very far away. Not a bird's-whistle, which would have a sort of friendliness, but a boy's whistle, determined, and somewhat aggressive. Sylvia left the cow to whatever sad fate might await her, and stepped discreetly aside into the bushes, but she was just too late. The enemy had discovered her, and called out in a very cheerful and persuasive tone, "Halloa, little girl, how far is it to the road?" and trembling Sylvia answered almost inaudibly, "A good ways."

She did not dare to look boldly at the tall young man, who carried a gun over his shoulder, but she came out of her bush and again followed the cow, while he walked alongside.

"I have been hunting for some birds," the stranger said kindly, "and I have lost my way, and need a friend very much. Don't be afraid," he added gallantly. "Speak up and tell me what your name is, and whether you think I can spend the night at your house, and go out gunning early in the morning."

Sylvia was more alarmed than before. Would not her grandmother consider her much to blame? But who could have foreseen such an accident as this? It did not seem to be her fault, and she hung her head as if the stem of it were broken, but managed to answer "Sylvy," with much effort when her companion again asked her name.

Mrs. Tilley was standing in the doorway when the trio came into view. The cow gave a loud moo by way of explanation.

"Yes, you'd better speak up for yourself, you old trial! Where'd she tucked herself away this time, Sylvy?" But Sylvia kept an awed silence; she knew by instinct that her grandmother did not comprehend the gravity of the situation. She must be mistaking the stranger for one of the farmer-lads of the region.

The young man stood his gun beside the door, and dropped a lumpy game-bag beside it; then he bade Mrs. Tilley good-evening, and repeated his wayfarer's story, and asked if he could have a night's lodging.

"Put me anywhere you like," he said. "I must be off early in the morning, before day; but I am very hungry, indeed. You can give me some milk at any rate, that's plain."

"Dear sakes, yes," responded the hostess, whose long slumbering hospitality seemed to be easily awakened. "You might fare better if you went out to the main road a mile or so, but you're welcome to what we've got. I'll milk right off, and you make yourself at home. You can sleep on husks or feathers," she proffered graciously. "I raised them all myself. There's good pasturing for geese just below here towards the ma'sh. Now step round and set a plate for the gentleman, Sylvy!" And Sylvia promptly stepped. She was glad to have something to do, and she was hungry herself.

It was a surprise to find so clean and comfortable a little dwelling in this New England wilderness. The young man had known the horrors of its most primitive housekeeping, and the dreary squalor of that level of society which does not rebel at the companionship of hens. This was the best thrift of an old-fashioned farmstead, though on such a small scale that it seemed like a hermitage. He listened eagerly to the old woman's quaint talk, he watched Sylvia's pale face and shining gray eyes with ever growing enthusiasm, and insisted that this was the best supper he had eaten for a month, and afterward the new-made friends sat down in the door-way together while the moon came up.

Soon it would be berry-time, and Sylvia was a great help at picking. The cow was a good milker, though a plaguy thing to keep track of, the hostess gossiped frankly, adding presently that she had buried four children, so Sylvia's mother, and a son (who might be dead) in California were all the children she had left. "Dan, my boy, was a great hand to go gunning," she explained sadly. "I never wanted for pa'tridges or gray squer'ls while he was to home. He's been a great wand'rer, I expect, and he's no hand to write letters. There, I don't blame him, I'd ha' seen the world myself if it had been so I could.

"Sylvy takes after him," the grandmother continued affectionately, after a minute's pause. "There ain't a foot o' ground she don't know her way over, and the wild creaturs counts her one o' themselves. Squer'ls she'll tame to come an' feed right out o' her hands, and all sorts o' birds. Last winter she got the jay-birds to bangeing here, and I believe she'd 'a' scanted herself of her own meals to have plenty to throw out amongst 'em, if I hadn't kep' watch. Anything but crows, I tell her, I'm willin' to help support—though Dan he had a tamed one o' them that did seem to have reason same as folks. It was round here a good spell after he went away. Dan an' his father they didn't hitch,—but he never held up his head ag'in after Dan had dared him an' gone off."

The guest did not notice this hint of family sorrows in his eager interest in something else.

"So Sylvy knows all about birds, does she?" he exclaimed, as he looked round at the little girl who sat, very demure but increasingly sleepy, in the moonlight. "I am making a collection of birds myself. I have been at it ever since I was a boy." (Mrs. Tilley smiled.) "There are two or three very rare ones I have been hunting for these five years. I mean to get them on my own ground if they can be found."

"Do you cage 'em up?" asked Mrs. Tilley doubtfully, in response to this enthusiastic announcement.

"Oh no, they're stuffed and preserved, dozens and dozens of them," said the ornithologist, "and I have shot or snared every one myself. I caught a glimpse of a white heron a few miles from here on Saturday, and I have followed it in this direction. They have never been found in this district at all. The little white heron, it is," and he turned again to look at Sylvia with the hope of discovering that the rare bird was one of her acquaintances.

But Sylvia was watching a hop-toad in the narrow footpath.

"You would know the heron if you saw it," the stranger continued eagerly. "A queer tall white bird with soft feathers and long thin legs. And it would have a nest perhaps in the top of a high tree, made of sticks, something like a hawk's nest."

Sylvia's heart gave a wild beat; she knew that strange white bird, and had once stolen softly near where it stood in some bright green swamp grass, away over at the other side of the woods. There was an open place where the sunshine always seemed strangely yellow and hot, where tall, nodding rushes grew, and her grandmother had warned her that she might sink in the soft black mud underneath and never be heard of more. Not far beyond were the salt marshes just this side the sea itself, which Sylvia wondered and dreamed much about, but never had seen, whose great voice could sometimes be heard above the noise of the woods on stormy nights.

"I can't think of anything I should like so much as to find that heron's nest," the handsome stranger was saying. "I would give ten dollars to anybody who could show it to me," he added desperately, "and I mean to spend my whole vacation hunting for it if need be. Perhaps it was only migrating, or had been chased out of its own region by some bird of prey."

Mrs. Tilley gave amazed attention to all this, but Sylvia still watched the toad, not divining, as she might have done at some calmer time, that the creature wished to get to its hole under the door-step, and was much hindered by the unusual spectators at that hour of the evening. No amount of thought, that night, could decide how many wished-for treasures the ten dollars, so lightly spoken of, would buy.

The next day the young sportsman hovered about the woods, and Sylvia kept him company, having lost her first fear of the friendly lad, who proved to be most kind and sympathetic. He told her many things about the birds and what they knew and where they lived and what they did with themselves. And he gave her a jack-knife, which she thought as great a treasure as if she were a desert-islander. All day long he did not once make her troubled or afraid except when he brought down some unsuspecting singing creature from its bough. Sylvia would have liked him vastly better without his gun; she could not understand why he killed the very birds he seemed to like so much. But as the day waned, Sylvia still watched the young man with loving admiration. She had never seen anybody so charming and delightful; the woman's heart, asleep in the child, was vaguely thrilled by a dream of love. Some premonition of that great power stirred and swayed these young creatures who traversed the solemn woodlands with soft-footed silent care. They stopped to listen to a bird's song; they pressed forward again eagerly, parting the branches—speaking to each other rarely and in whispers; the young man going first and Sylvia following, fascinated, a few steps behind, with her gray eyes dark with excitement.

She grieved because the longed-for white heron was elusive, but she did not lead the guest, she only followed, and there was no such thing as speaking first. The sound of her own unquestioned voice would have terrified her—it was hard enough to answer yes or no when there was need of that. At last evening began to fall, and they drove the cow home together, and Sylvia smiled with pleasure when they came to the place where she heard the whistle and was afraid only the night before.

II

Half a mile from home, at the farther edge of the woods, where the land was highest, a great pine-tree stood, the last of its generation. Whether it was left for a boundary mark, or for what reason, no one could say; the woodchoppers who had felled its mates were dead and gone long ago, and a whole forest of sturdy trees, pines and oaks and maples, had grown again. But the stately head of this old pine towered above them all and made a landmark for sea and shore miles and miles away. Sylvia knew it well. She had always believed that whoever climbed to the top of it could see the ocean; and the little girl had often laid her hand on the great rough trunk and looked up wistfully at those dark boughs that the wind always stirred, no matter how hot and still the air might be below. Now she thought of the tree with a new excitement, for why, if one climbed it at break of day, could not one see all the world, and easily discover from whence the white heron flew, and mark the place, and find the hidden nest?

What a spirit of adventure, what wild ambition! What fancied triumph and delight and glory for the later morning when she could make known the secret! It was almost too real and too great for the childish heart to bear.

All night the door of the little house stood open and the whippoorwills came and sang upon the very step. The young sportsman and his old hostess were sound asleep, but Sylvia's great design kept her broad awake and watching. She forgot to think of sleep. The short summer night seemed as long as the winter darkness, and at last when the whippoorwills ceased, and she was afraid the morning would after all come too soon, she stole out of the house and followed the pasture path through the woods, hastening toward the open ground beyond, listening with a sense of comfort and companionship to the drowsy twitter of a half-awakened bird, whose perch she had jarred in passing. Alas, if the great wave of human interest which flooded for the first time this dull little life should sweep away the satisfactions of an existence heart to heart with nature and the dumb life of the forest!

There was the huge tree asleep yet in the paling moonlight, and small and silly Sylvia began with utmost bravery to mount to the top of it, with tingling, eager blood coursing the channels of her whole frame, with her bare feet and fingers, that pinched and held like bird's claws to the monstrous ladder reaching up, up, almost to the sky itself. First she must mount the white oak tree that grew alongside, where she was almost lost among the dark branches and the green leaves heavy and wet with dew; a bird fluttered off its nest, and a red squirrel ran to and fro and scolded pettishly at the harmless housebreaker. Sylvia felt her way easily. She had often climbed there, and knew that higher still one of the oak's upper branches chafed against the pine trunk, just where its lower boughs were set close together. There, when she made the dangerous pass from one tree to the other, the great enterprise would really begin.

She crept out along the swaying oak limb at last, and took the daring step across into the old pine-tree. The way was harder than she thought; she must reach far and hold fast, the sharp dry twigs caught and held her and scratched her like angry talons, the pitch made her thin little fingers clumsy and stiff as she went round and round the tree's great stem, higher and higher upward. The sparrows and robins in the woods below were beginning to wake and twitter to the dawn, yet it seemed much lighter there aloft in the pine-tree, and the child knew she must hurry if her project were to be of any use.

The tree seemed to lengthen itself out as she went up, and to reach farther and farther upward. It was like a great main-mast to the voyaging earth; it must truly have been amazed that morning through all its ponderous frame as it felt this determined spark of human spirit wending its way from higher branch to branch. Who knows how steadily the least twigs held themselves to advantage this light, weak creature on her way! The old pine must have loved his new dependent. More than all the hawks, and bats, and moths, and even the sweet voiced thrushes, was the brave, beating heart of the solitary gray-eyed child. And the tree stood still and frowned away the winds that June morning while the dawn grew bright in the east.

Sylvia's face was like a pale star, if one had seen it from the ground, when the last thorny bough was past, and she stood trembling and tired but wholly triumphant, high in the tree-top. Yes, there was the sea with the dawning sun making a golden dazzle over it, and toward that glorious east flew two hawks with slow-moving pinions. How low they looked in the air from that height when one had only seen them before far up, and dark against the blue sky. Their gray feathers were as soft as moths; they seemed only a little way from the tree, and Sylvia felt as if she too could go flying away among the clouds. Westward, the woodlands and farms reached miles and miles into the distance; here and there were church steeples, and white villages, truly it was a vast and awesome world

The birds sang louder and louder. At last the sun came up bewilderingly bright. Sylvia could see the white sails of ships out at sea, and the clouds that were purple and rose-colored and yellow at first began to fade away. Where was the white heron's nest in the sea of green branches, and was this wonderful sight and pageant of the world the only reward for having climbed to such a giddy height? Now look down again, Sylvia, where the green marsh is set among the shining birches and dark hemlocks; there where you saw the white heron once you will see him again; look, look! a white spot of him like a single floating feather comes up from the dead hemlock and grows larger, and rises, and comes close at last, and goes by the landmark pine with steady sweep of wing and outstretched slender neck and crested head. And wait! wait! do not move a foot or a finger, little girl, do not send an arrow of light and consciousness from your two eager eyes, for the heron has perched on a pine bough not far beyond yours, and cries back to his mate on the nest and plumes his feathers for the new day!

The child gives a long sigh a minute later when a company of shouting cat-birds comes also to the tree, and vexed by their fluttering and lawlessness the solemn heron goes away. She knows his secret now, the wild, light, slender bird that floats and wavers, and goes back like an arrow presently to his home in the green world beneath. Then Sylvia, well satisfied, makes her perilous way down again, not daring to look far below the branch she stands on, ready to cry sometimes because her fingers ache and her lamed feet slip. Wondering over and over again what the stranger would say to her, and what he would think when she told him how to find his way straight to the heron's nest.

"Sylvy, Sylvy!" called the busy old grandmother again and again, but nobody answered, and the small husk bed was empty and Sylvia had disappeared.

The guest waked from a dream, and remembering his day's pleasure hurried to dress himself that it might sooner begin. He was sure from the way the shy little girl looked once or twice yesterday that she had at least seen the white heron, and now she must really be made to tell. Here she comes now, paler than ever, and her worn old frock is torn and tattered, and smeared with pine pitch. The grandmother and the sportsman stand in the door together and question her, and the splendid moment has come to speak of the dead hemlock-tree by the green marsh.

But Sylvia does not speak after all, though the old grandmother fretfully rebukes her, and the young man's kind, appealing eyes are looking straight in her own. He can make them rich with money; he has promised it, and they are poor now. He is so well worth making happy, and he waits to hear the story she can tell.

No, she must keep silence! What is it that suddenly forbids her and makes her dumb? Has she been nine years growing and now, when the great world for the first time puts out a hand to her, must she thrust it aside for a bird's sake? The murmur of the pine's green branches is in her ears, she remembers how the white heron came flying through the golden air and how they watched the sea and the morning together, and Sylvia cannot speak; she cannot tell the heron's secret and give its life away.

Dear loyalty, that suffered a sharp pang as the guest went away disappointed later in the day, that could have served and followed him and loved him as a dog loves! Many a night Sylvia heard the echo of his whistle haunting the pasture path as she came home with the loitering cow. She forgot even her sorrow at the sharp report of his gun and the sight of thrushes and sparrows dropping silent to the ground, their songs hushed and their pretty feathers stained and wet with blood. Were the birds better friends than their hunter might have been,—who can tell? Whatever treasures were lost to her, woodlands and summer-time, remember! Bring your gifts and graces and tell your secrets to this lonely country child!

The Sheriff's Children

Charles Waddell Chesnutt
1889

The story was first published in *The New York Independent*, November 7, 1889. Later, it was collected in *The Wife of His Youth*, 1899.

Branson County, North Carolina, is in a sequestered district of one of the staidest and most conservative States of the Union. Society in Branson County is almost primitive in its simplicity. Most of the white people own their own farms, and even before the War there were no very wealthy families to force their neighbors, by comparison, into the category of "poor whites."

To Branson County, as to most rural communities in the South, the War is the one historical event that overshadows all others. It is the era from which all local chronicles are dated—births, deaths, marriages, storms, freshets. No description of the life of any Southern community would be perfect that failed to emphasize the all-pervading influence of the great conflict.

And yet the fierce tide of war that had rushed through the cities and along the great highways of the country, had, comparatively speaking, but slightly disturbed the sluggish current of life in this region remote from railroads and navigable streams. To the north in Virginia, to the west in Tennessee, and all along the seaboard the war had raged; but the thunder of its cannon had not disturbed the echoes of Branson County, where the loudest sounds heard were the crack of some hunter's rifle, the baying of some deep-mouthed hound, or the yodel of some tuneful Negro on his way through the pine forest. To the east, Sherman's army had passed on its march to the sea; but no straggling band of "bummers" had penetrated the confines of Branson County. The war, it is true, had robbed the county of the flower of its young manhood; but the burden of taxation, the doubt and uncertainty of the conflict, and the sting of ultimate defeat, had been borne by the people with an apathy that robbed misfortune of half its sharpness.

The nearest approach to town life afforded by Branson County is found in the little village of Troy, the county-seat, a hamlet with a population of four or five hundred.

Ten years make little difference in the appearance of these remote Southern towns. If a railroad is built through one of them, it infuses some enterprise; the social corpse is galvanized by the fresh blood of civilization that pulses along the farthest ramifications of our great system of commercial highways. At the period of which I write, no railroad had come to Troy. If a traveler, accustomed to the bustling life of cities, could have ridden through Troy on a summer day, he might easily have fancied himself in a deserted village. Around him he would have seen weather-beaten houses, innocent of paint, the shingled roofs in many instances covered with a rich growth of moss. Here and there he would have met a razor-backed hog lazily rooting his way along the principal thoroughfare; and more than once be would probably have had to disturb the slumbers of some yellow dog, dozing away the hours in the ardent sunshine, and reluctantly yielding up his place in the middle of the dusty road.

On Saturdays the village presented a somewhat livelier appearance, and the shade-trees around the court-house square and along Front Street served as hitching-posts for a goodly number of horses and mules and stunted oxen, belonging to the farmer-folk who had come in to trade at the two or three local stores.

A murder was a rare event in Branson County. Every well-informed citizen could tell the number of homicides committed in the county for fifty years back, and whether the slayer, in any given instance, had escaped, either by flight or acquittal, or had suffered the penalty of the law. So, when it became known in Troy early one Friday morning in summer, about ten years after the war, that old Captain Walker, who had served in Mexico under Scott, and had left an arm on the field of Gettysburg, had been foully murdered during the night, there was intense excitement in the village. Business was practically suspended, and the citizens gathered in little groups to discuss the murder, and speculate upon the identity of the murderer. It transpired from testimony at the coroner's inquest, held during the morning, that a strange mulatto had been seen going in the direction of Captain Walker's house the night before, and had been met going away from Troy early Friday morning, by a farmer on his way to town. Other circumstances seemed to connect the stranger with the crime. The sheriff organized a posse to search for him, and early in the evening, when most of the citizens of Troy were at supper, the suspected man was brought in and lodged in the county jail.

By the following morning the news of the capture had spread to the farthest limits of the county. A much larger number of people than usual came to town that Saturday—bearded men in straw hats and blue homespun shirts, and butternut trousers of great amplitude of material and vagueness of outline; women in homespun frocks and slat-bonnets, with faces as expressionless as the dreary sandhills which gave them a meagre sustenance.

The murder was almost the sole topic of conversation. A steady stream of curious observers visited the house of mourning, and gazed upon the rugged face of the old veteran, now stiff and cold in death; and more than one eye dropped a tear at the remembrance of the cheery smile, and the joke—sometimes superannuated, generally feeble, but always good-natured—with which the captain had been wont to greet his acquaintances. There was a growing sentiment of anger among these stern men, toward the murderer who had thus cut down their friend, and a strong feeling that ordinary justice was too slight a punishment for such a crime

Toward noon there was an informal gathering of citizens in Dan Tyson's store.

"I hear it 'lowed that Square Kyahtah's too sick ter hole co'te this evenin'," said one, "an' that the purlim'nary hearin' 'll haf ter go over tel nex' week."

A look of disappointment went round the crowd.

"Hit 's the durndes', meanes' murder ever committed in this caounty," said another, with moody emphasis.

"I s'pose the Nigger 'lowed the Cap'n had some greenbacks," observed a third speaker.

"The Cap'n," said another, with an air of superior information, "has left two bairls of Confedrit money, which he 'spected 'ud be good some day er nuther."

This statement gave rise to a discussion of the speculative value of Confederate money; but in a little while the conversation returned to the murder.

"Hangin' air too good fer the murderer," said one; "he oughter be burnt, stidier bein' hung."

There was an impressive pause at this point, during which a jug of moonlight whiskey went the round of the crowd.

"Well," said a round-shouldered farmer, who, in spite of his peaceable expression and faded gray eye, was known to have been one of the most daring followers of a rebel guerrilla chieftain, "what air yer gwine ter do about it? Ef you fellers air gwine ter set down an' let a wuthless Nigger kill the bes' white man in Branson, an' not say nuthin' ner do nuthin', I 'll move outen the caounty."

This speech gave tone and direction to the rest of the conversation. Whether the fear of losing the round-shouldered farmer operated to bring about the result or not is immaterial to this narrative; but, at all events, the crowd decided to lynch the Negro. They agreed that this was the least that could be done to avenge the death of their murdered friend, and that it was a becoming way in which to honor his memory. They had some vague notions of the majesty of the law and the rights of the citizen, but in the passion of the moment these sunk into oblivion; a white man had been killed by a Negro.

"The Cap'n was an ole sodger," said one of his friends, solemnly. "He 'll sleep better when he knows that a co'te-martial has be'n hilt an' jestice done."

By agreement the lynchers were to meet at Tyson's store at five o'clock in the afternoon, and proceed thence to the jail, which was situated down the Lumberton Dirt Road (as the old turnpike antedating the plank-road was called), about half a mile south of the court-house. When the preliminaries of the lynching had been arranged, and a committee appointed to manage the affair, the crowd dispersed, some to go to their dinners, and some to quietlysecure recruits for the lynching party.

It was twenty minutes to five o'clock, when an excited Negro, panting and perspiring, rushed up to the back door of Sheriff Campbell's dwelling, which stood at a little distance from the jail and somewhat farther than the latter building from the court house. A turbaned colored woman came to the door in response to the egro's knock.

"Hoddy, Sis' Nance."

"Hoddy, Brer Sam."

"Is de shurff in," inquired the Negro.

"Yas, Brer Sam, he's eatin' his dinner," was the answer.

"Will yer ax 'im ter step ter de do' a minute, Sis' Nance?"

The woman went into the dining-room, and a moment later the sheriff came to the door. He was a tall, muscular man, of a ruddier complexion than is usual among Southerners. A pair of keen, deep-set gray eyes looked out from under bushy eye-brows, and about his mouth was a masterful expression, which a full beard, once sandy in color, but now profusely sprinkled with gray, could not entirely conceal. The day was hot; the sheriff had discarded his coat and vest, and had his white shirt open at the throat.

"What do you want, Sam?" he inquired of the Negro, who stood hat in hand, wiping the moisture from his face with a ragged shirt-sleeve.

"Shurff, dey gwine ter hang de pris'ner w'at's lock' up in de jail. Dey 're comin' dis a-way now. I wuz layin' down on a sack er corn down at de sto', behine a pile er flour-bairls, w'en I hearn Doc' Cain en Kunnel Wright talkin' erbout it. I slip' outen de back do', en run here as fas' as I could. I hearn you say down ter de sto' once't dat you wouldn't let nobody take a pris'ner 'way fum you widout walkin' over yo' dead body, en I thought I'd let you know 'fo dey come, so yer could pertec' de pris'ner."

The sheriff listened calmly, but his face grew firmer, and a determined gleam lit up his gray eyes. His frame grew more erect, and he unconsciously assumed the attitude of a soldier who momentarily expects to meet the enemy face to face.

"Much obliged, Sam," he answered. "I'll protect the prisoner. Who 's coming?"

"I dunno who-all is comin'," replied the Negro. "Dere's Mistah McSwayne, en Doc' Cain, en Maje' McDonal', en Kunnel Wright, en a heap er yuthers. I wuz so skeered I done furgot mo'd'n half un em. I spec' dey mus' be mos' here by dis time, so I'll git outen de way; fer I doan want nobody fer ter think I wuz mix' up in dis business." The Negro glanced nervously down the road toward the town, and made a movement as if to go away.

"Won't you have some dinner first?" asked the sheriff.

The Negro looked longingly in at the open door, and sniffed the appetizing odor of boiled pork and collards.

"I ain't got no time fer ter tarry, Shurff," he said, "but Sis' Nance mought gin me sump'n I could kyar in my han' en eat on de way."

A moment later Nancy brought him a huge sandwich, consisting of split corn-pone, with a thick slice of fat bacon inserted between the halves, and a couple of baked yams. The Negro hastily replaced his ragged hat on his head, dropped the yams in the pocket of his capacious trousers, and taking the sandwich in his hand, hurried across the road and disappeared in the woods beyond.

The sheriff re-entered the house, and put on his coat and hat. He then took down a double-barreled shot-gun and loaded it with buckshot. Filling the chambers of a revolver with fresh cartridges, he slipped it into the pocket of the sack-coat which he wore.

A comely young woman in a calico dress watched these proceedings with anxious surprise.

"Where are you goin', Pa," she asked. She had not heard the conversation with the Negro.

"I am goin' over to the jail," responded the sheriff. "There's a mob comin' this way to lynch the Nigger we've got locked up. But they won't do it," he added, with emphasis.

"Oh, Pa! don't go!" pleaded the girl, clinging to his arm; "they'll shoot you if you don't give him up."

"You never mind me, Polly," said her father re-assuringly, as he gently unclasped her hands from his arm. " I'll take care of myself and the prisoner, too. There ain't a man in Branson County that would shoot me. Besides, I have faced fire too often to be scared away from my duty. You keep close in the house," he continued, "and if any one disturbs you just use the old horse-pistol in the top bureau drawer. It 's a little old-fashioned, but it did good work a few years ago."

The young girl shuddered at this sanguinary allusion, but made no further objection to her father's departure.

The sheriff of Branson was a man far above the average of the community in wealth, education and social position. His had been one of the few families in the county that before the war had owned large estates and numerous slaves. He had graduated at the State University at Chapel Hill, and had kept up some acquaintance with current literature and advanced thought. He had traveled some in his youth, and was looked up to in the county as an authority on all subjects connected with the outer world. At first an ardent supporter of the Union, he had opposed the secession movement in his native State as long as opposition availed to stem the tide of public opinion. Yielding at last to the force of circumstances, he had entered the Confederate service rather late in the war, and served with distinction through several campaigns, rising in time to the rank of colonel. After the war he had taken the oath of allegiance, and had been chosen by the people as the most available candidate for the office of sheriff, to which he had been elected without opposition. He had filled the office for several terms, and was universally popular with his constituents.

Colonel, or Sheriff Campbell, as he was indifferently called, as the military or civil title happened to be most important in the opinion of the person addressing him, had a high sense of the responsibility attaching to his office. He had sworn to do his duty faithfully, and he knew what his duty was, as sheriff, perhaps more clearly than he had apprehended it in other passages of his life. It was, therefore, with no uncertainty in regard to his course that he prepared his weapons and went over to the jail. He had no fears for Polly's safety.

The sheriff had just locked the heavy front door of the jail behind him when a half-dozen horsemen, followed by a crowd of men on foot, came round a bend in the road and drew near the jail. They halted in front of the picket fence that surrounded the building, while several of the committee of arrangements rode on a few rods farther to the sheriff's house. One of them dismounted and rapped on the door with his riding-whip.

"Is the sheriff at home?" he inquired.

"No, he has just gone out," replied Polly, who had come to the door.

"We want the jail keys," he continued.

"They are not here," said Polly. "The sheriff has them himself." And then she added, with assumed indifference, "He is at the jail now."

The man turned away, and Polly went into the front room, from which she peered anxiously between the slats of the green blinds of a window that looked toward the jail. Meanwhile the messenger returned to his companions and announced his discovery. It looked as tho the sheriff had got wind of their design and was preparing to resist it.

One of them stepped forward and rapped on the jail door.

"Well, what is it?" said the sheriff, from within.

"We want to talk to you, Sheriff," replied the spokesman.

There was a little wicket in the door, this the sheriff opened, and answered through it.

"All right, boys, talk away. You are all strangers to me, and I don't know what business you can have." The sheriff did not think it necessary to recognize anybody in particular on such an occasion; the question of identity sometimes comes up in the investigation of these extra-judicial executions.

"We're a committee of citizens and we want to get into the jail."

"What for? It ain't much trouble to get into jail. Most people are anxious to keep out."

The mob was in no humor to appreciate a joke, and the sheriff's witticism fell dead upon an unresponsive audience.

"We want to have a talk with the Nigger that killed Cap'n Walker."

"You can talk to that Nigger in the court-house, when he 's brought out for trial. Court will be in session here next week. I know what you fellows want; but you can't get my prisoner to-day. Do you want to take the bread out of a poor man's mouth? I get seventy-five cents a day for keeping this prisoner, and he's the only one in jail. I can't have my family suffer just to please you fellows."

One or two young men in the crowd laughed at the idea of Sheriff Campbell's suffering for want of seventy-five cents a day; but they were frowned into silence by those who stood near them.

"Ef yer don't let us in," cried a voice, "we'll bu's' the do' open."

"Bu'st away," answered the sheriff, raising his voice so that all could hear. "But I give you fair warning. The first man that tries it will be filled with buckshot. I'm sheriff of this county, and I know my duty, and I mean to do it."

"What's the use of kicking, Sheriff," argued one of the leaders of the mob. "The Nigger is sure to hang anyhow; he richly deserves it; and we 've got to do something to teach the Niggers their places, or white people won't be able to live in the county."

"There 's no use talking, boys," responded the sheriff. "I'm a white man outside, but in this jail I'm sheriff; and if this Nigger's to be hung in this county, I propose to do the hanging. So you fellows might as well right-about-face, and march back to Troy. You've had a pleasant trip, and the exercise will be good for you. You know me. I've got powder and ball, and I've faced fire before now, with nothing between me and the enemy, and I don't mean to surrender this jail while I 'm able to shoot." Having thus announced his determination the sheriff closed and fastened the wicket, and looked around for the best position from which to defend the building.

The crowd drew off a little, and the leaders conversed together in low tones.

The Branson County jail was a small, two-story brick building, strongly constructed, with no attempt at architectural ornamentation. Each story was divided into two large cells by a passage running from front to rear. A grated iron door gave entrance from the passage to each of the four cells. The jail seldom had many prisoners in it, and the lower windows had been boarded up. When the sheriff had closed the wicket, he ascended the steep wooden stair to the upper floor. There was no window at the front of the upper passage, and the most available position from which to watch the movements of the crowd below was the front window of the cell occupied by the solitary prisoner.

The sheriff unlocked the door and entered the cell. The prisoner was crouched in a corner, his yellow face, blanched with terror, looking ghastly in the semi-darkness of the room. A cold perspiration had gathered on his forehead, and his teeth were chattering with affright.

"For God's sake, Sheriff," he murmured hoarsely, "don't let 'em lynch me; I didn't kill the old man."

The sheriff glanced at the cowering wretch with a look of mingled contempt and loathing.

"Get up," he said sharply. "You will probably be hung sooner or later, but it will not be to-day, if I can help it. I will unlock your fetters, and if I can't hold the jail, you will have to make the best fight you can. If I am shot, I will consider my responsibility at an end."

There were iron fetters on the prisoner's ankles, and handcuffs on his wrist. These the sheriff unlocked, and they fell clanking to the floor.

"Keep back from the window," said the sheriff. "They might shoot if they saw you."

The sheriff drew toward the window a pine bench which formed a part of the scanty furniture of the cell, and laid his revolver upon it. Then he took his gun in hand, and took his stand at the side of the window where he could with least exposure of himself watch the movements of the crowd below.

The lynchers had not anticipated any determined resistance. Of course they had looked for a formal protest, and perhaps a sufficient show of opposition to excuse the sheriff in the eye of any stickler for legal formalities. But they had not come prepared to fight a battle, and no one of them seemed willing to lead an attack upon the jail. The leaders of the party conferred together with a good deal of animated gesticulation, which was visible to the sheriff from his outlook, tho the distance was too great for him to hear what was said. At length one of them broke away from the group, and rode back to the main body of the lynchers, who were restlessly awaiting orders.

"Well, boys," said the messenger, "we'll have to let it go for the present. The sheriff says he'll shoot, and he's got the drop on us this time. There ain't any of us that want to follow Cap'n Walker jest yet. Besides, the sheriff is a good fellow, and we don't want to hurt 'im. But," he added, as if to re-assure the crowd, which began to show signs of disappointment, "the Nigger might as well say his prayers, for he ain't got long to live."

There was a murmur of dissent from the mob, and several voices insisted that an attack be made on the jail. But pacific counsels finally prevailed, and the mob sullenly withdrew.

The sheriff stood at the window until they had disappeared around the bend in the road. He did not relax his watchfulness when the last one was out of sight. Their withdrawal might be a mere feint, to be followed by a further attempt. So closely, indeed, was his attention drawn to the outside, that he neither saw nor heard the prisoner creep stealthily across the floor, reach out his hand and secure the revolver which lay on the bench behind the sheriff, and creep as noiselessly back to his place in the corner of the room.

A moment after the last of the lynching party had disappeared there was a shot fired from the woods across the road; a bullet whistled by the window and buried itself in the wooden casing a few inches from where the sheriff was standing. Quick as thought, with the instinct born of a semi-guerrilla army experience, he raised his gun and fired twice at the point from which a faint puff of smoke showed the hostile bullet to have been sent. He stood a moment watching, and then rested his gun against the window, and reached behind him mechanically for the other weapon. It was not on the bench. As the sheriff realized this fact, he turned his head and looked into the muzzle of the revolver.

"Stay where you are, Sheriff," said the prisoner, his eyes glistening, his face almost ruddy with excitement.

The sheriff mentally cursed his own carelessness for allowing him to be caught in such a predicament. He had not expected anything of the kind. He had relied on the Negro's cowardice and subordination in the presence of an armed white man as a matter of course. The sheriff was a brave man, but realized that the prisoner had him at an immense disadvantage. The two men stood thus for a moment, fighting a harmless duel with their eyes.

"Well, what do you mean to do?" asked the sheriff, with apparent calmness.

"To get away, of course," said the prisoner, in a tone which caused the sheriff to look at him more closely, and with an involuntary feeling of apprehension; if the man was not mad, he was in a state of mind akin to madness, and quite as dangerous. The sheriff felt that he must speak the prisoner fair, and watch for a chance to turn the tables on him. The keen-eyed, desperate man before him was a different being altogether from the groveling wretch who had begged so piteously for life a few minutes before.

At length the sheriff spoke:

"Is this your gratitude to me for saving your life at the risk of my own? If I had not done so, you would now be swinging from the limb of some neighboring tree."

"True," said the prisoner, "you saved my life, but for how long? When you came in, you said Court would sit next week. When the crowd went away they said I had not long to live. It is merely a choice of two ropes."

"While there's life there's hope," replied the sheriff. He uttered this commonplace mechanically, while his brain was busy in trying to think out some way of escape. "If you are innocent you can prove it."

The mulatto kept his eye upon the sheriff. "I didn't kill the old man," he replied; "but I shall never be able to clear myself. I was at his house at nine o'clock. I stole from it the coat that was on my back when I was taken. I would be convicted, even with a fair trial, unless the real murderer were discovered beforehand."

The sheriff knew this only too well. While he was thinking what argument next to use, the prisoner continued:

"Throw me the keys—no, unlock the door."

The sheriff stood a moment irresolute. The mulatto's eye glittered ominously. The sheriff crossed the room and unlocked the door leading into the passage.

"Now go down and unlock the outside door."

The heart of the sheriff leaped within him. Perhaps he might make a dash for liberty, and gain the outside. He descended the narrow stair, the prisoner keeping close behind him.

The sheriff inserted the huge iron key into the lock. The rusty bolt yielded slowly. It still remained for him to pull the door open.

"Stop!" thundered the mulatto, who seemed to divine the sheriff's purpose. "Move a muscle, and I 'll blow your brains out."

The sheriff obeyed; he realized that his chance had not yet come.

"Now keep on that side of the passage, and go back up-stairs."

Keeping the sheriff in front of him, the mulatto followed the other up the stairs. The sheriff expected the prisoner to lock him into the cell and make his own escape. He had about come to the conclusion that the best thing he could do under the circumstances was to submit quietly, and take his chances of recapturing the prisoner after the alarm had been given. The sheriff had faced death more than once upon the battle-field. A few minutes before, well armed, and with a brick wall between him and them he had dared a hundred men to fight; but he felt instinctively that the desperate man in front of him was not to be trifled with, and he was too prudent a man to risk his life against such heavy odds. He had Polly to look after, and there was a limit beyond which devotion to duty would be quixotic and even foolish.

"I want to get away," said the prisoner, "and I don't want to be captured; for if I am, I know I will be hung on the spot. I am afraid," he added somewhat reflectively, "that in order to save myself I shall have to kill you."

"Good God!" exclaimed the sheriff, in involuntary terror; "you would not kill the man to whom you owe your own life."

"You speak more truly than you know," replied the mulatto. "I indeed owe my life to you."

The sheriff started. He was capable of surprise, even in that moment of extreme peril. "Who are you?" he asked in amazement.

"Tom, Cicely's son," returned the other. He had closed the door and stood talking to the sheriff through the grated opening. "Don't you remember Cicely—Cicely, whom you sold, with her child, to the speculator on his way to Alabama?"

The sheriff did remember. He had been sorry for it many a time since. It had been the old story of debts, mortgages and bad crops. He had quarreled with the mother. The price offered for her and her child had been unusually large, and he had yielded to the combination of anger and pecuniary stress.

"Good God!" he gasped, "you would not murder your own father?"

"My father?" replied the mulatto. "It were well enough for me to claim the relationship, but it comes with poor grace from you to ask anything by reason of it. What father's duty have you ever performed for me? Did you give me your name, or even your protection? Other white men gave their colored sons freedom and money, and sent them to the free States. You sold me to the rice swamps."

"I at least gave you the life you cling to," murmured the sheriff.

"Life?" said the prisoner, with a sarcastic laugh. "What kind of a life? You gave me your own blood, your own features—no man need look at us together twice to see that—and you gave me a black mother. Poor wretch! She died under the lash, because she had enough womanhood to call her soul her own. You gave me a white man's spirit, and you made me a slave, and crushed it out."

"But you are free now," said the sheriff. He had not doubted, could not doubt, the mulatto's word. He knew whose passions coursed beneath that swarthy skin and burned in the black eyes opposite his own. He saw in this mulatto what he himself might have become had not the safeguards of parental restraint and public opinion been thrown around him.

"Free to do what?" replied the mulatto. "Free in name, but despised and scorned and set aside by the people to whose race I belong far more than to that of my mother."

"There are schools," said the sheriff. "You have been to school." He had noticed that the mulatto spoke more eloquently and used better language than most Branson County people.

"I have been to school and dreamed when I went that it would work some marvelous change in my condition. But what did I learn? I learned to feel that no degree of learning or wisdom will change the color of my skin and that I shall always wear what in my own country is a badge of degradation. When I think about it seriously I do not care particularly for such a life. It is the animal in me, not the man, that flees the gallows. I owe you nothing," he went on, "and expect nothing of you; and it would be no more than justice if I were to avenge upon you my mother's wrongs and my own. But still I hate to shoot you; I have never yet taken human life—for I did not kill the old captain. Will you promise to give no alarm and make no attempt to capture me until morning, if I do not shoot?"

So absorbed were the two men in their colloquy and their own tumultuous thoughts that neither of them had heard the door below move upon its hinges. Neither of them had heard a light step come stealthily up the stair, nor seen a slender form creep along the darkening passage toward the mulatto.

The sheriff hesitated. The struggle between his love of life and his sense of duty was a terrific one. It may seem strange that a man who could sell his own child into slavery should hesitate at such a moment when his life was trembling in the balance. But the baleful influence of human slavery poisoned the very fountains of life, and created new standards of right. The sheriff was conscientious; his conscience had merely been warped by his environment. Let no one ask what his answer would have been; he was spared the necessity of a decision.

"Stop," said the mulatto, "you need not promise. I could not trust you if you did. It is your life for mine; there is but one safe way for me; you must die."

He raised his arm to fire, when there was a flash—a report from the passage behind him. His arm fell heavily at his side, and the pistol dropped at his feet.

The sheriff recovered first from his surprise, and throwing open the door secured the fallen weapon. Then seizing the prisoner he thrust him into the cell and locked the door upon him; after which he turned to Polly, who leaned half-fainting against the wall, her hands clasped over her heart.

"Oh, Pa, I was just in time!" she cried hysterically, and, wildly sobbing, threw herself into her father's arms.

"I watched until they all went away," she said. "I heard the shot from the woods and I saw you shoot. Then when you did not come out I feared something had happened, that perhaps you had been wounded. I got out the other pistol and ran over here. When I found the door open, I knew something was wrong, and when I heard voices I crept up-stairs, and reached the top just in time to hear him say he would kill you. Oh, it was a narrow escape!"

When she had grown somewhat calmer, the sheriff left her standing there and went back into the cell. The prisoner's arm was bleeding from a flesh wound. His bravado had given place to a stony apathy. There was no sign in his face of fear or disappointment or feeling of any kind. The sheriff sent Polly to the house for cloth, and bound up the prisoner's wound with a rude skill acquired during his army life.

"I will have a doctor come and dress the wound in the morning," he said to the prisoner. "It will do very well until then, if you will keep quiet. If the doctor asks you how the wound was caused, you can say that you were struck by the bullet fired from the woods. It would do you no good to have it known that you were shot while attempting to escape."

The prisoner uttered no word of thanks or apology, but sat in sullen silence. When the wounded arm had been bandaged, Polly and her father returned to the house.

The sheriff was in an unusually thoughtful mood that evening. He put salt in his coffee at supper, and poured vinegar over his pancakes. To many of Polly's questions he returned random answers. When he had gone to bed he lay awake for several hours.

In the silent watches of the night, when he was alone with God, there came into his mind a flood of unaccustomed thoughts. An hour or two before, standing face to face with death, he had experienced a sensation similar to that which drowning men are said to feel—a kind of clarifying of the moral faculty, in which the veil of the flesh, with its obscuring passions and prejudices, is pushed aside for a moment, and all the acts of one's life stand out, in the clear light of truth, in their correct proportions and relations—a state of mind in which one sees himself as God may be supposed to see him. In the reaction following his rescue, this feeling had given place for a time to far different emotions. But now, in the silence of midnight, something of this clearness of spirit returned to the sheriff. He saw that he had owed some duty to this son of his—that neither law nor custom could destroy a responsibility inherent in the nature of mankind. He could not thus, in the eyes of God at least, shake off the consequences of his sin. Had he never sinned, this wayward spirit would never have come back from the vanished past to haunt him. And as he thought, his anger against the mulatto died away, and in its place there sprang up a great, an ineffable pity. The hand of parental authority might have restrained the passions he had seen burning in the prisoner's eyes when the desperate man spoke the words which had seemed to doom his father to death. The sheriff felt that he might have saved this fiery spirit from the slough of slavery; that he might have sent him to the free North, and given him there, or in some other land, an opportunity to turn to usefulness and honorable pursuits the talents that had run to crime, perhaps to madness; he might, still less, have given this son of his the poor simulacrum of liberty which men of his caste could possess in a slave-holding community; or least of all, but still something, he might have kept the boy on the plantation, where the burdens of slavery would have fallen lightly upon him.

The sheriff recalled his own youth. He had inherited an honored name to keep untarnished; he had had a future to make; the picture of a fair young bride had beckoned him on to happiness. The poor wretch now stretched upon a pallet of straw between the brick walls of the jail had had none of these things—no name, no father, no mother—in the true meaning of motherhood—and until the past few years no possible future, and then one vague and shadowy in its outline, and dependent for form and substance upon the slow solution of a problem in which there were many unknown quantities.

From what he might have done to what he might yet do was an easy transition for the awakened conscience of the sheriff. It occurred to him, purely as a hypothesis, that he might permit his prisoner to escape; but his oath of office, his duty as sheriff, stood in the way of such a course, and the sheriff dismissed the idea from his mind. But he could investigate the circumstances of the murder, and move Heaven and earth to discover the real criminal, for he no longer doubted the prisoner's innocence; he could employ counsel for the accused, and perhaps influence public opinion in his favor. An acquittal once secured, some plan could be devised by which the sheriff might in some degree atone for his neglect of what he now clearly perceived to have been a duty.

When the sheriff had reached this conclusion he fell into an unquiet slumber, from which he awoke late the next morning.

He went over to the jail before breakfast and found the prisoner lying on his pallet; his face turned to the wall: he did not move when the sheriff rattled the door.

"Good-morning," said the latter, in a tone intended to waken the prisoner.

There was no response. The sheriff looked more keenly at the recumbent figure; there was an unnatural rigidity about its attitude.

He hastily unlocked the door and, entering the cell, bent over the prostrate form. There was no sound of breathing; he turned the body over, it was cold and stiff. The prisoner had torn the bandage from his wound and bled to death during the night. He had evidently been dead several hours.

The Boarded Window

Ambrose Bierce
1891

The story was first published in the *San Francisco Examiner* on April 12th, 1891.

In 1820, only a few miles away from what is now the great city of Cincinnati, lay an immense and almost unbroken forest. The whole region was sparsely settled by people of the frontier—restless souls who no sooner had hewn fairly habitable homes out of the wilderness and attained to that degree of prosperity which today we should call indigence, than, impelled by some mysterious impulse of their nature, they abandoned all and pushed farther westward, to encounter new perils and privations in the effort to regain the meager comforts which they had voluntarily renounced. Many of them had already forsaken that region for the remoter settlements, but among those remaining was one who had been of those first arriving. He lived alone in a house of logs surrounded on all sides by the great forest, of whose gloom and silence he seemed a part, for no one had ever known him to smile nor speak a needless word. His simple wants were supplied by the sale or barter of skins of wild animals in the river town, for not a thing did he grow upon the land which, if needful, he might have claimed by right of undisturbed possession. There were evidences of "improvement"—a few acres of ground immediately about the house had once been cleared of its trees, the decayed stumps of which were half concealed by the new growth that had been suffered to repair the ravage wrought by the ax. Apparently the man's zeal for agriculture had burned with a failing flame, expiring in penitential ashes.

The little log house, with its chimney of sticks, its roof of warping clapboards weighted with traversing poles and its "chinking" of clay, had a single door and, directly opposite, a window. The latter, however, was boarded up—nobody could remember a time when it was not. And none knew why it was so closed; certainly not because of the occupant's dislike of light and air, for on those rare occasions when a hunter had passed that lonely spot the recluse had commonly been seen sunning himself on his doorstep if heaven had provided sunshine for his need. I fancy there are few persons living today who ever knew the secret of that window, but I am one, as you shall see.

The man's name was said to be Murlock. He was apparently seventy years old, actually about fifty. Something besides years had had a hand in his aging. His hair and long, full beard were white, his gray, lusterless eyes sunken, his face singularly seamed with wrinkles which appeared to belong to two intersecting systems. In figure he was tall and spare, with a stoop of the shoulders—a burden bearer. I never saw him; these particulars I learned from my grandfather, from whom also I got the man's story when I was a lad. He had known him when living near by in that early day.

One day Murlock was found in his cabin, dead. It was not a time and place for coroners and newspapers, and I suppose it was agreed that he had died from natural causes or I should have been told, and should remember. I know only that with what was probably a sense of the fitness of things the body was buried near the cabin, alongside the grave of his wife, who had preceded him by so many years that local tradition had retained hardly a hint of her existence. That closes the final chapter of this true story—excepting, indeed, the circumstance that many years afterward, in company with an equally intrepid spirit, I penetrated to the place and ventured near enough to the ruined cabin to throw a stone against it, and ran away to avoid the ghost which every well-informed boy thereabout knew haunted the spot. But there is an earlier chapter—that supplied by my grandfather.

FICTION

When Murlock built his cabin and began laying sturdily about with his ax to hew out a farm—the rifle, meanwhile, his means of support—he was young, strong and full of hope. In that eastern country whence he came he had married, as was the fashion, a young woman in all ways worthy of his honest devotion, who shared the dangers and privations of his lot with a willing spirit and light heart. There is no known record of her name; of her charms of mind and person tradition is silent and the doubter is at liberty to entertain his doubt; but God forbid that I should share it! Of their affection and happiness there is abundant assurance in every added day of the man's widowed life; for what but the magnetism of a blessed memory could have chained that venturesome spirit to a lot like that?

One day Murlock returned from gunning in a distant part of the forest to find his wife prostrate with fever, and delirious. There was no physician within miles, no neighbor; nor was she in a condition to be left, to summon help. So he set about the task of nursing her back to health, but at the end of the third day she fell into unconsciousness arid so passed away, apparently, with never a gleam of returning reason.

From what we know of a nature like his we may venture to sketch in some of the details of the outline picture drawn by my grandfather. When convinced that she was dead, Murlock had sense enough to remember that the dead must be prepared for burial. In performance of this sacred duty he blundered now and again, did certain things incorrectly, and others which he did correctly were done over and over. His occasional failures to accomplish some simple and ordinary act filled him with astonishment, like that of a drunken man who wonders at the suspension of familiar natural laws. He was surprised, too, that he did not weep—surprised and a little ashamed; surely it is unkind not to weep for the dead. "Tomorrow," he said aloud, "I shall have to make the coffin arid dig the grave; and then I shall miss her, when she is no longer in sight; but now—she is dead, of course, but it is all right—it must be all right, somehow. Things cannot be so bad as they seem."

He stood over the body in the fading light, adjusting the hair and putting the finishing touches to the simple toilet, doing all mechanically, with soulless care. And still through his consciousness ran an undersense of conviction that all was right—that he should have her again as before, and everything explained. He had had no experience in grief; his capacity had not been enlarged by use. His heart could not contain it all, nor his imagination rightly conceive it. He did not know he was so hard struck; that knowledge would come later, and never go. Grief is an artist of powers as various as the instruments upon which he plays his dirges for the dead, evoking from some the sharpest, shrillest notes, from others the low, grave chords that throb recurrent like the slow beating of a distant drum. Some natures it startles; some it stupefies. To one it comes like the stroke of an arrow, stinging all the sensibilities to a keener life; to another as the blow of a bludgeon, which in crushing benumbs. We may conceive Murlock to have been that way affected, for (and here we are upon surer ground than that of conjecture) no sooner had he finished his pious work than, sinking into a chair by the side of the table upon which the body lay, and noting how white the profile showed in the deepening gloom, he laid his arms upon the table's edge, and dropped his face into them, tearless yet and unutterably weary. At that moment came in through the open window a long, wailing sound like the cry of a lost child in the far deeps of the darkening woods! But the man did not move. Again, and nearer than before, sounded that unearthly cry upon his failing sense. Perhaps it was a wild beast; perhaps it was a dream. For Murlock was asleep.

Some hours later, as it afterward appeared, this unfaithful watcher awoke and lifting his head from his arms intently listened—he knew not why. There in the black darkness by the side of the dead, recalling all without a shock, he strained his eyes to see—he knew not what. His senses were all alert, his breath was suspended, his blood had stilled its tides as if to assist the silence. Who—what had waked him, and where was it?

Suddenly the table shook beneath his arms, and at the same moment he heard, or fancied that he heard, a light, soft step—another—sounds as of bare feet upon the floor!

He was terrified beyond the power to cry out or move. Perforce he waited—waited there in the darkness through seeming centuries of such dread as one may know, yet live to tell. He tried vainly to speak the dead woman's name, vainly to stretch forth his hand across the table to learn if she were there. His throat was powerless, his arms and hands were like lead. Then occurred something most frightful. Some heavy body seemed hurled against the table with an impetus that pushed it against his breast so sharply as nearly to overthrow him, and at the same instant he heard and felt the fall of something upon the floor with so violent a thump that the whole house was shaken by the impact. A scuffling ensued, and a confusion of sounds impossible to describe. Murlock had risen to his feet. Fear had by excess forfeited control of his faculties. He flung his hands upon the table. Nothing was there!

There is a point at which terror may turn to madness; and madness incites to action. With no definite intent, from no motive but the wayward impulse of a madman, Murlock sprang to the wall, with a little groping seized his loaded rifle, and without aim discharged it. By the flash which lit up the room with a vivid illumination, he saw an enormous panther dragging the dead woman toward the window, its teeth fixed in her throat! Then there were darkness blacker than before, and silence; and when he returned to consciousness the sun was high and the wood vocal with songs of birds.

The body lay near the window, where the beast had left it when frightened away by the flash and report of the rifle. The clothing was deranged, the long hair in disorder, the limbs lay anyhow. From the throat, dreadfully lacerated, had issued a pool of blood not yet entirely coagulated. The ribbon with which he had bound the wrists was broken; the hands were tightly clenched. Between the teeth was a fragment of the animal's ear.

The Yellow Wallpaper

Charlotte Perkins Gilman
1892

The story was first published in the *New England Magazine,* January, 1892.

It is very seldom that mere ordinary people like John and myself secure ancestral halls for the summer.

A colonial mansion, a hereditary estate, I would say a haunted house, and reach the height of romantic felicity,—but that would be asking too much of fate!

Still I will proudly declare that there is something queer about it.

Else, why should it be let so cheaply? And why have stood so long untenanted?

John laughs at me, of course, but one expects that in marriage.

John is practical in the extreme. He has no patience with faith, an intense horror of superstition, and he scoffs openly at any talk of things not to be felt and seen and put down in figures.

John is a physician, and perhaps—(I would not say it to a living soul, of course, but this is dead paper and a great relief to my mind)—perhaps that is one reason I do not get well faster.

You see, he does not believe I am sick!

And what can one do?

If a physician of high standing, and one's own husband, assures friends and relatives that there is really nothing the matter with one but temporary nervous depression,—a slight hysterical tendency,—what is one to do?

My brother is also a physician, and also of high standing, and he says the same thing.

So I take phosphates or phosphites,—whichever it is,—and tonics, and journeys, and air, and exercise, and am absolutely forbidden to "work" until I am well again.

Personally I disagree with their ideas.

Personally I believe that congenial work, with excitement and change, would do me good.

But what is one to do?

I did write for a while in spite of them; but it does exhaust me a good deal—having to be so sly about it, or else meet with heavy opposition.

I sometimes fancy that in my condition if I had less opposition and more society and stimulus—but John says the very worst thing I can do is to think about my condition, and I confess it always makes me feel bad.

So I will let it alone and talk about the house.

The most beautiful place! It is quite alone, standing well back from the road, quite three miles from the village. It makes me think of English places that you read about, for there are hedges and walls and gates that lock, and lots of separate little houses for the gardeners and people.

There is a delicious garden! I never saw such a garden—large and shady, full of box-bordered paths, and lined with long grape-covered arbors with seats under them.

There were greenhouses, too, but they are all broken now.

There was some legal trouble, I believe, something about the heirs and co-heirs; anyhow, the place has been empty for years.

That spoils my ghostliness, I am afraid; but I don't care—there is something strange about the house—I can feel it.

I even said so to John one moonlight evening, but he said what I felt was a draught, and shut the window.

I get unreasonably angry with John sometimes. I'm sure I never used to be so sensitive. I think it is due to this nervous condition.

But John says if I feel so I shall neglect proper self-control; so I take pains to control myself,—before him, at least,—and that makes me very tired.

I don't like our room a bit. I wanted one downstairs that opened on the piazza and had roses all over the window, and such pretty, old-fashioned chintz hangings! but John would not hear of it.

He said there was only one window and not room for two beds, and no near room for him if he took another.

He is very careful and loving, and hardly lets me stir without special direction.

I have a schedule prescription for each hour in the day; he takes all care from me, and so I feel basely ungrateful not to value it more.

He said we came here solely on my account, that I was to have perfect rest and all the air I could get. "Your exercise depends on your strength, my dear," said he, "and your food somewhat on your appetite; but air you can absorb all the time." So we took the nursery, at the top of the house.

It is a big, airy room, the whole floor nearly, with windows that look all ways, and air and sunshine galore. It was nursery first and then playground and gymnasium, I should judge; for the windows are barred for little children, and there are rings and things in the walls.

The paint and paper look as if a boys' school had used it. It is stripped off—the paper—in great patches all around the head of my bed, about as far as I can reach, and in a great place on the other side of the room low down. I never saw a worse paper in my life.

One of those sprawling flamboyant patterns committing every artistic sin.

It is dull enough to confuse the eye in following, pronounced enough to constantly irritate, and provoke study, and when you follow the lame, uncertain curves for a little distance they suddenly commit suicide—plunge off at outrageous angles, destroy themselves in unheard-of contradictions.

The color is repellant, almost revolting; a smouldering, unclean yellow, strangely faded by the slow-turning sunlight.

It is a dull yet lurid orange in some places, a sickly sulphur tint in others.

No wonder the children hated it! I should hate it myself if I had to live in this room long.

There comes John, and I must put this away,—he hates to have me write a word.

We have been here two weeks, and I haven't felt like writing before, since that first day.

I am sitting by the window now, up in this atrocious nursery, and there is nothing to hinder my writing as much as I please, save lack of strength.

John is away all day, and even some nights when his cases are serious.

I am glad my case is not serious!

But these nervous troubles are dreadfully depressing.

John does not know how much I really suffer. He knows there is no reason to suffer, and that satisfies him.

Of course it is only nervousness. It does weigh on me so not to do my duty in any way!

I meant to be such a help to John, such a real rest and comfort, and here I am a comparative burden already!

Nobody would believe what an effort it is to do what little I am able—to dress and entertain, and order things.

It is fortunate Mary is so good with the baby. Such a dear baby!

And yet I cannot be with him, it makes me so nervous.

I suppose John never was nervous in his life. He laughs at me so about this wall paper!

At first he meant to repaper the room, but afterwards he said that I was letting it get the better of me, and that nothing was worse for a nervous patient than to give way to such fancies.

He said that after the wall paper was changed it would be the heavy bedstead, and then the barred windows, and then that gate at the head of the stairs, and so on.

"You know the place is doing you good," he said, "and really, dear, I don't care to renovate the house just for a three months' rental."

"Then do let us go downstairs," I said, "there are such pretty rooms there."

Then he took me in his arms and called me a blessed little goose, and said he would go down cellar if I wished, and have it whitewashed into the bargain.

But he is right enough about the beds and windows and things.

It is as airy and comfortable a room as any one need wish, and, of course, I would not be so silly as to make him uncomfortable just for a whim.

I'm really getting quite fond of the big room, all but that horrid paper.

Out of one window I can see the garden, those mysterious deep-shaded arbors, the riotous old-fashioned flowers, and bushes and gnarly trees.

Out of another I get a lovely view of the bay and a little private wharf belonging to the estate. There is a beautiful shaded lane that runs down there from the house. I always fancy I see people walking in these numerous paths and arbors, but John has cautioned me not to give way to fancy in the least. He says that with my imaginative power and habit of story-making a nervous weakness like mine is sure to lead to all manner of excited fancies, and that I ought to use my will and good sense to check the tendency. So I try.

I think sometimes that if I were only well enough to write a little it would relieve the press of ideas and rest me.

But I find I get pretty tired when I try.

It is so discouraging not to have any advice and companionship about my work. When I get really well John says we will ask Cousin Henry and Julia down for a long visit; but he says he would as soon put fire-works in my pillow-case as to let me have those stimulating people about now.

I wish I could get well faster.

But I must not think about that. This paper looks to me as if it knew what a vicious influence it had!

There is a recurrent spot where the pattern lolls like a broken neck and two bulbous eyes stare at you upside-down.

I got positively angry with the impertinence of it and the everlastingness. Up and down and sideways they crawl, and those absurd, unblinking eyes are everywhere. There is one place where two breadths didn't match, and the eyes go all up and down the line, one a little higher than the other.

I never saw so much expression in an inanimate thing before, and we all know how much expression they have! I used to lie awake as a child and get more entertainment and terror out of blank walls and plain furniture than most children could find in a toy-store.

I remember what a kindly wink the knobs of our big old bureau used to have, and there was one chair that always seemed like a strong friend.

I used to feel that if any of the other things looked too fierce I could always hop into that chair and be safe.

The furniture in this room is no worse than inharmonious, however, for we had to bring it all from downstairs. I suppose when this was used as a playroom they had to take the nursery things out, and no wonder! I never saw such ravages as the children have made here.

The wall paper, as I said before, is torn off in spots, and it sticketh closer than a brother—they must have had perseverance as well as hatred.

Then the floor is scratched and gouged and splintered, the plaster itself is dug out here and there, and this great heavy bed, which is all we found in the room, looks as if it had been through the wars.

But I don't mind it a bit—only the paper.

There comes John's sister. Such a dear girl as she is, and so careful of me! I must not let her find me writing.

She is a perfect, an enthusiastic housekeeper, and hopes for no better profession. I verily believe she thinks it is the writing which made me sick!

But I can write when she is out, and see her a long way off from these windows.

There is one that commands the road, a lovely, shaded, winding road, and one that just looks off over the country. A lovely country, too, full of great elms and velvet meadows.

This wall paper has a kind of sub-pattern in a different shade, a particularly irritating one, for you can only see it in certain lights, and not clearly then.

But in the places where it isn't faded, and where the sun is just so, I can see a strange, provoking, formless sort of figure, that seems to sulk about behind that silly and conspicuous front design.

There's sister on the stairs!

Well, the Fourth of July is over! The people are all gone and I am tired out. John thought it might do me good to see a little company, so we just had mother and Nellie and the children down for a week.

Of course I didn't do a thing. Jennie sees to everything now.

But it tired me all the same.

John says if I don't pick up faster he shall send me to Weir Mitchell in the fall.

But I don't want to go there at all. I had a friend who was in his hands once, and she says he is just like John and my brother, only more so!

Besides, it is such an undertaking to go so far.

I don't feel as if it was worth while to turn my hand over for anything, and I'm getting dreadfully fretful and querulous.

I cry at nothing, and cry most of the time.

Of course I don't when John is here, or anybody else, but when I am alone.

And I am alone a good deal just now. John is kept in town very often by serious cases, and Jennie is good and lets me alone when I want her to.

So I walk a little in the garden or down that lovely lane, sit on the porch under the roses, and lie down up here a good deal.

I'm getting really fond of the room in spite of the wall paper. Perhaps because of the wall paper.

It dwells in my mind so!

I lie here on this great immovable bed—it is nailed down, I believe—and follow that pattern about by the hour. It is as good as gymnastics, I assure you. I start, we'll say, at the bottom, down in the corner over there where it has not been touched, and I determine for the thousandth time that I will follow that pointless pattern to some sort of a conclusion.

I know a little of the principles of design, and I know this thing was not arranged on any laws of radiation, or alternation, or repetition, or symmetry, or anything else that I ever heard of.

It is repeated, of course, by the breadths, but not otherwise.

Looked at in one way, each breadth stands alone, the bloated curves and flourishes—a kind of "debased Romanesque" with delirium tremens—go waddling up and down in isolated columns of fatuity.

But, on the other hand, they connect diagonally, and the sprawling outlines run off in great slanting waves of optic horror, like a lot of wallowing seaweeds in full chase.

The whole thing goes horizontally, too, at least it seems so, and I exhaust myself in trying to distinguish the order of its going in that direction.

They have used a horizontal breadth for a frieze, and that adds wonderfully to the confusion.

There is one end of the room where it is almost intact, and there, when the cross-lights fade and the low sun shines directly upon it, I can almost fancy radiation, after all,—the interminable grotesques seem to form around a common centre and rush off in headlong plunges of equal distraction.

It makes me tired to follow it. I will take a nap, I guess.

I don't know why I should write this.

I don't want to.

I don't feel able.

And I know John would think it absurd. But I must say what I feel and think in some way—it is such a relief!

But the effort is getting to be greater than the relief.

Half the time now I am awfully lazy, and lie down ever so much.

John says I mustn't lose my strength, and has me take cod-liver oil and lots of tonics and things, to say nothing of ale and wine and rare meat.

Dear John! He loves me very dearly, and hates to have me sick. I tried to have a real earnest reasonable talk with him the other day, and tell him how I wished he would let me go and make a visit to Cousin Henry and Julia.

But he said I wasn't able to go, nor able to stand it after I got there; and I did not make out a very good case for myself, for I was crying before I had finished.

It is getting to be a great effort for me to think straight. Just this nervous weakness, I suppose.

And dear John gathered me up in his arms, and just carried me upstairs and laid me on the bed, and sat by me and read to me till he tired my head.

He said I was his darling and his comfort and all he had, and that I must take care of myself for his sake, and keep well.

He says no one but myself can help me out of it, that I must use my will and self-control and not let my silly fancies run away with me.

There's one comfort, the baby is well and happy, and does not have to occupy this nursery with the horrid wall paper.

If we had not used it that blessed child would have! What a fortunate escape! Why, I wouldn't have a child of mine, an impressionable little thing, live in such a room for worlds.

I never thought of it before, but it is lucky that John kept me here, after all. I can stand it so much easier than a baby, you see.

Of course I never mention it to them any more,—I am too wise,—but I keep watch of it all the same.

There are things in that paper that nobody knows but me, or ever will.

Behind that outside pattern the dim shapes get clearer every day.

It is always the same shape, only very numerous.

And it is like a woman stooping down and creeping about behind that pattern. I don't like it a bit. I wonder—I begin to think—I wish John would take me away from here!

It is so hard to talk with John about my case, because he is so wise, and because he loves me so.

But I tried it last night.

It was moonlight. The moon shines in all around, just as the sun does.

I hate to see it sometimes, it creeps so slowly, and always comes in by one window or another.

John was asleep and I hated to waken him, so I kept still and watched the moonlight on that undulating wall paper till I felt creepy.

The faint figure behind seemed to shake the pattern, just as if she wanted to get out.

I got up softly and went to feel and see if the paper did move, and when I came back John was awake.

"What is it, little girl?" he said. "Don't go walking about like that—you'll get cold."

I thought it was a good time to talk, so I told him that I really was not gaining here, and that I wished he would take me away.

"Why, darling!" said he, "our lease will be up in three weeks, and I can't see how to leave before.

"The repairs are not done at home, and I cannot possibly leave town just now. Of course if you were in any danger I could and would, but you really are better, dear, whether you can see it or not. I am a doctor, dear, and I know. You are gaining flesh and color, your appetite is better. I feel really much easier about you."

"I don't weigh a bit more," said I, "nor as much; and my appetite may be better in the evening, when you are here, but it is worse in the morning, when you are away."

"Bless her little heart!" said he with a big hug; "she shall be as sick as she pleases. But now let's improve the shining hours by going to sleep, and talk about it in the morning."

"And you won't go away?" I asked gloomily.

THE YELLOW WALLPAPER   **81**

"Why, how can I, dear? It is only three weeks more and then we will take a nice little trip of a few days while Jennie is getting the house ready. Really, dear, you are better!"

"Better in body, perhaps"—I began, and stopped short, for he sat up straight and looked at me with such a stern, reproachful look that I could not say another word.

"My darling," said he, "I beg of you, for my sake and for our child's sake, as well as for your own, that you will never for one instant let that idea enter your mind! There is nothing so dangerous, so fascinating, to a temperament like yours. It is a false and foolish fancy. Can you not trust me as a physician when I tell you so?"

So of course I said no more on that score, and we went to sleep before long. He thought I was asleep first, but I wasn't,—I lay there for hours trying to decide whether that front pattern and the back pattern really did move together or separately.

On a pattern like this, by daylight, there is a lack of sequence, a defiance of law, that is a constant irritant to a normal mind.

The color is hideous enough, and unreliable enough, and infuriating enough, but the pattern is torturing.

You think you have mastered it, but just as you get well under way in following, it turns a back somersault, and there you are. It slaps you in the face, knocks you down, and tramples upon you. It is like a bad dream.

The outside pattern is a florid arabesque, reminding one of a fungus. If you can imagine a toadstool in joints, an interminable string of toadstools, budding and sprouting in endless convolutions,—why, that is something like it.

That is, sometimes!

There is one marked peculiarity about this paper, a thing nobody seems to notice but myself, and that is that it changes as the light changes.

When the sun shoots in through the east window—I always watch for that first long, straight ray—it changes so quickly that I never can quite believe it.

That is why I watch it always.

By moonlight—the moon shines in all night when there is a moon—I wouldn't know it was the same paper.

At night in any kind of light, in twilight, candlelight, lamplight, and worst of all by moonlight, it becomes bars! The outside pattern, I mean, and the woman behind it is as plain as can be.

I didn't realize for a long time what the thing was that showed behind,— that dim sub-pattern,—but now I am quite sure it is a woman.

By daylight she is subdued, quiet. I fancy it is the pattern that keeps her so still. It is so puzzling. It keeps me quiet by the hour.

I lie down ever so much now. John says it is good for me, and to sleep all I can.

Indeed, he started the habit by making me lie down for an hour after each meal.

It is a very bad habit, I am convinced, for, you see, I don't sleep.

And that cultivates deceit, for I don't tell them I'm awake,—oh, no!

The fact is, I am getting a little afraid of John.

He seems very queer sometimes, and even Jennie has an inexplicable look.

It strikes me occasionally, just as a scientific hypothesis, that perhaps it is the paper!

I have watched John when he did not know I was looking, and come into the room suddenly on the most innocent excuses, and I've caught him several times looking at the paper! And Jennie too. I caught Jennie with her hand on it once.

She didn't know I was in the room, and when I asked her in a quiet, a very quiet voice, with the most restrained manner possible, what she was doing with the paper she turned around as if she had been caught stealing, and looked quite angry—asked me why I should frighten her so!

Then she said that the paper stained everything it touched, that she had found yellow smooches on all my clothes and John's, and she wished we would be more careful!

Did not that sound innocent? But I know she was studying that pattern, and I am determined that nobody shall find it out but myself!

Life is very much more exciting now than it used to be. You see I have something more to expect, to look forward to, to watch. I really do eat better, and am more quiet than I was.

John is so pleased to see me improve! He laughed a little the other day, and said I seemed to be flourishing in spite of my wall paper.

I turned it off with a laugh. I had no intention of telling him it was because of the wall paper—he would make fun of me. He might even want to take me away.

I don't want to leave now until I have found it out. There is a week more, and I think that will be enough.

I'm feeling ever so much better! I don't sleep much at night, for it is so interesting to watch developments; but I sleep a good deal in the daytime.

In the daytime it is tiresome and perplexing.

There are always new shoots on the fungus, and new shades of yellow all over it. I cannot keep count of them, though I have tried conscientiously.

It is the strangest yellow, that wall paper! It makes me think of all the yellow things I ever saw—not beautiful ones like buttercups, but old foul, bad yellow things.

But there is something else about that paper—the smell! I noticed it the moment we came into the room, but with so much air and sun it was not bad. Now we have had a week of fog and rain, and whether the windows are open or not the smell is here.

It creeps all over the house.

I find it hovering in the dining-room, skulking in the parlor, hiding in the hall, lying in wait for me on the stairs.

It gets into my hair.

Even when I go to ride, if I turn my head suddenly and surprise it—there is that smell!

Such a peculiar odor, too! I have spent hours in trying to analyze it, to find what it smelled like.

It is not bad—at first, and very gentle, but quite the subtlest, most enduring odor I ever met.

In this damp weather it is awful. I wake up in the night and find it hanging over me.

It used to disturb me at first. I thought seriously of burning the house—to reach the smell.

But now I am used to it. The only thing I can think of that it is like is the color of the paper—a yellow smell!

There is a very funny mark on this wall, low down, near the mopboard. A streak that runs around the room. It goes behind every piece of furniture, except the bed, a long, straight, even smooch, as if it had been rubbed over and over.

I wonder how it was done and who did it, and what they did it for. Round and round and round—round and round and round—it makes me dizzy!

I really have discovered something at last.

Through watching so much at night, when it changes so, I have finally found out.

The front pattern does move—and no wonder! The woman behind shakes it!

Sometimes I think there are a great many women behind, and sometimes only one, and she crawls around fast, and her crawling shakes it all over.

Then in the very bright spots she keeps still, and in the very shady spots she just takes hold of the bars and shakes them hard.

And she is all the time trying to climb through. But nobody could climb through that pattern—it strangles so; I think that is why it has so many heads.

They get through, and then the pattern strangles them off and turns them upside-down, and makes their eyes white!

If those heads were covered or taken off it would not be half so bad.

I think that woman gets out in the daytime!

And I'll tell you why—privately—I've seen her!

I can see her out of every one of my windows!

It is the same woman, I know, for she is always creeping, and most women do not creep by daylight.

I see her in that long shaded lane, creeping up and down. I see her in those dark grape arbors, creeping all around the garden.

I see her on that long road under the trees, creeping along, and when a carriage comes she hides under the blackberry vines.

I don't blame her a bit. It must be very humiliating to be caught creeping by daylight!

I always lock the door when I creep by daylight. I can't do it at night, for I know John would suspect something at once.

And John is so queer, now, that I don't want to irritate him. I wish he would take another room! Besides, I don't want anybody to get that woman out at night but myself.

I often wonder if I could see her out of all the windows at once.

But, turn as fast as I can, I can only see out of one at one time.

And though I always see her she may be able to creep faster than I can turn!

I have watched her sometimes away off in the open country, creeping as fast as a cloud shadow in a high wind.

If only that top pattern could be gotten off from the under one! I mean to try it, little by little.

I have found out another funny thing, but I shan't tell it this time! It does not do to trust people too much.

There are only two more days to get this paper off, and I believe John is beginning to notice. I don't like the look in his eyes.

And I heard him ask Jennie a lot of professional questions about me. She had a very good report to give.

She said I slept a good deal in the daytime.

John knows I don't sleep very well at night, for all I'm so quiet!

He asked me all sorts of questions, too, and pretended to be very loving and kind.

As if I couldn't see through him!

Still, I don't wonder he acts so, sleeping under this paper for three months.

It only interests me, but I feel sure John and Jennie are secretly affected by it.

Hurrah! This is the last day, but it is enough. John is to stay in town over night, and won't be out until this evening.

Jennie wanted to sleep with me—the sly thing! but I told her I should undoubtedly rest better for a night all alone.

That was clever, for really I wasn't alone a bit! As soon as it was moonlight, and that poor thing began to crawl and shake the pattern, I got up and ran to help her.

I pulled and she shook, I shook and she pulled, and before morning we had peeled off yards of that paper.

A strip about as high as my head and half around the room.

And then when the sun came and that awful pattern began to laugh at me I declared I would finish it today!

We go away to-morrow, and they are moving all my furniture down again to leave things as they were before.

Jennie looked at the wall in amazement, but I told her merrily that I did it out of pure spite at the vicious thing.

She laughed and said she wouldn't mind doing it herself, but I must not get tired.

How she betrayed herself that time!

But I am here, and no person touches this paper but me—not alive!

She tried to get me out of the room—it was too patent! But I said it was so quiet and empty and clean now that I believed I would lie down again and sleep all I could; and not to wake me even for dinner—I would call when I woke.

So now she is gone, and the servants are gone, and the things are gone, and there is nothing left but that great bed-stead nailed down, with the canvas mattress we found on it.

We shall sleep downstairs to-night, and take the boat home to-morrow.

I quite enjoy the room, now it is bare again.

How those children did tear about here!

This bedstead is fairly gnawed!

But I must get to work.

I have locked the door and thrown the key down into the front path.

I don't want to go out, and I don't want to have anybody come in, till John comes.

I want to astonish him.

I've got a rope up here that even Jennie did not find. If that woman does get out, and tries to get away, I can tie her!

But I forgot I could not reach far without anything to stand on!

This bed will not move!

I tried to lift and push it until I was lame, and then I got so angry I bit off a little piece at one corner—but it hurt my teeth.

Then I peeled off all the paper I could reach standing on the floor. It sticks horribly and the pattern just enjoys it! All those strangled heads and bulbous eyes and waddling fungus growths just shriek with derision!

I am getting angry enough to do something desperate. To jump out of the window would be admirable exercise, but the bars are too strong even to try.

Besides, I wouldn't do it. Of course not. I know well enough that a step like that is improper and might be misconstrued.

I don't like to look out of the windows even—there are so many of those creeping women, and they creep so fast.

I wonder if they all come out of that wall paper, as I did?

But I am securely fastened now by my well-hidden rope—you don't get me out in the road there!

I suppose I shall have to get back behind the pattern when it comes night, and that is hard!

It is so pleasant to be out in this great room and creep around as I please!

I don't want to go outside. I won't, even if Jennie asks me to.

For outside you have to creep on the ground, and everything is green instead of yellow.

But here I can creep smoothly on the floor, and my shoulder just fits in that long smooch around the wall, so I cannot lose my way.

Why, there's John at the door!

It is no use, young man, you can't open it!

How he does call and pound!

Now he's crying for an axe.

It would be a shame to break down that beautiful door!

"John, dear!" said I in the gentlest voice, "the key is down by the front steps, under a plantain leaf!"

That silenced him for a few moments.

Then he said—very quietly indeed, "Open the door, my darling!"

"I can't," said I. "The key is down by the front door, under a plantain leaf!"

And then I said it again, several times, very gently and slowly, and said it so often that he had to go and see, and he got it, of course, and came in. He stopped short by the door.

"What is the matter?" he cried. "For God's sake, what are you doing?"

I kept on creeping just the same, but I looked at him over my shoulder.

"I've got out at last," said I, "in spite of you and Jane! And I've pulled off most of the paper, so you can't put me back!"

Now why should that man have fainted? But he did, and right across my path by the wall, so that I had to creep over him every time!

The Fulness of Life

Edith Wharton
1893

The story was first published in *Scribner's* 14 (December 1893): 699-704.

I

For hours she had lain in a kind of gentle torpor, not unlike that sweet lassitude which masters one in the hush of a midsummer noon, when the heat seems to have silenced the very birds and insects, and, lying sunk in the tasselled meadow-grasses, one looks up through a level roofing of maple-leaves at the vast shadowless, and unsuggestive blue. Now and then, at ever-lengthening intervals, a flash of pain darted through her, like the ripple of sheet-lightning across such a midsummer sky; but it was too transitory to shake her stupor, that calm, delicious, bottomless stupor into which she felt herself sinking more and more deeply, without a disturbing impulse of resistance, an effort of reattachment to the vanishing edges of consciousness.

The resistance, the effort, had known their hour of violence; but now they were at an end. Through her mind, long harried by grotesque visions, fragmentary images of the life that she was leaving, tormenting lines of verse, obstinate presentments of pictures once beheld, indistinct impressions of rivers, towers, and cupolas, gathered in the length of journeys half forgotten-through her mind there now only moved a few primal sensations of colorless well-being; a vague satisfaction in the thought that she had swallowed her noxious last draught of medicine . . . and that she should never again hear the creaking of her husband's boots—those horrible boots—and that no one would come to bother her about the next day's dinner . . . or the butcher's book. . . .

At last even these dim sensations spent themselves in the thickening obscurity which enveloped her; a dusk now filled with pale geometric roses, circling softly, interminably before her, now darkened to a uniform blue-blackness, the hue of a summer night without stars. And into this darkness she felt herself sinking, sinking, with the gentle sense of security of one upheld from beneath. Like a tepid tide it rose around her, gliding ever higher and higher, folding in its velvety embrace her relaxed and tired body, now submerging her breast and shoulders, now creeping gradually, with soft inexorableness, over her throat to her chin, to her ears, to her mouth. . . . Ah, now it was rising too high; the impulse to struggle was renewed;. . . her mouth was full;. . . she was choking. . . . Help!

"It is all over," said the nurse, drawing down the eyelids with official composure.

The clock struck three. They remembered it afterward. Someone opened the window and let in a blast of that strange, neutral air which walks the earth between darkness and dawn; someone else led the husband into another room. He walked vaguely, like a blind man, on his creaking boots.

II

She stood, as it seemed, on a threshold, yet no tangible gateway was in front of her. Only a wide vista of light, mild yet penetrating as the gathered glimmer of innumerable stars, expanded gradually before her eyes, in blissful contrast to the cavernous darkness from which she had of late emerged.

She stepped forward, not frightened, but hesitating, and as her eyes began to grow more familiar with the melting depths of light about her, she distinguished the outlines of a landscape, at first swimming in the opaline uncertainty of Shelley's vaporous creations, then gradually resolved into distincter shape—the vast unrolling of a sunlit plain, aerial forms of mountains, and presently the silver crescent of a river in the valley, and a blue stencilling of trees along its curve—something suggestive in its ineffable hue of an azure background of Leonardo's, strange, enchanting, mysterious, leading on the eye and the imagination into regions of fabulous delight. As she gazed, her heart beat with a soft and rapturous surprise; so exquisite a promise she read in the summons of that hyaline distance.

"And so death is not the end after all," in sheer gladness she heard herself exclaiming aloud. "I always knew that it couldn't be. I believed in Darwin, of course. I do still; but then Darwin himself said that he wasn't sure about the soul—at least, I think he did—and Wallace was a spiritualist; and then there was St. George Mivart —"

Her gaze lost itself in the ethereal remoteness of the mountains.

"How beautiful! How satisfying!" she murmured. "Perhaps now I shall really know what it is to live."

As she spoke she felt a sudden thickening of her heart-beats, and looking up she was aware that before her stood the Spirit of Life.

"Have you never really known what it is to live?" the Spirit of Life asked her.

"I have never known," she replied, "that fulness of life which we all feel ourselves capable of knowing; though my life has not been without scattered hints of it, like the scent of earth which comes to one sometimes far out at sea."

"And what do you call the fulness of life?" the Spirit asked again.

"Oh, I can't tell you, if you don't know," she said, almost reproachfully. "Many words are supposed to define it—love and sympathy are those in commonest use, but I am not even sure that they are the right ones, and so few people really know what they mean."

"You were married," said the Spirit, "yet you did not find the fulness of life in your marriage?"

"Oh, dear, no," she replied, with an indulgent scorn, "my marriage was a very incomplete affair."

"And yet you were fond of your husband?"

"You have hit upon the exact word; I was fond of him, yes, just as I was fond of my grandmother, and the house that I was born in, and my old nurse. Oh, I was fond of him, and we were counted a very happy couple. But I have sometimes thought that a woman's nature is like a great house full of rooms: there is the hall, through which everyone passes in going in and out; the drawingroom, where one receives formal visits; the sitting-room, where the members of the family come and go as they list; but beyond that, far beyond, are other rooms, the handles of whose doors perhaps are never turned; no one knows the way to them, no one knows whither they lead; and in the innermost room, the holy of holies, the soul sits alone and waits for a footstep that never comes."

"And your husband," asked the Spirit, after a pause, "never got beyond the family sitting-room?"

"Never," she returned, impatiently; "and the worst of it was that he was quite content to remain there. He thought it perfectly beautiful, and sometimes, when he was admiring its commonplace furniture, insignificant as the chairs and tables of a hotel parlor, I felt like crying out to him: 'Fool, will you never guess that close at hand are rooms full of treasures and wonders, such as the eye of man hath not seen, rooms that no step has crossed, but that might be yours to live in, could you but find the handle of the door?'"

"Then," the Spirit continued, "those moments of which you lately spoke, which seemed to come to you like scattered hints of the fulness of life, were not shared with your husband?"

"Oh, no—never. He was different. His boots creaked, and he always slammed the door when he went out, and he never read anything but railway novels and the sporting advertisements in the papers—and—and, in short, we never understood each other in the least."

"To what influence, then, did you owe those exquisite sensations?"

"I can hardly tell. Sometimes to the perfume of a flower; sometimes to a verse of Dante or of Shakespeare; sometimes to a picture or a sunset, or to one of those calm days at sea, when one seems to be lying in the hollow of a blue pearl; sometimes, but rarely, to a word spoken by someone who chanced to give utterance, at the right moment, to what I felt but could not express."

"Someone whom you loved?" asked the Spirit.

"I never loved anyone, in that way," she said, rather sadly, "nor was I thinking of any one person when I spoke, but of two or three who, by touching for an instant upon a certain chord of my being, had called forth a single note of that strange melody which seemed sleeping in my soul. It has seldom happened, however, that I have owed such feelings to people; and no one ever gave me a moment of such happiness as it was my lot to feel one evening in the Church of Or San Michele, in Florence."

"Tell me about it," said the Spirit.

"It was near sunset on a rainy spring afternoon in Easter week. The clouds had vanished, dispersed by a sudden wind, and as we entered the church the fiery panes of the high windows shone out like lamps through the dusk. A priest was at the high altar, his white cope a livid spot in the incense-laden obscurity, the light of the candles flickering up and down like fireflies about his head; a few people knelt near by. We stole behind them and sat down on a bench close to the tabernacle of Orcagna.

"Strange to say, though Florence was not new to me, I had never been in the church before; and in that magical light I saw for the first time the inlaid steps, the fluted columns, the sculptured bas-reliefs and canopy of the marvellous shrine. The marble, worn and mellowed by the subtle hand of time, took on an unspeakable rosy hue, suggestive in some remote way of the honeycolored columns of the Parthenon, but more mystic, more complex, a color not born of the sun's inveterate kiss, but made up of cryptal twilight, and the flame of candles upon martyrs' tombs, and gleams of sunset through symbolic panes of chrysoprase and ruby; such a light as illumines the missals in the library of Siena, or burns like a hidden fire through the Madonna of Gian Bellini in the Church of the Redeemer, at Venice; the light of the Middle Ages, richer, more solemn, more significant than the limpid sunshine of Greece.

"The church was silent, but for the wail of the priest and the occasional scraping of a chair against the floor, and as I sat there, bathed in that light, absorbed in rapt contemplation of the marble miracle which rose before me, cunningly wrought as a casket of ivory and enriched with jewel-like incrustations and tarnished gleams of gold, I felt myself borne onward along a mighty current, whose source seemed to be in the very beginning of things, and whose tremendous waters gathered as they went all the mingled streams of human passion and endeavor. Life in all its varied manifestations of beauty and strangeness seemed weaving a rhythmical dance around me as I moved, and wherever the spirit of man had passed I knew that my foot had once been familiar.

"As I gazed the mediaeval bosses of the tabernacle of Orcagna seemed to melt and flow into their primal forms so that the folded lotus of the Nile and the Greek acanthus were braided with the runic knots and fish-tailed monsters of the North, and all the plastic terror and beauty born of man's hand from the Ganges to the Baltic quivered and mingled in Orcagna's apotheosis of Mary. And so the river bore me on, past the alien face of antique civilizations and the familiar wonders of Greece, till I swam upon the fiercely rushing tide of the Middle Ages, with its swirling eddies of passion, its heaven-reflecting pools of poetry and art; I heard the rhythmic blow of the craftsmen's hammers in the goldsmiths' workshops and on the walls of churches, the party-cries of armed factions in the narrow streets, the organroll of Dante's verse, the crackle of the fagots around Arnold of Brescia, the twitter of the swallows to which St. Francis preached, the laughter of the ladies listening on the hillside to the quips of the Decameron, while plague-struck Florence howled beneath them—all this and much more I heard, joined in strange unison with voices earlier and more remote, fierce, passionate, or tender, yet subdued to such awful harmony that I thought of the song that the morning stars sang together and felt as though it were sounding in my ears. My heart beat to suffocation, the tears burned my lids, the joy, the mystery of it seemed too intolerable to be borne. I could not understand even then the words of the song; but I knew that if there had been someone at my side who could have heard it with me, we might have found the key to it together.

"I turned to my husband, who was sitting beside me in an attitude of patient dejection, gazing into the bottom of his hat; but at that moment he rose, and stretching his stiffened legs, said, mildly: 'Hadn't we better be going? There doesn't seem to be much to see here, and you know the table d'hote dinner is at half-past six o'clock.'"

Her recital ended, there was an interval of silence; then the Spirit of Life said: "There is a compensation in store for such needs as you have expressed."

"Oh, then you do understand?" she exclaimed. "Tell me what compensation, I entreat you!"

"It is ordained," the Spirit answered, "that every soul which seeks in vain on earth for a kindred soul to whom it can lay bare its inmost being shall find that soul here and be united to it for eternity."

A glad cry broke from her lips. "Ah, shall I find him at last?" she cried, exultant.

"He is here," said the Spirit of Life.

She looked up and saw that a man stood near whose soul (for in that unwonted light she seemed to see his soul more clearly than his face) drew her toward him with an invincible force.

"Are you really he?" she murmured.

"I am he," he answered.

She laid her hand in his and drew him toward the parapet which overhung the valley.

"Shall we go down together," she asked him, "into that marvellous country; shall we see it together, as if with the self-same eyes, and tell each other in the same words all that we think and feel?"

"So," he replied, "have I hoped and dreamed."

"What?" she asked, with rising joy. "Then you, too, have looked for me?"

"All my life."

"How wonderful! And did you never, never find anyone in the other world who understood you?"

"Not wholly—not as you and I understand each other."

"Then you feel it, too? Oh, I am happy," she sighed.

They stood, hand in hand, looking down over the parapet upon the shimmering landscape which stretched forth beneath them into sapphirine space, and the Spirit of Life, who kept watch near the threshold, heard now and then a floating fragment of their talk blown backward like the stray swallows which the wind sometimes separates from their migratory tribe.

"Did you never feel at sunset —"

"Ah, yes; but I never heard anyone else say so. Did you?"

"Do you remember that line in the third canto of the 'Inferno?'"

"Ah, that line—my favorite always. Is it possible —"

"You know the stooping Victory in the frieze of the Nike Apteros?"

"You mean the one who is tying her sandal? Then you have noticed, too, that all Botticelli and Mantegna are dormant in those flying folds of her drapery?"

"After a storm in autumn have you never seen —"

"Yes, it is curious how certain flowers suggest certain painters-the perfume of the incarnation, Leonardo; that of the rose, Titian; the tuberose, Crivelli —"

"I never supposed that anyone else had noticed it."

"Have you never thought —"

"Oh, yes, often and often; but I never dreamed that anyone else had."

"But surely you must have felt —"

"Oh, yes, yes; and you, too —"

"How beautiful! How strange —"

Their voices rose and fell, like the murmur of two fountains answering each other across a garden full of flowers. At length, with a certain tender impatience, he turned to her and said: "Love, why should we linger here? All eternity lies before us. Let us go down into that beautiful country together and make a home for ourselves on some blue hill above the shining river."

FICTION

As he spoke, the hand she had forgotten in his was suddenly withdrawn, and he felt that a cloud was passing over the radiance of her soul.

"A home," she repeated, slowly, "a home for you and me to live in for all eternity?"

"Why not, love? Am I not the soul that yours has sought?"

"Y-yes—yes, I know—but, don't you see, home would not be like home to me, unless —"

"Unless?" he wonderingly repeated.

She did not answer, but she thought to herself, with an impulse of whimsical inconsistency, "Unless you slammed the door and wore creaking boots."

But he had recovered his hold upon her hand, and by imperceptible degrees was leading her toward the shining steps which descended to the valley.

"Come, O my soul's soul," he passionately implored; "why delay a moment? Surely you feel, as I do, that eternity itself is too short to hold such bliss as ours. It seems to me that I can see our home already. Have I not always seem it in my dreams? It is white, love, is it not, with polished columns, and a sculptured cornice against the blue? Groves of laurel and oleander and thickets of roses surround it; but from the terrace where we walk at sunset, the eye looks out over woodlands and cool meadows where, deep-bowered under ancient boughs, a stream goes delicately toward the river. Indoors our favorite pictures hang upon the walls and the rooms are lined with books. Think, dear, at last we shall have time to read them all. With which shall we begin? Come, help me to choose. Shall it be 'Faust' or the 'Vita Nuova,' the 'Tempest' or 'Les Caprices de Marianne,' or the thirty-first canto of the 'Paradise,' or 'Epipsychidion' or "Lycidas'? Tell me, dear, which one?"

As he spoke he saw the answer trembling joyously upon her lips; but it died in the ensuing silence, and she stood motionless, resisting the persuasion of his hand.

"What is it?" he entreated.

"Wait a moment," she said, with a strange hesitation in her voice. "Tell me first, are you quite sure of yourself? Is there no one on earth whom you sometimes remember?"

"Not since I have seen you," he replied; for, being a man, he had indeed forgotten.

Still she stood motionless, and he saw that the shadow deepened on her soul.

"Surely, love," he rebuked her, "it was not that which troubled you? For my part I have walked through Lethe. The past has melted like a cloud before the moon. I never lived until I saw you."

She made no answer to his pleadings, but at length, rousing herself with a visible effort, she turned away from him and moved toward the Spirit of Life, who still stood near the threshold.

"I want to ask you a question," she said, in a troubled voice.

"Ask," said the Spirit.

"A little while ago," she began, slowly, "you told me that every soul which has not found a kindred soul on earth is destined to find one here."

"And have you not found one?" asked the Spirit.

"Yes; but will it be so with my husband's soul also?"

"No," answered the Spirit of Life, "for your husband imagined that he had found his soul's mate on earth in you; and for such delusions eternity itself contains no cure."

She gave a little cry. Was it of disappointment or triumph?

"Then—then what will happen to him when he comes here?"

"That I cannot tell you. Some field of activity and happiness he will doubtless find, in due measure to his capacity for being active and happy."

She interrupted, almost angrily: "He will never be happy without me."

"Do not be too sure of that," said the Spirit.

She took no notice of this, and the Spirit continued: "He will not understand you here any better than he did on earth."

"No matter," she said; "I shall be the only sufferer, for he always thought that he understood me."

"His boots will creak just as much as ever —"

"No matter."

"And he will slam the door —"

"Very likely."

"And continue to read railway novels —"

She interposed, impatiently: "Many men do worse than that."

"But you said just now," said the Spirit, "that you did not love him."

"True," she answered, simply; "but don't you understand that I shouldn't feel at home without him? It is all very well for a week or two—but for eternity! After all, I never minded the creaking of his boots, except when my head ached, and I don't suppose it will ache here; and he was always so sorry when he had slammed the door, only he never could remember not to. Besides, no one else would know how to look after him, he is so helpless. His inkstand would never be filled, and he would always be out of stamps and visiting-cards. He would never remember to have his umbrella re-covered, or to ask the price of anything before he bought it. Why, he wouldn't even know what novels to read. I always had to choose the kind he liked, with a murder or a forgery and a successful detective."

She turned abruptly to her kindred soul, who stood listening with a mien of wonder and dismay.

"Don't you see," she said, "that I can't possibly go with you?"

"But what do you intend to do?" asked the Spirit of Life.

"What do I intend to do?" she returned, indignantly. "Why, I mean to wait for my husband, of course. If he had come here first he would have waited for me for years and years; and it would break his heart not to find me here when he comes." She pointed with a contemptuous gesture to the magic vision of hill and vale sloping away to the translucent mountains. "He wouldn't give a fig for all that," she said, "if he didn't find me here."

"But consider," warned the Spirit, "that you are now choosing for eternity. It is a solemn moment."

"Choosing!" she said, with a half-sad smile. "Do you still keep up here that old fiction about choosing? I should have thought that you knew better than that. How can I help myself? He will expect to find me here when he comes, and he would never believe you if you told him that I had gone away with someone else-never, never."

"So be it," said the Spirit. "Here, as on earth, each one must decide for himself."

She turned to her kindred soul and looked at him gently, almost wistfully. "I am sorry," she said. "I should have liked to talk with you again; but you will understand, I know, and I dare say you will find someone else a great deal cleverer —"

And without pausing to hear his answer she waved him a swift farewell and turned back toward the threshold.

"Will my husband come soon?" she asked the Spirit of Life.

"That you are not destined to know," the Spirit replied.

"No matter," she said, cheerfully; "I have all eternity to wait in."

And still seated alone on the threshold, she listens for the creaking of his boots.

FICTION

The Red Room

H. G. Wells
1894

Written in 1894 and first published in the March 1896 edition of *The Idler* magazine.

"I can assure you," said I, "that it will take a very tangible ghost to frighten me." And I stood up before the fire with my glass in my hand.

"It is your own choosing," said the man with the withered arm, and glanced at me askance.

"Eight-and-twenty years," said I, "I have lived, and never a ghost have I seen as yet."

The old woman sat staring hard into the fire, her pale eyes wide open. "Ay," she broke in; "and eight-and-twenty years you have lived and never seen the likes of this house, I reckon. There's a many things to see, when one's still but eight-and-twenty." She swayed her head slowly from side to side. "A many things to see and sorrow for."

I half suspected the old people were trying to enhance the spiritual terrors of their house by their droning insistence. I put down my empty glass on the table and looked about the room, and caught a glimpse of myself, abbreviated and broadened to an impossible sturdiness, in the queer old mirror at the end of the room. "Well," I said, "if I see anything to-night, I shall be so much the wiser. For I come to the business with an open mind."

"It's your own choosing," said the man with the withered arm once more.

I heard the sound of a stick and a shambling step on the flags in the passage outside, and the door creaked on its hinges as a second old man entered, more bent, more wrinkled, more aged even than the first. He supported himself by a single crutch, his eyes were covered by a shade, and his lower lip, half averted, hung pale and pink from his decaying yellow teeth. He made straight for an arm-chair on the opposite side of the table, sat down clumsily, and began to cough. The man with the withered arm gave this new-comer a short glance of positive dislike; the old woman took no notice of his arrival, but remained with her eyes fixed steadily on the fire.

"I said—it's your own choosing," said the man with the withered arm, when the coughing had ceased for a while.

"It's my own choosing," I answered.

The man with the shade became aware of my presence for the first time, and threw his head back for a moment and sideways, to see me. I caught a momentary glimpse of his eyes, small and bright and inflamed. Then he began to cough and splutter again.

"Why don't you drink?" said the man with the withered arm, pushing the beer towards him. The man with the shade poured out a glassful with a shaky hand that splashed half as much again on the deal table. A monstrous shadow of him crouched upon the wall and mocked his action as he poured and drank. I must confess I had scarce expected these grotesque custodians. There is to my mind something inhuman in senility, something crouching and atavistic; the human qualities seem to drop from old people insensibly day by day. The three of them made me feel uncomfortable, with their gaunt silences, their bent carriage, their evident unfriendliness to me and to one another.

"If," said I, "you will show me to this haunted room of yours, I will make myself comfortable there."

The old man with the cough jerked his head back so suddenly that it startled me, and shot another glance of his red eyes at me from under the shade; but no one answered me. I waited a minute, glancing from one to the other.

"If," I said a little louder, "if you will show me to this haunted room of yours, I will relieve you from the task of entertaining me."

"There's a candle on the slab outside the door," said the man with the withered arm, looking at my feet as he addressed me. "But if you go to the red room to-night——"

("This night of all nights!" said the old woman.)

"You go alone."

"Very well," I answered. "And which way do I go?"

"You go along the passage for a bit," said he, "until you come to a door, and through that is a spiral staircase, and half-way up that is a landing and another door covered with baize. Go through that and down the long corridor to the end, and the red room is on your left up the steps."

"Have I got that right?" I said, and repeated his directions. He corrected me in one particular.

"And are you really going?" said the man with the shade, looking at me again for the third time, with that queer, unnatural tilting of the face.

("This night of all nights!" said the old woman.)

"It is what I came for," I said, and moved towards the door. As I did so, the old man with the shade rose and staggered round the table, so as to be closer to the others and to the fire. At the door I turned and looked at them, and saw they were all close together, dark against the firelight, staring at me over their shoulders, with an intent expression on their ancient faces.

"Good-night," I said, setting the door open.

"It's your own choosing," said the man with the withered arm.

I left the door wide open until the candle was well alight, and then I shut them in and walked down the chilly, echoing passage.

I must confess that the oddness of these three old pensioners in whose charge her ladyship had left the castle, and the deep-toned, old-fashioned furniture of the housekeeper's room in which they foregathered, affected me in spite of my efforts to keep myself at a matter-of-fact phase. They seemed to belong to another age, an older age, an age when things spiritual were different from this of ours, less certain; an age when omens and witches were credible, and ghosts beyond denying. Their very existence was spectral; the cut of their clothing, fashions born in dead brains. The ornaments and conveniences of the room about them were ghostly—the thoughts of vanished men, which still haunted rather than participated in the world of to-day. But with an effort I sent such thoughts to the right-about. The long, draughty subterranean passage was chilly and dusty, and my candle flared and made the shadows cower and quiver. The echoes rang up and down the spiral staircase, and a shadow came sweeping up after me, and one fled before me into the darkness overhead. I came to the landing and stopped there for a moment, listening to a rustling that I fancied I heard; then, satisfied of the absolute silence, I pushed open the baize-covered door and stood in the corridor.

The effect was scarcely what I expected, for the moonlight, coming in by the great window on the grand staircase, picked out everything in vivid black shadow or silvery illumination. Everything was in its place: the house might have been deserted on the yesterday instead of eighteen months ago. There were candles in the sockets of the sconces, and whatever dust had gathered on the carpets or upon the polished flooring was distributed so evenly as to be invisible in the moonlight. I was about to advance, and stopped abruptly. A bronze group stood upon the landing, hidden from me by the corner of the wall, but its shadow fell with marvellous distinctness upon the white panelling, and gave me the impression of someone crouching to waylay me. I stood rigid for half a minute perhaps. Then, with my hand in the pocket that held my revolver, I advanced, only to discover a Ganymede and Eagle glistening in the moonlight. That incident for a time restored my nerve, and a porcelain Chinaman on a buhl table, whose head rocked silently as I passed him, scarcely startled me.

The door to the red room and the steps up to it were in a shadowy corner. I moved my candle from side to side, in order to see clearly the nature of the recess in which I stood before opening the door. Here it was, thought I, that my predecessor was found, and the memory of that story gave me a sudden twinge of apprehension. I glanced over my shoulder at the Ganymede in the moonlight, and opened the door of the red room rather hastily, with my face half turned to the pallid silence of the landing.

I entered, closed the door behind me at once, turned the key I found in the lock within, and stood with the candle held aloft, surveying the scene of my vigil, the great red room of Lorraine Castle, in which the young duke had died. Or, rather, in which he had begun his dying, for he had opened the door and fallen headlong down the steps I had just ascended. That had been the end of his vigil, of his gallant attempt to conquer the ghostly tradition of the place, and never, I thought, had apoplexy better served the ends of superstition. And there were other and older stories that clung to the room, back to the half-credible beginning of it all, the tale of a timid wife and the tragic end that came to her husband's jest of frightening her. And looking around that large sombre room, with its shadowy window bays, its recesses and alcoves, one could well understand the legends that had sprouted in its black corners, its germinating darkness. My candle was a little tongue of light in its vastness, that failed to pierce the opposite end of the room, and left an ocean of mystery and suggestion beyond its island of light.

I resolved to make a systematic examination of the place at once, and dispel the fanciful suggestions of its obscurity before they obtained a hold upon me. After satisfying myself of the fastening of the door, I began to walk about the room, peering round each article of furniture, tucking up the valances of the bed, and opening its curtains wide. I pulled up the blinds and examined the fastenings of the several windows before closing the shutters, leant forward and looked up the blackness of the wide chimney, and tapped the dark oak panelling for any secret opening. There were two big mirrors in the room, each with a pair of sconces bearing candles, and on the mantelshelf, too, were more candles in china candlesticks. All these I lit one after the other. The fire was laid, an unexpected consideration from the old housekeeper,—and I lit it, to keep down any disposition to shiver, and when it was burning well, I stood round with my back to it and regarded the room again. I had pulled up a chintz-covered arm-chair and a table, to form a kind of barricade before me, and on this lay my revolver ready to hand. My precise examination had done me good, but I still found the remoter darkness of the place, and its perfect stillness, too stimulating for the imagination. The echoing of the stir and crackling of the fire was no sort of comfort to me. The shadow in the alcove at the end in particular, had that undefinable quality of a presence, that odd suggestion of a lurking, living thing, that comes so easily in silence and solitude. At last, to reassure myself, I walked with a candle into it, and satisfied myself that there was nothing tangible there. I stood that candle upon the floor of the alcove, and left it in that position.

By this time I was in a state of considerable nervous tension, although to my reason there was no adequate cause for the condition. My mind, however, was perfectly clear. I postulated quite unreservedly that nothing supernatural could happen, and to pass the time I began to string some rhymes together, Ingoldsby fashion, of the original legend of the place. A few I spoke aloud, but the echoes were not pleasant. For the same reason I also abandoned, after a time, a conversation with myself upon the impossibility of ghosts and haunting. My mind reverted to the three old and distorted people downstairs, and I tried to keep it upon that topic. The sombre reds and blacks of the room troubled, me; even with seven candles the place was merely dim. The one in the alcove flared in a draught, and the fire-flickering kept the shadows and penumbra perpetually shifting and stirring. Casting about for a remedy, I recalled the candles I had seen in the passage, and, with a slight effort, walked out into the moonlight, carrying a candle and leaving the door open, and presently returned with as many as ten. These I put in various knick-knacks of china with which the room was sparsely adorned, lit and placed where the shadows had lain deepest, some on the floor, some in the window recesses, until at last my seventeen candles were so arranged that not an inch of the room but had the direct light of at least one of them. It occurred to me that when the ghost came, I could warn him not to trip over them. The room was now quite brightly illuminated. There was something very cheery and reassuring in these little streaming flames, and snuffing them gave me an occupation, and afforded a helpful sense of the passage of time. Even with that, however, the brooding expectation of the vigil weighed heavily upon me. It was after midnight that the candle in the alcove suddenly went out, and the black shadow sprang back to its place there. I did not see the candle go out; I simply turned and saw that the darkness was there, as one might start and see the unexpected presence of a stranger. "By Jove!" said I aloud; "that draught's a strong one!" and, taking the matches from the table, I walked across the room in a leisurely manner, to relight the corner again. My first match would not strike, and as I succeeded with the second, something seemed to blink on the wall before me. I turned my head involuntarily, and saw that the two candles on the little table by the fireplace were extinguished. I rose at once to my feet.

"Odd!" I said. "Did I do that myself in a flash of absent-mindedness?"

I walked back, relit one, and as I did so, I saw the candle in the right sconce of one of the mirrors wink and go right out, and almost immediately its companion followed it. There was no mistake about it. The flame vanished, as if the wicks had been suddenly nipped between a finger and a thumb, leaving the wick neither glowing nor smoking, but black. While I stood gaping, the candle at the foot of the bed went out, and the shadows seemed to take another step towards me.

"This won't do!" said I, and first one and then another candle on the mantelshelf followed.

"What's up?" I cried, with a queer high note getting into my voice somehow. At that the candle on the wardrobe went out, and the one I had relit in the alcove followed.

"Steady on!" I said. "These candles are wanted," speaking with a half-hysterical facetiousness, and scratching away at a match the while for the mantel candlesticks. My hands trembled so much that twice I missed the rough paper of the matchbox. As the mantel emerged from darkness again, two candles in the remoter end of the window were eclipsed. But with the same match I also relit the larger mirror candles, and those on the floor near the doorway, so that for the moment I seemed to gain on the extinctions. But then in a volley there vanished four lights at once in different corners of the room, and I struck another match in quivering haste, and stood hesitating whither to take it.

As I stood undecided, an invisible hand seemed to sweep out the two candles on the table. With a cry of terror, I dashed at the alcove, then into the corner, and then into the window, relighting three, as two more vanished by the fireplace; then, perceiving a better way, I dropped the matches on the iron-bound deed-box in the corner, and caught up the bedroom candlestick. With this I avoided the delay of striking matches; but for all that the steady process of extinction went on, and the shadows I feared and fought against returned, and crept in upon me, first a step gained on this side of me and then on that. It was like a ragged storm-cloud sweeping out the stars. Now and then one returned for a minute, and was lost again. I was now almost frantic with the horror of the coming darkness, and my self-possession deserted me. I leaped panting and dishevelled from candle to candle, in a vain struggle against that remorseless advance.

I bruised myself on the thigh against the table, I sent a chair headlong, I stumbled and fell and whisked the cloth from the table in my fall. My candle rolled away from me, and I snatched another as I rose. Abruptly this was blown out, as I swung it off the table by the wind of my sudden movement, and immediately the two remaining candles followed. But there was light still in the room, a red light that staved off the shadows from me. The fire! Of course I could still thrust my candle between the bars and relight it!

I turned to where the flames were still dancing between the glowing coals, and splashing red reflections upon the furniture, made two steps towards the grate, and incontinently the flames dwindled and vanished, the glow vanished, the reflections rushed together and vanished, and as I thrust the candle between the bars darkness closed upon me like the shutting of an eye, wrapped about me in a stifling embrace, sealed my vision, and crushed the last vestiges of reason from my brain. The candle fell from my hand. I flung out my arms in a vain effort to thrust that ponderous blackness away from me, and, lifting up my voice, screamed with all my might—once, twice, thrice. Then I think I must have staggered to my feet. I know I thought suddenly of the moonlit corridor, and, with my head bowed and my arms over my face, made a run for the door.

But I had forgotten the exact position of the door, and struck myself heavily against the corner of the bed. I staggered back, turned, and was either struck or struck myself against some other bulky furniture. I have a vague memory of battering myself thus, to and fro in the darkness, of a cramped struggle, and of my own wild crying as I darted to and fro, of a heavy blow at last upon my forehead, a horrible sensation of falling that lasted an age, of my last frantic effort to keep my footing, and then I remember no more.

I opened my eyes in daylight. My head was roughly bandaged, and the man with the withered arm was watching my face. I looked about me, trying to remember what had happened, and for a space I could not recollect. I rolled my eyes into the corner, and saw the old woman, no longer abstracted, pouring out some drops of medicine from a little blue phial into a glass. "Where am I?" I asked; "I seem to remember you, and yet I cannot remember who you are."

They told me then, and I heard of the haunted Red Room as one who hears a tale. "We found you at dawn," said he, "and there was blood on your forehead and lips."

It was very slowly I recovered my memory of my experience. "You believe now," said the old man, "that the room is haunted?" He spoke no longer as one who greets an intruder, but as one who grieves for a broken friend.

"Yes," said I; "the room is haunted."

"And you have seen it. And we, who have lived here all our lives, have never set eyes upon it. Because we have never dared . . . Tell us, is it truly the old earl who——"

"No," said I; "it is not."

"I told you so," said the old lady, with the glass in her hand. "It is his poor young countess who was frightened——"

"It is not," I said. "There is neither ghost of earl nor ghost of countess in that room, there is no ghost there at all; but worse, far worse——"

"Well?" they said.

"The worst of all the things that haunt poor mortal man," said I; "and that is, in all its nakedness—Fear that will not have light nor sound, that will not bear with reason, that deafens and darkens and overwhelms. It followed me through the corridor, it fought against me in the room——"

I stopped abruptly. There was an interval of silence. My hand went up to my bandages.

Then the man with the shade sighed and spoke. "That is it," said he. "I knew that was it. A power of darkness. To put such a curse upon a woman! It lurks there always. You can feel it even in the daytime, even of a bright summer's day, in the hangings, in the curtains, keeping behind you however you face about. In the dusk it creeps along the corridor and follows you, so that you dare not turn. There is Fear in that room of hers—black Fear, and there will be—so long as this house of sin endures."

The Bride Comes to Yellow Sky

Stephen Crane
1898

An 1898 western short story by American author Stephen Crane (1871–1900). Originally published in *McClure's Magazine*, it was written in England.

I

The great Pullman was whirling onward with such dignity of motion that a glance from the window seemed simply to prove that the plains of Texas were pouring eastward. Vast flats of green grass, dull-hued spaces of mesquite and cactus, little groups of frame houses, woods of light and tender trees, all were sweeping into the east, sweeping over the horizon, a precipice.

A newly married pair had boarded this coach at San Antonio. The man's face was reddened from many days in the wind and sun, and a direct result of his new black clothes was that his brick-colored hands were constantly performing in a most conscious fashion. From time to time he looked down respectfully at his attire. He sat with a hand on each knee, like a man waiting in a barber's shop. The glances he devoted to other passengers were furtive and shy.

The bride was not pretty, nor was she very young. She wore a dress of blue cashmere, with small reservations of velvet here and there and with steel buttons abounding. She continually twisted her head to regard her puff sleeves, very stiff, straight, and high. They embarrassed her. It was quite apparent that she had cooked, and that she expected to cook, dutifully. The blushes caused by the careless scrutiny of some passengers as she had entered the car were strange to see upon this plain, under-class countenance, which was drawn in placid, almost emotionless lines.

They were evidently very happy. "Ever been in a parlor-car before?" he asked, smiling with delight.

"No," she answered, "I never was. It's fine, ain't it?"

"Great! And then after a while we'll go forward to the diner and get a big layout. Finest meal in the world. Charge a dollar."

"Oh, do they?" cried the bride. "Charge a dollar? Why, that's too much — for us—ain't it, Jack?"

"Not this trip, anyhow," he answered bravely. "We're going to go the whole thing."

Later, he explained to her about the trains. "You see, it's a thousand miles from one end of Texas to the other, and this train runs right across it and never stops but four times." He had the pride of an owner. He pointed out to her the dazzling fittings of the coach, and in truth her eyes opened wider as she contemplated the sea-green figured velvet, the shining brass, silver, and glass, the wood that gleamed as darkly brilliant as the surface of a pool of oil. At one end a bronze figure sturdily held a support for a separated chamber, and at convenient places on the ceiling were frescoes in olive and silver.

To the minds of the pair, their surroundings reflected the glory of their marriage that morning in San Antonio. This was the environment of their new estate, and the man's face in particular beamed with an elation that made him appear ridiculous to the negro porter. This individual at times surveyed them from afar with an amused and superior grin. On other occasions he bullied them with skill in ways that did not make it exactly plain to them that they were being bullied. He subtly used all the manners of the most unconquerable kind of snobbery. He oppressed them, but of this oppression they had small knowledge, and they speedily forgot that infrequently a number of travelers covered them with stares of derisive enjoyment. Historically there was supposed to be something infinitely humorous in their situation.

"We are due in Yellow Sky at 3:42," he said, looking tenderly into her eyes.

"Oh, are we?" she said, as if she had not been aware of it. To evince surprise at her husband's statement was part of her wifely amiability. She took from a pocket a little silver watch, and as she held it before her and stared at it with a frown of attention, the new husband's face shone.

"I bought it in San Anton' from a friend of mine," he told her gleefully.

"It's seventeen minutes past twelve," she said, looking up at him with a kind of shy and clumsy coquetry. A passenger, noting this play, grew excessively sardonic, and winked at himself in one of the numerous mirrors.

At last they went to the dining-car. Two rows of negro waiters, in glowing white suits, surveyed their entrance with the interest and also the equanimity of men who had been forewarned. The pair fell to the lot of a waiter who happened to feel pleasure in steering them through their meal. He viewed them with the manner of a fatherly pilot, his countenance radiant with benevolence. The patronage, entwined with the ordinary deference, was not plain to them. And yet, as they returned to their coach, they showed in their faces a sense of escape.

To the left, miles down a long purple slope, was a little ribbon of mist where moved the keening Rio Grande. The train was approaching it at an angle, and the apex was Yellow Sky. Presently it was apparent that, as the distance from Yellow Sky grew shorter, the husband became commensurately restless. His brick-red hands were more insistent in their prominence. Occasionally he was even rather absent-minded and far-away when the bride leaned forward and addressed him.

As a matter of truth, Jack Potter was beginning to find the shadow of a deed weigh upon him like a leaden slab. He, the town marshal of Yellow Sky, a man known, liked, and feared in his corner, a prominent person, had gone to San Antonio to meet a girl he believed he loved, and there, after the usual prayers, had actually induced her to marry him, without consulting Yellow Sky for any part of the transaction. He was now bringing his bride before an innocent and unsuspecting community.

Of course, people in Yellow Sky married as it pleased them, in accordance with a general custom; but such was Potter's thought of his duty to his friends, or of their idea of his duty, or of an unspoken form which does not control men in these matters, that he felt he was heinous. He had committed an extraordinary crime. Face to face with this girl in San Antonio, and spurred by his sharp impulse, he had gone headlong over all the social hedges. At San Antonio he was like a man hidden in the dark. A knife to sever any friendly duty, any form, was easy to his hand in that remote city. But the hour of Yellow Sky, the hour of daylight, was approaching.

He knew full well that his marriage was an important thing to his town. It could only be exceeded by the burning of the new hotel. His friends could not forgive him. Frequently he had reflected on the advisability of telling them by telegraph, but a new cowardice had been upon him.

He feared to do it. And now the train was hurrying him toward a scene of amazement, glee, and reproach. He glanced out of the window at the line of haze swinging slowly in towards the train.

Yellow Sky had a kind of brass band, which played painfully, to the delight of the populace. He laughed without heart as he thought of it. If the citizens could dream of his prospective arrival with his bride, they would parade the band at the station and escort them, amid cheers and laughing congratulations, to his adobe home.

He resolved that he would use all the devices of speed and plains-craft in making the journey from the station to his house. Once within that safe citadel he could issue some sort of a vocal bulletin, and then not go among the citizens until they had time to wear off a little of their enthusiasm.

The bride looked anxiously at him. "What's worrying you, Jack?"

He laughed again. "I'm not worrying, girl. I'm only thinking of Yellow Sky."

She flushed in comprehension.

A sense of mutual guilt invaded their minds and developed a finer tenderness. They looked at each other with eyes softly aglow. But Potter often laughed the same nervous laugh. The flush upon the bride's face seemed quite permanent.

The traitor to the feelings of Yellow Sky narrowly watched the speeding landscape. "We're nearly there," he said.

Presently the porter came and announced the proximity of Potter's home. He held a brush in his hand and, with all his airy superiority gone, he brushed Potter's new clothes as the latter slowly turned this way and that way. Potter fumbled out a coin and gave it to the porter, as he had seen others do. It was a heavy and muscle-bound business, as that of a man shoeing his first horse.

The porter took their bag, and as the train began to slow they moved forward to the hooded platform of the car. Presently the two engines and their long string of coaches rushed into the station of Yellow Sky.

"They have to take water here," said Potter, from a constricted throat and in mournful cadence, as one announcing death. Before the train stopped, his eye had swept the length of the platform, and he was glad and astonished to see there was none upon it but the station-agent, who, with a slightly hurried and anxious air, was walking toward the water-tanks. When the train had halted, the porter alighted first and placed in position a little temporary step.

"Come on, girl," said Potter hoarsely. As he helped her down they each laughed on a false note. He took the bag from the negro, and bade his wife cling to his arm. As they slunk rapidly away, his hang-dog glance perceived that they were unloading the two trunks, and also that the station-agent far ahead near the baggage-car had turned and was running toward him, making gestures. He laughed, and groaned as he laughed, when he noted the first effect of his marital bliss upon Yellow Sky. He gripped his wife's arm firmly to his side, and they fled. Behind them the porter stood chuckling fatuously.

II

The California Express on the Southern Railway was due at Yellow Sky in twenty-one minutes. There were six men at the bar of the "Weary Gentleman" saloon. One was a drummer who talked a great deal and rapidly; three were Texans who did not care to talk at that time; and two were Mexican sheep-herders who did not talk as a general practice in the "Weary Gentleman" saloon. The barkeeper's dog lay on the board walk that crossed in front of the door. His head was on his paws, and he glanced drowsily here and there with the constant vigilance of a dog that is kicked on occasion. Across the sandy street were some vivid green grass plots, so wonderful in appearance amid the sands that burned near them in a blazing sun that they caused a doubt in the mind. They exactly resembled the grass mats used to represent lawns on the stage. At the cooler end of the railway station a man without a coat sat in a tilted chair and smoked his pipe. The fresh-cut bank of the Rio Grande circled near the town, and there could be seen beyond it a great, plum-colored plain of mesquite.

Save for the busy drummer and his companions in the saloon, Yellow Sky was dozing. The new-comer leaned gracefully upon the bar, and recited many tales with the confidence of a bard who has come upon a new field.

"—and at the moment that the old man fell down stairs with the bureau in his arms, the old woman was coming up with two scuttles of coal, and, of course—"

The drummer's tale was interrupted by a young man who suddenly appeared in the open door. He cried: "Scratchy Wilson's drunk, and has turned loose with both hands." The two Mexicans at once set down their glasses and faded out of the rear entrance of the saloon.

The drummer, innocent and jocular, answered: "All right, old man. S'pose he has. Come in and have a drink, anyhow."

But the information had made such an obvious cleft in every skull in the room that the drummer was obliged to see its importance. All had become instantly solemn. "Say," said he, mystified, "what is this?" His three companions made the introductory gesture of eloquent speech, but the young man at the door forestalled them.

"It means, my friend," he answered, as he came into the saloon, "that for the next two hours this town won't be a health resort."

The barkeeper went to the door and locked and barred it. Reaching out of the window, he pulled in heavy wooden shutters and barred them. Immediately a solemn, chapel-like gloom was upon the place. The drummer was looking from one to another.

"But, say," he cried, "what is this, anyhow? You don't mean there is going to be a gun-fight?"

"Don't know whether there'll be a fight or not," answered one man grimly. "But there'll be some shootin'—some good shootin'."

The young man who had warned them waved his hand. "Oh, there'll be a fight fast enough if anyone wants it. Anybody can get a fight out there in the street. There's a fight just waiting."

The drummer seemed to be swayed between the interest of a foreigner and a perception of personal danger.

"What did you say his name was?" he asked.

"Scratchy Wilson," they answered in chorus.

"And will he kill anybody? What are you going to do? Does this happen often? Does he rampage around like this once a week or so? Can he break in that door?"

"No, he can't break down that door," replied the barkeeper. "He's tried it three times. But when he comes you'd better lay down on the floor, stranger. He's dead sure to shoot at it, and a bullet may come through."

Thereafter the drummer kept a strict eye upon the door. The time had not yet been called for him to hug the floor, but, as a minor precaution, he sidled near to the wall. "Will he kill anybody?" he said again.

The men laughed low and scornfully at the question.

"He's out to shoot, and he's out for trouble. Don't see any good in experimentin' with him."

"But what do you do in a case like this? What do you do?"

A man responded: "Why, he and Jack Potter—"

"But," in chorus, the other men interrupted, "Jack Potter's in San Anton'."

"Well, who is he? What's he got to do with it?"

"Oh, he's the town marshal. He goes out and fights Scratchy when he gets on one of these tears."

"Wow," said the drummer, mopping his brow. "Nice job he's got."

The voices had toned away to mere whisperings. The drummer wished to ask further questions which were born of an increasing anxiety and bewilderment; but when he attempted them, the men merely looked at him in irritation and motioned him to remain silent. A tense waiting hush was upon them. In the deep shadows of the room their eyes shone as they listened for sounds from the street. One man made three gestures at the barkeeper, and the latter, moving like a ghost, handed him a glass and a bottle. The man poured a full glass of whisky, and set down the bottle noiselessly. He gulped the whisky in a swallow, and turned again toward the door in immovable silence. The drummer saw that the barkeeper, without a sound, had taken a Winchester from beneath the bar. Later he saw this individual beckoning to him, so he tiptoed across the room.

"You better come with me back of the bar."

"No, thanks," said the drummer, perspiring. "I'd rather be where I can make a break for the back door."

Whereupon the man of bottles made a kindly but peremptory gesture. The drummer obeyed it, and finding himself seated on a box with his head below the level of the bar, balm was laid upon his soul at sight of various zinc and copper fittings that bore a resemblance to armor-plate. The barkeeper took a seat comfortably upon an adjacent box.

"You see," he whispered, "this here Scratchy Wilson is a wonder with a gun—a perfect wonder—and when he goes on the war trail, we hunt our holes—naturally. He's about the last one of the old gang that used to hang out along the river here. He's a terror when he's drunk. When he's sober he's all right—kind of simple—wouldn't hurt a fly—nicest fellow in town. But when he's drunk—whoo!"

There were periods of stillness. "I wish Jack Potter was back from San Anton'," said the barkeeper. "He shot Wilson up once—in the leg—and he would sail in and pull out the kinks in this thing."

Presently they heard from a distance the sound of a shot, followed by three wild yowls. It instantly removed a bond from the men in the darkened saloon. There was a shuffling of feet. They looked at each other. "Here he comes," they said.

III

A man in a maroon-colored flannel shirt, which had been purchased for purposes of decoration and made, principally, by some Jewish women on the east side of New York, rounded a corner and walked into the middle of the main street of Yellow Sky. In either hand the man held a long, heavy, blue-black revolver. Often he yelled, and these cries rang through a semblance of a deserted village, shrilly flying over the roofs in a volume that seemed to have no relation to the ordinary vocal strength of a man. It was as if the surrounding stillness formed the arch of a tomb over him. These cries of ferocious challenge rang against walls of silence. And his boots had red tops with gilded imprints, of the kind beloved in winter by little sledding boys on the hillsides of New England.

The man's face flamed in a rage begot of whisky. His eyes, rolling and yet keen for ambush, hunted the still doorways and windows. He walked with the creeping movement of the midnight cat. As it occurred to him, he roared menacing information. The long revolvers in his hands were as easy as straws; they were moved with an electric swiftness. The little fingers of each hand played sometimes in a musician's way. Plain from the low collar of the shirt, the cords of his neck straightened and sank, straightened and sank, as passion moved him. The only sounds were his terrible invitations. The calm adobes preserved their demeanor at the passing of this small thing in the middle of the street.

There was no offer of fight; no offer of fight. The man called to the sky. There were no attractions. He bellowed and fumed and swayed his revolvers here and everywhere.

The dog of the barkeeper of the "Weary Gentleman" saloon had not appreciated the advance of events. He yet lay dozing in front of his master's door. At sight of the dog, the man paused and raised his revolver humorously. At sight of the man, the dog sprang up and walked diagonally away, with a sullen head, and growling. The man yelled, and the dog broke into a gallop. As it was about to enter an alley, there was a loud noise, a whistling, and something spat the ground directly before it. The dog screamed, and, wheeling in terror, galloped headlong in a new direction.

Again there was a noise, a whistling, and sand was kicked viciously before it. Fear-stricken, the dog turned and flurried like an animal in a pen. The man stood laughing, his weapons at his hips.

Ultimately the man was attracted by the closed door of the "Weary Gentleman" saloon. He went to it, and hammering with a revolver, demanded drink.

The door remaining imperturbable, he picked a bit of paper from the walk and nailed it to the framework with a knife. He then turned his back contemptuously upon this popular resort, and walking to the opposite side of the street, and spinning there on his heel quickly and lithely, fired at the bit of paper. He missed it by a half inch. He swore at himself, and went away. Later, he comfortably fusilladed the windows of his most intimate friend. The man was playing with this town. It was a toy for him.

But still there was no offer of fight. The name of Jack Potter, his ancient antagonist, entered his mind, and he concluded that it would be a glad thing if he should go to Potter's house and by bombardment induce him to come out and fight. He moved in the direction of his desire, chanting Apache scalp-music.

When he arrived at it, Potter's house presented the same still front as had the other adobes. Taking up a strategic position, the man howled a challenge. But this house regarded him as might a great stone god. It gave no sign. After a decent wait, the man howled further challenges, mingling with them wonderful epithets.

Presently there came the spectacle of a man churning himself into deepest rage over the immobility of a house. He fumed at it as the winter wind attacks a prairie cabin in the North. To the distance there should have gone the sound of a tumult like the fighting of 200 Mexicans. As necessity bade him, he paused for breath or to reload his revolvers.

IV

Potter and his bride walked sheepishly and with speed. Sometimes they laughed together shamefacedly and low.

"Next corner, dear," he said finally.

They put forth the efforts of a pair walking bowed against a strong wind. Potter was about to raise a finger to point the first appearance of the new home when, as they circled the corner, they came face to face with a man in a maroon-colored shirt who was feverishly pushing cartridges into a large revolver. Upon the instant the man dropped his revolver to the ground, and, like lightning, whipped another from its holster. The second weapon was aimed at the bridegroom's chest.

There was silence. Potter's mouth seemed to be merely a grave for his tongue. He exhibited an instinct to at once loosen his arm from the woman's grip, and he dropped the bag to the sand. As for the bride, her face had gone as yellow as old cloth. She was a slave to hideous rites gazing at the apparitional snake.

The two men faced each other at a distance of three paces. He of the revolver smiled with a new and quiet ferocity.

"Tried to sneak up on me," he said. "Tried to sneak up on me!" His eyes grew more baleful. As Potter made a slight movement, the man thrust his revolver venomously forward. "No, don't you do it, Jack Potter. Don't you move a finger toward a gun just yet. Don't you move an eyelash. The time has come for me to settle with you, and I'm goin' to do it my own way and loaf along with no interferin'. So if you don't want a gun bent on you, just mind what I tell you."

Potter looked at his enemy. "I ain't got a gun on me, Scratchy," he said. "Honest, I ain't." He was stiffening and steadying, but yet somewhere at the back of his mind a vision of the Pullman floated, the sea-green figured velvet, the shining brass, silver, and glass, the wood that gleamed as darkly brilliant as the surface of a pool of oil—all the glory of the marriage, the environment of the new estate. "You know I fight when it comes to fighting, Scratchy Wilson, but I ain't got a gun on me. You'll have to do all the shootin' yourself."

His enemy's face went livid. He stepped forward and lashed his weapon to and fro before Potter's chest. "Don't you tell me you ain't got no gun on you, you whelp. Don't tell me no lie like that. There ain't a man in Texas ever seen you without no gun. Don't take me for no kid." His eyes blazed with light, and his throat worked like a pump.

"I ain't takin' you for no kid," answered Potter. His heels had not moved an inch backward. "I'm takin' you for a———fool. I tell you I ain't got a gun, and I ain't. If you're goin' to shoot me up, you better begin now. You'll never get a chance like this again."

So much enforced reasoning had told on Wilson's rage. He was calmer. "If you ain't got a gun, why ain't you got a gun?" he sneered. "Been to Sunday-school?"

"I ain't got a gun because I've just come from San Anton' with my wife. I'm married," said Potter. "And if I'd thought there was going to be any galoots like you prowling around when I brought my wife home, I'd had a gun, and don't you forget it."

"Married!" said Scratchy, not at all comprehending.

"Yes, married. I'm married," said Potter distinctly.

"Married?" said Scratchy. Seemingly for the first time he saw the drooping, drowning woman at the other man's side. "No!" he said. He was like a creature allowed a glimpse of another world. He moved a pace backward, and his arm with the revolver dropped to his side. "Is this the lady?" he asked.

"Yes, this is the lady," answered Potter.

There was another period of silence.

"Well," said Wilson at last, slowly, "I s'pose it's all off now."

"It's all off if you say so, Scratchy. You know I didn't make the trouble." Potter lifted his valise.

"Well, I 'low it's off, Jack," said Wilson. He was looking at the ground. "Married!" He was not a student of chivalry; it was merely that in the presence of this foreign condition he was a simple child of the earlier plains. He picked up his starboard revolver, and placing both weapons in their holsters, he went away. His feet made funnel-shaped tracks in the heavy sand.

The Law of Life

Jack London
1901

The story was first published in *McClure's Magazine*, Vol.16, March, 1901. It was collected in London's 1902 *The Children of the Frost*, published by Macmillan Publishers.

Old Koskoosh listened greedily. Though his sight had long since faded, his hearing was still acute, and the slightest sound penetrated to the glimmering intelligence which yet abode behind the withered forehead, but which no longer gazed forth upon the things of the world. Ah! that was Sit-cum-to-ha, shrilly anathematizing the dogs as she cuffed and beat them into the harnesses. Sit-cum-to-ha was his daughter's daughter, but she was too busy to waste a thought upon her broken grandfather, sitting alone there in the snow, forlorn and helpless. Camp must be broken. The long trail waited while the short day refused to linger. Life called her, and the duties of life, not death. And he was very close to death now.

The thought made the old man panicky for the moment, and he stretched forth a palsied hand which wandered tremblingly over the small heap of dry wood beside him. Reassured that it was indeed there, his hand returned to the shelter of his mangy furs, and he again fell to listening. The sulky crackling of half-frozen hides told him that the chief's moose-skin lodge had been struck, and even then was being rammed and jammed into portable compass. The chief was his son, stalwart and strong, head man of the tribesmen, and a mighty hunter. As the women toiled with the camp luggage, his voice rose, chiding them for their slowness. Old Koskoosh strained his ears. It was the last time he would hear that voice. There went Geehow's lodge! And Tusken's! Seven, eight, nine; only the shaman's could be still standing. There! They were at work upon it now. He could hear the shaman grunt as he piled it on the sled. A child whimpered, and a woman soothed it with soft, crooning gutturals. Little Koo-tee, the old man thought, a fretful child, and not overstrong. It would die soon, perhaps, and they would burn a hole through the frozen tundra and pile rocks above to keep the wolverines away. Well, what did it matter? A few years at best, and as many an empty belly as a full one. And in the end, Death waited, ever-hungry and hungriest of them all.

What was that? Oh, the men lashing the sleds and drawing tight the thongs. He listened, who would listen no more. The whip-lashes snarled and bit among the dogs. Hear them whine! How they hated the work and the trail! They were off! Sled after sled churned slowly away into the silence. They were gone. They had passed out of his life, and he faced the last bitter hour alone. No. The snow crunched beneath a moccasin; a man stood beside him; upon his head a hand rested gently. His son was good to do this thing. He remembered other old men whose sons had not waited after the tribe. But his son had. He wandered away into the past, till the young man's voice brought him back.

"Is it well with you?" he asked.

And the old man answered, "It is well."

"There be wood beside you," the younger man continued, "and the fire burns bright. The morning is gray, and the cold has broken. It will snow presently. Even now is it snowing."

"Ay, even now is it snowing."

"The tribesmen hurry. Their bales are heavy, and their bellies flat with lack of feasting. The trail is long and they travel fast. I go now. It is well?"

"It is well. I am as a last year's leaf, clinging lightly to the stem. The first breath that blows, and I fall. My voice is become like an old woman's. My eyes no longer show me the way of my feet, and my feet are heavy, and I am tired. It is well."

He bowed his head in content till the last noise of the complaining snow had died away, and he knew his son was beyond recall. Then his hand crept out in haste to the wood. It alone stood between him and the eternity that yawned in upon him. At last the measure of his life was a handful of fagots. One by one they would go to feed the fire, and just so, step by step, death would creep upon him. When the last stick had surrendered up its heat, the frost would begin to gather strength. First his feet would yield, then his hands; and the numbness would travel, slowly, from the extremities to the body. His head would fall forward upon his knees, and he would rest. It was easy. All men must die.

He did not complain. It was the way of life, and it was just. He had been born close to the earth, close to the earth had he lived, and the law thereof was not new to him. It was the law of all flesh. Nature was not kindly to the flesh. She had no concern for that concrete thing called the individual. Her interest lay in the species, the race. This was the deepest abstraction old Koskoosh's barbaric mind was capable of, but he grasped it firmly. He saw it exemplified in all life. The rise of the sap, the bursting greenness of the willow bud, the fall of the yellow leaf—in this alone was told the whole history. But one task did Nature set the individual. Did he not perform it, he died. Did he perform it, it was all the same, he died. Nature did not care; there were plenty who were obedient, and it was only the obedience in this matter, not the obedient, which lived and lived always. The tribe of Koskoosh was very old. The old men he had known when a boy, had known old men before them. Therefore it was true that the tribe lived, that it stood for the obedience of all its members, way down into the forgotten past, whose very resting-places were unremembered. They did not count; they were episodes. They had passed away like clouds from a summer sky. He also was an episode, and would pass away. Nature did not care. To life she set one task, gave one law. To perpetuate was the task of life, its law was death. A maiden was a good creature to look upon, full-breasted and strong, with spring to her step and light in her eyes. But her task was yet before her. The light in her eyes brightened, her step quickened, she was now bold with the young men, now timid, and she gave them of her own unrest. And ever she grew fairer and yet fairer to look upon, till some hunter, able no longer to withhold himself, took her to his lodge to cook and toil for him and to become the mother of his children. And with the coming of her offspring her looks left her. Her limbs dragged and shuffled, her eyes dimmed and bleared, and only the little children found joy against the withered cheek of the old squaw by the fire. Her task was done. But a little while, on the first pinch of famine or the first long trail, and she would be left, even as he had been left, in the snow, with a little pile of wood. Such was the law.

He placed a stick carefully upon the fire and resumed his meditations. It was the same everywhere, with all things. The mosquitoes vanished with the first frost. The little tree-squirrel crawled away to die. When age settled upon the rabbit it became slow and heavy, and could no longer outfoot its enemies. Even the big bald-face grew clumsy and blind and quarrelsome, in the end to be dragged down by a handful of yelping huskies. He remembered how he had abandoned his own father on an upper reach of the Klondike one winter, the winter before the missionary came with his talk-books and his box of medicines. Many a time had Koskoosh smacked his lips over the recollection of that box, though now his mouth refused to moisten. The "painkiller" had been especially good. But the missionary was a bother after all, for he brought no meat into the camp, and he ate heartily, and the hunters grumbled. But he chilled his lungs on the divide by the Mayo, and the dogs afterwards nosed the stones away and fought over his bones.

Koskoosh placed another stick on the fire and harked back deeper into the past. There was the time of the Great Famine, when the old men crouched empty-bellied to the fire, and let fall from their lips dim traditions of the ancient day when the Yukon ran wide open for three winters, and then lay frozen for three summers. He had lost his mother in that famine. In the summer the salmon run had failed, and the tribe looked forward to the winter and the coming of the caribou. Then the winter came, but with it there were no caribou. Never had the like been known, not even in the lives of the old men. But the caribou did not come, and it was the seventh year, and the rabbits had not replenished, and the dogs were naught but bundles of bones. And through the long darkness the children wailed and died, and the women, and the old men; and not one in ten of the tribe lived to meet the sun when it came back in the spring. That was a famine!

But he had seen times of plenty, too, when the meat spoiled on their hands, and the dogs were fat and worthless with overeating—times when they let the game go unkilled, and the women were fertile, and the lodges were cluttered with sprawling men-children and women-children. Then it was the men became high-stomached, and revived ancient quarrels, and crossed the divides to the south to kill the Pellys, and to the west that they might sit by the dead fires of the Tananas. He remembered, when a boy, during a time of plenty, when he saw a moose pulled down by the wolves. Zing-ha lay with him in the snow and watched—Zing-ha, who later became the craftiest of hunters, and who, in the end, fell through an air-hole on the

Yukon. They found him, a month afterward, just as he had crawled halfway out and frozen stiff to the ice.

But the moose. Zing-ha and he had gone out that day to play at hunting after the manner of their fathers. On the bed of the creek they struck the fresh track of a moose, and with it the tracks of many wolves. "An old one," Zing-ha, who was quicker at reading the sign, said—"an old one who cannot keep up with the herd. The wolves have cut him out from his brothers, and they will never leave him." And it was so. It was their way. By day and by night, never resting, snarling on his heels, snapping at his nose, they would stay by him to the end. How Zing-ha and he felt the blood-lust quicken! The finish would be a sight to see!

Eager-footed, they took the trail, and even he, Koskoosh, slow of sight and an unversed tracker, could have followed it blind, it was so wide. Hot were they on the heels of the chase, reading the grim tragedy, fresh-written, at every step. Now they came to where the moose had made a stand. Thrice the length of a grown man's body, in every direction, had the snow been stamped about and uptossed. In the midst were the deep impressions of the splay-hoofed game, and all about, everywhere, were the lighter footmarks of the wolves. Some, while their brothers harried the kill, had lain to one side and rested. The full-stretched impress of their bodies in the snow was as perfect as though made the moment before. One wolf had been caught in a wild lunge of the maddened victim and trampled to death. A few bones, well picked, bore witness.

Again, they ceased the uplift of their snowshoes at a second stand. Here the great animal had fought desperately. Twice had he been dragged down, as the snow attested, and twice had he shaken his assailants clear and gained footing once more. He had done his task long since, but none the less was life dear to him. Zing-ha said it was a strange thing, a moose once down to get free again; but this one certainly had. The shaman would see signs and wonders in this when they told him.

And yet again, they come to where the moose had made to mount the bank and gain the timber. But his foes had laid on from behind, till he reared and fell back upon them, crushing two deep into the snow. It was plain the kill was at hand, for their brothers had left them untouched. Two more stands were hurried past, brief in time-length and very close together. The trail was red now, and the clean stride of the great beast had grown short and slovenly. Then they heard the first sounds of the battle—not the full-throated chorus of the chase, but the short, snappy bark which spoke of close quarters and teeth to flesh. Crawling up the wind, Zing-ha bellied it through the snow, and with him crept he, Koskoosh, who was to be chief of the tribesmen in the years to come. Together they shoved aside the under branches of a young spruce and peered forth. It was the end they saw.

The picture, like all of youth's impressions, was still strong with him, and his dim eyes watched the end played out as vividly as in that far-off time. Koskoosh marvelled at this, for in the days which followed, when he was a leader of men and a head of councillors, he had done great deeds and made his name a curse in the mouths of the Pellys, to say naught of the strange white man he had killed, knife to knife, in open fight.

For long he pondered on the days of his youth, till the fire died down and the frost bit deeper. He replenished it with two sticks this time, and gauged his grip on life by what remained. If Sit-cum-to-ha had only remembered her grandfather, and gathered a larger armful, his hours would have been longer. It would have been easy. But she was ever a careless child, and honored not her ancestors from the time the Beaver, son of the son of Zing-ha, first cast eyes upon her. Well, what mattered it? Had he not done likewise in his own quick youth? For a while he listened to the silence. Perhaps the heart of his son might soften, and he would come back with the dogs to take his old father on with the tribe to where the caribou ran thick and the fat hung heavy upon them.

He strained his ears, his restless brain for the moment stilled. Not a stir, nothing. He alone took breath in the midst of the great silence. It was very lonely. Hark! What was that? A chill passed over his body. The familiar, long-drawn howl broke the void, and it was close at hand. Then on his darkened eyes was projected the vision of the moose—the old bull moose—the torn flanks and bloody sides, the riddled mane, and the great branching horns, down low and tossing to the last. He saw the flashing forms of gray, the gleaming eyes, the lolling tongues, the slavered fangs. And he saw the inexorable circle close in till it became a dark point in the midst of the stamped snow.

A cold muzzle thrust against his cheek, and at its touch his soul leaped back to the present. His hand shot into the fire and dragged out a burning faggot. Overcome for the nonce by his hereditary fear of man, the brute retreated, raising a prolonged call to his brothers; and greedily they answered, till a ring of crouching, jaw-slobbered gray was stretched round about. The old man listened to the drawing in of this circle. He waved his brand wildly, and sniffs turned to snarls; but the panting brutes refused to scatter. Now one wormed his chest forward, dragging his haunches after, now a second, now a third; but never a one drew back. Why should he cling to life? he asked, and dropped the blazing stick into the snow. It sizzled and went out. The circle grunted uneasily, but held its own. Again he saw the last stand of the old bull moose, and Koskoosh dropped his head wearily upon his knees. What did it matter after all? Was it not the law of life?

Editha

William Dean Howells
1905

The story was first published in *Harper's Monthly* 110 (Jan. 1905) and was later collected in *Between the Dark and the Daylight* (New York: Harper and Brothers, 1907).

The air was thick with the war feeling, like the electricity of a storm which has not yet burst. Editha sat looking out into the hot spring afternoon, with her lips parted, and panting with the intensity of the question whether she could let him go. She had decided that she could not let him stay, when she saw him at the end of the still leafless avenue, making slowly up towards the house, with his head down and his figure relaxed. She ran impatiently out on the veranda, to the edge of the steps, and imperatively demanded greater haste of him with her will before she called aloud to him: "George!"

He had quickened his pace in mystical response to her mystical urgence, before he could have heard her; now he looked up and answered, "Well?"

"Oh, how united we are!" she exulted, and then she swooped down the steps to him. "What is it?" she cried.

"It's war," he said, and he pulled her up to him and kissed her.

She kissed him back intensely, but irrelevantly, as to their passion, and uttered from deep in her throat. "How glorious!"

"It's war," he repeated, without consenting to her sense of it; and she did not know just what to think at first. She never knew what to think of him; that made his mystery, his charm. All through their courtship, which was contemporaneous with the growth of the war feeling, she had been puzzled by his want of seriousness about it. He seemed to despise it even more than he abhorred it. She could have understood his abhorring any sort of bloodshed; that would have been a survival of his old life when he thought he would be a minister, and before he changed and took up the law. But making light of a cause so high and noble seemed to show a want of earnestness at the core of his being. Not but that she felt herself able to cope with a congenital defect of that sort, and make his love for her save him from himself. Now perhaps the miracle was already wrought in him. In the presence of the tremendous fact that he announced, all triviality seemed to have gone out of him; she began to feel that. He sank down on the top step, and wiped his forehead with his handkerchief, while she poured out upon him her question of the origin and authenticity of his news.

All the while, in her duplex emotioning, she was aware that now at the very beginning she must put a guard upon herself against urging him, by any word or act, to take the part that her whole soul willed him to take, for the completion of her ideal of him. He was very nearly perfect as he was, and he must be allowed to perfect himself. But he was peculiar, and he might very well be reasoned out of his peculiarity. Before her reasoning went her emotioning: her nature pulling upon his nature, her womanhood upon his manhood, without her knowing the means she was using to the end she was willing. She had always supposed that the man who won her would have done something to win her; she did not know what, but something. George Gearson had simply asked her for her love, on the way home from a concert, and she gave her love to him, without, as it were, thinking. But now, it flashed upon her, if he could do something worthy to have won her—be a hero, her hero—it would be even better than if he had done it before asking her; it would be grander. Besides, she had believed in the war from the beginning.

"But don't you see, dearest," she said, "that it wouldn't have come to this if it hadn't been in the order of Providence? And I call any war glorious that is for the liberation of people who have been struggling for years against the cruelest oppression. Don't you think so, too?"

"I suppose so," he returned, languidly. "But war! Is it glorious to break the peace of the world?"

"That ignoble peace! It was no peace at all, with that crime and shame at our very gates." She was conscious of parroting the current phrases of the newspapers, but it was no time to pick and choose her words. She must sacrifice anything to the high ideal she had for him, and after a good deal of rapid argument she ended with the climax: "But now it doesn't matter about the how or why. Since the war has come, all that is gone. There are no two sides any more. There is nothing now but our country."

He sat with his eyes closed and his head leant back against the veranda, and he remarked, with a vague smile, as if musing aloud, "Our country—right or wrong."

"Yes, right or wrong!" she returned, fervidly. "I'll go and get you some lemonade." She rose rustling, and whisked away; when she came back with two tall glasses of clouded liquid on a tray, and the ice clucking in them, he still sat as she had left him, and she said, as if there had been no interruption: "But there is no question of wrong in this case. I call it a sacred war. A war for liberty and humanity, if ever there was one. And I know you will see it just as I do, yet."

He took half the lemonade at a gulp, and he answered as he set the glass down: "I know you always have the highest ideal. When I differ from you I ought to doubt myself."

A generous sob rose in Editha's throat for the humility of a man, so very nearly perfect, who was willing to put himself below her.

Besides, she felt, more subliminally, that he was never so near slipping through her fingers as when he took that meek way.

"You shall not say that! Only, for once I happen to be right." She seized his hand in her two hands, and poured her soul from her eyes into his. "Don't you think so?" she entreated him.

He released his hand and drank the rest of his lemonade, and she added, "Have mine, too," but he shook his head in answering, "I've no business to think so, unless I act so, too."

Her heart stopped a beat before it pulsed on with leaps that she felt in her neck. She had noticed that strange thing in men: they seemed to feel bound to do what they believed, and not think a thing was finished when they said it, as girls did. She knew what was in his mind, but she pretended not, and she said, "Oh, I am not sure," and then faltered.

He went on as if to himself, without apparently heeding her: "There's only one way of proving one's faith in a thing like this."

She could not say that she understood, but she did understand.

He went on again. "If I believed—if I felt as you do about this war—Do you wish me to feel as you do?"

Now she was really not sure; so she said: "George, I don't know what you mean."

He seemed to muse away from her as before.

"There is a sort of fascination in it. I suppose that at the bottom of his heart every man would like at times to have his courage tested, to see how he would act."

"How can you talk in that ghastly way?"

"It is rather morbid. Still, that's what it comes to, unless you're swept away by ambition or driven by conviction. I haven't the conviction or the ambition, and the other thing is what it comes to with me. I ought to have been a preacher, after all; then I couldn't have asked it of myself, as I must, now I'm a lawyer. And you believe it's a holy war, Editha?" he suddenly addressed her. "Oh, I know you do! But you wish me to believe so, too?"

She hardly knew whether he was mocking or not, in the ironical way he always had with her plainer mind. But the only thing was to be outspoken with him.

"George, I wish you to believe whatever you think is true, at any and every cost. If I've tried to talk you into anything, I take it all back."

"Oh, I know that, Editha. I know how sincere you are, and how—I wish I had your undoubting spirit! I'll think it over; I'd like to believe as you do. But I don't, now; I don't, indeed. It isn't this war alone; though this seems peculiarly wanton and needless; but it's every war—so stupid; it makes me sick. Why shouldn't this thing have been settled reasonably?"

"Because," she said, very throatily again, "God meant it to be war."

"You think it was God? Yes, I suppose that is what people will say."

"Do you suppose it would have been war if God hadn't meant it?"

"I don't know. Sometimes it seems as if God had put this world into men's keeping to work it as they pleased."

"Now, George, that is blasphemy."

"Well, I won't blaspheme. I'll try to believe in your pocket Providence," he said, and then he rose to go.

"Why don't you stay to dinner?" Dinner at Balcom's Works was at one o'clock.

"I'll come back to supper, if you'll let me. Perhaps I shall bring you a convert."

"Well, you may come back, on that condition."

"All right. If I don't come, you'll understand."

He went away without kissing her, and she felt it a suspension of their engagement. It all interested her intensely; she was undergoing a tremendous experience, and she was being equal to it. While she stood looking after him, her mother came out through one of the long windows onto the veranda, with a catlike softness and vagueness.

"Why didn't he stay to dinner?"

"Because—because—war has been declared," Editha pronounced, without turning.

Her mother said, "Oh, my!" and then said nothing more until she had sat down in one of the large Shaker chairs and rocked herself for some time.

Then she closed whatever tacit passage of thought there had been in her mind with the spoken words: "Well, I hope he won't go."

"And I hope he will," the girl said, and confronted her mother with a stormy exaltation that would have frightened any creature less unimpressionable than a cat.

Her mother rocked herself again for an interval of cogitation. What she arrived at in speech was: "Well, I guess you've done a wicked thing, Editha Balcom."

The girl said, as she passed indoors through the same window her mother had come out by: "I haven't done anything—yet."

* * * * *

In her room, she put together all her letters and gifts from Gearson, down to the withered petals of the first flower he had offered, with that timidity of his veiled in that irony of his. In the heart of the packet she enshrined her engagement ring which she had restored to the pretty box he had brought it her in. Then she sat down, if not calmly yet strongly, and wrote:

GEORGE:—I understood when you left me. But I think we had better emphasize your meaning that if we cannot be one in everything we had better be one in nothing. So I am sending these things for your keeping till you have made up your mind.

I shall always love you, and therefore I shall never marry any one else. But the man I marry must love his country first of all, and be able to say to me, I could not love thee, dear, so much,
Loved I not honor more.'
There is no honor above America with me. In this great hour there is no other honor.

Your heart will make my words clear to you. I had never expected to say so much, but it has come upon me that I must say the utmost.

EDITHA.

She thought she had worded her letter well, worded it in a way that could not be bettered; all had been implied and nothing expressed.

She had it ready to send with the packet she had tied with red, white, and blue ribbon, when it occurred to her that she was not just to him, that she was not giving him a fair chance. He had said he would go and think it over, and she was not waiting. She was pushing, threatening, compelling. That was not a woman's part. She must leave him free, free, free. She could not accept for her country or herself a forced sacrifice.

In writing her letter she had satisfied the impulse from which it sprang; she could well afford to wait till he had thought it over. She put the packet and the letter by, and rested serene in the consciousness of having done what was laid upon her by her love itself to do, and yet used patience, mercy, justice.

She had her reward. Gearson did not come to tea, but she had given him till morning, when, late at night there came up from the village the sound of a fife and drum, with a tumult of voices, in shouting, singing, and laughing. The noise drew nearer and nearer; it reached the street end of the avenue; there it silenced itself, and one voice, the voice she knew best, rose over the silence. It fell; the air was filled with cheers; the fife and drum struck up, with the shouting, singing, and laughing again, but now retreating; and a single figure came hurrying up the avenue.

She ran down to meet her lover and clung to him. He was very gay, and he put his arm round her with a boisterous laugh. "Well, you must call me Captain now; or Cap, if you prefer; that's what the boys call me. Yes, we've had a meeting at the town-hall, and everybody has volunteered; and they selected me for captain, and I'm going to the war, the big war, the glorious war, the holy war ordained by the pocket Providence that blesses butchery.

Come along; let's tell the whole family about it. Call them from their downy beds, father, mother, Aunt Hitty, and all the folks!"

But when they mounted the veranda steps he did not wait for a larger audience; he poured the story out upon Editha alone.

"There was a lot of speaking, and then some of the fools set up a shout for me. It was all going one way, and I thought it would be a good joke to sprinkle a little cold water on them. But you can't do that with a crowd that adores you. The first thing I knew I was sprinkling hell-fire on them. 'Cry havoc, and let slip the dogs of war.' That was the style. Now that it had come to the fight, there were no two parties; there was one country, and the thing was to fight to a finish as quick as possible. I suggested volunteering then and there, and I wrote my name first of all on the roster. Then they elected me—that's all. I wish I had some ice-water."

She left him walking up and down the veranda, while she ran for the ice-pitcher and a goblet, and when she came back he was still walking up and down, shouting the story he had told her to her father and mother, who had come out more sketchily dressed than they commonly were by day. He drank goblet after goblet of the ice-water without noticing who was giving it, and kept on talking, and laughing through his talk wildly. "It's astonishing," he said, "how well the worse reason looks when you try to make it appear the better. Why, I believe I was the first convert to the war in that crowd to-night! I never thought I should like to kill a man; but now I shouldn't care; and the smokeless powder lets you see the man drop that you kill. It's all for the country! What a thing it is to have a country that can't be wrong, but if it is, is right, anyway!"

Editha had a great, vital thought, an inspiration. She set down the ice-pitcher on the veranda floor, and ran up-stairs and got the letter she had written him. When at last he noisily bade her father and mother, "Well, goodnight. I forgot I woke you up; I sha'n't want any sleep myself," she followed him down the avenue to the gate. There, after the whirling words that seemed to fly away from her thoughts and refuse to serve them, she made a last effort to solemnize the moment that seemed so crazy, and pressed the letter she had written upon him.

"What's this?" he said. "Want me to mail it?"

"No, no. It's for you. I wrote it after you went this morning. Keep it—keep it—and read it sometime—" She thought, and then her inspiration came: "Read it if ever you doubt what you've done, or fear that I regret your having done it. Read it after you've started."

They strained each other in embraces that seemed as ineffective as their words, and he kissed her face with quick, hot breaths that were so unlike him, that made her feel as if she had lost her old lover and found a stranger in his place. The stranger said: "What a gorgeous flower you are, with your red hair, and your blue eyes that look black now, and your face with the color painted out by the white moonshine! Let me hold you under the chin, to see whether I love blood, you tiger-lily!" Then he laughed Gearson's laugh, and released her, scared and giddy. Within her wilfulness she had been frightened by a sense of subtler force in him, and mystically mastered as she had never been before.

She ran all the way back to the house, and mounted the steps panting. Her mother and father were talking of the great affair. Her mother said: "Wa'n't Mr. Gearson in rather of an excited state of mind? Didn't you think he acted curious?"

"Well, not for a man who'd just been elected captain and had set 'em up for the whole of Company A," her father chuckled back.

"What in the world do you mean, Mr. Balcom? Oh! There's Editha!" She offered to follow the girl indoors.

"Don't come, mother!" Editha called, vanishing.

Mrs. Balcom remained to reproach her husband. "I don't see much of anything to laugh at."

"Well, it's catching. Caught it from Gearson. I guess it won't be much of a war, and I guess Gearson don't think so, either. The other fellows will back down as soon as they see we mean it. I wouldn't lose any sleep over it. I'm going back to bed, myself."

* * * * *

Gearson came again next afternoon, looking pale and rather sick, but quite himself, even to his languid irony. "I guess I'd better tell you, Editha, that I consecrated myself to your god of battles last night by pouring too many libations to him down my own throat. But I'm all right now. One has to carry off the excitement, somehow."

"Promise me," she commanded, "that you'll never touch it again!"

"What! Not let the cannikin clink? Not let the soldier drink? Well, I promise."

"You don't belong to yourself now; you don't even belong to me. You belong to your country, and you have a sacred charge to keep yourself strong and well for your country's sake. I have been thinking, thinking all night and all day long."

"You look as if you had been crying a little, too," he said, with his queer smile.

"That's all past. I've been thinking, and worshipping you. Don't you suppose I know all that you've been through, to come to this? I've followed you every step from your old theories and opinions."

"Well, you've had a long row to hoe."

"And I know you've done this from the highest motives—"

"Oh, there won't be much pettifogging to do till this cruel war is—"

"And you haven't simply done it for my sake. I couldn't respect you if you had."

"Well, then we'll say I haven't. A man that hasn't got his own respect intact wants the respect of all the other people he can corner. But we won't go into that. I'm in for the thing now, and we've got to face our future. My idea is that this isn't going to be a very protracted struggle; we shall just scare the enemy to death before it comes to a fight at all. But we must provide for contingencies, Editha. If anything happens to me—"

"Oh, George!" She clung to him, sobbing.

"I don't want you to feel foolishly bound to my memory. I should hate that, wherever I happened to be."

"I am yours, for time and eternity—time and eternity." She liked the words; they satisfied her famine for phrases.

"Well, say eternity; that's all right; but time's another thing; and I'm talking about time. But there is something! My mother! If anything happens—"

She winced, and he laughed. "You're not the bold soldier-girl of yesterday!" Then he sobered. "If anything happens, I want you to help my mother out. She won't like my doing this thing. She brought me up to think war a fool thing as well as a bad thing. My father was in the Civil War; all through it; lost his arm in it." She thrilled with the sense of the arm round her; what if that should be lost? He laughed as if divining her: "Oh, it doesn't run in the family, as far as I know!" Then he added, gravely: "He came home with misgivings about war, and they grew on him. I guess he and mother agreed between them that I was to be brought up in his final mind about it; but that was before my time. I only knew him from my mother's report of him and his opinions; I don't know whether they were hers first; but they were hers last. This will be a blow to her. I shall have to write and tell her—"

He stopped, and she asked: "Would you like me to write, too, George?"

"I don't believe that would do. No, I'll do the writing. She'll understand a little if I say that I thought the way to minimize it was to make war on the largest possible scale at once—that I felt I must have been helping on the war somehow if I hadn't helped keep it from coming, and I knew I hadn't; when it came, I had no right to stay out of it."

Whether his sophistries satisfied him or not, they satisfied her. She clung to his breast, and whispered, with closed eyes and quivering lips: "Yes, yes, yes!"

"But if anything should happen, you might go to her and see what you could do for her. You know? It's rather far off; she can't leave her chair—"

"Oh, I'll go, if it's the ends of the earth! But nothing will happen! Nothing can! I—"

She felt herself lifted with his rising, and Gearson was saying, with his arm still round her, to her father: "Well, we're off at once, Mr. Balcom. We're to be formally accepted at the capital, and then bunched up with the rest somehow, and sent into camp somewhere, and got to the front as soon as possible. We all want to be in the van, of course; we're the first company to report to the Governor. I came to tell Editha, but I hadn't got round to it."

* * * * *

She saw him again for a moment at the capital, in the station, just before the train started southward with his regiment. He looked well, in his uniform, and very soldierly, but somehow girlish, too, with his clean-shaven face and slim figure. The manly eyes and the strong voice satisfied her, and his preoccupation with some unexpected details of duty flattered her. Other girls were weeping and bemoaning themselves, but she felt a sort of noble distinction in the abstraction, the almost unconsciousness, with which they parted. Only at the last moment he said: "Don't forget my mother. It mayn't be such a walk-over as I supposed," and he laughed at the notion.

He waved his hand to her as the train moved off—she knew it among a score of hands that were waved to other girls from the platform of the car, for it held a letter which she knew was hers. Then he went inside the car to read it, doubtless, and she did not see him again. But she felt safe for him through the strength of what she called her love. What she called her God, always speaking the name in a deep voice and with the implication of a mutual understanding, would watch over him and keep him and bring him back to her. If with an empty sleeve, then he should have three arms instead of two, for both of hers should be his for life. She did not see, though, why she should always be thinking of the arm his father had lost.

There were not many letters from him, but they were such as she could have wished, and she put her whole strength into making hers such as she imagined he could have wished, glorifying and supporting him. She wrote to his mother glorifying him as their hero, but the brief answer she got was merely to the effect that Mrs. Gearson was not well enough to write herself, and thanking her for her letter by the hand of some one who called herself "Yrs truly, Mrs. W.J. Andrews."

Editha determined not to be hurt, but to write again quite as if the answer had been all she expected. Before it seemed as if she could have written, there came news of the first skirmish, and in the list of the killed, which was telegraphed as a trifling loss on our side, was Gearson's name. There was a frantic time of trying to make out that it might be, must be, some other Gearson; but the name and the company and the regiment and the State were too definitely given.

Then there was a lapse into depths out of which it seemed as if she never could rise again; then a lift into clouds far above all grief, black clouds, that blotted out the sun, but where she soared with him, with George—George! She had the fever that she expected of herself, but she did not die in it; she was not even delirious, and it did not last long. When she was well enough to leave her bed, her one thought was of George's mother, of his strangely worded wish that she should go to her and see what she could do for her. In the exaltation of the duty laid upon her—it buoyed her up instead of burdening her—she rapidly recovered.

Her father went with her on the long railroad journey from northern New York to western Iowa; he had business out at Davenport, and he said he could just as well go then as any other time; and he went with her to the little country town where George's mother lived in a little house on the edge of the illimitable cornfields, under trees pushed to a top of the rolling prairie. George's father had settled there after the Civil War, as so many other old soldiers had done; but they were Eastern people, and Editha fancied touches of the East in the June rose overhanging the front door, and the garden with early summer flowers stretching from the gate of the paling fence.

It was very low inside the house, and so dim, with the closed blinds, that they could scarcely see one another: Editha tall and black in her crapes which filled the air with the smell of their dyes; her father standing decorously apart with his hat on his forearm, as at funerals; a woman rested in a deep arm-chair, and the woman who had let the strangers in stood behind the chair.

The seated woman turned her head round and up, and asked the woman behind her chair: "Who did you say?"

Editha, if she had done what she expected of herself, would have gone down on her knees at the feet of the seated figure and said, "I am George's Editha," for answer.

But instead of her own voice she heard that other woman's voice, saying: "Well, I don't know as I did get the name just right. I guess I'll have to make a little more light in here," and she went and pushed two of the shutters ajar.

Then Editha's father said, in his public will-now-address-a-few-remarks tone: "My name is Balcom, ma'am—Junius H. Balcom, of Balcom's Works, New York; my daughter—"

"Oh!" the seated woman broke in, with a powerful voice, the voice that always surprised Editha from Gearson's slender frame. "Let me see you. Stand round where the light can strike on your face," and Editha dumbly obeyed. "So, you're Editha Balcom," she sighed.

"Yes," Editha said, more like a culprit than a comforter.

"What did you come for?" Mrs. Gearson asked.

Editha's face quivered and her knees shook. "I came—because—because George—" She could go no further.

"Yes," the mother said, "he told me he had asked you to come if he got killed. You didn't expect that, I suppose, when you sent him."

"I would rather have died myself than done it!" Editha said, with more truth in her deep voice than she ordinarily found in it. "I tried to leave him free—"

"Yes, that letter of yours, that came back with his other things, left him free."

Editha saw now where George's irony came from.

"It was not to be read before—unless—until—I told him so," she faltered.

"Of course, he wouldn't read a letter of yours, under the circumstances, till he thought you wanted him to. Been sick?" the woman abruptly demanded.

"Very sick," Editha said, with self-pity.

"Daughter's life," her father interposed, "was almost despaired of, at one time."

Mrs. Gearson gave him no heed. "I suppose you would have been glad to die, such a brave person as you! I don't believe he was glad to die. He was always a timid boy, that way; he was afraid of a good many things; but if he was afraid he did what he made up his mind to. I suppose he made up his mind to go, but I knew what it cost him by what it cost me when I heard of it. I had been through one war before. When you sent him you didn't expect he would get killed."

The voice seemed to compassionate Editha, and it was time. "No," she huskily murmured.

"No, girls don't; women don't, when they give their men up to their country. They think they'll come marching back, somehow, just as gay as they went, or if it's an empty sleeve, or even an empty pantaloon, it's all the more glory, and they're so much the prouder of them, poor things!"

The tears began to run down Editha's face; she had not wept till then; but it was now such a relief to be understood that the tears came.

"No, you didn't expect him to get killed," Mrs. Gearson repeated, in a voice which was startlingly like George's again. "You just expected him to kill some one else, some of those foreigners, that weren't there because they had any say about it, but because they had to be there, poor wretches—conscripts, or whatever they call 'em. You thought it would be all right for my George, your George, to kill the sons of those miserable mothers and the husbands of those girls that you would never see the faces of." The woman lifted her powerful voice in a psalmlike note. "I thank my God he didn't live to do it! I thank my God they killed him first, and that he ain't livin' with their blood on his hands!" She dropped her eyes, which she had raised with her voice, and glared at Editha. "What you got that black on for?" She lifted herself by her powerful arms so high that her helpless body seemed to hang limp its full length. "Take it off, take it off, before I tear it from your back!"

* * * * *

The lady who was passing the summer near Balcom's Works was sketching Editha's beauty, which lent itself wonderfully to the effects of a colorist. It had come to that confidence which is rather apt to grow between artist and sitter, and Editha had told her everything.

"To think of your having such a tragedy in your life!" the lady said. She added: "I suppose there are people who feel that way about war. But when you consider the good this war has done—how much it has done for the country! I can't understand such people, for my part. And when you had come all the way out there to console her—got up out of a sick-bed! Well!"

"I think," Editha said, magnanimously, "she wasn't quite in her right mind; and so did papa."

"Yes," the lady said, looking at Editha's lips in nature and then at her lips in art, and giving an empirical touch to them in the picture. "But how dreadful of her! How perfectly—excuse me—how vulgar!"

A light broke upon Editha in the darkness which she felt had been without a gleam of brightness for weeks and months. The mystery that had bewildered her was solved by the word; and from that moment she rose from grovelling in shame and self-pity, and began to live again in the ideal.

To Build a Fire

Jack London
1908

The story was first published in *The Youth's Companion* on May 29, 1902 with an ending possibly better suited for children. Later, however, the story's ending was re-written, and the story was republished in *The Century Magazine*, v.76, August, 1908.

Day had broken cold and gray, exceedingly cold and gray, when the man turned aside from the main Yukon trail and climbed the high earth-bank, where a dim and little traveled trail led eastward through the fat spruce timberland. It was a steep bank, and he paused for breath at the top, excusing the act to himself by looking at his watch. It was nine o'clock. There was no sun nor hint of sun, though there was not a cloud in the sky. It was a clear day, and yet there seemed an intangible pall over the face of things, a subtle gloom that made the day dark, and that was due to the absence of sun. This fact did not worry the man. He was used to the lack of sun. It had been days since he had seen the sun, and he knew that a few more-days must pass before that cheerful orb, due south, would just peep above the sky-line and dip immediately from view.

The man flung a look back along the way he had come. The Yukon lay a mile wide and hidden under three feet of ice. On top of this ice were as many feet of snow. It was all pure white, rolling in gentle, undulations where the ice jams of the freeze-up had formed. North and south, as far as his eye could see, it was unbroken white, save for a dark hairline that curved and twisted from around the spruce-covered island to the south, and that curved and twisted away into the north, where it disappeared behind another spruce-covered island. This dark hair-line was the trail—the main trail—that led south five hundred miles to the Chilcoot Pass, Dyea, and salt water; and that led north seventy miles to Dawson, and still on to the north a thousand miles to Nulato, and finally to St. Michael on Bering Sea, a thousand miles and half a thousand more.

But all this—the mysterious, far-reaching hair-line trail. the absence of sun from the sky, the tremendous cold, and the strangeness and weirdness of it all—made no impression on the man. It was not because he was long used to it. He was a newcomer! in the land, a *chechaquo*, and this was his first winter. The trouble with him was that he was without imagination. He was quick and alert in the things of life, but only in the things, and not in the significances. Fifty degrees below zero meant eighty-odd degrees of frost. Such fact impressed him as being cold and uncomfortable, and that was all. It did not lead him to meditate upon his frailty as a creature of temperature, and upon man's frailty in general, able only to live within certain narrow limits of heat and cold; and from there on it did not lead him to the conjectural field of immortality and man's place in the universe. Fifty degrees below zero stood forte bite of frost that hurt and that must be guarded against by the use of mittens, ear-flaps, warm moccasins, and thick socks. Fifty degrees below zero was to him just precisely fifty degrees below zero. That there should be anything more to it than that was a thought that never entered his head.

As he turned to go on, he spat speculatively. There was a sharp, explosive crackle that startled him. He spat again. And again, in the air, before it could fall to the snow, the spittle crackled. He knew that at fifty below spittle crackled on the snow, but this spittle had crackled in the air. Undoubtedly it was colder than fifty below—how much colder he did not know. But the temperature did not matter. He was bound for the old claim on the left fork of Henderson Creek, where the boys were already. They had come over across the divide from the Indian Creek country, while he had come the roundabout way to take; a look at the possibilities of getting out logs in the spring from the islands in the Yukon. He would be in to camp by six o'clock; a bit after dark, it was true, but the boys would be there, a fire would be going, and a hot supper would be ready. As for lunch, he pressed his hand against the protruding bundle under his jacket. It was also under his shirt, wrapped up in a handkerchief and lying against the naked skin. It was the only way to keep the biscuits from freezing. He smiled agreeably to himself as he thought of those biscuits, each cut open and sopped in bacon grease, and each enclosing a generous slice of fried bacon.

He plunged in among the big spruce trees. The trail was faint. A foot of snow had fallen since the last sled had passed over, and he was glad he was without a sled, traveling light. In fact, he carried nothing but the lunch wrapped in the handkerchief. He was surprised, however, at the cold. It certainly was cold, he concluded as he rubbed his numb nose and cheek-bones with his mittened hand. He was a warm-whiskered man, but the hair on his face did not protect the high cheek-bones and the eager nose that thrust itself aggressively into the frosty air.

At the man's heels trotted a dog, a big native husky, the proper wolfdog, gray-coated and without any visible or temperamental difference from its brother, the wild wolf. The animal was depressed by the tremendous cold. It knew that it was no time for traveling. Its instinct told it a truer tale than was told to the man by the man's judgment. In reality, it was not merely colder than fifty below zero; it was colder than sixty below, than seventy below. It was seventy-five below zero. Since the freezing point is thirty-two above zero, it meant that one hundred and seven degrees of frost obtained. The dog did not know anything about thermometers. Possibly in its brain there was no sharp consciousness of a condition of very cold such as was in the man's brain. But the brute had its instinct. It experienced a vague but menacing apprehension that subdued it and made it slink along at the man's heels, and that made it question eagerly every unwonted movement of the man as if expecting him to go into camp or to seek shelter somewhere and build a fire. The dog had learned fire, and it wanted fire, or else to burrow under the snow and cuddle its warmth away from the air.

The frozen moisture of its breathing had settled on its fur in a fine powder of frost, and especially were its jowls, muzzle, and eyelashes whitened by its crystalled breath. The man's red beard and mustache were likewise frosted, but more solidly, the deposit taking the form of ice and increasing with every warm, moist breath he exhaled. Also, the man was chewing tobacco, and the muzzle of ice held his lips so rigidly that he was unable to clear his chin when he expelled the juice. The result was that a crystal beard of the color and solidity of amber was increasing its length on his chin. If he fell down it would shatter itself, like glass, into brittle fragments. But he did not mind the appendage. It was the penalty all tobacco-chewers paid in that country, and he had been out before in two cold snaps. They had not been so cold as this, he knew, but by the spirit thermometer at Sixty Mile he knew they had been registered at fifty below and at fifty-five.

He held on through the level stretch of woods for several miles, crossed a wide flat of rigger-heads, and dropped down a bank to the frozen bed of a small stream. This was Henderson Creek, and he knew he was ten miles from the forks. He looked at his watch. It was ten o'clock. He was making four miles an hour, and he calculated that he would arrive at the forks at half-past twelve. He decided to celebrate that event by eating his lunch there.

The dog dropped in again at his heels, with a tail drooping discouragement, as the man swung along the creek-bed. The furrow of the old sled-trail was plainly visible, but a dozen inches of snow covered the marks of the last runners. In a month no man had come up or down that silent creek. The man held steadily on. He was not much given to thinking, and just then particularly he had nothing to think about save that he would eat lunch at-the forks and that at six o'clock he would be in camp with the boys. There was nobody to talk to; and, had there been, speech would have been impossible because of the ice-muzzle on his mouth. So he continued monotonously to chew tobacco and to increase the length of his amber beard.

Once in a while the thought reiterated itself that it was very cold and that he had never experienced such cold. As he walked along he rubbed his cheek-bones and nose with the back of his mittened hand. He did this automatically, now and again changing hands. But rub as he would, the instant he stopped his cheek-bones went numb, and the following instant the end of his nose went numb. He was sure to frost his cheeks; he knew that, and experienced a pang of regret that he had not devised a nose-strap of the sort Bud wore in cold snaps. Such a strap passed across the cheeks, as well, and saved them. But it didn't matter much, after all. What were frosted cheeks? A bit painful, that was all; they were never serious.

Empty as the man's mind was of thoughts, he was keenly observant, and he noticed the changes in the creek, the curves and bends and timber jams, and always he sharply noted where he placed his feet. Once coming around a bend, he shied abruptly, like a startled horse, curved away from the place where he had been walking, and retreated several paces back along the trail. The creek he knew was frozen clear to the bottom,—no creek could contain water in that arctic winter,—but he knew also that there were springs that bubbled out from the hillsides and ran along under the snow and on top the ice of the creek. He knew that the coldest snaps never froze these springs, and he knew likewise their danger. They were traps. They hid pools of water under the snow that might be three inches deep, or three feet. Sometimes a skin of ice. half an inch thick covered them, and in turn was covered by the snow. Sometimes there were alternate layers of water and ice-skin, so that when one broke through he kept on breaking through for a while, sometimes wetting himself to the waist.

That was why he had shied in such panic. He had felt the give under his feet and heard the crackle of a snow-hidden ice-skin. And to get his feet wet in such a temperature meant trouble and danger. At the very least it meant delay, for he would be forced to stop and build a fire, and under its protection to bare his feet while he dried his socks and moccasins. He stood and studied the creek-bed and its banks, and decided that the flow of water came from the right. He reflected a while, rubbing his nose and cheeks, then skirted to the left, stepping gingerly and testing the footing for each step. Once clear of the danger, he took a fresh chew of tobacco and swung along at his four-mile gait.

In the course of the next two hours he came upon several similar traps. Usually the snow above the hidden pools had a sunken, candied appearance that advertised the danger. Once again, however, he had a close call; and once, suspecting danger, he compelled the dog to go on in front. The dog did not want to go. It hung back until the man shoved it forward, and then it went quickly across the white, unbroken surface. Suddenly it broke through, floundered to one side, and got away to firmer footing. It had wet its forefeet and legs, and almost immediately the water that clung to it turned to ice. It made quick efforts to lick the ice off its legs, then dropped down in the snow and began to bite out the ice that had formed between the toes. I his was a matter of instinct. To permit the ice to remain would mean sore feet. It did not know this. It merely obeyed the mysterious prompting that arose from the deep crypts of its being. But the man knew, having achieved a judgment on the subject, and he removed the mitten from his right hand and helped tear out the ice-particles. He did not expose his fingers more than a minute, and was astonished at the swift numbness that smote them. It certainly was cold. He pulled on the mitten hastily, and beat the hand savagely across his chest.

At twelve o'clock the day was at its brightest. Yet the sun was too; far south an its winter journey to clear the horizon. The bulge of the earth intervened between it arid Henderson Creek, where the man walked under a clear sky at noon and cast no shadow. At half-past twelve, to the minute, he arrived at the forks of the creek. He was. pleased at the speed he had made. If he kept it up, he would certainly be with the boys by six. He unbuttoned his jacket and shirt and drew forth his lunch. The action consumed no more than a quarter of a minute, yet in that brief moment the numbness laid hold of the exposed fingers. He did not put the mitten on, but, instead struck the fingers a dozen sharp smashes against his leg. Then he sat down on a snow-covered log to eat. The sting that followed upon the striking of his fingers against his leg ceased so quickly that he was startled. He had had no chance to take a bite of biscuit. He struck the fingers repeatedly and returned them to the mitten, baring the other hand for the purpose of eating, He tried to take a mouthful, but the ice-muzzle prevented. He had forgotten to build a fire and thaw out. He chuckled at his foolishness, and as he chuckled he noted the numbness creeping into the exposed fingers. Also, he noted that the stinging which had first come to his toes when he sat down was already passing away. He wandered whether the toes were warm or numb. He moved them inside the moccasins and decided that they were numb.

He pulled the mitten on hurriedly and stood up. He was a bit frightened. He stamped up and down until the stinging returned into the feet. It certainly was cold, was his thought. That man from Sulphur Creek had spoken the truth when telling how cold it sometimes got in the country. And he had laughed at him at the time! That showed one must not be too sure of things. There was no mistake about it, it was cold. He strode up and down, stamping his feet and threshing his arms, until reassured by the returning warmth. Then he got out matches and proceeded to make a fire. From the undergrowth, where high water of the previous spring had lodged a supply of seasoned twigs, he got his firewood. Working carefully from a small beginning, he soon had a roaring fire, over which he thawed the ice from his face and in the protection of which he ate his biscuits. For the moment the cold space was outwitted. The dog took satisfaction in the fire, stretching out close enough for warmth and far enough away to escape being singed.

When the man had finished, be filled his pipe and took his comfortable time over a smoke. Then he pulled on his mittens, settled the ear-flaps of his cap firmly about his ears, and took the creek trail up the left fork. The dog was disappointed and yearned back toward the fire. This man did not know cold. Possibly all the generations of his ancestry had been ignorant of cold of real cold, of cold one hundred and seven degrees below freezing point. But the dog knew; all its ancestry knew, and it had inherited the knowledge. And it knew that it was not good to walk abroad in such fearful cold. It was the time to lie snug in a hole in the snow and wait for a curtain of cloud to be drawn across the face of outer space whence this cold came. On the other hand, there was no keen intimacy between the dog and the man. The one was the toil-slave of the other, and the only caresses it had ever received were the caresses of the whiplash and of harsh and menacing throat-sounds that threatened the whiplash. So, the dog made no effort to communicate its apprehension to the man. It was not concerned in the welfare of the man, it was for its own sake that it yearned back toward the fire. But the man whistled, and spoke to it with the sound of whiplashes and the dog swung in at the man's heel and followed after.

The man took a chew of tobacco and proceeded to start a new amber beard. Also, his moist breath quickly powdered with white his mustache, eyebrows, and lashes. There did not seem to be so many springs on the left fork of the Henderson, and for half an hour the man saw no signs of any. And then it happened. At a place where there were no signs, where the soft, unbroken snow seemed to advertise solidity beneath, tee man broke through. It was not deep. He wet himself halfway to the knees before he floundered out to the firm crust.

He was angry, and cursed his luck aloud. He had hoped to get into camp with the boys at six o'clock, and this would delay him an hour, for he would have to build a fire and dry out his foot-gear. This was imperative at that low temperature—he knew that much; and he turned aside to the bank, which he climbed. On top, tangled in the underbrush about the trunks of several small spruce trees, was a high-water deposit of dry firewood—sticks and twigs, principally, but also larger portions of seasoned branches and fine, dry, last-year's grasses. He threw down several large pieces on top of the snow. This served for a foundation and prevented the young flame from drowning itself in the snow it otherwise would melt. The flame he got by touching a match to a small shred of birch bark that he took from his pocket. This burned even more readily than paper. Placing it on the foundation, he fed the young flame with wisps of dry grass and with the tiniest dry twigs.

He worked slowly and carefully, keenly aware of his danger. Gradually, as the flame grew stronger, he increased the size of the twigs with which he fed it. He squatted in the snow, pulling the twigs out from their entanglement in the brush and feeding directly to the flame. He knew there must be no failure. When it is seventy-five below zero, a man must not fail in his first attempt to build a fire—that is, if his feet are wet. If his feet are dry, and he fails, he can run along the trail for half a mile and restore his circulation. But the circulation of wet and freezing feet cannot be restored by running when it is seventy-five below. No matter how fast he runs, the wet feet will freeze the harder.

All this the man knew. The old-timer on Sulphur Creek had told him about it the previous fall, and now he was appreciating the advice. Already all sensation had gone out of his feet. To build the fire he had been forced to remove his mittens, and the fingers had quickly gone numb. His pace of four miles an hour had kept his heart pumping blood to the surface of his body and to all the extremities. But the instant he stopped, the action of the pump eased down. The cold of space smote the unprotected tip of the planet, and he, being on that unprotected tip, received the full force of the blow. The blood of his body recoiled before it. The blood was alive, like the dog, and like the dog it wanted to hide away and cover itself up from the fearful cold. So long as he walked four miles an hour, he pumped that blood, willy-nilly, to the surface; but now it ebbed away and sank down into the recesses of his body. The extremities were the first to feel its absence. His wet feet froze the faster, and his exposed fingers numbed the faster, though they had not yet begun to freeze. Nose and cheeks were already freezing, while the skin of all his body chilled as it lost its blood.

But he was safe. Toes and nose and cheeks would be only touched by the frost, for the fire was beginning to burn with strength. He was feeding it with twigs the size of his finger. In another minute he would be able to feed it with branches the size of his wrier, and then he could remove his wet toot-gear, and, while it dried, he could keep his naked feet warm by the fire, rubbing them at first, of course, with snow. The fire was a success. He was safe. He remembered the advice of the old timer on Sulphur Creek, and smiled. The old-timer had been very serious in laying down the law that no man must travel alone in the Klondike after fifty below. Well, here he was; he had had the accident; he was alone; and he had saved himself. Those old-timers were rather womanish, some of them, he thought. All a man had to do was to keep his head, and he was all right. Any man who was a man could travel alone. But it was surprising, the rapidity with which his cheeks and nose were freezing. And he had not thought his fingers could go lifeless in so short a time. Lifeless they were, for he could scarcely make them move together to grip a twig, and they seemed remote from his body and from him. When he touched a twig, he had to look and see whether or not he had hold of it. The wires were pretty well down between him and his finger-ends.

All of which counted for little. There was the fire, snapping and crackling and promising life with every dancing flame. He started to untie his moccasins. They were coated with ice; the thick German socks were like sheaths of iron halfway to the knees; and the moccasin strings were like rods of steel all twisted and knotted as by some conflagration. For a moment he tugged with his numb fingers, then, realizing the folly of it, he drew his sheath-knife.

But before he could cut the strings, it happened. It was his own fault or, rather, his mistake. He should not have built the fire under the spruce tree. He should have built it in the open. But it had been easier to pull the twigs from the brush and drop them directly on the fire. Now the tree under which he had done this carried a weight of snow on its boughs. No wind had blown for weeks, and each bough was fully freighted. Each time he had pulled a twig he had communicated a slight agitation to the tree—an imperceptible agitation, so far as he was concerned, but an agitation sufficient to bring about the disaster. High up in the tree one bough capsized its load of snow. This fell on the boughs beneath, capsizing them. This process continued, spreading out and involving the whole tree. It grew like an avalanche, and it descended without warning upon the man and the fire, and the fire was blotted out! Where it had burned was a mantle of fresh and disordered snow.

The man was shocked. It was as though he had just heard his own sentence of death. For a moment he sat and stared at the spot where the fire had been. Then he grew very calm. Perhaps the old-timer on Sulphur Creek was right. If he had only had a trail-mate he would have been in no danger now. The trail-mate could have built the fire. Well, it was up to him to build the fire over again, and this second time there must be no failure. Even if he succeeded, he would most likely lose some toes His feet must be badly frozen by now, and there would be some time before the second fire Was ready.

Such were his thoughts, but he did not sit and think them. He was busy all the time they were passing through his mind. He made a new foundation for a fire, this time in the open, where no treacherous tree could blot it out. Next, he gathered dry grasses and tiny twigs from the high-water flotsam. He could not bring his fingers together to pull them out, but he was able to gather them by the handful. In this way he got many rotten twigs and bits of green moss that were undesirable, but it was the best he could do. He worked methodically, even collecting an armful of the larger branches to be used later when the fire gathered strength. And all the while the dog sat and watched him, a certain yearning wistfulness in its eyes, for it looked upon him as the fire-provider, and the fire was slow in coming.

When all was ready, the man reached in his pocket for a second piece of birch bark. He knew the bark was there, and, though he could not feel it with his fingers, he could hear its crisp rustling as he fumbled for it. Try as he would, he could not clutch hold of it. And all the time in his consciousness, was the knowledge that each instant his feet were freezing. This thought tended to put him in a panic, but he fought against it and kept calm. He pulled on his mittens with his teeth, and threshed his arms back and forth, beating his hands with all his might against his sides. He did this sitting down, and he stood up to do it; and all the while the do,g sat in the snow, its wolf-brush of a tail curled around warmly over its forefeet, its sharp wolf-ears pricked forward intently as it watched the man And the man, as he beat and threshed with his arms and hands, felt a great surge of envy as he regarded the creature that was warm ant secure in its natural covering.

After a time he was aware of the first far-away signals of sensation in his beaten fingers. The faint tingling grew stronger till it evolved into a stinging ache that was excruciating, but which the man hailed with satisfaction. He stripped the mitten from his right hand and fetched forth the birch bark. The exposed fingers were quickly going numb again. Next he brought out his bunch of sulphur matches. But the tremendous cold had already driven the life out of his fingers. In his effort to separate one match from the others, the whole bunch fell in the snow. He tried to pick it out of the snow, but failed. The dead fingers could neither touch nor clutch. He was very careful. He drove the thought of his freezing feet, and nose, and cheeks, out of his mind, devoting his whole soul to the matches. He watched, using the sense of vision in place of that of touch, and when he saw his fingers on each side the bunch, he dosed them—that is, he willed to close them, for the wires were down, and the fingers did not obey. He pulled the mitten on the right hand and beat it fiercely against his knee. Then. with both mittened hands, he scooped the bunch of matches, along with much snow, into his lap. Yet he was no better off.

After some manipulation he managed to get the bunch between the heels of his mittened hands. In this fashion he carried it to his mouth. The ice crackled and snapped when by a violent effort he opened his mouth. He drew the lower jaw in, curled the upper lip out of the way, and scraped the bunch with his upper teeth in order to separate a match. He succeeded in getting one, which he dropped on his lap. He was no better off. He could not pick it up. Then he devised a way. He picked it up in his teeth and scratched it on his leg. Twenty times he scratched before he succeeded in lighting it. As it flamed he held it with his teeth to the birch bark. But the burning brimstone went up his nostrils and into his lungs, causing him to cough spasmodically. The match fell into the snow and went out.

The old-timer an Sulphur Creek was right, he thought in the moment of controlled despair that ensued after fifty below, a man should travel with a partner. He beat his hands, but failed in exciting any sensation. Suddenly he bared both hands, removing the mittens with his teeth. He caught the whole bunch between the heels of his hands. His arm muscles not being frozen enabled him to press the hand-heels tightly against the matches. Then he scratched the bunch along his leg It flared into flame, seventy sulphur matches at once! There was no wind to blow them out He kept his head to one side to escape the strangling fumes, and held the blazing bunch to the birth bark. As he so held it, he became aware of sensation in his hand. His flesh was burning. He could smell it. Deep down below the surface he could feel it. The sensation developed into pain that grew acute. And still he endured, it holding the flame of the matches clumsily to the bark that would not light readily because his own burning hands were in the way, absorbing most of the flame.

At last, when he could endure no more, he jerked his hands apart. The blazing matches fell sizzling into the snow, but the birch bark was alight. He began laying dry grasses and the tiniest twigs on the flame. He could not pick and choose, for he had to lift the fuel between the heels of his hands. Small pieces of rotten wood and green moss clung to the twigs, and he bit them off as well as he could with his teeth. He cherished the flame carefully and awkwardly. It meant life, and it must not perish. The withdrawal of blood from the surface of his body now made him begin to shiver, and he grew more awkward. A large piece of green moss fell squarely on the little fire. He tried to poke it out with his fingers, but his shivering frame made him poke too far and he disrupted the nucleus of the little fire, the burning grasses and tiny twigs separating and scattering. He tried to poke them together again, but in spite of the tenseness of the effort, his shivering got away with him, and the twigs were hopelessly scattered. Each twig gushed a puff of smoke and went out. The fire-provider had failed. As he looked apathetically about him, his eyes chanced on the dog, sitting across the ruins of the fire from him, in the snow, making restless, hunching movements, slightly lifting one forefoot and then the other, shifting its weight back and forth on them with wistful eagerness.

The sight of the dog put a wild idea into his head. He remembered the tale of the man, caught in a blizzard, who killed a steer and crawled inside the carcass, and so was saved. He would kill the dog and bury his hands in the warm body until the numbness went out of them. Then he could build another fire. He spoke to the dog, calling it to him; but in his voice was a strange note of fear that frightened the animal, who had never known the man to speak in such way before. Something was the matter, and its suspicious nature sensed danger—it knew not what danger, but somewhere, somehow, in its brain arose an apprehension of the man. It flattened its ears down at the sound of the man's voice, and its restless, hunching movements and the liftings and shiftings of its forefeet became more pronounced; but it would not come to the man. He got on his hands and knees and crawled toward the dog. This unusual posture again excited suspicion, and the animal sidled mincingly away.

The man sat up in the snow for a moment and struggled for calmness. Then he pulled on his mittens, by means of his teeth, and got upon his feet. He glanced down at first in order to assure himself that he was really standing up, for the absence of sensation in his feet left him unrelated to the earth. His erect position in itself started to drive the webs of suspicion from the dog's mind; and when he spoke peremptorily, with the sound of whiplashes in his voice, the dog rendered its customary allegiance and came to him. As it came within reaching distance, the man lost his control. His arms flashed out to the dog, and he experienced genuine surprise when he discovered that his hands could not clutch, that there was neither bend nor feeling in the fingers. He had forgotten for the moment that they were frozen and that they were freezing more and more. All this happened quickly, and before the animal could get away, he encircled its body with his arms. He sat down in the snow, and in this fashion held the dog, while it snarled and whined and struggled.

But it was all he could do, hold its body encircled in his arms and sit there. He realized that he could not kill the dog. There was no way to do it. With his helpless hands he could neither draw nor hold his sheath knife nor throttle the animal. He released it, and it plunged wildly away, with tail between its legs, and still snarling. It halted forty feet away and surveyed him curiously, with ears sharply pricked forward. The man looked down at his hands in order to locate them, and found them hanging on the ends of his arms. It struck him as curious that one should have to use his eyes in order to find out where his hands were. He began threshing his arms back and forth, beating the mittened hands against his sides. He did this for five minutes, violently, and his heart pumped enough blood up to the surface to put a stop to his shivering. But no sensation was aroused in the hands. He had an impression that they hung like weights on the ends of his arms, but when he tried to run the impression down, he could not find it.

A certain fear of death, dull and oppressive, came to him. This fear quickly became poignant as he realized that it was no longer a mere matter of freezing his fingers and toes, or of losing his hands and feet, but that it was a matter of life and death with the chances against him. This threw him into a panic, and he turned and ran up the creek-bed along the old, dim trail. The dog joined in behind and kept up with him. He ran blindly, without intention, in fear such as he had never known in his life. Slowly, as he plowed and floundered through the snow, he began to see things again, the banks of the creek, the old timber-jams, the leafless aspens, and the sky. The running made him feel better. He did not shiver. Maybe, if he ran on, his feet would thaw out; and, anyway, if he ran far enough, he would reach camp and the boys. Without doubt he would lose some fingers and toes and some of his face; but the boys would take care of him, and save the rest of him when he got there. And at the same time there was another thought in his mind that said he would never get to the camp and the boys; that it was too many miles away, that the freezing had too great a start on him, and that he would soon be stiff and dead. This thought he kept in the background and refused to consider. Sometimes it pushed itself forward and demanded to be heard, but he thrust it back and strove to think of other things.

It struck him as curious that he could run at all on feet so frozen that he could not feel them when they struck the earth and took the weigh. of his body. He seemed to himself to skim along above the surface, and to have no connection with the earth. Somewhere he had once seen a winged Mercury, and he wondered if Mercury felt as he felt when skimming over the earth.

His theory of running until he reached camp and the boys had one flaw in it: he lacked the endurance. Several times he stumbled, and finally he tottered, crumpled up, and fell. When he tried to rise, he failed. He must sit and rest, he decided, and next time he would merely walk and keep on going. As he sat and regained his breath, he noted that he was feeling quite warm and comfortable He was not shivering, and it even seemed that a warm glow had come to his chest and trunk. And yet, when he touched his nose or cheeks, there was no sensation. Running would not thaw them out. Nor would it thaw out his hands and feet. Then the thought came to him that the frozen portions of his body must be extending. He tried to keep this thought down, to forget it, to think of something else; he was aware of the panicky feeling that it caused, and he was afraid of the panic. But the thought asserted itself, and persisted, until it produced a vision of his body totally frozen. This was too much, and he made another wild run along the trail. Once he slowed down to a walk, but the thought of the freezing extending itself made him run again.

And all the time the dog ran with him, at his heels. When he fell down a second time, it curled its tad! over its forefeet and sat in front of him, facing him, curiously eager and intent The warmth and security of the animal angered him, and he cursed it till it flattened down its ears appealingly. This time the shivering came more quickly upon the man. He was losing in his battle with the frost. It was creeping into his body from all sides. The thought of it drove him on, but he ran no more than a hundred feet, when he staggered and pitched headlong. It was his last panic. When he had recovered his breath and control, he sat up and entertained in his mind the conception of meeting death with dignity. However, the conception did not come to him in such terms. His idea of it was that he had been making a fool of himself, running around like a chicken with its head cut off—such was the simile that occurred to him. Well, he was bound to freeze anyway, and he might as well take it decently. With this new-found peace of mind came the first glimmerings of drowsiness. A good idea, he thought, to sleep off to death. It was like salting an anaesthetic. Freezing was not so bad as people thought. There were lots worse ways to die.

He pictured the boys finding his body next day. Suddenly he found himself with them, coming along the trail and looking for himself. And, still with them, he came around a turn in the trail and found himself lying in the snow. He did not belong with himself any more, for even then he was out of himself, standing with the boys and looking at himself in the snow. It certainly was cold, was his thought. When he got back to the States he could tell the folks what real cold was He drifted on from this to a vision of the old-timer on Sulphur Creek He could see him quite clearly, warm and comfortable, and smoking a pipe.

"You were right, old hoss; you were right," the man mumbled to the old-timer of Sulphur Creek.

Then the man drowsed off into what seemed to him the most comfortable and satisfying sleep he had ever known. The dog sat facing him and waiting. The brief day drew to a close in a long, slow twilight. There were no signs of a fire to be made, and, besides, never in the dog's experience had it known a man to sit like that in the snow and make no fire. As the twilight drew on, its eager yearning for the fire mastered it, and with a great lifting and shifting of forefeet, it whined softly, then flattened its ears down in anticipation of being chidden by the man. But the man remained silent. Later, the dog whined loudly. And still later it crept close to the man and caught the scent of death. This made the animal bristle and back away. A little longer it delayed, howling under the stars that leaped and danced and shone brightly in the cold sky. Then it turned and trotted up the trail in the direction of the camp it knew, where were the other food-providers and fire-providers.

Dracula's Guest

Bram Stoker
1914

"Dracula's Guest" was excised from the original *Dracula* manuscript by his publisher because of the length of the original book MSS. It was published as a short story in 1914, two years after Stoker's death.

When we started for our drive the sun was shining brightly on Munich, and the air was full of the joyousness of early summer. Just as we were about to depart, Herr Delbruck (the maitre d'hotel of the Quatre Saisons,[1] where I was staying) came down bareheaded to the carriage and, after wishing me a pleasant drive, said to the coachman, still holding his hand on the handle of the carriage door, "Remember you are back by nightfall. The sky looks bright but there is a shiver in the north wind that says there may be a sudden storm. But I am sure you will not be late." Here he smiled and added,"for you know what night it is."

Johann answered with an emphatic, "*Ja, mein Herr*,"[2] and, touching his hat, drove off quickly. When we had cleared the town, I said, after signalling to him to stop:

"Tell me, Johann, what is tonight?"

He crossed himself, as he answered laconically: "*Walpurgis nacht*."[3] Then he took out his watch, a great, old-fashioned German silver thing as big as a turnip and looked at it, with his eyebrows gathered together and a little impatient shrug of his shoulders. I realized that this was his way of respectfully protesting against the unnecessary delay and sank back in the carriage, merely motioning him to proceed. He started off rapidly, as if to make up for lost time. Every now and then the horses seemed to throw up their heads and sniff the air suspiciously. On such occasions I often looked round in alarm. The road was pretty bleak, for we were traversing a sort of high windswept plateau. As we drove, I saw a road that looked but little used and which seemed to dip through a little winding valley. It looked so inviting that, even at the risk of offending him, I called Johann to stop—and when he had pulled up, I told him I would like to drive down that road. He made all sorts of excuses and frequently crossed himself as he spoke. This somewhat piqued my curiosity, so I asked him various questions. He answered fencingly and repeatedly looked at his watch in protest.

Finally I said, "Well, Johann, I want to go down this road. I shall not ask you to come unless you like; but tell me why you do not like to go, that is all I ask." For answer he seemed to throw himself off the box, so quickly did he reach the ground. Then he stretched out his hands appealingly to me and implored me not to go. There was just enough of English mixed with the German for me to understand the drift of his talk. He seemed always just about to tell me something—the very idea of which evidently frightened him; but each time he pulled himself up saying, "Walpurgis nacht!"

I tried to argue with him, but it was difficult to argue with a man when I did not know his language. The advantage certainly rested with him, for although he began to speak in English, of a very crude and broken kind, he

---

[1] The maître d'hôtel, head waiter, host or maître d' manages the public part or "front of the house" of a formal restaurant. The responsibilities of a maître d'hôtel generally include supervising the waiting staff, welcoming guests and assigning tables to them, taking reservations, and ensuring that guests are satisfied. *Quatre Saisons* means Four Seasons.

[2] Yes, my lord.

[3] Walpurgis Night (*Walpurgisnacht*) is a traditional spring festival on 30 April or 1 May in large parts of Central and Northern Europe. It is often celebrated with dancing and bonfires. It is exactly six months from All Hallows' Eve. In Germany, *Walpurgisnacht*, is the night when witches are reputed to hold a large celebration on the Brocken and await the arrival of spring.

always got excited and broke into his native tongue—and every time he did so, he looked at his watch. Then the horses became restless and sniffed the air. At this he grew very pale, and, looking around in a frightened way, he suddenly jumped forward, took them by the bridles, and led them on some twenty feet. I followed and asked why he had done this. For an answer he crossed himself, pointed to the spot we had left, and drew his carriage in the direction of the other road, indicating a cross, and said, first in German, then in English, "Buried him—him what killed themselves."

I remembered the old custom of burying suicides at cross roads: "Ah! I see, a suicide. How interesting!" But for the life of me I could not make out why the horses were frightened.

Whilst we were talking, we heard a sort of sound between a yelp and a bark. It was far away; but the horses got very restless, and it took Johann all his time to quiet them. He was pale and said, "It sounds like a wolf—but yet there are no wolves here now."

"No?" I said, questioning him. "Isn't it long since the wolves were so near the city?"

"Long, long," he answered, "in the spring and summer; but with the snow the wolves have been here not so long."

Whilst he was petting the horses and trying to quiet them, dark clouds drifted rapidly across the sky. The sunshine passed away, and a breath of cold wind seemed to drift over us. It was only a breath, however, and more of a warning than a fact, for the sun came out brightly again.

Johann looked under his lifted hand at the horizon and said, "The storm of snow, he comes before long time." Then he looked at his watch again, and, straightway holding his reins firmly—for the horses were still pawing the ground restlessly and shaking their heads—he climbed to his box as though the time had come for proceeding on our journey.

I felt a little obstinate and did not at once get into the carriage.

"Tell me," I said, "about this place where the road leads," and I pointed down.

Again he crossed himself and mumbled a prayer before he answered, "It is unholy."

"What is unholy?" I enquired.

"The village."

"Then there is a village?"

"No, no. No one lives there hundreds of years."

My curiosity was piqued, "But you said there was a village."

"There was."

"Where is it now?"

Whereupon he burst out into a long story in German and English, so mixed up that I could not quite understand exactly what he said. Roughly I gathered that long ago, hundreds of years, men had died there and been buried in their graves; but sounds were heard under the clay, and when the graves were opened, men and women were found rosy with life and their mouths red with blood. And so, in haste to save their lives (aye, and their souls!—and here he crossed himself)those who were left fled away to other places, where the living lived and the dead were dead and not—not something. He was evidently afraid to speak the last words. As he proceeded with his narration, he grew more and more excited. It seemed as if his imagination had got hold of him, and he ended in a perfect paroxysm of fear—white-faced, perspiring, trembling, and looking round him as if expecting that some dreadful presence would manifest itself there in the bright sunshine on the open plain.

Finally, in an agony of desperation, he cried, "Walpurgis nacht!" and pointed to the carriage for me to get in.

All my English blood rose at this, and standing back I said, "You are afraid, Johann—you are afraid. Go home, I shall return alone, the walk will do me good." The carriage door was open. I took from the seat my oak walking stick—which I always carry on my holiday excursions—and closed the door, pointing back to Munich, and said, "Go home, Johann—Walpurgis nacht doesn't concern Englishmen."

The horses were now more restive than ever, and Johann was trying to hold them in, while excitedly imploring me not to do anything so foolish. I pitied the poor fellow, he was so deeply in earnest; but all the same I could not help laughing. His English was quite gone now. In his anxiety he had forgotten that his only means of making me understand was to talk my language, so he jabbered away in his native German. It began to be a little tedious. After giving the direction, "Home!" I turned to go down the cross road into the valley.

With a despairing gesture, Johann turned his horses towards Munich. I leaned on my stick and looked after him. He went slowly along the road for a while, then there came over the crest of the hill a man tall and thin. I could see so much in the distance. When he drew near the horses, they began to jump and kick about, then to scream with terror. Johann could not hold them in; they bolted down the road, running away madly. I watched them out of sight, then looked for the stranger; but I found that he, too, was gone.

With a light heart I turned down the side road through the deepening valley to which Johann had objected. There was not the slightest reason, that I could see, for his objection; and I daresay I tramped for a couple of hours without thinking of time or distance and certainly without seeing a person or a house. So far as the place was concerned, it was desolation itself. But I did not notice this particularly till, on turning a bend in the road, I came upon a scattered fringe of wood; then I recognized that I had been impressed unconsciously by the desolation of the region through which I had passed.

I sat down to rest myself and began to look around. It struck me that it was considerably colder than it had been at the commencement of my walk—a sort of sighing sound seemed to be around me with, now and then, high overhead, a sort of muffled roar. Looking upwards I noticed that great thick clouds were drafting rapidly across the sky from north to south at a great height. There were signs of a coming storm in some lofty stratum of the air. I was a little chilly, and, thinking that it was the sitting still after the exercise of walking, I resumed my journey.

The ground I passed over was now much more picturesque. There were no striking objects that the eye might single out, but in all there was a charm of beauty. I took little heed of time, and it was only when the deepening twilight forced itself upon me that I began to think of how I should find my way home. The air was cold, and the drifting of clouds high overhead was more marked. They were accompanied by a sort of far away rushing sound, through which seemed to come at intervals that mysterious cry which the driver had said came from a wolf. For a while I hesitated. I had said I would see the deserted village, so on I went and presently came on a wide stretch of open country, shut in by hills all around. Their sides were covered with trees which spread down to the plain, dotting in clumps the gentler slopes and hollows which showed here and there. I followed with my eye the winding of the road and saw that it curved close to one of the densest of these clumps and was lost behind it.

As I looked there came a cold shiver in the air, and the snow began to fall. I thought of the miles and miles of bleak country I had passed, and then hurried on to seek shelter of the wood in front. Darker and darker grew the sky, and faster and heavier fell the snow, till the earth before and around me was a glistening white carpet the further edge of which was lost in misty vagueness. The road was here but crude, and when on the level its boundaries were not so marked as when it passed through the cuttings; and in a little while I found that I must have strayed from it, for I missed underfoot the hard surface, and my feet sank deeper in the grass and moss. Then the wind grew stronger and blew with ever increasing force, till I was fain to run before it. The air became icy-cold, and in spite of my exercise I began to suffer. The snow was now falling so thickly and whirling around me in such rapid eddies that I could hardly keep my eyes open. Every now and then the heavens were torn asunder by vivid lightning, and in the flashes I could see ahead of me a great mass of trees, chiefly yew and cypress all heavily coated with snow.

I was soon amongst the shelter of the trees, and there in comparative silence I could hear the rush of the wind high overhead. Presently the blackness of the storm had become merged in the darkness of the night. By-and-by the storm seemed to be passing away, it now only came in fierce puffs or blasts. At such moments the weird sound of the wolf appeared to be echoed by many similar sounds around me.

Now and again, through the black mass of drifting cloud, came a straggling ray of moonlight which lit up the expanse and showed me that I was at the edge of a dense mass of cypress and yew trees. As the snow had ceased to fall, I walked out from the shelter and began to investigate more closely. It appeared to me that, amongst so many old foundations as I had passed, there might be still standing a house in which, though in ruins, I could find some sort of shelter for a while. As I skirted the edge of the copse, I found that a low wall encircled it, and following this I presently found an opening. Here the cypresses formed an alley leading up to a square mass of some kind of building. Just as I caught sight of this, however, the drifting clouds obscured the moon, and I passed up the path in darkness. The wind must have grown colder, for I felt myself shiver as I walked; but there was hope of shelter, and I groped my way blindly on.

I stopped, for there was a sudden stillness. The storm had passed; and, perhaps in sympathy with nature's silence, my heart seemed to cease to beat. But this was only momentarily; for suddenly the moonlight broke through the clouds showing me that I was in a graveyard and that the square object before me was a great massive tomb of marble, as white as the snow that lay on and all around it. With the moonlight there came a fierce sigh of the storm which appeared to resume its course with a long, low howl, as of many dogs or wolves. I was awed and shocked, and I felt the cold perceptibly grow upon me till it seemed to grip me by the heart. Then while the flood of moonlight still fell on the marble tomb, the storm gave further evidence of renewing, as though it were returning on its track. Impelled by some sort of fascination, I approached the sepulchre to see what it was and why such a thing stood alone in such a place. I walked around it and read, over the Doric door, in German—

COUNTESS DOLINGEN OF GRATZ
IN STYRIA
SOUGHT AND FOUND DEATH
1801

On the top of the tomb, seemingly driven through the solid marble—for the structure was composed of a few vast blocks of stone—was a great iron spike or stake. On going to the back I saw, graven in great Russian letters: "The dead travel fast."

There was something so weird and uncanny about the whole thing that it gave me a turn and made me feel quite faint. I began to wish, for the first time, that I had taken Johann's advice. Here a thought struck me, which came under almost mysterious circumstances and with a terrible shock. This was Walpurgis Night!

Walpurgis Night was when, according to the belief of millions of people, the devil was abroad—when the graves were opened and the dead came forth and walked. When all evil things of earth and air and water held revel. This very place the driver had specially shunned. This was the depopulated village of centuries ago.This was where the suicide lay; and this was the place where I was alone—unmanned, shivering with cold in a shroud of snow with a wild storm gathering again upon me! It took all my philosophy, all the religion I had been taught, all my courage, not to collapse in a paroxysm of fright.

And now a perfect tornado burst upon me. The ground shook as though thousands of horses thundered across it; and this time the storm bore on its icy wings, not snow, but great hailstones which drove with such violence that they might have come from the thongs of Balearic slingers—hailstones that beat down leaf and branch and made the shelter of the cypresses of no more avail than though their stems were standing corn. At the first I had rushed to the nearest tree; but I was soon fain to leave it and seek the only spot that seemed to afford refuge, the deep Doric doorway of the marble tomb. There, crouching against the massive bronze door, I gained a certain amount of protection from the beating of the hailstones, for now they only drove against me as they ricocheted from the ground and the side of the marble.

As I leaned against the door, it moved slightly and opened inwards. The shelter of even a tomb was welcome in that pitiless tempest and I was about to enter it when there came a flash of forked lightning that lit up the whole expanse of the heavens. In the instant, as I am a living man, I saw, as my my eyes turned into the darkness of the tomb, a beautiful woman with rounded cheeks and red lips, seemingly sleeping on a bier. As the thunder broke overhead, I was grasped as by the hand of a giant and hurled out into the storm. The whole thing was so sudden that, before I could realize the shock, moral as well as physical, I found the hailstones beating me down. At the same time I had a strange, dominating feeling that I was not alone. I looked towards the tomb. Just then there came another blinding flash which seemed to strike the iron stake that surmounted the tomb and to pour through to the earth, blasting and crumbling the marble, as in a burst of flame. The dead woman rose for a moment of agony while she was lapped in the flame, and her bitter scream of pain was drowned in the thunder crash. The last thing I heard was this mingling of dreadful sound, as again I was seized in the giant grasp and dragged away, while the hailstones beat on me and the air around seemed reverberant with the howling of wolves. The last sight that I remembered was a vague, white, moving mass, as if all the graves around me had sent out the phantoms of their sheeted dead, and that they were closing in on me through the white cloudiness of the driving hail.

Gradually there came a sort of vague beginning of consciousness, then a sense of weariness that was dreadful. For a time I remembered nothing, but slowly my senses returned. My feet seemed positively racked with pain, yet I could not move them. They seemed to be numbed. There was an icy feeling at the back of my neck and all down my spine, and my ears, like my feet, were dead yet in torment; but there was in my breast a sense of warmth which was by comparison delicious. It was as a nightmare—a physical nightmare, if one may use such an expression; for some heavy weight on my chest made it difficult for me to breathe.

This period of semi-lethargy seemed to remain a long time, and as it faded away I must have slept or swooned. Then came a sort of loathing, like the first stage of seasickness, and a wild desire to be free of something—I knew not what. A vast stillness enveloped me, as though all the world were asleep or dead—only broken by the low panting as of some animal close to me. I felt a warm rasping at my throat, then came a consciousness of the awful truth which chilled me to the heart and sent the blood surging up through my brain. Some great animal was lying on me and now licking my throat. I feared to stir, for some instinct of prudence bade me lie still; but the brute seemed to realize that there was now some change in me, for it raised its head. Through my eyelashes I saw above me the two great flaming eyes of a gigantic wolf. Its sharp white teeth gleamed in the gaping red mouth, and I could feel its hot breath fierce and acrid upon me.

For another spell of time I remembered no more. Then I became conscious of a low growl, followed by a yelp, renewed again and again. Then seemingly very far away, I heard a "Holloa! holloa!" as of many voices calling in unison. Cautiously I raised my head and looked in the direction whence the sound came, but the cemetery blocked my view. The wolf still continued to yelp in a strange way, and a red glare began to move round the grove of cypresses, as though following the sound. As the voices drew closer, the wolf yelped faster and louder. I feared to make either sound or motion. Nearer came the red glow over the white pall which stretched into the darkness around me. Then all at once from beyond the trees there came at a trot a troop of horsemen bearing torches. The wolf rose from my breast and made for the cemetery. I saw one of the horsemen (soldiers by their caps and their long military cloaks) raise his carbine and take aim. A companion knocked up his arm, and I heard the ball whiz over my head. He had evidently taken my body for that of the wolf. Another sighted the animal as it slunk away, and a shot followed. Then, at a gallop, the troop rode forward—some towards me, others following the wolf as it disappeared amongst the snow-clad cypresses.

As they drew nearer I tried to move but was powerless, although I could see and hear all that went on around me. Two or three of the soldiers jumped from their horses and knelt beside me. One of them raised my head and placed his hand over my heart.

"Good news, comrades!" he cried. "His heart still beats!"

Then some brandy was poured down my throat; it put vigor into me, and I was able to open my eyes fully and look around. Lights and shadows were moving among the trees, and I heard men call to one another. They drew together, uttering frightened exclamations; and the lights flashed as the others came pouring out of the cemetery pell-mell, like men possessed. When the further ones came close to us, those who were around me asked them eagerly, "Well, have you found him?"

The reply rang out hurriedly, "No! no! Come away quick-quick! This is no place to stay, and on this of all nights!"

"What was it?" was the question, asked in all manner of keys. The answer came variously and all indefinitely as though the men were moved by some common impulse to speak yet were restrained by some common fear from giving their thoughts.

"It—it—indeed!" gibbered one, whose wits had plainly given out for the moment.

"A wolf—and yet not a wolf!" another put in shudderingly.

"No use trying for him without the sacred bullet," a third remarked in a more ordinary manner.

"Serve us right for coming out on this night! Truly we have earned our thousand marks!" were the ejaculations of a fourth.

"There was blood on the broken marble," another said after a pause, "the lightning never brought that there. And for him—is he safe? Look at his throat! See comrades, the wolf has been lying on him and keeping his blood warm."

The officer looked at my throat and replied, "He is all right, the skin is not pierced. What does it all mean? We should never have found him but for the yelping of the wolf."

"What became of it?" asked the man who was holding up my head and who seemed the least panic-stricken of the party, for his hands were steady and without tremor. On his sleeve was the chevron of a petty officer.

"It went home," answered the man, whose long face was pallid and who actually shook with terror as he glanced around him fearfully. "There are graves enough there in which it may lie. Come, comrades—come quickly! Let us leave this cursed spot."

The officer raised me to a sitting posture, as he uttered a word of command; then several men placed me upon a horse. He sprang to the saddle behind me, took me in his arms, gave the word to advance; and, turning our faces away from the cypresses, we rode away in swift military order.

As yet my tongue refused its office, and I was perforce silent. I must have fallen asleep; for the next thing I remembered was finding myself standing up, supported by a soldier on each side of me. It was almost broad daylight, and to the north a red streak of sunlight was reflected like a path of blood over the waste of snow. The officer was telling the men to say nothing of what they had seen, except that they found an English stranger, guarded by a large dog.

"Dog! that was no dog," cut in the man who had exhibited such fear. "I think I know a wolf when I see one."

The young officer answered calmly, "I said a dog."

"Dog!" reiterated the other ironically. It was evident that his courage was rising with the sun; and, pointing to me, he said, "Look at his throat. Is that the work of a dog, master?"

Instinctively I raised my hand to my throat, and as I touched it I cried out in pain. The men crowded round to look, some stooping down from their saddles; and again there came the calm voice of the young officer, "A dog, as I said. If aught else were said we should only be laughed at."

I was then mounted behind a trooper, and we rode on into the suburbs of Munich. Here we came across a stray carriage into which I was lifted , and it was driven off to the Quatre Saisons—the young officer accompanying me, whilst a trooper followed with his horse, and the others rode off to their barracks.

When we arrived, Herr Delbruck rushed so quickly down the steps to meet me, that it was apparent he had been watching within. Taking me by both hands he solicitously led me in.The officer saluted me and was turning to withdraw, when I recognized his purpose and insisted that he should come to my rooms. Over a glass of wine I warmly thanked him and his brave comrades for saving me. He replied simply that he was more than glad, and that Herr Delbruck had at the first taken steps to make all the searching party pleased; at which ambiguous utterance the maitre d'hotel smiled, while the officer plead duty and withdrew.

"But Herr Delbruck," I enquired, "how and why was it that the soldiers searched for me?"

He shrugged his shoulders, as if in depreciation of his own deed, as he replied, "I was so fortunate as to obtain leave from the commander of the regiment in which I serve, to ask for volunteers."

"But how did you know I was lost?" I asked.

"The driver came hither with the remains of his carriage, which had been upset when the horses ran away."

"But surely you would not send a search party of soldiers merely on this account?"

"Oh, no!" he answered, "but even before the coachman arrived, I had this telegram from the Boyar whose guest you are," and he took from his pocket a telegram which he handed to me, and I read:

> Bistritz. Be careful of my guest—his safety is most precious to me. Should aught happen to him, or if he be missed, spare nothing to find him and ensure his safety. He is English and therefore adventurous. There are often dangers from snow and wolves and night. Lose not a moment if you suspect harm to him. I answer your zeal with my fortune.
>
> —Dracula.

As I held the telegram in my hand, the room seemed to whirl around me, and if the attentive maitre d'hotel had not caught me, I think I should have fallen. There was something so strange in all this, something so weird and impossible to imagine, that there grew on me a sense of my being in some way the sport of opposite forces—the mere vague idea of which seemed in a way to paralyze me. I was certainly under some form of mysterious protection. From a distant country had come, in the very nick of time, a message that took me out of the danger of the snow sleep and the jaws of the wolf.

Araby

James Joyce
1914

The story was first published in his 1914 collection *Dubliners.*

North Richmond Street, being blind, was a quiet street except at the hour when the Christian Brothers' School set the boys free. An uninhabited house of two storeys stood at the blind end, detached from its neighbours in a square ground. The other houses of the street, conscious of decent lives within them, gazed at one another with brown imperturbable faces.

The former tenant of our house, a priest, had died in the back drawing-room. Air, musty from having been long enclosed, hung in all the rooms, and the waste room behind the kitchen was littered with old useless papers. Among these I found a few paper-covered books, the pages of which were curled and damp: The Abbot, by Walter Scott, The Devout Communicant, and The Memoirs of Vidocq. I liked the last best because its leaves were yellow. The wild garden behind the house contained a central apple-tree and a few straggling bushes, under one of which I found the late tenant's rusty bicycle-pump. He had been a very charitable priest; in his will he had left all his money to institutions and the furniture of his house to his sister.

When the short days of winter came, dusk fell before we had well eaten our dinners. When we met in the street the houses had grown sombre. The space of sky above us was the colour of ever-changing violet and towards it the lamps of the street lifted their feeble lanterns. The cold air stung us and we played till our bodies glowed. Our shouts echoed in the silent street. The career of our play brought us through the dark muddy lanes behind the houses, where we ran the gauntlet of the rough tribes from the cottages, to the back doors of the dark dripping gardens where odours arose from the ashpits, to the dark odorous stables where a coachman smoothed and combed the horse or shook music from the buckled harness. When we returned to the street, light from the kitchen windows had filled the areas. If my uncle was seen turning the corner, we hid in the shadow until we had seen him safely housed. Or if Mangan's sister came out on the doorstep to call her brother in to his tea, we watched her from our shadow peer up and down the street. We waited to see whether she would remain or go in and, if she remained, we left our shadow and walked up to Mangan's steps resignedly. She was waiting for us, her figure defined by the light from the half-opened door. Her brother always teased her before he obeyed, and I stood by the railings looking at her. Her dress swung as she moved her body, and the soft rope of her hair tossed from side to side.

Every morning I lay on the floor in the front parlour watching her door. The blind was pulled down to within an inch of the sash so that I could not be seen. When she came out on the doorstep my heart leaped. I ran to the hall, seized my books and followed her. I kept her brown figure always in my eye and, when we came near the point at which our ways diverged, I quickened my pace and passed her. This happened morning after morning. I had never spoken to her, except for a few casual words, and yet her name was like a summons to all my foolish blood.

Her image accompanied me even in places the most hostile to romance. On Saturday evenings when my aunt went marketing I had to go to carry some of the parcels. We walked through the flaring streets, jostled by drunken men and bargaining women, amid the curses of labourers, the shrill litanies of shop-boys who stood on guard by the barrels of pigs' cheeks, the nasal chanting of street-singers, who sang a come-all-you about O'Donovan Rossa, or a ballad about the troubles in our native land. These noises converged in a single sensation of life for me: I imagined that I bore my chalice safely through a throng of foes. Her name sprang to my lips at moments in strange prayers and praises which I myself did not understand. My eyes were often full of tears (I could not tell why) and at times a flood from my heart seemed to pour itself out into my bosom. I thought little of the future. I did not know whether I would ever speak to her or not or, if I spoke to her, how I could tell her of my confused adoration. But my body was like a harp and her words and gestures were like fingers running upon the wires.

One evening I went into the back drawing-room in which the priest had died. It was a dark rainy evening and there was no sound in the house. Through one of the broken panes I heard the rain impinge upon the earth, the fine incessant needles of water playing in the sodden beds. Some distant lamp or lighted window gleamed below me. I was thankful that I could see so little. All my senses seemed to desire to veil themselves and, feeling that I was about to slip from them, I pressed the palms of my hands together until they trembled, murmuring: 'O love! O love!' many times.

At last she spoke to me. When she addressed the first words to me I was so confused that I did not know what to answer. She asked me was I going to Araby. I forgot whether I answered yes or no. It would be a splendid bazaar; she said she would love to go.

'And why can't you?' I asked.

While she spoke she turned a silver bracelet round and round her wrist. She could not go, she said, because there would be a retreat that week in her convent. Her brother and two other boys were fighting for their caps, and I was alone at the railings. She held one of the spikes, bowing her head towards me. The light from the lamp opposite our door caught the white curve of her neck, lit up her hair that rested there and, falling, lit up the hand upon the railing. It fell over one side of her dress and caught the white border of a petticoat, just visible as she stood at ease.

'It's well for you,' she said.

'If I go,' I said, 'I will bring you something.'

What innumerable follies laid waste my waking and sleeping thoughts after that evening! I wished to annihilate the tedious intervening days. I chafed against the work of school. At night in my bedroom and by day in the classroom her image came between me and the page I strove to read. The syllables of the word Araby were called to me through the silence in which my soul luxuriated and cast an Eastern enchantment over me. I asked for leave to go to the bazaar on Saturday night. My aunt was surprised, and hoped it was not some Freemason affair. I answered few questions in class. I watched my master's face pass from amiability to sternness; he hoped I was not beginning to idle. I could not call my wandering thoughts together. I had hardly any patience with the serious work of life which, now that it stood between me and my desire, seemed to me child's play, ugly monotonous child's play.

On Saturday morning I reminded my uncle that I wished to go to the bazaar in the evening. He was fussing at the hallstand, looking for the hat-brush, and answered me curtly:

'Yes, boy, I know.'

As he was in the hall I could not go into the front parlour and lie at the window. I felt the house in bad humour and walked slowly towards the school. The air was pitilessly raw and already my heart misgave me.

When I came home to dinner my uncle had not yet been home. Still it was early. I sat staring at the clock for some time and, when its ticking began to irritate me, I left the room. I mounted the staircase and gained the upper part of the house. The high, cold, empty, gloomy rooms liberated me and I went from room to room singing. From the front window I saw my companions playing below in the street. Their cries reached me weakened and indistinct and, leaning my forehead against the cool glass, I looked over at the dark house where she lived. I may have stood there for an hour, seeing nothing but the brown-clad figure cast by my imagination, touched discreetly by the lamplight at the curved neck, at the hand upon the railings and at the border below the dress.

When I came downstairs again I found Mrs Mercer sitting at the fire. She was an old, garrulous woman, a pawnbroker's widow, who collected used stamps for some pious purpose. I had to endure the gossip of the tea-table. The meal was prolonged beyond an hour and still my uncle did not come. Mrs Mercer stood up to go: she was sorry she couldn't wait any longer, but it was after eight o'clock and she did not like to be out late, as the night air was bad for her. When she had gone I began to walk up and down the room, clenching my fists. My aunt said:

'I'm afraid you may put off your bazaar for this night of Our Lord.'

At nine o'clock I heard my uncle's latchkey in the hall door. I heard him talking to himself and heard the hallstand rocking when it had received the weight of his overcoat. I could interpret these signs. When he was midway through his dinner I asked him to give me the money to go to the bazaar. He had forgotten.

'The people are in bed and after their first sleep now,' he said.

I did not smile. My aunt said to him energetically:

'Can't you give him the money and let him go? You've kept him late enough as it is.'

My uncle said he was very sorry he had forgotten. He said he believed in the old saying: 'All work and no play makes Jack a dull boy.' He asked me where I was going and, when I told him a second time, he asked me did I know The Arab's Farewell to his Steed. When I left the kitchen he was about to recite the opening lines of the piece to my aunt.

I held a florin tightly in my hand as I strode down Buckingham Street towards the station. The sight of the streets thronged with buyers and glaring with gas recalled to me the purpose of my journey. I took my seat in a third-class carriage of a deserted train. After an intolerable delay the train moved out of the station slowly. It crept onward among ruinous houses and over the twinkling river. At Westland Row Station a crowd of people pressed to the carriage doors; but the porters moved them back, saying that it was a special train for the bazaar. I remained alone in the bare carriage. In a few minutes the train drew up beside an improvised wooden platform. I passed out on to the road and saw by the lighted dial of a clock that it was ten minutes to ten. In front of me was a large building which displayed the magical name.

I could not find any sixpenny entrance and, fearing that the bazaar would be closed, I passed in quickly through a turnstile, handing a shilling to a weary-looking man. I found myself in a big hall girded at half its height by a gallery. Nearly all the stalls were closed and the greater part of the hall was in darkness. I recognized a silence like that which pervades a church after a service. I walked into the centre of the bazaar timidly. A few people were gathered about the stalls which were still open. Before a curtain, over which the words Café Chantant were written in coloured lamps, two men were counting money on a salver. I listened to the fall of the coins. Remembering with difficulty why I had come, I went over to one of the stalls and examined porcelain vases and flowered tea-sets. At the door of the stall a young lady was talking and laughing with two young gentlemen. I remarked their English accents and listened vaguely to their conversation.

'O, I never said such a thing!'

'O, but you did!'

'O, but I didn't!'

'Didn't she say that?'

'Yes. I heard her.'

'O, there's a . . . fib!'

Observing me, the young lady came over and asked me did I wish to buy anything. The tone of her voice was not encouraging; she seemed to have spoken to me out of a sense of duty. I looked humbly at the great jars that stood like eastern guards at either side of the dark entrance to the stall and murmured:

'No, thank you.'

The young lady changed the position of one of the vases and went back to the two young men. They began to talk of the same subject. Once or twice the young lady glanced at me over her shoulder.

I lingered before her stall, though I knew my stay was useless, to make my interest in her wares seem the more real. Then I turned away slowly and walked down the middle of the bazaar. I allowed the two pennies to fall against the sixpence in my pocket. I heard a voice call from one end of the gallery that the light was out. The upper part of the hall was now completely dark.

Gazing up into the darkness I saw myself as a creature driven and derided by vanity; and my eyes burned with anguish and anger.

The Crushed Flower

Leonid Andreyev
1916

The story was first published in *The Crushed Flower and Other Stories*. Trans. Herman Bernstein. New York: Harper & Brothers, 1916.

CHAPTER I

His name was Yura.

He was six years old, and the world was to him enormous, alive and bewitchingly mysterious. He knew the sky quite well. He knew its deep azure by day, and the white-breasted, half silvery, half golden clouds slowly floating by. He often watched them as he lay on his back upon the grass or upon the roof. But he did not know the stars so well, for he went to bed early. He knew well and remembered only one star—the green, bright and very attentive star that rises in the pale sky just before you go to bed, and that seemed to be the only star so large in the whole sky.

But best of all, he knew the earth in the yard, in the street and in the garden, with all its inexhaustible wealth of stones, of velvety grass, of hot sand and of that wonderfully varied, mysterious and delightful dust which grown people did not notice at all from the height of their enormous size. And in falling asleep, as the last bright image of the passing day, he took along to his dreams a bit of hot, rubbed off stone bathed in sunshine or a thick layer of tenderly tickling, burning dust.

When he went with his mother to the centre of the city along the large streets, he remembered best of all, upon his return, the wide, flat stones upon which his steps and his feet seemed terribly small, like two little boats. And even the multitude of revolving wheels and horses' heads did not impress themselves so clearly upon his memory as this new and unusually interesting appearance of the ground.

Everything was enormous to him—the fences, the dogs and the people— but that did not at all surprise or frighten him; that only made everything particularly interesting; that transformed life into an uninterrupted miracle. According to his measures, various objects seemed to him as follows:

His father—ten yards tall.

His mother—three yards.

The neighbour's angry dog—thirty yards.

Their own dog—ten yards, like papa.

Their house of one story was very, very tall—a mile.

The distance between one side of the street and the other—two miles.

Their garden and the trees in their garden seemed immense, infinitely tall.

The city—a million—just how much he did not know.

And everything else appeared to him in the same way. He knew many people, large and small, but he knew and appreciated better the little ones with whom he could speak of everything. The grown people behaved so foolishly and asked such absurd, dull questions about things that everybody knew, that it was necessary for him also to make believe that he was foolish. He had to lisp and give nonsensical answers; and, of course, he felt like running away from them as soon as possible. But there were over him and around him and within him two entirely extraordinary persons, at once big and small, wise and foolish, at once his own and strangers—his father and mother.

They must have been very good people, otherwise they could not have been his father and mother; at any rate, they were charming and unlike other people. He could say with certainty that his father was very great, terribly wise, that he possessed immense power, which made him a person to be feared somewhat, and it was interesting to talk with him about unusual things, placing his hand in father's large, strong, warm hand for safety's sake.

Mamma was not so large, and sometimes she was even very small; she was very kind hearted, she kissed tenderly; she understood very well how he felt when he had a pain in his little stomach, and only with her could he relieve his heart when he grew tired of life, of his games or when he was the victim of some cruel injustice. And if it was unpleasant to cry in father's presence, and even dangerous to be capricious, his tears had an unusually pleasant taste in mother's presence and filled his soul with a peculiar serene sadness, which he could find neither in his games nor in laughter, nor even in the reading of the most terrible fairy tales.

It should be added that mamma was a beautiful woman and that everybody was in love with her. That was good, for he felt proud of it, but that was also bad—for he feared that she might be taken away. And every time one of the men, one of those enormous, invariably inimical men who were busy with themselves, looked at mamma fixedly for a long time, Yura felt bored and uneasy. He felt like stationing himself between him and mamma, and no matter where he went to attend to his own affairs, something was drawing him back.

Sometimes mamma would utter a bad, terrifying phrase:

"Why are you forever staying around here? Go and play in your own room."

There was nothing left for him to do but to go away. He would take a book along or he would sit down to draw, but that did not always help him. Sometimes mamma would praise him for reading but sometimes she would say again:

"You had better go to your own room, Yurochka. You see, you've spilt water on the tablecloth again; you always do some mischief with your drawing."

And then she would reproach him for being perverse. But he felt worst of all when a dangerous and suspicious guest would come when Yura had to go to bed. But when he lay down in his bed a sense of easiness came over him and he felt as though all was ended; the lights went out, life stopped; everything slept.

In all such cases with suspicious men Yura felt vaguely but very strongly that he was replacing father in some way. And that made him somewhat like a grown man—he was in a bad frame of mind, like a grown person, but, therefore, he was unusually calculating, wise and serious. Of course, he said nothing about this to any one, for no one would understand him; but, by the manner in which he caressed father when he arrived and sat down on his knees patronizingly, one could see in the boy a man who fulfilled his duty to the end. At times father could not understand him and would simply send him away to play or to sleep—Yura never felt offended and went away with a feeling of great satisfaction. He did not feel the need of being understood; he even feared it. At times he would not tell under any circumstances why he was crying; at times he would make believe that he was absent minded, that he heard nothing, that he was occupied with his own affairs, but he heard and understood.

And he had a terrible secret. He had noticed that these extraordinary and charming people, father and mother, were sometimes unhappy and were hiding this from everybody. Therefore he was also concealing his discovery, and gave everybody the impression that all was well. Many times he found mamma crying somewhere in a corner in the drawing room, or in the bedroom—his own room was next to her bedroom—and one night, very late, almost at dawn, he heard the terribly loud and angry voice of father and the weeping voice of mother. He lay a long time, holding his breath, but then he was so terrified by that unusual conversation in the middle of the night that he could not restrain himself and he asked his nurse in a soft voice:

"What are they saying?"

And the nurse answered quickly in a whisper:

"Sleep, sleep. They are not saying anything."

"I am coming over to your bed."

"Aren't you ashamed of yourself? Such a big boy!"

"I am coming over to your bed."

Thus, terribly afraid lest they should be heard, they spoke in whispers and argued in the dark; and the end was that Yura moved over to nurse's bed, upon her rough, but cosy and warm blanket.

In the morning papa and mamma were very cheerful and Yura pretended that he believed them and it seemed that he really did believe them. But that same evening, and perhaps it was another evening, he noticed his father crying. It happened in the following way: He was passing his father's study, and the door was half open; he heard a noise and he looked in quietly—father lay face downward upon his couch and cried aloud. There was no one else in the room. Yura went away, turned about in his room and came back—the door was still half open, no one but father was in the room, and he was still sobbing. If he cried quietly, Yura could understand it, but he sobbed loudly, he moaned in a heavy voice and his teeth were gnashing terribly. He lay there, covering the entire couch, hiding his head under his broad shoulders, sniffing heavily—and that was beyond his understanding. And on the table, on the large table covered with pencils, papers and a wealth of other things, stood the lamp burning with a red flame, and smoking—a flat, greyish black strip of smoke was coming out and bending in all directions.

Suddenly father heaved a loud sigh and stirred. Yura walked away quietly. And then all was the same as ever. No one would have learned of this; but the image of the enormous, mysterious and charming man who was his father and who was crying remained in Yura's memory as something dreadful and extremely serious. And, if there were things of which he did not feel like speaking, it was absolutely necessary to say nothing of this, as though it were something sacred and terrible, and in that silence he must love father all the more. But he must love so that father should not notice it, and he must give the impression that it is very jolly to live on earth.

And Yura succeeded in accomplishing all this. Father did not notice that he loved him in a special manner; and it was really jolly to live on earth, so there was no need for him to make believe. The threads of his soul stretched themselves to all—to the sun, to the knife and the cane he was peeling; to the beautiful and enigmatic distance which he saw from the top of the iron roof; and it was hard for him to separate himself from all that was not himself. When the grass had a strong and fragrant odour it seemed to him that it was he who had such a fragrant odour, and when he lay down in his bed, however strange it may seem, together with him in his little bed lay down the enormous yard, the street, the slant threads of the rain and the muddy pools and the whole, enormous, live, fascinating, mysterious world. Thus all fell asleep with him and thus all awakened with him, and together with him they all opened their eyes. And there was one striking fact, worthy of the profoundest reflection—if he placed a stick somewhere in the garden in the evening it was there also in the morning; and the knuckle-bones which he hid in a box in the barn remained there, although it was dark and he went to his room for the night. Because of this he felt a natural need for hiding under his pillow all that was most valuable to him. Since things stood or lay there alone, they might also disappear of their accord, he reasoned. And in general it was so wonderful and pleasant that the nurse and the house and the sun existed not only yesterday, but every day; he felt like laughing and singing aloud when he awoke.

When people asked him what his name was he answered promptly:
"Yura."

But some people were not satisfied with this alone, and they wanted to know his full name—and then he replied with a certain effort:
"Yura Mikhailovich."
And after a moment's thought he added:
"Yura Mikhailovich Pushkarev."

CHAPTER II

An unusual day arrived. It was mother's birthday. Guests were expected in the evening; military music was to play, and in the garden and upon the terrace parti-coloured lanterns were to burn, and Yura need not go to bed at 9 o'clock but could stay up as late as he liked.

Yura got up when all were still sleeping. He dressed himself and jumped out quickly with the expectation of miracles. But he was unpleasantly surprised—the rooms were in the same disorder as usual in the morning; the cook and the chambermaid were still sleeping and the door was closed with a hook—it was hard to believe that the people would stir and commence to run about, and that the rooms would assume a holiday appearance, and he feared for the fate of the festival. It was still worse in the garden. The paths were not swept and there was not a single lantern there. He grew very uneasy. Fortunately, Yevmen, the coachman, was washing the carriage behind the barn in the back yard and though he had done this frequently before, and though there was nothing unusual about his appearance, Yura clearly felt something of the holiday in the decisive way in which the coachman splashed the water from the bucket with his sinewy arms, on which the sleeves of his red blouse were rolled up to his elbows. Yevmen only glanced askance at Yura, and suddenly Yura seemed to have noticed for the first time his broad, black, wavy beard and thought respectfully that Yevmen was a very worthy man. He said:
"Good morning, Yevmen."

Then all moved very rapidly. Suddenly the janitor appeared and started to sweep the paths, suddenly the window in the kitchen was thrown open and women's voices were heard chattering; suddenly the chambermaid rushed out with a little rug and started to beat it with a stick, as though it were a dog. All commenced to stir; and the events, starting simultaneously in different places, rushed with such mad swiftness that it was impossible to catch up with them. While the nurse was giving Yura his tea, people were beginning to hang up the wires for the lanterns in the garden, and while the wires were being stretched in the garden, the furniture was rearranged completely in the drawing room, and while the furniture was rearranged in the drawing room, Yevmen, the coachman, harnessed the horse and drove out of the yard with a certain special, mysterious mission.

Yura succeeded in concentrating himself for some time with the greatest difficulty. Together with father he was hanging up the lanterns. And father was charming; he laughed, jested, put Yura on the ladder; he himself climbed the thin, creaking rungs of the ladder, and finally both fell down together with the ladder upon the grass, but they were not hurt. Yura jumped up, while father remained lying on the grass, hands thrown back under his head, looking with half-closed eyes at the shining, infinite azure of the sky. Thus lying on the grass, with a serious expression on his face, apparently not in the mood for play, father looked very much like Gulliver longing for his land of giants. Yura recalled something unpleasant; but to cheer his father up he sat down astride upon his knees and said:

"Do you remember, father, when I was a little boy I used to sit down on your knees and you used to shake me like a horse?"

But before he had time to finish he lay with his nose on the grass; he was lifted in the air and thrown down with force—father had thrown him high up with his knees, according to his old habit. Yura felt offended; but father, entirely ignoring his anger, began to tickle him under his armpits, so that Yura had to laugh against his will; and then father picked him up like a little pig by the legs and carried him to the terrace. And mamma was frightened.

"What are you doing? The blood will rush to his head!"

After which Yura found himself standing on his legs, red faced, dishevelled, feeling very miserable and terribly happy at the same time.

The day was rushing fast, like a cat that is chased by a dog. Like forerunners of the coming great festival, certain messengers appeared with notes, wonderfully tasty cakes were brought, the dressmaker came and locked herself in with mamma in the bedroom; then two gentlemen arrived, then another gentleman, then a lady—evidently the entire city was in a state of agitation. Yura examined the messengers as though they were strange people from another world, and walked before them with an air of importance as the son of the lady whose birthday was to be celebrated; he met the gentlemen, he escorted the cakes, and toward midday he was so exhausted that he suddenly started to despise life. He quarrelled with the nurse and lay down in his bed face downward in order to have his revenge on her; but he fell asleep immediately. He awoke with the same feeling of hatred for life and a desire for revenge, but after having looked at things with his eyes, which he washed with cold water, he felt that both the world and life were so fascinating that they were even funny.

When they dressed Yura in a red silk rustling blouse, and he thus clearly became part of the festival, and he found on the terrace a long, snow white table glittering with glass dishes, he again commenced to spin about in the whirlpool of the onrushing events.

"The musicians have arrived! The musicians have arrived!" he cried, looking for father or mother, or for any one who would treat the arrival of the musicians with proper seriousness. Father and mother were sitting in the garden—in the arbour which was thickly surrounded with wild grapes— maintaining silence; the beautiful head of mother lay on father's shoulder; although father embraced her, he seemed very serious, and he showed no enthusiasm when he was told of the arrival of the musicians. Both treated their arrival with inexplicable indifference, which called forth a feeling of sadness in Yura. But mamma stirred and said:

"Let me go. I must go."

"Remember," said father, referring to something Yura did not understand but which resounded in his heart with a light, gnawing alarm.

"Stop. Aren't you ashamed?" mother laughed, and this laughter made Yura feel still more alarmed, especially since father did not laugh but maintained the same serious and mournful appearance of Gulliver pining for his native land . . . .

But soon all this was forgotten, for the wonderful festival had begun in all its glory, mystery and grandeur. The guests came fast, and there was no longer any place at the white table, which had been deserted but a while before. Voices resounded, and laughter and merry jests, and the music began to play. And on the deserted paths of the garden where but a while ago Yura had wandered alone, imagining himself a prince in quest of the sleeping princess, now appeared people with cigarettes and with loud free speech. Yura met the first guests at the front entrance; he looked at each one carefully, and he made the acquaintance and even the friendship of some of them on the way from the corridor to the table.

Thus he managed to become friendly with the officer, whose name was Mitenka—a grown man whose name was Mitenka—he said so himself. Mitenka had a heavy leather sword, which was as cold as a snake, which could not be taken out—but Mitenka lied; the sword was only fastened at the handle with a silver cord, but it could be taken out very nicely; and Yura felt vexed because the stupid Mitenka instead of carrying his sword, as he always did, placed it in a corner in the hallway as a cane. But even in the corner the sword stood out alone—one could see at once that it was a sword. Another thing that displeased Yura was that another officer came with Mitenka, an officer whom Yura knew and whose name was also Yura Mikhailovich. Yura thought that the officer must have been named so for fun. That wrong Yura Mikhailovich had visited them several times; he even came once on horseback; but most of the time he came just before little Yura had to go to bed. And little Yura went to bed, while the unreal Yura Mikhailovich remained with mamma, and that caused him to feel alarmed and sad; he was afraid that mamma might be deceived. He paid no attention to the real Yura Mikhailovich: and now, walking beside Mitenka, he did not seem to realise his guilt; he adjusted his moustaches and maintained silence. He kissed mamma's hand, and that seemed repulsive to little Yura; but the stupid Mitenka also kissed mamma's hand, and thereby set everything aright.

But soon the guests arrived in such numbers, and there was such a variety of them, as if they had fallen straight from the sky. And some of them seemed to have fallen near the table, while others seemed to have fallen into the garden. Suddenly several students and ladies appeared in the path. The ladies were ordinary, but the students had holes cut at the left side of their white coats—for their swords. But they did not bring their swords along, no doubt because of their pride—they were all very proud. And the ladies rushed over to Yura and began to kiss him. Then the most beautiful of the ladies, whose name was Ninochka, took Yura to the swing and swung him until she threw him down. He hurt his left leg near the knee very painfully and even stained his little white pants in that spot, but of course he did not cry, and somehow his pain had quickly disappeared somewhere. At this time father was leading an important-looking bald-headed old man in the garden, and he asked Yurochka,

"Did you get hurt?"

But as the old man also smiled and also spoke, Yurochka did not kiss father and did not even answer him; but suddenly he seemed to have lost his mind—he commenced to squeal for joy and to run around. If he had a bell as large as the whole city he would have rung that bell; but as he had no such bell he climbed the linden tree, which stood near the terrace, and began to show off. The guests below were laughing and mamma was shouting, and suddenly the music began to play, and Yura soon stood in front of the orchestra, spreading his legs apart and, according to his old but long forgotten habit, put his finger into his mouth. The sounds seemed to strike at him all at once; they roared and thundered; they made his legs tingle, and they shook his jaw. They played so loudly that there was nothing but the orchestra on the whole earth—everything else had vanished. The brass ends of some of the trumpets even spread apart and opened wide from the great roaring; Yura thought that it would be interesting to make a military helmet out of such a trumpet.

Suddenly Yura grew sad. The music was still roaring, but now it was somewhere far away, while within him all became quiet, and it was growing ever more and more quiet. Heaving a deep sigh, Yura looked at the sky—it was so high—and with slow footsteps he started out to make the rounds of the holiday, of all its confused boundaries, possibilities and distances. And everywhere he turned out to be too late; he wanted to see how the tables for card playing would be arranged, but the tables were ready and people had been playing cards for a long time when he came up. He touched the chalk and the brush near his father and his father immediately chased him away. What of that, what difference did that make to him? He wanted to see how they would start to dance and he was sure that they would dance in the parlour, but they had already commenced to dance, not in the parlour, but under the linden trees. He wanted to see how they would light the lanterns, but the lanterns had all been lit already, every one of them, to the very last of the last. They lit up of themselves like stars.

Mamma danced best of all.

CHAPTER III

Night arrived in the form of red, green and yellow lanterns. While there were no lanterns, there was no night. And now it lay everywhere. It crawled into the bushes; it covered the entire garden with darkness, as with water, and it covered the sky. Everything looked as beautiful as the very best fairy tale with coloured pictures. At one place the house had disappeared entirely; only the square window made of red light remained. And the chimney of the house was visible and there a certain spark glistened, looked down and seemed to think of its own affairs. What affairs do chimneys have? Various affairs.

Of the people in the garden only their voices remained. As long as some one walked near the lanterns he could be seen; but as soon as he walked away all seemed to melt, melt, melt, and the voice above the ground laughed, talked, floating fearlessly in the darkness. But the officers and the students could be seen even in the dark—a white spot, and above it a small light of a cigarette and a big voice.

And now the most joyous thing commenced for Yura—the fairy tale. The people and the festival and the lanterns remained on earth, while he soared away, transformed into air, melting in the night like a grain of dust. The great mystery of the night became his mystery, and his little heart yearned for still more mystery; in its solitude his heart yearned for the fusion of life and death. That was Yura's second madness that evening—he became invisible. Although he could enter the kitchen as others did, he climbed with difficulty upon the roof of the cellar over which the kitchen window was flooded with light and he looked in; there people were roasting something, busying themselves, and did not know that he was looking at them—and yet he saw everything! Then he went away and looked at papa's and mamma's bedroom; the room was empty; but the beds had already been made for the night and a little image lamp was burning—he saw that. Then he looked into his own room; his own bed was also ready, waiting for him. He passed the room where they were playing cards, also as an invisible being, holding his breath and stepping so lightly, as though he were soaring in the air. Only when he reached the garden, in the dark, he drew a proper breath. Then he resumed his quest. He came over to people who were talking so near him that he could touch them with his hand, and yet they did not know that he was there, and they continued to speak undisturbed. He watched Ninochka for a long time until he learned all her life—he was almost trapped. Ninochka even exclaimed:

"Yurochka, is that you?"

He lay down behind a bush and held his breath. Thus Ninochka was deceived. And she had almost caught him! To make things more mysterious, he started to crawl instead of walk—now the alleys seemed full of danger. Thus a long time went by—according to his own calculations at the time, ten years went by, and he was still hiding and going ever farther away from the people. And thus he went so far that he was seized with dread—between him and the past, when he was walking like everybody else, an abyss was formed over which it seemed to him impossible to cross. Now he would have come out into the light but he was afraid—it was impossible; all was lost. And the music was still playing, and everybody had forgotten him, even mamma. He was alone. There was a breath of cold from the dewy grass; the gooseberry bush scratched him, the darkness could not be pierced with his eyes, and there was no end to it. O Lord!

Without any definite plan, in a state of utter despair, Yura now crawled toward a mysterious, faintly blinking light. Fortunately it turned out to be the same arbour which was covered with wild grapes and in which father and mother had sat that day. He did not recognise it at first! Yes, it was the same arbour. The lights of the lanterns everywhere had gone out, and only two were still burning; a yellow little lantern was still burning brightly, and the other, a yellow one, too, was already beginning to blink. And though there was no wind, that lantern quivered from its own blinking, and everything seemed to quiver slightly. Yura was about to get up to go into the arbour and there begin life anew, with an imperceptible transition from the old, when suddenly he heard voices in the arbour. His mother and the wrong Yura Mikhailovich, the officer, were talking. The right Yura grew petrified in his place; his heart stood still; and his breathing ceased.

Mamma said:

"Stop. You have lost your mind! Somebody may come in here."

Yura Mikhailovich said:

"And you?"

Mamma said:

"I am twenty-six years old to-day. I am old!"

Yura Mikhailovich said:

"He does not know anything. Is it possible that he does not know anything? He does not even suspect? Listen, does he shake everybody's hand so firmly?"

Mamma said:

"What a question! Of course he does! That is—no, not everybody."

Yura Mikhailovich said:

"I feel sorry for him."

Mamma said:

"For him?"

And she laughed strangely. Yurochka understood that they were talking of him, of Yurochka—but what did it all mean, O Lord? And why did she laugh?

Yura Mikhailovich said:

"Where are you going? I will not let you go."

Mamma said:

"You offend me. Let me go! No, you have no right to kiss me. Let me go!"

They became silent. Now Yurochka looked through the leaves and saw that the officer embraced and kissed mamma. Then they spoke of something, but he understood nothing; he heard nothing; he suddenly forgot the meaning of words. And he even forgot the words which he knew and used before. He remembered but one word, "Mamma," and he whispered it uninterruptedly with his dry lips, but that word sounded so terrible, more terrible than anything. And in order not to exclaim it against his will, Yura covered his mouth with both hands, one upon the other, and thus remained until the officer and mamma went out of the arbour.

When Yura came into the room where the people were playing cards, the serious, bald-headed man was scolding papa for something, brandishing the chalk, talking, shouting, saying that father did not act as he should have acted, that what he had done was impossible, that only bad people did such things, that the old man would never again play with father, and so on. And father was smiling, waving his hands, attempting to say something, but the old man would not let him, and he commenced to shout more loudly. And the old man was a little fellow, while father was big, handsome and tall, and his smile was sad, like that of Gulliver pining for his native land of tall and handsome people.

Of course, he must conceal from him—of course, he must conceal from him that which happened in the arbour, and he must love him, and he felt that he loved him so much. And with a wild cry Yura rushed over to the bald-headed old man and began to beat him with his fists with all his strength.

"Don't you dare insult him! Don't you dare insult him!"

O Lord, what has happened! Some one laughed; some one shouted. Father caught Yura in his arms, pressed him closely, causing him pain, and cried:

"Where is mother? Call mother."

Then Yura was seized with a whirlwind of frantic tears, of desperate sobs and mortal anguish. But through his frantic tears he looked at his father to see whether he had guessed it, and when mother came in he started to shout louder in order to divert any suspicion. But he did not go to her arms; he clung more closely to father, so that father had to carry him into his room. But it seemed that he himself did not want to part with Yura. As soon as he carried him out of the room where the guests were he began to kiss him, and he repeated:

"Oh, my dearest! Oh, my dearest!"

And he said to mamma, who walked behind him:

"Just think of the boy!"

Mamma said:

"That is all due to your whist. You were scolding each other so, that the child was frightened."

Father began to laugh, and answered:

"Yes, he does scold harshly. But Yura, oh, what a dear boy!"

In his room Yura demanded that father himself undress him. "Now, you are getting cranky," said father. "I don't know how to do it; let mamma undress you."

"But you stay here."

Mamma had deft fingers and she undressed him quickly, and while she was removing his clothes Yura held father by the hand. He ordered the nurse out of the room; but as father was beginning to grow angry, and he might guess what had happened in the arbour, decided to let him go. But while kissing him he said cunningly:

"He will not scold you any more, will he?"

Papa smiled. Then he laughed, kissed Yura once more and said:

"No, no. And if he does I will throw him across the fence."

"Please, do," said Yura. "You can do it. You are so strong."

"Yes, I am pretty strong. But you had better sleep! Mamma will stay here with you a while."

Mamma said:

"I will send the nurse in. I must attend to the supper."

Father shouted:

"There is plenty of time for that! You can stay a while with the child."

But mamma insisted:

"We have guests! We can't leave them that way."

But father looked at her steadfastly, and shrugged his shoulders. Mamma decided to stay.

"Very well, then, I'll stay here. But see that Maria does not mix up the wines."

Usually it was thus: when mamma sat near Yura as he was falling asleep she held his hand until the last moment—that is what she usually did. But now she sat as though she were all alone, as though Yura, her son, who was falling asleep, was not there at all—she folded her hands in her lap and looked into the distance. To attract her attention Yura stirred, but mamma said briefly:

"Sleep."

And she continued to look. But when Yura's eyes had grown heavy and he was falling asleep with all his sorrow and his tears, mamma suddenly went down on her knees before the little bed and kissed Yura firmly many, many times. But her kisses were wet—hot and wet.

"Why are your kisses wet? Are you crying?" muttered Yura.

"Yes, I am crying."

"You must not cry."

"Very well, I won't," answered mother submissively.

And again she kissed him firmly, firmly, frequently, frequently. Yura lifted both hands with a heavy movement, clasped his mother around the neck and pressed his burning cheek firmly to her wet and cold cheek. She was his mother, after all; there was nothing to be done. But how painful; how bitterly painful!

Miss Brill

Katherine Mansfield
1920

The story was first published in *Athenaeum* on 26 November 1920, and later reprinted in *The Garden Party and Other Stories*, 1922.

Although it was so brilliantly fine—the blue sky powdered with gold and great spots of light like white wine splashed over the Jardins Publiques—Miss Brill was glad that she had decided on her fur. The air was motionless, but when you opened your mouth there was just a faint chill, like a chill from a glass of iced water before you sip, and now and again a leaf came drifting—from nowhere, from the sky. Miss Brill put up her hand and touched her fur. Dear little thing! It was nice to feel it again. She had taken it out of its box that afternoon, shaken out the moth powder, given it a good brush, and rubbed the life back into the dim little eyes. "What has been happening to me?" said the sad little eyes. Oh, how sweet it was to see them snap at her again from the red eiderdown! . . . But the nose, which was of some black composition, wasn't at all firm. It must have had a knock, somehow. Never mind—a little dab of black sealing-wax when the time came—when it was absolutely necessary . . . Little rogue! Yes, she really felt like that about it. Little rogue biting its tail just by her left ear. She could have taken it off and laid it on her lap and stroked it. She felt a tingling in her hands and arms, but that came from walking, she supposed. And when she breathed, something light and sad—no, not sad, exactly—something gentle seemed to move in her bosom.

There were a number of people out this afternoon, far more than last Sunday. And the band sounded louder and gayer. That was because the Season had begun. For although the band played all the year round on

Sundays, out of season it was never the same. It was like some one playing with only the family to listen; it didn't care how it played if there weren't any strangers present. Wasn't the conductor wearing a new coat, too? She was sure it was new. He scraped with his foot and flapped his arms like a rooster about to crow, and the bandsmen sitting in the green rotunda blew out their cheeks and glared at the music. Now there came a little "flutey" bit—very pretty!—a little chain of bright drops. She was sure it would be repeated. It was; she lifted her head and smiled.

Only two people shared her "special" seat: a fine old man in a velvet coat, his hands clasped over a huge carved walking-stick, and a big old woman, sitting upright, with a roll of knitting on her embroidered apron. They did not speak. This was disappointing, for Miss Brill always looked forward to the conversation. She had become really quite expert, she thought, at listening as though she didn't listen, at sitting in other people's lives just for a minute while they talked round her.

She glanced, sideways, at the old couple. Perhaps they would go soon. Last Sunday, too, hadn't been as interesting as usual. An Englishman and his wife, he wearing a dreadful Panama hat and she button boots. And she'd gone on the whole time about how she ought to wear spectacles; she knew she needed them; but that it was no good getting any; they'd be sure to break and they'd never keep on. And he'd been so patient. He'd suggested everything—gold rims, the kind that curve round your ears, little pads inside the bridge. No, nothing would please her. "They'll always be sliding down my nose!" Miss Brill had wanted to shake her.

The old people sat on a bench, still as statues. Never mind, there was always the crowd to watch. To and fro, in front of the flower beds and the band rotunda, the couples and groups paraded, stopped to talk, to greet, to buy a handful of flowers from the old beggar who had his tray fixed to the railings. Little children ran among them, swooping and laughing; little boys with big white silk bows under their chins, little girls, little French dolls, dressed up in velvet and lace. And sometimes a tiny staggerer came suddenly rocking into the open from under the trees, stopped, stared, as suddenly sat down "flop," until its small high-stepping mother, like a young hen, rushed scolding to its rescue. Other people sat on the benches and green chairs, but they were nearly always the same, Sunday after Sunday, and–Miss Brill had often noticed–there was something funny about nearly all of them. They were odd, silent, nearly all old, and from the way they stared they looked as though they'd just come from dark little rooms or even–even cupboards!

Behind the rotunda the slender trees with yellow leaves down drooping, and through them just a line of sea, and beyond the blue sky with gold-veined clouds.

Tum-tum-tum tiddle-um! tiddle-um! tum tiddley-um tum ta! blew the band.

Two young girls in red came by and two young soldiers in blue met them, and they laughed and paired and went off arm-in-arm. Two peasant women with funny straw hats passed, gravely, leading beautiful smoke-coloured donkeys. A cold, pale nun hurried by. A beautiful woman came along and dropped her bunch of violets, and a little boy ran after to hand them to her, and she took them and threw them away as if they'd been poisoned. Dear me! Miss Brill didn't know whether to admire that or not! And now an ermine toque and a gentleman in gray met just in front of her. He was tall, stiff, dignified, and she was wearing the ermine toque she'd bought when her hair was yellow. Now everything, her hair, her face, even her eyes, was the same colour as the shabby ermine, and her hand, in its cleaned glove, lifted to dab her lips, was a tiny yellowish paw. Oh, she was so pleased to see him–delighted! She rather thought they were going to meet that afternoon. She described where she'd been–everywhere, here, there, along by the sea. The day was so charming–didn't he agree? And wouldn't he, perhaps? . . .

But he shook his head, lighted a cigarette, slowly breathed a great deep puff into her face, and even while she was still talking and laughing, flicked the match away and walked on. The ermine toque was alone; she smiled more brightly than ever. But even the band seemed to know what she was feeling and played more softly, played tenderly, and the drum beat, "The Brute! The Brute!" over and over. What would she do? What was going to happen now? But as Miss Brill wondered, the ermine toque turned, raised her hand as though she'd seen someone else, much nicer, just over there, and pattered away. And the band changed again and played more quickly, more gayly than ever, and the old couple on Miss Brill's seat got up and marched away, and such a funny old man with long whiskers hobbled along in time to the music and was nearly knocked over by four girls walking abreast.

Oh, how fascinating it was! How she enjoyed it! How she loved sitting here, watching it all! It was like a play. It was exactly like a play. Who could believe the sky at the back wasn't painted? But it wasn't till a little brown dog trotted on solemn and then slowly trotted off, like a little "theatre" dog, a little dog that had been drugged, that Miss Brill discovered what it was that made it so exciting. They were all on stage. They weren't only the audience, not only looking on; they were acting. Even she had a part and came every Sunday. No doubt somebody would have noticed if she hadn't been there; she was part of the performance after all. How strange she'd never thought of it like that before! And yet it explained why she made such point of starting from home at just the same time each week–so as not to be late for the performance–and it also explained why she had a queer, shy feeling at telling her English pupils how she spent her Sunday afternoons. No wonder! Miss Brill nearly laughed out loud. She was on the stage. She thought of the old invalid gentleman to whom she read the newspaper four afternoons a week while he slept in the garden. She had got quite used to the frail head on the cotton pillow, the hollowed eyes, the open mouth and the high pinched nose. If he'd been dead she mightn't have noticed for weeks; she wouldn't have minded. But suddenly he knew he was having the paper read to him by an actress! "An actress!" The old head lifted; two points of light quivered in the old eyes. "An actress–are ye?" And Miss Brill smoothed the newspaper as though it were the manuscript of her part and said gently; "Yes, I have been an actress for a long time."

The band had been having a rest. Now they started again. And what they played was warm, sunny, yet there was just a faint chill–a something, what was it?–not sadness–no, not sadness–a something that made you want to sing. The tune lifted, lifted, the light shone; and it seemed to Miss Brill that in another moment all of them, all the whole company, would begin singing. The young ones, the laughing ones who were moving together, they would begin and the men's voices, very resolute and brave, would join them. And then she too, she too, and the others on the benches–they would come in with a kind of accompaniment–something low, that scarcely rose or fell, something so beautiful–moving. . . . And Miss Brill's eyes filled with tears and she looked smiling at all the other members of the company. Yes, we understand, we understand, she thought–though what they understood she didn't know.

Just at that moment a boy and girl came and sat down where the old couple had been. They were beautifully dressed; they were in love. The hero and heroine, of course, just arrived from his father's yacht. And still soundlessly singing, still with that trembling smile, Miss Brill prepared to listen.

"No, not now," said the girl. "Not here, I can't."

"But why? Because of that stupid old thing at the end there?" asked the boy. "Why does she come here at all–who wants her? Why doesn't she keep her silly old mug at home?"

"It's her fu-ur which is so funny," giggled the girl. "It's exactly like a fried whiting."

"Ah, be off with you!" said the boy in an angry whisper. Then: "Tell me, ma petite chère–"

"No, not here," said the girl. "Not yet."

. . . .

On her way home she usually bought a slice of honeycake at the baker's. It was her Sunday treat. Sometimes there was an almond in her slice, sometimes not. It made a great difference. If there was an almond it was like carrying home a tiny present–a surprise–something that might very well not have been there. She hurried on the almond Sundays and struck the match for the kettle in quite a dashing way.

But to-day she passed the baker's by, climbed the stairs, went into the little dark room–her room like a cupboard–and sat down on the red eiderdown. She sat there for a long time. The box that the fur came out of was on the bed. She unclasped the necklet quickly; quickly, without looking, laid it inside. But when she put the lid on she thought she heard something crying.

The Horse Dealer's Daughter

D. H. Lawrence
1922

The story was first published in *English Review*, April 1922 and later collected in *England, My England and other stories* (1922) on October 24 by Thomas Seltzer in the US. The first UK edition of the collection was published by Martin Secker in 1924.

"Well, Mabel, and what are you going to do with yourself?" asked Joe, with foolish flippancy. He felt quite safe himself. Without listening for an answer, he turned aside, worked a grain of tobacco to the tip of his tongue, and spat it out. He did not care about anything, since he felt safe himself.

The three brothers and the sister sat round the desolate breakfast-table, attempting some sort of desultory consultation. The morning's post had given the final tap to the family fortunes, and all was over. The dreary dining-room itself, with its heavy mahogany furniture, looked as if it were waiting to be done away with.

But the consultation amounted to nothing. There was a strange air of ineffectuality about the three men, as they sprawled at table, smoking and reflecting vaguely on their own condition. The girl was alone, a rather short, sullen-looking young woman of twenty-seven. She did not share the same life as her brothers. She would have been good-looking, save for the impressive fixity of her face, "bull-dog," as her brothers called it.

There was a confused tramping of horses" feet outside. The three men all sprawled round in their chairs to watch. Beyond the dark holly bushes that separated the strip of lawn from the high-road, they could see a cavalcade of shire horses swinging out of their own yard, being taken for exercise. This was the last time. These were the last horses that would go through their hands. The young men watched with critical, callous look. They were all frightened at the collapse of their lives, and the sense of disaster in which they were involved left them no inner freedom.

Yet they were three fine, well-set fellows enough. Joe, the eldest, was a man of thirty-five, broad and handsome in a hot flushed way. His face was red, he twisted his black moustache over a thick finger, his eyes were shallow and restless. HE had a sensual way of uncovering his teeth when he laughed, and his bearing was stupid. Now he watched the horses with a glazed look of helplessness in his eyes, a certain stupor of downfall.

The great drought-horses swung past. They were tied head to tail, four of them, and they heaved along to where a lane branched off from the high-road, planting their great roofs flouting in the fine black mud, swinging their great rounded haunches sumptuously, and trotting a few sudden steps as they were led into the lane, round the corner. Every movement showed a massive, slumbrous strength, and a stupidity which held them in subjection. The groom at the head looked back, jerking the leading rope. And the cavalcade moved out of sight up the lane, the tail of the last horse, bobbed up tight and stiff, held out taut from the swinging great haunches as they rocked behind the hedges in a motion-like sleep.

Joe watched with glazed hopeless eyes. The horses were almost like his own body to him. He felt he was done for now. Luckily he was engaged to a woman as old as himself, and therefore her father, who was steward of a neighbouring estate, would provide him with a job. He would marry and go into harness. His life was over, he would be a subject animal now.

He turned uneasily aside, the retreating steps of the horses echoing in his ears. Then, with foolish restlessness, he reached for the scraps of bacon-rind from the plates, and making a faint whistling sound, flung them to the terrier that lay against the fender. He watched the dog swallow them, and waited till the creature looked into his eyes. Then a faint grin came on his face, and in a high, foolish voice he said:

"You won't get much more bacon, shall you, you little b——?"

The dog faintly and dismally wagged its tail, then lowered its haunches, circled round, and lay down again.

There was another hopeless silence at the table. Joe sprawled uneasily in his seat, not willing to go till the family conclave was dissolved. Fred Henry, the second brother, was erect, clean-limbed, alert. He had watched the passing of the horses with more sang-froid. If he was an animal, like Joe, he was an animal which controls, not one which is controlled. He was master of any horse, and he carried himself with a well-tempered air of mastery. But he was not master of the situation of life. He pushed his coarse brown moustache upwards, off his lip, and glanced irritably at his sister, who sat impassive and inscrutable.

"You'll go and stop with Lucy for a bit, shan't you?" he asked. The girl did not answer.

"I don't see what else you can do," persisted Fred Henry.

"Go as a skivvy," Joe interpolated laconically.

The girl did not move a muscle.

"If I was her, I should go in for training for a nurse," said Malcolm, the youngest of them all. He was the baby of the family, a young man of twenty-two, with a fresh, jaunty museau.

But Mabel did not take any notice of him. They had talked at her and round her for so many years, that she hardly heard them at all.

The marble clock on the mantel piece softly chimed the half-hour, the dog rose uneasily from the hearth-rug and looked at the party at the breakfast-table. But still they sat on in ineffectual conclave.

"Oh, all right," said Joe suddenly, apropos of nothing. "Ill get a move on."

He pushed back his chair, straddled his knees with a downward jerk, to get them free, in horsey fashion, and went to the fire. Still, he did not go out of the room; he was curious to know what the others would do or say. He began to charge his pipe, looking down at the dog and saying in a high affected voice:

"Going wi' me? Going wi' me are ter? Tha'rt goin' further than tha counts on just now, dost hear?"

The dog faintly wagged its tail, the man stuck out his jaw and covered his pipe with his hands, and puffed intently, losing himself in the tobacco, looking down all the while at the dog with an absent brown eye. The dog looked up at him in mournful distrust. Joe stood with his knees stuck out, in real horsey fashion.

"Have you had a letter from Lucy?" Fred Henry asked of his sister.

"Last week," came the neutral reply.

"And what does she say?"

There was no answer.

"Does she ask you to go and stop there ?" persisted Fred Henry.

"She says I can if I like."

"Well, then, you'd better. Tell her you'll come on Monday."

This was received in silence.

"That's what you'll do then, is it?" said Fred Henry, in some exasperation.

But she made no answer. There was a silence of futility and irritation in the room. Malcolm grinned fatuously.

"You'll have to make up your mind between now and next Wednesday," said Joe loudly, "or else find your lodgings on the kerbstone.

The face of the young woman darkened, but she sat on immutable.

"Here's Jack Fergusson!" exclaimed Malcolm, who was looking aimlessly out of the window.

"Where?" exclaimed Joe loudly.

"Just gone past."

"Coming in?"

Malcolm craned his neck to see the gate.

"Yes," he said.

There was a silence. Mabel sat on like one condemned, at the head of the table. Then a whistle was heard from the kitchen. The dog got up and barked sharply. Joe opened the door and shouted: "Come on."

After a moment a young man entered. He was muffled in overcoat and a purple woollen scarf, and his tweed cap, which he did not remove, was pulled down on his head. He was of medium height, his face was rather long and pale, his eyes looked tired.

"Hello, Jack! Well, Jack!" exclaimed Malcolm and Joe. Fred Henry merely said: "Jack."

"What's doing?" asked the newcomer, evidently addressing Fred Henry.

"Same. We've got to be out by Wednesday. Got a cold?"

"I have—got it bad, too."

"Why don't you stop in?"

"Me stop in ? When I can't stand on my legs, perhaps I shall have a chance." The young man spoke huskily. He had a slight Scotch accent.

"It's a knock-out, isn't it," said Joe, boisterously, "if a doctor goes round croaking with a cold. Looks bad for the patients, doesn't it?"

The young doctor looked at him slowly.

"Anything the matter with you then?" he asked sarcastically.

"Not as I know of. Damn your eyes, I hope not. Why?"

"I thought you were very concerned about the patients, wondered if you might be one yourself."

"Damn it, no, I've never been a patient to no flaming doctor, and hope I never shall be," returned Joe.

At this point Mabel rose from the table, and they all seemed to become aware of their existence. She began putting the dishes together. The young doctor looked at her, but did not address her. He had not greeted her. She went out the room with the tray, her face impassive and unchanged.

"When are you off then, all of you?" asked the doctor.

"I'm catching the eleven-forty," replied Malcolm. "Are you goin' down wi' th' trap, Joe?"

"Yes, I've told you I'm going down wi' th' trap, haven't I?"

"We'd better be getting in then. So long, Jack, if I don't see you before I go," said Malcolm, shaking hands.

He went out, followed by Joe, who seemed to have his tail between his legs.

"Well, this is the devil's own," exclaimed the doctor, when he was left alone with Fred Henry. "Going before Wednesday, are you?"

"That's the orders," replied the other.

"Where, to Northampton?"

"That's it."

"The devil!" exclaimed Fergusson, with quiet chagrin.

And there was silence between the two.

"All settled up, are you?" asked Fergusson.

"About."

There was another pause.

"Well, I shall miss yer, Freddy, boy," said the young doctor.

"And I shall miss thee, Jack," returned the other.

"Miss you like hell," mused the doctor.

Fred Henry turned aside. There was nothing to say. Mabel came in again, to finish clearing the table.

"What are you going to do, then, Miss Pervin?" asked Fergusson. "Going to your sister's, are you?"

Mabel looked at him with her steady, dangerous eyes, that always made him uncomfortable, unsettling his superficial ease.

"No," she said.

"Well, what in the name of fortune are you going to do? Say what you mean to do," cried Fred Henry, with futile intensity.

But she only averted her head, and continued her work. She folded the white table-cloth, and put on the chenille cloth.

"The sulkiest bitch that ever trod!" muttered her brother.

But she finished her task with perfectly impassive face, the young doctor watching her interestedly all the while. Then she went out.

Fred Henry stared after her, clenching his lips, his blue eyes fixing in sharp antagonism, as he made a grimace of sour exasperation.

"You could bray her into bits, and that's all you'd get out of her," he said, in a small, narrowed tone.

The doctor smiled faintly.

"What's she going to do, then?" he asked.

"Strike me if I know !" returned the other.

There was a pause. Then the doctor stirred.

"I'll be seeing you to-night, shall I?" he said to his friend.

"Ay—where's it to be? Are we going over to Jessdale?"

"I don't know. I've got such a cold on me. I'll come round to the 'Moon and Stars', anyway."

"Let Lizzie and May miss their night for once, eh?"

"That's it—if I feel as I do now."

"All's one—"

The two young men went through the passage and down to the back door together. The house was large, but it was servantless now, and desolate. At the back was a small bricked house-yard and beyond that a big square, gravelled fine and red, and having stables on two sides. Sloping, dank, winter-dark fields stretched away on the open sides.

But the stables were empty. Joseph Pervin, the father of the family, had been a man of no education, who had become a fairly large horse-dealer. The stables had been full of horses, there was a great turmoil and come-and-go of horses and of dealers and grooms. Then the kitchen was full of servants. But of late things has declined. The old man had married a second time, to retrieve his fortunes. Now he was dead and everything was gone to the dogs, there was nothing but debt and threatening.

For months, Mabel had been servantless in the big house, keeping the home together in penury for her ineffectual brothers. She had kept house for ten years. But previously it was with unstinted means. Then, however brutal and coarse everything was, the sense of money had kept her proud, confident. The men might be foul-mouthed, the women in the kitchens might have bad reputations, her brothers might have illegitimate children. But so long as there was money, the girl felt herself established, and brutally proud, reserved.

No company came to the house, save dealers and coarse men. Mabel had no associates of her own sex, after her sister went away. But she did not mind. She went regularly to church, she attended to her father. And she lived in the memory of her mother, who had died when she was fourteen, and whom she had loved. She had loved her father, too, in a different way, depending upon him, and feeling secure in him, until at the age of fifty-four he married again. And then she had set hard against him. Now he had died and left them all hopelessly in debt.

She had suffered badly during the period of poverty. Nothing, however, could shake the curious, sullen, animal pride that dominated each member of the family. Now, for Mabel, the end had come. Still she would not cast about her. She would follow her own way just the same. She would always hold the keys of her own situation. Mindless and persistent, she endured from day to day. Why should she think? Why should she answer anybody? It was enough that this was the end, and there was no way out. She need not pass any more darkly along the main street of the small town, avoiding every eye. She need not pass any more darkly along the main street of the small town, avoiding every eye. She need not demean herself any more, going into the shops and buying the cheapest food. This was at an end. She thought of nobody, not even herself. Mindless and persistent, she seemed in a sort of ecstasy to be coming nearer to her fulfilment, her own glorification, approaching her dead mother, who was glorified.

In the afternoon she took a little bag, with shears and sponge and a small scrubbing-brush, and went out. It was a grey, wintry day, with saddened, dark green fields and an atmosphere blackened by the smoke of foundries not far off. She went quickly, darkly along the causeway, heeding nobody, through the town to the churchyard.

There she always felt secure, as if no one could see her, although as a matter of fact she was exposed to the stare of everyone who passed along the churchyard wall. Nevertheless, once under the shadow of the great looming church, among the graves, she felt immune from the world, reserved within the thick churchyard wall as in another country.

Carefully she clipped the grass from the grave, and arranged the pinky white, small chrysanthemums in the tin cross. When this was done, she took an empty jar from a neighbouring grave, brought water, and carefully, most scrupulously sponged the marble headstone and the coping-stone.

It gave her sincere satisfaction to do this. She felt in immediate contact with the world of her mother. She took minute pains, went through the park in a state bordering on pure happiness, as if in performing this task she came into a subtle, intimate connection with her mother. For the life she followed here in the world was far less real than the world of death she inherited from her mother.

The doctor's house was just by the church. Fergusson, being a mere hired assistant, was slave to the country-side. As he hurried now to attend to the out-patients in the surgery, glancing across the graveyard with his quick eye, he saw the girl at task at the grave. She seemed so intent and remote, it was looking into another world. Some mystical element was touched in him. He slowed down as he walked, watching her as if spellbound.

She lifted her eyes, feeling him looking. Their eyes met. And each looked again at once, each feeling, in some way, found out by the other. He lifted his cap and passed on down the road. There remained distinct in consciousness, like a vision, the memory of her face, lifted from the tombstone in the churchyard, and looking at him with slow, large, portentous eyes. It was portentous, her face. It seemed to mesmerise him. There was a heavy power in her eyes which laid hold of his whole being, as if he had drunk some powerful drug. He had been feeling weak and done before. Now the life came back into him, he felt delivered from his own fretted, daily self.

He finished his duties at the surgery as quickly as might be, hastily filling up the bottles of the waiting people with cheap drugs. Then, in perpetual haste, he set off again to visit several cases in another part of his round, before tea-time. At all times he preferred to walk if he could, but particularly, when he was not well. He fancied the motion restored him.

The afternoon was falling. It was grey, deadened, and wintry, with a slow, moist, heavy coldness sinking in and deadening all the faculties. But why should he think or notice? He hastily climbed the hill and turned across the dark green fields, following the black cinder-track. In the distance, across a shallow dip in the country, the small town was clustered like smouldering ash, a tower, a spire, a heap of low, raw, extinct houses. And on the nearest fringe of the town, sloping into the dip, was Oldmeadow, the Pervins' house. He could see the stables and the outbuildings distinctly, as they lay towards him on the slope. Well, he would not go there many more times ! Another resource would be lost to him, another place gone: the only company he cared for in the alien, ugly little town he was losing. Nothing but work, drudgery, constant hastening from dwelling to dwelling among the colliers and the iron-workers. It wore him out, but at the same time he had a craving for it. It was a stimulant to him to be in the bones of the working people, moving, as it were, through the innermost body of their life. His nerves were excited and gratified. He could come so near, into the very lives of the rough, inarticulate, powerfully emotional men and women. He grumbled, he said he hated the hellish hole. But as a matter of fact it excited him, the contact with the rough, strongly-feeling people was a stimulant applied direct to his nerves.

Below Oldmeadow, in the green, shallow, soddened hollow of fields, lay a square, deep pond. Roving across the landscape, the doctor's quick eye detected a figure in black passing through the gate of the field, down towards the pond. He looked again. It would be Mabel Pervin. His mind suddenly became alive and attentive.

Why was she going down there? He pulled up on the path on the slope above, and stood staring. He could just make sure of the small black figure moving in the hollow of the failing day. He seemed to see her in the midst of such obscurity, that he was like a clairvoyant, seeing rather with the mind's eye that with ordinary sight. Yet he could see her positively enough, whilst he kept his eye attentive. He felt, if he looked away from her, in the thick, ugly falling dusk, he would lose her altogether.

He followed her minutely as she moved, direct and intent, like something transmitted rather than stirring in voluntary activity, straight down the field towards the pond. There she stood on the bank for a moment. She never raised her head. Then she waded slowly into the water.

He stood motionless as the small black figure walked slowly and deliberately towards the centre of the pond, very slowly, gradually moving deeper into the motionless water, and still moving forward as the water got up to her breast. Then he could see her no more in the dusk of the dead afternoon.

"There!" he exclaimed. "Would you believe it?"

And he hastened straight down, running over the wet, soddened fields, pushing through the hedges, down into the depression of callous wintry obscurity. It took him several minutes to come to the pond. He stood on the bank, breathing heavily. He could see nothing. His eyes seemed to penetrate the dead water. Yes, perhaps that was the dark shadow of her black clothing beneath the surface of water.

He slowly ventured into the pond. The bottom was deep, soft clay, he sank in, and the water clasped dead cold round his legs. As he stirred he could smell the cold, rotten clay that fouled up into the water. It was objectionable in his lungs. Still, repelled and yet not heeding, he moved deeper into the pond. The cold water rose over his thighs, over his loins, upon his abdomen The lower part of body was all sunk in the hideous cold element. And the bottom was so deeply soft and uncertain, he was afraid of pitching with his mouth underneath. He could not swim, and was afraid.

He crouched a little, spreading his hands under the water and moving them round, trying to feel for her. The dead cold pond swayed upon his chest. He moved again, a little deeper, and again, with his hands underneath, he felt all around under the water. And he touched her clothing. But it evaded his fingers. He made a desperate effort to grasp it.

And so doing her lost his balance and went under, horribly, suffocating in the foul earthy water, struggling madly for a few moments. At last, after what seemed an eternity, he got his footing, rose again into the air and looked around. He gasped, and knew he was in the world. Then he looked at the water. She had risen near him. He grasped her clothing, and drawing her nearer, turned to take his way to land again.

He went very slowly, carefully, absorbed in the slow process. He rose higher, climbing out of the pond. The water was now only about his legs; he was thankful, full of relief to be out of the clutches of the pond. He lifted her and staggered on to the bank, out of the horror of wet, grey clay.

He laid her down on the bank. She was quite unconscious and running with water. He made the water come from her mouth, he worked to restore her. He did not have to work very long before he could feel the breathing begin again in her; she was breathing heavily naturally. He worked a little longer. He could feel her live beneath his hands; she was coming back. He wiped her face, wrapped her in his overcoat, looked round into the dim, dark grey world, then lifted her and staggered down the bank and across the fields.

It seemed an unthinkably long way, and his burden so heavy he felt he would never get to the house. But at last he was in the stable-yard, and then in the house-yard. He opened the door and went into the house. In the kitchen he laid her down on the hearth-rug and called. The house was empty. But the fire was burning in the grate.

Then again he kneeled to attend to her. She was breathing regularly, her eyes wide open and as if conscious, but there seemed something missing in her look. She was conscious in herself, but unconscious of her surroundings.

He ran upstairs, took blankets from a bed and put them before the fire to warm. Then he removed her saturated, earthy-smelling clothing, rubbed her dry with a towel, and wrapped her naked in the blankets. Then he went into the dining-room, to look for spirits. There was a little whisky. He drank a gulp himself, and put some into her mouth.

The effect was instantaneous. She looked full into his face, as if she had been seeing him for some time, and yet had only just become conscious of him.

"Dr. Fergusson?" she said.

"What?" he answered.

He was divesting himself of his coat, intending to find some dry clothing upstairs. He could not bear the smell of the dead, clayey water, and he was mortally afraid for his own health.

"What did I do?" she asked.

"Walked into the pond," he replied. He had begun to shudder like one sick, and could hardly attend to her. Her eyes remained full on him, he seemed to be going dark in his mind, looking back at her helplessly. The shuddering became quieter in him, his life came back to him, dark and unknowing, but strong again.

"Was I out of my mind?" she asked, while her eyes were fixed on him all the time.

"Maybe, for the moment," he replied. He felt quiet, because his strength had come back. The strange fretful strain had left him.

"Am I out of my mind now?" she asked.

"Are you?" he reflected a moment. "No," he answered truthfully, "I don't see that you are." He turned his face aside. He was afraid now, because he felt dazed, and felt dimly that her power was stronger that his, in this issue. And she continued to look at him fixedly all the time. "Can you tell me where I shall find some dry things to put on?" he asked.

"Did you dive into the pond for me?" she asked."

"No," he answered. "I walked in. But I went in overhead as well.

There was silence for a moment. He hesitated. He very much wanted to go upstairs to get into dry clothing. But there was another desire in him. And she seemed to hold him. His will seemed to have gone to sleep, and left him, standing there slack before her. But he felt warm inside himself. He did not shudder at all, though his clothes were sodden on him.

"Why did you?" she asked.

"Because I didn't want you to do such a foolish thing," he said.

"It wasn't foolish," she said, still gazing at him as she lay on the floor, with a sofa cushion under her head. "It was the right thing to do. I knew best, then."

"I'll go and shift these wet things," he said. But still he had not the power to move out of her presence, until she sent him. It was as if she had the life of his body in her hands, and he could not extricate himself. Or perhaps he did not want to.

Suddenly she sat up. Then she became aware of her own immediate condition. She felt the blankets about her, she knew her own limbs. For a moment it seemed as if her reason were going. She looked round, with wild eye, as if seeking something. He stood still with fear. She saw her clothing lying scattered.

"Who undressed me?" she asked, her eyes resting full and inevitable on his face.

"I did," he replied, "to bring you round."

For some moments she sat and gazed at him awfully, her lips parted.

"Do you love me, then?" she asked.

He only stood and stared at her, fascinated. His soul seemed to melt.

She shuffled forward on her knees, and put her arms round him, round his legs, as he stood there, pressing her breasts against his knees and thighs, clutching him with strange, convulsive certainty, pressing his thighs against her, drawing him to her face, her throat, as she looked up at him with flaring, humble eyes and transfiguration, triumphant in first possession.

"You love me," she murmured, in strange transport, yearning and triumphant and confident. "You love me. I know you love me, I know."

And she was passionately kissing his knees, through the wet clothing, passionately and indiscriminately kissing his knees, his legs, as if unaware of everything.

He looked down at the tangled wet hair, the wild, bare, animal shoulders. He was amazed, bewildered and afraid. He had never thought of loving her. He had never wanted to love her. When he rescued her and restored her, he was a doctor, and she was a patient. He had had no single personal thought of her. Nay, this introduction of the personal element was very distasteful to him, a violation of his professional honour. It was horrible to have her there embracing his knees. It was horrible. He revolted from it, violently. And yet—and yet—he had not the power to break away.

She looked at him again, with the same supplication of powerful love, and that same transcendent, frightening light of triumph. In view of the delicate flame which seemed to come from her face like a light, he was powerless. And yet he had never intended to love her. He had never intended. And something stubborn in him could not give way.

"You love me," she repeated, in a murmur of deep, rhapsodic assurance. "You love me."

Her hands were drawing him, drawing him down to her. He was afraid, even a little horrified. For he had, really, no intention of loving her. Yet her hands were drawing him towards her. He put out his hand quickly to steady himself, and grasped her bare shoulder. He had no intention of loving her: his whole will was against his yielding. It was horrible. And yet wonderful was the touch of her shoulders, beautiful the shining of her face. Was she perhaps mad ? He had a horror of yielding to her. Yet something in him ached also.

He had been staring away at the door, away from her. But his hand remained on her shoulder. She had gone suddenly very still. He looked down at her. Her eyes were now wide with fear, with doubt, the light was dying from her face, a shadow of terrible greyness was returning. He could not bear the touch of her eyes' question upon him, and the look of death behind the question.

With an inward groan he gave way, and let his heart yield towards her. A sudden gentle smile came on his face. And her eyes, which never left his face, slowly, slowly filled with tears. He watched the strange water rise in her eyes, like some slow fountain coming up. And his heart seemed to burn and melt away in his breast.

He could not bear to look at her any more. He dropped on his knees and caught her head. with his arms and pressed her face against his throat. She was very still. His heart, which seemed to have broken, was burning with a kind of agony in his breast. And he felt her slow, hot tears wetting his throat. But he could not move.

He felt the hot tears wet his neck and the hollows of his neck, and he remained motionless, suspended through one of man's eternities. Only now it had become indispensable to him to have her face pressed close to him; he could never let her go again. He could never let her head go away from the close crutch of his arm. He wanted to remain like that for ever, with his heart hurting him in a pain that was also life to him. Without knowing, he was looking down on her damp, soft brown hair.

Then, as it were suddenly, he smelt the horrid stagnant smell of that water. And at the same moment she drew away from him and looked at him. Her eyes were wistful and unfathomable. He was afraid of them, and he fell to kissing her, not knowing what he was doing. He wanted her eyes not to have that terrible, wistful, unfathomable look.

When she turned her face to him again, a faint delicate flush was glowing, and there was again dawning that terrible shining of joy in her eyes, which really terrified him, and yet which he now wanted to see, because he feared the look of doubt still more.

"You love me?" she said, rather faltering.

"Yes." The word cost him a painful effort. Not because it wasn't true. But because it was too newly true, the saying seemed to tear open again his newly-torn heart. And he hardly wanted it to be true, even now.

She lifted her face to him, and he bent forward and kissed her on the mouth, gently, with the one kiss that is an eternal pledge. And as he kissed her his heart strained again in his breast. He never intended to love her. But now it was over. He had crossed over the gulf to her, and all that he had left behind had shriveled and become void.

After the kiss, her eyes again slowly filled with tears. She sat still, away from him, with her face drooped aside, and her hands folded in her lap. The tears fell very slowly. There was complete silence. He too sat there motionless and silent on the hearth-rug. The strange pain of his heart that was broken seemed to consume him. That he should love her? That this was love! That he should be ripped open in this way! Him, a doctor! How they would all jeer if they knew! It was agony to him to think they might know.

In the curious naked pain of the thought he looked again to her. She was sitting there drooped into a muse. He saw a tear fall, and his heart flared hot. He saw for the first time that one of her shoulders was quite uncovered, one arm bare, he could see one of her small breasts; dimly, because it had become almost dark in the room.

"Why are you crying?" he asked, in an altered voice.

She looked up at him, and behind her tears the consciousness of her situation for the first time brought a dark look of shame to her eyes.

"I'm not crying, really," she said, watching him, half-frightened.

He reached his hand, and softly closed it on her bare arm.

"I love you! I love you!" he said in a soft, low vibrating voice, unlike himself.

She shrank, and dropped her head. The soft, penetrating grip of his hand on her arm distressed her. She looked up at him.

"I want to go," she said. "I want to go and get you some dry things."

"Why?" he said. "I'm all right."

"But I want to go," she said. "And I want you to change your things."

He released her arm, and she wrapped herself in the blanket, looking at him rather frightened. And still she did not rise.

"Kiss me," she said wistfully.

He kissed her, but briefly, half in anger.

Then, after a second, she rose nervously, all mixed up in the blanket. He watched her in her confusion as she tried to extricate herself and wrap herself up so that she could walk. He watched her relentlessly, as she knew. And as she went, the blanket trailing, and he saw a glimpse of her feet and her white leg, he tried to remember her as she was when he had wrapped her up in the blanket. But then he didn't want to remember, because she had been nothing to him then, and his nature revolted from remembering her as she was when she was nothing to him.

A tumbling, muffled noise from within the dark house startled him. Then he heard her voice: "There are clothes." He rose and went to the foot of the stairs, and gathered up the garments she had thrown down. Then he came back to the

fire, to rub himself down and dress. He grinned at his own appearance when he had finished.

The fire was sinking, so he put on coal. The house was now quite dark, save for the light of a street-lamp that shone in faintly from beyond the holly trees. He lit the gas with matches he found on the mantelpiece. Then he emptied the pockets of his own clothes, and threw all his wet things in a heap into the scullery. After which he gathered up her sodden clothes, gently, and put them in a separate heap on the copper-top in the scullery.

It was six o"clock on the clock. His own watch had stopped. He ought to go back to the surgery. He waited, and still she did not come down. So he went to the foot of the stairs and called:

"I shall have to go."

Almost immediately he heard her coming down. She had on her best dress of black voile, and her hair was tidy, but still damp. She looked at him—and in spite of herself, smiled.

"I don't like you in those clothes," she said.

"Do I look a sight?" he answered.

They were shy of one another.

"I'll make you some tea," she said.

"No, I must go."

"Must you?" And she looked at him again with the wide, strained, doubtful eyes. And again, from the pain of his breast, he knew how he loved her. He went and bent to kiss her, gently, passionately, with his heart's painful kiss.

"And my hair smells so horrible," she murmured in distraction. "And I'm so awful, I'm so awful! Oh no, I'm too awful." And she broke into bitter, heart-broken sobbing. "You can't want to love me, I'm horrible."

"Don't be silly, don't be silly," he said, trying to comfort her, kissing her, holding her in his arms. "I want you, I want to marry you, we're going to be married, quickly, quickly— to-morrow if I can."

But she only sobbed terribly, and cried:

"I feel awful. I feel awful. I feel I'm horrible to you."

"No, I want you, I want you," was all he answered, blindly, with that terrible intonation which frightened her almost more than her horror lest he should not want her.

A Small Campfire

Michael S. Kelly
2000

Each grain of sand in the desert gulped down the last gasps of the sinking sun whose light struggled over the crumbling edges of the distant mountains. To the untrained eye only a slight wind stirred in the aftermath of daytime, twirling small dust clouds of sand in futile attempts to conjure larger mounds underneath the vast, dusk sky—while there was still time. Here, between the day and the dark, shadows yawned desperately across the dune sea, preparing to sleep, and in their somnolence, dream—still, they were unwilling to dissipate into the night's undefined, cold blackness—a void of terror and of unknown horror.

For, during the day, the sky could observe the land and the land the sky with each line drawn with certitude, each border limited by a proper boundary. But, at night, there was only the indefinite darkness that blurred edges into mirages of indecision with only the cold as its guide. The finale was inevitable. The night would take its place, supplanting the day dispassionately. So, when the sun's last glimmer fell mutely upon the barren stage over which it had once reigned supreme, each sandy pellet huddled up its thoughts into tight formations and the night's panoply began.

"Have you found the matches yet?" asked the man, his voice crackling across the desert stillness.

The woman foraged in a backpack, voiceless and quiet.

The man sighed, roughing the air past rattling lungs. "Wait, here they are. Ha! They were in my pocket all along."

There was a brief flare as the wooden match head burst into flame, consuming air and wood without mercy. The woman watched as the man knelt before the pile of twigs and branches they had brought with them. They were dry and caught fire quickly, or perhaps the fire was simply so hungry that it would have devoured anything just as readily.

"Ah, we'll have a good, warm fire in a few minutes now," the man said matter-of-factly. His eyes, glinting with images of the fire, watched the twigs burn under the heavier pieces of wood. He stared as if under a spell and tended the growing fire.

The woman looked away, strangely feeling at home in the desert, yet she was still afraid—not at the man, not at the night, but at what might come out of the night and into their camp amid the firelight. So, at each coyote howl, she gave brief starts, glancing quickly to see if the man noticed. He did not. His attention was on the fire.

She smiled.

"This is great. We haven't done this in—I don't know—how long?" inquired the man.

"We never have," the woman said, turning her attention back to the man but feeling curiously exposed despite her thick flannel shirt and felt coat.

"Hm!" It was more of a confirmation that he had not realized they had never taken the time to experience a campfire in the desert together. Other than that, there was nothing. "Well, we're doing it now. Sure feels nice to be out of the city even just for a few hours."

The woman's head, having turned it back to the night, looked up and found that her eyes had already adjusted to the darkness. Something in the night sky flashed briefly like a streaking line. "Look!" She said with excitement.

The man looked at the woman then quickly upward. "What?" But, his eyes were used to the flames, so he saw nothing but spots.

"A shooting star," she said, wishing he had seen it, too.

"Way to go! Now make a wish."

The woman bit her lip pensively, looking at the fire and the man beside it.

"Have you got it?" He asked expectantly.

"No . . . yes—" she said abruptly and smiled to reassure him, but he was tending to the fire.

They Shall Seek Peace

Dennis Humphrey
2012

Dr. Dennis Humphrey chairs the English and Fine Arts Division at Arkansas State University—Beebe and holds a PhD in English with Creative Writing emphasis from the University of Louisiana at Lafayette. His fiction publications include stories in *storySouth*,*Southern Hum, Clapboard House, Prick of the Spindle, BloodLotus, Spilt Milk, SN Review, Fried Chicken and Coffee,* and a story forthcoming in the next issue of *Toad Suck Review.* "They Shall Seek Peace" was first published in *friedchickenandcoffee.com.*

Destruction cometh; and they shall seek peace, and there shall be none.

Ezekiel 7:25
Izard County, Arkansas
November, 1861

If Lemuel Clump had been just a little bit quicker, he'd have known when to act just a little bit slower. It might have put off Ab Swinson in the first place when he'd come around with his fevered ideas about the war, about the bushwhackers and jayhawkers that were riding all up and down the country, about protecting their homes from the likes of either of them. It might have led the young Confederate officer to consider him pitiful enough to be harmless if Lemuel had simply stared back slack jawed in a mute plea of ignorance when the officer had questioned him about the yellow strip of cloth tied to the front porch post of his shack.

The plain truth was, Lemuel hadn't any more idea what Ab or the Confederate officer were in such a sweat about than his rawboned mule knew why it dragged his rickety plow through the red dirt and rocks year after year after year on the plot of ground that was Lemuel's mostly because no one else wanted it. Ab had always been a decent enough neighbor, a mite pushy maybe, but Lemuel would never have suspected him of trying to play anything on him. He had seemed square enough about it that day in the fall when he'd interrupted Lemuel's preparations for hog killing with his pitch for his "Peace Society," as he called it. Still, Lemuel was habitually leery of society of any kind, content to stay out of the world's way on his ridge. He bothered no one and expected nothing more from the world than to have the favor returned. As Ab stood beside him, shifting from foot to foot, Lemuel sat astride his chopping block, honing the blade of his axe with a hunk of native whetstone. His slender face was placid as he attended to his task with the whetstone, though his lean features were worn by a life of hard toil for mere survival, for all that he was still under thirty.

"See, Lem, it ain't nothing but a way for all us up here in the hills to sort of band together for protection. I mean, if bushwhackers or jayhawkers was to come through and burn you out, would it really matter what flag they claimed they did it under?" Ab's round, bearded face was even more flushed than usual with the energy of his conviction, and it was plain it took considerable effort for him to wait for Lemuel's response.

Lemuel rolled the quid of tobacco in his cheek. He'd heard about the bushwhackers' and jayhawkers' raids all over the Ozarks. Lawless bands of riders, murdering and taking as they pleased in the name of one flag or another. The rocky ridge he scraped for what life it could give him wasn't much compared to bottom land farms like Ab's down in the valley below the ridge, but he'd buried his pa and his ma in it after they'd worked to clear it. It had soaked up his sweat and his flesh and his blood. He couldn't bear to think of it driven beneath the heels of murderers and thieves, northern or southern. He lifted his heavy eyelids enough to glance up at Ab, who seemed beside himself waiting for Lemuel to answer. It had been a long time since Lemuel had had a decent chaw of good tobacco, and he was just thinking that Ab was about as good a fellow as one might wish for in a neighbor, pushiness and all. He felt the edge of the axe blade with his calloused thumb, and resumed applying the stone in slow elliptical rhythm. "I reckon not, Ab."

"'Deed not!" Ab's pitch shot forth again as though popped from behind a cork. "And see, that's why we need this here Peace Society, to keep the peace. We ain't looking for no trouble. We're just convincing trouble to let us alone is all."

Lemuel spat a stream of tobacco juice and paused his sharpening to wipe his stubbled chin. He wiped the juice from his hand on the patched knee of his overalls, and then tested the edge of the axe blade again. Lemuel nodded his narrow head with grim slowness, and he set the axe aside. Then he pulled his Arkansas Toothpick from its sheath on his belt, and went to work on it with the whetstone. "What do I got to do?"

"Nothin much. Just be ready to come help if any of our farms is attacked, and swear as you won't tell our society's secrets to no one."

"Reckon I can't tell no secrets I don't know, Ab."

"That's good enough for me, Lem." Ab waddled over to Lemuel's porch, skirting a sow and her squealing brood of shoats which had no idea what was about to befall them, and he tied a strip of yellow cloth to the rough cedar post that supported the porch roof.

"What's that for?"

"It shows you're a member of the Peace Society, Lem, and only other members will know it."

"Well, now, I got me a secret to keep after all."

Ab strode back over from tying the yellow cloth a changed man. All the fever had left him, and his face shone now with a warm satisfaction. He looked at Lemuel, still honing the knife, and then he looked at the shoats, two of which were fighting over a bare corn cob. "Reckon it's cold enough for hog killing, Lem?"

Lemuel stopped honing the blade and plucked a hair from his head. He dragged the hair across the blade, and the hair fell in two. "Reckon it's a mite cooler up here on the ridge come morning than it is down the valley."

Lemuel thought little of it when the Confederate officer rode up the narrow road with a column of dismounted troops in trail. Lemuel had no quarrel with them, and might have joined them despite his lack of personal stake in the economic or political issues of the war, but Ola was near ready to birth again, and his oldest boy, Seth, was still too small to handle a plow. Lemuel stood with an armload of fire wood halfway across the bare, packed earth between the unpainted clapboard house and the smokehouse near the wood line, prepared to watch the column pass by along the road. It did not even occur to him to wonder where the unit could possibly be going on a road that led only a few more miles out into the wilderness after passing Lemuel's place. Then the officer rode right into Lemuel's yard, up to the front of Lemuel's shack, and tore the yellow strip of cloth from its post without so much as a "howdy," as the dismounted column halted and made a facing movement toward Lemuels's yard. Lemuel did think that was a little odd. Looking closer, he saw a dismal looking string of men on a chain, straggling at the rear of the column, bearing the distinct look of men who heartily wish to be elsewhere. Lemuel looked back toward the offier. "Something I can help you boys with?"

The officer held the yellow strip of cloth in his gloved hand and thrust it toward Lemuel. "What is this?"

"Well it ain't no secret sign if that's what you're thinking."

"Corporal."

One of the dismounted troops in the small detachment accompanying the officer stepped forward. "Sir?"

"Put this man with the others and have a squad search the premises."

The corporal saluted. "Yessir." He motioned two other confederate enlisted men toward Lemuel and directed several more toward the house.

"Say, what's this about?" Lemuel dropped his load of firewood and tried to pull free as one of the soldiers grasped his shoulder.

"Quiet you!" The soldier holding his shoulder gave him a shake as he secured a better hold on Lemuel. He pulled the knife from the sheath on Lemuel's belt and held it up. "Well looky here boys. Now who was you aiming to skin with that, you traitor?"

Lemuel ceased struggling turned his slow gaze to the man in disbelief. "Traitor? Traitor to what?"

"Blue belly scum." The man thrust the knife into his own belt and began pushing Lemuel toward the chain gang at the rear of the column.

Lemuel was about to explain he had to tend the smokehouse, or his meat would not cure, when a woman's voice cried out as several of the soldiers burst through the front door of the house. "Lem!"

"Ola!" Lemuel pulled free from the two soldiers holding him and made for the shack, but he was tackled from behind. He kept scrambling for the house long enough to see Seth jump out the side window. He stood and looked toward Lemuel, his eyes wide.

"Pa?"

"Run boy! Run! You take them woods and run far as you can!" The boy hesitated, and Lemuel shouted "Go!"

Seth jumped and began sprinting toward the woods. When Lemuel rolled on his back to try to throw the men off, he saw the raised rifle aimed at his boy silhouetted against the iron gray sky, hesitating there. Lemuel kicked the knee of the soldier, sending the aim high and wide as the piece fired. The soldier looked down at him, raising the rifle butt above Lemuel's head, where it seemed to hang in the dissipating smoke of the missed shot.

Lemuel's mind retreated to a warm, green day when his father first showed him how to snag panfish from the creek below the ridge where they were carving out a farm in the raw wilderness. Now that Seth was old enough, he'd planned to show his boy that same fishing hole the coming spring. He could see it, his boy, dragging his flopping catch onto the bank, slick scales swapping colors as they turn this way or that to the sunlight, purple and green, the boy poised over it like a fish hawk before pouncing to pin it down and get a hold so it won't get away, just as Lemuel had done all those years before, holding his catch up for his father's approval. He saw it so clearly that he was only vaguely aware of the rifle butt coming down, down. Then all was black.

Headwaters of the Sacred Heart

Dennis Humphrey
2013

Dr. Dennis Humphrey chairs the English and Fine Arts Division at Arkansas State University—Beebe and holds a PhD in English with Creative Writing emphasis from the University of Louisiana at Lafayette. His fiction publications include stories in *storySouth*, *Southern Hum, Clapboard House, Prick of the Spindle, BloodLotus, Spilt Milk, SN Review, Fried Chicken and Coffee,* and a story forthcoming in the next issue of *Toad Suck Review.* "Headwaters of the Sacred Heart" was first published online in *Milk Sugar*, August/September 2013.

The hillsides along the trail lay exposed and humiliated, stripped of their clothing of soaring southern pines by the lumber company's machines. Clumps of underbrush pushed toward the sunlight through the brown and gray criss-crossing tangle of mangled young trees that had been run over by the skidders as they bulled their way through small hardwoods to get to the pines they were harvesting. It had the bleak look of old photos of World War I battlefields. Tad watched a line of gray clouds slouching above the horizon as though they meant to sidle up to their campsite without him or Wyatt noticing. It occurred to him that if the forest had still stood as tall and as thick as it once had, he might never have noticed the clouds through the former canopy of evergreen boughs.

"Great," Wyatt kicked a stone down the steep path. "Your spring break finally comes, and we have the worst weather in a month."

"You sound like one of my students. At least it's warm." Tad shifted his pack on his shoulders. "Besides, that's why we brought a tent, right?" Tad was a little short of breath. He could tell he'd aged since he and Wyatt had last made the hike to the old campsite.

"Smart-ass, I'm quite aware how warm it is. That's a March cold front coming. When that cold dry air hits this warm humid air, it's going to get messy." Wyatt paused to wipe his forehead, but he didn't seem winded. "How much further?"

They reached the bottom of the draw they were traversing and began up the other side. Tad looked up the trail and at what remained of the surrounding woods. "*Farther*, and I don't know. With all the logging that's been done here, I can't tell one draw from the next."

Wyatt frowned. "You think it's still there?"

"The old blue hole campsite?" Tad shrugged. "Well, the lumber companies aren't supposed to clearcut close to rivers and streams—something about erosion prevention."

"I was afraid you'd say something like that."

Tad only smiled. He was looking for a landmark, something to let him know he was on the right trail. Everything was too wide open, as though he had walked into his childhood home to find it gutted, the ceiling, roof, and interior walls all gone. Still, he'd been down the trail often enough. The loggers must have missed something he would recognize.

"So," Wyatt began. It was almost a full minute before he continued. "You hear from Anna lately?"

Tad stopped as they approached the crest of the ridge. To the left of where the trail crossed a saddle in the ridge was an area thick with tall grass and brambles, a stark contrast to the denuded landscape surrounding it. There was also a lone oak, its four foot thick trunk rising like a pillar supporting a vast network of limbs draped in the glossy pale green of new leaves not yet toughened and darkened by summer sun. It was the old home site on the south face of the ridge just below the saddle where the trail crossed the last ridge before it wound down the steep approach to the river. The lone oak had grown to tremendous size with its unimpeded access to open sky and sunlight in the shaded midst of the high pines. He hadn't recognized the home site before because its appearance was exactly opposite to what it used to be. When the forest stood around it, it was the only clearing for miles, hacked out of virgin forest more than century earlier so long-gone settlers could build in the deep woods. Tad recalled a time when he and Anna had hiked the trail down to the campsite, and they had stopped to explore the old clearing, before they were married, before they'd had little Gracie, before it all crumbled to ash.

"Look, Tad. Daffodils." Anna bent and gathered a handful of yellow blossoms by their deep green stems. She pushed her honey colored hair back behind her left ear and put one of the flower stems through the long strands so the blossom rested just above and in front of the ear. "What would they be doing way out here in the wilderness?"

"It's an old home site. The settlers who made this clearing must have planted them."

"Old home site?" She looked around. "How old?"

Tad shrugged and surveyed the clearing. "Well, according to my papaw, his papaw's family got to the foot of these mountains in the mid 1800's when his grandfather was just a baby. They were some of the first to try to settle the territory for more than just hunting and trapping. My papaw was the first one who brought me here. Even he didn't remember when the house was here." Tad could still see himself as a child, tramping down weeds in the clearing, looking for treasures: old medicine bottles, buttons, rusted remnants of old tools.

"Tad, come out of that clearing. It's bad luck to disturb old home sites."

Tad looked up. "Why papaw?"

"Could be an abandoned well in there somewheres. Could be something bad happened here. Something we don't want to get in the middle of."

Anna looked around the clearing. "I wonder what made them leave?"

Tad kicked at the rocky ground. "Probably had to move to better farming land. The soil up here doesn't look much good for farming."

"The bark of that old oak tree looks charred a bit. Maybe the house burned down."

"Maybe," Tad said. "Hard to say. That charring on the tree could be from a controlled burn. The forestry service does them from time to time to keep the underbrush down."

Anna pushed through some weeds near the base of the massive oak to reveal an oblong mound of stones a couple feet high, four or so feet in length, about three feet across. "What do you suppose this means, Tad?"

"I think it means this ground wasn't so good for digging graves in either. Must have been a child for the mound to be so short."

She caressed the stones. "Maybe that's why they had to leave. Maybe there just wasn't any staying."

"Why don't you come out of there, babe? There could be an abandoned well or something."

She placed the remaining daffodils in the pile of stones and rose, walking back to him out of the weeds, the yellow flower bright beside her dark eyes.

"Tad?"

Tad turned to look at Wyatt, who was looking at him quizzically. "I'm sorry, Wyatt. What were you saying?"

"Oh, nothing. What are you staring at?"

"That lone oak over there," he pointed. "It's the old home site that marks the turn down to the river."

"Oh yeah. I guess we're on the right trail." Wyatt's tone was flat, distracted.

As they crested the ridge just past the home site, they could look down into the deep river valley cut by the swift headwaters of the Sacre Coure River.

"Looks like you were right," Wyatt said, sounding mildly surprised.

The tall evergreen forest stood in the narrow valley of the Sacre Coure River like an army massed for its last line of defense. Tad stopped to take a drink from his canteen before starting down. "Anna doesn't answer my e-mails anymore, or my letters. Seems she's got a new beau these days. I don't suppose he likes it much."

"I thought you didn't hear me," Wyatt said. "Any idea who the new guy is?"

Tad took another drink. "I figured you'd know more than me about that since you both live down in Texarkana." When Wyatt didn't answer, Tad screwed the cap back on the canteen, and set off down the trail.

As the trail descended into the pines, Tad felt a tension ease out from between his shoulders and wash down his back in a shiver. He'd felt a nagging urge to make this trip for some time, to trek up to the headwaters, to get into the clean air and clear water near the origin of the river that slopped languid and muddy through his hometown far downstream. Finally, the dance of dappled sun on the forest floor, the hushed roar of wind in the boughs, the gin-like fragrance of loblolly pine needles flushed through his nerves, soothing. Of course, he always felt a certain sense of soothing there, but on that particular trip, after crossing through the lumber company clear cuts, he was especially relieved to find the forest still standing at all. All of the place's usual effects were magnified by his recent fear he'd never experience them again.

When they reached the bottom of the Sacre Coure River Valley, they had to work their way downstream a few hundred yards to reach the camp site. Clear water gurgled over rounded stones in a rushing tumble.

"Around this bend," Tad said. Wyatt nodded. Where the river turned against a rock bluff, the water had scoured out a deep pool. The current that seemed in such a turbulent rush to get over the stones in the rapids slowed and smoothed, and a mirror image of bluff, pines, and blue sky backed by towering thunderheads wavered on the barely rippling surface. Opposite the bluff on the inside of the curve was the sandy spit where the campsite hid under a stand of beech trees.

They walked into the campsite in silence. Empty beer cans littered the cleared area around the fire pit's circle of stones. The remains of a fire smoldered under a pile of assorted trash, much of which consisted of plastic and cans. A broken and twisted lawn chair lay tangled against the base of a tree, and several scrap boards were nailed between two trees and topped with old planks to create a makeshift table.

"Nice." Wyatt kicked one of the beer cans into the fire pit.

Tad took off his backpack and rummaged inside. After a moment he pulled out a roll of plastic trash bags.

Wyatt dropped his own backpack to the ground. "There's the old Boy Scout."

Tad popped a bag in the air to open it, and stooped to pick up the nearest cans. "Always leave a campsite cleaner than you found it."

"Well, that should be no problem." He bent to join Tad's cleanup efforts. When they had all of the cans picked up, Wyatt added, "We'd better stoke that fire some to burn off that trash, or we'll be sucking in fumes from that smoldering plastic all day."

"Right." Tad wandered into the woods in search of downed limbs and driftwood. Near the slope down the final sandy bank to the river, an ancient beech leaned out over the river channel, but not quite over the water. The smooth, pale bark was a perfect medium for carving, and the old beech had always borne a variety of markings. Some were fairly recent—initials of fellow modern explorers leaving their marks in the wilderness; proclamations of undying love like TJ+AW 2gether 4ever; demonstrations of team spirit: Go Hornets! Beat Wolves! and what looked like the newest addition: "Van Halen Rules!" There were also older markings, just discernable by their darker scarring under the more recent cuts. He guessed the tree must have been hundreds of years old, and some of the symbols seemed archetypal, like stars, stick figure people, animals, and daggers, speaking from past even the earliest white settlements in the area. He ran his fingers over a spot where criss-crossing newer cuts nearly obscured three stick figures, which seemed to represent a man, a woman, and a child. He peered at the scars in the bark, wondering what might be lost beneath the confusion of the newer etchings, wondering whether even older etchings had been lost beneath old ones he could make out, and wondering what messages the symbols were trying to convey anyway. He recalled one of his literature professors once saying there were always at least two meanings for every symbol: the one the author intended, and the one the reader perceived.

"Whatcha doing?" Wyatt said from behind him. Tad jumped.

"Looking at the markings on this old tree."

"Yeah. I've seen that one before. My Uncle Jeb told me it was an old treasure tree."

"Treasure tree?"

"Yeah. We're only about ten miles from the Oklahoma border. Uncle Jeb said outlaws and civil war bushwhackers used to bury their loot out in these mountains before ducking into the Indian Territories to hide. They'd mark the spots by carving trees and bending them to point in particular directions."

"Huh. My papaw told me these were Indian trail marker trees." Tad mused still fingering the most ancient looking symbols. "This tree looks way older than the civil war."

"Well, anyway, I got the fire stoked up, but I couldn't figure out that tent of yours."

"Sorry." Tad still didn't look up from the carvings. "I didn't realize I'd been taking so long. I'll pitch the tent when I get back to camp."

"It's okay. I'd kind of like to jump in the river while the sun is still high enough to hit the water. I mean it may be warm out here, but it's still March"

"Good idea. I'm a bit grimy myself after the hike. You go ahead. I'll be along in a minute." Tad continued to run his fingers over shapes etched into the bark. It was a couple of minutes before he heard Wyatt walk away. He knew that when Wyatt went into the water, he would swim across the blue hole to the bluff on the far side. He would climb up the bluff to the rock outcropping about ten feet up, and he would dive off. When Tad heard the splash, he turned from the tree and walked back to camp.

When the tent was up, he put on his swimming trunks and walked out on the sand bar across the blue hole from the bluff. He'd heard the splash of Wyatt diving a couple more times, and Tad got there just in time to see him dive again. While neither of them was as fit as they'd been when they used to come to the campsite more often, Wyatt had kept himself in better shape. When Tad stepped from the trees toward the water, Wyatt made a show of the form on his next dive with broad sweeping movements of his arms before launching from the rock into a jackknife. He stayed underwater long enough for Tad to wonder what was taking so long, when he resurfaced with a beer can in his hand.

"Nice tuck."

"Looks like we missed one." Wyatt held the can up as he side stroked toward Tad. "I saw it on the bottom from the diving rock."

"Why'd you wait til this dive to get it?"

"'Cause before I couldn't do this." Wyatt hurled the can toward Tad from the pool. It thumped on the sand at Tad's feet, and the water in it began chugging out.

"Thanks." Tad bent to pick up the can. He recalled when he and Wyatt were boys, maybe ten or eleven. They were swinging on muscadine vines in the bottoms downstream of where the Sacre Coure River's muddy and sluggish waters passed through Riverdown, far downstream of the blue hole campsite, past where the man-made dam of Église Reservoir held the waters to turn the turbines that powered the town below.

"Bet you can't beat this one!" Wyatt said, taking a running leap at one of the vines they'd cut at the bottom so they could swing on them. His momentum carried him in a slow arc out over the cut bank that dropped straight down to the river. At the point where he was farthest from the bank, the vine slipped a little, but the tendrils that intermeshed the branches of the trees caught and held, swinging him back over the bank again, where he landed in a tangle of smaller vines.

"Whoa! You almost went swimming that time."

Wyatt laughed. "Well, how about it Tad-pole?"

Tad backed up the hill to get a better run. He ran as fast as he could, jumping and grabbing a vine. "Woo hoo!" He knew he had a good swing going. He went out over the water, out past where Wyatt's last swing carried him. "Yeah! Beat that, Wyatt-burp!"

Before he could hear Wyatt's reply, the limb that supported the vine he'd chosen snapped. He felt a momentary weightlessness before he plunged into the murk of the water. Caught by surprise, he didn't have a good breath before submerging, and he broke surface again sputtering and coughing brown water.

"Tad! Don't let go of the vine! I got the other end!"Wyatt pulled Tad toward the tangle of tree roots where the undercut bank rose five feet straight up from the water. Snagged amidst the roots was an assortment of every type of plastic garbage imaginable: soda bottles, grocery sacks, milk jugs, even a naked plastic baby doll, crusted with river mud, staring with blue eyes at the sky. He wondered what other, less obvious pollutants were in the water as he continued to cough out the water he'd sucked in. Wyatt kept pulling as Tad held on to the vine with one hand and clawed at the muddy bank with the other hand and both feet. As Wyatt hauled him over the rim of the embankment, they rolled away from the drop-off in a muddy heap.

Wyatt was laughing again. "Jeeze, Tad. I thought I lost you there for a minute."

Tad had caught his breath enough to smell the river mud that caked him. He rolled onto his hands and knees and retched into the dank leaves.

Tad poured out the remaining water from the beer can Wyatt had thrown to him. "It's good to know all the logging across the ridge hasn't affected the water clarity up here."

"Saw it so plain I could almost read the label through eight feet of water." Wyatt rolled over and backstroked out to the center of the pool, spitting an arcing stream of water as he went. He stopped at the center of the hole, treading water. "Your turn on the diving rock."

"No thanks. I'll pass." Tad waded out into the clear water, wincing from the chill. They were only three miles from where the river gushed from the raw rock halfway down the easternmost side of Trinity Mountain's triple peaks, tumbling through the air and over bare stone into the narrow river gorge. Even in midsummer, the water there was as clear and cold as water straight from a well. He eased in until he was waist deep and couldn't stand the suspense any longer. He plunged forward in a shallow dive calculated to bring him to the surface beside Wyatt. He sputtered through chattering teeth, "Jesus, how are you standing this?"

"Aw, it's not so bad once you get used to it."

"Get used to it hell. I'm rinsed off; I'm going back to camp. I'm just glad you got the fire stoked up before we got in here."

"Lightweight."

Tad smiled and stroked for the sandbar, slogging straight up to the camp fire. After a minute he heard the sound of Wyatt plunging from the diving rock again. Though the water was cold, the afternoon was still unseasonably warm, and the heat from the fire soon stopped his shivering. He added more sticks of wood to the fire and poked at them absently with a piece of metal tubing from one of the mangled lawn chairs left by the previous campers. As the fire flared, images of Anna, not really coherent memories but rather disjointed clips, wavered in and out of his mind like dancing shadows. Anna by a campfire in that very fire pit, shivering, dripping as he was now, laughing. Anna by the fireplace in the cabin they'd rented on their honeymoon. Anna dancing around a bonfire at her parents' farm, their baby, Gracie, cradled in the crook of her arm. Anna wrapped in a blanket outside their rented home, lit by flickering firelight and blue and red strobes that reflected off the wet surfaces of the night in the drizzling rain, as Tad, just returning from another long night at the library, pushed through the police securing the scene. Anna lying half unconscious on the ambulance stretcher, her honey-colored hair plastered against her soot-streaked face as the firefighter asked, "*Ma'am, is there anyone else inside*?"

When Wyatt walked up to the fire, still dripping, Tad looked up from the flames. "Feel better now?"

"I was about to ask you the same thing."

"Now that I'm reasonably dry, I'm going to put some dry clothes on." Tad went into the tent. After dressing, he put on a light jacket, anticipating a drop in temperature after sunset. Before leaving the tent, he went though his pack. He emerged with a skillet and a couple cans of beef stew. Wyatt was poking at the fire the same way Tad had been.

"Hey." Tad held up the cans of stew and the skillet. "If you want to go change into something dry, I'll get supper started."

Wyatt looked up slowly, like he'd been in the middle of a thought he was reluctant to leave. "Sure."

Tad arranged the skillet on the edge of the circle of stones around the fire pit and set to opening the cans with his Swiss Army Knife. By the time Wyatt emerged from the tent in dry clothes and a jacket, the stew was steaming in the skillet, and the narrow valley was in shadow as the sun dipped below the ridge to the west. A distant rumble rolled through the woods, barely audible over the sound of the rapids above the pool and the wind in the trees.

"You want to just eat from the skillet? We won't have to dirty dishes that way."

Wyatt nodded. "Sure."

Tad slid his hand back up into his jacket sleeve so he could grasp the skillet handle without burning himself. He transferred the skillet to a flat topped rock a few feet from the fire pit so he and Wyatt could pull up logs to sit on either side and eat from the pan. Tad produced two spoons from his jacket pocket and handed one to Wyatt. "Bon appetite."

Wyatt took the spoon. "Yummy."

They sat opposite each other and began eating. Wyatt sucked air around the first spoonful he put in his mouth.

"Hot?" Tad blew on his spoon's contents.

Wyatt smiled as best he could as he reached for his canteen. The rest of the meal passed in silence, and as they scraped their last spoonfuls from the pan, Tad looked up at Wyatt, who looked away.

Tad sat back from the skillet "So, what's on your mind, Wyatt?"

"Huh?" Wyatt looked up from the pan like he was surprised to find anyone else sitting there. The dusk had darkened enough that they were lit mostly by firelight.

"We've known each other since we were kids, Wyatt-burp. Something's been bugging you since we linked up at the trail head."

Wyatt looked down. "Yeah. I was hoping it would come up without being so brought up."

"What?"

"So what do you know about Anna's new fiancée?"

"Fiancée? I didn't know *that*." Tad fidgeted. "Like I said, I figured you know more about that since you both live down in Texarkana."

Wyatt looked down toward the river. A flicker of light lit the valley, and ten seconds later a low rumble rolled through.

"So, do you know him?"

Wyatt nodded. "Yeah."

"Is he a good man?
Wyatt laughed, half hearted. "I like to think so."

Tad looked vacantly at the fire a moment, then fixed Wyatt with eyes that seemed drawn straight from the heart of the fire. "You're shitting me."

Wyatt took a deep breath.

"You."

Wyatt let the breath out. His upper body seemed to deflate and sag under his hunched shoulders.

Tad bolted to his feet and strode away from the fire before wheeling back. "Here? You have something like this to tell me, and you bring me here? Really?"

"Tad…"

"No. No, no, *no.* I don't even want to know." He turned from the fire again and walked into the dark toward the river.

There was enough light for him to tell where the sand bar ended and the water began, but not much more. He turned downstream at the water's edge and started walking. The third time he tripped over something in the dark, he stopped getting mad and wondered for the first time where he was going anyway. He heard something stirring in the darkness up ahead. Another bright flash lit the narrow valley like a strobe, and he saw the freeze-frame image of a raccoon at the edge of the water. This time the thunder crashed after only three or four seconds. He heard the wind picking up in the treetops. He looked back upstream. The campfire glowed about a hundred yards away.

"Damn it." He turned back toward the camp.

When he arrived, Wyatt was gone. He stared at the skillet for several minutes without moving, without a single thought stirring in his head before he picked up the skillet and took it to the water's edge, dipping it into the water and rubbing a handful of clean sand around it with the palm of his hand. When he returned to camp, there was still no sign of Wyatt. He went into the tent and rolled out his sleeping bag. He looked at the air mattress he'd brought. In his younger days, he had never needed such comforts, and he remembered thinking as he packed it, he wasn't just older but considerably wiser than he had been then. Somehow the thought of inflating it then was as daunting as running the entire hundred miles home. He left it where it was and crawled into the sleeping bag.

He heard the first splatters of rain hit the rain fly of the tent and felt the satisfaction all humans have felt since they first learned to keep the weather off themselves. It was a good tent. He'd ridden out storms in it before and stayed completely dry. A brief image of him and Anna patting the tent floor to feel the water sloshing under it flashed into his mind like the lightning outside, but other images forced it out as quickly: a numbness everywhere except the ache deep behind his eye sockets as he stared, shocked stupid, at a casket so tiny it didn't seem real, but a sick joke from a tasteless novelty shop. The steady patter in the leaves and on the tent blended into a hiss of white noise, punctuated occasionally with the rumble and crash of thunder. Somewhere between the meanders of his memories, he thought he heard the baby crying and mumbled to Anna, "Go check on Gracie, baby."

He didn't know he had slept until a steady roar caught the attention of his sleeping mind. As it was, only half his mind took notice and pondered the roar's meaning as the other half continued sleeping. Opening one eye, he could see dawn already in progress. As he lay on his back, staring up at the top of the tent in the dim light, only his face showing from his zipped up sleeping bag, he still heard and even felt the steady roar. He tried to remember what people said tornadoes sounded like. He'd heard various comparisons: jet engines, trains, iron wheels rushing over cobblestones. This didn't sound like any of those. It sounded more like running water. He zipped open his sleeping bag and sat up. When he put his hand down on the floor of the tent, it splashed. While he was still wondering about that, the tent started to shift and distort around him. Any portion of his mind that was still sleeping snapped into full alert.

"What?" Tad grabbed his hiking boots and jacket, and he wriggled out just as the tent was collapsing as the current pushed it against a tree. What he saw in the place of the clear stream of the Sacre Coure River was something that looked like it belonged in a brochure for extreme whitewater rafting. The tent had been pitched a good twenty five yards from the edge of the water and at least eight feet higher in elevation. Now the water was wrapping the tent around a tree, and across the main channel the rolling torrent was just below the level of the diving rock.

"Holy shit." A light but steady rain was still falling. He knew that meant the river was not done rising. He tossed his boots up the hill and waded in to grab the tent, dragging it and its waterlogged contents out of the water and up the hill another ten feet to keep it from washing away while he thought about what to do. The rain had thoroughly drowned the campfire, and there was nothing dry enough in the vicinity to start another one. He sat on the wet log beside the soggy fire pit and pulled on his now soaked boots.

"Good morning."

Tad looked up. Wyatt stood, soaked, just uphill from the camp site.

"Thought you were gone," Tad grumbled.

"I got turned around in the dark. It took me most of the night to find the trailhead to get to my car."

"So? Why aren't you on your way back to Texarkana?"

"That's the thing. I tried to drive out—do you remember that low water bridge we had to cross to get back in here?"

"Oh." The low water bridge was a glorified ford, a strip of concrete poured straight across the riverbed with enough culverts through it to handle normal water volume. When the river was up, it simply washed over the top.

"The water's not so low right now," Wyatt said. "Driving out is not an option."

Tad rose and went to the tent. He pulled his waterlogged pack from the soggy heap and began going through the outside pockets. He found his cell phone and a topographic map of the wilderness area, both in Zip Locked bags. He opened the one with his cell phone in it and opened the phone.

"No service."

Wyatt shook his head. "I already tried mine at the top of the ridge by the old home site. Nothing."

"I bet the only ground nearby high enough to get line of sight on a cell tower is Trinity Mountain."

Wyatt nodded. "If we could get across that river, we could walk out the road to find a house with a land line."

Tad looked at the foaming flood. "How do you suggest we do that?"

"Swim."

Tad snorted. "You go right ahead. I'll watch from here to critique your form."

"Look, we have to do something. In case you haven't noticed, it's getting colder out here."

Tad realized Wyatt was right about at least that much. As the sun rose higher above the rain clouds, it had continued getting cooler instead of warming up.

"We could go back to the cars for shelter."

Wyatt frowned. "We could do that. I don't know about you, but I have maybe four gallons of fuel above what it will take to drive back to civilization, whenever we get to do that. How long do you think it will be before the water goes down enough to cross that low water bridge?"

Tad shrugged.

Wyatt continued, "There's no guarantee it will be passable even then without repair after this volume of water has run over it."

Tad nodded, pulling the map from its plastic bag. "Look, I don't relish the prospect of hypothermia, but if I go into that swollen river, it will only be to end it all more quickly. I know you're a better swimmer than I am, but I doubt you'd fare much better. You're not a twenty-five year old tri-athlete anymore." Tad studied the map.

Wyatt was nodding. "Okay, so what do you propose?"

Tad pointed to the map. "We're trapped south of the Sacre Coure River. We could try hiking overland to the south, but the nearest place we might find help in that direction is a good ten miles, and we'd have to cross several valleys that probably have streams that look a lot like this one does right now."

Wyatt nodded. "So we can't go south."

Tad nodded. "If we went downstream to the east, we'd be cut off by swollen tributaries we couldn't cross either."

"So east is out."

"North is blocked by the river itself, so that leaves west."

"Upstream?"

Tad nodded. "We're only about three or so miles from the headwater where the river comes out the side of Trinity Mountain. If we can't cross the river, we can go around it."

"We might even be able to get a cell phone signal up there."

Tad folded the map, put it back in its bag, and stuffed it in his pocket. "We'd better pack all this stuff up and get going."

"Whoa, what do we need all of it for? I can see taking some clean water and some food, but the rest will just slow us down."

"Do you have any idea how much that tent and the sleeping bags are worth to me?"

"If you want to lug that waterlogged crap up the side of Trinity Mountain, be my guest. Maybe the National Guard rescue party can use it to sling your corpse down off the mountain after you collapse from exhaustion and die of exposure. Jesus, Tad. Have you been paying attention? If we don't get our asses three miles up hill to the head of this river, three miles back down to the road, and at least two miles up the road to the nearest house before sundown, we could die out here."

"You don't get it. I've had this gear for years. Anna and I used this gear, on this very campsite. Damn it, I can't believe you brought me out here to tell me about you and her."

Wyatt stood silent as Tad panted in fury as rain ran down both of their faces. "Get whatever you can't live without. We can pack it out to the cars and then take the cars as far as the low water bridge, but don't tell me every can of pork and beans we packed in here has irreplaceable sentimental value. If you want to fight about Anna, can we wait until we're on the move? We're burning daylight."

Tad walked to the pile of gear and separated out the things he meant to keep. The tent. The sleeping bags. The skillet. Ready-to-eat food. In their water-swollen condition, the sleeping bags were impossible to roll small enough to get in the backpacks, so Tad tied them to the outside. The tent wouldn't fit in its bag either. Tad looked up after two frustrated attempts to squeeze enough water out to get it in the bag.

"Just put all the parts inside and zip it shut. We can carry it between us as far as the cars. We have got to get moving."

Tad nodded, and they were on their way, Wyatt in the lead with one end of the tent, Tad trailing with the other. The path up the side of the valley was steep, and their load was not only heavy, but awkward. Each of them slipped and fell at different times, but neither spoke except to curse after slipping and falling. After they crested the ridge, the old home site came into view. The denuded landscape all around it was a quagmire of mud, but the home site, with its massive oak and tall weeds and flowers and wild rose vines was unchanged aside from the drenching.

"Wyatt."

Wyatt stopped and turned around. His face was flushed and his eyes red. "Yeah?"

"You were right. This stuff is too heavy to carry any further. We can stash it over there in the old home site. I can come back for it later."

"You sure?"

Tad wiped his face. "Yeah."

They carried to gear over to the base of the old oak. Tad put the sleeping bags and backpacks inside the tent and zipped it up. He borrowed a few rocks from the oblong pile near the base of the tree. Not many—just enough to weight the tent so the wind would not blow it away before Tad could come back for it. They kept only their canteens, what food they could stuff in their jacket pockets, their cell phones in their baggies, the map, and Tad's Swiss Army Knife.

Wyatt took a drink from his canteen as Tad finished stashing the gear. He replaced the cap. "Funny being so thirsty with all this water."

In the brief pause in their efforts, Tad could see Wyatt already shivering, and he felt a chill coming over himself as well. "We'd better get moving again."

"Yeah."

The mud that clogged the trail through the clearcut area between the home site and the trailhead sucked at their boots and accumulated in layers on the soles. By the time they reached the cars, Tad's boots felt like they weighed ten pounds each. He checked the trunk of his car to see if he had any other shoes in there, anything dry and not caked in clay. "No such luck," he muttered, closing the trunk. Wyatt was in his car already, a newish Land

Rover, waiting for Tad to get in the old GTO he'd bought and restored after his divorce was final. He scraped two inches of mud off the bottoms of his feet before getting in his car and starting it. The radio emitted only static. He switched the stereo from FM to CD. His home-made compilation Rolling Stones disc was in the player, and "You Can't Always Get What You Want" started playing.

"Aw gimme a break." Tad forwarded through the playlist and stopped on "Paint It Black." "Now we're talking."

Wyatt started on the narrow logging road back to the low water bridge, and Tad pulled out behind him. The steady *whump-whir* of the windshield wipers had a mesmerizing effect. The night of the fire, he'd hardly noticed. He was driving home from the library, and for some reason there was traffic backed up on the street into his subdivision.

"What now?" Tad ejected the book on tape, knowing he couldn't concentrate on it and the unexpected traffic at the same time. He craned to see better through the windshield. The wiper blades were worn out, like a lot of things, and the streaks made it difficult to tell what was up ahead. He knew Anna would already be pissed he'd stayed so late. "Hell," he muttered to himself, "she was pissed when I left."

"Where are you going?" Anna had a screaming Gracie over her left shoulder, patting her little back and bouncing her in the futile way any parent of a colicky baby would recognize immediately.

"To the library. I can't concentrate here." Tad was stuffing books and notebooks into his backpack like they were live snakes that might try to escape if he handled them gently.

"Again?"

"Anna, my comps are in two weeks."

"I know, I know, believe me I know. Any chance you'll be available any time soon to help raise your child?"

"Anna, if I don't pass comps, I don't graduate. How can I support my child while I'm paying off student loans for a degree I never completed? When I get through comps, I'll be mainly working on my dissertation. My schedule will be more flexible." He strode to the door and opened it.

"Uh huh. While you're studying, make sure you look up the *Ubi sunt* motif."

"Actually I already know that one." Tad was pulling the door closed behind him as she replied.

"Do you?"

Tad could see the red and blue strobes of emergency vehicles ahead. "Come on, come on. I don't have time for this."

As Wyatt stopped up the hill from the low water bridge, Tad pulled in behind him. "Gimme Shelter" was just starting as he shut off the car. As he stepped out of his car, Wyatt was closing his door.

"I think we should leave the cars up the hill to make sure they're well clear of the flood water."

Tad nodded. "You think we're far enough over on the side of the road?"

"Well, anyone who has trouble getting around us can feel free to call the cops."

Tad almost smiled, until he remembered how pissed off he was. He took out his map and spread it on the hood of his car. "Okay, so we're here." He pointed at the map. "We need to follow up this side of the river to the headwater, go around and come back down to this road to walk out."

"Do we have to go all the way to the headwater? It's halfway up the freaking mountain."

Tad shrugged. "Could be when we get part way there, the river will be crossable before we reach the actual headwater."

"Guess we better get started." Wyatt was shivering again.

The brief time in their cars was enough to warm up a bit, but Tad wasn't sure how much good it did them. He folded up the map and secured it in its bag. "Yeah. If we get idle too long after all this exertion in this cold and wet, we'll get stiff in no time."

"Real stiff. Should we take the top of the ridge from here?"

"Yeah. We've just got to make sure to keep the river in sight on our right. We don't want to take a wrong turn out here."

The ridge on the south side of the Sacre Coure River Valley was as rocky as it was steep. Before they got two hundred yards from their cars, they reached a formation of rock columns jutting from the ridge top as though carelessly thrust there by some colossal hand.

Wyatt stood atop one of the rock columns. Tad could see that if he were to try to get to the next one, he'd have to jump a gap at least ten feet wide. Wyatt turned back to look at him. "Dude, even if we could get across these rocks without breaking our necks with them all slick from the rain, it would take all day to get the next half mile."

Tad eased to the northernmost edge of the rock to look. Maybe sixty feet below them, the river was still crashing through its course. The rock formation dropped straight down a little less than half that distance. From there, the side of the ridge tapered down to the river at a shallower angle, still steep, but not vertical. At the base of the vertical rock, just before the slope angled down to the river, Tad thought he could see a bit of a shoulder. "Hey Wyatt. Come look at this."

Wyatt looked over the edge beside him. "What am I looking at?"

"Does that look like a trail at the base of the rock? Maybe a game trail or something?"

"Yeah, maybe. Anyway, it looks more passable than this mess up here."

"We'll need to double back to find a place to get down to it."

They'd gone back maybe seventy yards when Wyatt pointed out a smooth rock face sloping down to the base of the rocks. "Here we go."

"What are you talking about? It's only another hundred and twenty yards back to the road. We can get down to the trail there now that we know where to look for it."

Instead of debating, Wyatt sat down and began sliding down the rock face toward a small tree growing at the bottom of the rock. When he got to it, he grabbed the tree and swung around it to stop himself from tumbling on down the slope to the river.

"You're crazy."

Wyatt smiled up at him. "I'm also on the trail."

"I hate you. I want you to know that." Tad sat down and started sliding. His trajectory did not take him as directly toward the small tree as Wyatt's had. Halfway down the rock face, he saw he wasn't going to be able to reach the tree. "Wyatt..."

Wyatt grasped the tree with one hand a lay his body out to stretch his other hand far enough out for Tad to reach it. Tad grabbed the hand as he slid off the rock. He tried to find traction on the steep sloping ground, but his feet slipped in the wet leaves.

"Just hang on." Wyatt didn't try to stop Tad's weight and momentum. He swung Tad smoothly around, in a wider arc than he had made, of course, and directed the momentum back up the slope to the narrow shoulder of ground that formed the trail.

"There. See?"

"Alright, that was *not* fun. No more sliding."

"Okay. No more sliding."

The path was so narrow that they had to walk single file, and Wyatt took the lead. They moved at a good pace, and Tad began to feel more confident that the plan would work. As his hands began feeling a bit numb, he unconsciously pulled them up into his sleeves when he didn't need them to aid in his climbing. In places, however, the path was so narrow and so close to the rock face that it was difficult to maintain balance as their center of gravity leaned out from the rock. They managed by steadying themselves against trees that grew alongside the trail, but in one such place the trees were more sparse—too far apart to reach from one to the next without letting go. Tad stopped, his arm hooked around a small tree like the forelimb of a praying mantis, since his hands were drawn up inside his sleeves. He noticed as he paused that the sound of the precipitation seemed different—crisp. "Wait up."

Wyatt stopped at a tree up ahead. "What's wrong?"

"Is that sleet?"

Wyatt listened and looked around. "Sounds like it. The temperature aloft must be below freezing. I don't think it's freezing here at ground level yet. There's no ice on the trees."

"What do we do?"

Wyatt looked at Tad like he was examining him. "We keep moving. This was your plan, remember?"

"It's too far from this tree to the next one. I'll fall." Tad panted.

"I made it."

"I'm telling you I can't make it."

"We've hiked trails more difficult than this, Tad. What's the matter with you?"

"I can't."

"Look, just keep moving. The faster you go the easier it is to keep your balance, just like riding a bike. Swing your weight upslope as you release one tree and keep moving quickly so you can grab the next one before your weight shifts back down slope, then swing your weight upslope from that one. It's just like skipping a bar on the monkey bars. There's no way to do it without using your momentum."

"How do I do that if I can't reach the next tree?"

"You have to let go." Wyatt demonstrated, swinging his way across a difficult stretch of the trail.

Tad looked down the slope and hugged the tree tighter.

"Tell me again about the night of the fire."

Tad stared down at the Mondrian pattern of red, blue, yellow, and white squares and rectangles on his therapist's rug. "What about it?"

"Where were you when the fire started?"

"At the library."

"And why were you there?"

"I was studying."

"For your comprehensive exams."

"Yes."

"Who was watching the baby?"

"Anna."

"And how did the fire start?"

"They said it was a malfunction in the water heater."

"I see. Do you think Anna did anything that would have contributed to the malfunction?"

"I don't see how." Tad went over that morning in his mind. He remembered shouting from the shower.

"Anna! Why isn't there any hot water, damn it!"

"How should I know? I don't know how those things work."

"I've got class in thirty minutes."

"I'll call the landlord, but you know he won't be in any rush to come look at it."

"I'll try to look at it this evening."

"Those gas appliances scare me. Can't you look at it now?"

"Anna, I told you, I have class in thirty minutes."

He looked up and right, at the bust of some ancient Greek goddess on the bookshelf. "No, I can't think of anything she did that would have caused the fire."

"Has Anna ever said she thought that something you did might have caused the fire?"

Tad looked down from the Greek statue to look directly at the doctor. "No. Never. Not once."

"How long after the fire did the two of you divorce?"

"A year."

"Irreconcilable differences?"

"Yeah. How'd you know?"

"Just a guess."

Tad saw Wyatt stop and look back. When Tad didn't budge from his tree, Wyatt began swinging his way back toward him. When he was a couple of trees away, he stopped. "Tad, you can't stay here. Swing your weight upslope and let go."

Tad was already beginning to tremble. "I can't."

"This isn't like you."

Tad looked back down the slope. "What is like me? To see you do something crazy and follow right behind you?"

"This isn't some kind of dare. This is survival."

"Survival."

"Tad!"

Tad looked up, his teeth chattering.

"Don't do this. Keep moving." Wyatt swung himself over to the tree Tad was hugging. He grabbed a fistful of the middle of the back of Tad's jacket. "Let go of the tree, Tad."

"Why?" Tad let his arms drop.

Wyatt shoved him in the direction of the next tree. "That's why."

Tad screamed all the way to the next tree, wrapping it in both arms when he reached it.

"Damn it! Don't stop! Swing to the next one!"

"I told you I can't."

"You just did. Now you're going to the next tree if I have to punt you." Wyatt swung toward the tree where Tad stood, grabbing him again.

Tad looked up at him. "Why are you doing this?"

"Why wouldn't I?"

"I just thought you must hate me."

"Why would I—oh what the hell am I arguing with you for? We don't have time for this. Get your ass moving." Wyatt shoved him ahead again and repeated the process until they were past the difficult stretch of trail and they could walk it again. Tad's gait was getting clumsy, even on the best parts of the trail.

"Eat one of your granola bars, Tad." Wyatt pulled one out of his own pocket and tore it open with his teeth. Tad tried to follow suit, but he dropped the bar he took out, and they watched its green foil package tumble down the slope. Wyatt took out another of his, opened it, and went back to Tad. "Here."

Tad took it and began to eat. "Guess I've let myself go in recent years, huh? A few years ago, I'd actually have enjoyed a little adventure like this."

"You're doing fine. We need to get moving again."

"I know."

They rounded a bend in the river valley, and for the first time, they had a straight view of Trinity Mountain, maybe a mile further ahead, though the headwater itself was shrouded in mist.

"Look at that," Wyatt said. "Almost there."

Tad laughed. "No sweat."

Just ahead of them was an area where a shelf of the rock on the ridge top had broken free in the distant past, but it had not tumbled or slid down the slope. Rather, it had embedded itself in the slope, creating a twenty-yard stretch of slope that was bare rock, no shoulder to walk on and no trees to swing from. There was a lip of rock along the crack where the slab had separated from the rest of the rock, but it was too narrow and too close to the rock face for them to walk it. Wyatt looked it over.

"We'll have to go across using the crack at the top, hand over hand."

Tad laughed. "You must be joking. We won't be able to get more than our fingertips on that lip of rock. I can't hold myself up with my fingertips."

"Our finger tips won't have to hold all our weight. This rock is rough enough to hold most of it. We just need the crack at the top to keep us from slipping, that's all."

Tad sat down on the trail and leaned into the rock face, a deep sob shaking his chest and shoulders.

Wyatt grabbed the front of Tad's jacket and shook him. "Oh no you don't."

Tad just looked up at him. "Why, Wyatt? Why'd you do it?"

Wyatt still held him by the front of the jacket. "Why'd I talk to her in the first place? Because of you, you idiot. It's been ten years for Christ sake. I couldn't figure out what kept you trapped in what happened. She lived in Texarkana; I lived in Texarkana, so I went to ask her why she wouldn't just let you be. You know what she told me?" Tad didn't answer, so he shook him before asking again, "You know what she told me? It was you. You kept making the phone calls, the e-mails, the letters, trying to fight with her, picking at it so it could never heal. She showed me some of the e-mails, Tad. Cruel. Hateful. Spiteful. She didn't know what to do either."

Tad listened, silent except for his sobbing.

"I talked to her more, and then more. We both tried to figure out how to get the two of you out of the endless cycle, and then one day it occurred to me, I was caught in the cycle too, and not just because I cared about you. Because I cared about her, and I am *not* going to let you stop me from doing what I can to make things better for her." Wyatt shook him on the *not*.

Tad stopped sobbing to look up at Wyatt. "I can't let you do that. I can't."

Wyatt let go of Tad's jacket to let him slump back against the rock. "Well you're going to have to catch me to stop me, Tad-pole." Wyatt strode over to the slab and lay flat against its surface, hooking his fingers in the crack along the top. With one more look back at Tad, he began scooting sideways across the slab.

When Wyatt was halfway across it, Tad shouted, "Damn you, Wyatt!"

Wyatt kept on scooting. Tad crawled over to the rock slab and started edging across himself, watching Wyatt instead of where he was going. Less than half way across, his numb fingers fumbled on the lip of rock. Before he realized he'd missed the crack, he slipped. He shot a look toward Wyatt, who was all the way across and on the trail again, looking back at Tad. "Come on, Tad-pole. Think you can catch me just hanging there?"

"Wyatt, I lost my grip on the crack. There's nothing holding me here but friction."

Tad could see Wyatt craning his neck to look closer. "Your fingertips are just a couple inches from the crack. Try to stretch up and grab it."

Tad stretched, and slid another inch down before stopping. "I can't. If I move, it makes me slip."

"Don't move. I'm coming."

Tad watched him lie back down against the slab and begin scooting back toward him. When Wyatt was beside him, he said, "Tad, I have a good grip on the crack. Grab me and use me to pull yourself back up."

Tad tried, but his stiff fingers lacked the strength. "My fingers—I can't grip."

Wyatt let go with one hand, grasped him by the right wrist, and began pulling him upward. Tad heard him groan as he strained, "Just three inches."

Wyatt's pull gave Tad the support he needed to thy stretching again. He got his left hand up to the crack. His effort coupled with Wyatt's got him the three inches, and knowing his fingers had failed him before, he jammed the side of his hand into the crack. The last surge of effort Wyatt used to get him pulled up caused Wyatt's own fingers to slip, and he began sliding down the rock face, not fast, but not stopping as Tad had. Tad looked down and saw that if Wyatt could angle his slide a little to his right as he slid face down, feet first down the slope, there was one tree limb that stretched over and just brushed the edge of the slab.

"Wyatt, the tree! To your right!"

"I'm trying!"

Wyatt was pushing sideways with the palms of his hands, but Tad could see it wouldn't be enough. Wyatt was about halfway down the slab, with about fifteen feet to go before reaching the edge and a steep drop to the river which had continued to rise and rolled with even more wild power than before. There was no time then for anything, no words, no explanations. Tad pushed himself away from the rock to break the friction and let go, rolling sideways to gain momentum and overtake Wyatt on the way down. He collided with Wyatt and kicked him as savagely as he had wanted to kick him all day, since the night before. Newton's third law of motion changed both of their trajectories. Wyatt was angling now for the tree limb, and Tad toward the other bottom corner of the slab. He had just enough time to see Wyatt grab the limb before sliding over the edge. In the weightless space of the fall, Tad thought briefly of Gracie, just long enough to be glad he would see her soon, but the thought he dwelled on was of Anna, of the time before, when he'd have sworn he'd die for her a thousand times. He'd never know if he'd have really died for Gracie, but he knew his answer now for Anna, and for Wyatt, and for himself, and in that sense, he felt sure Gracie would be glad to see him too.

Seven Years Later

Anna bent over a bed of yellow daffodils in the clearing of the old home site. The new seedlings re-planted by the lumber companies were almost shoulder high all around it, and the weeds of the clearing were mowed short. The roses that had gone wild were pruned and trained over a white new arbor. A small girl, maybe four or five years old, in a yellow sundress and with her gold hair up in pigtails, was skipping through the clearing from the tire swing under the old oak toward a platform of sturdy boards flush with the ground. Anna looked up, and pushed her honey colored hair back behind her left ear. A simple gold band circled the third finger.

"Eva honey, come away from that old well."

"Oh mommy, it's all boarded up. How can I fall in?"

"Never mind, baby, and do as mommy says."

"Yes mommy." The girl skipped over to Anna. "Is it time to pick the flowers now?"

"Let's wait for daddy."

Wyatt strode up from the trail with a bag of three-in-one fertilizer over one shoulder. He dropped the bag beside Anna and stooped to kiss the back of her neck. "Go ahead and pick some good ones, sweetheart."

The child clapped and began gathering an assortment of blossoms, some of the daffodils, and the jonquils Anna had added, a handful of the brown-eyed susans, and one of the black speckled orange tiger lilies. "Is this good, mommy?"

"That's just fine, baby." Anna knelt next to an oblong mound of stones beneath the oak. "Bring some over here."

The girl went to Anna and placed the tiger lily and brown-eyed susans on the stones.

"Okay, let's go down to the river." Wyatt reached down and scooped up the giggling girl to put her on his shoulders, and the three of them walked down the path to the blue hole. The girl darted to the water's edge as soon as Wyatt put her on the sand bar, and she tossed the daffodils and jonquils as far out over the pool as she could manage. The flowers scattered and landed on the clear surface. A few sank immediately, their bright spots of yellow and white and orange still visible as they settled to the rounded stones below. The rest spun lazily in the eddies of the pool as they glided toward the rapids just downstream.

Theme: Male Domination **LITERARY STUDIES**

KATE CHOPIN

Story of an Hour

Kate Chopin
1894

women = ∅ money
∅ land
had to have a husband

Written on April 19, 1894, and first published in *Vogue* on December 6, 1894 as "The Dream of an Hour." Later, it was reprinted in *St. Louis Life* on January 5, 1895 as "The Story of an Hour."[1]

Knowing that Mrs. Mallard was afflicted with a heart trouble, great care was taken to break to her as gently as possible the news of her husband's death.

It was her sister Josephine who told her, in broken sentences; veiled hints that revealed in half concealing. Her husband's friend Richards was there, too, near her. It was he who had been in the newspaper office when intelligence of the railroad disaster was received, with Brently Mallard's name leading the list of "killed." He had only taken the time to assure himself of its truth by a second telegram, and had hastened to forestall any less careful, less tender friend in bearing the sad message.

She did not hear the story as many women have heard the same, with a paralyzed inability to accept its significance. She wept at once, with sudden, wild abandonment, in her sister's arms. When the storm of grief had spent itself she went away to her room alone. She would have no one follow her.

There stood, facing the open window, a comfortable, roomy armchair. Into this she sank, pressed down by a physical exhaustion that haunted her body and seemed to reach into her soul.

She could see in the open square before her house the tops of trees that were all aquiver with the new spring life. The delicious breath of rain was in the air. In the street below a peddler was crying his wares. The notes of a distant song which some one was singing reached her faintly, and countless sparrows were twittering in the eaves.

There were patches of blue sky showing here and there through the clouds that had met and piled one above the other in the west facing her window.

She sat with her head thrown back upon the cushion of the chair, quite motionless, except when a sob came up into her throat and shook her, as a child who has cried itself to sleep continues to sob in its dreams.

She was young, with a fair, calm face, whose lines bespoke repression and even a certain strength. But now there was a dull stare in her eyes, whose gaze was fixed away off yonder on one of those patches of blue sky. It was not a glance of reflection, but rather indicated a suspension of intelligent thought.

There was something coming to her and she was waiting for it, fearfully. What was it? She did not know; it was too subtle and elusive to name. But she felt it, creeping out of the sky, reaching toward her through the sounds, the scents, the color that filled the air.

---

[1] Schulster, Patricia J. "Story of an Hour, The."*The Facts on File Companion to the American Short Story*. Abby H. P. Werlock, ed. 2nd ed. New York: Facts on File, 2010. 619. and the New York Public Library Website: Lois Moore, Senior Librarian, Mid-Manhattan Library. "Story Time for Grown-Ups: "The Story of An Hour" by Kate Chopin."

Now her bosom rose and fell tumultuously. She was beginning to recognize this thing that was approaching to possess her, and she was striving to beat it back with her will—as powerless as her two white slender hands would have been. When she abandoned herself a little whispered word escaped her slightly parted lips. She said it over and over under hte breath: "free, free, free!" The vacant stare and the look of terror that had followed it went from her eyes. They stayed keen and bright. Her pulses beat fast, and the coursing blood warmed and relaxed every inch of her body.

She did not stop to ask if it were or were not a monstrous joy that held her. A clear and exalted perception enabled her to dismiss the suggestion as trivial. She knew that she would weep again when she saw the kind, tender hands folded in death; the face that had never looked save with love upon her, fixed and gray and dead. But she saw beyond that bitter moment a long procession of years to come that would belong to her absolutely. And she opened and spread her arms out to them in welcome.

There would be no one to live for during those coming years; she would live for herself.[2] There would be no powerful will bending hers in that blind persistence with which men and women believe they have a right to impose a private will upon a fellow-creature. A kind intention or a cruel intention made the act seem no less a crime as she looked upon it in that brief moment of illumination.

And yet she had loved him—sometimes. Often she had not. What did it matter! What could love, the unsolved mystery, count for in the face of this possession of self-assertion which she suddenly recognized as the strongest impulse of her being!

"Free! Body and soul free!" she kept whispering.

Josephine was kneeling before the closed door with her lips to the keyhole, imploring for admission. "Louise, open the door! I beg; open the door—you will make yourself ill. What are you doing, Louise? For heaven's sake open the door."

"Go away. I am not making myself ill." No; she was drinking in a very elixir of life through that open window.

Her fancy was running riot along those days ahead of her. Spring days, and summer days, and all sorts of days that would be her own. She breathed a quick prayer that life might be long. It was only yesterday she had thought with a shudder that life might be long.

She arose at length and opened the door to her sister's importunities. There was a feverish triumph in her eyes, and she carried herself unwittingly like a goddess of Victory. She clasped her sister's waist, and together they descended the stairs. Richards stood waiting for them at the bottom.

Some one was opening the front door with a latchkey. It was Brently Mallard who entered, a little travel-stained, composedly carrying his grip-sack and umbrella. He had been far from the scene of the accident, and did not even know there had been one. He stood amazed at Josephine's piercing cry; at Richards' quick motion to screen him from the view of his wife.

When the doctors came they said she had died of heart disease—of the joy that kills.

---

[2] *KateChopin.org* contends that a word is missing in the public domain texts of the story. The website says the sentence should read: "There would be no one to live for her during those coming years; she would live for herself."

A Respectable Woman

Kate Chopin
1894

The story was written on January 20, 1894, and published in *Vogue* on February 15, 1894, one of nineteen Kate Chopin stories that *Vogue* published. It was reprinted in Chopin's collection of stories *A Night in Acadie* in 1897.[3]

Mrs. Baroda was a little provoked to learn that her husband expected his friend, Gouvernail, up to spend a week or two on the plantation.

They had entertained a good deal during the winter; much of the time had also been passed in New Orleans in various forms of mild dissipation. She was looking forward to a period of unbroken rest, now, and undisturbed tete-a-tete with her husband, when he informed her that Gouvernail was coming up to stay a week or two.

This was a man she had heard much of but never seen. He had been her husband's college friend; was now a journalist, and in no sense a society man or "a man about town," which were, perhaps, some of the reasons she had never met him. But she had unconsciously formed an image of him in her mind. She pictured him tall, slim, cynical; with eye-glasses, and his hands in his pockets; and she did not like him. Gouvernail was slim enough, but he wasn't very tall nor very cynical; neither did he wear eyeglasses nor carry his hands in his pockets. And she rather liked him when he first presented himself.

But why she liked him she could not explain satisfactorily to herself when she partly attempted to do so. She could discover in him none of those brilliant and promising traits which Gaston, her husband, had often assured her that he possessed. On the contrary, he sat rather mute and receptive before her chatty eagerness to make him feel at home and in face of Gaston's frank and wordy hospitality. His manner was as courteous toward her as the most exacting woman could require; but he made no direct appeal to her approval or even esteem.

Once settled at the plantation he seemed to like to sit upon the wide portico in the shade of one of the big Corinthian pillars, smoking his cigar lazily and listening attentively to Gaston's experience as a sugar planter.

"This is what I call living," he would utter with deep satisfaction, as the air that swept across the sugar field caressed him with its warm and scented velvety touch. It pleased him also to get on familiar terms with the big dogs that came about him, rubbing themselves sociably against his legs. He did not care to fish, and displayed no eagerness to go out and kill grosbecs when Gaston proposed doing so.

Gouvernail's personality puzzled Mrs. Baroda, but she liked him. Indeed, he was a lovable, inoffensive fellow. After a few days, when she could understand him no better than at first, she gave over being puzzled and remained piqued. In this mood she left her husband and her guest, for the most part, alone together. Then finding that Gouvernail took no manner of exception to her action, she imposed her society upon him, accompanying him in his idle strolls to the mill and walks along the batture. She persistently sought to penetrate the reserve in which he had unconsciously enveloped himself.

"When is he going—your friend?" she one day asked her husband. "For my part, he tires me frightfully."

"Not for a week yet, dear. I can't understand; he gives you no trouble."

---

[3] Introduction from KateChopin.org.

"No. I should like him better if he did; if he were more like others, and I had to plan somewhat for his comfort and enjoyment."

Gaston took his wife's pretty face between his hands and looked tenderly and laughingly into her troubled eyes.

They were making a bit of toilet sociably together in Mrs. Baroda's dressing-room.

"You are full of surprises, ma belle," he said to her. "Even I can never count upon how you are going to act under given conditions." He kissed her and turned to fasten his cravat before the mirror.

"Here you are," he went on, "taking poor Gouvernail seriously and making a commotion over him, the last thing he would desire or expect."

"Commotion!" she hotly resented. "Nonsense! How can you say such a thing? Commotion, indeed! But, you know, you said he was clever."

"So he is. But the poor fellow is run down by overwork now. That's why I asked him here to take a rest."

"You used to say he was a man of ideas," she retorted, unconciliated. "I expected him to be interesting, at least. I'm going to the city in the morning to have my spring gowns fitted. Let me know when Mr. Gouvernail is gone; I shall be at my Aunt Octavie's."

That night she went and sat alone upon a bench that stood beneath a live oak tree at the edge of the gravel walk.

She had never known her thoughts or her intentions to be so confused. She could gather nothing from them but the feeling of a distinct necessity to quit her home in the morning.

Mrs. Baroda heard footsteps crunching the gravel; but could discern in the darkness only the approaching red point of a lighted cigar. She knew it was Gouvernail, for her husband did not smoke. She hoped to remain unnoticed, but her white gown revealed her to him. He threw away his cigar and seated himself upon the bench beside her; without a suspicion that she might object to his presence.

"Your husband told me to bring this to you, Mrs. Baroda," he said, handing her a filmy, white scarf with which she sometimes enveloped her head and shoulders. She accepted the scarf from him with a murmur of thanks, and let it lie in her lap.

He made some commonplace observation upon the baneful effect of the night air at the season. Then as his gaze reached out into the darkness, he murmured, half to himself:

"'Night of south winds—night of the large few stars!

Still nodding night—'"

She made no reply to this apostrophe to the night, which, indeed, was not addressed to her.

Gouvernail was in no sense a diffident man, for he was not a self-conscious one. His periods of reserve were not constitutional, but the result of moods. Sitting there beside Mrs. Baroda, his silence melted for the time.

He talked freely and intimately in a low, hesitating drawl that was not unpleasant to hear. He talked of the old college days when he and Gaston had been a good deal to each other; of the days of keen and blind ambitions and large intentions. Now there was left with him, at least, a philosophic acquiescence to the existing order—only a desire to be permitted to exist, with now and then a little whiff of genuine life, such as he was breathing now.

Her mind only vaguely grasped what he was saying. Her physical being was for the moment predominant. She was not thinking of his words, only drinking in the tones of his voice. She wanted to reach out her hand in the darkness and touch him with the sensitive tips of her fingers upon the face or the lips. She wanted to draw close to him and whisper against his cheek—she did not care what—as she might have done if she had not been a respectable woman.

The stronger the impulse grew to bring herself near him, the further, in fact, did she draw away from him. As soon as she could do so without an appearance of too great rudeness, she rose and left him there alone.

Before she reached the house, Gouvernail had lighted a fresh cigar and ended his apostrophe to the night.

Mrs. Baroda was greatly tempted that night to tell her husband—who was also her friend—of this folly that had seized her. But she did not yield to the temptation. Beside being a respectable woman she was a very sensible one; and she knew there are some battles in life which a human being must fight alone.

When Gaston arose in the morning, his wife had already departed. She had taken an early morning train to the city. She did not return till Gouvernail was gone from under her roof.

There was some talk of having him back during the summer that followed. That is, Gaston greatly desired it; but this desire yielded to his wife's strenuous opposition.

However, before the year ended, she proposed, wholly from herself, to have Gouvernail visit them again. Her husband was surprised and delighted with the suggestion coming from her.

"I am glad, chere amie, to know that you have finally overcome your dislike for him; truly he did not deserve it."

"Oh," she told him, laughingly, after pressing a long, tender kiss upon his lips, "I have overcome everything! you will see. This time I shall be very nice to him."

The Blind Man

Kate Chopin
1897

The story was written in July 1896 and first published in *Vogue*, 13 May 1897.

A man carrying a small red box in one hand walked slowly down the street. His old straw hat and faded garments looked as if the rain had often beaten upon them, and the sun had as many times dried them upon his person. He was not old, but he seemed feeble; and he walked in the sun, along the blistering asphalt pavement. On the opposite side of the street there were trees that threw a thick and pleasant shade: people were all walking on that side. But the man did not know, for he was blind, and moreover he was stupid.

In the red box were lead pencils, which he was endeavoring to sell. He carried no stick, but guided himself by trailing his foot along the stone copings or his hand along the iron railings. When he came to the steps of a house he would mount them. Sometimes, after reaching the door with great difficulty, he could not find the electric button, whereupon he would patiently descend and go his way. Some of the iron gates were locked, their owners being away for the summer, and he would consume much time striving to open them, which made little difference, as he had all the time there was at his disposal.

At times he succeeded in finding the electric button: but the man or maid who answered the bell needed no pencil, nor could they be induced to disturb the mistress of the house about so small a thing.

The man had been out long and had walked far, but had sold nothing. That morning someone who had finally grown tired of having him hanging around had equipped him with this box of pencils, and sent him out to make his living. Hunger, with sharp fangs, was gnawing at his stomach and a consuming thirst parched his mouth and tortured him. The sun was broiling. He wore too much clothing — a vest and coat over his shirt. He might have removed these and carried them on his arm or thrown them away; but he did not think of it. A kind woman who saw him from an upper window felt sorry for him, and wished that he would cross over into the shade.

The man drifted into a side street, where there was a group of noisy, excited children at play. The color of the box which he carried attracted them and they wanted to know what was in it. One of them attempted to take it away from him. With the instinct to protect his own and his only means of sustenance, he resisted, shouted at the children and called them names. A policeman coming round the corner and seeing that he was the centre of a disturbance, jerked him violently around by the collar; but upon perceiving that he was blind, considerably refrained from clubbing him and sent him on his way. He walked on in the sun.

During his aimless rambling he turned into a street where there were monster electric cars thundering up and down, clanging wild bells and literally shaking the ground beneath his feet with their terrific impetus. He started to cross the street.

Then something happened — something horrible happened that made the women faint and the strongest men who saw it grow sick and dizzy. The motorman's lips were as gray as his face, and that was ashen gray; and he shook and staggered from the superhuman effort he had put forth to stop his car.

Where could the crowds have come from so suddenly, as if by magic? Boys on the run, men and women tearing up on their wheels to see the sickening sight: doctors dashing up in buggies as if directed by Providence.

And the horror grew when the multitude recognized in the dead and mangled figure one of the wealthiest, most useful and most influential men of the town, a man noted for his prudence and foresight. How could such a terrible fate have overtaken him? He was hastening from his business house, for he was late, to join his family, who were to start in an hour or two for their summer home on the Atlantic coast. In his hurry he did not perceive the other car coming from the opposite direction and the common, harrowing thing was repeated.

The blind man did not know what the commotion was all about. He had crossed the street, and there he was, stumbling on in the sun, trailing his foot along the coping.

WILLA CATHER

A Wagner Matinée

Willa Cather
1904

The story was first published in *Everybody's Magazine*, 10 (March 1904): 325-328. Collected in her 1905 *The Troll Garden*.

I received one morning a letter, written in pale ink, on glassy, blue-lined note-paper, and bearing the postmark of a little Nebraska village. This communication, worn and rubbed, looking as though it had been carried for some days in a coat-pocket that was none too clean, was from my Uncle Howard. It informed me that his wife had been left a small legacy by a bachelor relative who had recently died, and that it had become necessary for her to come to Boston to attend to the settling of the estate. He requested me to meet her at the station, and render her whatever services might prove necessary. On examining the date indicated as that of her arrival, I found it no later than to-morrow. He had characteristically delayed writing until, had I been away from home for a day, I must have missed the good woman altogether.

The name of my Aunt Georgiana called up not alone her own figure, at once pathetic and grotesque, but opened before my feet a gulf of recollections so wide and deep that, as the letter dropped from my hand, I felt suddenly a stranger to all the present conditions of my existence, wholly ill at ease and out of place amid the surroundings of my study. I became, in short, the gangling farmer-boy my aunt had known, scourged with chilblains and bashfulness, my hands cracked and raw from the corn husking. I felt the knuckles of my thumb tentatively, as though they were raw again. I sat again before her parlor organ, thumbing the scales with my stiff, red hands, while she beside me made canvas mittens for the huskers.

The next morning, after preparing my landlady somewhat, I set out for the station. When the train arrived I had some difficulty in finding my aunt. She was the last of the passengers to alight, and when I got her into the carriage she looked not unlike one of those charred, smoked bodies that firemen lift from the débris of a burned building. She had come all the way in a day coach; her linen duster had become black with soot and her black bonnet gray with dust during the journey. When we arrived at my boarding-house the landlady put her to bed at once, and I did not see her again until the next morning.

Whatever shock Mrs. Springer experienced at my aunt's appearance she considerately concealed. Myself, I saw my aunt's misshapened figure with that feeling of awe and respect with which we behold explorers who have left their ears and fingers north of Franz Josef Land, or their health somewhere along the Upper Congo. My Aunt Georgiana had been a music-teacher at the Boston Conservatory, somewhere back in the latter sixties. One summer, which she had spent in the little village in the Green Mountains where her ancestors had dwelt for generations, she had kindled the callow fancy of the most idle and shiftless of all the village lads, and had conceived for this Howard Carpenter one of those absurd and extravagant passions which a handsome country boy of twenty-one sometimes inspires in a plain, angular, spectacled woman of thirty. When she returned to her duties in Boston, Howard followed her; and the upshot of this inexplicable infatuation was that she eloped with him, eluding the reproaches of her family and the criticism of her friends by going with him to the Nebraska frontier. Carpenter, who of course had no money, took a homestead in Red Willow County, fifty miles from the railroad. There they measured off their eighty acres by driving across the prairie in a wagon, to the wheel of which they had tied a red cotton handkerchief, and counting off its revolutions. They built a dugout in the red hillside, one of those cave dwellings whose inmates usually reverted to the conditions of primitive savagery. Their water they got from the lagoons where the buffalo drank, and their slender stock of provisions was always at the mercy of bands of roving Indians. For thirty years my aunt had not been farther than fifty miles from the homestead.

But Mrs. Springer knew nothing of all this, and must have been considerably shocked at what was left of my kinswoman. Beneath the soiled linen duster, which on her arrival was the most conspicuous feature of her costume, she wore a black stuff dress whose ornamentation showed that she had surrendered herself unquestioningly into the hands of a country dressmaker. My poor aunt's figure, however, would have presented astonishing difficulties to any dressmaker. Her skin was yellow as a Mongolian's from constant exposure to a pitiless wind, and to the alkaline water, which transforms the most transparent cuticle into a sort of flexible leather. She wore ill-fitting false teeth. The most striking thing about her physiognomy, however, was an incessant twitching of the mouth and eyebrows, a form of nervous disorder resulting from isolation and monotony, and from frequent physical suffering.

In my boyhood this affliction had possessed a sort of horrible fascination for me, of which I was secretly very much ashamed, for in those days I owed to this woman most of the good that ever came my way, and had a reverential affection for her. During the three winters when I was riding herd for my uncle, my aunt, after cooking three meals for half a dozen farm-hands, and putting the six children to bed, would often stand until midnight at her ironing-board, hearing me at the kitchen table beside her recite Latin declensions and conjugations, and gently shaking me when my drowsy head sank down over a page of irregular verbs. It was to her, at her ironing or mending, that I read my first Shakespere; and her old text-book of mythology was the first that ever came into my empty hands. She taught me my scales and exercises, too, on the little parlor organ which her husband had bought her after fifteen years, during which she had not so much as seen any instrument except an accordion, that belonged to one of the Norwegian farm-hands. She would sit beside me by the hour, darning and counting, while I struggled with the "Harmonious Blacksmith"; but she seldom talked to me about music, and I understood why. She was a pious woman; she had the consolation of religion; and to her at least her martyrdom was not wholly sordid. Once when I had been doggedly beating out some easy passages from an old score of "Euryanthe" I had found among her music-books, she came up to me and, putting her hands over my eyes, gently drew my head back upon her shoulder, saying tremulously, "Don't love it so well, Clark, or it may be taken from you. Oh! dear boy, pray that whatever your sacrifice be it is not that."

When my aunt appeared on the morning after her arrival, she was still in a semi-somnambulant state. She seemed not to realize that she was in the city where she had spent her youth, the place longed for hungrily half a lifetime. She had been so wretchedly train-sick throughout the journey that she had no recollection of anything but her discomfort, and, to all intents and purposes, there were but a few hours of nightmare between the farm in Red Willow County and my study on Newbury Street. I had planned a little pleasure for her that afternoon, to repay her for some of the glorious moments she had given me when we used to milk together in the straw-thatched cow-shed, and she, because I was more than usually tired, or because her husband had spoken sharply to me, would tell me of the splendid performance of Meyerbeer's "Huguenots" she had seen in Paris in her youth. At two o'clock the Boston Symphony Orchestra was to give a Wagner programme, and I intended to take my aunt, though as I conversed with her I grew doubtful about her enjoyment of it. Indeed, for her own sake, I could only wish her taste for such things quite dead, and the long struggle mercifully ended at last. I suggested our visiting the Conservatory and the Common before lunch, but she seemed altogether too timid to wish to venture out. She questioned me absently about various changes in the city, but she was chiefly concerned that she had forgotten to leave instructions about feeding half-skimmed milk to a certain weakling calf, "Old Maggie's calf, you know, Clark," she explained, evidently having forgotten how long I had been away. She was further troubled because she had neglected to tell her daughter about the freshly opened kit of mackerel in the cellar, that would spoil if it were not used directly.

I asked her whether she had ever heard any of the Wagnerian operas, and found that she had not, though she was perfectly familiar with their respective situations and had once possessed the piano score of "The Flying Dutchman." I began to think it would have been best to get her back to Red Willow County without waking her, and regretted having suggested the concert.

From the time we entered the concert-hall, however, she was a trifle less passive and inert, and seemed to begin to perceive her surroundings. I had felt some trepidation lest she might become aware of the absurdities of her attire, or might experience some painful embarrassment at stepping suddenly into the world to which she had been dead for a quarter of a century. But again I found how superficially I had judged her. She sat looking about her with eyes as impersonal, almost as stony, as those with which the granite Rameses in a museum watches the froth and fret that ebbs and flows about his pedestal, separated from it by the lonely stretch of centuries. I have seen this same aloofness in old miners who drift into the Brown Hotel at Denver, their pockets full of bullion, their linen soiled, their haggard faces unshorn, and who stand in the thronged corridors as solitary as though they were still in a frozen camp on the Yukon, or in the yellow blaze of the Arizona desert, conscious that certain experiences have isolated them from their fellows by a gulf no haberdasher could conceal.

The audience was made up chiefly of women. One lost the contour of faces and figures, indeed any effect of line whatever, and there was only the color contrast of bodices past counting, the shimmer and shading of fabrics soft and firm, silky and sheer, resisting and yielding: red, mauve, pink, blue, lilac, purple, écru, rose, yellow, cream, and white, all the colors that an impressionist finds in a sunlit landscape, with here and there the dead black shadow of a frock-coat. My Aunt Georgiana regarded them as though they had been so many daubs of tube paint on a palette.

When the musicians came out and took their places, she gave a little stir of anticipation, and looked with quickening interest down over the rail at that invariable grouping; perhaps the first wholly familiar thing that had greeted her eye since she had left old Maggie and her weakling calf. I could feel how all those details sank into her soul, for I had not forgotten how they had sunk into mine when I came fresh from ploughing forever and forever between green aisles of corn, where, as in a treadmill, one might walk from daybreak to dusk without perceiving a shadow of change in one's environment. I reminded myself of the impression made on me by the clean profiles of the musicians, the gloss of their linen, the dull black of their coats, the beloved shapes of the instruments, the patches of yellow light thrown by the green-shaded stand-lamps on the smooth, varnished bellies of the 'cellos and the bass viols in the rear, the restless, wind-tossed forest of fiddle necks and bows; I recalled how, in the first orchestra I had ever heard, those long bow strokes seemed to draw the soul out of me, as a conjurer's stick reels out paper ribbon from a hat.

The first number was the Tannhäuser overture. When the violins drew out the first strain of the Pilgrim's chorus, my Aunt Georgiana clutched my coat-sleeve. Then it was that I first realized that for her this singing of basses and stinging frenzy of lighter strings broke a silence of thirty years, the inconceivable silence of the plains. With the battle between the two motifs, with the bitter frenzy of the Venusberg theme and its ripping of strings, came to me an overwhelming sense of the waste and wear we are so powerless to combat. I saw again the tall, naked house on the prairie, black and grim as a wooden fortress; the black pond where I had learned to swim, the rain-gullied clay about the naked house; the four dwarf ash-seedlings on which the dishcloths were always hung to dry before the kitchen door. The world there is the flat world of the ancients; to the east, a cornfield that stretched to daybreak; to the west, a corral that stretched to sunset; between, the sordid conquests of peace, more merciless than those of war.

The overture closed. My aunt released my coat-sleeve, but she said nothing. She sat staring at the orchestra through a dullness of thirty years, through the films made little by little, by each of the three hundred and sixty-five days in every one of them. What, I wondered, did she get from it? She had been a good pianist in her day, I knew, and her musical education had been broader than that of most music-teachers of a quarter of a century ago. She had often told me of Mozart's operas and Meyerbeer's, and I could remember hearing her sing, years ago, certain melodies of Verdi's. When I had fallen ill with a fever she used to sit by my cot in the evening, while the cool night wind blew in through the faded mosquito-netting tacked over the window, and I lay watching a bright star that burned red above the cornfield, and sing "Home to our mountains, oh, let us return!" in a way fit to break the heart of a Vermont boy near dead of homesickness already.

I watched her closely through the prelude to Tristan and Isolde, trying vainly to conjecture what that warfare of motifs, that seething turmoil of strings and winds, might mean to her. Had this music any message for her? Did or did not a new planet swim into her ken? Wagner had been a sealed book to Americans before the sixties. Had she anything left with which to comprehend this glory that had flashed around the world since she had gone from it? I was in a fever of curiosity, but Aunt Georgiana sat silent upon her peak in Darien. She preserved this utter immobility throughout the numbers from the "Flying Dutchman," though her fingers worked mechanically upon her black dress, as though of themselves they were recalling the piano score they had once played. Poor old hands! They were stretched and pulled and twisted into mere tentacles to hold, and lift, and knead with; the palms unduly swollen, the fingers bent and knotted, on one of them a thin worn band that had once been a wedding-ring. As I pressed and gently quieted one of those groping hands, I remembered, with quivering eyelids, their services for me in other days.

Soon after the tenor began the Prize Song, I heard a quick-drawn breath, and turned to my aunt. Her eyes were closed, but the tears were glistening on her cheeks, and I think in a moment more they were in my eyes as well. It never really dies, then, the soul? It withers to the outward eye only, like that strange moss which can lie on a dusty shelf half a century and yet, if placed in water, grows green again. My aunt wept gently throughout the development and elaboration of the melody.

During the intermission before the second half of the concert, I questioned my aunt and found that the Prize Song was not new to her. Some years before there had drifted to the farm in Red Willow County a young German, a tramp cow-puncher, who had sung in the chorus at Baireuth, when he was a boy, along with the other peasant boys and girls. Of a Sunday morning he used to sit on his gingham-sheeted bed in the hands' bedroom, which opened off the kitchen, cleaning the leather of his boots and saddle, and singing the Prize Song, while my aunt went about her work in the kitchen. She had hovered about him until she had prevailed upon him to join the country church, though his sole fitness for this step, so far as I could gather, lay in his boyish face and his possession of this divine melody. Shortly afterward he had gone to town on the Fourth of July, been drunk for several days, lost his money at a faro-table, ridden a saddled Texan steer on a bet, and disappeared with a fractured collar-bone.

"Well, we have come to better things than the old Trovatore at any rate, Aunt Georgie?" I queried, with well-meant jocularity.

Her lip quivered and she hastily put her handkerchief up to her mouth. From behind it she murmured, "And you have been hearing this ever since you left me, Clark?" Her question was the gentlest and saddest of reproaches.

"But do you get it, Aunt Georgiana, the astonishing structure of it all?" I persisted.

"Who could?" she said, absently; "why should one?"

The second half of the programme consisted of four numbers from the Ring. This was followed by the forest music from Siegfried, and the programme closed with Siegfried's funeral march. My aunt wept quietly, but almost continuously. I was perplexed as to what measure of musical comprehension was left to her, to her who had heard nothing but the singing of gospel hymns in Methodist services at the square frame school-house on

Section Thirteen. I was unable to gauge how much of it had been dissolved in soapsuds, or worked into bread, or milked into the bottom of a pail.

The deluge of sound poured on and on; I never knew what she found in the shining current of it; I never knew how far it bore her, or past what happy islands, or under what skies. From the trembling of her face I could well believe that the Siegfried march, at least, carried her out where the myriad graves are, out into the gray, burying-grounds of the sea; or into some world of death vaster yet, where, from the beginning of the world, hope has lain down with hope, and dream with dream and, renouncing, slept.

The concert was over; the people filed out of the hall chattering and laughing, glad to relax and find the living level again, but my kinswoman made no effort to rise. I spoke gently to her. She burst into tears and sobbed pleadingly, "I don't want to go, Clark, I don't want to go!"

I understood. For her, just outside the door of the concert-hall, lay the black pond with the cattle-tracked bluffs, the tall, unpainted house, naked as a tower, with weather-curled boards; the crook-backed ash-seedlings where the dishcloths hung to dry, the gaunt, moulting turkeys picking up refuse about the kitchen door.

The Enchanted Bluff

Willa Cather
1905

The story was first published in *Harper's* in April 1909.

We had our swim before sundown, and while we were cooking our supper the oblique rays of light made a dazzling glare on the white sand about us. The translucent red ball itself sank behind the brown stretches of cornfield as we sat down to eat, and the warm layer of air that had rested over the water and our clean sand bar grew fresher and smelled of the rank ironweed and sunflowers growing on the flatter shore. The river was brown and sluggish, like any other of the half-dozen streams that water the Nebraska corn lands. On one shore was an irregular line of bald clay bluffs where a few scrub oaks with thick trunks and flat, twisted tops threw light shadows on the long grass. The western shore was low and level, with cornfields that stretched to the skyline, and all along the water's edge were little sandy coves and beaches where slim cottonwoods and willow saplings flickered.

The turbulence of the river in springtime discouraged milling, and, beyond keeping the old red bridge in repair, the busy farmers did not concern themselves with the stream; so the Sandtown boys were left in undisputed possession. In the autumn we hunted quail through the miles of stubble and fodder land along the flat shore, and, after the winter skating season was over and the ice had gone out, the spring freshets and flooded bottoms gave us our great excitement of the year. The channel was never the same for two successive seasons. Every spring the swollen stream undermined a bluff to the east, or bit out a few acres of cornfield to the west and whirled the soil away, to deposit it in spumy mud banks somewhere else. When the water fell low in midsummer, new sand bars were thus exposed to dry and whiten in the August sun. Sometimes these were banked so firmly that the fury of the next freshet failed to unseat them; the little willow seedlings emerged triumphantly from the yellow froth, broke into spring leaf, shot up into summer growth, and with their mesh of roots bound together the moist sand beneath them against the batterings of another April. Here and there a cottonwood soon glittered among them, quivering in the low current of air that, even on breathless days when the dust hung like smoke above the wagon road, trembled along the face of the water.

It was on such an island, in the third summer of its yellow green, that we built our watch fire; not in the thicket of dancing willow wands, but on the level terrace of fine sand which had been added that spring; a little new bit of world, beautifully ridged with ripple marks, and strewn with the tiny skeletons of turtles and fish, all as white and dry as if they had been expertly cured. We had been careful not to mar the freshness of the place, although we often swam to it on summer evenings and lay on the sand to rest.

This was our last watch fire of the year, and there were reasons why I should remember it better than any of the others. Next week the other boys were to file back to their old places in the Sandtown High School, but I was to go up to the Divide to teach my first country school in the Norwegian district. I was already homesick at the thought of quitting the boys with whom I had always played; of leaving the river, and going up into a windy plain that was all windmills and cornfields and big pastures; where there was nothing wilful or unmanageable in the landscape, no new islands, and no chance of unfamiliar birds—such as often followed the watercourses.

Other boys came and went and used the river for fishing or skating, but we six were sworn to the spirit of the stream, and we were friends mainly because of the river. There were the two Hassler boys, Fritz and Otto, sons of the little German tailor. They were the youngest of us; ragged boys of ten and twelve, with sunburned hair, weather-stained faces, and pale blue eyes. Otto, the elder, was the best mathematician in school, and clever at his books, but he always dropped out in the spring term as if the river could not get on without him. He and Fritz caught the fat, horned catfish and sold them about the town, and they lived so much in the water that they were as brown and sandy as the river itself.

There was Percy Pound, a fat, freckled boy with chubby cheeks, who took half a dozen boys' story-papers and was always being kept in for reading detective stories behind his desk. There was Tip Smith, destined by his freckles and red hair to be the buffoon in all our games, though he walked like a timid little old man and had a funny, cracked laugh. Tip worked hard in his father's grocery store every afternoon, and swept it out before school in the morning. Even his recreations were laborious. He collected cigarette cards and tin tobacco-tags indefatigably, and would sit for hours humped up over a snarling little scroll-saw which he kept in his attic. His dearest possessions were some little pill bottles that purported to contain grains of wheat from the Holy Land, water from the Jordan and the Dead Sea, and earth from the Mount of Olives. His father had bought these dull things from a Baptist missionary who peddled them, and Tip seemed to derive great satisfaction from their remote origin.

The tall boy was Arthur Adams. He had fine hazel eyes that were almost too reflective and sympathetic for a boy, and such a pleasant voice that we all loved to hear him read aloud. Even when he had to read poetry aloud at school, no one ever thought of laughing. To be sure, he was not at school very much of the time. He was seventeen and should have finished the High School the year before, but he was always off somewhere with his gun. Arthur's mother was dead, and his father, who was feverishly absorbed in promoting schemes, wanted to send the boy away to school and get him off his hands; but Arthur always begged off for another year and promised to study. I remember him as a tall, brown boy with an intelligent face, always lounging among a lot of us little fellows, laughing at us oftener than with us, but such a soft, satisfied laugh that we felt rather flattered when we provoked it. In after-years people said that Arthur had been given to evil ways as a lad, and it is true that we often saw him with the gambler's sons and with old Spanish Fanny's boy, but if he learned anything ugly in their company he never betrayed it to us. We would have followed Arthur anywhere, and I am bound to say that he led us into no worse places than the cattail marshes and the stubble fields. These, then, were the boys who camped with me that summer night upon the sand bar.

After we finished our supper we beat the willow thicket for driftwood. By the time we had collected enough, night had fallen, and the pungent, weedy smell from the shore increased with the coolness. We threw ourselves down about the fire and made another futile effort to show Percy Pound the Little Dipper. We had tried it often before, but he could never be got past the big one.

"You see those three big stars just below the handle, with the bright one in the middle?" said Otto Hassler; "that's Orion's belt, and the bright one is the clasp." I crawled behind Otto's shoulder and sighted up his arm to the star that seemed perched upon the tip of his steady forefinger. The Hassler boys did seine-fishing at night, and they knew a good many stars.

Percy gave up the Little Dipper and lay back on the sand, his hands clasped under his head. "I can see the North Star," he announced, contentedly, pointing toward it with his big toe. "Anyone might get lost and need to know that."

We all looked up at it.

"How do you suppose Columbus felt when his compass didn't point north any more?" Tip asked.

Otto shook his head. "My father says that there was another North Star once, and that maybe this one won't last always. I wonder what would happen to us down here if anything went wrong with it?"

Arthur chuckled. "I wouldn't worry, Ott. Nothing's apt to happen to it in your time. Look at the Milky Way! There must be lots of good dead Indians."

We lay back and looked, meditating, at the dark cover of the world. The gurgle of the water had become heavier. We had often noticed a mutinous, complaining note in it at night, quite different from its cheerful daytime chuckle, and seeming like the voice of a much deeper and more powerful stream. Our water had always these two moods: the one of sunny complaisance, the other of inconsolable, passionate regret.

"Queer how the stars are all in sort of diagrams," remarked Otto. "You could do most any proposition in geometry with 'em. They always look as if they meant something. Some folks say everybody's fortune is all written out in the stars, don't they?"

"They believe so in the old country," Fritz affirmed.

But Arthur only laughed at him. "You're thinking of Napoleon, Fritzey. He had a star that went out when he began to lose battles. I guess the stars don't keep any close tally on Sandtown folks."

We were speculating on how many times we could count a hundred before the evening star went down behind the cornfields, when someone cried, "There comes the moon, and it's as big as a cart wheel!"

We all jumped up to greet it as it swam over the bluffs behind us. It came up like a galleon in full sail; an enormous, barbaric thing, red as an angry heathen god.

"When the moon came up red like that, the Aztecs used to sacrifice their prisoners on the temple top," Percy announced.

"Go on, Perce. You got that out of Golden Days. Do you believe that, Arthur?" I appealed.

Arthur answered, quite seriously: "Like as not. The moon was one of their gods. When my father was in Mexico City he saw the stone where they used to sacrifice their prisoners."

As we dropped down by the fire again some one asked whether the Mound-Builders were older than the Aztecs. When we once got upon the Mound-Builders we never willingly got away from them, and we were still conjecturing when we heard a loud splash in the water.

"Must have been a big cat jumping," said Fritz. "They do sometimes. They must see bugs in the dark. Look what a track the moon makes!"

There was a long, silvery streak on the water, and where the current fretted over a big log it boiled up like gold pieces.

"Suppose there ever was any gold hid away in this old river?" Fritz asked. He lay like a little brown Indian, close to the fire, his chin on his hand and his bare feet in the air. His brother laughed at him, but Arthur took his suggestion seriously.

"Some of the Spaniards thought there was gold up here somewhere. Seven cities chuck full of gold, they had it, and Coronado and his men came up to hunt it. The Spaniards were all over this country once."

Percy looked interested. "Was that before the Mormons went through?"

We all laughed at this.

"Long enough before. Before the Pilgrim Fathers, Perce. Maybe they came along this very river. They always followed the watercourses."

"I wonder where this river really does begin?" Tip mused. That was an old and a favorite mystery which the map did not clearly explain. On the map the little black line stopped somewhere in western Kansas; but since rivers generally rose in mountains, it was only reasonable to suppose that ours came from the Rockies. Its destination, we knew, was the Missouri, and the Hassler boys always maintained that we could embark at Sandtown in floodtime, follow our noses, and eventually arrive at New Orleans. Now they took up their old argument. "If us boys had grit enough to try it, it wouldn't take no time to get to Kansas City and St. Joe."

We began to talk about the places we wanted to go to. The Hassler boys wanted to see the stockyards in Kansas City, and Percy wanted to see a big store in Chicago. Arthur was interlocutor and did not betray himself.

"Now it's your turn, Tip."

Tip rolled over on his elbow and poked the fire, and his eyes looked shyly out of his queer, tight little face. "My place is awful far away. My Uncle Bill told me about it."

Tip's Uncle Bill was a wanderer, bitten with mining fever, who had drifted into Sandtown with a broken arm, and when it was well had drifted out again.

"Where is it?"

"Aw, it's down in New Mexico somewheres. There aren't no railroads or anything. You have to go on mules, and you run out of water before you get there and have to drink canned tomatoes."

"Well, go on, kid. What's it like when you do get there?"

Tip sat up and excitedly began his story.

"There's a big red rock there that goes right up out of the sand for about nine hundred feet. The country's flat all around it, and this here rock goes up all by itself, like a monument. They call it the Enchanted Bluff down there, because no white man has ever been on top of it. The sides are smooth rock, and straight up, like a wall. The Indians say that hundreds of years ago, before the Spaniards came, there was a village away up there in the air. The tribe that lived there had some sort of steps, made out of wood and bark, hung down over the face of the bluff, and the braves went down to hunt and carried water up in big jars swung on their backs. They kept a big supply of water and dried meat up there, and never went down except to hunt. They were a peaceful tribe that made cloth and pottery, and they went up there to get out of the wars. You see, they could pick off any war party that tried to get up their little steps. The Indians say they were a handsome people, and they had some sort of queer religion. Uncle Bill thinks they were Cliff-Dwellers who had got into trouble and left home. They weren't fighters, anyhow.

"One time the braves were down hunting and an awful storm came up—a kind of waterspout—and when they got back to their rock they found their little staircase had been all broken to pieces, and only a few steps were left hanging away up in the air. While they were camped at the foot of the rock, wondering what to do, a war party from the north came along and massacred 'em to a man, with all the old folks and women looking on from the rock. Then the war party went on south and left the village to get down the best way they could. Of course they never got down. They starved to death up there, and when the war party came back on their way north, they could hear the children crying from the edge of the bluff where they had crawled out, but they didn't see a sign of a grown Indian, and nobody has ever been up there since."

We exclaimed at this dolorous legend and sat up.

"There couldn't have been many people up there," Percy demurred. "How big is the top, Tip?"

"Oh, pretty big. Big enough so that the rock doesn't look nearly as tall as it is. The top's bigger than the base. The bluff is sort of worn away for several hundred feet up. That's one reason it's so hard to climb."

I asked how the Indians got up, in the first place.

"Nobody knows how they got up or when. A hunting party came along once and saw that there was a town up there, and that was all."

Otto rubbed his chin and looked thoughtful. "Of course there must be some way to get up there. Couldn't people get a rope over someway and pull a ladder up?"

Tip's little eyes were shining with excitement. "I know a way. Me and Uncle Bill talked it over. There's a kind of rocket that would take a rope over—lifesavers use 'em—and then you could hoist a rope ladder and peg it down at the bottom and make it tight with guy ropes on the other side. I'm going to climb that there bluff, and I've got it all planned out."

Fritz asked what he expected to find when he got up there.

"Bones, maybe, or the ruins of their town, or pottery, or some of their idols. There might be 'most anything up there. Anyhow, I want to see."

"Sure nobody else has been up there, Tip?" Arthur asked.

"Dead sure. Hardly anybody ever goes down there. Some hunters tried to cut steps in the rock once, but they didn't get higher than a man can reach. The Bluff's all red granite, and Uncle Bill thinks it's a boulder the glaciers left. It's a queer place, anyhow. Nothing but cactus and desert for hundreds of miles, and yet right under the Bluff there's good water and plenty of grass. That's why the bison used to go down there."

Suddenly we heard a scream above our fire, and jumped up to see a dark, slim bird floating southward far above us—a whooping crane, we knew by her cry and her long neck. We ran to the edge of the island, hoping we might see her alight, but she wavered southward along the rivercourse until we lost her. The Hassler boys declared that by the look of the heavens it must be after midnight, so we threw more wood on our fire, put on our jackets, and curled down in the warm sand. Several of us pretended to doze, but I fancy we were really thinking about Tip's Bluff and the extinct people. Over in the wood the ring doves were calling mournfully to one another, and once we heard a dog bark, far away. "Somebody getting into old Tommy's melon patch," Fritz murmured sleepily, but nobody answered him. By and by Percy spoke out of the shadows.

"Say, Tip, when you go down there will you take me with you?"

"Maybe."

"Suppose one of us beats you down there, Tip?"

"Whoever gets to the Bluff first has got to promise to tell the rest of us exactly what he finds," remarked one of the Hassler boys, and to this we all readily assented.

Somewhat reassured, I dropped off to sleep. I must have dreamed about a race for the Bluff, for I awoke in a kind of fear that other people were getting ahead of me and that I was losing my chance. I sat up in my damp clothes and looked at the other boys, who lay tumbled in uneasy attitudes about the dead fire. It was still dark, but the sky was blue with the last wonderful azure of night. The stars glistened like crystal globes, and trembled as if they shone through a depth of clear water. Even as I watched, they began to pale and the sky brightened. Day came suddenly, almost instantaneously. I turned for another look at the blue night, and it was gone. Everywhere the birds began to call, and all manner of little insects began to chirp and hop about in the willows. A breeze sprang up from the west and brought the heavy smell of ripened corn. The boys rolled over and shook themselves. We stripped and plunged into the river just as the sun came up over the windy bluffs.

When I came home to Sandtown at Christmas time, we skated out to our island and talked over the whole project of the Enchanted Bluff, renewing our resolution to find it.

Although that was twenty years ago, none of us have ever climbed the Enchanted Bluff. Percy Pound is a stockbroker in Kansas City and will go nowhere that his red touring car cannot carry him. Otto Hassler went on the railroad and lost his foot braking; after which he and Fritz succeeded their father as the town tailors.

Arthur sat about the sleepy little town all his life—he died before he was twenty-five. The last time I saw him, when I was home on one of my college vacations, he was sitting in a steamer chair under a cottonwood tree in the little yard behind one of the two Sandtown saloons. He was very untidy and his hand was not steady, but when he rose, unabashed, to greet me, his eyes were as clear and warm as ever. When I had talked with him for an hour and heard him laugh again, I wondered how it was that when Nature had taken such pains with a man, from his hands to the arch of his long foot, she had ever lost him in Sandtown. He joked about Tip Smith's Bluff, and declared he was going down there just as soon as the weather got cooler; he thought the Grand Canyon might be worth while, too.

I was perfectly sure when I left him that he would never get beyond the high plank fence and the comfortable shade of the cottonwood. And, indeed, it was under that very tree that he died one summer morning.

Tip Smith still talks about going to New Mexico. He married a slatternly, unthrifty country girl, has been much tied to a perambulator, and has grown stooped and grey from irregular meals and broken sleep. But the worst of his difficulties are now over, and he has, as he says, come into easy water. When I was last in Sandtown I walked home with him late one moonlight night, after he had balanced his cash and shut up his store. We took the long way around and sat down on the schoolhouse steps, and between us we quite revived the romance of the lone red rock and the extinct people. Tip insists that he still means to go down there, but he thinks now he will wait until his boy Bert is old enough to go with him. Bert has been let into the story, and thinks of nothing but the Enchanted Bluff.

A Death in the Desert

Willa Cather
1903, 1905, 1920

The story was first published in *The Scribner's* in January 1903: 109-21. In the original 1903 publication, Everett Hilgarde's name was Windermere Hilgarde. It was changed to "Everett" for the publication of *The Troll Garden*, 1905. Four of these stories—"The Sculptor's Funeral," "A Death in the Desert," "A Wagner Matinee," and "Paul's Case"—were revised and included in Cather's next collection of short fiction *Youth and the Bright Medusa*, published in 1920. Our text is from the 1920 version.

Everett Hilgarde was conscious that the man in the seat across the aisle was looking at him intently. He was a large, florid man, wore a conspicuous diamond solitaire upon his third finger, and Everett judged him to be a travelling salesman of some sort. He had the air of an adaptable fellow who had been about the world and who could keep cool and clean under almost any circumstances.

The "High Line Flyer," as this train was derisively called among railroad men, was jerking along through the hot afternoon over the monotonous country between Holdredge and Cheyenne. Besides the blond man and himself the only occupants of the car were two dusty, bedraggled-looking girls who had been to the Exposition at Chicago, and who were earnestly discussing the cost of their first trip out of Colorado. The four uncomfortable passengers were covered with a sediment of fine, yellow dust which clung to their hair and eyebrows like gold powder. It blew up in clouds from the bleak, lifeless country through which they passed, until they were one colour with the sage-brush and sand-hills. The grey and yellow desert was varied only by occasional ruins of deserted towns, and the little red boxes of station-houses, where the spindling trees and sickly vines in the blue-grass yards made little green reserves fenced off in that confusing wilderness of sand.

As the slanting rays of the sun beat in stronger and stronger through the car-windows, the blond gentleman asked the ladies' permission to remove his coat, and sat in his lavender striped shirtsleeves, with a black silk handkerchief tucked about his collar. He had seemed interested in Everett since they had boarded the train at Holdredge; kept glancing at him curiously and then looking reflectively out of the window, as though he were trying to recall something. But wherever Everett went, some one was almost sure to look at him with that curious interest, and it had ceased to embarrass or annoy him. Presently the stranger, seeming satisfied with his observation, leaned back in his seat, half closed his eyes, and began softly to whistle the Spring Song from *Proserpine*, the cantata that a dozen years before had made its young composer famous in a night. Everett had heard that air on guitars in Old Mexico, on mandolins at college glees, on cottage organs in New England hamlets, and only two weeks ago he had heard it played on sleigh-bells at a variety theatre in Denver. There was literally no way of escaping his brother's precocity. Adriance could live on the other side of the Atlantic, where his youthful indiscretions were forgotten in his mature achievements, but his brother had never been able to outrun *Proserpine*,— and here he found it again, in the Colorado sand-hills. Not that Everett was exactly ashamed of *Proserpine*; only a man of genius could have written it, but it was the sort of thing that a man of genius outgrows as soon as he can.

Everett unbent a trifle, and smiled at his neighbour across the aisle. Immediately the large man rose and coming over dropped into the seat facing Hilgarde, extending his card.

"Dusty ride, isn't it? I don't mind it myself; I'm used to it. Born and bred in de briar patch, like Br'er Rabbit. I've been trying to place you for a long time; I think I must have met you before."

"Thank you," said Everett, taking the card; "my name is Hilgarde. You've probably met my brother, Adriance; people often mistake me for him."

The travelling-man brought his hand down upon his knee with such vehemence that the solitaire blazed.

"So I was right after all, and if you're not Adriance Hilgarde you're his double. I thought I couldn't be mistaken. Seen him? Well, I guess! I never missed one of his recitals at the Auditorium, and he played the piano score of *Proserpine* through to us once at the Chicago Press Club. I used to be on the *Commercial* there before I began to travel for the publishing department of the concern. So you're Hilgarde's brother, and here I've run into you at the jumping-off place. Sounds like a newspaper yarn, doesn't it?"

The travelling-man laughed and offering Everett a cigar plied him with questions on the only subject that people ever seemed to care to talk to him about. At length the salesman and the two girls alighted at a Colorado way station, and Everett went on to Cheyenne alone.

The train pulled into Cheyenne at nine o'clock, late by a matter of four hours or so; but no one seemed particularly concerned at its tardiness except the station agent, who grumbled at being kept in the office over time on a summer night. When Everett alighted from the train he walked down the platform and stopped at the track crossing, uncertain as to what direction he should take to reach a hotel. A phaeton stood near the crossing and a woman held the reins. She was dressed in white, and her figure was clearly silhouetted against the cushions, though it was too dark to see her face. Everett had scarcely noticed her, when the switch-engine came puffing up from the opposite direction, and the head-light threw a strong glare of light on his face. The woman in the phaeton uttered a low cry and dropped the reins. Everett started forward and caught the horse's head, but the animal only lifted its ears and whisked its tail in impatient surprise. The woman sat perfectly still, her head sunk between her shoulders and her handkerchief pressed to her face. Another woman came out of the depot and hurried toward the phaeton, crying, "Katharine, dear, what is the matter?"

Everett hesitated a moment in painful embarrassment, then lifted his hat and passed on. He was accustomed to sudden recognitions in the most impossible places, especially from women.

While he was breakfasting the next morning, the head waiter leaned over his chair to murmur that there was a gentleman waiting to see him in the parlour. Everett finished his coffee, and went in the direction indicated, where he found his visitor restlessly pacing the floor. His whole manner betrayed a high degree of agitation, though his physique was not that of a man whose nerves lie near the surface. He was something below medium height, square-shouldered and solidly built. His thick, closely cut hair was beginning to show grey about the ears, and his bronzed face was heavily lined. His square brown hands were locked behind him, and he held his shoulders like a man conscious of responsibilities, yet, as he turned to greet Everett, there was an incongruous diffidence in his address.

"Good-morning, Mr. Hilgarde," he said, extending his hand; "I found your name on the hotel register. My name is Gaylord. I'm afraid my sister startled you at the station last night, and I've come around to explain."

"Ah! the young lady in the phaeton? I'm sure I didn't know whether I had anything to do with her alarm or not. If I did, it is I who owe an apology."

The man coloured a little under the dark brown of his face.

"Oh, it's nothing you could help, sir, I fully understand that. You see, my sister used to be a pupil of your brother's, and it seems you favour him; when the switch-engine threw a light on your face, it startled her."

Everett wheeled about in his chair. "Oh! *Katharine* Gaylord! Is it possible! Why, I used to know her when I was a boy. What on earth—"

"Is she doing here?" Gaylord grimly filled out the pause. "You've got at the heart of the matter. You know my sister had been in bad health for a long time?"

"No. The last I knew of her she was singing in London. My brother and I correspond infrequently, and seldom get beyond family matters. I am deeply sorry to hear this."

The lines in Charley Gaylord's brow relaxed a little.

"What I'm trying to say, Mr. Hilgarde, is that she wants to see you. She's set on it. We live several miles out of town, but my rig's below, and I can take you out any time you can go."

"At once, then. I'll get my hat and be with you in a moment."

When he came downstairs Everett found a cart at the door, and Charley Gaylord drew a long sigh of relief as he gathered up the reins and settled back into his own element.

"I think I'd better tell you something about my sister before you see her, and I don't know just where to begin. She travelled in Europe with your brother and his wife, and sang at a lot of his concerts; but I don't know just how much you know about her."

"Very little, except that my brother always thought her the most gifted of his pupils. When I knew her she was very young and very beautiful, and quite turned my head for a while."

Everett saw that Gaylord's mind was entirely taken up by his grief.

"That's the whole thing," he went on, flecking his horses with the whip.

"She was a great woman, as you say, and she didn't come of a great family. She had to fight her own way from the first. She got to Chicago, and then to New York, and then to Europe, and got a taste for it all; and now she's dying here like a rat in a hole, out of her own world, and she can't fall back into ours. We've grown apart, some way—miles and miles apart—and I'm afraid she's fearfully unhappy."

"It's a tragic story you're telling me, Gaylord," said Everett. They were well out into the country now, spinning along over the dusty plains of red grass, with the ragged blue outline of the mountains before them.

"Tragic!" cried Gaylord, starting up in his seat, "my God, nobody will ever know how tragic! It's a tragedy I live with and eat with and sleep with, until I've lost my grip on everything. You see she had made a good bit of money, but she spent it all going to health resorts. It's her lungs. I've got money enough to send her anywhere, but the doctors all say it's no use. She hasn't the ghost of a chance. It's just getting through the days now. I had no notion she was half so bad before she came to me. She just wrote that she was run down. Now that she's here, I think she'd be happier anywhere under the sun, but she won't leave. She says it's easier to let go of life here. There was a time when I was a brakeman with a run out of Bird City, Iowa, and she was a little thing I could carry on my shoulder, when I could get her everything on earth she wanted, and she hadn't a wish my $80 a month didn't cover; and now, when I've got a little property together, I can't buy her a night's sleep!"

Everett saw that, whatever Charley Gaylord's present status in the world might be, he had brought the brakeman's heart up the ladder with him.

The reins slackened in Gaylord's hand as they drew up before a showily painted house with many gables and a round tower. "Here we are," he said, turning to Everett, "and I guess we understand each other."

They were met at the door by a thin, colourless woman, whom Gaylord introduced as "My sister, Maggie." She asked her brother to show Mr. Hilgarde into the music-room, where Katharine would join him.

When Everett entered the music-room he gave a little start of surprise, feeling that he had stepped from the glaring Wyoming sunlight into some New York studio that he had always known. He looked incredulously out of the window at the grey plain that ended in the great upheaval of the Rockies.

The haunting air of familiarity perplexed him. Suddenly his eye fell upon a large photograph of his brother above the piano. Then it all became clear enough: this was veritably his brother's room. If it were not an exact copy of one of the many studios that Adriance had fitted up in various parts of the world, wearying of them and leaving almost before the renovator's varnish had dried, it was at least in the same tone. In every detail Adriance's taste was so manifest that the room seemed to exhale his personality.

Among the photographs on the wall there was one of Katharine Gaylord, taken in the days when Everett had known her, and when the flash of her eye or the flutter of her skirt was enough to set his boyish heart in a tumult. Even now, he stood before the portrait with a certain degree of embarrassment. It was the face of a woman already old in her first youth, a trifle hard, and it told of what her brother had called her fight. The *camaraderie* of her frank, confident eyes was qualified by the deep lines about her mouth and the curve of the lips, which was both sad and cynical. Certainly she had more good-will than confidence toward the world. The chief charm of the woman, as Everett had known her, lay in her superb figure and in her eyes, which possessed a warm, life-giving quality like the sunlight; eyes which glowed with a perpetual *salutat* to the world.

Everett was still standing before the picture, his hands behind him and his head inclined, when he heard the door open. A tall woman advanced toward him, holding out her hand. As she started to speak she coughed slightly, then, laughing, said, in a low, rich voice, a trifle husky: "You see I make the traditional Camille entrance. How good of you to come, Mr. Hilgarde."

Everett was acutely conscious that while addressing him she was not looking at him at all, and, as he assured her of his pleasure in coming, he was glad to have an opportunity to collect himself. He had not reckoned upon the ravages of a long illness. The long, loose folds of her white gown had been especially designed to conceal the sharp outlines of her body, but the stamp of her disease was there; simple and ugly and obtrusive, a pitiless fact that could not be disguised or evaded. The splendid shoulders were stooped, there was a swaying unevenness in her gait, her arms seemed disproportionately long, and her hands were transparently white, and cold to the touch. The changes in her face were less obvious; the proud carriage of the head, the warm, clear eyes, even the delicate flush of colour in her cheeks, all defiantly remained, though they were all in a lower key—older, sadder, softer.

She sat down upon the divan and began nervously to arrange the pillows. "Of course I'm ill, and I look it, but you must be quite frank and sensible about that and get used to it at once, for we've no time to lose. And if I'm a trifle irritable you won't mind?—for I'm more than usually nervous."

"Don't bother with me this morning, if you are tired," urged Everett. "I can come quite as well tomorrow."

"Gracious, no!" she protested, with a flash of that quick, keen humour that he remembered as a part of her. "It's solitude that I'm tired to death of—solitude and the wrong kind of people. You see, the minister called on me this morning. He happened to be riding by on his bicycle and felt it his duty to stop. The funniest feature of his conversation is that he is always excusing my own profession to me. But how we are losing time! Do tell me about New York; Charley says you're just on from there. How does it look and taste and smell just now? I think a whiff of the Jersey ferry would be as flagons of cod-liver oil to me. Are the trees still green in Madison Square, or have they grown brown and dusty? Does the chaste Diana still keep her vows through all the exasperating changes of weather? Who has your brother's old studio now, and what misguided aspirants practise their scales in the rookeries about Carnegie Hall? What do people go to see at the theatres, and what do they eat and drink in the world nowadays? Oh, let me die in Harlem!" she was interrupted by a violent attack of coughing, and Everett, embarrassed by her discomfort, plunged into gossip about the professional people he had met in town during the summer, and the musical outlook for the winter. He was diagramming with his pencil some new mechanical device to be used at the Metropolitan in the production of the *Rheingold*, when he became conscious that she was looking at him intently, and that he was talking to the four walls.

Katharine was lying back among the pillows, watching him through half-closed eyes, as a painter looks at a picture. He finished his explanation vaguely enough and put the pencil back in his pocket. As he did so, she said, quietly: "How wonderfully like Adriance you are!"

He laughed, looking up at her with a touch of pride in his eyes that made them seem quite boyish. "Yes, isn't it absurd? It's almost as awkward as looking like Napoleon—But, after all, there are some advantages. It has made some of his friends like me, and I hope it will make you."

POETRY

Katharine gave him a quick, meaning glance from under her lashes. "Oh, it did that long ago. What a haughty, reserved youth you were then, and how you used to stare at people, and then blush and look cross. Do you remember that night you took me home from a rehearsal, and scarcely spoke a word to me?"

"It was the silence of admiration," protested Everett, "very crude and boyish, but certainly sincere. Perhaps you suspected something of the sort?"

"I believe I suspected a pose; the one that boys often affect with singers. But it rather surprised me in you, for you must have seen a good deal of your brother's pupils." Everett shook his head. "I saw my brother's pupils come and go. Sometimes I was called on to play accompaniments, or to fill out a vacancy at a rehearsal, or to order a carriage for an infuriated soprano who had thrown up her part. But they never spent any time on me, unless it was to notice the resemblance you speak of."

"Yes," observed Katharine, thoughtfully, "I noticed it then, too; but it has grown as you have grown older. That is rather strange, when you have lived such different lives. It's not merely an ordinary family likeness of features, you know, but the suggestion of the other man's personality in your face— like an air transposed to another key. But I'm not attempting to define it; it's beyond me; something altogether unusual and a trifle—well, uncanny," she finished, laughing.

Everett sat looking out under the red window-blind which was raised just a little. As it swung back and forth in the wind it revealed the glaring panorama of the desert—a blinding stretch of yellow, flat as the sea in dead calm, splotched here and there with deep purple shadows; and, beyond, the ragged blue outline of the mountains and the peaks of snow, white as the white clouds. "I remember, when I was a child I used to be very sensitive about it. I don't think it exactly displeased me, or that I would have had it otherwise, but it seemed like a birthmark, or something not to be lightly spoken of. It came into even my relations with my mother. Ad went abroad to study when he was very young, and mother was all broken up over it. She did her whole duty by each of us, but it was generally understood among us that she'd have made burnt-offerings of us all for him any day. I was a little fellow then, and when she sat alone on the porch on summer evenings, she used sometimes to call me to her and turn my face up in the light that streamed out through the shutters and kiss me, and then I always knew she was thinking of Adriance."

"Poor little chap," said Katharine, in her husky voice. "How fond people have always been of Adriance! Tell me the latest news of him. I haven't heard, except through the press, for a year or more. He was in Algiers then, in the valley of the Chelif, riding horseback, and he had quite made up his mind to adopt the Mahometan faith and become an Arab. How many countries and faiths has he adopted, I wonder?"

"Oh, that's Adriance," chuckled Everett. "He is himself barely long enough to write checks and be measured for his clothes. I didn't hear from him while he was an Arab; I missed that."

"He was writing an Algerian *suite* for the piano then; it must be in the publisher's hands by this time. I have been too ill to answer his letter, and have lost touch with him."

Everett drew an envelope from his pocket. "This came a month ago. Read it at your leisure."

"Thanks. I shall keep it as a hostage. Now I want you to play for me. Whatever you like; but if there is anything new in the world, in mercy let me hear it."

He sat down at the piano, and Katharine sat near him, absorbed in his remarkable physical likeness to his brother, and trying to discover in just what it consisted. He was of a larger build than Adriance, and much heavier. His face was of the same oval mould, but it was grey, and darkened about the mouth by continual shaving. His eyes were of the same inconstant April colour, but they were reflective and rather dull; while Adriance's were always points of high light, and always meaning another thing than the thing they meant yesterday. It was hard to see why this earnest man should so continually suggest that lyric, youthful face, as gay as his was grave. For Adriance, though he was ten years the elder, and though his hair was streaked with silver, had the face of a boy of twenty, so mobile that it told his thoughts before he could put them into words. A contralto, famous for the extravagance of her vocal methods and of her affections, once said that the shepherd-boys who sang in the Vale of Tempe must certainly have looked like young Hilgarde.

Everett sat smoking on the veranda of the Inter-Ocean House that night, the victim of mournful recollections. His infatuation for Katharine Gaylord, visionary as it was, had been the most serious of his boyish love-affairs. The fact that it was all so done and dead and far behind him, and that the woman had lived her life out since then, gave him an oppressive sense of age and loss.

He remembered how bitter and morose he had grown during his stay at his brother's studio when Katharine Gaylord was working there, and how he had wounded Adriance on the night of his last concert in New York. He had sat there in the box—while his brother and Katherine were called back again and again, and the flowers went up over the footlights until they were stacked half as high as the piano—brooding in his sullen boy's heart upon the pride those two felt in each other's work—spurring each other to their best and beautifully contending in song. The footlights had seemed a hard, glittering line drawn sharply between their life and his. He walked back to his hotel alone, and sat in his window staring out on Madison Square until long after midnight, resolved to beat no more at doors that he could never enter.

* * * * *

Everett's week in Cheyenne stretched to three, and he saw no prospect of release except through the thing he dreaded. The bright, windy days of the Wyoming autumn passed swiftly. Letters and telegrams came urging him to hasten his trip to the coast, but he resolutely postponed his business engagements. The mornings he spent on one of Charley Gaylord's ponies, or fishing in the mountains. In the afternoon he was usually at his post of duty. Destiny, he reflected, seems to have very positive notions about the sort of parts we are fitted to play. The scene changes and the compensation varies, but in the end we usually find that we have played the same class of business from first to last. Everett had been a stop-gap all his life. He remembered going through a looking-glass labyrinth when he was a boy, and trying gallery after gallery, only at every turn to bump his nose against his own face—which, indeed, was not his own, but his brother's. No matter what his mission, east or west, by land or sea, he was sure to find himself employed in his brother's business, one of the tributary lives which helped to swell the shining current of Adriance Hilgarde's. It was not the first time that his duty had been to comfort, as best he could, one of the broken things his brother's imperious speed had cast aside and forgotten. He made no attempt to analyse the situation or to state it in exact terms; but he accepted it as a commission from his brother to help this woman to die. Day by day he felt her need for him grow more acute and positive; and day by day he felt that in his peculiar relation to her, his own individuality played a smaller part. His power to minister to her comfort lay solely in his link with his brother's life. He knew that she sat by him always watching for some trick of gesture, some familiar play of expression, some illusion of light and shadow, in which he should seem wholly Adriance. He knew that she lived upon this, and that in the exhaustion which followed this turmoil of her dying senses, she slept deep and sweet, and dreamed of youth and art and days in a certain old Florentine garden, and not of bitterness and death.

A few days after his first meeting with Katharine Gaylord, he had cabled his brother to write her. He merely said that she was mortally ill; he could depend on Adriance to say the right thing—that was a part of his gift. Adriance always said not only the right thing, but the opportune, graceful, exquisite thing. He caught the lyric essence of the moment, the poetic suggestion of every situation. Moreover, he usually did the right thing,—except, when he did very cruel things—bent upon making people happy when their existence touched his, just as he insisted that his material environment should be beautiful; lavishing upon those near him all the warmth and radiance of his rich nature, all the homage of the poet and troubadour, and, when they were no longer near, forgetting—for that also was a part of Adriance's gift.

Three weeks after Everett had sent his cable, when he made his daily call at the gaily painted ranch-house, he found Katharine laughing like a girl. "Have you ever thought," she said, as he entered the music-room, "how much these séances of ours are like Heine's 'Florentine Nights,' except that I don't give you an opportunity to monopolize the conversation?" She held his hand longer than usual as she greeted him. "You are the kindest man living, the kindest," she added, softly.

Everett's grey face coloured faintly as he drew his hand away, for he felt that this time she was looking at him, and not at a whimsical caricature of his brother.

She drew a letter with a foreign postmark from between the leaves of a book and held it out, smiling. "You got him to write it. Don't say you didn't, for it came direct, you see, and the last address I gave him was a place in Florida. This deed shall be remembered of you when I am with the just in Paradise. But one thing you did not ask him to do, for you didn't know about it. He has sent me his latest work, the new sonata, and you are to play it for me directly. But first for the letter; I think you would better read it aloud to me."

Everett sat down in a low chair facing the window-seat in which she reclined with a barricade of pillows behind her. He opened the letter, his lashes half-veiling his kind eyes, and saw to his satisfaction that it was a long one; wonderfully tactful and tender, even for Adriance, who was tender with his valet and his stable-boy, with his old gondolier and the beggar-women who prayed to the saints for him.

The letter was from Granada, written in the Alhambra, as he sat by the fountain of the Patio di Lindaraxa. The air was heavy with the warm fragrance of the South and full of the sound of splashing, running water, as it had been in a certain old garden in Florence, long ago. The sky was one great turquoise, heated until it glowed. The wonderful Moorish arches threw graceful blue shadows all about him. He had sketched an outline of them on the margin of his note-paper. The letter was full of confidences about his work, and delicate allusions to their old happy days of study and comradeship.

As Everett folded it he felt that Adriance had divined the thing needed and had risen to it in his own wonderful way. The letter was consistently egotistical, and seemed to him even a trifle patronizing, yet it was just what she had wanted. A strong realization of his brother's charm and intensity and power came over him; he felt the breath of that whirlwind of flame in which Adriance passed, consuming all in his path, and himself even more resolutely than he consumed others. Then he looked down at this white, burnt-out brand that lay before him.

"Like him, isn't it?" she said, quietly. "I think I can scarcely answer his letter, but when you see him next you can do that for me. I want you to tell him many things for me, yet they can all be summed up in this: I want him to grow wholly into his best and greatest self, even at the cost of what is half his charm to you and me. Do you understand me?"

"I know perfectly well what you mean," answered Everett, thoughtfully. "And yet it's difficult to prescribe for those fellows; so little makes, so little mars."

Katharine raised herself upon her elbow, and her face flushed with feverish earnestness. "Ah, but it is the waste of himself that I mean; his lashing himself out on stupid and uncomprehending people until they take him at their own estimate."

"Come, come," expostulated Everett, now alarmed at her excitement. "Where is the new sonata? Let him speak for himself."

He sat down at the piano and began playing the first movement, which was indeed the voice of Adriance, his proper speech. The sonata was the most ambitious work he had done up to that time, and marked the transition from his early lyric vein to a deeper and nobler style. Everett played intelligently and with that sympathetic comprehension which seems peculiar to a certain lovable class of men who never accomplish anything in particular. When he had finished he turned to Katharine.

"How he has grown!" she cried. "What the three last years have done for him! He used to write only the tragedies of passion; but this is the tragedy of effort and failure, the thing Keats called hell. This is my tragedy, as I lie here, listening to the feet of the runners as they pass me—ah, God! the swift feet of the runners!"

She turned her face away and covered it with her hands. Everett crossed over to her and knelt beside her. In all the days he had known her she had never before, beyond an occasional ironical jest, given voice to the bitterness of her own defeat. Her courage had become a point of pride with him.

"Don't do it," he gasped. "I can't stand it, I really can't, I feel it too much."

When she turned her face back to him there was a ghost of the old, brave, cynical smile on it, more bitter than the tears she could not shed. "No, I won't; I will save that for the night, when I have no better company. Run over that theme at the beginning again, will you? It was running in his head when we were in Venice years ago, and he used to drum it on his glass at the dinner-table. He had just begun to work it out when the late autumn came on, and he decided to go to Florence for the winter. He lost touch with his idea, I suppose, during his illness. Do you remember those frightful days? All the people who have loved him are not strong enough to save him from himself! When I got word from Florence that he had been ill, I was singing at Monte Carlo. His wife was hurrying to him from Paris, but I reached him first. I arrived at dusk, in a terrific storm. They had taken an old palace there for the winter, and I found him in the library—a long, dark room full of old Latin books and heavy furniture and bronzes. He was sitting by a wood fire at one end of the room, looking, oh, so worn and pale!—as he always does when he is ill, you know. Ah, it is so good that you do know! Even his red smoking-jacket lent no colour to his face. His first words were not to tell me how ill he had been, but that that morning he had been well enough to put the last strokes to the score of his *'Souvenirs d' Automne,'* and he was as I most like to remember him; calm and happy, and tired with that heavenly tiredness that comes after a good work done at last. Outside, the rain poured down in torrents, and the wind moaned and sobbed in the garden and about the walls of that desolated old palace. How that night comes back to me! There were no lights in the room, only the wood fire. It glowed on the black walls and floor like the reflection of purgatorial flame. Beyond us it scarcely penetrated the gloom at all. Adriance sat staring at the fire with the weariness of all his life in his eyes, and of all the other lives that must aspire and suffer to make up one such life as his. Somehow the wind with all its world-pain had got into the room, and the cold rain was in our eyes, and the wave came up in both of us at once—that awful vague, universal pain, that cold fear of life and death and God and hope—and we were like two clinging together on a spar in mid-ocean after the shipwreck of everything. Then we heard the front door open with a great gust of wind that shook even the walls, and the servants came running with lights, announcing that Madame had returned, *'and in the book we read no more that night.'"*

She gave the old line with a certain bitter humour, and with the hard, bright smile in which of old she had wrapped her weakness as in a glittering garment. That ironical smile, worn through so many years, had gradually changed the lines of her face, and when she looked in the mirror she saw not herself, but the scathing critic, the amused observer and satirist of herself.

Everett dropped his head upon his hand. "How much you have cared!" he said.

"Ah, yes, I cared," she replied, closing her eyes. "You can't imagine what a comfort it is to have you know how I cared, what a relief it is to be able to tell it to some one."

Everett continued to look helplessly at the floor. "I was not sure how much you wanted me to know," he said.

"Oh, I intended you should know from the first time I looked into your face, when you came that day with Charley. You are so like him, that it is almost like telling him himself. At least, I feel now that he will know some day, and then I will be quite sacred from his compassion."

"And has he never known at all?" asked Everett, in a thick voice.

"Oh! never at all in the way that you mean. Of course, he is accustomed to looking into the eyes of women and finding love there; when he doesn't find it there he thinks he must have been guilty of some discourtesy. He has a genuine fondness for every woman who is not stupid or gloomy, or old or preternaturally ugly. I shared with the rest; shared the smiles and the gallantries and the droll little sermons. It was quite like a Sunday-school picnic; we wore our best clothes and a smile and took our turns. It was his kindness that was hardest."

"Don't; you'll make me hate him," groaned Everett.

Katherine laughed and began to play nervously with her fan. "It wasn't in the slightest degree his fault; that is the most grotesque part of it. Why, it had really begun before I ever met him. I fought my way to him, and I drank my doom greedily enough."

Everett rose and stood hesitating. "I think I must go. You ought to be quiet, and I don't think I can hear any more just now."

She put out her hand and took his playfully.

"You've put in three weeks at this sort of thing, haven't you? Well, it ought to square accounts for a much worse life than yours will ever be."

He knelt beside her, saying, brokenly: "I stayed because I wanted to be with you, that's all. I have never cared about other women since I knew you in New York when I was a lad. You are a part of my destiny, and I could not leave you if I would."

She put her hands on his shoulders and shook her head. "No, no; don't tell me that. I have seen enough tragedy. It was only a boy's fancy, and your divine pity and my utter pitiableness have recalled it for a moment. One does not love the dying, dear friend. Now go, and you will come again tomorrow, as long as there are tomorrows." She took his hand with a smile that was both courage and despair, and full of infinite loyalty and tenderness, as she said softly:

"For ever and for ever, farewell, Cassius; If we do meet again, why, we shall smile; If not, why then, this parting was well made."

The courage in her eyes was like the clear light of a star to him as he went out.

On the night of Adriance Hilgarde's opening concert in Paris, Everett sat by the bed in the ranch-house in Wyoming, watching over the last battle that we have with the flesh before we are done with it and free of it for ever. At times it seemed that the serene soul of her must have left already and found some refuge from the storm, and only the tenacious animal life were left to do battle with death. She laboured under a delusion at once pitiful and merciful, thinking that she was in the Pullman on her way to New York, going back to her life and her work. When she roused from her stupor, it was only to ask the porter to waken her half an hour out of Jersey City, or to remonstrate about the delays and the roughness of the road. At midnight Everett and the nurse were left alone with her. Poor Charley Gaylord had lain down on a couch outside the door. Everett sat looking at the sputtering night-lamp until it made his eyes ache. His head dropped forward, and he sank into heavy, distressful slumber. He was dreaming of Adriance's concert in Paris, and of Adriance, the troubadour. He heard the applause and he saw the flowers going up over the footlights until they were stacked half as high as the piano, and the petals fell and scattered, making crimson splotches on the floor. Down this crimson pathway came Adriance with his youthful step, leading his singer by the hand; a dark woman this time, with Spanish eyes.

The nurse touched him on the shoulder, he started and awoke. She screened the lamp with her hand. Everett saw that Katharine was awake and conscious, and struggling a little. He lifted her gently on his arm and began to fan her. She looked into his face with eyes that seemed never to have wept or doubted. "Ah, dear Adriance, dear, dear!" she whispered.

Everett went to call her brother, but when they came back the madness of art was over for Katharine.

Two days later Everett was pacing the station siding, waiting for the west-bound train. Charley Gaylord walked beside him, but the two men had nothing to say to each other. Everett's bags were piled on the truck, and his step was hurried and his eyes were full of impatience, as he gazed again and again up the track, watching for the train. Gaylord's impatience was not less than his own; these two, who had grown so close, had now become painful and impossible to each other, and longed for the wrench of farewell.

As the train pulled in, Everett wrung Gaylord's hand among the crowd of alighting passengers. The people of a German opera company, *en route* for the coast, rushed by them in frantic haste to snatch their breakfast during the stop. Everett heard an exclamation, and a stout woman rushed up to him, glowing with joyful surprise and caught his coat-sleeve with her tightly gloved hands.

"*Herr Gott*, Adriance, *lieber Freund*,"[1] she cried.

Everett lifted his hat, blushing. "Pardon me, madame, I see that you have mistaken me for Adriance Hilgarde. I am his brother." Turning from the crestfallen singer he hurried into the car.

---

[1] German: *Lord, Adriance, dear friend*.

POETRY—17TH CENTURY

Matsuo Bashō

A Collection of Haiku

17th Century

Matsuo Bashō was the most famous poet of the Edo period in Japan. During his lifetime, Bashō was recognized for his works in the collaborative *haikai no renga* form; today, after centuries of commentary, he is recognized as the greatest master of haiku (at the time called hokku).

Translated by Sam Hamill, Donald Keene, Robert Hass and others online at Classical Japanese Database.

	Japanese:
Ah! The ancient pond	古池
As a frog takes the plunge	蛙飛び込む
Sound of the water.	水の音
The summer grasses—	夏草や
Of the brave soldiers' dreams	兵どもが
The aftermath.	夢の跡
Spring passes	行く春や
and the birds cry out—tears	鳥啼き魚の
in the eyes of fishes	目は泪
Sick on a journey,	旅に病で
my dreams wander	夢は枯野を
the withered fields.	かけ廻る
This pervasive silence	静けさや
Enhanced yet by cicadas simmering	岩に滲み入る
Into the Temple Rocks dissipating	蝉の声

Still to be Neat

Ben Jonson
1609

Published in Act I as part of his play *Epicoene; or, The Silent Woman*, 1609.

Still to be neat, still to be drest,
As you were going to a feast;
Still to be powdr'd, still perfumed:
Lady, it is to be presumed,
Though art's hid causes are not found,   5
All is not sweet, all is not sound.

Give me a look, give me a face
That makes simplicity a grace;
Robes loosely flowing, hair as free:
Such sweet neglect more taketh me   10
Than all th' adulteries of art;
They strike mine eyes, but not my heart.

Shall I Compare Thee to a Summer's Day?

William Shakespeare
1609

First published in a 1609 quarto entitled *Shake-Speares Sonnets.*
Never before imprinted as Sonnet 18.

Shall I compare thee to a summer's day?
Thou art more lovely and more temperate;
Rough winds do shake the darling buds of May,
And summer's lease hath all too short a date:
Sometime too hot the eye of heaven shines,   5
And often is his gold complexion dimm'd:
And every fair from fair sometime declines,
By chance, or nature's changing course, untrimm'd.
But thy eternal summer shall not fade,
Nor lose possession of that fair thou owest;   10
Nor shall Death brag thou wanderest in his shade
When in eternal lines to time thou growest.
  So long as men can breathe, or eyes can see
  So long lives this, and this gives life to thee.

My Mistress' Eyes Are Nothing Like the Sun

William Shakespeare
1609

First published in a 1609 quarto entitled *Shake-Speares Sonnets.*
Never before imprinted as Sonnet 130.

My mistress' eyes are nothing like the sun
Coral is far more red than her lips' red:
If snow be white, why then her breasts are dun;
If hairs be wires, black wires grow on her head.
I have seen roses damask'd, red and white,   5
But no such roses see I in her cheeks;
And in some perfumes is there more delight
Than in the breath that from my mistress reeks.
I love to hear her speak, yet well I know
That music hath a far more pleasing sound: 10
I grant I never saw a goddess go,—
My mistress, when she walks, treads on the ground:
  And yet, by heaven, I think my love as rare
  As any she belied with false compare.

Death Be Not Proud

John Donne
1611

Written around 1610 and first published posthumously in 1633.

Death be not proud, though some have called thee
Mighty and dreadfull, for, thou art not so,
For, those, whom thou think'st, thou dost overthrow,
Die not, poore death, nor yet canst thou kill me.
From rest and sleepe, which but thy pictures bee,   5
Much pleasure, then from thee, much more must flow,

And soonest our best men with thee doe goe,
Rest of their bones, and soules deliverie.
Thou art slave to Fate, Chance, kings, and desperate men,
And dost with poyson, warre, and sicknesse dwell,   10
And poppie, or charmes can make us sleepe as well,
And better then thy stroake; why swell'st thou then;
One short sleepe past, wee wake eternally,
And death shall be no more; death, thou shalt die.

A Valediction: Forbidding Mourning

John Donne
1611/1612

Written in 1611/1612 and then first published posthumously in the
collection *Songs and Sonnets*, 1633.

AS virtuous men pass mildly away,
 And whisper to their souls to go;
While some of their sad friends do say,
 Now his breath goes, and some say, No;
So let us melt, and make no noise,   5
 No tear-floods, nor sigh-tempests move;
'Twere profanation of our joys
 To tell the laity our love.

Moving of th' earth brings harms and fears
 Men reckon what it did and meant;   10
But trepidations of the spheres,
 Though greater far, are innocent.

Dull sublunary lovers' love,
 Whose soul is sense, cannot admit
Absence; for that it doth remove   15
 Those things which elemented it.

But we, by a love so far refined,
 That ourselves know not what it is,
Inter-assurèd of the mind,
 Careless, eyes, lips and hands to miss,   20

—Our two souls therefore, which are one,
 Though I must go, endure not yet
A breach, but an expansion,
 Like gold to airy thinness beat.
If they be two, they are two so   25
 As stiff twin compasses are two;
Thy soul, the fixt foot, makes no show
 To move, but doth if th' other do.

And though it in the centre sit,
 Yet when the other far doth roam,   30
It leans and hearkens after it,
 And grows erect as that comes home.

Such wilt thou be to me, who must,
 Like th' other foot, obliquely run;
Thy firmness makes my circles just,   35
 And makes me end where I begun.

The Flea

John Donne
1633

First published posthumously in 1633.

Mark but this flea, and mark in this,
How little that which thou deniest me is;
It suck'd me first, and now sucks thee,
And in this flea our two bloods mingled be.
Thou know'st that this cannot be said   5
A sin, nor shame, nor loss of maidenhead;
  Yet this enjoys before it woo,
  And pamper'd swells with one blood made of two;
  And this, alas! is more than we would do.
O stay, three lives in one flea spare,   10
Where we almost, yea, more than married are.
This flea is you and I, and this
Our marriage bed, and marriage temple is.
Though parents grudge, and you, we're met,
And cloister'd in these living walls of jet.   15
  Though use make you apt to kill me,
  Let not to that self-murder added be,
  And sacrilege, three sins in killing three.

Cruel and sudden, hast thou since
Purpled thy nail in blood of innocence?   20
Wherein could this flea guilty be,
Except in that drop which it suck'd from thee?
Yet thou triumph'st, and say'st that thou
Find'st not thyself nor me the weaker now.
  'Tis true; then learn how false fears be;   25
  Just so much honour, when thou yield'st to me,
  Will waste, as this flea's death took life from thee.

Delight in Disorder

Robert Herrick
1648

Published in *The Works Both Humane & Divine of Robert Herrick Esq.*
London: Printed for John Williams and Francis Eglesfield, 1648.

A sweet disorder in the dress
Kindles in clothes a wantonness;
A lawn about the shoulders thrown
Into a fine distraction;
An erring lace, which here and there   5
Enthrals the crimson stomacher;
A cuff neglectful, and thereby
Ribbons to flow confusedly;
A winning wave, deserving note,
In the tempestuous petticoat;   10
A careless shoe-string, in whose tie
I see a wild civility;—
Do more bewitch me, than when art
Is too precise in every part.

To the Virgins, to Make Much of Time

Robert Herrick
1648

First published in 1648 as number 208 in *Hesperides.*

Gather ye rosebuds while ye may,
 Old Time is still a-flying:
And this same flower that smiles to-day
 To-morrow will be dying.
The glorious lamp of heaven, the sun,   5
 The higher he 's a-getting,
The sooner will his race be run,
 And nearer he 's to setting.

That age is best which is the first,
 When youth and blood are warmer;   10
But being spent, the worse, and worst
 Times still succeed the former.

Then be not coy, but use your time,
 And while ye may, go marry:
For having lost but once your prime,   15
 You may for ever tarry.

Upon Julia's Clothes

Robert Herrick
1648

Published in *The Works Both Humane & Divine of Robert Herrick Esq.*
London: Printed for John Williams and Francis Eglesfield, 1648.

Whenas in silks my Julia goes,
Then, then, methinks, how sweetly flows
That liquefaction of her clothes.

Next, when I cast mine eyes and see
That brave vibration each way free;   5
O how that glittering taketh me!

To His Coy Mistress

Andrew Marvell
1649-60

Written some time between 1649-1660.

Had we but World enough, and Time,
This coyness Lady were no crime.
We would sit down, and think which way
To walk, and pass our long Loves Day.
Thou by the Indian Ganges side.   5
Should'st Rubies find: I by the Tide
Of Humber would complain. I would
Love you ten years before the Flood:
And you should if you please refuse
Till the Conversion of the Jews.   10

My vegetable Love should grow
Vaster then Empires, and more slow.
An hundred years should go to praise
Thine Eyes, and on thy Forehead Gaze.
Two hundred to adore each Breast.   15
But thirty thousand to the rest.
An Age at least to every part,
And the last Age should show your Heart.
For Lady you deserve this State;
Nor would I love at lower rate.   20
But at my back I alwaies hear
Times winged Charriot hurrying near:
And yonder all before us lye
Desarts of vast Eternity.
Thy Beauty shall no more be found;   25
Nor, in thy marble Vault, shall sound
My ecchoing Song: then Worms shall try
That long preserv'd Virginity:
And your quaint Honour turn to durst;
And into ashes all my Lust.   30
The Grave's a fine and private place,
But none I think do there embrace.
Now therefore, while the youthful hew
Sits on thy skin like morning glew,
And while thy willing Soul transpires   35
At every pore with instant Fires,
Now let us sport us while we may;
And now, like am'rous birds of prey,
Rather at once our Time devour,
Than languish in his slow-chapt pow'r.   40
Let us roll all our Strength, and all
Our sweetness, up into one Ball:
And tear our Pleasures with rough strife,
Thorough the Iron gates of Life.
Thus, though we cannot make our Sun   45
Stand still, yet we will make him run.

from The Winter Evening

William Cowper
1785

Published in *The Task: A Poem, in Six Books* (1785). This selection is taken from Book IV, The Winter Evening.

'Tis pleasant, through the loopholes of retreat,
To peep at such a world; to see the stir
Of the great Babel, and not feel the crowd;
To hear the roar she sends through all her gates,
At a safe distance, where the dying sound   5
Falls a soft murmur on the uninjured ear.
Thus sitting and surveying thus at ease
The globe and its concerns, I seem advanced
To some secure and more than mortal height,
That liberates and exempts me from them all.   10
It turns submitted to my view, turns round
With all its generations; I behold
The tumult, and am still. The sound of war
Has lost its terrors ere it reaches me;

Grieves, but alarms me not. I mourn the pride   15
And avarice that make man a wolf to man,
Hear the faint echo of those brazen throats,
By which he speaks the language of his heart,
And sigh, but never tremble at the sound.
He travels and expatiates, as the bee   20
From flower to flower, so he from land to land:
The manners, customs, policy of all
Pay contribution to the store he gleans;
He sucks intelligence in every clime,
And spreads the honey of his deep research   25
At his return,—a rich repast for me.
He travels, and I too. I tread his deck,
Ascend his topmast, through his peering eyes
Discover countries, with a kindred heart
Suffer his woes, and share in his escapes;   30
While fancy, like the finger of a clock,
Runs the great circuit, and is still at home.

The Lamb

William Blake
1789

Published in *Songs of Innocence* in 1789.

Little lamb, who made thee?
 Dost thou know who made thee?
Gave thee life, and bid thee feed,
By the stream and o'er the mead;
Gave thee clothing of delight,   5
Softest clothing, woolly, bright;
Gave thee such a tender voice,
Making all the vales rejoice?
 Little Lamb, who made thee?
 Dost thou know who made thee?   10

 Little Lamb, I'll tell thee,
 Little Lamb, I'll tell thee:
He is callèd by thy name,
For He calls Himself a Lamb.
He is meek, and He is mild;   15
He became a little child.
I a child, and thou a lamb,
We are callèd by His name.
 Little Lamb, God bless thee!
 Little Lamb, God bless thee!   20

The Tyger

William Blake
1789

Published in *Songs of Experience* in 1789.

Tyger, tyger, burning bright
In the forests of the night,
What immortal hand or eye
Could frame thy fearful symmetry?

In what distant deeps or skies   5
Burnt the fire of thine eyes?

On what wings dare he aspire?
What the hand dare seize the fire?

And what shoulder and what art
Could twist the sinews of thy heart?   10
And, when thy heart began to beat,
What dread hand and what dread feet?

What the hammer? What the chain?
In what furnace was thy brain?
What the anvil? What dread grasp   15
Dare its deadly terrors clasp?

When the stars threw down their spears,
And water'd heaven with their tears,
Did He smile His work to see?
Did He who made the lamb make thee?   20

Tyger, tyger, burning bright
In the forests of the night,
What immortal hand or eye
Dare frame thy fearful symmetry?

Infant Sorrow

William Blake
1789

Published in *Songs of Experience* in 1789.

My mother groan'd, my father wept,
Into the dangerous world I leapt;
Helpless, naked, piping loud,
Like a fiend hid in a cloud.

Struggling in my father's hands,   5
Striving against my swaddling-bands,
Bound and weary, I thought best
To sulk upon my mother's breast.

Earth's Answer

William Blake
1794

Published as part of his collection *Songs of Experience* (1794).

Earth rais'd up her head
From the darkness dread and drear.
Her light fled,
Stony dread!
And her locks cover'd with grey despair.   5

'Prison'd on wat'ry shore,
Starry Jealousy does keep my den:
Cold and hoar,
Weeping o'er,
I hear the Father of the Ancient Men.   10

'Selfish Father of Men!
Cruel, jealous, selfish Fear!

Can delight,
Chain'd in night,
The virgins of youth and morning bear?   15

'Does spring hide its joy
When buds and blossoms grow?
Does the sower
Sow by night,
Or the ploughman in darkness plough?   20

'Break this heavy chain
That does freeze my bones around.
Selfish! vain!
Eternal bane!
That free Love with bondage bound.'   25

A Red, Red Rose

Robert Burns
1794

Produced as a 1794 song and often made into a poem.

O my Luve's like a red, red rose,
 That's newly sprung in June:
O my Luve's like the melodie,
 That's sweetly play'd in tune.
As fair art thou, my bonie lass,   5
 So deep in luve am I;
And I will luve thee still, my dear,
 Till a' the seas gang dry.

Till a' the seas gang dry, my dear,
 And the rocks melt wi' the sun;   10
And I will luve thee still, my dear,
 While the sands o' life shall run.

And fare-thee-weel, my only Luve!
 And fare-thee-weel, a while!
And I will come again, my Luve,   15
 Tho' 'twere ten thousand mile!

London's Summer Morning

Mary Robinson
1795

Who has not waked to list the busy sounds
Of summer's morning, in the sultry smoke
Of noisy London? On the pavement hot
The sooty chimney-boy, with dingy face
And tattered covering, shrilly bawls his trade,   5
Rousing the sleepy housemaid. At the door
The milk-pail rattles, and the tinkling bell
Proclaims the dustman's office; while the street
Is lost in clouds impervious. Now begins
The din of hackney-coaches, waggons, carts;   10
While tinmen's shops, and noisy trunk-makers,
Knife-grinders, coopers, squeaking cork-cutters,
Fruit-barrows, and the hunger-giving cries

Of vegetable-vendors, fill the air.
Now every shop displays its varied trade,   15
And the fresh-sprinkled pavement cools the feet
Of early walkers. At the private door
The ruddy housemaid twirls the busy mop,
Annoying the smart 'prentice, or neat girl,
Tripping with band-box lightly. Now the sun   20
Darts burning splendor on the glittering pane,
Save where the canvas awning throws a shade
On the gay merchandise. Now, spruce and trim,
In shops (where beauty smiles with industry)
Sits the smart damsel; while the passenger   25
Peeps through the window, watching every charm.
Now pastry dainties catch the eye minute
Of humming insects, while the limy snare
Waits to enthrall them. Now the lamp-lighter
Mounts the tall ladder, nimbly venturous,   30
To trim the half-filled lamps, while at his feet
The pot-boy yells discordant! All along
The sultry pavement, the old-clothes-man cries
In tone monotonous, while sidelong views
The area for his traffic: now the bag   35
Is slyly opened, and the half-worn suit
(Sometimes the pilfered treasure of the base
Domestic spoiler), for one half its worth,
Sinks in the green abyss. The porter now
Bears his huge load along the burning way;   40
And the poor poet wakes from busy dreams,
To paint the summer morning.

Kubla Khan

Samuel Taylor Coleridge
1797, 1816

Written in 1797, the poem was first published in *Christabel, Kubla Khan, and the Pains of Sleep* (1816).

In Xanadu did Kubla Khan
　A stately pleasure-dome decree:
Where Alph, the sacred river, ran
Through caverns measureless to man
　Down to a sunless sea.   5
So twice five miles of fertile ground
　With walls and towers were girdled round:
And there were gardens bright with sinuous rills
Where blossom'd many an incense-bearing tree;
And here were forests ancient as the hills,   10
Enfolding sunny spots of greenery.

But O, that deep romantic chasm which slanted
Down the green hill athwart a cedarn cover!
A savage place! as holy and enchanted
As e'er beneath a waning moon was haunted   15
By woman wailing for her demon-lover!
And from this chasm, with ceaseless turmoil seething,
As if this earth in fast thick pants were breathing,
A mighty fountain momently was forced;
Amid whose swift half-intermitted burst   20
Huge fragments vaulted like rebounding hail,

Or chaffy grain beneath the thresher's flail:
And 'mid these dancing rocks at once and ever
It flung up momently the sacred river.
Five miles meandering with a mazy motion   25
Through wood and dale the sacred river ran,
Then reach'd the caverns measureless to man,
And sank in tumult to a lifeless ocean:
And 'mid this tumult Kubla heard from far
Ancestral voices prophesying war!   30

  The shadow of the dome of pleasure
    Floated midway on the waves;
  Where was heard the mingled measure
    From the fountain and the caves.
It was a miracle of rare device,   35
A sunny pleasure-dome with caves of ice!

  A damsel with a dulcimer
    In a vision once I saw:
  It was an Abyssinian maid,
    And on her dulcimer she play'd,   40
  Singing of Mount Abora.
  Could I revive within me,
  Her symphony and song,
To such a deep delight 'twould win me,
That with music loud and long,   45
I would build that dome in air,
That sunny dome! those caves of ice!
And all who heard should see them there,

And all should cry, Beware! Beware!
His flashing eyes, his floating hair!   50
Weave a circle round him thrice,
  And close your eyes with holy dread,
  For he on honey-dew hath fed,
And drunk the milk of Paradise.

POETRY—1800-1850

She Walks in Beauty

George Gordon, Lord Byron
1814

Written in 1814 and collected in *Hebrew Melodies* in 1815.

She walks in beauty, like the night
Of cloudless climes and starry skies,
And all that's best of dark and bright
Meet in her aspect and her eyes;
Thus mellow'd to that tender light   5
Which heaven to gaudy day denies.

One shade the more, one ray the less,
Had half impair'd the nameless grace
Which waves in every raven tress
Or softly lightens o'er her face,   10
Where thoughts serenely sweet express
How pure, how dear their dwelling-place.

And on that cheek and o'er that brow
So soft, so calm, yet eloquent,
The smiles that win, the tints that glow   15
But tell of days in goodness spent,—
A mind at peace with all below,
A heart whose love is innocent.

The Ballad of Dead Ladies

Dante Gabriel Rossetti
1817

An 1869 translation of François Villon's poem "Ballade des dames du temps jadis" written in 1450.

Tell me now in what hidden way is
  Lady Flora the lovely Roman?
Where 's Hipparchia, and where is Thais,
  Neither of them the fairer woman
  Where is Echo, beheld of no man,   5
Only heard on river and mere,—
  She whose beauty was more than human? . . .
But where are the snows of yester-year?

Where 's Héloise, the learned nun,
  For whose sake Abeillard, I ween,   10
Lost manhood and put priesthood on?
  (From Love he won such dule and teen!)
  And where, I pray you, is the Queen
Who will'd that Buridan should steer
  Sew'd in a sack's mouth down the Seine? . . .   15
But where are the snows o yester-year?

White Queen Blanche, like a queen of lilies,
  With a voice like any mermaiden,—
Bertha Broadfoot, Beatrice, Alice,
  And Ermengarde the lady of Maine,—   20
  And that good Joan whom English-men
At Rouen doom'd and burn'd her there,—
  Mother of God, where are they then? . . .
But where are the snows of yester-year?

Nay, never ask this week, fair lord,   25
  Where they are gone, nor yet this year,
Save with thus much for an overword,—
  But where are the snows of yester-year?

Ozymandias

Percy Bysshe Shelley
1817

Published in the 11 January 1818 issue of *The Examiner* in London.

I met a traveller from an antique land
Who said:—Two vast and trunkless legs of stone
Stand in the desert. Near them on the sand,
Half sunk, a shatter'd visage lies, whose frown
And wrinkled lip and sneer of cold command   5
Tell that its sculptor well those passions read

Which yet survive, stamp'd on these lifeless things,
The hand that mock'd them and the heart that fed.
And on the pedestal these words appear:
"My name is Ozymandias, king of kings: 10
Look on my works, ye mighty, and despair!"
Nothing beside remains: round the decay
Of that colossal wreck, boundless and bare,
The lone and level sands stretch far away.

To Autumn

John Keats
1819

Composed on September 19, 1819 and then revised for publication in
his 1820 collection of poetry titled *Lamia, Isabella, the Eve of St.
Agnes, and Other Poems.*

Season of mists and mellow fruitfulness,
Close bosom-friend of the maturing sun;
Conspiring with him how to load and bless
With fruit the vines that round the thatch-eaves run;
To bend with apples the moss'd cottage-trees,   5
And fill all fruit with ripeness to the core;
To swell the gourd, and plump the hazel shells
With a sweet kernel; to set budding more,
And still more, later flowers for the bees,
Until they think warm days will never cease;   10
For Summer has o'erbrimm'd their clammy cells.

Who hath not seen Thee oft amid thy store?
Sometimes whoever seeks abroad may find
Thee sitting careless on a granary floor,
Thy hair soft-lifted by the winnowing wind;   15
Or on a half-reap'd furrow sound asleep,
Drowsed with the fume of poppies, while thy hook
Spares the next swath and all its twine'd flowers:
And sometimes like a gleaner thou dost keep
Steady thy laden head across a brook;   20
Or by a cider-press, with patient look,
Thou watchest the last oozings, hours by hours.

Where are the songs of Spring? Ay, where are they?
Think not of them, thou hast thy music too,
While barre'd clouds bloom the soft-dying day   25
And touch the stubble-plains with rosy hue;
Then in a wailful choir the small gnats mourn
Among the river-sallows, borne aloft
Or sinking as the light wind lives or dies;
And full-grown lambs loud bleat from hilly bourn;   30
Hedge-crickets sing, and now with treble soft
The redbreast whistles from a garden-croft;
And gathering swallows twitter in the skies.

Ode to the West Wind

Percy Bysshe Shelley
1819

Written in 1819 near Florence, Italy and published in *Prometheus
Unbound, A Lyrical Drama in Four Acts, With Other Poems*, 1820.

I

O wild West Wind, thou breath of Autumn's being
  Thou from whose unseen presence the leaves dead
Are driven like ghosts from an enchanter fleeing,

  Yellow, and black, and pale, and hectic red,
Pestilence-stricken multitudes! O thou   5
  Who chariotest to their dark wintry bed

The wingèd seeds, where they lie cold and low,
  Each like a corpse within its grave, until
Thine azure sister of the Spring shall blow

  Her clarion o'er the dreaming earth, and fill   10
(Driving sweet buds like flocks to feed in air)
  With living hues and odours plain and hill;

Wild Spirit, which art moving everywhere;
Destroyer and preserver; hear, O hear!

II

Thou on whose stream, 'mid the steep sky's commotion,   15
  Loose clouds like earth's decaying leaves are shed,
Shook from the tangled boughs of heaven and ocean,

  Angels of rain and lightning! there are spread
On the blue surface of thine airy surge,
  Like the bright hair uplifted from the head   20

Of some fierce Mænad, even from the dim verge
  Of the horizon to the zenith's height,
The locks of the approaching storm. Thou dirge

  Of the dying year, to which this closing night
Will be the dome of a vast sepulchre,   25
  Vaulted with all thy congregated might

Of vapours, from whose solid atmosphere
Black rain, and fire, and hail, will burst: O hear!

III

Thou who didst waken from his summer dreams
  The blue Mediterranean, where he lay,   30
Lull'd by the coil of his crystàlline streams,

  Beside a pumice isle in Baiæ's bay,
And saw in sleep old palaces and towers
  Quivering within the wave's intenser day,

All overgrown with azure moss, and flowers   35
  So sweet, the sense faints picturing them! Thou
For whose path the Atlantic's level powers

  Cleave themselves into chasms, while far below
The sea-blooms and the oozy woods which wear
  The sapless foliage of the ocean, know   40

Thy voice, and suddenly grow gray with fear,
And tremble and despoil themselves: O hear!

IV

If I were a dead leaf thou mightest bear;
  If I were a swift cloud to fly with thee;
A wave to pant beneath thy power, and share   45

  The impulse of thy strength, only less free
Than thou, O uncontrollable! if even
  I were as in my boyhood, and could be

The comrade of thy wanderings over heaven,
  As then, when to outstrip thy skiey speed   50
Scarce seem'd a vision—I would ne'er have striven

  As thus with thee in prayer in my sore need.
O! lift me as a wave, a leaf, a cloud!
  I fall upon the thorns of life! I bleed!

A heavy weight of hours has chain'd and bow'd   55
One too like thee—tameless, and swift, and proud.

V

Make me thy lyre, even as the forest is:
  What if my leaves are falling like its own?
The tumult of thy mighty harmonies

  Will take from both a deep autumnal tone,   60
Sweet though in sadness. Be thou, Spirit fierce,
  My spirit! Be thou me, impetuous one!

Drive my dead thoughts over the universe,
  Like wither'd leaves, to quicken a new birth;
And, by the incantation of this verse,   65

  Scatter, as from an unextinguish'd hearth
Ashes and sparks, my words among mankind!
  Be through my lips to unawaken'd earth

The trumpet of a prophecy! O Wind,
If Winter comes, can Spring be far behind?   70

Ode on a Grecian Urn

John Keats
1820

Written in May 1819, the poem was first published anonymously in the
January 1820, Number 15 issue of the magazine *Annals of the Fine Arts*.

Thou still unravish'd bride of quietness,
  Thou foster-child of silence and slow time,
Sylvan historian, who canst thus express
  A flowery tale more sweetly than our rhyme:
What leaf-fring'd legend haunts about thy shape   5
  Of deities or mortals, or of both,
    In Tempe or the dales of Arcady?
  What men or gods are these? What maidens loth?
What mad pursuit? What struggle to escape?
    What pipes and timbrels? What wild ecstasy?   10

Heard melodies are sweet, but those unheard
  Are sweeter; therefore, ye soft pipes, play on;
Not to the sensual ear, but, more endear'd,

Pipe to the spirit ditties of no tone:
Fair youth, beneath the trees, thou canst not leave   15
    Thy song, nor ever can those trees be bare;
        Bold Lover, never, never canst thou kiss,
Though winning near the goal yet, do not grieve;
    She cannot fade, though thou hast not thy bliss,
        For ever wilt thou love, and she be fair!   20

Ah, happy, happy boughs! that cannot shed
    Your leaves, nor ever bid the Spring adieu;
And, happy melodist, unwearied,
    For ever piping songs for ever new;
More happy love! more happy, happy love!   25
    For ever warm and still to be enjoy'd,
        For ever panting, and for ever young;
All breathing human passion far above,
    That leaves a heart high-sorrowful and cloy'd,
        A burning forehead, and a parching tongue.   30

Who are these coming to the sacrifice?
    To what green altar, O mysterious priest,
Lead'st thou that heifer lowing at the skies,
    And all her silken flanks with garlands drest?
What little town by river or sea shore,   35
    Or mountain-built with peaceful citadel,
        Is emptied of this folk, this pious morn?
And, little town, thy streets for evermore
    Will silent be; and not a soul to tell
        Why thou art desolate, can e'er return.   40

O Attic shape! Fair attitude! with brede
    Of marble men and maidens overwrought,
With forest branches and the trodden weed;
    Thou, silent form, dost tease us out of thought
As doth eternity: Cold Pastoral!   45
    When old age shall this generation waste,
        Thou shalt remain, in midst of other woe
Than ours, a friend to man, to whom thou say'st,
    "Beauty is truth, truth beauty,—that is all
        Ye know on earth, and all ye need to know."   50

La Belle Dame Sans Merci
John Keats
1820

Published in the *Indicator* on 10 May 1820.

O what can ail thee, knight-at-arms,
Alone and palely loitering?
The sedge has withered from the lake,
And no birds sing.

O what can ail thee, knight-at-arms,   5
So haggard and so woe-begone?
The squirrel's granary is full,
And the harvest's done.

I see a lily on thy brow,
With anguish moist and fever-dew,   10
And on thy cheeks a fading rose
Fast withereth too.

I met a lady in the meads,
Full beautiful—a faery's child,
Her hair was long, her foot was light,
And her eyes were wild.   15

I made a garland for her head,
And bracelets too, and fragrant zone;
She looked at me as she did love,
And made sweet moan   20

I set her on my pacing steed,
And nothing else saw all day long,
For sidelong would she bend, and sing
A faery's song.

She found me roots of relish sweet,   25
And honey wild, and manna-dew,
And sure in language strange she said—
'I love thee true'.

She took me to her Elfin grot,
And there she wept and sighed full sore,   30
And there I shut her wild wild eyes
With kisses four.

And there she lullèd me asleep,
And there I dreamed—Ah! woe betide!—
The latest dream I ever dreamt   35
On the cold hill side.

I saw pale kings and princes too,
Pale warriors, death-pale were they all;
They cried—'La Belle Dame sans Merci
Hath thee in thrall!'   40

I saw their starved lips in the gloam,
With horrid warning gapèd wide,
And I awoke and found me here,
On the cold hill's side.

And this is why I sojourn here,   45
Alone and palely loitering,
Though the sedge is withered from the lake,
And no birds sing.

Porphyria's Lover

Robert Browning
1836

First published as "Porphyria" in the January 1836 issue of *Monthly Repository*. Browning later republished it as "Porphyria's Lover" in *Dramatic Lyrics*, 1842.

The rain set early in to-night,
  The sullen wind was soon awake,
It tore the elm-tops down for spite,[1]
  And did its worst to vex[2] the lake:
  I listen'd with heart fit to break.   5

---

[1] spite: a desire to hurt, annoy, or offend someone

[2] vex: make (someone) feel annoyed, frustrated, or worried, esp. with trivial matters.

When glided in Porphyria;[3] straight
  She shut the cold out and the storm,
And kneel'd and made the cheerless grate[4]
  Blaze up, and all the cottage warm;
  Which done, she rose, and from her form   10
Withdrew the dripping cloak and shawl,[5]
  And laid her soil'd[6] gloves by, untied
Her hat and let the damp hair fall,
  And, last, she sat down by my side
  And call'd me. When no voice replied,   15
She put my arm about her waist,
  And made her smooth white shoulder bare,
And all her yellow hair displaced,
  And, stooping, made my cheek lie there,
  And spread, o'er all, her yellow hair,   20
Murmuring how she loved me—she
  Too weak, for all her heart's endeavour,
To set its struggling passion free
  From pride, and vainer[7] ties dissever,[8]
  And give herself to me for ever.   25
But passion sometimes would prevail,
  Nor could to-night's gay[9] feast restrain
A sudden thought of one so pale
  For love of her, and all in vain:
  So, she was come through wind and rain.   30
Be sure I look'd up at her eyes
  Happy and proud; at last I knew
Porphyria worshipp'd me; surprise
  Made my heart swell, and still it grew
  While I debated what to do.   35
That moment she was mine, mine, fair,
  Perfectly pure and good: I found
A thing to do, and all her hair
  In one long yellow string I wound
  Three times her little throat around,   40
And strangled her. No pain felt she;
  I am quite sure she felt no pain.
As a shut bud that holds a bee,
  I warily oped[10] her lids: again
  Laugh'd the blue eyes without a stain.   45
And I untighten'd next the tress[11]
  About her neck; her cheek once more
Blush'd bright beneath my burning kiss:
  I propp'd her head up as before,

---

[3] Porphyria: the name of the lady but also a rare hereditary disease in which the blood pigment hemoglobin is abnormally metabolized. Porphyrins are excreted in the urine, which becomes dark; other symptoms include mental disturbances and extreme sensitivity of the skin to light.

[4] grate: a metal frame confining fuel in a fireplace or furnace. Also as a verb: 1) make an unpleasant rasping sound, 2) have an irritating effect.

[5] shawl: a piece of fabric worn by women over the shoulders or head or wrapped around a baby.

[6] soil'd: dirty

[7] vainer: 1) having or showing an excessively high opinion of one's appearance, abilities, or worth, 2) producing no result; useless, 3) having no meaning or likelihood of fulfillment

[8] dissever: divide or sever (something).

[9] gay: lighthearted and carefree

[10] oped: opened

[11] tress: a long lock of a woman's hair

Only, this time my shoulder bore　　　　　　　　　50
Her head, which droops upon it still:
　The smiling rosy little head,
So glad it has its utmost will,
　That all it scorn'd at once is fled,
　And I, its love, am gain'd instead!　　　　　　55
Porphyria's love: she guess'd not how
　Her darling one wish would be heard.
And thus we sit together now,
　And all night long we have not stirr'd,
　And yet God has not said a word!　　　　　　　60

The Deserted Garden

Elizabeth Barrett Browning
1838

Collected in *The Seraphim, and Other Poems*. London: Saunders and
Otley, 1838.

I mind me in the days departed,
How often underneath the sun
With childish bounds I used to run
　To a garden long deserted.
The beds and walks were vanish'd quite;　　　　5
And wheresoe'er had struck the spade,
The greenest grasses Nature laid,
　To sanctify her right.
I call'd the place my wilderness,
For no one enter'd there but I.　　　　　　　　　10
The sheep look'd in, the grass to espy,
　And pass'd it ne'ertheless.
The trees were interwoven wild,
And spread their boughs enough about
To keep both sheep and shepherd out,　　　　　15
　But not a happy child.
Adventurous joy it was for me!
I crept beneath the boughs, and found
A circle smooth of mossy ground
　Beneath a poplar-tree.　　　　　　　　　　　　20
Old garden rose-trees hedged it in,
Bedropt with roses waxen-white,
Well satisfied with dew and light,
　And careless to be seen.
Long years ago, it might befall,　　　　　　　　25
When all the garden flowers were trim,
The grave old gardener prided him
　On these the most of all.
Some Lady, stately overmuch,
Here moving with a silken noise,　　　　　　　　30
Has blush'd beside them at the voice
　That liken'd her to such.
Or these, to make a diadem,
She often may have pluck'd and twined;
Half-smiling as it came to mind,　　　　　　　　35
　That few would look at them.
O, little thought that Lady proud,
A child would watch her fair white rose,
When buried lay her whiter brows,

And silk was changed for shroud!—   40
Nor thought that gardener (full of scorns
For men unlearn'd and simple phrase)
A child would bring it all its praise,
  By creeping through the thorns!
To me upon my low moss seat,   45
Though never a dream the roses sent
Of science or love's compliment,
  I ween they smelt as sweet.
It did not move my grief to see
The trace of human step departed: 50
Because the garden was deserted,
  The blither place for me!
Friends, blame me not! a narrow ken
Hath childhood 'twixt the sun and sward:
We draw the moral afterward—   55
  We feel the gladness then.
And gladdest hours for me did glide
In silence at the rose-tree wall:
A thrush made gladness musical
  Upon the other side.   60
Nor he nor I did e'er incline
To peck or pluck the blossoms white:—
How should I know but that they might
  Lead lives as glad as mine?
To make my hermit-home complete,   65
I brought clear water from the spring
Praised in its own low murmuring,
  And cresses glossy wet.
And so, I thought, my likeness grew
(Without the melancholy tale)   70
To 'gentle hermit of the dale,'
  And Angelina too.
For oft I read within my nook
Such minstrel stories; till the breeze
Made sounds poetic in the trees,   75
  And then I shut the book.
If I shut this wherein I write,
I hear no more the wind athwart
Those trees, nor feel that childish heart
  Delighting in delight.   80
My childhood from my life is parted,
My footstep from the moss which drew
Its fairy circle round: anew
  The garden is deserted.
Another thrush may there rehearse   85
The madrigals which sweetest are;
No more for me!—myself afar
  Do sing a sadder verse.
Ah me! ah me! when erst I lay
In that child's-nest so greenly wrought,   90
I laugh'd unto myself and thought,
  'The time will pass away.'
And still I laugh'd, and did not fear
But that, whene'er was pass'd away
The childish time, some happier play   95
  My womanhood would cheer.
I knew the time would pass away;
And yet, beside the rose-tree wall,
Dear God, how seldom, if at all,

Did I look up to pray!   100
The time is past: and now that grows
The cypress high among the trees,
And I behold white sepulchres
  As well as the white rose,—
When wiser, meeker thoughts are given,   105
And I have learnt to lift my face,
Reminded how earth's greenest place
  The colour draws from heaven,—
It something saith for earthly pain,
But more for heavenly promise free,   110
That I who was, would shrink to be
  That happy child again.

The Haunted Palace

Edgar Allan Poe
1839

First published in April 1839, *American Museum*. Lator, it was added to
"The Fall of the House of Usher" as a song written by Roderick Usher.

In the greenest of our valleys
  By good angels tenanted,
Once a fair and stately palace—
  Radiant palace—reared its head.
In the monarch Thought's dominion—   5
  It stood there!
Never seraph spread a pinion
  Over fabric half so fair!

Banners yellow, glorious, golden,
  On its roof did float and flow,   10
(This—all this—was in the olden
  Time long ago,)
And every gentle air that dallied,
  In that sweet day,
Along the ramparts plumed and pallid,   15
  A wingèd odor went away.

Wanderers in that happy valley,
  Through two luminous windows, saw
Spirits moving musically,
  To a lute's well-tunèd law,   20
Round about a throne where, sitting,
  (Porphyrogene!)
In state his glory well befitting,
  The ruler of the realm was seen.
And all with pearl and ruby glowing   25
  Was the fair palace door,
Through which came flowing, flowing, flowing,
  And sparkling evermore,
A troop of Echoes, whose sweet duty
  Was but to sing,   30
In voices of surpassing beauty,
  The wit and wisdom of their king.

But evil things, in robes of sorrow,
  Assailed the monarch's high estate.
(Ah, let us mourn!—for never morrow   35

   Shall dawn upon him desolate!)
And round about his home the glory
  That blushed and bloomed,
Is but a dim-remembered story
  Of the old time entombed.   40

And travellers, now, within that valley,
  Through the red-litten windows see
Vast forms, that move fantastically
  To a discordant melody,
While, like a ghastly rapid river,   45
  Through the pale door
A hideous throng rush out forever
  And laugh—but smile no more.

My Last Duchess

Robert Browning
1842

Collected in *Dramatic Lyrics*, 1842.

That's my last Duchess painted on the wall,
Looking as if she were alive. I call
That piece a wonder, now: Frà Pandolf's hands
Worked busily a day, and there she stands.
Will't please you sit and look at her? I said   5
"Frà Pandolf" by design, for never read
Strangers like you that pictured countenance,
The depth and passion of its earnest glance,
But to myself they turned (since none puts by
The curtain I have drawn for you, but I)   10
And seemed as they would ask me, if they durst,
How such a glance came there; so, not the first
Are you to turn and ask thus. Sir, 'twas not
Her husband's presence only, called that spot
Of joy into the Duchess' cheek: perhaps   15
Frà Pandolf chanced to say, "Her mantle laps
Over my lady's wrist too much," or "Paint
Must never hope to reproduce the faint
Half-flush that dies along her throat:" such stuff
Was courtesy, she thought, and cause enough   20
For calling up that spot of joy. She had
A heart—how shall I say?—too soon made glad.
Too easily impressed: she liked whate'er
She looked on, and her looks went everywhere.
Sir, 'twas all one! My favor at her breast,   25
The dropping of the daylight in the West,
The bough of cherries some officious fool
Broke in the orchard for her, the white mule
She rode with round the terrace—all and each
Would draw from her alike the approving speech, 30
Or blush, at least. She thanked men,—good! but thanked
Somehow—I know not how—as if she ranked
My gift of a nine-hundred-years-old name
With anybody's gift. Who'd stoop to blame
This sort of trifling? Even had you skill   35
In speech—(which I have not)—to make your will
Quite clear to such an one, and say, "Just this

Or that in you disgusts me; here you miss,
Or there exceed the mark"—and if she let
Herself be lessoned so, nor plainly set   40
Her wits to yours, forsooth, and made excuse,
—E'en then would be some stooping; and I choose
Never to stoop. Oh sir, she smiled, no doubt,
Whene'er I passed her; but who passed without
Much the same smile? This grew; I gave commands;   45
Then all smiles stopped together. There she stands
As if alive. Will't please you rise? We'll meet
The company below, then. I repeat,
The Count your master's known munificence
Is ample warrant that no just pretence   50
Of mine for dowry will be disallowed;
Though his fair daughter's self, as I avowed
At starting, is my object. Nay, we'll go
Together down, sir. Notice Neptune, though,
Taming a sea-horse, thought a rarity,   55
Which Claus of Innsbruck cast in bronze for me!

The Night-wind

Emily Brontë
1846

Bronte, A., Bronte, C., and Bronte, E. (1846). *Poems by Currer, Ellis, and Acton Bell*. London, England: Aylott and Jones.

In summer's mellow midnight,
  A cloudless moon shone through
Our open parlour window,
  And rose-trees wet with dew.
I sat in silent musing,   5
  The soft wind waved my hair;
It told me heaven was glorious,
  And sleeping earth was fair.
I needed not its breathing
  To bring such thoughts to me;   10
But still it whispered lowly,
  How dark the woods will be!
"The thick leaves in my murmur
  Are rustling like a dream,
And all their myriad voices   15
  Instinct with spirit seem."
I said, "Go, gentle singer,
  Thy wooing voice is kind:
But do not think its music
  Has power to reach my mind.   20
"Play with the scented flower,
  The young tree's supple bough,
And leave my human feelings
  In their own course to flow."
The wanderer would not heed me;   25
  Its kiss grew warmer still.
"Oh come!" it sighed so sweetly;
  "I'll win thee 'gainst thy will.
"Were we not friends from childhood?
  Have I not loved thee long?   30
As long as thou, the solemn night,

Whose silence wakes my song.
"And when thy heart is resting
   Beneath the church-aisle stone,
I shall have time for mourning,   35
   And thou for being alone."

Bacchus

Ralph Waldo Emerson
1847

Published in *Poems,* 1847.

Bring me wine, but wine which never grew
In the belly of the grape,
Or grew on vine whose tap-roots, reaching through
Under the Andes to the Cape,
Suffer'd no savour of the earth to 'scape.   5
Let its grapes the morn salute
From a nocturnal root,
Which feels the acrid juice
Of Styx and Erebus;
And turns the woe of Night,   10
By its own craft, to a more rich delight.
We buy ashes for bread;
We buy diluted wine;
Give me of the true,
Whose ample leaves and tendrils curl'd   15
Among the silver hills of heaven
Draw everlasting dew;
Wine of wine,
Blood of the world,
Form of forms, and mould of statures,   20
That I intoxicated,
And by the draught assimilated,
May float at pleasure through all natures;
The bird-language rightly spell,
And that which roses say so well: 25
Wine that is shed
Like the torrents of the sun
Up the horizon walls,
Or like the Atlantic streams, which run
When the South Sea calls.   30
Water and bread,
Food which needs no transmuting,
Rainbow-flowering, wisdom-fruiting,
Wine which is already man,
Food which teach and reason can.   35
Wine which Music is,—
Music and wine are one,—
That I, drinking this,
Shall hear far Chaos talk with me;
Kings unborn shall walk with me;   40
And the poor grass shall plot and plan
What it will do when it is man.
Quicken'd so, will I unlock
Every crypt of every rock.
I thank the joyful juice   45
For all I know;

Winds of remembering
Of the ancient being blow,
And seeming-solid walls of use
Open and flow.   50
Pour, Bacchus! the remembering wine;
Retrieve the loss of me and mine!
Vine for vine be antidote,
And the grape requite the lote!
Haste to cure the old despair;   55
Reason in Nature's lotus drench'd—
The memory of ages quench'd—
Give them again to shine;
Let wine repair what this undid;
And where the infection slid,   60
A dazzling memory revive;
Refresh the faded tints,
Recut the aged prints,
And write my old adventures with the pen
Which on the first day drew,   65
Upon the tablets blue,
The dancing Pleiads and eternal men.

Annabel Lee

Edgar Allan Poe
1849

Rufus Wilmot Griswold, Poe's literary executor and personal rival, was
the first to publish the poem on October 9, 1849, two days after Poe's
death as part of his obituary of Poe in the New York *Daily Tribune*.[12]

It was many and many a year ago,
    In a kingdom by the sea,
That a maiden there lived whom you may know
    By the name of Annabel Lee;
And this maiden she lived with no other thought   5
    Than to love and be loved by me.

I was a child and she was a child,
    In this kingdom by the sea,
But we loved with a love that was more than love,
    I and my Annabel Lee;   10
With a love that the wingèd seraphs of heaven
    Coveted her and me.

And this was the reason that, long ago,
    In this kingdom by the sea,
A wind blew out of a cloud, chilling   15
    My beautiful Annabel Lee;
So that her highborn kinsmen came
    And bore her away from me,
To shut her up in a sepulchre
    In this kingdom by the sea.   20
The angels, not half so happy in heaven,
    Went envying her and me;
Yes! that was the reason (as all men know,

---

[12] Meyers, Jeffrey. *Edgar Allan Poe: His Life and Legacy*. New York: Cooper Square Press, 1992. p. 244.
ISBN 0-8154-1038-7.

In this kingdom by the sea)
That the wind came out of the cloud by night,   25
   Chilling and killing my Annabel Lee.

But our love it was stronger by far than the love
   Of those who were older than we,
   Of many far wiser than we;
And neither the angels in heaven above,   30
   Nor the demons down under the sea,
Can ever dissever my soul from the soul
   Of the beautiful Annabel Lee:

For the moon never beams, without bringing me dreams
   Of the beautiful Annabel Lee;   35
And the stars never rise, but I feel the bright eyes
   Of the beautiful Annabel Lee;
And so, all the night-tide, I lie down by the side
Of my darling—my darling—my life and my bride,
   In her sepulchre there by the sea,   40
   In her tomb by the sounding sea.

POETRY—1850-1922

The Author to Her Book

Anne Bradstreet
1850's

Possibly written in the 1850's.

Thou ill-form'd offspring of my feeble brain,
Who after birth didst by my side remain,
Till snatcht from thence by friends, less wise then true
Who thee abroad, expos'd to publick view,
Made thee in raggs, halting to th' press to trudg,   5
Where errors were not lessened (all may judg)
At thy return my blushing was not small,
My rambling brat (in print,) should mother call,
I cast thee by as one unfit for light,
Thy Visage was so irksome in my sight;   10
Yet being mine own, at length affection would
Thy blemishes amend, if so I could:
I wash'd thy face, but more defects I saw,
And rubbing off a spot, still made a flaw.
I stretcht thy joynts to make thee even feet,   15
Yet still thou run'st more hobling then is meet;
In better dress to trim thee was my mind,
But nought save home-spun Cloth, i' th' house I find
In this array, mong'st Vulgars mayst thou roam
In Critick's hands, beware thou dost not come;   20
And take thy way where yet thou art not known,
If for thy Father askt, say, thou hadst none;
And for thy Mother, she alas is poor.
Which caused her thus to turn thee out of door.

In a London Drawingroom

George Eliot, Mary Ann Evans
1860-70's

Probably written between 1860-1870 but published after Evans' death in 1879.

The sky is cloudy, yellowed by the smoke.
For view there are the houses opposite
Cutting the sky with one long line of wall
Like solid fog: far as the eye can stretch
Monotony of surface & of form   5
Without a break to hang a guess upon.
No bird can make a shadow as it flies,
For all is shadow, as in ways o'erhung
By thickest canvass, where the golden rays
Are clothed in hemp. No figure lingering   10
Pauses to feed the hunger of the eye
Or rest a little on the lap of life.
All hurry on & look upon the ground,
Or glance unmarking at the passers by
The wheels are hurrying too, cabs, carriages   15
All closed, in multiplied identity.
The world seems one huge prison-house & court
Where men are punished at the slightest cost,
With lowest rate of colour, warmth & joy.

Hap

Thomas Hardy
1866

Collected in Wessex Poems and Other Verses, 1898.

If but some vengeful god would call to me
  From up the sky, and laugh: "Thou suffering thing,
Know that thy sorrow is my ecstasy,
  That thy love's loss is my hate's profiting!"
Then would I bear, and clench myself, and die,   5
  Steeled by the sense of ire unmerited;
Half-eased, too, that a Powerfuller than I
  Had willed and meted me the tears I shed.
But not so. How arrives it joy lies slain,
  And why unblooms the best hope ever sown?   10
—Crass Casualty obstructs the sun and rain,
  And dicing Time for gladness casts a moan. . . .
  These purblind Doomsters had as readily strown
Blisses about my pilgrimage as pain.

Dover Beach

Matthew Arnold
1867

First published in 1867 in the collection *New Poems*.

The sea is calm to-night.
The tide is full, the moon lies fair
Upon the straits;[1]—on the French coast the light
Gleams and is gone; the cliffs of England stand,
Glimmering and vast, out in the tranquil bay.   5
Come to the window, sweet is the night-air!
Only, from the long line of spray
Where the sea meets the moon-blanch'd sand,[2]
Listen! you hear the grating roar
Of pebbles which the waves draw back, and fling,   10
At their return, up the high strand,
Begin, and cease, and then again begin,
With tremulous cadence[3] slow, and bring
The eternal note of sadness in.
Sophocles[4] long ago   15
Heard it on the Ægæan,[5] and it brought
Into his mind the turbid[6] ebb and flow
Of human misery; we
Find also in the sound a thought,
Hearing it by this distant northern sea.   20
The sea of faith
Was once, too, at the full, and round earth's shore
Lay like the folds of a bright girdle furl'd.[7]
But now I only hear
Its melancholy, long, withdrawing roar,   25
Retreating, to the breath
Of the night-winds, down the vast edges drear
And naked shingles of the world.
Ah, love, let us be true
To one another! for the world, which seems   30
To lie before us like a land of dreams,
So various, so beautiful, so new,
Hath really neither joy, nor love, nor light,
Nor certitude, nor peace, nor help for pain;
And we are here as on a darkling plain   35
Swept with confus'd alarms of struggle and flight,
Where ignorant armies clash by night.

---

[1] straits: 1) a comparatively narrow passageway connecting two large bodies of water, 2) a situation of perplexity or distress

[2] moon-blanch'd sand: the sand has no color because of the moon

[3] tremulous cadence: trembling or sensitive rhythmical motion or activity

[4] Sophocles: A Greek playwright and a distinguished public figure in Athens, he served successively in important posts as a treasurer, commander, and adviser. His most popular play is *Oedipus the King*.

[5] Ægæan: The Aegean Sea lies between Greece and Turkey and is part of the Mediterranean Sea.

[6] turbid: confused, lacking in purity and clarity

[7] girdle: a woman's close-fitting undergarment often boned and usually elasticized that extends from the waist to below the hips—in this case, the girdle is unfurled.

Vigil Strange I Kept on the Field One Night

Walt Whitman
1867

Published in *Leaves of Grass*, 1867 collection.

Vigil strange I kept on the field one night;
When you my son and my comrade dropt at my side that day,
One look I but gave which your dear eyes return'd with a look I shall never
        forget,
One touch of your hand to mine O boy, reach'd up as you lay on the ground,
Then onward I sped in the battle, the even-contested battle,   5
Till late in the night reliev'd to the place at last again I made my way,
Found you in death so cold dear comrade, found your body son of responding
        kisses (never again on earth responding),
Bared your face in the starlight, curious the scene, cool blew the moderate
        night-wind,
Long there and then in vigil I stood, dimly around me the battle-field
        spreading,
Vigil wondrous and vigil sweet there in the fragrant silent night,   10
But not a tear fell, not even a long-drawn sigh, long, long I gazed.
Then on the earth partially reclining sat by your side leaning my chin in my
        hands,
Passing sweet hours, immortal and mystic hours with you dearest comrade—
        not a tear, not a word.
Vigil of silence, love and death, vigil for you my son and my soldier,
As onward silently stars aloft, eastward new ones upward stole,   15
Vigil final for you brave boy, (I could not save you, swift was your death,
I faithfully loved you and cared for you living, I think we shall surely meet
        again,)
Till at latest lingering of the night, indeed just as the dawn appear'd,
My comrade I wrapt in his blanket, envelop'd well his form,
Folded the blanket well, tucking it carefully over head and carefully under feet, 20
And there and then and bathed by the rising sun, my son in his grave, in his
        rude-dug grave I deposited,
Ending my vigil strange with that, vigil of night and battlefield dim,
Vigil for boy of responding kisses (never again on earth responding),
Vigil for comrade swiftly slain, vigil I never forget, how as day brighten'd,
I rose from the chill ground and folded my soldier well in his blanket,   25
And buried him where he fell.

When I heard the Learn'd Astronomer

Walt Whitman
1867

Published in *Leaves of Grass*, 1867 collection.

When I heard the learn'd astronomer;
When the proofs, the figures, were ranged in columns before me;
When I was shown the charts and the diagrams, to add, divide, and measure
        them;
When I, sitting, heard the astronomer, where he lectured with much applause in
        the lecture-room,
How soon, unaccountable, I became tired and sick;   5
Till rising and gliding out, I wander'd off by myself,
In the mystical moist night-air, and from time to time,
Look'd up in perfect silence at the stars.

Jabberwocky

Lewis Carroll
1872

Written in his 1871 novel *Through the Looking-Glass, and What Alice Found There*, a sequel to *Alice's Adventures in Wonderland*.

`Twas brillig, and the slithy toves
  Did gyre and gimble in the wabe:
All mimsy were the borogoves,
  And the mome raths outgrabe.

"Beware the Jabberwock, my son!   5
  The jaws that bite, the claws that catch!
Beware the Jubjub bird, and shun
  The frumious Bandersnatch!"

He took his vorpal sword in hand:
  Long time the manxome foe he sought —   10
So rested he by the Tumtum tree,
  And stood awhile in thought.

And, as in uffish thought he stood,
  The Jabberwock, with eyes of flame,
Came whiffling through the tulgey wood,   15
  And burbled as it came!

One, two! One, two! And through and through
  The vorpal blade went snicker-snack!
He left it dead, and with its head
  He went galumphing back.   20

"And, has thou slain the Jabberwock?
  Come to my arms, my beamish boy!
O frabjous day! Callooh! Callay!'
  He chortled in his joy.

`Twas brillig, and the slithy toves   25
  Did gyre and gimble in the wabe;
All mimsy were the borogoves,
  And the mome raths outgrabe.

Pied Beauty

Gerard Manley Hopkins
1877

Written in 1877, but not published until 1918, when it was included as part of the collection *Poems of Gerard Manley Hopkins*.

Glory be to God for dappled things—
For skies of couple-colour as a brinded cow;
For rose-moles all in stipple upon trout that swim;
Fresh-firecoal chestnut-falls; finches' wings;
  Landscape plotted and pieced—fold, fallow, and plough;   5
  And áll trádes, their gear and tackle and trim.
All things counter, original, spare, strange;
  Whatever is fickle, freckled (who knows how?)
  With swift, slow; sweet, sour; adazzle, dim;
He fathers-forth whose beauty is past change: 10
  Praise him.

God's Grandeur

Gerard Manley Hopkins
1877

Written in 1877 and published posthumously in *Poems of Gerard Manley Hopkins* and edited by his friend and fellow poet Robert Bridges. Published: London: Humphrey Milford, 1918.

The world is charged with the grandeur of God.
  It will flame out, like shining from shook foil;[8]
  It gathers to a greatness, like the ooze of oil
Crushed. Why do men then now not reck[9] his rod?[10]
Generations have trod, have trod, have trod;[11]   5
  And all is seared with trade; bleared, smeared with toil;
  And wears man's smudge and shares man's smell: the soil
Is bare now, nor can foot feel, being shod.[12]
And for all this, nature is never spent;
  There lives the dearest freshness deep down things;   10
And though the last lights off the black West went
  Oh, morning, at the brown brink eastward, springs—
Because the Holy Ghost[13] over the bent
  World broods with warm breast and with ah! bright wings.

Spring and Fall

Gerard Manley Hopkins
1880, 1918

Written in 1880 and published posthumously in *Poems of Gerard Manley Hopkins Now First Published*. Ed. Robert Bridges. London: Humphry Milford, 1918.

Márgarét, áre you gríeving
Over Goldengrove unleaving?
Leáves, líke the things of man, you
With your fresh thoughts care for, can you?
Áh! ás the heart grows older   5
It will come to such sights colder
By and by, nor spare a sigh
Though worlds of wanwood leafmeal lie;
And yet you wíll weep and know why.
Now no matter, child, the name: 10
Sórrow's spríngs áre the same.
Nor mouth had, no nor mind, expressed
What heart heard of, ghost guessed:
It ís the blight man was born for,
It is Margaret you mourn for.

---

[8] shook foil: There are many interpretations, but it is likely a reference to the 19th century use of a candle and the foil put into the bottom of a lantern to reflect light. Over time, the foil cracks a part; any light from striking the foil would be splintered or shaken.

[9] reck: to take heed, to reckon, to acknowledge, to regard

[10] rod: Dating back to ancient times, the rod was associated with rularship and royalty.

[11] trod: walking

[12] shod: 1) an external covering for the human foot, 2) a horseshoe or a similar plate for the hoof of some other animal

[13] part of the Christian Holy Trinity; a divine aspect of Yah-weh

Quantum Mutata

Oscar Wilde
1881

Published in *Poems.* Boston: Robert Brothers, 1881.

There was a time in Europe long ago

    Where no man died for freedom anywhere,
    But England's lion leaping from its lair

Laid hands on the oppressor! it was so
While England could a great Republic show.   5

    Witness the men of Piedmont, chiefest care
    Of Cromwell, when with impotent despair

The Pontiff in his painted portico
Trembled before our stern ambassadors.

    How comes it then that from such high estate   10
    We have thus fallen save that Luxury

With barren merchandise pils up at the gate
Where noble thoughts and noble deeds should enter by:

    Else might we still be Milton's heritors.

When You Are Old

William Butler Yeats
1893

Published in *The Rose, 1893*.

When you are old and grey and full of sleep,
And nodding by the fire, take down this book,
And slowly read, and dream of the soft look
Your eyes had once, and of their shadows deep;

How many loved your moments of glad grace,   5
And loved your beauty with love false or true,
But one man loved the pilgrim Soul in you,
And loved the sorrows of your changing face;

And bending down beside the glowing bars,
Murmur, a little sadly, how Love fled   10
And paced upon the mountains overhead
And hid his face amid a crowd of stars.

The House on the Hill

Edwin Arlington Robinson
1894, 1897

Collected in *The Children of the Night*. Boston: Richard G. Badger &
Company, 1897.

They are all gone away,
  The House is shut and still,
There is nothing more to say.

Through broken walls and gray
  The winds blow bleak and shrill: 5
They are all gone away.

Nor is there one to-day
  To speak them good or ill:
There is nothing more to say.
Why is it then we stray   10
  Around the sunken sill?
They are all gone away,

And our poor fancy-play
  For them is wasted skill:
There is nothing more to say.   15

There is ruin and decay
  In the House on the Hill:
They are all gone away,
There is nothing more to say.

Loveliest of Trees, The Cherry Now

A. E. Housman
1896

Published in *A Shropshire Lad,* 1896.

Loveliest of trees, the cherry now
Is hung with bloom along the bough,
And stands about the woodland ride
Wearing white for Eastertide.
Now, of my threescore years and ten,   5
Twenty will not come again,
And take from seventy springs a score,
It only leaves me fifty more.

And since to look at things in bloom
Fifty springs are little room,   10
About the woodlands I will go
To see the cherry hung with snow.

To an Athlete Dying Young

A. E. Housman
1896

Published in A.E. Housman's *A Shropshire Lad* (1896).

The time you won your town the race,
We chaired they through the market-place;
Man and boy stood cheering by,
And home we brought you shoulder-high.
To-day, the road all runners come,   5
Shoulder-high we bring you home,
And set you at your threshold down,
Townsman of a stiller town.

Smart lad, to slip betimes away
From fields where glory does not stay   10
And early though the laurel grows
It withers quicker than the rose.

Eyes the shady night has shut
Cannot see the record cut,
And silence sounds no worse than cheers   15
After earth has stopped the ears:

Now you will not swell the rout
Of lads that wore their honours out,
Runners whom renown outran
And the name died before the man.   20

So set, before its echoes fade,
The fleet foot on the sill of shade,
And hold to the low lintel up
The still-defended challenge-cup.
And round that early-laurelled head   25
Will flock to gaze the strengthless dead,
And find unwithered on its curls
The garland briefer than a girl's.

Richard Cory

Edwin Arlington Robinson
1897

First published in 1897, as part of *The Children of the Night.*

Whenever Richard Cory went down town,
We people on the pavement looked at him:
He was a gentleman from sole to crown,
Clean favored, and imperially slim.
And he was always quietly arrayed,   5
And he was always human when he talked;
But still he fluttered pulses when he said,
"Good-morning," and he glittered when he walked.

And he was rich—yes, richer than a king—
And admirably schooled in every grace: 10
In fine, we thought that he was everything
To make us wish that we were in his place.

So on we worked, and waited for the light,
And went without the meat, and cursed the bread;
And Richard Cory, one calm summer night,   15
Went home and put a bullet through his head.

A Man Said to the Universe

Stephen Crane
1899

Collected in *War is Kind,* 1899.

A man said to the universe:
"Sir, I exist!"
"However," replied the universe,
"The fact has not created in me
"A sense of obligation."   5

There Was a Man with Tongue of Wood

Stephen Crane
1899

Collected in *War is Kind* (1899).

There was a man with tongue of wood
Who essayed to sing,
And in truth it was lamentable.[14]
But there was one who heard
The clip-clapper of this tongue of wood   5
And knew what the man
Wished to sing,
And with that the singer was content.

The Haunted Oak

Paul Laurence Dunbar
1900

First published in the *Century Magazine* in 1900 and later collected in
Lyrics of Love and Laughter, 1903. According to Anne P. Rice
(*Witnessing Lynching: American Writers Respond*, 2003), Dunbar's
editor in 1900 declined to publish the poem with the last two stanzas.

Pray why are you so bare, so bare,
  Oh, bough of the old oak-tree;
And why, when I go through the shade you throw,
  Runs a shudder over me?

My leaves were green as the best, I trow,   5
  And sap ran free in my veins,
But I saw in the moonlight dim and weird
  A guiltless victim's pains.

I bent me down to hear his sigh;
  I shook with his gurgling moan,   10
And I trembled sore when they rode away,
  And left him here alone.

They'd charged him with the old, old crime,
  And set him fast in jail:
Oh, why does the dog howl all night long,   15
  And why does the night wind wail?

He prayed his prayer and he swore his oath,
  And he raised his hand to the sky;
But the beat of hoofs smote on his ear,
  And the steady tread drew nigh.   20

Who is it rides by night, by night,
  Over the moonlit road?
And what is the spur that keeps the pace,
  What is the galling goad?

And now they beat at the prison door,   25
  "Ho, keeper, do not stay!

---

[14] lamentable: (of circumstances or conditions) deplorably bad or unsatisfactory.

We are friends of him whom you hold within,
 And we fain would take him away

"From those who ride fast on our heels
 With mind to do him wrong;   30
They have no care for his innocence,
 And the rope they bear is long."

They have fooled the jailer with lying words,
 They have fooled the man with lies;
The bolts unbar, the locks are drawn,   35
 And the great door open flies.

Now they have taken him from the jail,
 And hard and fast they ride,
And the leader laughs low down in his throat,
 As they halt my trunk beside.   40

Oh, the judge, he wore a mask of black,
 And the doctor one of white,
And the minister, with his oldest son,
 Was curiously bedight.

Oh, foolish man, why weep you now?   45
 'Tis but a little space,
And the time will come when these shall dread
 The mem'ry of your face.

I feel the rope against my bark,
 And the weight of him in my grain,   50
I feel in the throe of his final woe
 The touch of my own last pain.

And never more shall leaves come forth
 On a bough that bears the ban;
I am burned with dread, I am dried and dead,   55
 From the curse of a guiltless man.

And ever the judge rides by, rides by,
 And goes to hunt the deer,
And ever another rides his soul
 In the guise of a mortal fear.   60

And ever the man he rides me hard,
 And never a night stays he;
For I feel his curse as a haunted bough
 On the trunk of a haunted tree.

Ah, Are You Digging on My Grave?

Thomas Hardy
1913

First published September 27, 1913, Saturday Review and then collected in *Satires of Circumstance: Lyrics and Reveries with Miscellaneous Pieces,* 1914.

"Ah, are you digging on my grave
My loved one?—planting rue?"
—"No: yesterday he went to wed
One of the brightest wealth has bred.
'It cannot hurt her now,' he said,   5
'That I should not be true.'"

"Then who is digging on my grave?
My nearest dearest kin?"
—"Ah, no; they sit and think, 'What use!
What good will planting flowers produce?   10
No tendance of her mound can loose
Her spirit from Death's gin.'"

"But some one digs upon my grave?
My enemy?—prodding sly?"
—"Nay: when she heard you had passed the Gate   15
That shuts on all flesh soon or late,
She thought you no more worth her hate,
And cares not where you lie."

"Then, who is digging on my grave?
Say—since I have not guessed!"   20
—"O it is I, my mistress dear,
Your little dog, who still lives near,
And much I hope my movements here
Have not disturbed your rest?"
"Ah, yes! YOU dig upon my grave . . .   25
Why flashed it not on me
That one true heart was left behind!
What feeling do we ever find
To equal among human kind
A dog's fidelity!"   30

"Mistress, I dug upon your grave
To bury a bone, in case
I should be hungry near this spot
When passing on my daily trot.
I am sorry, but I quite forgot   35
It was your resting-place."

Theology

Paul Laurence Dunbar
1913

Published in *The Complete Poems of Paul Laurence Dunbar*. New York:
Dodd, Mead, and Company, 1913.

There is a heaven, for ever, day by day,
The upward longing of my soul doth tell me so.
There is a hell, I 'm quite as sure; for pray,
If there were not, where would my neighbours go?

A Woman and Her Dead Husband

D. H. Lawrence
1914

First published in *Poetry Magazine*, January 1914.

Ah stern cold man,
How can you lie so relentless hard
While I wash you with weeping water!
Ah face, carved hard and cold,
You have been like this, on your guard   5
Against me, since death began.

You masquerader![15]
How can you shame to act this part
Of unswerving indifference to me?
It is not you; why disguise yourself   10
Against me, to break my heart,
You evader?
You've a warm mouth,
A good warm mouth always sooner to soften
Even than your sudden eyes.   15
Ah cruel, to keep your mouth
Relentless, however often
I kiss it in drouth.[16]
You are not he.
Who are you, lying in his place on the bed   20
And rigid and indifferent to me?
His mouth, though he laughed or sulked,
Was always warm and red
And good to me.
And his eyes could see   25
The white moon hang like a breast revealed
By the slipping shawl of stars,
Could see the small stars tremble
As the heart beneath did wield
Systole, diastole.[17]   30
And he showed it me
So, when he made his love to me;
And his brows like rocks on the sea jut out,
And his eyes were deep like the sea
With shadow, and he looked at me,   35
Till I sank in him like the sea,
Awfully.
Oh, he was multiform—
Which then was he among the manifold?[18]
The gay, the sorrowful, the seer?   40
I have loved a rich race of men in one—
But not this, this never-warm
Metal-cold—!
Ah masquerader!
With your steel face white-enamelled,   45
Were you he, after all, and I never
Saw you or felt you in kissing?
—Yet sometimes my heart was trammelled[19]
With fear, evader!
Then was it you   50
After all, this cold, hard man?
—Ah no, look up at me,
Tell me it isn't true,
That you're only frightening me!

---

[15] masquerader: someone or something that gives a false show or pretense

[16] drouth: dialect or poetic form of drought (a prolonged period of abnormally low rainfall; a shortage of water resulting from this)

[17] Systole, diastole: Systole: the phase of the heartbeat when the heart muscle contracts and pumps blood from the chambers into the arteries. Diastole: the phase of the heartbeat when the heart muscle relaxes and allows the chambers to fill with blood.

[18] manifold: 1) many and various, 2) a pipe or chamber branching into several openings, 3) (in an internal combustion engine) the part conveying air and fuel from the carburetor to the cylinders or that leading from the cylinders to the exhaust pipe.

[19] trammelled: deprive of freedom of action.

You will not stir,   55
Nor hear me, not a sound.
—Then it was you—
And all this time you were
Like this when I lived with you.
It is not true,   60
I am frightened, I am frightened of you
And of everything.
O God!—God too
Has deceived me in everything,
In everything.   65

The Convergence of the Twain
Thomas Hardy
1915

Published in 1915 in response to the sinking of the *Titanic* on April 15, 1912.

(Lines on the loss of the "Titanic")

I

In a solitude of the sea
 Deep from human vanity,
And the Pride of Life that planned her, stilly couches she.

II

Steel chambers, late the pyres
 Of her salamandrine fires,   5
Cold currents thrid, and turn to rhythmic tidal lyres.

III

Over the mirrors meant
 To glass the opulent
The sea-worm crawls—grotesque, slimed, dumb, indifferent.

IV

Jewels in joy designed   10
 To ravish the sensuous mind
Lie lightless, all their sparkles bleared and black and blind.

V

Dim moon-eyed fishes near
 Gaze at the gilded gear
And query: "What does this vaingloriousness down here?". . .

VI

Well: while was fashioning
 This creature of cleaving wing,
The Immanent Will that stirs and urges everything

VII

Prepared a sinister mate
 For her—so gaily great—   20
A Shape of Ice, for the time far and dissociate.

VIII

And as the smart ship grew
 In stature, grace, and hue,
In shadowy silent distance grew the Iceberg too.

IX

Alien they seemed to be;   25
 No mortal eye could see
The intimate welding of their later history,

X

Or sign that they were bent
 By paths coincident
On being anon twin halves of one august event,   30

XI

Till the Spinner of the Years
 Said "Now!" And each one hears,
And consummation comes, and jars two hemispheres.

Portrait of a Lady

T. S. Eliot
1915

First published in September 1915 in *Others: A Magazine of the New Verse.*

I

Among the smoke and fog of a December afternoon
You have the scene arrange itself—as it will seem to do—
With "I have saved this afternoon for you";
And four wax candles in the darkened room,
Four rings of light upon the ceiling overhead: 5
An atmosphere of Juliet's tomb[20]
Prepared for all the things to be said, or left unsaid.
We have been, let us say, to hear the latest Pole
Transmit the Preludes,[21] through his hair and finger-tips.
"So intimate, this Chopin, that I think his soul   10
Should be resurrected only among friends—
Some two or three, who will not touch the bloom
That is rubbed and questioned in the concert room."
And so the conversation slips
Among velleities[22] and carefully caught regrets,   15
Through attenuated[23] tones of violins
Mingled with remote cornets,[24]
And begins:
"You do not know how much they mean to me, my friends;
And how, how rare and strange it is, to find,   20
In a life composed so much, so much of odds and ends—
(For indeed I do not love it … you knew? you are not blind! How keen[25] you are!)
To find a friend who has these qualities,
Who has, and gives
Those qualities upon which friendship lives: 25

[20] Juliet's tomb: the tomb of Juliet in Shakespeare's *Romeo and Juliet*

[21] Pole / Transmit the Preludes: Referring to Frédérik Chopin (1810-1849), and his preludes. Chopin was a Polish composer and pianist.

[22] velleities: wishes or inclinations not strong enough to lead to action.

[23] attenuated: reduce the force, effect, or value of.

[24] cornets: 1) a brass instrument resembling a trumpet but shorter and wider, played chiefly in bands, 2) a cone-shaped wafer, esp. one filled with ice cream

[25] keen: 1) having or showing eagerness or enthusiasm, 2) (of mental faculties) quick to understand or function

How much it means that I say this to you—
Without these friendships-life, what cauchemar!"[26]
Among the windings of the violins,
And the ariettes[27]
Of cracked cornets,   30
Inside my brain a dull tom-tom begins
Absurdly hammering a prelude of its own—
Capricious monotone[28]
That is at least one definite "false note."
Let us take the air, in a tobacco trance,   35
Admire the monuments,
Discuss the late events,
Correct our watches by the public clocks;
Then sit for half an hour and drink our bocks.[29]

II

Now that lilacs[30] are in bloom   40
She has a bowl of lilacs in her room
And twists one in her fingers while she talks.
"Ah my friend, you do not know, you do not know
What life is, you who hold it in your hands—"
(Slowly twisting the lilac stalks);   45
"You let it flow from you, you let it flow,
And youth is cruel, and has no remorse,
And smiles at situations which it cannot see."
I smile, of course,
And go on drinking tea.   50
"Yet with these April sunsets, that somehow recall
My buried life, and Paris in the spring,
I feel immeasurably at peace, and find the world
To be wonderful and youthful, after all."
The voice returns like the insistent out-of-tune   55
Of a broken violin on an August afternoon:
"I am always sure that you understand
My feelings, always sure that you feel,
Sure that across the gulf[31] you reach your hand.
"You are invulnerable, you have no Achilles' heel.[32]   60
You will go on, and when you have prevailed
You can say: 'At this point many a one has failed.'
But what have I, but what have I, my friend,
To give you, what can you receive from me?
Only the friendship and the sympathy   65
Of one about to reach her journey's end.
"I shall sit here, serving tea to friends ..."

---

[26] cauchemar: A vampire who feeds exclusively on sleeping victims

[27] ariettes: A short aria. Aria: a long, accompanied song for a solo voice, typically one in an opera or oratorio.

[28] Capricious: given to sudden and unaccountable changes of mood or behavior; monotone: 1) a continuing sound, esp. of someone's voice, that is unchanging in pitch and without intonation, 2) without vividness or variety; dull

[29] bocks: a strong dark beer brewed in the fall and drunk in the spring

[30] lilacs: a Eurasian shrub or small tree of the olive family, that has fragrant violet, pink, or white blossoms and is widely cultivated as an ornamental

[31] gulf: 1) a deep inlet of the sea almost surrounded by land, with a narrow mouth, 2) a deep ravine, chasm, or abyss

[32] Achilles' heel: a weakness or vulnerable point (according to various sources of Greek mythology, the Greek warrior Achilles was invulnerable except at the heel, where his mother, Thetis, held him as a baby to dip him into the River Styx to make him invulnerable)

I take my hat: how can I make a cowardly amends[33]
For what she has said to me?
You will see me any morning in the park   70
Reading the comics and the sporting page.
Particularly I remark
An English countess[34] goes upon the stage,
A Greek was murdered at a Polish dance,
Another bank defaulter has confessed.   75
I keep my countenance,[35]
I remain self-possessed
Except when a street piano, mechanical and tired,
Reiterates some worn-out common song,
With the smell of hyacinths[36] across the garden   80
Recalling things that other people have desired.
Are these ideas right or wrong?

III

The October night comes down. Returning as before,
Except for a slight sensation of being ill at ease,
I mount the stairs and turn the handle of the door   85
And feel as if I had mounted on my hands and knees.
"And so you are going abroad; and when do you return?
But that's a useless question.
You hardly know when you are coming back,
You will find so much to learn."   90
My smile falls heavily among the bric-a-brac.[37]
"Perhaps you can write to me."
My self-possession flares up for a second;
This is as I had reckoned.
"I have been wondering frequently of late   95
(But our beginnings never know our ends!)
Why we have not developed into friends."
I feel like one who smiles, and turning shall remark
Suddenly, his expression in a glass.
My self-possession gutters;[38] we are really in the dark.   100
"For everybody said so, all our friends,
They all were sure our feelings would relate
So closely! I myself can hardly understand.
We must leave it now to fate.[39]
You will write, at any rate.   105
Perhaps it is not too late.
I shall sit here, serving tea to friends."
And I must borrow every changing shape
To find expression . . . dance, dance

---

[33] amends: reparation or compensation, to come to a mutual agreement

[34] countess: a woman holding the rank of count or earl in her own right (an approximate rank between the highest and lowest titles of nobility)

[35] countenance: 1) a person's face or facial expression, 2) support

[36] hyacinths: 1) a bulbous plant of the lily family, with straplike leaves and a compact spike of bell-shaped fragrant flowers; native to western Asia, 2) a light purplish-blue color typical of some hyacinth flowers, 3) In Greek mythology, Hyacinth was a beautiful youth loved by both the god Apollo and the West Wind, Zephyr. Like many flowers, Hyacinths are sometimes associated with rebirth.

[37] bric-a-brac: miscellaneous objects and ornaments of little value

[38] gutters: as a verb 1) (of a candle or flame) flicker and burn unsteadily, 2) channel or furrow with something such as streams or tears, 3) stream down

[39] fate: 1) the development of events beyond a person's control, regarded as determined by a supernatural power, 2) the three goddesses who preside over the birth and life of humans. Each person's destiny was thought of as a thread spun, measured, and cut by the three Fates, Clotho, Lachesis, and Atropos.

Like a dancing bear,   110
Cry like a parrot, chatter like an ape.
Let us take the air, in a tobacco trance …
Well! and what if she should die some afternoon,
Afternoon gray and smoky, evening yellow and rose;
Should die and leave me sitting pen in hand   115
With the smoke coming down above the house tops;
Doubtful, for quite a while
Not knowing what to feel or if I understand
Or whether wise or foolish, tardy or too soon. . . .
Would she not have the advantage, after all?   120
This music is successful with a "dying fall"
Now that we talk of dying—
And should I have the right to smile?

That the Night Come

William Butler Yeats
1916

Collected in *Responsibilities and Other Poems*, 1916.

She lived in storm and strife,
Her soul had such desire
For what proud death may bring
That it could not endure
The common good of life,   5
But lived as 'twere a king
That packed his marriage day
With banneret and pennon,
Trumpet and kettledrum,
And the outrageous cannon,   10
To bundle time away
That the night come.

Dulce et Decorum est[40]

Wilfred Owen
1920

Written in 1917 during World War I, and collected posthumously in
Poems by Wifred Owen. With an Introduction by Siegfried Sassoon.
Published by London, Chatto & Windus. Printed by Morrison and Gibb
Ltd. Edinburgh. First Edition. (1920).

Bent double, like old beggars under sacks,
Knock-kneed, coughing like hags, we cursed through sludge,
Till on the haunting flares we turned our backs
And towards our distant rest began to trudge.
Men marched asleep. Many had lost their boots   5
But limped on, blood-shod. All went lame; all blind;
Drunk with fatigue; deaf even to the hoots
Of disappointed shells that dropped behind.

GAS! Gas! Quick, boys!— An ecstasy of fumbling,
Fitting the clumsy helmets just in time;   10

---

[40] *Dulce et Decorum est*: Latin for "It is sweet and right." Dulce is pronounced Dul-kay.

But someone still was yelling out and stumbling
And floundering like a man in fire or lime.—
Dim, through the misty panes and thick green light
As under a green sea, I saw him drowning.
In all my dreams, before my helpless sight,   15
He plunges at me, guttering, choking, drowning.

If in some smothering dreams you too could pace
Behind the wagon that we flung him in,
And watch the white eyes writhing in his face,
His hanging face, like a devil's sick of sin;   20
If you could hear, at every jolt, the blood
Come gargling from the froth-corrupted lungs,
Obscene as cancer, bitter as the cud
Of vile, incurable sores on innocent tongues,—
My friend, you would not tell with such high zest   25
To children ardent for some desperate glory,
The old Lie: Dulce et decorum est
Pro patria mori.[41]

The Hunting of the Dragon

G. K. Chesterton
1922

Published in *The Ballad of St. Barbara and Other Poems* (1922).

When we went hunting the Dragon
In the days when we were young,
We tossed the bright world over our shoulder
As bugle and baldrick slung;[1]
Never was world so wild and fair   5
As what went by on the wind,
Never such fields of paradise
As the fields we left behind:
For this is the best of a rest for men
That men should rise and ride   10
Making a flying fairyland
Of market and country-side,
Wings on the cottage, wings on the wood,
Wings upon pot and pan,
For the hunting of the Dragon   15
That is the life of a man.
For men grow weary of fairyland
When the Dragon is a dream,
And tire of the talking bird in the tree,
The singing fish in the stream;   20

And the wandering stars grow stale, grow stale,
And the wonder is stiff with scorn;[2]
For this is the honour of fairyland
And the following of the horn;
Beauty on beauty called us back   25
When we could rise and ride,

---

[41] *Dulce et decorum est Pro patria mori*: "it is sweet and right to die for your country"

[1] bugle and baldrick: A bugle is a brass instrument like a small trumpet, typically without valves or keys and used for military signals. A baldrick (also baldric) is a wide (ornamented) belt worn over the right shoulder to support a sword or bugle by the left hip.

[2] scorn: the feeling or belief that someone or something is worthless or despicable; contempt.

And a woman looked out of every window
As wonderful as a bride:
And the tavern-sign as a tabard[1] blazed,
And the children cheered and ran,   30
For the love of the hate of the Dragon
That is the pride of a man.
The sages called him a shadow
And the light went out of the sun:
And the wise men told us that all was well   35
And all was weary and one:
And then, and then, in the quiet garden,
With never a weed to kill,

We knew that his shining tail had shone
In the white road over the hill: 40
We knew that the clouds were flakes of flame,
We knew that the sunset fire
Was red with the blood of the Dragon
Whose death is the world's desire.
For the horn was blown in the heart of the night   45
That men should rise and ride,
Keeping the tryst[2] of a terrible jest[3]
Never for long untried;
Drinking a dreadful blood for wine,
Never in cup or can,   50
The death of a deathless Dragon,
That is the life of a man.

LITERARY STUDIES

WILLIAM WORDSWORTH

Lines Written in Early Spring

William Wordsworth
1798

Published in *Lyrical Ballads, with a Few Other Poems* (1798) by William
Wordsworth and Samuel Taylor Coleridge.

I heard a thousand blended notes,
While in a grove I sate reclined,
In that sweet mood when pleasant thoughts
Bring sad thoughts to the mind.
To her fair works did Nature link   5
The human soul that through me ran;
And much it grieved my heart to think
What man has made of man.

Through primrose tufts, in that green bower,
The periwinkle trailed its wreaths;   10
And 'tis my faith that every flower
Enjoys the air it breathes.

---

[1] tabard: 1) a coarse sleeveless garment worn as the outer dress of medieval peasants and clerics, or worn as a surcoat over armor, 2) a herald's official coat emblazoned with the arms of the sovereign

[2] tryst: a private, romantic rendezvous between lovers.

[3] jest: 1) a thing said or done for amusement; a joke, 2) speak or act in a joking manner.

The birds around me hopped and played,
Their thoughts I cannot measure:—
But the least motion which they made   15
It seemed a thrill of pleasure.

The budding twigs spread out their fan,
To catch the breezy air;
And I must think, do all I can,
That there was pleasure there.   20

If this belief from heaven be sent,
If such be Nature's holy plan,
Have I not reason to lament
What man has made of man?

The Tables Turned
An Evening Scene on the Same Subject

William Wordsworth
1798

Published in *Lyrical Ballads, with a Few Other Poems* (1798) by William Wordsworth and Samuel Taylor Coleridge.

Up! up! my Friend, and quit your books;
Or surely you'll grow double:
Up! up! my Friend, and clear your looks;
Why all this toil and trouble?
The sun, above the mountain's head,   5
A freshening lustre mellow
Through all the long green fields has spread,
His first sweet evening yellow.

Books! 'tis a dull and endless strife:
Come, hear the woodland linnet,   10
How sweet his music! on my life,
There's more of wisdom in it.

And hark! how blithe the throstle sings!
He, too, is no mean preacher:
Come forth into the light of things,   15
Let Nature be your teacher.

She has a world of ready wealth,
Our minds and hearts to bless—
Spontaneous wisdom breathed by health,
Truth breathed by cheerfulness.   20

One impulse from a vernal wood
May teach you more of man,
Of moral evil and of good,
Than all the sages can.
Sweet is the lore which Nature brings;   25
Our meddling intellect
Mis-shapes the beauteous forms of things:—
We murder to dissect.

Enough of Science and of Art;
Close up those barren leaves;   30
Come forth, and bring with you a heart
That watches and receives.

Michael

William Wordsworth
1800

Published in the second volume of *Lyrical Ballads, with a Few Other Poems* (1800) by William Wordsworth and Samuel Taylor Coleridge.

If from the public way you turn your steps
Up the tumultuous brook of Greenhead Ghyll,
You will suppose that with an upright path
Your feet must struggle; in such bold ascent
The pastoral mountains front you, face to face.   5
But, courage! for around that boisterous brook
The mountains have all opened out themselves,
And made a hidden valley of their own.
No habitation can be seen; but they
Who journey thither find themselves alone   10
With a few sheep, with rocks and stones, and kites
That overhead are sailing in the sky.
It is in truth an utter solitude;
Nor should I have made mention of this Dell
But for one object which you might pass by,   15
Might see and notice not. Beside the brook
Appears a straggling heap of unhewn stones!
And to that simple object appertains
A story—unenriched with strange events,
Yet not unfit, I deem, for the fireside,   20
Or for the summer shade. It was the first
Of those domestic tales that spake to me
Of shepherds, dwellers in the valleys, men
Whom I already loved; not verily
For their own sakes, but for the fields and hills   25
Where was their occupation and abode.
And hence this Tale, while I was yet a Boy
Careless of books, yet having felt the power
Of Nature, by the gentle agency
Of natural objects, led me on to feel   30
For passions that were not my own, and think
(At random and imperfectly indeed)
On man, the heart of man, and human life.
Therefore, although it be a history
Homely and rude, I will relate the same   35
For the delight of a few natural hearts;
And, with yet fonder feeling, for the sake
Of youthful Poets, who among these hills
Will be my second self when I am gone.
  Upon the forest-side in Grasmere Vale   40
There dwelt a Shepherd, Michael was his name;
An old man, stout of heart, and strong of limb.
His bodily frame had been from youth to age
Of an unusual strength: his mind was keen,
Intense, and frugal, apt for all affairs,   45
And in his shepherd's calling he was prompt
And watchful more than ordinary men.
Hence had he learned the meaning of all winds,
Of blasts of every tone; and, oftentimes,
When others heeded not, He heard the South   50
Make subterraneous music, like the noise

Of bagpipers on distant Highland hills.
The Shepherd, at such warning, of his flock
Bethought him, and he to himself would say,
"The winds are now devising work for me!"   55
And, truly, at all times, the storm, that drives
The traveller to a shelter, summoned him
Up to the mountains: he had been alone
Amid the heart of many thousand mists,
That came to him, and left him, on the heights.   60
So lived he till his eightieth year was past.
And grossly that man errs, who should suppose
That the green valleys, and the streams and rocks,
Were things indifferent to the Shepherd's thoughts.
Fields, where with cheerful spirits he had breathed   65
The common air; hills, which with vigorous step
He had so often climbed; which had impressed
So many incidents upon his mind
Of hardship, skill or courage, joy or fear;
Which, like a book, preserved the memory   70
Of the dumb animals, whom he had saved,
Had fed or sheltered, linking to such acts
The certainty of honourable gain;
Those fields, those hills—what could they less? had laid
Strong hold on his affections, were to him   75
A pleasurable feeling of blind love,
The pleasure which there is in life itself.

  His days had not been passed in singleness.
His Helpmate was a comely matron, old—
Though younger than himself full twenty years.   80
She was a woman of a stirring life,
Whose heart was in her house: two wheels she had
Of antique form; this large, for spinning wool;
That small, for flax; and if one wheel had rest
It was because the other was at work.   85
The Pair had but one inmate in their house,
An only Child, who had been born to them
When Michael, telling o'er his years, began
To deem that he was old,—in shepherd's phrase,
With one foot in the grave. This only Son,   90
With two brave sheep-dogs tried in many a storm,
The one of an inestimable worth,
Made all their household. I may truly say,
That they were as a proverb in the vale
For endless industry. When day was gone   95
And from their occupations out of doors
The Son and Father were come home, even then,
Their labour did not cease; unless when all
Turned to the cleanly supper-board, and there,
Each with a mess of pottage and skimmed milk,   100
Sat round the basket piled with oaten cakes,
And their plain home-made cheese. Yet when the meal
Was ended, Luke (for so the Son was named)
And his old Father both betook themselves
To such convenient work as might employ   105
Their hands by the fireside; perhaps to card
Wool for the Housewife's spindle, or repair
Some injury done to sickle, flail, or scythe,
Or other implement of house or field.
  Down from the ceiling, by the chimney's edge,   110

That in our ancient uncouth country style
With huge and black projection overbrowed
Large space beneath, as duly as the light
Of day grew dim the Housewife hung a lamp;
An aged utensil, which had performed   115
Service beyond all others of its kind.
Early at evening did it burn—and late,
Surviving comrade of uncounted hours,
Which, going by from year to year, had found,
And left, the couple neither gay perhaps   120
Nor cheerful, yet with objects and with hopes,
Living a life of eager industry.
And now, when Luke had reached his eighteenth year,
There by the light of this old lamp they sate,
Father and Son, while far into the night   125
The Housewife plied her own peculiar work,
Making the cottage through the silent hours
Murmur as with the sound of summer flies.
This light was famous in its neighbourhood,
And was a public symbol of the life   130
That thrifty Pair had lived. For, as it chanced,
Their cottage on a plot of rising ground
Stood single, with large prospect, north and south,
High into Easedale, up to Dunmail-Raise,
And westward to the village near the lake;   135
And from this constant light, so regular
And so far seen, the House itself, by all
Who dwelt within the limits of the vale,
Both old and young, was named THE EVENING STAR.
  Thus living on through such a length of years,   140
The Shepherd, if he loved himself, must needs
Have loved his Helpmate; but to Michael's heart
This son of his old age was yet more dear—
Less from instinctive tenderness, the same
Fond spirit that blindly works in the blood of all—   145
Than that a child, more than all other gifts
That earth can offer to declining man,
Brings hope with it, and forward-looking thoughts,
And stirrings of inquietude, when they
By tendency of nature needs must fail.   150
Exceeding was the love he bare to him,
His heart and his heart's joy! For oftentimes
Old Michael, while he was a babe in arms,
Had done him female service, not alone
For pastime and delight, as is the use   155
Of fathers, but with patient mind enforced
To acts of tenderness; and he had rocked
His cradle, as with a woman's gentle hand.

  And, in a later time, ere yet the Boy
Had put on boy's attire, did Michael love,   160
Albeit of a stern unbending mind,
To have the Young-one in his sight, when he
Wrought in the field, or on his shepherd's stool
Sate with a fettered sheep before him stretched
Under the large old oak, that near his door   165
Stood single, and, from matchless depth of shade,
Chosen for the Shearer's covert from the sun,
Thence in our rustic dialect was called
The CLIPPING TREE, a name which yet it bears.

There, while they two were sitting in the shade,   170
With others round them, earnest all and blithe,
Would Michael exercise his heart with looks
Of fond correction and reproof bestowed
Upon the Child, if he disturbed the sheep
By catching at their legs, or with his shouts   175
Scared them, while they lay still beneath the shears.

   And when by Heaven's good grace the boy grew up
A healthy Lad, and carried in his cheek
Two steady roses that were five years old;
Then Michael from a winter coppice cut   180
With his own hand a sapling, which he hooped
With iron, making it throughout in all
Due requisites a perfect shepherd's staff,
And gave it to the Boy; wherewith equipt
He as a watchman oftentimes was placed   185
At gate or gap, to stem or turn the flock;
And, to his office prematurely called,
There stood the urchin, as you will divine,
Something between a hindrance and a help;
And for this cause not always, I believe,   190
Receiving from his Father hire of praise;
Though nought was left undone which staff, or voice,
Or looks, or threatening gestures, could perform.

   But soon as Luke, full ten years old, could stand
Against the mountain blasts; and to the heights,   195
Not fearing toil, nor length of weary ways,
He with his Father daily went, and they
Were as companions, why should I relate
That objects which the Shepherd loved before
Were dearer now? that from the Boy there came   200
Feelings and emanations—things which were
Light to the sun and music to the wind;
And that the old Man's heart seemed born again?

   Thus in his Father's sight the Boy grew up:
And now, when he had reached his eighteenth year,   205
He was his comfort and his daily hope.

   While in this sort the simple household lived
From day to day, to Michael's ear there came
Distressful tidings. Long before the time
Of which I speak, the Shepherd had been bound   210
In surety for his brother's son, a man
Of an industrious life, and ample means;
But unforeseen misfortunes suddenly
Had prest upon him; and old Michael now
Was summoned to discharge the forfeiture,   215
A grievous penalty, but little less
Than half his substance. This unlooked-for claim,
At the first hearing, for a moment took
More hope out of his life than he supposed
That any old man ever could have lost.   220
As soon as he had armed himself with strength
To look his trouble in the face, it seemed
The Shepherd's sole resource to sell at once
A portion of his patrimonial fields.
Such was his first resolve; he thought again,   225
And his heart failed him. "Isabel," said he,
Two evenings after he had heard the news,

"I have been toiling more than seventy years,
And in the open sunshine of God's love
Have we all lived; yet if these fields of ours   230
Should pass into a stranger's hand, I think
That I could not lie quiet in my grave.
Our lot is a hard lot; the sun himself
Has scarcely been more diligent than I;
And I have lived to be a fool at last   235
To my own family. An evil man
That was, and made an evil choice, if he
Were false to us; and if he were not false,
There are ten thousand to whom loss like this
Had been no sorrow. I forgive him;—but   240
'Twere better to be dumb than to talk thus.

  When I began, my purpose was to speak
Of remedies and of a cheerful hope.
Our Luke shall leave us, Isabel; the land
Shall not go from us, and it shall be free;   245
He shall possess it, free as is the wind
That passes over it. We have, thou know'st,
Another kinsman—he will be our friend
In this distress. He is a prosperous man,
Thriving in trade—and Luke to him shall go,   250
And with his kinsman's help and his own thrift
He quickly will repair this loss, and then
He may return to us. If here he stay,
What can be done? Where every one is poor,
What can be gained?"   255
At this the old Man paused,
And Isabel sat silent, for her mind
Was busy, looking back into past times.
There's Richard Bateman, thought she to herself,
He was a parish-boy—at the church-door   260
They made a gathering for him, shillings, pence
And halfpennies, wherewith the neighbours bought
A basket, which they filled with pedlar's wares;
And, with this basket on his arm, the lad
Went up to London, found a master there,   265
Who, out of many, chose the trusty boy
To go and overlook his merchandise
Beyond the seas; where he grew wondrous rich,
And left estates and monies to the poor,
And, at his birth-place, built a chapel, floored   270
With marble which he sent from foreign lands.
These thoughts, and many others of like sort,
Passed quickly through the mind of Isabel,
And her face brightened. The old Man was glad,
And thus resumed:—"Well, Isabel! this scheme   275
These two days, has been meat and drink to me.
Far more than we have lost is left us yet.
—We have enough—I wish indeed that I
Were younger;—but this hope is a good hope.
—Make ready Luke's best garments, of the best   280
Buy for him more, and let us send him forth
To-morrow, or the next day, or to-night:
—If he 'could' go, the Boy should go tonight."

  Here Michael ceased, and to the fields went forth
With a light heart. The Housewife for five days   285
Was restless morn and night, and all day long

Wrought on with her best fingers to prepare
Things needful for the journey of her son.
But Isabel was glad when Sunday came
To stop her in her work: for, when she lay   290
By Michael's side, she through the last two nights
Heard him, how he was troubled in his sleep:
And when they rose at morning she could see
That all his hopes were gone. That day at noon
She said to Luke, while they two by themselves   295
Were sitting at the door, "Thou must not go:
We have no other Child but thee to lose
None to remember—do not go away,
For if thou leave thy Father he will die."
The Youth made answer with a jocund voice;   300
And Isabel, when she had told her fears,
Recovered heart. That evening her best fare
Did she bring forth, and all together sat
Like happy people round a Christmas fire.
  With daylight Isabel resumed her work;   305
And all the ensuing week the house appeared
As cheerful as a grove in Spring: at length
The expected letter from their kinsman came,
With kind assurances that he would do
His utmost for the welfare of the Boy;   310
To which, requests were added, that forthwith
He might be sent to him. Ten times or more
The letter was read over; Isabel
Went forth to show it to the neighbours round;
Nor was there at that time on English land   315
A prouder heart than Luke's. When Isabel
Had to her house returned, the old Man said,
"He shall depart to-morrow." To this word
The Housewife answered, talking much of things
Which, if at such short notice he should go,   320
Would surely be forgotten. But at length
She gave consent, and Michael was at ease.

  Near the tumultuous brook of Greenhead Ghyll,
In that deep valley, Michael had designed
To build a Sheepfold; and, before he heard   325
The tidings of his melancholy loss,
For this same purpose he had gathered up
A heap of stones, which by the streamlet's edge
Lay thrown together, ready for the work.
With Luke that evening thitherward he walked: 330
And soon as they had reached the place he stopped,
And thus the old Man spake to him:—"My Son,
To-morrow thou wilt leave me: with full heart
I look upon thee, for thou art the same
That wert a promise to me ere thy birth,   335
And all thy life hast been my daily joy.
I will relate to thee some little part
Of our two histories; 'twill do thee good
When thou art from me, even if I should touch
On things thou canst not know of.—After thou   340
First cam'st into the world—as oft befalls
To new-born infants—thou didst sleep away
Two days, and blessings from thy Father's tongue
Then fell upon thee. Day by day passed on,
And still I loved thee with increasing love.   345

Never to living ear came sweeter sounds
Than when I heard thee by our own fireside
First uttering, without words, a natural tune;
While thou, a feeding babe, didst in thy joy
Sing at thy Mother's breast. Month followed month,   350
And in the open fields my life was passed
And on the mountains; else I think that thou
Hadst been brought up upon thy Father's knees.
But we were playmates, Luke: among these hills,
As well thou knowest, in us the old and young   355
Have played together, nor with me didst thou
Lack any pleasure which a boy can know."
Luke had a manly heart; but at these words
He sobbed aloud. The old Man grasped his hand,
And said, "Nay, do not take it so—I see   360
That these are things of which I need not speak.
—Even to the utmost I have been to thee
A kind and a good Father: and herein
I but repay a gift which I myself
Received at others' hands; for, though now old   365
Beyond the common life of man, I still
Remember them who loved me in my youth.
Both of them sleep together: here they lived,
As all their Forefathers had done; and when
At length their time was come, they were not loth   370
To give their bodies to the family mould.
I wished that thou should'st live the life they lived:
But, 'tis a long time to look back, my Son,
And see so little gain from threescore years.
These fields were burthened when they came to me;   375
Till I was forty years of age, not more
Than half of my inheritance was mine.
I toiled and toiled; God blessed me in my work,
And till these three weeks past the land was free.
—It looks as if it never could endure   380
Another Master. Heaven forgive me, Luke,
If I judge ill for thee, but it seems good
That thou should'st go."

  At this the old Man paused;
Then, pointing to the stones near which they stood,   385
Thus, after a short silence, he resumed:
"This was a work for us; and now, my Son,
It is a work for me. But, lay one stone—
Here, lay it for me, Luke, with thine own hands.
Nay, Boy, be of good hope;—we both may live   390
To see a better day. At eighty-four
I still am strong and hale;—do thou thy part;
I will do mine.—I will begin again
With many tasks that were resigned to thee:
Up to the heights, and in among the storms,   395
Will I without thee go again, and do
All works which I was wont to do alone,
Before I knew thy face.—Heaven bless thee, Boy!
Thy heart these two weeks has been beating fast
With many hopes; it should be so—yes—yes—   400
I knew that thou could'st never have a wish
To leave me, Luke: thou hast been bound to me
Only by links of love: when thou art gone,
What will be left to us!—But, I forget

My purposes. Lay now the corner-stone,   405
As I requested; and hereafter, Luke,
When thou art gone away, should evil men
Be thy companions, think of me, my Son,
And of this moment; hither turn thy thoughts,
And God will strengthen thee: amid all fear   410
And all temptation, Luke, I pray that thou
May'st bear in mind the life thy Fathers lived,
Who, being innocent, did for that cause
Bestir them in good deeds. Now, fare thee well—
When thou return'st, thou in this place wilt see   415
A work which is not here: a covenant
'Twill be between us; but, whatever fate
Befall thee, I shall love thee to the last,
And bear thy memory with me to the grave."
  The Shepherd ended here; and Luke stooped down,   420
And, as his Father had requested, laid
The first stone of the Sheepfold. At the sight
The old Man's grief broke from him; to his heart
He pressed his Son, he kissed him and wept;
And to the house together they returned.   425
—Hushed was that House in peace, or seeming peace,
Ere the night fell:—with morrow's dawn the Boy
Began his journey, and when he had reached
The public way, he put on a bold face;
And all the neighbours, as he passed their doors,   430
Came forth with wishes and with farewell prayers,
That followed him till he was out of sight.

  A good report did from their Kinsman come,
Of Luke and his well-doing: and the Boy
Wrote loving letters, full of wondrous news,   435
Which, as the Housewife phrased it, were throughout
"The prettiest letters that were ever seen."
Both parents read them with rejoicing hearts.
So, many months passed on: and once again
The Shepherd went about his daily work   440
With confident and cheerful thoughts; and now
Sometimes when he could find a leisure hour
He to that valley took his way, and there
Wrought at the Sheepfold. Meantime Luke began
To slacken in his duty; and, at length,   445
He in the dissolute city gave himself
To evil courses: ignominy and shame
Fell on him, so that he was driven at last
To seek a hiding-place beyond the seas.
  There is a comfort in the strength of love;   450
'Twill make a thing endurable, which else
Would overset the brain, or break the heart:
I have conversed with more than one who well
Remember the old Man, and what he was
Years after he had heard this heavy news.   455
His bodily frame had been from youth to age
Of an unusual strength. Among the rocks
He went, and still looked up to sun and cloud,
And listened to the wind; and, as before,
Performed all kinds of labour for his sheep,   460
And for the land, his small inheritance.
And to that hollow dell from time to time
Did he repair, to build the Fold of which

His flock had need. 'Tis not forgotten yet
The pity which was then in every heart   465
For the old Man—and 'tis believed by all
That many and many a day he thither went,
And never lifted up a single stone.

   There, by the Sheepfold, sometimes was he seen
Sitting alone, or with his faithful Dog,   470
Then old, beside him, lying at his feet.
The length of full seven years, from time to time,
He at the building of this Sheepfold wrought,
And left the work unfinished when he died.
Three years, or little more, did Isabel   475
Survive her Husband: at her death the estate
Was sold, and went into a stranger's hand.
The Cottage which was named the EVENING STAR
Is gone—the ploughshare has been through the ground
On which it stood; great changes have been wrought   480
In all the neighbourhood:—yet the oak is left
That grew beside their door; and the remains
Of the unfinished Sheepfold may be seen
Beside the boisterous brook of Greenhead Ghyll.

My Heart Leaps Up

William Wordsworth
1802

Written March 26, 1802 and collected in *Poems, in Two Volumes*, 1807.

My heart leaps up when I behold
 A rainbow in the sky:
So was it when my life began,
So is it now I am a man,
So be it when I shall grow old   5
 Or let me die!
The Child is father of the Man:
And I could wish my days to be
Bound each to each by natural piety.

The Solitary Reaper

William Wordsworth
1807

Published in *Poems, in Two Volumes* (1807).

Behold her, single in the field,
Yon solitary Highland Lass!
Reaping and singing by herself;
Stop here, or gently pass!
Alone she cuts and binds the grain,   5
And sings a melancholy strain;
O listen! for the Vale profound
Is overflowing with the sound.

No Nightingale did ever chaunt
More welcome notes to weary bands   10
Of travellers in some shady haunt,
Among Arabian sands:

A voice so thrilling ne'er was heard
In spring-time from the Cuckoo-bird,
Breaking the silence of the seas   15
Among the farthest Hebrides.

Will no one tell me what she sings?—
Perhaps the plaintive numbers flow
For old, unhappy, far-off things,
And battles long ago: 20
Or is it some more humble lay,
Familiar matter of to-day?
Some natural sorrow, loss, or pain,
That has been, and may be again?
Whate'er the theme, the Maiden sang   25
As if her song could have no ending;
I saw her singing at her work,
And o'er the sickle bending;—
I listened, motionless and still;
And, as I mounted up the hill   30
The music in my heart I bore,
Long after it was heard no more.

The World Is Too Much with Us

William Wordsworth
1807

Published in *Poems, in Two Volumes* (1807).

The world is too much with us; late and soon,
  Getting and spending, we lay waste our powers:
  Little we see in Nature that is ours;
We have given our hearts away, a sordid boon![4]
This sea that bares her bosom to the moon;   5
  The winds that will be howling at all hours,
  And are up-gather'd now like sleeping flowers;
For this, for everything, we are out of tune;
It moves us not.—Great God! I'd rather be
  A Pagan[5] suckled in a creed[6] outworn;   10
So might I, standing on this pleasant lea,
  Have glimpses that would make me less forlorn;
Have sight of Proteus[7] rising from the sea;
  Or hear old Triton[8] blow his wreathèd horn.

---

[4] sordid boon: Essentially a "dirty blessing." *Sordid* refers to dirty or soiled or unsavory character. *Boon* is a gift or blessing.

[5] Pagan: a person holding religious beliefs other than those of the main world religions. In Europe and the West, it is often associated with non-Christian beliefs.

[6] creed: a brief authoritative formula or statement of religious belief

[7] Proteus: a Greek sea god capable of assuming different forms; first known use in 15th century

[8] Triton: a son of Poseidon described as a demigod of the sea with the lower part of his body like that of a fish

EMILY DICKINSON

Her first collection of poetry was published in 1890 by personal
acquaintances Thomas Wentworth Higginson and Mabel Loomis Todd,
both of whom heavily edited the content. A complete and mostly
unaltered collection of her poetry became available for the first time in
1955 when *The Poems of Emily Dickinson* was published by scholar
Thomas H. Johnson.

Wild Nights—Wild Nights!

Emily Dickinson

Wild nights! Wild nights!
Were I with thee,
Wild nights should be
Our luxury!
Futile the winds   5
To a heart in port,—
Done with the compass,
Done with the chart.

Rowing in Eden!
Ah! the sea!   10
Might I but moor
To-night in thee!

A Bird came down the Walk—

Emily Dickinson

A bird came down the walk:
He did not know I saw;
He bit an angle-worm in halves
And ate the fellow, raw.

And then he drank a dew   5
From a convenient grass,
And then hopped sidewise to the wall
To let a beetle pass.

He glanced with rapid eyes
That hurried all abroad,—   10
They looked like frightened beads, I thought
He stirred his velvet head

Like one in danger; cautious,
I offered him a crumb,
And he unrolled his feathers   15
And rowed him softer home

Than oars divide the ocean,
Too silver for a seam,
Or butterflies, off banks of noon,
Leap, plashless, as they swim.   20

I like a look of agony

Emily Dickinson

I like a look of agony,
Because I know it 's true;
Men do not sham convulsion,
Nor simulate a throe.[1]
The eyes glaze once, and that is death.   5
Impossible to feign
The beads upon the forehead
By homely anguish strung.

Because I could not stop for Death

Emily Dickinson

Because I could not stop for Death,
He kindly stopped for me;
The carriage[2] held but just ourselves
And Immortality.
We slowly drove, he knew no haste,   5
And I had put away
My labor, and my leisure too,
For his civility.[3]
We passed the school where children played
At wrestling in a ring;   10
We passed the fields of gazing grain,
We passed the setting sun.
We paused before a house that seemed
A swelling of the ground;
The roof was scarcely visible,   15
The cornice[4] but a mound.
Since then 'tis centuries; but each
Feels shorter than the day
I first surmised the horses' heads[5]
Were toward eternity.   20

---

[1] throe: severe spasm of pain

[2] carriage: a four-wheeled passenger vehicle pulled by two or more horses

[3] civility: formal politeness and courtesy in behavior or speech.

[4] cornice: 1) an ornamental molding around the wall of a room just below the ceiling, 2) a horizontal molded projection crowning a building or structure, esp. the uppermost member of the entablature of an order, surmounting the frieze, 3) an overhanging mass of hardened snow at the edge of a mountain precipice.

[5] horses' heads: 1) any of several silvery marine fishes with very flat bodies, 2) Also called: kingfish

The Soul selects her own Society—

Emily Dickinson

The Soul selects her own Society—
Then—shuts the Door—
To her divine Majority—
Present no more—
Unmoved—she notes the Chariots—pausing— 5
At her low Gate—
Unmoved—an Emperor be kneeling
Upon her Mat—
I've known her—from an ample nation—
Choose One— 10
Then—close the Valves of her attention—
Like Stone—

Each life converges to some centre

Emily Dickinson

Each life converges to some centre
Expressed or still;
Exists in every human nature
A goal,

Admitted scarcely to itself, it may be, 5
Too fair
For credibility's temerity
To dare.

Adored with caution, as a brittle heaven,
To reach 10
Were hopeless as the rainbow's raiment
To touch,

Yet persevered toward, surer for the distance;
How high
Unto the saints' slow diligence 15
The sky!

Ungained, it may be, by a life's low venture,
But then,
Eternity enables the endeavoring
Again.

ROBERT FROST

The Death of the Hired Man

Robert Frost
1915

Published in *North of Boston*. New York: Henry Holt and Company, 1915.

Mary sat musing on the lamp-flame at the table
Waiting for Warren. When she heard his step,
She ran on tip-toe down the darkened passage
To meet him in the doorway with the news
And put him on his guard. "Silas is back."   5
She pushed him outward with her through the door
And shut it after her. "Be kind," she said.
She took the market things from Warren's arms
And set them on the porch, then drew him down
To sit beside her on the wooden steps.   10

"When was I ever anything but kind to him?
But I'll not have the fellow back," he said.
"I told him so last haying, didn't I?
'If he left then,' I said, 'that ended it.'
What good is he? Who else will harbour him   15
At his age for the little he can do?
What help he is there's no depending on.
Off he goes always when I need him most.
'He thinks he ought to earn a little pay,
Enough at least to buy tobacco with,   20
So he won't have to beg and be beholden.'
'All right,' I say, 'I can't afford to pay
Any fixed wages, though I wish I could.'
'Someone else can.' 'Then someone else will have to.'
I shouldn't mind his bettering himself   25
If that was what it was. You can be certain,
When he begins like that, there's someone at him
Trying to coax him off with pocket-money,—
In haying time, when any help is scarce.
In winter he comes back to us. I'm done."   30
"Sh! not so loud: he'll hear you," Mary said.

"I want him to: he'll have to soon or late."
"He's worn out. He's asleep beside the stove.
When I came up from Rowe's I found him here,
Huddled against the barn-door fast asleep,   35
A miserable sight, and frightening, too—
You needn't smile—I didn't recognise him—
I wasn't looking for him—and he's changed.
Wait till you see."

"Where did you say he'd been?"   40

"He didn't say. I dragged him to the house,
And gave him tea and tried to make him smoke.
I tried to make him talk about his travels.
Nothing would do: he just kept nodding off."

"What did he say? Did he say anything?"   45

"But little."

"Anything? Mary, confess
He said he'd come to ditch the meadow for me."

"Warren!"

"But did he? I just want to know."   50

"Of course he did. What would you have him say?
Surely you wouldn't grudge the poor old man
Some humble way to save his self-respect.
He added, if you really care to know,
He meant to clear the upper pasture, too.   55
That sounds like something you have heard before?
Warren, I wish you could have heard the way
He jumbled everything. I stopped to look
Two or three times—he made me feel so queer—
To see if he was talking in his sleep.   60
He ran on Harold Wilson—you remember—
The boy you had in haying four years since.
He's finished school, and teaching in his college.
Silas declares you'll have to get him back.
He says they two will make a team for work: 65
Between them they will lay this farm as smooth!
The way he mixed that in with other things.
He thinks young Wilson a likely lad, though daft
On education—you know how they fought
All through July under the blazing sun,   70
Silas up on the cart to build the load,
Harold along beside to pitch it on."

"Yes, I took care to keep well out of earshot."

"Well, those days trouble Silas like a dream.
You wouldn't think they would. How some things linger!   75
Harold's young college boy's assurance piqued him.
After so many years he still keeps finding
Good arguments he sees he might have used.
I sympathise. I know just how it feels
To think of the right thing to say too late.   80
Harold's associated in his mind with Latin.
He asked me what I thought of Harold's saying
He studied Latin like the violin
Because he liked it—that an argument!
He said he couldn't make the boy believe   85
He could find water with a hazel prong—
Which showed how much good school had ever done him.
He wanted to go over that. But most of all
He thinks if he could have another chance
To teach him how to build a load of hay——"   90

"I know, that's Silas' one accomplishment.

He bundles every forkful in its place,
And tags and numbers it for future reference,
So he can find and easily dislodge it
In the unloading. Silas does that well.   95
He takes it out in bunches like big birds' nests.
You never see him standing on the hay
He's trying to lift, straining to lift himself."

"He thinks if he could teach him that, he'd be
Some good perhaps to someone in the world.   100
He hates to see a boy the fool of books.
Poor Silas, so concerned for other folk,

And nothing to look backward to with pride,
And nothing to look forward to with hope,
So now and never any different."   105

Part of a moon was falling down the west,
Dragging the whole sky with it to the hills.
Its light poured softly in her lap. She saw
And spread her apron to it. She put out her hand
Among the harp-like morning-glory strings,   110
Taut with the dew from garden bed to eaves,
As if she played unheard the tenderness
That wrought on him beside her in the night.
"Warren," she said, "he has come home to die:
You needn't be afraid he'll leave you this time."   115

"Home," he mocked gently.

"Yes, what else but home?
It all depends on what you mean by home.
Of course he's nothing to us, any more
Than was the hound that came a stranger to us   120
Out of the woods, worn out upon the trail."

"Home is the place where, when you have to go there,
They have to take you in."

"I should have called it
Something you somehow haven't to deserve."   125

Warren leaned out and took a step or two,
Picked up a little stick, and brought it back
And broke it in his hand and tossed it by.
"Silas has better claim on us you think
Than on his brother? Thirteen little miles   130
As the road winds would bring him to his door.
Silas has walked that far no doubt to-day.
Why didn't he go there? His brother's rich,
A somebody—director in the bank."

"He never told us that."   135

"We know it though."

"I think his brother ought to help, of course.
I'll see to that if there is need. He ought of right
To take him in, and might be willing to—
He may be better than appearances.   140
But have some pity on Silas. Do you think
If he'd had any pride in claiming kin
Or anything he looked for from his brother,
He'd keep so still about him all this time?"

"I wonder what's between them."   145

"I can tell you.

Silas is what he is—we wouldn't mind him—
But just the kind that kinsfolk can't abide.
He never did a thing so very bad.
He don't know why he isn't quite as good   150
As anyone. He won't be made ashamed
To please his brother, worthless though he is."

"I can't think Si ever hurt anyone."

"No, but he hurt my heart the way he lay

And rolled his old head on that sharp-edged chair-back.   155
He wouldn't let me put him on the lounge.
You must go in and see what you can do.
I made the bed up for him there to-night.
You'll be surprised at him—how much he's broken.
His working days are done; I'm sure of it."   160

"I'd not be in a hurry to say that."

"I haven't been. Go, look, see for yourself.

But, Warren, please remember how it is:
He's come to help you ditch the meadow.
He has a plan. You mustn't laugh at him.   165
He may not speak of it, and then he may.
I'll sit and see if that small sailing cloud
Will hit or miss the moon."

It hit the moon.
Then there were three there, making a dim row,   170
The moon, the little silver cloud, and she.

Warren returned—too soon, it seemed to her,
Slipped to her side, caught up her hand and waited.

"Warren," she questioned.

"Dead," was all he answered.   175

Home Burial

Robert Frost
1915

Published in *North of Boston*. New York: Henry Holt and Company, 1915.

He saw her from the bottom of the stairs
Before she saw him. She was starting down,
Looking back over her shoulder at some fear.
She took a doubtful step and then undid it
To raise herself and look again. He spoke   5
Advancing toward her: 'What is it you see
From up there always—for I want to know.'
She turned and sank upon her skirts at that,
And her face changed from terrified to dull.
He said to gain time: 'What is it you see,'   10
Mounting until she cowered under him.
'I will find out now—you must tell me, dear.'
She, in her place, refused him any help
With the least stiffening of her neck and silence.
She let him look, sure that he wouldn't see,   15
Blind creature; and awhile he didn't see.
But at last he murmured, 'Oh,' and again, 'Oh.'

'What is it—what?' she said.

                        'Just that I see.'

'You don't,' she challenged. 'Tell me what it is.'

'The wonder is I didn't see at once.   20
I never noticed it from here before.
I must be wonted to it—that's the reason.
The little graveyard where my people are!

So small the window frames the whole of it.
Not so much larger than a bedroom, is it?   25
There are three stones of slate and one of marble,
Broad-shouldered little slabs there in the sunlight
On the sidehill. We haven't to mind *those*.
But I understand: it is not the stones,
But the child's mound—'

              'Don't, don't, don't, don't,' she cried.

She withdrew shrinking from beneath his arm
That rested on the banister, and slid downstairs;
And turned on him with such a daunting look,
He said twice over before he knew himself:
'Can't a man speak of his own child he's lost?'   35

'Not you! Oh, where's my hat? Oh, I don't need it!
I must get out of here. I must get air.
I don't know rightly whether any man can.'

'Amy! Don't go to someone else this time.
Listen to me. I won't come down the stairs.'   40
He sat and fixed his chin between his fists.
'There's something I should like to ask you, dear.'

'You don't know how to ask it.'

              'Help me, then.'

Her fingers moved the latch for all reply.

'My words are nearly always an offense.   45
I don't know how to speak of anything
So as to please you. But I might be taught
I should suppose. I can't say I see how.
A man must partly give up being a man
With women-folk. We could have some arrangement   50
By which I'd bind myself to keep hands off
Anything special you're a-mind to name.
Though I don't like such things 'twixt those that love.
Two that don't love can't live together without them.
But two that do can't live together with them.'   55
She moved the latch a little. 'Don't—don't go.
Don't carry it to someone else this time.
Tell me about it if it's something human.
Let me into your grief. I'm not so much
Unlike other folks as your standing there   60
Apart would make me out. Give me my chance.
I do think, though, you overdo it a little.
What was it brought you up to think it the thing
To take your mother-loss of a first child
So inconsolably—in the face of love.   65
You'd think his memory might be satisfied—'

'There you go sneering now!'

              'I'm not, I'm not!
You make me angry. I'll come down to you.
God, what a woman! And it's come to this,
A man can't speak of his own child that's dead.'   70

'You can't because you don't know how to speak.
If you had any feelings, you that dug
With your own hand—how could you?—his little grave;

I saw you from that very window there,
Making the gravel leap and leap in air,   75
Leap up, like that, like that, and land so lightly
And roll back down the mound beside the hole.
I thought, Who is that man? I didn't know you.
And I crept down the stairs and up the stairs
To look again, and still your spade kept lifting.   80
Then you came in. I heard your rumbling voice
Out in the kitchen, and I don't know why,
But I went near to see with my own eyes.
You could sit there with the stains on your shoes
Of the fresh earth from your own baby's grave   85
And talk about your everyday concerns.
You had stood the spade up against the wall
Outside there in the entry, for I saw it.'

'I shall laugh the worst laugh I ever laughed.
I'm cursed. God, if I don't believe I'm cursed.'   90

'I can repeat the very words you were saying:
"Three foggy mornings and one rainy day
Will rot the best birch fence a man can build."
Think of it, talk like that at such a time!
What had how long it takes a birch to rot   95
To do with what was in the darkened parlor?
You *couldn't* care! The nearest friends can go
With anyone to death, comes so far short
They might as well not try to go at all.
No, from the time when one is sick to death,   100
One is alone, and he dies more alone.
Friends make pretense of following to the grave,
But before one is in it, their minds are turned
And making the best of their way back to life
And living people, and things they understand.   105
But the world's evil. I won't have grief so
If I can change it. Oh, I won't, I won't!'

'There, you have said it all and you feel better.
You won't go now. You're crying. Close the door.
The heart's gone out of it: why keep it up.   110
Amy! There's someone coming down the road!'

'*You*—oh, you think the talk is all. I must go—
Somewhere out of this house. How can I make you—'

'If—you—do!' She was opening the door wider.
'Where do you mean to go? First tell me that.   115
I'll follow and bring you back by force. I *will!*—'

Mending Wall

Robert Frost
1915

Published in *North of Boston*. New York: Henry Holt and Company, 1915.

Something there is that doesn't love a wall,
That sends the frozen-ground-swell under it,
And spills the upper boulders in the sun;
And makes gaps even two can pass abreast.
The work of hunters is another thing: 5

I have come after them and made repair
Where they have left not one stone on a stone,
But they would have the rabbit out of hiding,
To please the yelping dogs. The gaps I mean,
No one has seen them made or heard them made, 10
But at spring mending-time we find them there.
I let my neighbor know beyond the hill;
And on a day we meet to walk the line
And set the wall between us once again.
We keep the wall between us as we go. 15
To each the boulders that have fallen to each.
And some are loaves and some so nearly balls
We have to use a spell to make them balance:
"Stay where you are until our backs are turned!"
We wear our fingers rough with handling them. 20
Oh, just another kind of out-door game,
One on a side. It comes to little more:
There where it is we do not need the wall:
He is all pine and I am apple orchard.
My apple trees will never get across 25
And eat the cones under his pines, I tell him.
He only says, "Good fences make good neighbors."
Spring is the mischief in me, and I wonder
If I could put a notion in his head:
"Why do they make good neighbors? Isn't it 30
Where there are cows? But here there are no cows.
Before I built a wall I'd ask to know
What I was walling in or walling out,
And to whom I was like to give offense.
Something there is that doesn't love a wall, 35
"That wants it down." I could say "Elves" to him,
But it's not elves exactly, and I'd rather
He said it for himself. I see him there
Bringing a stone grasped firmly by the top
In each hand, like an old-stone savage armed. 40
He moves in darkness as it seems to me,
Not of woods only and the shade of trees.
He will not go behind his father's saying,
And he likes having thought of it so well
He says again, "Good fences make good neighbors." 45

Bereft

Robert Frost
1915

Published in *West-Running Brook*. New York: Henry Holt and Company, 1928, containing woodcuts by J.J. Lankes.

Where had I heard this wind before
Change like this to a deeper roar?
What would it take my standing there for,
Holding open a restive door,
Looking down hill to a frothy shore? 5
Summer was past and the day was past.
Sombre clouds in the west were massed.
Out on the porch's sagging floor,
Leaves got up in a coil and hissed,

Blindly struck at my knee and missed.   10
Something sinister in the tone
Told me my secret must be known:
Word I was in the house alone
Somehow must have gotten abroad,
Word I was in my life alone,   15
Word I had no one left but God.

Stopping by Woods on a Snowy Evening

Robert Frost
1915

Published in *New Hampshire*, a 1923 Pulitzer Prize-winning volume of poems.

Whose woods these are I think I know.
His house is in the village though;
He will not see me stopping here
To watch his woods fill up with snow.

My little horse must think it queer   5
To stop without a farmhouse near
Between the woods and frozen lake
The darkest evening of the year.

He gives his harness bells a shake
To ask if there is some mistake.   10
The only other sound's the sweep
Of easy wind and downy flake.

The woods are lovely, dark and deep,
But I have promises to keep,
And miles to go before I sleep,   15
And miles to go before I sleep.

The Road Not Taken

Robert Frost
1915

Published in North *of Boston*. New York: Henry Holt and Company, 1915.

Two roads diverged in a yellow wood,
And sorry I could not travel both
And be one traveler, long I stood
And looked down one as far as I could
To where it bent in the undergrowth;   5

Then took the other, as just as fair,
And having perhaps the better claim,
Because it was grassy and wanted wear;
Though as for that the passing there
Had worn them really about the same,   10

And both that morning equally lay
In leaves no step had trodden black.
Oh, I kept the first for another day!
Yet knowing how way leads on to way,
I doubted if I should ever come back.   15

I shall be telling this with a sigh
Somewhere ages and ages hence:
Two roads diverged in a wood, and I—
I took the one less traveled by,
And that has made all the difference.   20

Birches

Robert Frost
1916

Collected in Frost's third collection of poetry *Mountain Interval*, 1916.

When I see birches[1] bend to left and right
Across the lines of straighter darker trees,
I like to think some boy's been swinging them.
But swinging doesn't bend them down to stay
As ice-storms do. Often you must have seen them   5
Loaded with ice a sunny winter morning
After a rain. They click upon themselves
As the breeze rises, and turn many-colored
As the stir cracks and crazes their enamel.[2]
Soon the sun's warmth makes them shed crystal shells   10
Shattering and avalanching on the snow-crust—
Such heaps of broken glass to sweep away
You'd think the inner dome of heaven had fallen.
They are dragged to the withered bracken[3] by the load,
And they seem not to break; though once they are bowed
So low for long, they never right themselves:
You may see their trunks arching in the woods
Years afterwards, trailing their leaves on the ground
Like girls on hands and knees that throw their hair
Before them over their heads to dry in the sun.   20
But I was going to say when Truth broke in
With all her matter-of-fact about the ice-storm
I should prefer to have some boy bend them
As he went out and in to fetch the cows—
Some boy too far from town to learn baseball,   25
Whose only play was what he found himself,
Summer or winter, and could play alone.
One by one he subdued[4] his father's trees
By riding them down over and over again
Until he took the stiffness out of them,   30
And not one but hung limp, not one was left
For him to conquer. He learned all there was
To learn about not launching out too soon
And so not carrying the tree away
Clear to the ground. He always kept his poise   35
To the top branches, climbing carefully
With the same pains you use to fill a cup

---

[1] birches: 1) a slender, fast-growing tree that has thin bark (often peeling) and bears catkins. Birch trees grow chiefly in north temperate regions, some reaching the northern limit of tree growth, 2) historically, a formal punishment in which a person is flogged with a bundle of birch twigs

[2] enamel: an opaque or semitransparent glassy substance applied to metallic or other hard surfaces for ornament or as a protective coating

[3] bracken: a tall fern with coarse lobed fronds that occurs worldwide and can cover large areas

[4] subdued: overcome, quieten, or bring under control

Up to the brim, and even above the brim.
Then he flung outward, feet first, with a swish,
Kicking his way down through the air to the ground.   40
So was I once myself a swinger of birches.
And so I dream of going back to be.
It's when I'm weary of considerations,
And life is too much like a pathless wood
Where your face burns and tickles with the cobwebs   45
Broken across it, and one eye is weeping
From a twig's having lashed across it open.
I'd like to get away from earth awhile
And then come back to it and begin over.
May no fate willfully misunderstand me   50
And half grant what I wish and snatch me away
Not to return. Earth's the right place for love:
I don't know where it's likely to go better.
I'd like to go by climbing a birch tree,
And climb black branches up a snow-white trunk   55
Toward heaven, till the tree could bear no more,
But dipped its top and set me down again.
That would be good both going and coming back.
One could do worse than be a swinger of birches.

DRAMA

Prometheus Bound

Aeschylus
c. 525 BCE

Translation by Ian Johnston, 2012

Vancouver Island University, Nanaimo, BC, Canada. Nearly all footnotes are by the translator (often with the help of F. A. Paley's commentary on the play).

Background Note

Aeschylus (c.525 BC to c.456 BC) was one of the three great Greek tragic dramatists whose works have survived. Of his many plays, seven still remain. Aeschylus may have fought against the Persians at Marathon (490 BC), and he did so again at Salamis (480 BC). According to tradition, he died from being hit with a tortoise dropped by an eagle. After his death, the Athenians, as a mark of respect, permitted his works to be restaged in their annual competitions.

Prometheus Bound was apparently the first play in a trilogy (the other two plays, now lost except for some fragments, were *Prometheus Unbound* and *Prometheus the Fire-Bringer*). Although a number of modern scholars have questioned whether Aeschylus was truly the author of the play, it has always been included among his works.

In Greek mythology, Prometheus was a Titan, a descendant of the original gods, Gaia and Ouranos (Earth and Heaven). The Titans were defeated in a battle with Zeus, who fought against his own father, Cronos, imprisoned him deep in the earth, and became the new ruling power in heaven. Although he was a Titan, Prometheus assisted Zeus in this conflict, but later offended him by stealing fire from heaven and giving it to human beings, for whom he had a special affection. Aeschylus' play begins after Zeus has assumed control of heaven and learned about the theft.

Dramatis Personae

POWER	divine agent of Zeus
FORCE	divine agent of Zeus
HEPHAESTUS	divine son of Zeus, the artisan god, also a metalsmith
PROMETHEUS	a Titan
CHORUS	daughters of Oceanus[1]
OCEANUS	a god of the sea
IO	daughter of Inachus
HERMES	divine son of Zeus

Power & Hephaestus

[In a remote mountainous region of Scythia.[2] HEPHAESTUS enters with POWER and FORCE dragging PROMETHEUS with them in chains.]

POWER   We have just reached the land of Scythia,
at the most distant limits of the world,
remote and inaccessible. Hephaestus,
now it is your duty to carry out
those orders you received from Father Zeus—   5
to nail this troublemaker firmly down
against these high, steep cliffs, shackling him
in adamantine chains that will not break.[3]
For he in secret stole your pride and joy
and handed it to men—the sacred fire   10

---

[1] All choral speeches and chants are assigned to the character named CHORUS. However, depending on the context, some of these will be spoken by the Chorus Leader, some by the full Chorus, and some by selected members of the Chorus.

[2] Scythia: a reference to an ancient tribe of horsemen, who inhabited the vast plains of southeast Europe and northeast of Greece. The mountainous region is likely the Caucasus Mountains.

[3] Since Hephaestus is god of the forge and the craftsman god (especially with metals), it is part of his work to make sure that the chains and rivets holding Prometheus to the rock are securely fixed. Hephaestus was a son of Zeus and one of the new Olympian gods, who supplanted the Titans.

which fosters all the arts. For such a crime,
he must pay retribution to the gods,
so he will learn to bear the rule of Zeus
and end that love he has for humankind.

HEPHAESTUS   Power and Force, where you two are concerned,
what Zeus commanded us has now been done.
There are no further obstacles to face.
I am not bold enough to use sheer force
against a kindred god and nail him down
here on this freezing rock. But nonetheless,   20
I must steel myself to finish off our work,
for it is dangerous to disregard
the words of Father Zeus.

[HEPHAESTUS addresses PROMETHEUS]

                              High-minded son
of our wise counsellor, goddess Themis,
against my will and yours, I must bind you   25
with chains of brass which no one can remove
on this cliff face, far from all mortal men,
where you will never hear a human voice
or glimpse a human shape and sun's hot rays
will scorch and age your youthful flesh.[4] For you,   30
the sparkling stars high in the sky at night
will hide those rays and offer some relief.
Then, in the morning, once again the sun
will melt the frost. This never-ending burden
of your present agony will wear you down,   35
for the one who is to rescue you someday
is not yet even born. This is your reward
for acting as a friend to human beings.
Though you are a god, you were not deterred
by any fear of angering the gods.   40
You gave men honours they did not deserve,
possessions they were not entitled to.
Because of that, you will remain on guard,
here on this joyless rock, standing upright
with your legs straight, and you will never sleep.   45
You will often scream in pain and sorrow,
for Zeus' heart is pitilessly harsh,
and everyone whose ruling power is new
is cruel and ruthless.

POWER   Come on. Why wait
and mope around like this so uselessly?   50
Why do you not despise this deity
who is so hateful to the other gods?
He gave your special gift to mortal men.

HEPHAESTUS   We are comrades—we share strong common bonds.[5]

POWER   That may be true, but can you disobey   55
your father's words? Do you not fear him more?

---

[4] Themis, a Titan, was goddess of order, law, traditions, and divine justice. In other accounts, Prometheus is the son of Clymene.

[5] The common bond they share is not a particularly close family link. Prometheus was a Titan and Hephaestus was a son of Zeus. The words may perhaps refer to the fact that both Hephaestus and Prometheus were well known for their inventive minds and thus perhaps shared an appreciation for each other's characters and talents.

HEPHAESTUS   Ah yes! You always lack a sense of pity
  and are so full of cruel self-confidence.

POWER   There is no point in wailing a lament
  for this one here. You should stop wasting time   60
  on things that bring no benefits to you.

HEPHAESTUS   How much I hate the special work I do!

POWER   Why hate it? It's clear enough your artistry
  had nothing at all to do with causing
  what we are facing here.

HEPHAESTUS   That may be true,   65
  but still I wish my lot as artisan
  had gone to someone else.

POWER   Well, every task
  is burdensome, except to rule the gods.
  No one is truly free except for Zeus.

HEPHAESTUS   I know. This work is proof enough of that.   70
  I cannot deny it.

POWER   Then hurry up
  and get these chains around him, just in case
  Zeus sees you stalling.

HEPHAESTUS   All right. These shackles here
  are ready. Take a look.

[Hephaestus starts chaining Prometheus' arm to the cliff]

POWER   Bind his hands.
  Use some heavy hammer blows and rivet him   75
  against the rock.

HEPHAESTUS   There! This part is finished.
  It looks all right.

POWER   Strike harder. Make sure
  he is securely fixed, with nothing slack.
  He is an expert at devising ways
  to wriggle out of hopeless situations.   80

HEPHAESTUS   Well, this arm, at least, is firmly nailed here.
  No one will get this out.

POWER   Now drive a spike
  in here as well—make sure it won't come loose.
  No matter how intelligent he is,
  he has to learn he is nothing but a fool   85
  compared to Zeus.

HEPHAESTUS   No one could justly fault
  this work I do, except for him.

POWER   Now smash
  the blunt tip of this adamantine wedge
  straight through his chest—use all your force.

HEPHAESTUS   Alas!
  O Prometheus, this suffering of yours—   90
  how it makes me weep![6]

POWER   Why are you so slow
  and sighing over Zeus' enemy?
  Be careful, or soon you may be groaning
  for yourself.

---

[6] As a Titan, Prometheus is immortal. Hence, the metal piercing his chest will not kill him.

HEPHAESTUS   This sight is difficult to watch,
    as you can see.

POWER   I see this criminals   95
    is getting just what he deserves. Come on,
    wrap these chains around his ribs.

HEPHAESTUS   Look, I know
    I have to carry out this work, so stop
    ordering me about so much.

POWER   Hold on—
    I'll give you orders as often as I please   100
    and keep on badgering you. Move down,
    and use your strength to fix his legs in place.

HEPHAESTUS   Our work is done. That did not take too long.

POWER   Hit the fetters really hard—those ones there,
    around his feet. The one who's watching us,   105
    inspecting what we do, can turn vicious.

HEPHAESTUS   The words you speak well match the way you look.

POWER   Well, your soft heart can sympathize with him,
    but do not criticize my stubborn will
    and my harsh temper.

HEPHAESTUS   We should be going.   110
    His limbs are all securely fixed in place.

[Exit Hephaestus]

POWER   *[To Prometheus]* Now you can flaunt your arrogance up here,
    by stealing honours given to the gods
    and offering them to creatures of a day.
    Are mortal beings strong enough to ease   115
    the burden of your pain? The gods were wrong
    to give that name 'Prometheus' to you,
    'someone who thinks ahead,' for now you need
    a real Prometheus to help you out
    and find a way to free you from these chains.[7]   120

[Exit Power and Force]

PROMETHEUS   O you heavenly skies and swift-winged winds,
    you river springs, you countless smiling waves
    on ocean seas, and Earth, you mother of all,
    and you as well, the all-seeing circle
    of the celestial sun—I summon you   125
    to see what I, a god, am suffering
    at the hands of gods. Look here and witness
    how I am being worn down with torments
    which I will undergo for countless years.
    This is the kind of shameful punishment   130
    the new ruler of the gods imposed on me.
    Alas! Alas! I groan under the pain
    of present torments and those yet to come.
    Who will deliver me from such harsh pain?
    From what part of the sky will he appear?   135
    And yet, why talk like this? For I possess
    a detailed knowledge of what lies in store
    before it happens—none of my tortures
    will come as a surprise. I must endure,
    as best I can, the fate I have been given,   140
    for I know well that no one can prevail

---

[7] The name Prometheus is a combination of two words which, when put together, mean forethought.

against the strength of harsh Necessity.
And yet it is not possible for me
to speak or not to speak about my fate.[8]
I have been compelled to bear the yoke   145
of punishment because I gave a gift
to mortal beings—I searched out and stole
the source of fire concealed in fennel stalks,
and that taught men the use of all the arts
and gave them ways to make amazing things.   150
Now chained and nailed beneath the open sky,
I am paying the price for what I did.
But wait! What noise and what invisible scent
is drifting over me? Is it divine
or human or both of these? Has someone   155
travelled to the very edges of the world
to watch my suffering. What do they want?

[Prometheus shouts out to whoever is watching him]

Here I am, an ill-fated god! You see
an enemy of Zeus shackled in chains,
hated by all those gods who spend their time   160
in Zeus' court! They think my love for men
is too excessive! What is that sound I hear?
The whirling noise of birds nearby—the air
is rustling with their lightly beating wings!
Whatever comes too close alarms me.   165

Prometheus & the Chorus

[Enter the Chorus of nymphs, daughters of Oceanus, in a winged chariot, which hovers beside Prometheus][9]

CHORUS   You need not fear us. We are your friends.
The rapid beating of these eager wings
has borne our company to this sheer cliff.
We worked to get our father to agree,
and he did so, although that was not easy.   170
The swiftly moving breezes bore us on,
for the echoing clang of hammer blows
pierced right into the corners of our cave
and beat away my bashful modesty.
And so, without tying any sandals on,   175
I rushed here in this chariot with wings.

PROMETHEUS   Aaaiii! Alas! O you daughters
born from fertile Tethys, children
of your father Oceanus, whose current
circles the entire world and never rests,   180
look at me! See how I am chained here,
nailed on this cliff above a deep ravine,
where I maintain my dreary watch.[10]

CHORUS   I see that, Prometheus, and a cloud
of tears and terror moves across my eyes   185
to observe your body being worn away
in these outrageous adamantine chains.

---

[8] This thought would seem to mean that Prometheus cannot help protesting what has happened to him because it is inherently unjust, while at the same time he cannot speak because there is no point in protesting against Necessity—he knows that his words will have no effect on what he is fated to suffer.

[9] The Chorus remains in the chariot until asked to alight by Prometheus.

[10] Oceanus and Tethys, who are brother and sister, are children of the original gods Gaia and Ouranos. They are both gods of the sea.

New gods now rule on Mount Olympus,
and, like a tyrant, Zeus is governing
with new-fangled laws, overpowering   190
those gods who were so strong before.

PROMETHEUS   If only he had thrown me underground,
down there in Hades, which receives the dead,
in Tartarus, through which no one can pass,
and cruelly bound me there in fetters   195
no one could break, so that none of the gods
or anyone else could gloat at my distress.
But now the blowing winds toy with me here,
and the pain I feel delights my enemies.

CHORUS   What god is so hard hearted he would find   200
this scene enjoyable? Who would not feel
compassion for these sufferings of yours,
apart from Zeus, who, in his angry mood,
has set his rigid mind inflexibly
on conquering the race of Ouranos.   205
And he will never stop until his heart
is fully satisfied or someone else
overthrows his power by trickery,
hard as that may be, and rules instead.

PROMETHEUS   Yes, and even though I am being tortured,   210
bound in these strong chains, the day is coming
when that ruler of those sacred beings
will truly need me to reveal to him
a new intrigue by which he will be stripped
of all his honours and his sceptre, too.[11]   215
He will not charm that secret out of me
with sweet honeyed phrases of persuasion,
nor, for all his savage threats, will I ever
cringe down in front of him and let him know
the answer—no!—not until he frees me   220
from these cruel shackles and is willing
to pay me compensation for his crime!

CHORUS   With that audacious confidence of yours,
you do not cower before these bitter pains,
but you allow your tongue to speak too freely.   225
A piercing fear knifes through my heart,
my dread about your fate, how you must
steer your ship to find safe haven
and see an end to all your troubles.
For the son of Cronos has a heart   230
that is inflexible—his character
will not be moved by prayer.

PROMETHEUS   Yes, I know.
Zeus is a harsh god and holds the reins
of justice in his hands. But nonetheless,
I can see the day approaching when his mind   235
will soften, once that secret I described
has led to his collapse. Then he will abate
his stubborn rage and enter eagerly
into a bond of friendship with me.
By then I will be eager for that, too.   240

---

[11] The 'plot' mentioned here and later was the secret knowledge Prometheus had of the prophecy that the nymph Thetis would give birth to a son greater than his father. Zeus was ignorant of this secret and would put his rule in danger by pursuing a sexual liaison with Thetis.

CHORUS   Tell us the whole story of what happened.
How did Zeus have you seized and on what charge?
Why does he so shamefully abuse you
in this painful way? Give us the details,
unless you would be harmed by telling us.   245

PROMETHEUS   I find these matters truly unbearable
to talk about, but remaining silent
pains me, too. The events that led to this
are all so miserably unfortunate.
When the powers in heaven got angry,   250
they started quarrelling amongst themselves.
Some wanted to hurl Cronos from his throne,
so Zeus could rule instead, but then others
wanted the reverse—to ensure that Zeus
would never rule the gods. I tried my best   255
to give them good advice, but I could not
convince the Titans, offspring of the Earth
and Heaven, who, despising trickery,
insisted stubbornly they would prevail
without much effort, by using force.   260
Both mother Themis and the goddess Earth
(who has a single form but many names)
had often uttered prophecies to me
about how Fate would make events unfold,
how those who would seize power and control   265
would need, not brutal might and violence,
but sly deception. I went through all this,
but they were not concerned—they thought
everything I said a waste of time.
So then, when I considered what to do,   270
the wisest course of action seemed to be
to join my mother and take Zeus' side.
I did so eagerly, and he was keen
to have me with him. Thanks to my advice,
the gloomy pit of Tartarus now hides   275
old Cronos and his allies.[12] I helped Zeus,
that tyrant of the gods—now he repays me
with this foul torment. It is a sickness
which somehow comes with every tyranny
to place no trust in friends. But you asked   280
why Zeus is torturing me like this.
I will explain. As soon as he was seated
on his father's throne, he quickly set about
assigning gods their various honours
and organizing how he meant to rule.   285
But for those sad wretched human beings,
he showed no concern at all. He wanted
to wipe out the entire race and grow
a new one in its place. None of the gods
objected to his plan except for me.   290
I was the only one who had the courage.
So I saved those creatures from destruction
and a trip to Hades. And that is why
I have been shackled here and have to bear
such agonizing pain, so pitiful to see.   295
I set compassion for the human race

---

[12] Since Cronos and the Titans were immortals, they could not be killed. Tartarus was the deepest pit in
the Underworld.

above the way I felt about myself,
so now I am unworthy of compassion.
This is how he seeks to discipline me,
without a shred of mercy—the spectacle   300
disgraces Zeus' name.

CHORUS   But anyone
who shows no pity for your agonies,
Prometheus, has a heart of iron
and is made out of rock. As for myself,
I had no wish to see them, and now I have,   305
my heart is full of grief.

PROMETHEUS   Yes, to my friends
I make a most distressing sight.

CHORUS   Was there more?
Or were you guilty of just one offence?

PROMETHEUS   I stopped men thinking of their future deaths.

CHORUS   What cure for this disease did you discover?   310

PROMETHEUS   Inside their hearts I put blind hope.

CHORUS   With that
you gave great benefits to humankind.

PROMETHEUS   And in addition to hope, I gave them fire.

CHORUS   You did that for those creatures of a day?
Do they have fire now?

PROMETHEUS   They do. And with it   315
they will soon master many arts.

CHORUS   So Zeus
charged you with this . . .

PROMETHEUS   [interrupting] . . . and he torments me
and gives me no relief from suffering!

CHORUS   And has no time been set when your ordeal
comes to an end?

PROMETHEUS   No. None at all,   320
except when it seems suitable to Zeus.

CHORUS   How will he ever think it suitable?
What hope is there in that? Do you not see
where you went wrong? But I do not enjoy
discussing those mistakes you made, and you   325
must find it painful. Let us leave that point,
so in this anguish you find some release.

PROMETHEUS   It is easy for someone whose foot remains
unsnared by suffering to give advice
and criticize another in distress.   330
I was well aware of all these matters,
and those mistakes I made quite willingly—
I freely chose to do the things I did.
I will not deny that. By offering help
to mortal beings I brought on myself   335
this suffering. But still, I did not think
I would receive this kind of punishment,
wasting away on these high rocky cliffs,
fixed on this remote and desolate crag.
But do not mourn the troubles I now face.   340
Step down from your chariot and listen
to those misfortunes I must still confront,
so you will learn the details of my story
from start to finish. Accept my offer.

Agree to hear me out, and share with me   345
the pain I feel right now. For misery,
shifting around from place to place, settles
on different people at different times.

CHORUS   *[leaving the chariot]*
Your request does not fall on deaf ears,
Prometheus. My lightly stepping foot   350
has moved down from the swift-winged chariot
and sacred air, the pathway of the birds,
to walk along this rugged rock towards you.
I want to hear your tale, a full account
of all your suffering.

Oceanus

[Enter OCEANUS on a flying monster]

OCEANUS   I have now reached   355
the end of my long journey, travelling
to visit you, Prometheus, on the wings
of this swift beast, and using my own mind
instead of any reins to guide it here.
You know I feel great sympathy for you   360
and for your suffering. It seems to me
our ties of kinship make me feel that way.
But even if there were no family bonds,
no one wins more respect from me than you.
You will soon realize I speak the truth   365
and do not simply prattle empty words.
So come, show me how I can be of help,
for you will never say you have a friend
more loyal to you than Oceanus.

PROMETHEUS   What is this? What am I looking at?   370
Have you, too, travelled here to gaze upon
my agonies? How were you brave enough
to leave that flowing stream which shares your name
and those rock arches of the cave you made,
to journey to this land, the womb of iron?[13]   375
Or have you come to see how I am doing,
to sympathize with me in my distress?
Behold this spectacle—a friend of Zeus,
who helped him win his way to sovereignty!
See how his torments weigh me down!

OCEANUS   I see that,   380
Prometheus, and although you do possess
a subtle mind, I would like to offer you
some good advice. You have to understand
your character and adopt new habits.
For even gods have a new ruler now.   385
If you keep hurling out offensive words,
with such insulting and abusive language,
Zeus may well hear you, even though his throne
is far away, high in the heavenly sky,
and then this present heap of anguished pain   390
will seem mere childish play. Instead of that,
you poor suffering creature, set aside
this angry mood of yours and seek relief

---

[13] The Ocean, a river flowing around the world, has the same name as Oceanus, who lives in a cave in the sea. Scythia was famous for its rich iron deposits.

from all this misery. These words of mine
may seem to you perhaps too old and trite,   395
but this is what you get, Prometheus,
for having such a proud and boastful tongue.
You show no modesty in what you say
and will not bow down before misfortune,
for you prefer to add more punishments   400
to those you have already. You should hear me
as your teacher and stop this kicking out
against the whip. You know our present king,
who rules all by himself and has no one
he must answer to, is harsh. I will go   405
and, if I can, attempt to ease your pain.
You must stay quiet—do not keep shouting
such intemperate things. Do you not know,
with all that shrewd intelligence of yours,
your thoughtless tongue can get you punished?   410

PROMETHEUS   I am happy things turned out so well for you.
You had the courage to support my cause,
but you escaped all blame.[14] Now let me be,
and do not make my suffering your concern.
Whatever you may say will be in vain—   415
persuading Zeus is not an easy task.
You should take care this journey you have made
does not get you in trouble.

OCEANUS   Your nature
makes you far better at giving good advice
to neighbours rather than yourself. I judge   420
by looking at the facts, not by listening
to what others say. You should not deter
a person who is eager to help out.
For I am sure—yes, I am confident—
there is one gift which Zeus will offer me,   425
and he will free you from this suffering.

PROMETHEUS   You have my thanks—and I will not forget.
There is in you no lack of willingness
to offer aid. But spare yourself the trouble,
which will be useless and no help to me,   430
if, in fact, you want to make the effort.
Just keep quiet, and do not interfere.
I may be miserable, but my distress
does not make me desire to see such pain
imposed on everyone—no, not at all.   435
What my brother Atlas has to suffer
hurts my heart. In some region to the west
he has to stand, bearing on his shoulders
the pillar of earth and heaven, a load
even his arms find difficult to carry.[15]   440
And I feel pity when I contemplate
the creature living in Cilician caves,
that fearful monster with a hundred heads,
born from the earth, impetuous Typhon,

---

[14] These lines strongly suggest that Oceanus supported Prometheus in his desire to save mankind and that Prometheus was not acting entirely alone.

[15] Paley notes that Aeschylus has here combined two visions of Atlas, one which has him looking after the pillars which separate heaven and earth and one which has Atlas himself holding heaven apart from earth. In either case, Atlas was suffering punishment for fighting against Zeus.

curbed by Zeus' force.[16] He held out against   445
the might of all the gods. His hideous jaws
produced a terrifying hiss, and his eyes
flashed a ferocious stare, as if his strength
could utterly destroy the rule of Zeus.
But Zeus' thunderbolt, which never sleeps,   450
that swooping, fire-breathing lightning stroke,
came down and drove the arrogant boasting
right out of him. Struck to his very heart,
he was reduced to ash, and all his might
was blasted away by rolls of thunder.   455
Now his helpless and immobile body
lies close beside a narrow ocean strait,
pinned down beneath the roots of Aetna,
while on that mountain, at the very top,
Hephaestus sits and forges red-hot iron.   460
But one day that mountain peak will blow out
rivers of fire, whose savage jaws devour
the level fruitful fields of Sicily.
Though Typhon may have been burned down to ash
by Zeus' lightning bolt, his seething rage   465
will then erupt and shoot out molten arrows,
belching horrifying streams of liquid fire.
But you are not without experience
and have no need of me to teach you this.
So save yourself the way you think is best,   470
and I will bear whatever I must face,
until the rage in Zeus' heart subsides.

OCEANUS   Surely you realize, Prometheus,
that in the case of a disordered mood
words act as healers.

PROMETHEUS   Yes, but only if   475
one uses them at the appropriate time
to soften up the heart and does not try
to calm its swollen rage too forcefully.

OCEANUS   What dangers do you see if someone blends
his courage and his eagerness to act?   480
Tell me that.

PROMETHEUS   Simple stupidity
and wasted effort.

OCEANUS   Well, let me fall ill
from this disease, for someone truly wise
profits most when he is thought a fool.

PROMETHEUS   But they will think that I made the mistake.   485

OCEANUS   Those words of yours are clearly telling me
to go back home.

PROMETHEUS   Yes, in case concern for me
gets you in serious trouble.

OCEANUS   You mean with Zeus,
now seated on his new all-powerful throne?

PROMETHEUS   Take care, in case one day that heart of his   490
vents its rage on you.

[16] Aeschylus places Typhon here in Cilicia, a region of Asia Minor and, a few lines further on, under Mount Aetna in Sicily. The anger of this monster buried underground evidently led people to locate him in areas of high volcanic activity and frequent earthquakes. There was a major eruption of Aetna in 479 BC.

OCEANUS   What you are suffering,
  Prometheus, will teach me that.
PROMETHEUS   Then go.
  Be on your way. Keep to your present plans.

OCEANUS   These words of yours are telling me to leave,
  and I am eager to depart. The wings   495
  on this four-footed beast will brush the air
  and make our pathway smooth. He will rejoice
  to rest his limbs back in his stall at home.

  [Exit OCEANUS]

Prometheus & the Chorus

CHORUS   I groan for your accursed fate,
  Prometheus, and floods of tears   500
  are streaming from my weeping eyes
  and moisture wets my tender cheeks.
  For Zeus, who rules by his own laws,
  has set your wretched destiny and shows
  towards the gods of earlier days   505
  an overweening sense of power.
  Now every region cries in one lament.
  They mourn the lost magnificence,
  so honoured long ago, the glorious fame
  you and your brothers once possessed.   510
  And all those mortal beings who live
  in sacred Asia sense your pain,
  those agonies all men find pitiful . . .
  . . . including those young girls who dwell
  in Colchis and have no fear of war,   515
  and Scythian hordes who occupy
  the furthest regions of the world
  along the shores of lake Maeotis . . .
  . . . and in Arabian lands the warlike tribes
  from those high rocky fortress towns   520
  in regions near the Caucasus,
  a horde of warriors who scream
  to heft their lethal sharpened spears.[17]
  Only once before have I beheld
  another Titan god in such distress   525
  bound up in adamantine chains—
  great Atlas, whose enormous strength
  was unsurpassed and who now groans
  to bear the vault of heaven on his back.
  The sea waves, as they fall, cry out,   530
  the ocean depths lament, while down below
  the deep black pits of Hades growl,
  and limpid flowing rivers moan,
  to see the dreadful pain you undergo.

PROMETHEUS   You must not think it is my stubbornness   535
  that keeps me quiet, or a sense of pride,
  for bitter thoughts keep gnawing at my heart
  to see how foully I am being abused.
  And yet who else but I assigned clear rights

---

[17] The word designating Arabian lands has been challenged, since the region in question (near the Caucasus) is nowhere near Arabia, as the Greeks knew very well.

and privileges to these new deities?[18]   540
But I make no complaint about such things,
for if I spoke, I would be telling you
what you already know. So listen now
to all the miseries of mortal men—
how they were simple fools in earlier days,   545
until I gave them sense and intellect.
I will not speak of them to criticize,
but in a spirit of goodwill to show
I did them many favours. First of all,
they noticed things, but did not really see   550
and listened, too, but did not really hear.
They spent their lives confusing everything,
like random shapes in dreams. They knew nothing
of brick-built houses turned towards the sun
or making things with wood. Instead, they dug   555
their dwelling places underneath the earth,
like airy ants in cracks of sunless caves.
They had no signs on which they could rely
to show when winter came or flowery spring
or fruitful summer. Everything they did   560
betrayed their total lack of understanding,
until I taught them all about the stars
and pointed out the way they rise and set,
which is not something easy to discern.
Then I invented arithmetic for them,   565
the most ingenious acquired skill,
and joining letters to write down words,
so they could store all things in Memory,
the working mother of the Muses' arts.[19]
I was the first to set wild animals   570
beneath the yoke, and I made them submit
to collars and to packs, so mortal men
would find relief from bearing heavy loads.
I took horses trained to obey the reins
and harnessed them to chariots, a sign   575
of luxurious wealth and opulence.
And I was the one who designed their ships,
those mariners' vessels which sail on wings
across the open sea. Yes, those are the things
which I produced for mortal men, and yet,   580
as I now suffer here, I cannot find
a way to free myself from this distress.

CHORUS   You have had to bear appalling pain.
  You lost your wits and now are at a loss.
  Like some bad doctor who has fallen ill,   585
  you are now desperate and cannot find
  the medicine to cure your own disease.

PROMETHEUS   Just listen to what else I have to say,
  and you will be astonished even more
  by the ideas and skills I came up with.   590
  The greatest one was this: if anyone
  was sick, they had no remedies at all,

---

[18] Prometheus is presumably referring here to advice he gave Zeus about how to assign each god his or her appropriate privileges (since he never had sufficient power to organize the gods, as he is claiming here, all on his own), although he may also simply be overstating his own case.

[19] The nine Muses, the patron deities of the arts and sciences, were the daughters of Mnemosyne, goddess of memory.

no healing potions, food, or liniments.
Without such things, they simply withered up.
But then I showed them how to mix mild cures,   595
which they now use to fight off all disease.
I set up many forms of prophecy
and was the first to organize their dreams,
to say which ones were fated to come true.
I taught them about omens—vocal sounds   600
hard to understand, as well as random signs
encountered on the road. The flights of birds
with crooked talons I classified for them—
both those which by their nature are auspicious
and those whose prophecies are ominous—   605
observing each bird's different way of life,
its enemies, its friends, and its companions,
as well as the smooth texture of its entrails,
what colour the gall bladder ought to have
to please the gods, and the best symmetry   610
for speckled lobes on livers.[20] I roasted
thigh bones wrapped in fat and massive cuts of meat
and showed those mortal beings the right way
to read the omens which are hard to trace.
I opened up their eyes to fiery symbols   615
which previously they could not understand.
Yes, I did all that. And then I helped them
with what lay hidden in the earth—copper,
iron, silver, gold. Who could ever claim
he had discovered these before I did?   620
No one. I am quite confident of that,
unless he wished to waste his time in chat.
To sum up everything in one brief word,
know this—all the artistic skills men have
come from Prometheus.

CHORUS   But you should not   625
be giving help like that to human beings
beyond the proper limits, ignoring
your own troubles, for I have every hope
you will be liberated from these chains
and be as powerful as Zeus himself.   630

PROMETHEUS   It is not destined that almighty Fate
will ever end these matters in that way.
I will lose these chains, but only after
I have been left twisting here in agony,
bowed down by countless pains. Artistic skill   635
has far less strength than sheer Necessity.

CHORUS   Then who is the one who steers Necessity?

PROMETHEUS   The three-formed Fates and unforgetting Furies.[21]

CHORUS   Are they more powerful than Zeus?

---

[20] The prophetic significance of large birds of prey, especially eagles, depended upon where they appeared in the sky, the pattern of their flight, and the condition of their entrails. The appearance of the bird's liver was important—a missing or deformed lobe was a very inauspicious omen.

[21] Traditionally there were three Fates (Clotho, Lachesis, and Atropos) and three Furies (Alecto, Tissiphone, and Megaera), although the number does vary. The Fates determined the length of one's life in advance, and the Furies were the goddesses of revenge, especially blood revenge within the family. The relationship between the Olympian gods and Fate was often very ambiguous, as it is here, for Prometheus does not answer directly the Chorus' question about who finally has the most power.

PROMETHEUS   Well, Zeus
  will not at any rate escape his destiny.   640
CHORUS   But what has destiny foretold for Zeus,
  except to rule eternally?
PROMETHEUS   That point
  you must not know quite yet. Do not pursue it.
CHORUS   It is some holy secret you conceal.
PROMETHEUS   Think of something else. It is not yet time   645
  to talk of this. The matter must remain
  completely hidden, for if I can keep
  the secret safe, then I shall be released
  from torment and lose these shameful fetters.

CHORUS   May Zeus, who governs everything,   650
  never direct his power at me
  and fight against my purposes.
  And may I never ease my efforts
  to approach the gods with offerings
  of oxen slain in sacrifice   655
  beside my father's restless stream,
  the ceaseless flow of Oceanus.
  May I not speak a profane word.
  Instead let this resolve remain
  and never melt away from me.   660
  It is sweet to spend a lengthy life
  with hope about what lies in store,
  feeding one's heart with happy thoughts.
  But when I look at you, Prometheus,
  tormented by these countless pains,   665
  I shiver in fear—with your self-will
  you show no reverence for Zeus
  and honour mortal beings too much.
  Come, my friend, those gifts you gave—
  what gifts did you get in return?   670
  Tell me how they could offer help?
  What can such creatures of a day provide?
  Do you not see how weak they are,
  the impotent and dream-like state,
  in which the sightless human race   675
  is bound, with chains around their feet?
  Whatever mortal beings decide to do,
  they cannot overstep what Zeus has planned.
  I learned these things, Prometheus,
  by watching your destructive fate.   680
  The song which now steals over me
  is different from that nuptial chant
  I sang around your couch and bath
  to celebrate your wedding day,
  when with your dowry gifts you won   685
  Hesione, my sister, as your wife,
  and led her to your bridal bed.

Io

[Enter IO]²²

    IO   What land is this? What race of living beings?
    Who shall I say I see here bound in chains,
    exposed and suffering on these cold rocks?   690
    What crime has led to such a punishment
    and your destruction? Tell me where I am.
    Where has my wretched wandering brought me?
    To what part of the world?

[Io is suddenly in great pain]

                    Aaaaiiii! The pain!!!
    That gadfly stings me once again, the ghost   695
    of earth-born Argus! Get him away from me,
    O Earth, that herdsman with a thousand eyes—
    the very sight of him fills me with terror!
    Those crafty eyes of his keep following me.
    Though dead, he is not hidden underground,   700
    but moves out from the shades beneath the earth
    and hunts me down and, in my wretched state,
    drives me to wander without nourishment
    along the sandy shore beside the sea.
    A pipe made out of reeds and wax sings out   705
    a clear relaxing strain.²³ Alas for me!
    Where is this path of roaming far and wide
    now leading me? What did I ever do,
    O son of Cronos, how did I go wrong,
    that you should yoke me to such agonies . . .   710

[Io reacts to another attack]

    Aaaaiii!! . . . and by oppressing me like this,
    setting a fearful stinging fly to chase
    a helpless girl, drive me to this madness?
    Burn me with fire, or bury me in earth,
    or feed me to the monsters of the sea.   715
    Do not refuse these prayers of mine, my lord!
    I have had my fill of all this wandering,
    this roaming far and wide—and all this pain!
    I do not know how to escape the pain!
    Do you not hear the ox-horned maiden call?   720

    PROMETHEUS   How could I not hear that young girl's voice,
    the child of Inachus, in a frantic state
    from the gadfly's sting? She fires Zeus' heart
    with sexual lust, and now, worn down
    by Hera's hate, is forced to roam around   725
    on paths that never end.

---

²² Io was a nymph, daughter of the river god Inachus. Zeus had sexual designs on her, but had to transform her into a heifer, in order to conceal the girl from his wife, Hera. Hera was suspicious of the cow and made Zeus give it to her as a gift. She then set the monster Argus, who had hundreds of eyes, could see in all directions, and was always watchful, to act as a herdsman and guard Io. However, Hermes, acting on instructions from Zeus, killed Argus by lulling all the eyes to sleep at once. Hera punished Io by sending a stinging gadfly to torment the transformed girl, as she wandered around the world. At this point in her story Io has been transformed. It is not clear how she would have been presented on stage as a heifer, although line 828 below indicates that she has visible horns (unless her torment is all a hallucination).

²³ This rather odd detail may refer to the shepherd's pipe with which Hermes lulled Argus to sleep, just before he killed him. It is not clear whether Io is hallucinating the sound or whether the ghost of Argus (which may or may not appear) is accompanied by music.

IO   Why do you shout
  my father's name? Tell this unhappy girl
  just who you are, you wretched sufferer,
  and how, in my distress, you call to me,
  knowing who I am and naming my disease,   730
  the heaven-sent sickness which consumes me
  as it whips my skin with maddening stings . . .

*[Io is attacked again by the gadfly. She moves spasmodically as she wrestles with the
pain]*

  . . . Aaaiii! . . . I have come rushing here, wracked
  with driving pangs of hunger, overwhelmed
  by Hera's plans for her revenge. Of those   735
  who are in misery . . . Aaaiii! . . . which ones
  go through the sufferings I face? Give me
  some clear sign how much more agony
  I have to bear! Is there no remedy?
  Tell me the medicines for this disease,   740
  if you know any. Say something to me!
  Speak to a wretched wandering young girl!

PROMETHEUS   I will clarify for you all those things
  you wish to know—not by weaving riddles,
  but by using simple speech. For with friends   745
  our mouths should tell the truth quite openly.
  You are looking at the one who offered men
  the gift of fire. I am Prometheus.

IO   O you who have shown to mortal beings
  so many benefits they all can share,   750
  poor suffering Prometheus! What act
  has led you to be punished in this way?

PROMETHEUS   I have just finished mourning my own pain.

IO   Will you not grant this favour to me, then?

PROMETHEUS   Ask what you wish to know.   755
  For you will learn the details of it all from me.

IO   Tell me who chained you here against this rocky cleft.

PROMETHEUS   The will of Zeus and Hephaestus' hands.

IO   For what offence are you being punished?

PROMETHEUS   I have said enough. I will not tell you   760
  any more than that.

IO   But I need more.
  At least inform me when my wandering ends.
  How long will I be in this wretched state?

PROMETHEUS
  For you it would be better not to know
  than to have me answer.

IO   I'm begging you—   765
  do not conceal from me what I must bear.

PROMETHEUS   It is not that I begrudge that gift to you.

IO   Then why do you appear so hesitant
  to tell me everything?

PROMETHEUS   I am not unwilling,
  but I do not wish to break your spirit.   770

IO   Do not be more concerned for how I feel
  than I wish you to be.

PROMETHEUS   Since you insist,
  I am obliged to speak. So listen to me.

CHORUS   No, not yet. Give us a share in this, as well,
    so we may be content with what you say.   775
    We should first learn how she became diseased.
    So let the girl herself explain to us
    the things that led to her destructive fate.
    Then you can teach her what still lies in store.

PROMETHEUS   Well then, Io, it is now up to you   780
    to grace them with this favour—above all,
    because they are your father's sisters.[24]
    And whenever one is likely to draw tears
    from those who listen, it is well worthwhile
    to weep aloud, lamenting one's own fate.   785

IO   I do not know how I could now refuse you.
    From the plain tale I tell you will find out
    all things you wish to know, although to talk
    about the brutal storm sent by the gods,
    the cruel transformation of my shape,   790
    and where the trouble came from, as it swept
    down on a miserable wretch like me—
    that makes me feel ashamed. During the night
    visions were always strolling through my rooms
    calling me with smooth, seductive words: 795
    "You are a very fortunate young girl,
    so why remain a virgin all this time,
    when you could have the finest match of all?
    For Zeus, smitten by the shaft of passion,
    now burns for you and wishes to make love.   800
    My child, do not reject the bed of Zeus,
    but go to Lerna's fertile meadowlands,
    to your father's flocks and stalls of oxen,
    so Zeus' eyes can ease his fierce desire."
    Visions like that upset me every night,   805
    till I got brave enough to tell my father
    about what I was seeing in my dreams.
    He sent many messengers to Delphi
    and Dodona, to see if he could learn
    what he might do or say to please the gods.   810
    But his men all came back bringing reports
    of cryptic and confusing oracles,
    with wording difficult to comprehend.
    Inachus at last received a clear response,
    a simple order which he must obey—   815
    to drive me from my home and native land,
    to turn me out and force me into exile,
    roaming the remotest regions of the earth—
    and if he was unwilling, Zeus would send
    a flaming thunderbolt which would destroy   820
    his entire race, not leaving one alive.
    So he obeyed Apollo's oracles
    by forcing me away against my will
    and denying me entry to his home.
    He did not want to do it but was forced   825
    by the controlling majesty of Zeus.
    Immediately my mind and shape were changed.
    My head acquired these horns, as you can see,
    and a vicious fly began tormenting me
    with such ferocious stings I ran away,   830

---

[24] Inachus, the father of Io, was a son of Oceanus, the father of the Chorus members.

madly bounding off to the flowing stream
of sweet Cherchneia and then to Lerna's springs.
But the herdsman Argus, a child of Earth,
whose rage is violent, came after me,
with all those close-packed eyes of his, searching   835
for my tracks. But an unexpected fate
which no one could foresee robbed him of his life.
And now, tormented by this stinging gadfly,
a scourge from god, I am being driven
from place to place. So now you understand   840
the story of what I have had to suffer.
If you can talk about my future troubles,
then let me know. But do not pity me
and speak false words of reassurance,
for, in my view, to use deceitful speech   845
is the most shameful sickness of them all.

CHORUS   Alas, alas! Tell me no more! Alas!
    I never, never thought my ears
    would hear a story strange as this
    or suffering so hard to contemplate   850
    and terrible to bear, the outrage
    and the horror of that two-edged goad
    would pierce me to my soul. Alas!
    O Fate, Fate, how I shake with fear
    to see what has been done to Io.   855

PROMETHEUS   These cries and fears of yours are premature.
    Wait until you learn what lies in store for her.

CHORUS   Then speak, and tell us everything. The sick
    find solace when they clearly understand
    the pain they have to face before it comes.   860

PROMETHEUS   What you desired to learn about before
    you now have readily obtained from me,
    for you were eager first of all to hear
    Io herself tell you what she suffered.
    Now listen to what she has yet to face,   865
    the ordeals this girl must still experience
    at Hera's hands. You, too, child of Inachus,
    set what I have to say inside your heart,
    so you will find out how your roaming ends.
    First, turn from here towards the rising sun,   870
    then move across those lands as yet unploughed,
    and you will reach the Scythian nomads,
    who live in wicker dwellings which they raise
    on strong-wheeled wagons. These men possess
    far-shooting bows, so stay away from them.   875
    Keep moving on along the rocky shoreline
    beside the roaring sea, and pass their lands.
    The Chalybes, men who work with iron,
    live to your left.[25] You must beware of them,
    for they are wild and are not kind to strangers.   880
    Then you will reach the river Hubristes,
    correctly named for its great turbulence.
    Do not cross it, for that is dangerous,
    until you reach the Caucasus itself,
    the very highest of the mountains there,   885

---

[25] These directions indicate that Io is to wander eastward along the northern shore of the Euxine Sea (the Black Sea).

where the power of that flowing river
comes gushing from the slopes. Then cross those peaks,
which stretch up to the stars, and take the path
going south, until you reach the Amazons,
a tribe which hates all men. In days to come,   890
they will found settlements in Themiscyra,
beside the Thermodon, where the jagged rocks
of Salmydessus face the sea and offer
sailors and their ships a savage welcome.
They will be pleased to guide you on your way.   895
Next, you will reach the Cimmerian isthmus,
beside the narrow entrance to a lake.
You must be resolute and leave this place
and at Maeotis move across the stream,
a trip that will win you eternal fame   900
among all mortal men, for they will name
that place the Bosporus in praise of you.[26]
Once you leave behind the plains of Europe
you will arrive in Asian lands. And now,
does it not strike you that this tyrant god   905
is violent in everything he does?
Because this maiden was a mortal being
and he was eager to have sex with her,
he threw her out to wander the whole world.
Young girl, the one you found to seek your hand   910
is vicious. As for the story you just heard,
you should know this—I am not even past
the opening prelude.

IO   O no, no, no! Alas!

PROMETHEUS   Are you crying and moaning once again?
How will you act once you have learned from me   915
the agonies that still remain?

CHORUS   You mean
you have still more to say about her woes?

PROMETHEUS   I do—a wintry sea of dreadful pain.

IO   What point is there for me in living then?
Why do I not hurl myself this instant   920
from these rough rocks, fall to the plain below,
and put an end to all my misery?
I would prefer to die once and for all,
than suffer such afflictions every day.

PROMETHEUS   Then you would find it difficult to face   925
the torments I endure, for I am one
who cannot die, and death would offer me
relief from pain. But now no end is set
to tortures I must bear, until the day
when Zeus is toppled from his tyrant's throne.   930

IO   What's that? Will Zeus' power be overthrown?

PROMETHEUS   It seems to me that if that came about
you would be pleased.

---

26 The word Bosporus means the passing of the cow. The two major crossing points between Europe and
Asia Minor were the Hellespont, at the western end of the river flowing out of the Black Sea (near Troy),
and the Bosporus at the eastern end. Io will have moved back along the northern shore of the Black Sea
and across the river, thus leaving Europe and entering Asia Minor. Aeschylus' geography in these
descriptions of Io's route is not particularly reliable and in places appears confused.

IO   Why not? Because of him
  I suffer horribly.
PROMETHEUS   Then rest assured—
  these things are true.
IO   But who will strip away   935
  his tyrant's sceptre?
PROMETHEUS   He will do that himself
  with all those brainless purposes of his.
IO   But how? If it will do no harm, tell me.
PROMETHEUS   He will get married—a match he will regret.
IO   To someone mortal or divine? Tell me—   940
  if that is something you may talk about.
PROMETHEUS   Why ask me that? I cannot speak of it.
IO   His wife will force him from his throne?
PROMETHEUS   She will.
  For she will bear a child whose power
  is greater than his father's.
IO   Is there some way   945
  Zeus can avert this fate?
PROMETHEUS   No, none at all—
  except through me, once I lose these chains.
IO   Who will free you if Zeus does not consent?
PROMETHEUS   One of your grandchildren. So Fate decrees.
IO   What are you saying? Will a child of mine   950
  bring your afflictions to an end?
PROMETHEUS   He will—
  when thirteen generations have gone by.
IO   I find it difficult to understand
  what you foresee.
PROMETHEUS   You should not seek to know
  the details of the pain you still must bear.   955
IO   Do not say you will do me a favour
  and then withdraw it.
PROMETHEUS   I will offer you
  two possibilities, and you may choose.
IO   What are they? Tell me what the choices are.
  Then let me pick which one.
PROMETHEUS   All right, I will.   960
  Choose whether I should clarify for you
  the ordeals you still must face in days to come,
  or else reveal the one who will release me.
CHORUS   Do her a favour by disclosing one
  and me by telling us about the other.   965
  Do not refuse to tell us all the story.
  Describe her future wanderings to her,
  and speak to me of who will set you free.
  I long to hear that.
PROMETHEUS   Well, since you insist,
  I will not refuse to tell you everything   970
  you wish to know. First, Io, I will speak
  about the grievous wandering you face.
  Inscribe this on the tablets of your mind,
  deep in your memory. Once you have crossed
  the stream that separates two continents,   975

[select the route that] leads towards the east,
the flaming pathway of the rising son,
[and you will come, at first, to northern lands
where cold winds blow, and here you must beware
of gusting storms, in case a winter blast   980
surprises you and snatches you away.][27]
Then cross the roaring sea until you reach
the Gorgons' plains of Cisthene, the home
of Phorcys' daughters, three ancient women
shaped like swans, who possess a single eye   985
and just one tooth to share among themselves.
Rays from the sun do not look down on them,
nor does the moon at night. Beside them live
their sisters, three snake-haired, winged Gorgons,
whom human beings despise. No mortal man   990
can gaze at them and still continue breathing.[28]
I tell you this to warn you to take care.
Now hear about another fearful sight.
Keep watching out for gryphons, hounds of Zeus,
who have sharp beaks and never bark out loud,   995
and for that one-eyed Arimaspian horde
on horseback, who live beside the flow
of Pluto's gold-rich stream.[29] Do not go near them.
And later you will reach a distant land
of people with dark skins who live beside   1000
the fountains of the sun, where you will find
the river Aethiop.[30] Follow its banks,
until you move down to the cataract
where from the Bybline mountains the sweet Nile
sends out his sacred flow. He will guide you   1005
on your journey to the three-cornered land
of Nilotis, where destiny proclaims
you, Io, and your children will set up
a distant settlement. If any of this
remains obscure and hard to understand,   1010
question me again, and I will tell you.
For I have more leisure time than I desire.

CHORUS   If you have left out any incidents
or can say more about what lies ahead
in Io's cruel journeying, go on.   1015
But if that story has now reached an end,
then favour us, in turn, with what we asked,
if you by chance remember our request.

---

[27] The stream separating the continents is the Bosporus. Prometheus resumes the narrative he ended at line 904 above. Some editors believe that part of the Greek is missing here. The passage between square bracket is a translation of Paley's suggested interpolation, which, he notes, comes from a passage which Galen quotes, stating that it is part of Prometheus Bound. The geography of Io's wandering is somewhat confused in this passage, but it seems to indicate that she will be going east, and then north and west.

[28] Phorcys was a god of the sea and the father of many monsters. The three daughters who shared a single eye were called the Graiae. The Gorgons were so terrible to look at they turned human beings to stone. Two of them were immortal, but the third, Medusa, was slain by Perseus, who used her severed head to kill his enemies.

[29] The gryphons were fabulous creatures with the bodies of lions and the heads and wings of eagles. The Arimaspians were a one-eyed race who lived far to the north in Scythia.

[30] Paley suggests as one possible route for Io's journey a trip from Scythia in the north to Spain (known for its gold-bearing rivers), from there across the narrow strait in southern Spain to north Africa, and onto Egypt. His suggestion is, however, tentative, for Aeschylus' geographical details are still very confusing.

PROMETHEUS Io has now heard about her travels,
    a full account up to the very end.   1020
    But so she learns that what she heard from me
    was no mere empty tale, I will go through
    the troubles she endured before she came here,
    and thus provide a certain guarantee
    of what I have just said. I will omit   1025
    most of the details and describe for you
    the final stages of your journey here.
    Once you came to the Molossian plains
    and the steep mountain ridge beside Dodona,
    the home of the prophetic oracle   1030
    of Thesprotian Zeus, that miracle
    which defies belief, the talking oak trees,
    clearly and quite unambiguously
    saluted you as one who would become
    a celebrated bride of Zeus.[31] Is this   1035
    a memory that gives you some delight?
    From there, chased by the gadfly's sting, you rushed
    along the path beside the sea and reached
    the mighty gulf of Rhea and from there
    were driven back by storms. And you should know   1040
    an inner region of that sea will now,
    in days to come, be called Ionian,
    a name to make all mortal men recall
    how Io moved across it.[32] These details
    are tokens of how much I understand—   1045
    they show how my intelligence can see
    more things than what has been revealed.
    The rest I will describe for you and her to share,
    pursuing the same track I traced before.
    On the very edges of the mainland,   1050
    where at its mouth the Nile deposits soil,
    there is a city—Canopus. There Zeus
    will finally restore you to your senses
    by merely stroking and caressing you
    with his non-threatening hand. After that,   1055
    you will give birth to dark-skinned Epaphus,
    named from the way he was conceived by Zeus,
    and he will harvest all the fruit that grows
    in regions watered by the flowing Nile.[33]
    Five generations after Epaphus,   1060
    fifty young girls will return to Argos,
    not of their own free will, but to escape
    a marriage with their cousins, while the men,
    with passionate hearts, race after them,
    like hawks in close pursuit of doves, seeking   1065
    marriages they should not rightfully pursue.[34]

---

[31] The rustling sounds made by the branches of the oak trees at Zeus' oracle in Dodona were interpreted by priestesses as prophetic utterances. The Thesprotians were the group who first controlled the oracle. The details here place this stage of Io's roaming in north-western Greece.

[32] The Ionian Sea is that part of the Mediterranean between the west coast of mainland Greece and southern Italy. These details suggest that after leaving Dodona and moving out into the Adriatic, Io turned back in her journey westward and was on her way back east when she met Prometheus.

[33] Epaphus come from the Greek word meaning touch. Zeus' miraculous stroking of Io restored her mind and made her pregnant.

[34] The girls are the daughters of Danaus (the Danaïds), who were to marry the fifty sons of Aegyptus, the brother of Danaus and king of Egypt. The marriages were incestuous.Hence, the flight to Argos. Danaus,

But the gods will not allow them to enjoy
the young girls' bodies. They will be buried
in Pelasgian earth, for their new brides
keeping watch at night, will overpower   1070
and kill them all, in a daring murder,
and each young bride will take her husband's life,
bathing a two-edged sword in her man's blood.
I hope my enemies find love like that!
But passion will bewitch one of those wives   1075
to spare her husband's life, and her resolve
will fade. She will prefer to hear herself
proclaimed a coward than the alternative,
a murderess. And she will then give birth
in Argos to a royal line. To describe   1080
all these events in detail would require
a lengthy story. However, from her seed
a bold man will be born, who will become
a famous archer, and he is the one
who will deliver me from these afflictions.   1085
My primeval Titan mother, Themis,
revealed this prophecy to me in full,
but to describe how and when it happens
would take up too much time. And learning that
would bring no benefit to you at all.   1090

IO   Alas, alas for me! These spasms of pain,
these agonizing fits which drive me mad
are turning me to fire. That gadfly's string—
not forged in any flame—is piercing me.
My fearful heart is beating in my chest,   1095
my eyes are rolling in a frantic whirl,
and raging blasts of sheer insanity
are sweeping me away. This tongue of mine
is now beyond control—delirious words
beat aimlessly against the surging flood   1100
of my abhorred destruction.

[Exit IO]

Prometheus & the Chorus

CHORUS   That wise man was truly wise who first
devised that saying in his mind and then
whose tongue expressed the words aloud—
the finest marriages by far are those   1105
when both the parties have an equal rank.
The poor should never yearn to match themselves
with those whose wealth has made them indolent
or those who always praise their noble birth.
O you Fates, may you never, never see   1110
me going as Zeus' partner to his bed,
and may I never be the wedded bride
of anyone from heaven. I shake with fear
to look on this unmarried girl, young Io,
so devastated by the cruel journey,   1115
her punishment from goddess Hera.
For me, when a married couple stands
on equal footing, there is no cause to fear
and I am not afraid. So may the love

who had left with his daughters, agreed to the marriages only when the fifty sons threatened the citizens of Argos.

of mightier gods never cast on me   1120
that glance which no one can withstand.
That is a battle where there is no fight,
where what cannot be done is possible.
I do not know what would become of me,
for I can see no way I could escape   1125
the skilled resourcefulness of Zeus.

PROMETHEUS   And yet Zeus, for all his obdurate heart,
will be brought down, when he prepares a match
which will remove him from his tyrant's throne
and hurl him into deep obscurity.   1130
And then the curse his father, Cronos, spoke,
the one he uttered when he was deposed
and lost his ancient throne, will all come true.
None of the gods can clearly offer him
a certain way to stave off this defeat,   1135
except for me. I know what is involved
and how to save him. So for the moment
let him sit full of confidence, trusting
the rumbling he can make high in the sky
and waving in his hands that lightning bolt   1140
which breathes out fire. None of these will help.
They will not stop him falling in disgrace,
a setback he cannot withstand. For now
he is himself preparing the very one
who will oppose him, someone marvelous   1145
and irresistible, who will produce
a fiercer fire than Zeus' lightning flash,
and a roar to drown out Zeus' thunder.
Poseidon's trident he will split apart,
the spear which whips the sea and shakes the earth.[35]   1150
And when Zeus stumbles on this evil fate,
he will find out how great the difference is
between a sovereign king and abject slave.

CHORUS   You keep maligning Zeus because these things
fit in with your desires.

PROMETHEUS   They may be what I want,   1155
but they will come to pass.

CHORUS   So must we then
expect someone to lord it over Zeus?

PROMETHEUS   Yes. His neck will be weighed down with chains
more onerous than mine.

CHORUS   Why are you not afraid
to shout out taunts like this?

PROMETHEUS   Why should I fear   1160
when I am destined not to die?

CHORUS   But Zeus
could load you with afflictions worse than these.

PROMETHEUS   Then let him do it. I am quite prepared
for anything he may inflict.

CHORUS   But it is wise
to pay due homage to Necessity.   1165

PROMETHEUS   Well then, pay homage. Bow your heads in awe.
Flatter the one who has the power to rule,

---

[35] Poseidon, brother of Zeus, was god of the sea. He was also responsible for earthquakes.

at least for now. But as for me, I think
of Zeus as less than nothing. Let him act
however he wants and reign for a brief while.   1170
He will not rule the gods for very long.
But wait! I see the messenger of Zeus,
a servant of our brand new tyrant lord.
No doubt he has come here to give us news.

Hermes

[Enter Hermes]

HERMES   You devious, hot-tempered schemer, who sinned
   against the gods by giving their honours
   to creatures of a day, you thief of fire,
   I am here to speak to you. Father Zeus
   is ordering you to make known this marriage
   you keep boasting of and to provide the name   1180
   of who will bring on Zeus' fall from power.
   Do not speak in enigmatic riddles,
   but set down clearly each and every fact.
   And do not make me come a second time,
   Prometheus. What you are doing here,   1185
   as you well know, will not make Zeus relent.

PROMETHEUS   You speech is crammed with pride and arrogance,
   quite fitting for a servant of the gods.
   You all are young—so is your ruling power—
   and you believe the fortress where you live   1190
   lies far beyond all grief. But I have seen
   two tyrant rulers cast out from that place,
   and I will see a third, the present king,
   abruptly tossed from there in great disgrace.[36]
   Do you think I am afraid and cower down   1195
   before you upstart gods? The way I feel
   is far removed from any sense of fear.
   So you should hurry back the way you came,
   for you will not learn anything at all
   in answer to what you demand of me.   1200

HERMES   But earlier with this wilfulness of yours
   you brought these torments on yourself.

PROMETHEUS   Know this—
   I would not trade these harsh conditions of mine
   for the life you lead as Zeus' slave.

HERMES   I suppose
   you find it preferable to serve this rock   1205
   than be a trusted messenger of Father Zeus.

PROMETHEUS   Insolence like yours deserves such insults.

HERMES   It sounds as if you find your present state
   a source of pleasure.

PROMETHEUS   Of pleasure? How I wish
   I could see my foes enjoying themselves   1210
   the way I do. And I count you among them.

HERMES   You think I am to blame for your misfortune?

---

[36] The two deposed gods are Ouranos, an original god, and his son Cronos, who overthrew his father and
was, in turn, overthrown by his son Zeus.

PROMETHEUS   To put it bluntly—I hate all the gods
  who received my help and then abused me,
  perverting justice.

HERMES   From the words you speak   1215
  I see your madness is no mild disease.

PROMETHEUS   I may well be insane, if madness means
  one hates one's enemies.

HERMES   If you were well,
  you would be unendurable.

PROMETHEUS   Alas for me!

HERMES   Alas? That word is one Zeus does not recognize.   1220

PROMETHEUS   But time grows old and teaches everything.

HERMES   That well may be,
  and yet you have not learned to demonstrate
  a sense of self-control in how you think.

PROMETHEUS   If I had that, I would not talk to you—   1225
  to such a subservient slave.

HERMES   So then
  it seems, as far as what my father wants,
  you will say nothing.

PROMETHEUS   Well, obviously
  I owe him and should repay the favour.

HERMES   You taunt me now, as if I were a child.   1230

PROMETHEUS   Well, are you not a child, or even stupider,
  to think you will learn anything from me?
  There is no torture, no form of punishment,
  that Zeus can use to force my mouth to speak
  before these vicious chains are taken off.   1235
  So let him throw his fiery lightning bolt,
  and with his white-winged snow and thunderclaps
  and earthquakes underground shake everything,
  and hurl the world into complete disorder—
  for none of that will force me to submit   1240
  or even name the one who Fate decrees
  will cast him from his sovereignty.

HERMES   But now
  you should consider if this stance of yours
  will help your cause.

PROMETHEUS   What I am doing now
  has been foretold, determined long ago.   1245

HERMES   You self-willed fool, for once you should submit,
  given the present torments facing you.
  Let your mind be ruled by what is right.

PROMETHEUS   It is pointless to pester me this way—
  as if you were advising ocean waves.   1250
  For you should never entertain the thought
  that I will be afraid of Zeus' schemes,
  turn into a woman, and raise my hands,
  the way that supplicating females do,
  and beg an enemy I hate so much   1255
  to free me from these chains. To act like that
  is far beneath me.

HERMES   Well, it seems to me
  if I keep talking to you at great length
  my words will all be wasted—my appeals

do not improve your mood or calm you down.   1260
Like a young colt newly yoked, you bite the bit
and use your strength to fight against the reins.
But the vehement resistance you display
rests on a feeble scheme, for on its own
mere stubbornness in those with foolish minds   1265
is less than useless. If these words of mine
do not convince you, think about the storm,
the triple wave of torment which will fall
and you cannot escape. First, Father Zeus
will rip this mountain crag with thunder claps   1270
and bolts of flaming lightning, burying
your body in the rock, and yet this cleft
will hold you in its arms. When you have spent
a long time underground, you will return
into the light, and Zeus' winged hound,   1275
his ravenous eagle, will cruelly rip
your mutilated body into shreds
and, like an uninvited banqueter,
will feast upon your liver all day long,
until its chewing turns the organ black.   1280
Do not expect your suffering to end
until some god appears who will take on
your troubles and be willing to descend
to sunless Hades and the deep black pit
of Tartarus. And so you should think hard.   1285
What I have said is no fictitious boast,
but plain and simple truth. For Zeus' mouth
does not know how to utter something false.
No. Everything he says will be fulfilled.
Look around you and reflect. And never think   1290
self-will is preferable to prudent thought.

CHORUS   To us it seems that what Hermes has said
  is not unreasonable. His orders
  tell you to set aside your stubbornness
  and seek out wise advice. Do what he says.   1295
  It is dishonourable for someone wise
  to persevere in doing something wrong.

PROMETHEUS   Well, I already know about the news
  this fellow has announced with so much fuss.
  There is no shame in painful suffering   1300
  inflicted by one enemy on another.
  So let him hurl his twin-forked lightning bolts
  down on my head, convulse the air with thunder
  and frantic gusts of howling wind, and shake
  the earth with hurricanes until they shift   1305
  the very roots of its foundations. Let him
  make the wildly surging sea waves mingle
  with the pathways of the heavenly stars,
  then lift my body up and fling it down
  to pitch black Tartarus, into the whirl   1310
  of harsh Necessity. Let him do all that—
  he cannot make me die.

HERMES   [To the Chorus] Ideas like these,
  expressed the way he does, are what we hear
  from those who are quite mad. This prayer of his—
  how is that not delusion? When does it stop,   1315
  this senseless raving? Well, in any case,
  you who sympathize with his afflictions

    should move off with all speed to somewhere else,
    in case the roaring force of Zeus' thunder
    affects your minds and drives you all insane.   1320

CHORUS You will have give me different advice
    and try to urge me in some other way
    in order to convince me. For I believe
    your stream of words is unendurable.
    How can you order me to act so badly?   1325
    I wish to share with him whatever pain
    Fate has in store, for I have learned to hate
    those who betray—of all the sicknesses
    that is most despicable to me.

HERMES As you wish—but remember what I said.   1330
    Do not blame your luck when you are trapped
    in Ruin's nets, and never claim that Zeus
    flung you into torments without warning.
    No—you can blame yourselves. For now you know
    by your own folly you will be caught up   1335
    in Ruin's web, not by a secret ruse
    or unexpectedly. And from that net
    there will be no escape.

[Exit Hermes]

Conclusion

PROMETHEUS And now things are already being transformed
    from words to deeds—the earth is shuddering,   1340
    the roaring thunder from beneath the sea
    is rumbling past me, while bolts of lightning
    flash their twisting fire, whirlwinds toss the dust,
    and blasting winds rush out to launch a war
    of howling storms, one against another.   1345
    The sky is now confounded with the sea.
    This turmoil is quite clearly aimed at me
    and comes from Zeus to make me feel afraid.
    O sacred mother Earth and heavenly Sky,
    who rolls around the light that all things share,   1350
    you see these unjust wrongs I must endure![37]

[37] It is not clear whether there is some final stage direction. Some editors have suggested that Prometheus now sinks down into the earth, as Hermes has indicated earlier (line 1259 ff. above). It is equally unclear what happens to the Chorus, who have vowed to stay with Prometheus.

Much Ado about Nothing

William Shakespeare
1598-99

Edited by Michael S. Kelly

To create a more streamlined storyline, some dialogue has been omitted. In some cases, dialogue that was either extremely outdated or had little to do with the story was deleted. The text is based upon the *First Folio*, published in 1623.

Dramatis Personæ

SCENE

The town of MESSINA

ROYALTY

DON PEDRO	Prince of Arragon

SOLDIERS

CLAUDIO	a young lord of Florence
BENEDICK	a young lord of Padua
BALTHASAR	attendant on Don Pedro
DON JOHN	Don Pedro's bastard brother
CONRADE	follower of Don John
BORACHIO	follower of Don John

LEONATO'S FAMILY

LEONATO	Governor of Messina
ANTONIO	Leonato's brother
HERO	daughter to Leonato
BEATRICE	niece to Leonato
MARGARET	attendant to Hero
URSULA	attendant to Hero
	Messengers and Attendants

THE TOWN OF MESSINA

FRANCIS	Messina's Friar
DOGBERRY	a constable
VERGES	a headborough
SEXTON	a church official
WATCHMEN	The Night Watch

ACT I

Scene i

An orchard before Leonato's house. Enter LEONATO, HERO, and BEATRICE, with a Messenger.

LEONATO   I learn in this letter that Don Pedro of Arragon comes this night to Messina.

MESSENGER   He is very near by this: he was not three leagues off when I left him.

LEONATO   How many gentlemen have you lost in this action?   5

MESSENGER   But few of any sort, and none of name.

LEONATO   A victory is twice itself when the achiever brings home full
numbers. I find here that Don Pedro hath bestowed much honour on a
young Florentine called Claudio.

MESSENGER   Much deserved on his part. He hath borne himself beyond   10
the promise of his age, doing in the figure of a lamb the feats of a lion.

BEATRICE   I pray you, is Signior Mountanto returned from the wars or no?

MESSENGER   I know none of that name, lady: there was none such in the
army of any sort.

LEONATO   What is he that you ask for, niece?   15

HERO   My cousin means Signior Benedick of Padua.

MESSENGER   O! he is returned, and as pleasant as ever he was.

BEATRICE   I pray you, how many hath he killed and eaten in these wars?
But how many hath he killed? for, indeed, I promised to eat all of his
killing.   20

LEONATO   Faith, niece, you tax Signior Benedick too much.

MESSENGER   He hath done good service, lady, in these
wars. And a good soldier too, lady.

BEATRICE   And a good soldier to a lady; but what is he to a lord?

MESSENGER   A lord to a lord, a man to a man; stuffed with all honourable   25
virtues.

BEATRICE   It is so indeed; he is no less than a stuffed man; but for the
stuffing,—well, we are all mortal.

LEONATO   You must not, sir, mistake my niece. There is a kind of merry
war betwixt Signior Benedick and her; they never meet but there's a   30
skirmish of wit between them.

BEATRICE   Alas! he gets nothing by that. In our last conflict four of his
five wits went halting off, and now is the whole man governed with one!
so that if he have wit enough to keep himself warm, let him bear it for a
difference between himself and his horse; for it is all the wealth that he   35
hath left to be known a reasonable creature. Who is his companion now?
He hath every month a new sworn brother.

MESSENGER   He is most in the company of the right noble Claudio.

BEATRICE   O Lord, he will hang upon him like a disease: he is sooner
caught than the pestilence, and the taker runs presently mad. God help   40
the noble Claudio! If he have caught the Benedick, it will cost him a
thousand pound ere a' be cured.

MESSENGER   I will hold friends with you, lady.

BEATRICE   Do, good friend.

LEONATO   You will never run mad, niece.   45

BEATRICE   No, not till a hot January.

MESSENGER   Don Pedro is approached.

Enter DON PEDRO, DON JOHN, CLAUDIO, BENEDICK, BALTHAZAR, and Others.

DON PEDRO   Good Signior Leonato, you are come to meet your trouble:
the fashion of the world is to avoid cost, and you encounter it.

LEONATO   Never came trouble to my house in the likeness of your Grace,   50
for trouble being gone, comfort should remain; but when you depart
from me, sorrow abides and happiness takes his leave.

DON PEDRO   I think this is your daughter.

LEONATO   Her mother hath many times told me so.

BENEDICK   Were you in doubt, sir, that you asked her?   55

LEONATO   Signior Benedick, no; for then were you a child.

BENEDICK   If Signior Leonato be her father, she would not have his head on her shoulders for all Messina, as like him as she is.

BEATRICE   I wonder that you will still be talking, Signior Benedick: nobody marks you.   60

BENEDICK   What! my dear Lady Disdain, are you yet living?

BEATRICE   Is it possible Disdain should die while she hath such meet food to feed it as Signior Benedick? Courtesy itself must convert to disdain if you come in her presence.

BENEDICK   Then is courtesy a turncoat. But it is certain I am loved of all   65
ladies, only you excepted; and I would I could find in my heart that I had not a hard heart; for, truly, I love none.

BEATRICE   A dear happiness to women: they would else have been troubled with a pernicious suitor. I thank God and my cold blood, I am of your humour for that. I had rather hear my dog bark at a crow than a   70
man swear he loves me.

BENEDICK   God keep your ladyship still in that mind; so some gentleman or other shall scape a predestinate scratched face.

BEATRICE   Scratching could not make it worse, an 'twere such a face as yours were.   75

BENEDICK   Well, you are a rare parrot-teacher.

BEATRICE   A bird of my tongue is better than a beast of yours.

BENEDICK   I would my horse had the speed of your tongue. But keep your way, i' God's name; I have done.

BEATRICE   You always end with a jade's trick: I know you of old.   80

DON PEDRO   Signior Claudio, and Signior Benedick, my dear friend Leonato hath invited you all. I tell him we shall stay here at the least a month, and he heartily prays some occasion may detain us longer.

LEONATO   [To DON JOHN.] Let me bid you welcome, my lord: being reconciled to the prince your brother, I owe you all duty.   85

DON JOHN   I thank you: I am not of many words, but I thank you.

LEONATO   Please it your Grace lead on?

DON PEDRO   Your hand, Leonato; we will go together.

Exeunt all but BENEDICK and CLAUDIO.

CLAUDIO   Benedick, didst thou note the daughter of Signior Leonato?

BENEDICK   I noted her not; but I looked on her.   90

CLAUDIO   Is she not a modest young lady?

BENEDICK   Do you question me, as an honest man should do, for my simple true judgment; or would you have me speak after my custom, as being a professed tyrant to their sex?

CLAUDIO   No; I pray thee speak in sober judgment.   95

BENEDICK   Why, i' faith, methinks she's too low for a high praise, too brown for a fair praise, and too little for a great praise; only this commendation I can afford her, that were she other than she is, she were unhandsome, and being no other but as she is, I do not like her.

CLAUDIO   Thou thinkest I am in sport: I pray thee tell me truly how thou   100
likest her.

BENEDICK   Would you buy her, that you enquire after her?

CLAUDIO   Can the world buy such a jewel?

BENEDICK   Yea, and a case to put it into. But speak you this with a sad brow, or do you play the flouting Jack, to tell us Cupid is a good hare—   105
finder, and Vulcan a rare carpenter?

CLAUDIO   In mine eye she is the sweetest lady that ever I looked on.

BENEDICK   I can see yet without spectacles and I see no such
matter: there's her cousin an she were not possessed with a fury,
exceeds her as much in beauty as the first of May doth the last of
December. But I hope you have no intent to turn husband, have you?   110

CLAUDIO   I would scarce trust myself, though I had sworn to the
contrary, if Hero would be my wife.

BENEDICK   Is't come to this, i' faith? Shall I never see a bachelor of
threescore again? Go to, i' faith; an thou wilt needs thrust thy neck into a
yoke, wear the print of it and sigh away Sundays.   115

Re-enter DON PEDRO.

DON PEDRO   What secret hath held you here, that you followed not to
Leonato's?

BENEDICK   He is in love. With who? now that is your Grace's
part. Mark how short his answer is: with Hero, Leonato's short daughter.

DON PEDRO   Amen, if you love her; for the lady is very well worthy.   120

CLAUDIO   You speak this to fetch me in, my lord.

DON PEDRO   By my troth, I speak my thought.

CLAUDIO   And in faith, my lord, I spoke mine.

BENEDICK   And by my two faiths and troths, my lord, I spoke mine.

CLAUDIO   That I love her, I feel.   125

DON PEDRO   That she is worthy, I know.

BENEDICK   That I neither feel how she should be loved nor know how she
should be worthy, is the opinion that fire cannot melt out of me: I will die
in it at the stake.

DON PEDRO   Thou wast ever an obstinate heretic in the despite of beauty.   130

BENEDICK   That a woman conceived me, I thank her; that she brought
me up, I likewise give her most humble thanks; but that I will have a
recheat winded in my forehead, or hang my bugle in an invisible baldrick,
all women shall pardon me. Because I will not do them the wrong to
mistrust any, I will do myself the right to trust none; and the fine is—I   135
will live a bachelor.

DON PEDRO   I shall see thee, ere I die, look pale with love.

BENEDICK   With anger, with sickness, or with hunger, my lord; not with
love: prove that ever I lose more blood with love than I will get again
with drinking, pick out mine eyes with a ballad-maker's pen and hang me   140
up at the door of a brothel-house for the sign of blind Cupid.

DON PEDRO   Well, if ever thou dost fall from this faith, thou wilt prove a
notable argument.

BENEDICK   If I do, hang me in a bottle like a cat and shoot at me; and he
that hits me, let him be clapped on the shoulder and called Adam.   145

DON PEDRO   Well, as time shall try: 'In time the savage bull doth bear the
yoke.'

BENEDICK   The savage bull may; but if ever the sensible Benedick bear it,
pluck off the bull's horns and set them in my forehead; and let me be
vilely painted, and in such great letters as they write, 'Here is good horse   150
to hire,' let them signify under my sign 'Here you may see Benedick the
married man.'

DON PEDRO   Well, you will temporize with the hours. In the meantime,
good Signior Benedick, repair to Leonato's: commend me to him and tell
him I will not fail him at supper; for indeed he hath made great   155
preparation.

BENEDICK   *[To CLADUIO.]* Examine your conscience: and so I leave you.

[Exit.]

CLAUDIO   My liege, your highness now may do me good.

DON PEDRO   My love is thine to teach.

CLAUDIO   Hath Leonato any son, my lord?   160

DON PEDRO   No child but Hero;s he's his only heir.
  Dost thou affect her, Claudio?

CLAUDIO   O! my lord,
  When you went onward on this ended action,
   I looked upon her with a soldier's eye,   165
  That lik'd, but had a rougher task in hand
  Than to drive liking to the name of love;
  But now I am return'd, and that war-thoughts
  Have left their places vacant, in their rooms
  Come thronging soft and delicate desires,   170
  All prompting me how fair young Hero is,
  Saying, I lik'd her ere I went to wars.

DON PEDRO   Thou wilt be like a lover presently,
  And tire the hearer with a book of words.
  If thou dost love fair Hero, cherish it,   175
  And I will break with her, and with her father,
  And thou shalt have her. Was't not to this end
  That thou began'st to twist so fine a story?

CLAUDIO   How sweetly you do minister to love,
  That know love's grief by his complexion!   180
  But lest my liking might too sudden seem,
  I would have salv'd it with a longer treatise.

DON PEDRO   And I will fit thee with the remedy.
  I know we shall have revelling to-night: 185
  I will assume thy part in some disguise,
  And tell fair Hero I am Claudio;
  And in her bosom I'll unclasp my heart,
  And take her hearing prisoner with the force
  And strong encounter of my amorous tale:
  Then, after to her father will I break;   190
  And the conclusion is, she shall be thine.
  In practice let us put it presently.

  [Exeunt.]

Scene ii

A room in LEONATO's house. Enter LEONATO and ANTONIO, meeting.

LEONATO   How now, brother! Where is my cousin, your son? Hath he
  provided this music?

ANTONIO   He is very busy about it. But, brother, I can tell
  you strange news that you yet dreamt not of.
  The prince and Count   5
  Claudio, walking in a thick-pleached alley in mine
  orchard, were thus much overheard by a man of mine:
  the prince discovered to Claudio that he loved my
  niece your daughter and meant to acknowledge it
  this night in a dance: and if he found her   10
  accordant, he meant to take the present time by the
  top and instantly break with you of it.

LEONATO   No, no; we will hold it as a dream till it appear
  itself: but I will acquaint my daughter withal,
  that she may be the better prepared for an answer,   15
  if peradventure this be true. Go you and tell her of it.

Enter Attendants.

Cousins, you know what you have to do.

Exeunt

Scene iii

A room in LEONATO's house.   Enter DON JOHN and CONRADE.

CONRADE   What the good-year, my lord! why are you thus out of
measure sad?

DON JOHN   There is no measure in the occasion that breeds;
therefore the sadness is without limit.

CONRADE   You should hear reason.   5

DON JOHN   And when I have heard it, what blessing brings it?

CONRADE   If not a present remedy, at least a patient sufferance.

DON JOHN   I wonder that thou, being, as thou sayest thou art,
born under Saturn, goest about to apply a moral
medicine to a mortifying mischief. I cannot hide   10
what I am: I must be sad when I have cause and smile
at no man's jests, eat when I have stomach and wait
for no man's leisure, sleep when I am drowsy and
tend on no man's business, laugh when I am merry
and claw no man in his humour.   15

CONRADE   Yea, but you must not make the full show of this
till you may do it without controlment. You have of
late stood out against your brother, and he hath
ta'en you newly into his grace; where it is
impossible you should take true root but by the   20
fair weather that you make yourself: it is needful
that you frame the season for your own harvest.

DON JOHN   I had rather be a canker in a hedge than a rose in
his grace, and it better fits my blood to be
disdained of all than to fashion a carriage to rob   25
love from any: in this, though I cannot be said to
be a flattering honest man, it must not be denied
but I am a plain-dealing villain. I am trusted with
a muzzle and enfranchised with a clog; therefore I
have decreed not to sing in my cage. If I had my   30
mouth, I would bite; if I had my liberty, I would do
my liking: in the meantime let me be that I am and
seek not to alter me.

CONRADE   Can you make no use of your discontent?

DON JOHN   I make all use of it, for I use it only.   35
Who comes here?

Enter BORACHIO.

What news, Borachio?

BORACHIO   I came yonder from a great supper: the prince your brother is
royally entertained by Leonato: and I can give you intelligence of an
intended marriage.   40

DON JOHN   Will it serve for any model to build mischief on?
What is he for a fool that betroths himself to unquietness?

BORACHIO   Marry, it is your brother's right hand.

DON JOHN   Who? The most exquisite Claudio?

BORACHIO   Even he.   45

DON JOHN   A proper squire! And who, and who? Which way looks he?

BORACHIO   Marry, on Hero, the daughter and heir of Leonato.

DON JOHN   A very forward March-chick! How came you to this?

BORACHIO   Being entertained for a perfumer, as I was smoking a musty
   room, comes me the prince and Claudio, hand in hand in sad conference: 50
   I whipt me behind the arras; and there heard it agreed upon that the
   prince should woo Hero for himself, and having obtained her, give her to
   Count Claudio.

DON JOHN   Come, come, let us thither: this may prove food to
   my displeasure. That young start-up hath all the   55
   glory of my overthrow: if I can cross him any way, I
   bless myself every way. You are both sure, and will assist me?

CONRADE   To the death, my lord.

DON JOHN   Let us to the great supper: their cheer is the
   greater that I am subdued. Would the cook were of   60
   my mind! Shall we go prove what's to be done?

BORACHIO   We'll wait upon your lordship.

   Exeunt

ACT II

Scene i

A hall in LEONATO'S house. Enter LEONATO, ANTONIO, HERO, BEATRICE, and others.

LEONATO   Was not Count John here at supper?

ANTONIO   I saw him not.

BEATRICE   How tartly that gentleman looks! I never can see him but I am
   heart-burned an hour after.

HERO   He is of a very melancholy disposition.   5

BEATRICE   He were an excellent man that were made just in the midway
   between him and Benedick: the one is too like an image and says
   nothing, and the other too like my lady's eldest son, evermore tattling.

LEONATO   Then half Signior Benedick's tongue in Count John's mouth,
   and half Count John's melancholy in Signior Benedick's face,—   10

BEATRICE   With a good leg and a good foot, uncle, and money enough in
   his purse, such a man would win any woman in the world, if a' could get
   her good-will.

LEONATO   By my troth, niece, thou wilt never get thee a husband, if thou
   be so shrewd of thy tongue.   15

ANTONIO   In faith, she's too curst.

BEATRICE   Too curst is more than curst: I shall lessen God's sending that
   way; for it is said, 'God sends a curst cow short horns;' but to a cow too
   curst he sends none.

LEONATO   So, by being too curst, God will send you no horns.   20

BEATRICE   Just, if he send me no husband; for the which blessing I am at
   him upon my knees every morning and evening. Lord, I could not endure
   a husband with a beard on his face: I had rather lie in the woollen.

LEONATO   You may light on a husband that hath no beard.

BEATRICE   What should I do with him? dress him in my apparel and make   25
   him my waiting-gentlewoman? He that hath a beard is more than a youth,
   and he that hath no beard is less than a man: and he that is more than a
   youth is not for me, and he that is less than a man, I am not for him.

LEONATO   Well, then, go you into hell?

BEATRICE   No, but to the gate; and there will the devil meet me, like an   30
old cuckold, with horns on his head, and say 'Get you to heaven,
Beatrice, get you to heaven; here's no place for you maids:' and away to
Saint Peter for the heavens; he shows me where the bachelors sit, and
there live we as merry as the day is long.

ANTONIO   *[To HERO.]* Well, niece, I trust you will be ruled by your father.   35

BEATRICE   Yes, faith; it is my cousin's duty to make curtsy and say
'Father, as it please you.' But yet for all that, cousin, let him be a
handsome fellow, or else make another curtsy and say 'Father, as it
please me.'

LEONATO   Well, niece, I hope to see you one day fitted with a husband.   40

BEATRICE   Not till God make men of some other metal than earth. Would
it not grieve a woman to be overmastered with a pierce of valiant dust?
to make an account of her life to a clod of wayward marl? No, uncle, I'll
none: Adam's sons are my brethren.

LEONATO   Daughter, remember what I told you: if the prince do solicit   45
you in that kind, you know your answer.

BEATRICE   The fault will be in the music, cousin, if you be not wooed in
good time: if the prince be too important, tell him there is measure in
every thing and so dance out the answer.

LEONATO   Cousin, you apprehend passing shrewdly.   50

BEATRICE   I have a good eye, uncle; I can see a church by daylight.

LEONATO   The revellers are entering, brother: make good room.

[All put on their masks. Enter DON PEDRO, CLAUDIO, BENEDICK, BALTHASAR, DON JOHN, BORACHIO, MARGARET, URSULA and others, masked.]

DON PEDRO   Lady, will you walk about with your friend?

HERO   So you walk softly and look sweetly and say nothing,
I am yours for the walk; and especially when I walk away.   55

Drawing her aside.

BALTHASAR   Well, I would you did like me.

MARGARET   So would not I, for your own sake; for I have many ill-qualities.

BALTHASAR   Which is one?

MARGARET   I say my prayers aloud.

BALTHASAR   I love you the better: the hearers may cry, Amen.   60

MARGARET   God match me with a good dancer!

BALTHASAR   Amen.

[Another place in the party.]

URSULA   I know you well enough; you are Signior Antonio.

ANTONIO   At a word, I am not.

URSULA   I know you by the waggling of your head.   65

ANTONIO   To tell you true, I counterfeit him.

URSULA   You could never do him so ill-well, unless you were the very
man. Here's his dry hand up and down: you are he, you are he.

ANTONIO   At a word, I am not.

URSULA   Come, come, do you think I do not know you by your excellent   70
wit? can virtue hide itself? Go to, mum, you are he: graces will appear,
and there's an end.

[Another place in the party.]

BEATRICE   Will you not tell me who told you so?

BENEDICK   No, you shall pardon me.

BEATRICE   Nor will you not tell me who you are?   75

BENEDICK   Not now.

BEATRICE   That I was disdainful, and that I had my good wit out of the
'Hundred Merry Tales:'—well this was Signior Benedick that said so.

BENEDICK   What's he?

BEATRICE   I am sure you know him well enough.   80

BENEDICK   Not I, believe me.

BEATRICE   Did he never make you laugh?

BENEDICK   I pray you, what is he?

BEATRICE   Why, he is the prince's jester: a very dull fool; only his gift is
in devising impossible slanders: none but libertines delight in him; and   85
the commendation is not in his wit, but in his villany; for he both pleases
men and angers them, and then they laugh at him and beat him. I am
sure he is in the fleet: I would he had boarded me.

BENEDICK   When I know the gentleman, I'll tell him what you say.

BEATRICE   Do, do.   90

Music.

We must follow the leaders.

BENEDICK   In every good thing.

Dance. Then exeunt all except DON JOHN, BORACHIO, and CLAUDIO.

BORACHIO   And that is Claudio: I know him by his bearing.

DON JOHN   Are not you Signior Benedick?

CLAUDIO   You know me well; I am he.   95

DON JOHN   Signior, you are very near my brother in his love:
he is enamoured on Hero; I pray you, dissuade him
from her: she is no equal for his birth: you may
do the part of an honest man in it.

CLAUDIO   How know you he loves her?   100

DON JOHN   I heard him swear his affection.

BORACHIO   So did I too; and he swore he would marry her to-night.

DON JOHN   Come, let us to the banquet.

Exeunt DON JOHN and BORACHIO.

CLAUDIO   Thus answer I in the name of Benedick,
But hear these ill news with the ears of Claudio.   105
'Tis certain so; the prince wooes for himself.
Friendship is constant in all other things
Save in the office and affairs of love:
Therefore, all hearts in love use their own tongues;
Let every eye negotiate for itself   110
And trust no agent; for beauty is a witch
Against whose charms faith melteth into blood.
This is an accident of hourly proof,
Which I mistrusted not. Farewell, therefore, Hero!

Re-enter BENEDICK.

BENEDICK   Count Claudio?   115

CLAUDIO   Yea, the same.

BENEDICK   Come, will you go with me?

CLAUDIO   Whither?

BENEDICK   About your own business, for the prince hath got your Hero.

CLAUDIO   I wish him joy of her.   120

BENEDICK   Did you think the prince would have served you thus?

CLAUDIO   I pray you, leave me.

Exit CLAUDIO.

BENEDICK   Alas, poor hurt fowl! now will he creep into sedges.
But that my Lady Beatrice should know me, and not
know me! The prince's fool! Ha? It may be I go 125
under that title because I am merry. Yea, but so I
am apt to do myself wrong; I am not so reputed: it
is the base, though bitter, disposition of Beatrice
that puts the world into her person and so gives me
out. Well, I'll be revenged as I may. 130

Re-enter DON PEDRO.

DON PEDRO   Now, signior, where's the count? did you see him?

BENEDICK   Troth, my lord, I have played the part of Lady Fame.
I found him here as melancholy as a lodge in a
warren: I told him, and I think I told him true,
that your grace had got the good will of this young lady. 135

DON PEDRO   The Lady Beatrice hath a quarrel to you: the gentleman that
danced with her told her she is much wronged by you.

BENEDICK   O, she misused me past the endurance of a block!
She told me, not thinking I had been
myself, that I was the prince's jester, that I was 140
duller than a great thaw; huddling jest upon jest
with such impossible conveyance upon me that I stood
like a man at a mark, with a whole army shooting at
me. She speaks poniards, and every word stabs:
if her breath were as terrible as her terminations, 145
there were no living near her; she would infect to
the north star. So, indeed, all disquiet, horror
and perturbation follows her.

DON PEDRO   Look, here she comes.

Enter CLAUDIO, BEATRICE, HERO, and LEONATO.

BENEDICK   Will your grace command me any service to the 150
world's end? I will go on the slightest errand now
to the Antipodes that you can devise to send me on;
I will fetch you a tooth-picker now from the
furthest inch of Asia, bring you the length of
Prester John's foot, fetch you a hair off the great 155
Cham's beard, do you any embassage to the Pigmies,
rather than hold three words' conference with this
harpy. You have no employment for me?

DON PEDRO   None, but to desire your good company.

BENEDICK   O God, sir, here's a dish I love not: I cannot 160
endure my Lady Tongue.

Exit

DON PEDRO   Come, lady, come; you have lost the heart of Signior
Benedick.

BEATRICE   Indeed, my lord, he lent it me awhile; and I gave
him use for it, a double heart for his single one: 165
marry, once before he won it of me with false dice,
therefore your grace may well say I have lost it.

DON PEDRO   You have put him down, lady, you have put him down.

BEATRICE   So I would not he should do me, my lord, lest I
should prove the mother of fools. I have brought 170
Count Claudio, whom you sent me to seek.

DON PEDRO   Why, how now, count! wherefore are you sad?

CLAUDIO   Not sad, my lord.

DON PEDRO   How then? sick?

CLAUDIO   Neither, my lord.   175

BEATRICE   The count is neither sad, nor sick, nor merry, nor well; but civil
count, civil as an orange, and something of that jealous complexion.

DON PEDRO   I' faith, lady, I think your blazon to be true;
though, I'll be sworn, if he be so, his conceit is
false. Here, Claudio, I have wooed in thy name, and   180
fair Hero is won: I have broke with her father,
and his good will obtained: name the day of
marriage, and God give thee joy!

LEONATO   Count, take of me my daughter, and with her my fortunes: his
grace hath made the match, and an grace say Amen to it.   185

BEATRICE   Speak, count, 'tis your cue.

CLAUDIO   Silence is the perfectest herald of joy: I were
but little happy, if I could say how much. Lady, as
you are mine, I am yours: I give away myself for
you and dote upon the exchange.   190

BEATRICE   Speak, cousin; or, if you cannot, stop his mouth with a kiss,
and let not him speak neither.

DON PEDRO   In faith, lady, you have a merry heart.

BEATRICE   Yea, my lord; I thank it, poor fool, it keeps on the windy side
of care. My cousin tells him in his ear that he is in her heart.   195

CLAUDIO   And so she doth, cousin.

BEATRICE   Good Lord, for alliance! Thus goes every one to the world but I,
and I am sunburnt; I may sit in a corner and cry heigh-ho for a husband!

DON PEDRO   Lady Beatrice, I will get you one.

BEATRICE   I would rather have one of your father's getting. Hath your   200
grace ne'er a brother like you? Your father got excellent husbands, if a
maid could come by them.

DON PEDRO   Will you have me, lady?

BEATRICE   No, my lord, unless I might have another for working-days:
your grace is too costly to wear every day. But, I beseech your grace,   205
pardon me: I was born to speak all mirth and no matter.

DON PEDRO   Your silence most offends me, and to be merry best
becomes you; for, out of question, you were born in a merry hour.

BEATRICE   No, sure, my lord, my mother cried; but then there was a star
danced, and under that was I born. Cousins, God give you joy!   210

LEONATO   Niece, will you look to those things I told you of?

BEATRICE   I cry you mercy, uncle. By your grace's pardon.

Exit

DON PEDRO   By my troth, a pleasant-spirited lady.

LEONATO   There's little of the melancholy element in her, my lord: she is
never sad but when she sleeps, and not ever sad then; for I have heard   215
my daughter say, she hath often dreamed of unhappiness and waked
herself with laughing.

DON PEDRO   She cannot endure to hear tell of a husband.

LEONATO   O, by no means: she mocks all her wooers out of suit.

DON PEDRO   She were an excellent wife for Benedict.   220

LEONATO   O Lord, my lord, if they were but a week married,
they would talk themselves mad.

DON PEDRO   County Claudio, when mean you to go to church?

CLAUDIO   To-morrow, my lord: time goes on crutches till love have all his rites.

LEONATO   Not till Monday, my dear son, which is hence a just seven-   225
night; and a time too brief, too, to have all things answer my mind.

DON PEDRO   Come, you shake the head at so long a breathing:
but, I warrant thee, Claudio, the time shall not go
dully by us. I will in the interim undertake one of   230
Hercules' labours; which is, to bring Signior
Benedick and the Lady Beatrice into a mountain of
affection the one with the other. I would fain have
it a match, and I doubt not but to fashion it, if
you three will but minister such assistance as I   235
shall give you direction.

LEONATO   My lord, I am for you, though it cost me ten nights' watchings.

CLAUDIO   And I, my lord.

DON PEDRO   And you too, gentle Hero?

HERO   I will do any modest office, my lord, to help my cousin to a good
husband.   240

DON PEDRO   And Benedick is not the unhopefullest husband that
I know. Thus far can I praise him; he is of a noble
strain, of approved valour and confirmed honesty. I
will teach you how to humour your cousin, that she
shall fall in love with Benedick; and I, with your   245
two helps, will so practise on Benedick that, in
despite of his quick wit and his queasy stomach, he
shall fall in love with Beatrice. If we can do this,
Cupid is no longer an archer: his glory shall be
ours, for we are the only love-gods. Go in with me,   250
and I will tell you my drift.

Exeunt

Scene ii

The same.   Enter DON JOHN and BORACHIO.

DON JOHN   It is so; the Count Claudio shall marry the daughter of
Leonato.

BORACHIO   Yea, my lord; but I can cross it.

DON JOHN   Any bar, any cross, any impediment will be
medicinable to me: I am sick in displeasure to him,   5
and whatsoever comes athwart his affection ranges
evenly with mine. How canst thou cross this marriage?

BORACHIO   Not honestly, my lord; but so covertly that no dishonesty
shall appear in me.

DON JOHN   Show me briefly how.   10

BORACHIO   I think I told your lordship a year since, how much I am in the
favour of Margaret, the waiting gentlewoman to Hero.

DON JOHN   I remember.

BORACHIO   I can, at any unseasonable instant of the night, appoint her to
look out at her lady's chamber window.   15

DON JOHN   What life is in that, to be the death of this marriage?

BORACHIO   The poison of that lies in you to temper. Go you to the prince
your brother; spare not to tell him that he hath wronged his honour in
marrying the renowned Claudio—whose estimation do you mightily hold
up—to a contaminated stale, such a one as Hero.   15

DON JOHN   What proof shall I make of that?

BORACHIO   Proof enough to misuse the prince, to vex Claudio, to undo
  Hero and kill Leonato. Look you for any other issue?

DON JOHN   Only to despite them, I will endeavour any thing.

BORACHIO   Go, then; find me a meet hour to draw Don Pedro and the   20
  Count Claudio alone: tell them that you know that Hero loves me; intend
  a kind of zeal both to the prince and Claudio, as,—in love of your
  brother's honour, who hath made this match, and his friend's reputation,
  who is thus like to be cozened with the semblance of a maid,—that you
  have discovered thus. They will scarcely believe this without trial: 25
  offer them instances; which shall bear no less likelihood than to see me
  at her chamber-window, hear me call Margaret Hero, hear Margaret term
  me Claudio; and bring them to see this the very night before the
  intended wedding,—for in the meantime I will so fashion the matter that
  Hero shall be absent,—and there shall appear such seeming truth of   30
  Hero's disloyalty that jealousy shall be called assurance and all the
  preparation overthrown.

DON JOHN   Grow this to what adverse issue it can, I will put
  it in practise. Be cunning in the working this, and
  thy fee is a thousand ducats.   35

BORACHIO   Be you constant in the accusation, and my cunning shall not
  shame me.

DON JOHN   I will presently go learn their day of marriage.

  Exeunt

Scene iii

LEONATO'S orchard. Enter BENEDICK.

BENEDICK   I do much wonder that one man, seeing how much
  another man is a fool when he dedicates his
  behaviors to love, will, after he hath laughed at
  such shallow follies in others, become the argument
  of his own scorn by failing in love: and such a man   5
  is Claudio. I have known when there was no music
  with him but the drum and the fife; and now had he
  rather hear the tabour and the pipe: I have known
  when he would have walked ten mile a-foot to see a
  good armour; and now will he lie ten nights awake,   10
  carving the fashion of a new doublet. He was wont to
  speak plain and to the purpose, like an honest man
  and a soldier; and now is he turned orthography; his
  words are a very fantastical banquet, just so many
  strange dishes. May I be so converted and see with   15
  these eyes? I cannot tell; I think not: I will not
  be sworn, but love may transform me to an oyster; but
  I'll take my oath on it, till he have made an oyster
  of me, he shall never make me such a fool. One woman
  is fair, yet I am well; another is wise, yet I am   20
  well; another virtuous, yet I am well; but till all
  graces be in one woman, one woman shall not come in
  my grace. Rich she shall be, that's certain; wise,
  or I'll none; virtuous, or I'll never cheapen her;
  fair, or I'll never look on her; mild, or come not   25
  near me; noble, or not I for an angel; of good
  discourse, an excellent musician, and her hair shall
  be of what colour it please God. Ha! the prince and
  Monsieur Love! I will hide me in the arbour.

  Withdraws

  Enter DON PEDRO, CLAUDIO, and LEONATO.

DON PEDRO   Come, shall we hear this music?   30

CLAUDIO   Yea, my good lord. How still the evening is,
As hush'd on purpose to grace harmony!

DON PEDRO   See you where Benedick hath hid himself?

CLAUDIO   O, very well, my lord.

Enter BALTHASAR with Music.

DON PEDRO   Come, Balthasar, we'll hear that song again.   35

BALTHASAR   O, good my lord, tax not so bad a voice
To slander music any more than once.

DON PEDRO   It is the witness still of excellency
To put a strange face on his own perfection.
I pray thee, sing, and let me woo no more.   40

[Music]

BENEDICK   Now, divine air! now is his soul ravished! Is it not strange that
sheeps' guts should hale souls out of men's bodies?

The Song

BALTHASAR   "Sigh no more, ladies, sigh no more,
Men were deceivers ever,
One foot in sea and one on shore,   45
To one thing constant never:
Then sigh not so, but let them go,
And be you blithe and bonny,
Converting all your sounds of woe
Into Hey nonny, nonny.   50
Sing no more ditties, sing no moe,
Of dumps so dull and heavy;
The fraud of men was ever so,
Since summer first was leavy:
Then sigh not so,   55
But let them go,
And you be blithe and bonny
Converting all your sounds of woe
Into Hey nonny, nonny."

DON PEDRO   By my troth, a good song.   60

BALTHASAR   And an ill singer, my lord.

DON PEDRO   No, no, faith; thou singest well enough.

BENEDICK   *[Aside.]* An he had been a dog that should have howled thus,
they would have hanged him.

Exit BALTHASAR.

Come hither, Leonato. What was it you told me of   65
to-day, that your niece Beatrice was in love with
Signior Benedick?

CLAUDIO   *[Aside to Don Pedro.]* Stalk on, stalk on; the fowl sits.
[Aloud.] I did never think that lady would have loved any man.

LEONATO   No, nor I neither; but most wonderful that she   70
should so dote on Signior Benedick, whom she hath in
all outward behaviors seemed ever to abhor.

BENEDICK   *[Aside]* Is't possible?

LEONATO   By my troth, my lord, I cannot tell what to think
of it but that she loves him with an enraged   75
affection: it is past the infinite of thought.

DON PEDRO   May be she doth but counterfeit.

CLAUDIO   Faith, like enough.

LEONATO   O God, counterfeit! There was never counterfeit of
  passion came so near the life of passion as she discovers it.   80

DON PEDRO   Why, what effects of passion shows she?

CLAUDIO   *[Aside]* Bait the hook well; this fish will bite.

LEONATO   What effects, my lord?
  [To Claudio] You heard my daughter tell you how.

CLAUDIO   She did, indeed.   85

DON PEDRO   How pray you? You amaze me: I would have I thought her
  spirit had been invincible against all assaults of affection.

LEONATO   I would have sworn it had, my lord; especially against
  Benedick.

BENEDICK   *[Aside]* I should think this a gull, but that the white-bearded   90
  fellow speaks it: knavery cannot, sure, hide himself in such reverence.

CLAUDIO   *[Aside]* He hath ta'en the infection: hold it up.

DON PEDRO   Hath she made her affection known to Benedick?

LEONATO   No; and swears she never will: that's her torment.

CLAUDIO   'Tis true, indeed; so your daughter says: 'Shall   95
  I,' says she, 'that have so oft encountered him
  with scorn, write to him that I love him?'

LEONATO   This says she now when she is beginning to write to
  him; for she'll be up twenty times a night, and
  there will she sit in her smock till she have writ a   100
  sheet of paper: my daughter tells us all.

CLAUDIO   Then down upon her knees she falls, weeps, sobs,
  beats her heart, tears her hair, prays, curses; 'O
  sweet Benedick! God give me patience!'

LEONATO   She doth indeed; my daughter says so: and the ecstasy hath   105
  so much overborne her that my daughter is sometime afeared she will do
  a desperate outrage to herself.

DON PEDRO   It were good that Benedick knew of it by some other, if she
  will not discover it.

CLAUDIO   To what end? He would make but a sport of it and torment the   110
  poor lady worse.
  DON PEDRO   She's an excellent sweet lady; and, out of all suspicion,
  she is virtuous.

CLAUDIO   And she is exceeding wise.

DON PEDRO   In every thing but in loving Benedick. I pray you, tell   115
  Benedick of it, and hear what a' will say.

LEONATO   Were it good, think you?

CLAUDIO   Hero thinks surely she will die; for she says she
  will die, if he love her not, and she will die, ere
  she make her love known, and she will die, if he woo her.   120

DON PEDRO   If she should make tender of her
  love, 'tis very possible he'll scorn it; for the
  man, as you know all, hath a contemptible spirit.

DON PEDRO   Well, we will hear further of it by your daughter:
  let it cool the while. I love Benedick well; and I   125
  could wish he would modestly examine himself, to see
  how much he is unworthy so good a lady.

LEONATO   My lord, will you walk? dinner is ready.

CLAUDIO   *[Aside]* If he do not dote on her upon this,
  I will never trust my expectation.   130

DON PEDRO   *[Aside]* Let there be the same net spread for her; and that
must your daughter and her gentlewomen carry. The sport will be, when
they hold one an opinion of another's dotage. Let us send her to call him
in to dinner.

Exeunt DON PEDRO, CLAUDIO, and LEONATO.

BENEDICK   *[Coming forward.]*
The conference was sadly borne. They have the truth of   135
this from Hero. They seem to pity the lady: it
seems her affections have their full bent. Love me!
why, it must be requited. I hear how I am censured:
they say I will bear myself proudly, if I perceive
the love come from her; they say too that she will   140
rather die than give any sign of affection. I did
never think to marry: I must not seem proud: happy
are they that hear their detractions and can put
them to mending. They say the lady is fair; 'tis a
truth, I can bear them witness; and virtuous; 'tis   145
so, I cannot reprove it; and wise, but for loving
me; by my troth, it is no addition to her wit, nor
no great argument of her folly, for I will be
horribly in love with her. I may chance have some
odd quirks and remnants of wit broken on me,   150
because I have railed so long against marriage: but
doth not the appetite alter? a man loves the meat
in his youth that he cannot endure in his age.
Shall quips and sentences and these paper bullets of
the brain awe a man from the career of his humour?   155
No, the world must be peopled. When I said I would
die a bachelor, I did not think I should live till I
were married. Here comes Beatrice. By this day!
she's a fair lady: I do spy some marks of love in her.

Enter BEATRICE.

BEATRICE   Against my will I am sent to bid you come in to dinner.   160

BENEDICK   Fair Beatrice, I thank you for your pains.

BEATRICE   I took no more pains for those thanks than you take pains to
thank me: if it had been painful, I would not have come.

BENEDICK   You take pleasure then in the message?

BEATRICE   Yea, just so much as you may take upon a knife's point. You   165
have no stomach, signior: fare you well.

Exit

BENEDICK   Ha! 'Against my will I am sent to bid you come in to dinner;'
there's a double meaning in that. I will go get her picture.

Exit

ACT III

Scene i

LEONATO'S garden. Enter HERO and URSULA.

HERO   Now, Ursula, when Beatrice doth come,
  As we do trace this alley up and down,
  Our talk must only be of Benedick.
  When I do name him, let it be thy part
  To praise him more than ever man did merit: 5
  My talk to thee must be how Benedick
  Is sick in love with Beatrice. Of this matter
  Is little Cupid's crafty arrow made,
  That only wounds by hearsay.

Enter BEATRICE, behind, into the bower.

URSULA   But are you sure   10
  That Benedick loves Beatrice so entirely?

HERO   So says the prince and my new-trothed lord.

URSULA   And did they bid you tell her of it, madam?

HERO   They did entreat me to acquaint her of it;
  But I persuaded them, if they loved Benedick,   15
  To wish him wrestle with affection,
  And never to let Beatrice know of it.

URSULA   Why did you so? Doth not the gentleman
  Deserve as full as fortunate a bed
  As ever Beatrice shall couch upon?   20

HERO   O god of love! I know he doth deserve
  As much as may be yielded to a man:
  But Nature never framed a woman's heart
  Of prouder stuff than that of Beatrice;
  Disdain and scorn ride sparkling in her eyes,   25
  Misprising what they look on, and her wit
  Values itself so highly that to her
  All matter else seems weak: she cannot love,
  Nor take no shape nor project of affection,
  She is so self-endeared.   30

URSULA   Sure, I think so;
  And therefore certainly it were not good
  She knew his love, lest she make sport at it.

HERO   Why, you speak truth. I never yet saw man,
  How wise, how noble, young, how rarely featured,   35
  But she would spell him backward: if fair-faced.
  So turns she every man the wrong side out
  And never gives to truth and virtue that
  Which simpleness and merit purchaseth.
  But who dare tell her so? If I should speak,   40
  She would mock me into air; O, she would laugh me
  Out of myself, press me to death with wit.
  Therefore let Benedick, like cover'd fire,
  Consume away in sighs, waste inwardly.

URSULA   Yet tell her of it: hear what she will say.   45

HERO   No; rather I will go to Benedick
  And counsel him to fight against his passion.

URSULA   O, do not do your cousin such a wrong.
  She cannot be so much without true judgment—
  Having so swift and excellent a wit   50

As she is prized to have—as to refuse
So rare a gentleman as Signior Benedick.

HERO   He is the only man of Italy.
Always excepted my dear Claudio.

URSULA   *[To HERO]* She's limed, I warrant you: 55
we have caught her, madam.

HERO   *[To URSULA]* If it proves so, then loving goes by haps:
Some Cupid kills with arrows, some with traps.

Exeunt HERO and URSULA.

BEATRICE   *[Coming forward.]*
What fire is in mine ears? Can this be true?
Stand I condemn'd for pride and scorn so much?   60
Contempt, farewell! and maiden pride, adieu!
No glory lives behind the back of such.
And, Benedick, love on; I will requite thee,
Taming my wild heart to thy loving hand:
 If thou dost love, my kindness shall incite thee   65
To bind our loves up in a holy band;
For others say thou dost deserve, and I
Believe it better than reportingly.

Exit

Scene ii

A room in LEONATO'S house. Enter DON PEDRO, CLAUDIO, BENEDICK, and LEONATO.

BENEDICK   Gallants, I am not as I have been.

LEONATO   So say I methinks you are sadder.

CLAUDIO   I hope he be in love.

BENEDICK   Old signior, walk aside with me: I have studied eight or nine
wise words to speak to you, which these hobby-horses must not hear.   5

Exeunt BENEDICK and LEONATO.

DON PEDRO   For my life, to break with him about Beatrice.

CLAUDIO   'Tis even so. Hero and Margaret have by this
played their parts with Beatrice; and then the two
bears will not bite one another when they meet.

Enter DON JOHN.

DON JOHN   My lord and brother, God save you!   10

DON PEDRO   Good den, brother.

DON JOHN   If your leisure served, I would speak with you.

DON PEDRO   In private?

DON JOHN   If it please you: yet Count Claudio may hear; for what I would
speak of concerns him.   15

DON PEDRO   What's the matter?

DON JOHN   *[To CLAUDIO.]* Means your lordship to be married to-morrow?

DON PEDRO   You know he does.

DON JOHN   I know not that, when he knows what I know.

CLAUDIO   If there be any impediment, I pray you discover it.   20

DON JOHN   You may think I love you not: let that appear
hereafter, and aim better at me by that I now will manifest.

DON PEDRO   Why, what's the matter?

DON JOHN   I came hither to tell you; and, circumstances shortened, for
she has been too long a talking of, the lady is disloyal.   25

CLAUDIO   Who, Hero?

DON PEDRO   Even she; Leonato's Hero, your Hero, every man's Hero.

CLAUDIO   Disloyal?

DON JOHN   The word is too good to paint out her wickedness; I could say she were worse: think you of a worse title, and I will fit her to it. Wonder not till further warrant: go but with me to-night, you shall see her chamber-window entered, even the night before her wedding-day: if you love her then, to-morrow wed her; but it would better fit your honour to change your mind. 30

CLAUDIO   May this be so? 35

DON PEDRO   I will not think it.

DON JOHN   If you dare not trust that you see, confess not that you know: if you will follow me, I will show you enough; and when you have seen more and heard more, proceed accordingly.

CLAUDIO   If I see any thing to-night why I should not marry her tomorrow in the congregation, where I should wed, there will I shame her. 40

DON PEDRO   And, as I wooed for thee to obtain her, I will join with thee to disgrace her.

DON JOHN   I will disparage her no farther till you are my witnesses: bear it coldly but till midnight, and let the issue show itself. 45

Exeunt

Scene iii

A street. Enter DOGBERRY and VERGES with the Watch

DOGBERRY   Are you good men and true? Being chosen for the prince's watch, this is your charge: you shall comprehend all vagrom men; you are to bid any man stand, in the prince's name.

WATCHMAN 2   How if a' will not stand?

DOGBERRY   Why, then, take no note of him, but let him go; and presently call the rest of the watch together and thank God you are rid of a knave. 5

VERGES   If he will not stand when he is bidden, he is none of the prince's subjects.

DOGBERRY   True, and they are to meddle with none but the prince's subjects. You shall also make no noise in the streets; for, for the watch to babble and to talk is most tolerable and not to be endured. 10

WATCHMAN   We will rather sleep than talk.

DOGBERRY   Why, you speak like an ancient and most quiet watchman; for I cannot see how sleeping should offend: only, have a care that your bills be not stolen. Well, you are to call at all the ale-houses, and bid those that are drunk get them to bed. 15

WATCHMAN   How if they will not?

DOGBERRY   Why, then, let them alone till they are sober: if they make you not then the better answer, you may say they are not the men you took them for. If you meet a thief, you may suspect him, by virtue of your office, to be no true man; and, for such kind of men, the less you meddle or make with them, why the more is for your honesty. 20

WATCHMAN   If we know him to be a thief, shall we not lay hands on him?

DOGBERRY   Truly, by your office, you may; but I think they that touch pitch will be defiled: the most peaceable way for you, if you do take a thief, is to let him show himself what he is and steal out of your company. 30

VERGES   You have been always called a merciful man, partner.

DOGBERRY   Truly, I would not hang a dog by my will, much more a man who hath any honesty in him. 35

VERGES　'Tis very true.

DOGBERRY　This is the end of the charge. Come, neighbour.

WATCHMAN　Well, masters, we hear our charge: let us go sit here
upon the church-bench till two, and then all to bed.

DOGBERRY　One word more, honest neighbours. I pray you watch about　　40
Signior Leonato's door; for the wedding being there to-morrow, there is a
great coil to-night. Adieu: be vigitant,[1] I beseech you.

[Exeunt DOGBERRY and VERGES]

[Enter BORACHIO and CONRADE]

BORACHIO　What Conrade!

WATCHMAN　*[Aside]* Peace! stir not.

CONRADE　Here, man; I am at thy elbow.　　45

BORACHIO　Mass, and my elbow itched; I thought there would a scab
follow.

CONRADE　I will owe thee an answer for that: and now forward with thy
tale.

BORACHIO　Stand thee close, then, and I will, like a true drunkard, utter　　50
all to thee.

WATCHMAN　*[Aside]* Some treason, masters: yet stand close.

BORACHIO　Therefore know I have earned of Don John a thousand ducats.

CONRADE　Is it possible that any villany should be so dear?

BORACHIO　Know that I have to-night　　55
wooed Margaret, the Lady Hero's gentlewoman, by the
name of Hero: she leans me out at her mistress'
chamber-window, bids me a thousand times good
night,—I tell this tale vilely:—I should first
tell thee how the prince, Claudio and my master,　　60
planted and placed and possessed by my master Don
John, saw afar off in the orchard this amiable encounter.

CONRADE　And thought they Margaret was Hero?

BORACHIO　Two of them did, the prince and Claudio; but the
devil my master knew she was Margaret; and partly　　65
by his oaths, which first possessed them, partly by
the dark night, which did deceive them, but chiefly
by my villany, which did confirm any slander that
Don John had made, away went Claudio enraged; swore
he would meet her, as he was appointed, next morning　　70
at the temple, and there, before the whole
congregation, shame her with what he saw o'er night
and send her home again without a husband.

WATCHMAN 1　We charge you, in the prince's name, stand!

WATCHMAN 2　Call up the right master constable. We have here　　75
recovered the most dangerous piece of lechery that ever was known in
the commonwealth.

[Exeunt]

Scene iv

HERO's apartment. Enter HERO, MARGARET, and URSULA.

HERO　Good Ursula, wake my cousin Beatrice, and desire her to rise.

URSULA　I will, lady.

---

[1] Dogberry means to say "vigilant."

Exit URSULA. Enter BEATRICE.

HERO   Good morrow, coz.

BEATRICE   Good morrow, sweet Hero.

HERO   Why how now? do you speak in the sick tune?   5

BEATRICE   I am out of all other tune, methinks.
'Tis almost five o'clock, cousin; tis time you were
ready. By my troth, I am exceeding ill: heigh-ho!

MARGARET   If I would think my heart out of thinking, that you
are in love or that you will be in love or that you   10
can be in love. Yet Benedick was such another, and
now is he become a man: but methinks you look with
your eyes as other women do.

BEATRICE   What pace is this that thy tongue keeps?

MARGARET   Not a false gallop.   15

Re-enter URSULA.

URSULA   Madam, withdraw: the prince, the count, Signior
Benedick, Don John, and all the gallants of the
town, are come to fetch you to church.

HERO   Help to dress me, good coz, good Meg, good Ursula.

Exeunt

Scene v

Another room in LEONATO'S house. Enter LEONATO, with DOGBERRY and VERGES.

LEONATO   What would you with me, honest neighbour?

DOGBERRY   Marry, sir, I would have some confidence with you that
decerns you nearly.

LEONATO   Brief, I pray you; for you see it is a busy time with me.

DOGBERRY   Marry, this it is, sir.   5

VERGES   Yes, in truth it is, sir.

LEONATO   Neighbours, you are tedious.

DOGBERRY   It pleases your worship to say so, but we are the poor duke's
officers; but truly, for mine own part, if I were as tedious as a king, I
could find it in my heart to bestow it all of your worship.   10

LEONATO   All thy tediousness on me, ah? I would fain know what you
have to say.

VERGES   Marry, sir, our watch to-night, excepting your worship's
presence, ha' ta'en a couple of as arrant knaves as any in Messina.

DOGBERRY   A good old man, sir; he will be talking: as they say, when 15
the age is in, the wit is out: God help us! it is a world to see. Well said, i'
faith, neighbour Verges: well, God's a good man; an two men ride of a
horse, one must ride behind. An honest soul, i' faith, sir; by my troth he
is, as ever broke bread; but God is to be worshipped; all men are not
alike; alas, good neighbour!   20

LEONATO   Indeed, neighbour, he comes too short of you.

DOGBERRY   Gifts that God gives.

LEONATO   I must leave you.

DOGBERRY   One word, sir: our watch, sir, have indeed comprehended two
aspicious persons, and we would have them this morning examined   25
before your worship.

LEONATO   Take their examination yourself and bring it me: I am now in
great haste, as it may appear unto you. Drink some wine ere you go:
fare you well.

Exeunt LEONATO.

DOGBERRY We are now to examination these men. Get the learned   30
    writer to set down our excommunication and meet me at the gaol.

Exeunt

ACT IV

Scene i

*A church. Enter DON PEDRO, DON JOHN, LEONATO, FRIAR FRANCIS, CLAUDIO,
BENEDICK, HERO, BEATRICE, and Attendants.*

FRIAR FRANCIS   You come hither, my lord, to marry this lady.

CLAUDIO   No.

LEONATO   To be married to her: friar, you come to marry her.

FRIAR FRANCIS   Lady, you come hither to be married to this count.

HERO   I do.   5

FRIAR FRANCIS   If either of you know any inward impediment why you
    should not be conjoined, charge you, on your souls, to utter it.

CLAUDIO   Know you any, Hero?

HERO   None, my lord.

FRIAR FRANCIS   Know you any, count?   10

LEONATO   I dare make his answer, none.

CLAUDIO   Stand thee by, friar. Father, by your leave:
    Will you with free and unconstrained soul
    Give me this maid, your daughter?

LEONATO   As freely, son, as God did give her me.   15

CLAUDIO   And what have I to give you back, whose worth
    May counterpoise this rich and precious gift?

DON PEDRO   Nothing, unless you render her again.

CLAUDIO   Sweet prince, you learn me noble thankfulness.
    There, Leonato, take her back again: 20
    Give not this rotten orange to your friend;
    She's but the sign and semblance of her honour.
    Behold how like a maid she blushes here!
    O, what authority and show of truth
    Can cunning sin cover itself withal!   25
    Comes not that blood as modest evidence
    To witness simple virtue? Would you not swear,
    All you that see her, that she were a maid,
    By these exterior shows? But she is none:
    She knows the heat of a luxurious bed;   30
    Her blush is guiltiness, not modesty.

LEONATO   What do you mean, my lord?

CLAUDIO   Not to be married,
    Not to knit my soul to an approved wanton.

LEONATO   Dear my lord, if you, in your own proof,   35
    Have vanquish'd the resistance of her youth,
    And made defeat of her virginity,—

CLAUDIO   I never tempted her with word too large;
    But, as a brother to his sister, show'd
    Bashful sincerity and comely love.   40

HERO   And seem'd I ever otherwise to you?

CLAUDIO   You seem to me as Dian in her orb,
    As chaste as is the bud ere it be blown;

> But you are more intemperate in your blood
> Than Venus, or those pamper'd animals   45
> That rage in savage sensuality.

HERO   Is my lord well, that he doth speak so wide?

LEONATO   Sweet prince, why speak not you?

DON PEDRO   What should I speak?
> I stand dishonour'd, that have gone about   50
> To link my dear friend to a common stale.

LEONATO   Are these things spoken, or do I but dream?

DON JOHN   Sir, they are spoken, and these things are true.

HERO   True! O God!

CLAUDIO   Let me but move one question to your daughter;   55
> And, by that fatherly and kindly power
> That you have in her, bid her answer truly.

LEONATO   I charge thee do so, as thou art my child.

HERO   O, God defend me! how am I beset!
> What kind of catechising call you this?   60

CLAUDIO   To make you answer truly to your name.

HERO   Is it not Hero? Who can blot that name With any just reproach?

CLAUDIO   Marry, that can Hero;
> Hero itself can blot out Hero's virtue.
> What man was he talk'd with you yesternight   65
> Out at your window betwixt twelve and one?
> Now, if you are a maid, answer to this.

HERO   I talk'd with no man at that hour, my lord.

DON PEDRO   Why, then are you no maiden. Leonato,
> I am sorry you must hear: upon mine honour,   70
> Myself, my brother and this grieved count
> Did see her, hear her, at that hour last night
> Talk with a ruffian at her chamber-window
> Who hath indeed, most like a liberal villain,
> Confess'd the vile encounters they have had   75
> A thousand times in secret.

CLAUDIO   O Hero, what a Hero hadst thou been,
> If half thy outward graces had been placed
> About thy thoughts and counsels of thy heart!
> But fare thee well, most foul, most fair! farewell,   80
> Thou pure impiety and impious purity!
> For thee I'll lock up all the gates of love,
> And on my eyelids shall conjecture hang,
> To turn all beauty into thoughts of harm,
> And never shall it more be gracious.   85

LEONATO   Hath no man's dagger here a point for me?

HERO swoons.

BEATRICE   Why, how now, cousin! wherefore sink you down?

DON JOHN   Come, let us go. These things, come thus to light,
> Smother her spirits up.

Exeunt DON PEDRO, DON JOHN, and CLAUDIO.

BENEDICK   How doth the lady?   90

BEATRICE   Dead, I think. Help, uncle!

LEONATO   O Fate! take not away thy heavy hand.
> Death is the fairest cover for her shame
> That may be wish'd for.

BEATRICE   How now, cousin Hero!   95

FRIAR FRANCIS   Have comfort, lady.

LEONATO   Why, doth not every earthly thing
  Cry shame upon her? Could she here deny
  The story that is printed in her blood?
  Do not live, Hero; do not ope thine eyes: 100
  For, did I think thou wouldst not quickly die,
  Thought I thy spirits were stronger than thy shames,
  Myself would, on the rearward of reproaches,
  Strike at thy life. Grieved I, I had but one?
  Why had I one?   105
  Why ever wast thou lovely in my eyes?
  Why, she, O, she is fallen
  Into a pit of ink, that the wide sea
  Hath drops too few to wash her clean again
  And salt too little which may season give   110
  To her foul-tainted flesh!

BENEDICK   Sir, sir, be patient.
  For my part, I am so attired in wonder,
  I know not what to say.

BEATRICE   O, on my soul, my cousin is belied!   115

BENEDICK   Lady, were you her bedfellow last night?

BEATRICE   No, truly not; although, until last night,
  I have this twelvemonth been her bedfellow.

LEONATO   Confirm'd, confirm'd!
  Would the two princes lie, and Claudio lie?   120
  Hence from her! let her die.

FRIAR FRANCIS   Hear me a little; for I have only been
  Silent so long and given way unto
  This course of fortune
  By noting of the lady: I have mark'd   125
  A thousand blushing apparitions
  To start into her face; a thousand innocent shames
  In angel whiteness beat away those blushes;
  And in her eye there hath appear'd a fire,
  To burn the errors that these princes hold   130
  Against her maiden truth. Call me a fool,
  if this sweet lady lie not guiltless here
  Under some biting error.
  Lady, what man is he you are accused of?

HERO   They know that do accuse me; I know none!   135

FRIAR FRANCIS   There is some strange misprision in the princes.

BENEDICK   Two of them have the very bent of honour;
  And if their wisdoms be misled in this,
  The practise of it lives in John the bastard,
  Whose spirits toil in frame of villanies.   140

LEONATO   I know not. If they speak but truth of her,
  These hands shall tear her; if they wrong her honour,
  The proudest of them shall well hear of it.
  Time hath not yet so dried this blood of mine,
  Nor age so eat up my invention,   145
  Nor fortune made such havoc of my means,
  Nor my bad life reft me so much of friends,
  But they shall find, awaked in such a kind,
  Both strength of limb and policy of mind,
  Ability in means and choice of friends,   150
  To quit me of them throughly.

FRIAR FRANCIS Pause awhile,
  And let my counsel sway you in this case.
  Your daughter here the princes left for dead:
  Let her awhile be secretly kept in,   155
  And publish it that she is dead indeed;
  Maintain a mourning ostentation
  And on your family's old monument
  Hang mournful epitaphs and do all rites
  That appertain unto a burial.   160

LEONATO What shall become of this? what will this do?

FRIAR FRANCIS Marry, this well carried shall on her behalf
  Change slander to remorse; that is some good:
  But not for that dream I on this strange course,
  But on this travail look for greater birth.   165
  She dying, as it must so be maintain'd,
  Upon the instant that she was accused,
  Shall be lamented, pitied and excused
  Of every hearer: So will it fare with Claudio:
  When he shall hear she died upon his words,   170
  The idea of her life shall sweetly creep
  Into his study of imagination,
  And every lovely organ of her life
  Shall come apparell'd in more precious habit,
  More moving-delicate and full of life,   175
  Into the eye and prospect of his soul,
  Than when she lived indeed; then shall he mourn,
  But if all aim but this be levell'd false,
  The supposition of the lady's death
  Will quench the wonder of her infamy: 180
  And if it sort not well, you may conceal her,
  As best befits her wounded reputation,
  In some reclusive and religious life,
  Out of all eyes, tongues, minds and injuries.

BENEDICK Signior Leonato, let the friar advise you.   185

LEONATO Being that I flow in grief,
  The smallest twine may lead me.

FRIAR FRANCIS 'Tis well consented: presently away.
  Come, lady, die to live: this wedding-day
  Perhaps is but prolong'd: have patience and endure. 190

Exeunt all but BENEDICK and BEATRICE.

BENEDICK Lady Beatrice, have you wept all this while?

BEATRICE Yea, and I will weep a while longer.

BENEDICK I will not desire that.

BEATRICE You have no reason; I do it freely.

BENEDICK Surely I do believe your fair cousin is wronged.   195

BEATRICE Ah, how much might the man deserve of me that would right
her!

BENEDICK Is there any way to show such friendship?

BEATRICE A very even way, but no such friend.

BENEDICK May a man do it?   200

BEATRICE It is a man's office, but not yours.

BENEDICK I do love nothing in the world so well as you: is not that
strange?

BEATRICE   As strange as the thing I know not. It were as possible for me
to say I loved nothing so well as you: but believe me not; and yet I lie   205
not; I confess nothing, nor I deny nothing. I am sorry for my cousin.

BENEDICK   By my sword, Beatrice, thou lovest me.

BEATRICE   Do not swear, and eat it.

BENEDICK   I will swear by it that you love me; and I will make him eat it
that says I love not you.   210

BEATRICE   Will you not eat your word?

BENEDICK   I protest I love thee.

BEATRICE   Why, then, God forgive me!

BENEDICK   What offence, sweet Beatrice?

BEATRICE   You have stayed me in a happy hour: I was about to protest I   215
loved you.

BENEDICK   And do it with all thy heart.

BEATRICE   I love you with so much of my heart that none is left to
protest.

BENEDICK   Come, bid me do any thing for thee.   220

BEATRICE   Kill Claudio.

BENEDICK   Ha! not for the wide world.

BEATRICE   You kill me to deny it. Farewell.

BENEDICK   Tarry, sweet Beatrice. *[Holding her.]*

BEATRICE   I am gone, though I am here: there is no love in you: nay, I   225
pray you, let me go.

BENEDICK   Beatrice,—

BEATRICE   In faith, I will go.

BENEDICK   We'll be friends first.

BEATRICE   You dare easier be friends with me than fight with mine   230
enemy.

BENEDICK   Is Claudio thine enemy?

BEATRICE   Is he not approved in the height a villain, that hath slandered,
scorned, dishonoured my kinswoman? O that I were a man! What, bear
her in hand until they come to take hands; and then, with public   235
accusation, uncovered slander, unmitigated rancour, —O God, that I
were a man! I would eat his heart in the market-place.

BENEDICK   Hear me, Beatrice,—

BEATRICE   Talk with a man out at a window! A proper saying!

BENEDICK   Nay, but, Beatrice,—   240

BEATRICE   Sweet Hero! She is wronged, she is slandered, she is undone.

BENEDICK   Beatrice!

BEATRICE   O that I were a man for his sake! or that I had any friend
would be a man for my sake! But manhood is melted into courtesies,
valour into compliment, and men are only turned into tongue, and trim   245
ones too: he is now as valiant as Hercules that only tells a lie and swears
it. I cannot be a man with wishing, therefore I will die a woman with
grieving.

BENEDICK   Tarry, good Beatrice. By this hand, I love thee.

BEATRICE   Use it for my love some other way than swearing by it.   250

BENEDICK   Think you in your soul the Count Claudio hath wronged Hero?

BEATRICE   Yea, as sure as I have a thought or a soul.

BENEDICK   Enough, I am engaged; I will challenge him.
Claudio shall render me a dear account.

Go, comfort your cousin: 255
I must say she is dead: and so, farewell.

Exeunt

Scene ii

*A prison. Enter DOGBERRY, VERGES, and Sexton, in gowns; and the Watch, with
CONRADE and BORACHIO.*

DOGBERRY   Is our whole dissembly appeared?

SEXTON   Which be the malefactors?

DOGBERRY   Marry, that am I and my partner.

SEXTON   But which are the offenders that are to be examined? Let them
come before master constable.   5

DOGBERRY   Yea, marry, let them come before me. What is your name,
friend?

BORACHIO   Borachio.

DOGBERRY   Pray, write down, Borachio. Yours, sirrah?

CONRADE   I am a gentleman, sir, and my name is Conrade.   10

DOGBERRY   Write down, master gentleman Conrade.

[To BORACHIO and CONRADE.]

Masters, it is proved already that you are little better than false knaves.
How answer you for yourselves?

CONRADE   Marry, sir, we say we are none.

BORACHIO   Sir, I say to you we are none.   15

DOGBERRY   *[To SEXTON.]* Have you writ down, that they are none?

SEXTON   Master constable, you go not the way to examine: you must call
forth the watch that are their accusers.

DOGBERRY   Let the watch come forth. Masters, I charge you, in the
prince's name, accuse these men.   20

WATCHMAN 1   This man said, sir, that Don John, the prince's brother, was
a villain.

DOGBERRY   Write down Prince John a villain.

BORACHIO   Master constable,—

DOGBERRY   Pray thee, fellow, peace: I do not like thy look.   25

SEXTON   What heard you him say else?

WATCHMAN 2   Marry, that he had received a thousand ducats of Don John
for accusing the Lady Hero wrongfully.

DOGBERRY   Flat burglary as ever was committed.

VERGES   Yea, by mass, that it is.   30

SEXTON   What else, fellow?

WATCHMAN 1   And that Count Claudio did mean, upon his words, to
disgrace Hero before the whole assembly and not marry her.

DOGBERRY   O villain! thou wilt be condemned into everlasting redemption
for this.   35

SEXTON   What else?

WATCHMAN   This is all.

SEXTON   Prince John is this morning secretly stolen away; Hero was in
this manner accused, in this very manner refused, and upon the grief of
this suddenly died. Master constable, let these men be bound, and   40
brought to Leonato's: I will go before and show him their examination.

Exit

DOGBERRY Come, let them be opinioned.[1]

VERGES Let them be in the hands—

CONRADE Off, coxcomb!

DOGBERRY God's my life, where's the sexton? Let him write down the
prince's officer coxcomb. Come, bind them. Thou naughty varlet!   45

CONRADE Away! You are an ass, you are an ass.

DOGBERRY Dost thou not suspect my place? Dost thou not suspect my
years? O that he were here to write me down an ass! But, masters,
remember that I am an ass; though it be not written down, yet forget not
that I am an ass. Bring him away. O that I had been writ down an ass!   50

Exeunt

ACT V

Scene i

Before LEONATO'S house. Enter LEONATO and ANTONIO.

ANTONIO If you go on thus, you will kill yourself:
And 'tis not wisdom thus to second grief
Against yourself.

LEONATO Bring me a father that so loved his child,
Whose joy of her is overwhelm'd like mine,   5
And bid him speak of patience;
But there is no such man: for,
'tis all men's office to speak patience
To those that wring under the load of sorrow.

ANTONIO Yet bend not all the harm upon yourself;   10
Make those that do offend you suffer too.

LEONATO There thou speak'st reason: nay, I will do so.
My soul doth tell me Hero is belied;
And that shall Claudio know; so shall the prince
And all of them that thus dishonour her.   15

ANTONIO Here comes the prince and Claudio hastily.

Enter DON PEDRO and CLAUDIO.

DON PEDRO Good den, good den.

CLAUDIO Good day to both of you.

LEONATO Hear you. my lords,—

DON PEDRO We have some haste, Leonato.   20

LEONATO Some haste, my lord! well, fare you well, my lord:
Are you so hasty now? well, all is one.

DON PEDRO Nay, do not quarrel with us, good old man.

ANTONIO If he could right himself with quarreling,
Some of us would lie low.   25

CLAUDIO Who wrongs him?

LEONATO Marry, thou dost wrong me; thou dissembler, thou:—
Nay, never lay thy hand upon thy sword;
I fear thee not.

CLAUDIO Marry, beshrew my hand,   30
If it should give your age such cause of fear:
In faith, my hand meant nothing to my sword.

---

[1] Dogberry confuses *pinion* with *opinion*. Pinion means "to bind."

330 MUCH ADO ABOUT NOTHING – ACT V

LEONATO   Tush, tush, man; never fleer and jest at me:
   I speak not like a dotard nor a fool.
   I say thou hast belied mine innocent child;   35
   Thy slander hath gone through and through her heart,
   And she lies buried with her ancestors;
   O, in a tomb where never scandal slept,
   Save this of hers, framed by thy villany!

DON PEDRO   You say not right, old man.   40

LEONATO   My lord, my lord,
   I'll prove it on his body, if he dare,
   Despite his nice fence and his active practise,
   His May of youth and bloom of lustihood.

CLAUDIO   Away! I will not have to do with you.   45

LEONATO   Canst thou so daff me? Thou hast kill'd my child:
   If thou kill'st me, boy, thou shalt kill a man.

ANTONIO   He shall kill two of us, and men indeed:
   But that's no matter; let him kill one first;
   Win me and wear me; let him answer me.   50
   Come, follow me, boy; come, sir boy, come, follow me:
   Sir boy, I'll whip you from your foining fence;
   Nay, as I am a gentleman, I will.

LEONATO   Brother,—

ANTONIO   Content yourself. God knows I loved my niece;   55
   And she is dead, slander'd to death by villains,

DON PEDRO   Gentlemen both, we will not wake your patience.
   My heart is sorry for your daughter's death:
   But, on my honour, she was charged with nothing
   But what was true and very full of proof.   60

LEONATO   My lord, my lord,—

DON PEDRO   I will not hear you.

LEONATO   No? Come, brother; away! I will be heard.

ANTONIO   And shall, or some of us will smart for it.

Exeunt LEONATO and ANTONIO.

DON PEDRO   See, see; here comes the man we went to seek.   65

Enter BENEDICK.

CLAUDIO   Now, signior, what news?

BENEDICK   Good day, my lord.

DON PEDRO   Welcome, signior: you are almost come to part almost a
   fray.

CLAUDIO   We had like to have had our two noses snapped off with two old
   men without teeth.   70

BENEDICK   *[To CLAUDIO.]*
   Shall I speak a word in your ear? I will make it good how you dare, with
   what you dare, and when you dare. Do me right, or I will protest your
   cowardice. You have killed a sweet lady, and her death shall fall heavy on
   you. Let me hear from you. Fare you well, boy: you know my mind.

[To DON PEDRO.]

   My lord, for your many courtesies I thank you: I must discontinue your   75
   company: your brother the bastard is fled from Messina: you have
   among you killed a sweet and innocent lady. For my Lord Lackbeard
   there, he and I shall meet: and, till then, peace be with him.

Exit

DON PEDRO   He is in earnest.

CLAUDIO   In most profound earnest.   80

DON PEDRO   And hath challenged thee.

CLAUDIO   Most sincerely.

Enter DOGBERRY, VERGES, and the Watch, with CONRADE and BORACHIO.

DON PEDRO   Officers, what offence have these men done?

DOGBERRY   Marry, sir, they have committed false report; moreover, they
have spoken untruths; secondarily, they are slanders; sixth and lastly,   85
they have belied a lady; thirdly, they have verified unjust things; and, to
conclude, they are lying knaves.

DON PEDRO   Who have you offended, masters, that you are thus bound to
your answer? this learned constable is too cunning to be understood:
what's your offence?   90

BORACHIO   Sweet prince, let me go no farther to mine answer:
do you hear me, and let this count kill me. I have
deceived even your very eyes: what your wisdoms
could not discover, these shallow fools have brought
to light: who in the night overheard me confessing   95
to this man how Don John your brother incensed me
to slander the Lady Hero, how you were brought into
the orchard and saw me court Margaret in Hero's
garments, how you disgraced her, when you should
marry her: my villany they have upon record; which   100
I had rather seal with my death than repeat over
to my shame. The lady is dead upon mine and my
master's false accusation; and, briefly, I desire
nothing but the reward of a villain.

DON PEDRO   But did my brother set thee on to this?   105

BORACHIO   Yea, and paid me richly for the practise of it.

DON PEDRO   He is composed and framed of treachery:
And fled he is upon this villany.

CLAUDIO   Sweet Hero! Now thy image doth appear
In the rare semblance that I loved it first.   110

DOGBERRY   Come, bring away the plaintiffs: by this time our sexton hath
reformed Signior Leonato of the matter: and, masters, do not forget to
specify, when time and place shall serve, that I am an ass.

VERGES   Here, here.

Re-enter LEONATO and ANTONIO, with the Sexton.

LEONATO   Which is the villain? let me see his eyes,   115
That, when I note another man like him,
I may avoid him: which of these is he?

BORACHIO   If you would know your wronger, look on me.

LEONATO   Art thou the slave that with thy breath hast kill'd Mine innocent
child?   120

BORACHIO   Yea, even I alone.

LEONATO   No, not so, villain; thou beliest thyself:
Here stand a pair of honourable men;
A third is fled, that had a hand in it.
I thank you, princes, for my daughter's death: 125
Record it with your high and worthy deeds:
'Twas bravely done, if you bethink you of it.

CLAUDIO   I know not how to pray your patience;
Yet I must speak. Choose your revenge yourself;
Impose me to what penance your invention   130

> Can lay upon my sin: yet sinn'd I not
> But in mistaking.

DON PEDRO   By my soul, nor I.

LEONATO   I cannot bid you bid my daughter live;
> That were impossible: but, I pray you both,   135
> Possess the people in Messina here
> How innocent she died; and if your love
> Can labour ought in sad invention,
> Hang her an epitaph upon her tomb
> And sing it to her bones, sing it to-night: 140
> To-morrow morning come you to my house,
> And since you could not be my son-in-law,
> Be yet my nephew: my brother hath a daughter,
> Almost the copy of my child that's dead,
> And she alone is heir to both of us: 145
> Give her the right you should have given her cousin,
> And so dies my revenge.

CLAUDIO   O noble sir,
> Your over-kindness doth wring tears from me!
> I do embrace your offer; and dispose   150
> For henceforth of poor Claudio.

LEONATO   To-morrow then I will expect your coming;
> To-night I take my leave. This naughty man
> Shall face to face be brought to Margaret,
> Who I believe was pack'd in all this wrong,   155
> Hired to it by your brother.

BORACHIO   No, by my soul, she was not,
> Nor knew not what she did when she spoke to me,
> But always hath been just and virtuous
> In any thing that I do know by her.   160

DOGBERRY   Moreover, sir, which indeed is not under white and black, this
> plaintiff here, the offender, did call me ass: I beseech you, let it be
> remembered in his punishment.

LEONATO   I thank thee for thy care and honest pains.

DOGBERRY   Your worship speaks like a most thankful and reverend youth;   165
> and I praise God for you.

LEONATO   There's for thy pains.

DOGBERRY   God save the foundation!

LEONATO   Go, I discharge thee of thy prisoner, and I thank thee.

DOGBERRY   I leave an arrant knave with your worship; which I beseech   170
> your worship to correct yourself, for the example of others. God keep
> your worship! I wish your worship well; God restore you to health! I
> humbly give you leave to depart; and if a merry meeting may be wished,
> God prohibit it! Come, neighbour.

Exeunt DOGBERRY and VERGES.

LEONATO   Until to-morrow morning, lords, farewell.   175

ANTONIO   Farewell, my lords: we look for you to-morrow.

DON PEDRO   We will not fail.

CLAUDIO   To-night I'll mourn with Hero.

Exeunt, severally.

Scene ii

LEONATO'S garden. Enter BENEDICK.

Sings

BENEDICK   The god of love,
That sits above,
And knows me, and knows me,
How pitiful I deserve,—

Speaks

I mean in singing; but in loving, Leander the good   5
swimmer, Troilus the first employer of panders, and
a whole bookful of these quondam carpet-mangers,
whose names yet run smoothly in the even road of a
blank verse, why, they were never so truly turned
over and over as my poor self in love. Marry, I   10
cannot show it in rhyme; I have tried: I can find
out no rhyme to 'lady' but 'baby,' an innocent
rhyme; for 'scorn,' 'horn,' a hard rhyme; for,
'school,' 'fool,' a babbling rhyme; very ominous
endings: no, I was not born under a rhyming planet,   15
nor I cannot woo in festival terms.

Enter BEATRICE.

Sweet Beatrice, wouldst thou come when I called thee?

BEATRICE   Yea, signior, and depart when you bid me.

BENEDICK   O, stay but till then!

BEATRICE   'Then' is spoken; fare you well now: and yet, ere   20
I go, let me go with that I came; which is, with
knowing what hath passed between you and Claudio.

BENEDICK   Only foul words; and thereupon I will kiss thee.

BEATRICE   Foul words is but foul wind, and foul wind is but
foul breath, and foul breath is noisome; therefore I   25
will depart unkissed.

BENEDICK   Thou hast frighted the word out of his right sense,
so forcible is thy wit. But I must tell thee
plainly, Claudio undergoes my challenge; and either
I must shortly hear from him, or I will subscribe   30
him a coward. And, I pray thee now, tell me for
which of my bad parts didst thou first fall in love with me?

BEATRICE   For them all together; which maintained so politic
a state of evil that they will not admit any good
part to intermingle with them. But for which of my   35
good parts did you first suffer love for me?

BENEDICK   Suffer love! a good epithet! I do suffer love
indeed, for I love thee against my will.

BEATRICE   In spite of your heart, I think; alas, poor heart!
If you spite it for my sake, I will spite it for   40
yours; for I will never love that which my friend hates.

BENEDICK   Thou and I are too wise to woo peaceably.
And now tell me, how doth your cousin?

BEATRICE   Very ill.

BENEDICK   And how do you?   45

BEATRICE   Very ill too.

BENEDICK   Serve God, love me and mend. There will I leave
you too, for here comes one in haste.

Enter URSULA.

URSULA   Madam, you must come to your uncle.
It is proved my Lady Hero hath been   50
falsely accused, the prince and Claudio mightily
abused; and Don John is the author of all, who is
fed and gone. Will you come presently?

BEATRICE   Will you go hear this news, signior?

BENEDICK   I will live in thy heart, die in thy lap, and be   55
buried in thy eyes; and moreover I will go with
thee to thy uncle's.

Exeunt

Scene iii

A church. Enter DON PEDRO, CLAUDIO, and three or four with tapers.

CLAUDIO   [*Reading out of a scroll.*]
"Done to death by slanderous tongues
Was the Hero that here lies:
Death, in guerdon of her wrongs,
Gives her fame which never dies.
So the life that died with shame   5
Lives in death with glorious fame."

SONG.

"Pardon, goddess of the night,
Those that slew thy virgin knight;
For the which, with songs of woe,
Round about her tomb they go.   10
Midnight, assist our moan;
Help us to sigh and groan,
Heavily, heavily:
Graves, yawn and yield your dead,
Till death be uttered,   15
Heavily, heavily."

CLAUDIO   Now, unto thy bones good night!
Yearly will I do this rite.

DON PEDRO   Good morrow, masters; put your torches out:
The wolves have prey'd; and look, the gentle day,   20
Before the wheels of Phoebus, round about
Dapples the drowsy east with spots of grey.
Thanks to you all, and leave us: fare you well.

Exeunt

Scene iv

A room in LEONATO'S house. Enter LEONATO, ANTONIO, BENEDICK, BEATRICE, MARGARET, URSULA, FRIAR FRANCIS, and HERO.

FRIAR FRANCIS   Did I not tell you she was innocent?

LEONATO   So are the prince and Claudio, who accused her
Upon the error that you heard debated:
But Margaret was in some fault for this,
Although against her will, as it appears   5
In the true course of all the question.

ANTONIO   Well, I am glad that all things sort so well.

LEONATO   Well, daughter, and you gentle-women all,
Withdraw into a chamber by yourselves,
And when I send for you, come hither mask'd.   10

Exeunt Ladies.

The prince and Claudio promised by this hour
To visit me. You know your office, brother:
You must be father to your brother's daughter
And give her to young Claudio.

ANTONIO   Which I will do with confirm'd countenance.   15

BENEDICK   Friar, I must entreat your pains, I think.

FRIAR FRANCIS   To do what, signior?

BENEDICK   To bind me, or undo me; one of them.
Signior Leonato, truth it is, good signior,
Your niece regards me with an eye of favour.   20

LEONATO   That eye my daughter lent her: 'tis most true.

BENEDICK   And I do with an eye of love requite her.

LEONATO   The sight whereof I think you had from me,
From Claudio and the prince: but what's your will?

BENEDICK   Your answer, sir, is enigmatical: 25
But, for my will, my will is your good will
May stand with ours, this day to be conjoin'd
In the state of honourable marriage:
In which, good friar, I shall desire your help.

LEONATO   My heart is with your liking.   30

FRIAR FRANCIS   And my help.
Here comes the prince and Claudio.

Enter DON PEDRO and CLAUDIO, and two or three others.

CLAUDIO   Which is the lady I must seize upon?

ANTONIO   This same is she, and I do give you her.

CLAUDIO   Why, then she's mine. Sweet, let me see your face.   35

LEONATO   No, that you shall not, till you take her hand
Before this friar and swear to marry her.

CLAUDIO   Give me your hand: before this holy friar,
I am your husband, if you like of me.

HERO   And when I lived, I was your other wife: 40

HERO Unmasking.

And when you loved, you were my other husband.
One Hero died defiled, but I do live,
And surely as I live, I am a maid.

DON PEDRO   Hero that is dead!

LEONATO   She died, my lord, but whiles her slander lived.   45

FRIAR FRANCIS   All this amazement can I qualify:
When after that the holy rites are ended,
I'll tell you largely of fair Hero's death:

BENEDICK   Soft and fair, friar. Which is Beatrice?

BEATRICE Unmasking.

BENEDICK   Do not you love me?   50

BEATRICE   Why, no; no more than reason.

BENEDICK   Why, then your uncle and the prince and Claudio
Have been deceived; they swore you did.

BEATRICE   Do not you love me?

BENEDICK   Troth, no; no more than reason.   55

BEATRICE   Why, then my cousin Margaret and Ursula
Are much deceived; for they did swear you did.

BENEDICK   They swore that you were almost sick for me.

BEATRICE   They swore that you were well-nigh dead for me.

BENEDICK   'Tis no such matter. Then you do not love me?   60

BEATRICE   No, truly, but in friendly recompense.

LEONATO   Come, cousin, I am sure you love the gentleman.

CLAUDIO   And I'll be sworn upon't that he loves her;
For here's a paper written in his hand,
A halting sonnet of his own pure brain,   65
Fashion'd to Beatrice.

HERO   And here's another
Writ in my cousin's hand, stolen from her pocket,
Containing her affection unto Benedick.

BENEDICK   A miracle! here's our own hands against our hearts.   70
Come, I will have thee; but, by this light, I take
thee for pity.

BEATRICE   I would not deny you; but, by this good day, I yield
upon great persuasion; and partly to save your life,
for I was told you were in a consumption.   75

BENEDICK   Peace! I will stop your mouth.

Kissing her.

DON PEDRO   How dost thou, Benedick, the married man?

BENEDICK   I'll tell thee what, prince; a college of
wit-crackers cannot flout me out of my humour. Dost
thou think I care for a satire or an epigram? No.   80
In brief, since I do
purpose to marry, I will think nothing to any
purpose that the world can say against it; and
therefore never flout at me for what I have said
against it; for man is a giddy thing, and this is my   85
conclusion. For thy part, Claudio, I did think to
have beaten thee, but in that thou art like to be my
kinsman, live unbruised and love my cousin.
Come, come, we are friends: let's have a dance ere
we are married, that we may lighten our own hearts   90
and our wives' heels.

LEONATO   We'll have dancing afterward.

BENEDICK   First, of my word; therefore play, music. Prince,
thou art sad; get thee a wife, get thee a wife.

Enter a Messenger

MESSENGER   My lord, your brother John is ta'en in flight,   95
And brought with armed men back to Messina.

BENEDICK   Think not on him till to-morrow:
I'll devise thee brave punishments for him.
Strike up, pipers.

Dance

Exeunt.

A Doll's House

Henrik Ibsen
1879

First performed at the Royal Theatre in Copenhagen, Denmark, on December 21, 1879. From Ten Cent Pocket Series No. 353. Edited by E. Haldeman-Julius. Girard, Kansas: Haldeman-Julius Company, 1923.

Dramatis Personae

TORVALD, HELMER   bank executive

NORA wife of Torvald Helmer

RANK a doctor and friend of the family

MRS. LINDE old friend of Nora's

NILS KROGSTAD   disgraced banker looking for job

ANNE   a nurse

MAID and CHILDREN

[The action takes place in Helmer's house at Christmas.]

ACT I

Scene 1. Finance & Integrity

[SCENE.—A room furnished comfortably and tastefully, but not extravagantly. At the back, a door to the right leads to the entrance-hall, another to the left leads to Helmer's study. Between the doors stands a piano. In the middle of the left-hand wall is a door, and beyond it a window. Near the window are a round table, arm-chairs and a small sofa. In the right-hand wall, at the farther end, another door; and on the same side, nearer the footlights, a stove, two easy chairs and a rocking-chair; between the stove and the door, a small table. Engravings on the walls; a cabinet with china and other small objects; a small book-case with well-bound books. The floors are carpeted, and a fire burns in the stove.

It is winter. A bell rings in the hall; shortly afterwards the door is heard to open. Enter NORA, humming a tune and in high spirits. She is in outdoor dress and carries a number of parcels; these she lays on the table to the right. She leaves the outer door open after her, and through it is seen a PORTER who is carrying a Christmas Tree and a basket, which he gives to the MAID who has opened the door.]

NORA   Hide the Christmas Tree carefully, Helen. Be sure the children do not see it until this evening, when it is dressed. *[To the PORTER, taking out her purse.]* How much?

PORTER   Sixpence.

NORA   There is a shilling. No, keep the change.

[The PORTER thanks her, and goes out. NORA shuts the door. She is laughing to herself, as she takes off her hat and coat. She takes a packet of macaroons from her pocket and eats one or two; then goes cautiously to her husband's door and listens.]

Yes, he is in.

[Still humming, she goes to the table on the right.]

HELMER   *[calls out from his room.]* Is that my little lark twittering out there?

NORA   *[busy opening some of the parcels.]* Yes, it is!

HELMER   Is it my little squirrel bustling about?

NORA   Yes!

HELMER   When did my squirrel come home?

NORA   Just now. *[Puts the bag of macaroons[1] into her pocket and wipes her mouth.]* Come in here, Torvald, and see what I have bought.

HELMER   Don't disturb me. *[A little later, he opens the door and looks into the room, pen in hand.]* Bought, did you say? All these things? Has my little spendthrift been wasting money again?

NORA   Yes but, Torvald, this year we really can let ourselves go a little. This is the first Christmas that we have not needed to economise.

HELMER   Still, you know, we can't spend money recklessly.[2]

NORA   Yes, Torvald, we may be a wee bit more reckless now, mayn't we? Just a tiny wee bit! You are going to have a big salary and earn lots and lots of money.

HELMER   Yes, after the New Year; but then it will be a whole quarter before the salary is due.

NORA   Pooh! we can borrow until then.

HELMER   Nora! *[Goes up to her and takes her playfully by the ear.]* The same little featherhead! Suppose, now, that I borrowed fifty pounds[3] today, and you spent it all in the Christmas week, and then on New Year's Eve a slate fell on my head and killed me, and—

NORA   *[putting her hands over his mouth.]* Oh! don't say such horrid things.

HELMER   Still, suppose that happened,—what then?

NORA   If that were to happen, I don't suppose I should care whether I owed money or not.

HELMER   Yes, but what about the people who had lent it?

NORA   They? Who would bother about them? I should not know who they were.

HELMER   That is like a woman! But seriously, Nora, you know what I think about that. No debt, no borrowing. There can be no freedom or beauty about a home life that depends on borrowing and debt. We two have kept bravely on the straight road so far, and we will go on the same way for the short time longer that there need be any struggle.

NORA   *[moving towards the stove.]* As you please, Torvald.

HELMER   *[following her.]* Come, come, my little skylark must not droop her wings. What is this! Is my little squirrel out of temper? *[Taking out his purse.]* Nora, what do you think I have got here?

NORA   *[turning round quickly.]* Money!

HELMER   There you are. *[Gives her some money.]* Do you think I don't know what a lot is wanted for housekeeping at Christmas-time?

NORA   *[counting.]* Ten shillings—a pound—two pounds! Thank you, thank you, Torvald; that will keep me going for a long time.

HELMER   Indeed it must.

NORA   Yes, yes, it will. But come here and let me show you what I have bought. And all so cheap! Look, here is a new suit for Ivar, and a sword; and a horse and a trumpet for Bob; and a doll and dolly's bedstead for Emmy,—they are very plain, but anyway she will soon break them in pieces. And here are dress-lengths and handkerchiefs for the maids; old Anne ought really to have something better.

HELMER   And what is in this parcel?

NORA   *[crying out.]* No, no! you mustn't see that until this evening.

---

[1] macarooms: a small cookie

[2] In this time period, wives were to leave all financial matters to the husband. It was, unfortunately, generally perceived that women were somehow incapable of handling money in a responsible manner.

[3] fifty pounds: approximately $79 in 2012 (by comparison in 1870 United States, a 4-room house cost about $700)

HELMER   Very well. But now tell me, you extravagant little person, what would you like for yourself?

NORA   For myself? Oh, I am sure I don't want anything.

HELMER   Yes, but you must. Tell me something reasonable that you would particularly like to have.

NORA   No, I really can't think of anything—unless, Torvald—

HELMER   Well?

NORA   *[playing with his coat buttons, and without raising her eyes to his.]* If you really want to give me something, you might—you might—

HELMER   Well, out with it!

NORA   *[speaking quickly.]* You might give me money, Torvald. Only just as much as you can afford; and then one of these days I will buy something with it.

HELMER   But, Nora—

NORA   Oh, do! dear Torvald; please, please do! Then I will wrap it up in beautiful gilt paper and hang it on the Christmas Tree. Wouldn't that be fun?

HELMER   What are little people called that are always wasting money?

NORA   Spendthrifts—I know. Let us do as you suggest, Torvald, and then I shall have time to think what I am most in want of. That is a very sensible plan, isn't it?

HELMER   *[smiling.]* Indeed it is—that is to say, if you were really to save out of the money I give you, and then really buy something for yourself. But if you spend it all on the housekeeping and any number of unnecessary things, then I merely have to pay up again.

NORA   Oh but, Torvald—

HELMER   You can't deny it, my dear little Nora. *[Puts his arm round her waist.]* It's a sweet little spendthrift, but she uses up a deal of money. One would hardly believe how expensive such little persons are!

NORA   It's a shame to say that. I do really save all I can.

HELMER   *[laughing.]* That's very true,—all you can. But you can't save anything!

NORA   *[smiling quietly and happily.]* You haven't any idea how many expenses we skylarks and squirrels have, Torvald.

HELMER   You are an odd little soul. Very like your father. You always find some new way of wheedling money out of me, and, as soon as you have got it, it seems to melt in your hands. You never know where it has gone. Still, one must take you as you are. It is in the blood; for indeed it is true that you can inherit these things, Nora.

NORA   Ah, I wish I had inherited many of papa's qualities.

HELMER   And I would not wish you to be anything but just what you are, my sweet little skylark. But, do you know, it strikes me that you are looking rather—what shall I say—rather uneasy today?

NORA   Do I?

HELMER   You do, really. Look straight at me.

NORA   *[looks at him.]* Well?

HELMER   *[wagging his finger at her.]* Hasn't Miss Sweet Tooth been breaking rules in town today?

NORA   No; what makes you think that?

HELMER   Hasn't she paid a visit to the confectioner's?[4]

NORA   No, I assure you, Torvald—

HELMER   Not been nibbling sweets?

---

[4] Someone who makes candies and other sweets

NORA   No, certainly not.

HELMER   Not even taken a bite at a macaroon or two?

NORA   No, Torvald, I assure you really—

HELMER   There, there, of course I was only joking.

NORA   [going to the table on the right.] I should not think of going against your wishes.

HELMER   No, I am sure of that; besides, you gave me your word—[Going up to her.] Keep your little Christmas secrets to yourself, my darling. They will all be revealed tonight when the Christmas Tree is lit, no doubt.

NORA   Did you remember to invite Doctor Rank?

HELMER   No. But there is no need; as a matter of course he will come to dinner with us. However, I will ask him when he comes in this morning. I have ordered some good wine. Nora, you can't think how I am looking forward to this evening.

NORA   So am I! And how the children will enjoy themselves, Torvald!

HELMER   It is splendid to feel that one has a perfectly safe appointment, and a big enough income. It's delightful to think of, isn't it?

NORA   It's wonderful!

HELMER   Do you remember last Christmas? For a full three weeks beforehand you shut yourself up every evening until long after midnight, making ornaments for the Christmas Tree, and all the other fine things that were to be a surprise to us. It was the dullest three weeks I ever spent!

NORA   I didn't find it dull.

HELMER   [smiling.] But there was precious little result, Nora.

NORA   Oh, you shouldn't tease me about that again. How could I help the cat's going in and tearing everything to pieces?

HELMER   Of course you couldn't, poor little girl. You had the best of intentions to please us all, and that's the main thing. But it is a good thing that our hard times are over.

NORA   Yes, it is really wonderful.

HELMER   This time I needn't sit here and be dull all alone, and you needn't ruin your dear eyes and your pretty little hands—

NORA   [clapping her hands.] No, Torvald, I needn't any longer, need I! It's wonderfully lovely to hear you say so! [Taking his arm.] Now I will tell you how I have been thinking we ought to arrange things, Torvald. As soon as Christmas is over—[A bell rings in the hall.] There's the bell. [She tidies the room a little.] There's some one at the door. What a nuisance!

Scene 2. Christine Linde

HELMER   If it is a caller, remember I am not at home.

MAID   [in the doorway.] A lady to see you, ma'am,—a stranger.

NORA   Ask her to come in.

MAID   [to HELMER.] The doctor came at the same time, sir.

HELMER   Did he go straight into my room?

MAID   Yes, sir.

[HELMER goes into his room. The MAID ushers in Mrs Linde, who is in travelling dress, and shuts the door.]

MRS. LINDE   [in a dejected and timid voice.] How do you do, Nora?

NORA   [doubtfully.] How do you do—

MRS. LINDE   You don't recognise me, I suppose.

NORA   No, I don't know—yes, to be sure, I seem to—[Suddenly.] Yes! Christine! Is it really you?

MRS. LINDE   Yes, it is I.

NORA   Christine! To think of my not recognising you! And yet how could I—*[In a gentle voice.]* How you have altered, Christine!

MRS. LINDE   Yes, I have indeed. In nine, ten long years—

NORA   Is it so long since we met? I suppose it is. The last eight years have been a happy time for me, I can tell you. And so now you have come into the town, and have taken this long journey in winter—that was plucky[5] of you.

MRS. LINDE   I arrived by steamer[6] this morning.

NORA   To have some fun at Christmas-time, of course. How delightful! We will have such fun together! But take off your things. You are not cold, I hope. *[Helps her.]* Now we will sit down by the stove, and be cosy. No, take this armchair; I will sit here in the rocking-chair. *[Takes her hands.]* Now you look like your old self again; it was only the first moment—You are a little paler, Christine, and perhaps a little thinner.

MRS. LINDE   And much, much older, Nora.

NORA   Perhaps a little older; very, very little; certainly not much. *[Stops suddenly and speaks seriously.]* What a thoughtless creature I am, chattering away like this. My poor, dear Christine, do forgive me.

MRS. LINDE   What do you mean, Nora?

NORA   *[gently.]* Poor Christine, you are a widow.[7]

MRS. LINDE   Yes; it is three years ago now.

NORA   Yes, I knew; I saw it in the papers. I assure you, Christine, I meant ever so often to write to you at the time, but I always put it off and something always prevented me.

MRS. LINDE   I quite understand, dear.

NORA   It was very bad of me, Christine. Poor thing, how you must have suffered. And he left you nothing?

MRS. LINDE   No.

NORA   And no children?

MRS. LINDE   No.

NORA   Nothing at all, then.

MRS. LINDE   Not even any sorrow or grief to live upon.

NORA   *[looking incredulously at her.]* But, Christine, is that possible?

MRS. LINDE   *[smiles sadly and strokes her hair.]* It sometimes happens, Nora.

NORA   So you are quite alone. How dreadfully sad that must be. I have three lovely children. You can't see them just now, for they are out with their nurse. But now you must tell me all about it.

MRS. LINDE   No, no; I want to hear about you.

NORA   No, you must begin. I mustn't be selfish today; today I must only think of your affairs. But there is one thing I must tell you. Do you know we have just had a great piece of good luck?

MRS. LINDE   No, what is it?

NORA   Just fancy, my husband has been made manager of the Bank!

MRS. LINDE   Your husband? What good luck!

NORA   Yes, tremendous! A barrister's profession[8] is such an uncertain thing, especially if he won't undertake unsavoury cases; and naturally Torvald has never been willing to do that, and I quite agree with him. You may imagine how pleased

---

[5] Showing courage or determination

[6] A ship powered by one or more steam engines

[7] Both widows and spinsters were prominent in property ownership and in financing businesses as silent partners.

[8] A lawyer who speaks in the higher courts of law on behalf of either the defence or prosecution

we are! He is to take up his work in the Bank at the New Year, and then he will have a big salary and lots of commissions.[9] For the future we can live quite differently—we can do just as we like. I feel so relieved and so happy, Christine! It will be splendid to have heaps of money and not need to have any anxiety, won't it?

MRS. LINDE   Yes, anyhow I think it would be delightful to have what one needs.

NORA   No, not only what one needs, but heaps and heaps of money.

MRS. LINDE   [smiling.] Nora, Nora, haven't you learned sense yet? In our schooldays you were a great spendthrift.

NORA   [laughing.] Yes, that is what Torvald says now. [Wags her finger at her.] But "Nora, Nora" is not so silly as you think. We have not been in a position for me to waste money. We have both had to work.

MRS. LINDE   You too?

NORA   Yes; odds and ends, needlework, crotchet-work, embroidery, and that kind of thing.[10] [Dropping her voice.] And other things as well. You know Torvald left his office when we were married? There was no prospect of promotion there, and he had to try and earn more than before. But during the first year he over-worked himself dreadfully. You see, he had to make money every way he could, and he worked early and late; but he couldn't stand it, and fell dreadfully ill, and the doctors said it was necessary for him to go south.

MRS. LINDE   You spent a whole year in Italy, didn't you?

NORA   Yes. It was no easy matter to get away, I can tell you. It was just after Ivar was born; but naturally we had to go. It was a wonderfully beautiful journey, and it saved Torvald's life. But it cost a tremendous lot of money, Christine.

MRS. LINDE   So I should think.

NORA   It cost about two hundred and fifty pounds. That's a lot, isn't it?

MRS. LINDE   Yes, and in emergencies like that it is lucky to have the money.

NORA   I ought to tell you that we had it from papa.

MRS. LINDE   Oh, I see. It was just about that time that he died, wasn't it?

NORA   Yes; and, just think of it, I couldn't go and nurse him. I was expecting little Ivar's birth every day and I had my poor sick Torvald to look after. My dear, kind father—I never saw him again, Christine. That was the saddest time I have known since our marriage.

MRS. LINDE   I know how fond you were of him. And then you went off to Italy?

NORA   Yes; you see we had money then, and the doctors insisted on our going, so we started a month later.

MRS. LINDE   And your husband came back quite well?

NORA   As sound as a bell!

MRS. LINDE   But—the doctor?

NORA   What doctor?

MRS. LINDE   I thought your maid said the gentleman who arrived here just as I did, was the doctor?

NORA   Yes, that was Doctor Rank, but he doesn't come here professionally. He is our greatest friend, and comes in at least once everyday. No, Torvald has not had an hour's illness since then, and our children are strong and healthy and so am I. [Jumps up and claps her hands.] Christine! Christine! it's good to be alive and happy!—But how horrid of me; I am talking of nothing but my own affairs. [Sits on a stool near her, and rests her arms on her knees.] You mustn't be angry with

[9] A "rising barrister" in 1850 could have an annual income of £5,000. The 2008 relative value of these earnings was £428,200 via the CPI ("consumer price index"), comparable in 2012 to $681,266

[10] In 1870, women were allowed in Great Britain to keep money they had earned.

me. Tell me, is it really true that you did not love your husband? Why did you marry him?

MRS. LINDE   My mother was alive then, and was bedridden and helpless, and I had to provide for my two younger brothers; so I did not think I was justified in refusing his offer.

NORA   No, perhaps you were quite right. He was rich at that time, then?

MRS. LINDE   I believe he was quite well off. But his business was a precarious one;[11] and, when he died, it all went to pieces and there was nothing left.

NORA   And then?—

MRS. LINDE   Well, I had to turn my hand to anything I could find—first a small shop, then a small school, and so on. The last three years have seemed like one long working-day, with no rest. Now it is at an end, Nora. My poor mother needs me no more, for she is gone; and the boys do not need me either; they have got situations and can shift for themselves.

NORA   What a relief you must feel if—

MRS. LINDE   No, indeed; I only feel my life unspeakably empty. No one to live for anymore. *[Gets up restlessly.]* That was why I could not stand the life in my little backwater any longer. I hope it may be easier here to find something which will busy me and occupy my thoughts. If only I could have the good luck to get some regular work—office work of some kind—

NORA   But, Christine, that is so frightfully tiring, and you look tired out now. You had far better go away to some watering-place.

MRS. LINDE   *[walking to the window.]* I have no father to give me money for a journey, Nora.

NORA   *[rising.]* Oh, don't be angry with me!

MRS. LINDE   *[going up to her.]* It is you that must not be angry with me, dear. The worst of a position like mine is that it makes one so bitter. No one to work for, and yet obliged to be always on the lookout for chances. One must live, and so one becomes selfish. When you told me of the happy turn your fortunes have taken—you will hardly believe it—I was delighted not so much on your account as on my own.

NORA   How do you mean?—Oh, I understand. You mean that perhaps Torvald could get you something to do.

MRS. LINDE   Yes, that was what I was thinking of.

NORA   He must, Christine. Just leave it to me; I will broach the subject very cleverly—I will think of something that will please him very much. It will make me so happy to be of some use to you.

MRS. LINDE   How kind you are, Nora, to be so anxious to help me! It is doubly kind in you, for you know so little of the burdens and troubles of life.

NORA   I—? I know so little of them?

MRS. LINDE   *[smiling.]* My dear! Small household cares and that sort of thing!—You are a child, Nora.

NORA   *[tosses her head and crosses the stage.]* You ought not to be so superior.

MRS. LINDE   No?

NORA   You are just like the others. They all think that I am incapable of anything really serious—

MRS. LINDE   Come, come—

NORA   —that I have gone through nothing in this world of cares.

MRS. LINDE   But, my dear Nora, you have just told me all your troubles.

NORA   Pooh!—those were trifles. *[Lowering her voice.]* I have not told you the important thing.

---

[11] precarious: not securely held or in position; dangerously likely to fall or collapse.

MRS. LINDE   The important thing? What do you mean?

NORA   You look down upon me altogether, Christine—but you ought not to. You are proud, aren't you, of having worked so hard and so long for your mother?

MRS. LINDE   Indeed, I don't look down on anyone. But it is true that I am both proud and glad to think that I was privileged to make the end of my mother's life almost free from care.

NORA   And you are proud to think of what you have done for your brothers?

MRS. LINDE   I think I have the right to be.

NORA   I think so, too. But now, listen to this; I too have something to be proud and glad of.

MRS. LINDE   I have no doubt you have. But what do you refer to?

NORA   Speak low. Suppose Torvald were to hear! He mustn't on any account—no one in the world must know, Christine, except you.

MRS. LINDE   But what is it?

NORA   Come here. [Pulls her down on the sofa beside her.] Now I will show you that I too have something to be proud and glad of. It was I who saved Torvald's life.

MRS. LINDE   "Saved"? How?

NORA   I told you about our trip to Italy. Torvald would never have recovered if he had not gone there—

MRS. LINDE   Yes, but your father gave you the necessary funds.

NORA   [smiling.] Yes, that is what Torvald and all the others think, but—

MRS. LINDE   But—

NORA   Papa didn't give us a shilling. It was I who procured the money.

MRS. LINDE   You? All that large sum?

NORA   Two hundred and fifty pounds. What do you think of that?

MRS. LINDE   But, Nora, how could you possibly do it? Did you win a prize in the Lottery?

NORA   [contemptuously.] In the Lottery? There would have been no credit in that.

MRS. LINDE   But where did you get it from, then? Nora [humming and smiling with an air of mystery.] Hm, hm! Aha!

MRS. LINDE   Because you couldn't have borrowed it.

NORA   Couldn't I? Why not?

MRS. LINDE   No, a wife cannot borrow without her husband's consent.

NORA   [tossing her head.] Oh, if it is a wife who has any head for business—a wife who has the wit to be a little bit clever—

MRS. LINDE   I don't understand it at all, Nora.

NORA   There is no need you should. I never said I had borrowed the money. I may have got it some other way. [Lies back on the sofa.] Perhaps I got it from some other admirer. When anyone is as attractive as I am—

MRS. LINDE   You are a mad creature.

NORA   Now, you know you're full of curiosity, Christine.

MRS. LINDE   Listen to me, Nora dear. Haven't you been a little bit imprudent?

NORA   [sits up straight.] Is it imprudent to save your husband's life?

MRS. LINDE   It seems to me imprudent, without his knowledge, to—

NORA   But it was absolutely necessary that he should not know! My goodness, can't you understand that? It was necessary he should have no idea what a dangerous condition he was in. It was to me that the doctors came and said that his life was in danger, and that the only thing to save him was to live in the south. Do you suppose I didn't try, first of all, to get what I wanted as if it were for myself? I told him how much I should love to travel abroad like other young wives; I tried tears and entreaties with him; I told him that he ought to remember the condition I was in, and that he ought to be kind and indulgent to me; I even hinted that he might raise a loan. That nearly made him angry, Christine. He said I was thoughtless, and that it was his duty as my husband not to indulge me in my whims and caprices[12]—as I believe he called them. Very well, I thought, you must be saved—and that was how I came to devise a way out of the difficulty—

MRS. LINDE   And did your husband never get to know from your father that the money had not come from him?

NORA   No, never. Papa died just at that time. I had meant to let him into the secret and beg him never to reveal it. But he was so ill then—alas, there never was any need to tell him.

MRS. LINDE   And since then have you never told your secret to your husband?

NORA   Good Heavens, no! How could you think so? A man who has such strong opinions about these things! And besides, how painful and humiliating it would be for Torvald, with his manly independence, to know that he owed me anything! It would upset our mutual relations altogether; our beautiful happy home would no longer be what it is now.

MRS. LINDE   Do you mean never to tell him about it?

NORA   [meditatively, and with a half smile.] Yes—someday, perhaps, after many years, when I am no longer as nice-looking as I am now. Don't laugh at me! I mean, of course, when Torvald is no longer as devoted to me as he is now; when my dancing and dressing-up and reciting have palled on him; then it may be a good thing to have something in reserve—[Breaking off.] What nonsense! That time will never come. Now, what do you think of my great secret, Christine? Do you still think I am of no use? I can tell you, too, that this affair has caused me a lot of worry. It has been by no means easy for me to meet my engagements punctually. I may tell you that there is something that is called, in business, quarterly interest, and another thing called payment in installments, and it is always so dreadfully difficult to manage them. I have had to save a little here and there, where I could, you understand. I have not been able to put aside much from my housekeeping money, for Torvald must have a good table. I couldn't let my children be shabbily dressed; I have felt obliged to use up all he gave me for them, the sweet little darlings!

MRS. LINDE   So it has all had to come out of your own necessaries of life, poor Nora?

NORA   Of course. Besides, I was the one responsible for it. Whenever Torvald has given me money for new dresses and such things, I have never spent more than half of it; I have always bought the simplest and cheapest things. Thank Heaven, any clothes look well on me, and so Torvald has never noticed it. But it was often very hard on me, Christine—because it is delightful to be really well dressed, isn't it?

MRS. LINDE   Quite so.

NORA   Well, then I have found other ways of earning money. Last winter I was lucky enough to get a lot of copying to do; so I locked myself up and sat writing every evening until quite late at night. Many a time I was desperately tired; but all the same it was a tremendous pleasure to sit there working and earning money. It was like being a man.

MRS. LINDE   How much have you been able to pay off in that way?

NORA   I can't tell you exactly. You see, it is very difficult to keep an account of a business matter of that kind. I only know that I have paid every penny that I could scrape together. Many a time I was at my wits' end. [Smiles.] Then I used to sit here and imagine that a rich old gentleman had fallen in love with me—

MRS. LINDE   What! Who was it?

---

[12] caprices: sudden and unaccountable changes of mood or behavior.

NORA Be quiet!—that he had died; and that when his will was opened it contained, written in big letters, the instruction: "The lovely Mrs Nora Helmer is to have all I possess paid over to her at once in cash."

MRS. LINDE But, my dear Nora—who could the man be?

NORA Good gracious, can't you understand? There was no old gentleman at all; it was only something that I used to sit here and imagine, when I couldn't think of any way of procuring money. But it's all the same now; the tiresome old person can stay where he is, as far as I am concerned; I don't care about him or his will either, for I am free from care now. [Jumps up.] My goodness, it's delightful to think of, Christine! Free from care! To be able to be free from care, quite free from care; to be able to play and romp with the children; to be able to keep the house beautifully and have everything just as Torvald likes it! And, think of it, soon the spring will come and the big blue sky! Perhaps we shall be able to take a little trip—perhaps I shall see the sea again! Oh, it's a wonderful thing to be alive and be happy. [A bell is heard in the hall.]

MRS. LINDE [rising.] There is the bell; perhaps I had better go.

NORA No, don't go; no one will come in here; it is sure to be for Torvald.

SERVANT [at the hall door.] Excuse me, ma'am—there is a gentleman to see the master, and as the doctor is with him—

NORA Who is it?

KROGSTAD [at the door.] It is I, Mrs. Helmer [MRS. LINDE starts, trembles, and turns to the window.]

NORA [takes a step towards him, and speaks in a strained, low voice.] You? What is it? What do you want to see my husband about?

KROGSTAD Bank business—in a way. I have a small post in the Bank, and I hear your husband is to be our chief now—

NORA Then it is—

KROGSTAD Nothing but dry business matters, Mrs Helmer; absolutely nothing else.

NORA Be so good as to go into the study, then. [She bows indifferently to him and shuts the door into the hall; then comes back and makes up the fire in the stove.]

MRS. LINDE Nora—who was that man?

NORA A lawyer, of the name of Krogstad.

MRS. LINDE Then it really was he.

NORA Do you know the man?

MRS. LINDE I used to—many years ago. At one time he was a solicitor's clerk in our town.[13]

NORA Yes, he was.

MRS. LINDE He is greatly altered.

NORA He made a very unhappy marriage.

MRS. LINDE He is a widower now, isn't he?

NORA With several children. There now, it is burning up. [Shuts the door of the stove and moves the rocking-chair aside.]

MRS. LINDE They say he carries on various kinds of business.

NORA Really! Perhaps he does; I don't know anything about it. But don't let us think of business; it is so tiresome.

[13] solicitor's clerk: an apprentice in a professional firm; generally the term arises in the accountancy and legal professions

Scene 3. Doctor Rank

RANK   *[comes out of HELMER'S study. Before he shuts the door he calls to him].* No, my dear fellow, I won't disturb you; I would rather go in to your wife for a little while. *[Shuts the door and sees Mrs Linde.]* I beg your pardon; I am afraid I am disturbing you too.

NORA   No, not at all. *[Introducing him.]* Doctor Rank, Mrs Linde.

RANK   I have often heard Mrs Linde's name mentioned here. I think I passed you on the stairs when I arrived, Mrs Linde?

MRS. LINDE   Yes, I go up very slowly; I can't manage stairs well.

RANK   Ah! some slight internal weakness?

MRS. LINDE   No, the fact is I have been overworking myself.

RANK   Nothing more than that? Then I suppose you have come to town to amuse yourself with our entertainments?

MRS. LINDE   I have come to look for work.

RANK   Is that a good cure for overwork?

MRS. LINDE   One must live, Doctor Rank.

RANK   Yes, the general opinion seems to be that it is necessary.

NORA   Look here, Doctor Rank—you know you want to live.

RANK   Certainly. However wretched I may feel, I want to prolong the agony as long as possible. All my patients are like that. And so are those who are morally diseased; one of them, and a bad case too, is at this very moment with Helmer—

MRS. LINDE   *[sadly].* Ah!

NORA   Whom do you mean?

RANK   A lawyer of the name of Krogstad, a fellow you don't know at all. He suffers from a diseased moral character, Mrs Helmer; but even he began talking of its being highly important that he should live.

NORA   Did he? What did he want to speak to Torvald about?

RANK   I have no idea; I only heard that it was something about the Bank.

NORA   I didn't know this—what's his name—Krogstad had anything to do with the Bank.

RANK   Yes, he has some sort of appointment there. *[To Mrs Linde.]* I don't know whether you find also in your part of the world that there are certain people who go zealously snuffing about to smell out moral corruption, and, as soon as they have found some, put the person concerned into some lucrative position where they can keep their eye on him. Healthy natures are left out in the cold.

MRS. LINDE   Still I think the sick are those who most need taking care of.

RANK   *[shrugging his shoulders].* Yes, there you are. That is the sentiment that is turning Society into a sick-house.

[NORA, who has been absorbed in her thoughts, breaks out into smothered laughter and claps her hands.]

RANK   Why do you laugh at that? Have you any notion what Society really is?

NORA   What do I care about tiresome Society? I am laughing at something quite different, something extremely amusing. Tell me, Doctor Rank, are all the people who are employed in the Bank dependent on Torvald now?

RANK   Is that what you find so extremely amusing?

NORA   *[smiling and humming.]* That's my affair! *[Walking about the room.]* It's perfectly glorious to think that we have—that Torvald has so much power over so many people. *[Takes the packet from her pocket.]* Doctor Rank, what do you say to a macaroon?

RANK   What, macaroons? I thought they were forbidden here.

NORA   Yes, but these are some Christine gave me.

MRS. LINDE   What! I?—

NORA   Oh, well, don't be alarmed! You couldn't know that Torvald had forbidden them. I must tell you that he is afraid they will spoil my teeth. But, bah!—once in a way—That's so, isn't it, Doctor Rank? By your leave! *[Puts a macaroon into his mouth.]* You must have one too, Christine. And I shall have one, just a little one—or at most two. *[Walking about.]* I am tremendously happy. There is just one thing in the world now that I should dearly love to do.

RANK   Well, what is that?

NORA   It's something I should dearly love to say, if Torvald could hear me.

RANK   Well, why can't you say it?

NORA   No, I daren't; it's so shocking.

MRS. LINDE   Shocking?

RANK   Well, I should not advise you to say it. Still, with us you might. What is it you would so much like to say if Torvald could hear you?

NORA   I should just love to say—Well, I'm damned!

RANK   Are you mad?

MRS. LINDE   Nora, dear—!

RANK   Say it, here he is!

NORA   *[hiding the packet.]* Hush! Hush! Hush!

[HELMER comes out of his room, with his coat over his arm and his hat in his hand.]

NORA   Well, Torvald dear, have you got rid of him?

HELMER   Yes, he has just gone.

NORA   Let me introduce you—this is Christine, who has come to town.

HELMER   Christine—? Excuse me, but I don't know—

NORA   Mrs Linde, dear; Christine Linde.

HELMER   Of course. A school friend of my wife's, I presume?

MRS. LINDE   Yes, we have known each other since then.

NORA   And just think, she has taken a long journey in order to see you.

HELMER   What do you mean?

MRS. LINDE   No, really, I—

NORA   Christine is tremendously clever at book-keeping, and she is frightfully anxious to work under some clever man, so as to perfect herself—

HELMER   Very sensible, Mrs Linde.

NORA   And when she heard you had been appointed manager of the Bank—the news was telegraphed,[14] you know—she travelled here as quick as she could. Torvald, I am sure you will be able to do something for Christine, for my sake, won't you?

HELMER   Well, it is not altogether impossible. I presume you are a widow, Mrs Linde?

MRS. LINDE   Yes.

HELMER   And have had some experience of book-keeping?

MRS. LINDE   Yes, a fair amount.

HELMER   Ah! well, it's very likely I may be able to find something for you—

NORA   *[clapping her hands.]* What did I tell you? What did I tell you?

HELMER   You have just come at a fortunate moment, Mrs Linde.

MRS. LINDE   How am I to thank you?

HELMER   There is no need. *[Puts on his coat.]* But today you must excuse me—

---

[14] telegraph: a system for transmitting messages from a distance along a wire, esp. one creating signals by making and breaking an electrical connection.

RANK   Wait a minute; I will come with you. *[Brings his fur coat from the hall and warms it at the fire.]*

NORA   Don't be long away, Torvald dear.

HELMER   About an hour, not more.

NORA   Are you going too, Christine?

MRS. LINDE   *[putting on her cloak]*. Yes, I must go and look for a room.

HELMER   Oh, well then, we can walk down the street together.

NORA   *[helping her.]* What a pity it is we are so short of space here; I am afraid it is impossible for us—

MRS. LINDE   Please don't think of it! Goodbye, Nora dear, and many thanks.

NORA   Goodbye for the present. Of course you will come back this evening. And you too, Dr. Rank. What do you say? If you are well enough? Oh, you must be! Wrap yourself up well. *[They go to the door all talking together. Children's voices are heard on the staircase.]*

NORA   There they are! There they are! *[She runs to open the door. The NURSE comes in with the children.]* Come in! Come in! *[Stoops and kisses them.]* Oh, you sweet blessings! Look at them, Christine! Aren't they darlings?

RANK   Don't let us stand here in the draught.

HELMER   Come along, Mrs Linde; the place will only be bearable for a mother now!

[RANK, HELMER, and Mrs Linde go downstairs. The NURSE comes forward with the children; NORA shuts the hall door.]

NORA   How fresh and well you look! Such red cheeks like apples and roses. *[The children all talk at once while she speaks to them.]* Have you had great fun? That's splendid! What, you pulled both Emmy and Bob along on the sledge? — both at once?—that was good. You are a clever boy, Ivar. Let me take her for a little, Anne. My sweet little baby doll! *[Takes the baby from the MAID and dances it up and down.]* Yes, yes, mother will dance with Bob too. What! Have you been snowballing? I wish I had been there too! No, no, I will take their things off, Anne; please let me do it, it is such fun. Go in now, you look half frozen. There is some hot coffee for you on the stove.

[The NURSE goes into the room on the left. NORA takes off the children's things and throws them about, while they all talk to her at once.]

NORA   Really! Did a big dog run after you? But it didn't bite you? No, dogs don't bite nice little dolly children. You mustn't look at the parcels, Ivar. What are they? Ah, I daresay you would like to know. No, no—it's something nasty! Come, let us have a game! What shall we play at? Hide and Seek? Yes, we'll play Hide and Seek. Bob shall hide first. Must I hide? Very well, I'll hide first.

*[She and the children laugh and shout, and romp in and out of the room; at last NORA hides under the table, the children rush in and out for her, but do not see her; they hear her smothered laughter, run to the table, lift up the cloth and find her. Shouts of laughter. She crawls forward and pretends to frighten them. Fresh laughter.
Meanwhile there has been a knock at the hall door, but none of them has noticed it.
The door is half opened, and KROGSTAD appears, lie waits a little; the game goes on.]*

Scene 4. Krogstad

KROGSTAD   Excuse me, Mrs. Helmer.

NORA   *[with a stifled cry, turns round and gets up on to her knees]*. Ah! what do you want?

KROGSTAD   Excuse me, the outer door was ajar; I suppose someone forgot to shut it.

NORA   *[rising]*. My husband is out, Mr. Krogstad.

KROGSTAD   I know that.

NORA   What do you want here, then?

KROGSTAD   A word with you.

NORA   With me?—[*To the children, gently.*] Go in to nurse. What? No, the strange man won't do mother any harm. When he has gone we will have another game. [*She takes the children into the room on the left, and shuts the door after them.*] You want to speak to me?

KROGSTAD   Yes, I do.

NORA   Today? It is not the first of the month yet.

KROGSTAD   No, it is Christmas Eve, and it will depend on yourself what sort of a Christmas you will spend.

NORA   What do you mean? Today it is absolutely impossible for me—

KROGSTAD   We won't talk about that until later on. This is something different. I presume you can give me a moment?

NORA   Yes—yes, I can—although—

KROGSTAD   Good. I was in Olsen's Restaurant and saw your husband going down the street—

NORA   Yes?

KROGSTAD   With a lady.

NORA   What then?

KROGSTAD   May I make so bold as to ask if it was a Mrs Linde?

NORA   It was.

KROGSTAD   Just arrived in town?

NORA   Yes, today.

KROGSTAD   She is a great friend of yours, isn't she?

NORA   She is. But I don't see—

KROGSTAD   I knew her too, once upon a time.

NORA   I am aware of that.

KROGSTAD   Are you? So you know all about it; I thought as much. Then I can ask you, without beating about the bush—is Mrs Linde to have an appointment in the Bank?

NORA   What right have you to question me, Mr. Krogstad?—You, one of my husband's subordinates! But since you ask, you shall know. Yes, Mrs Linde is to have an appointment. And it was I who pleaded her cause, Mr. Krogstad, let me tell you that.

KROGSTAD   I was right in what I thought, then.

NORA   [*walking up and down the stage*]. Sometimes one has a tiny little bit of influence, I should hope. Because one is a woman, it does not necessarily follow that—. When anyone is in a subordinate position, Mr. Krogstad, they should really be careful to avoid offending anyone who—who—

KROGSTAD   Who has influence?

NORA   Exactly.

KROGSTAD   [*changing his tone*]. Mrs. Helmer, you will be so good as to use your influence on my behalf.

NORA   What? What do you mean?

KROGSTAD   You will be so kind as to see that I am allowed to keep my subordinate position in the Bank.

NORA   What do you mean by that? Who proposes to take your post away from you?

KROGSTAD   Oh, there is no necessity to keep up the pretence of ignorance. I can quite understand that your friend is not very anxious to expose herself to the chance of rubbing shoulders with me; and I quite understand, too, whom I have to thank for being turned off.

NORA   But I assure you—

KROGSTAD   Very likely; but, to come to the point, the time has come when I should advise you to use your influence to prevent that.

NORA   But, Mr. Krogstad, I have no influence.

KROGSTAD   Haven't you? I thought you said yourself just now—

NORA   Naturally I did not mean you to put that construction on it. I! What should make you think I have any influence of that kind with my husband?

KROGSTAD   Oh, I have known your husband from our student days. I don't suppose he is any more unassailable than other husbands.

NORA   If you speak slightingly of my husband, I shall turn you out of the house.

KROGSTAD   You are bold, Mrs. Helmer.

NORA   I am not afraid of you any longer. As soon as the New Year comes, I shall in a very short time be free of the whole thing.

KROGSTAD   [controlling himself]. Listen to me, Mrs. Helmer. If necessary, I am prepared to fight for my small post in the Bank as if I were fighting for my life.

NORA   So it seems.

KROGSTAD   It is not only for the sake of the money; indeed, that weighs least with me in the matter. There is another reason—well, I may as well tell you. My position is this. I daresay you know, like everybody else, that once, many years ago, I was guilty of an indiscretion.

NORA   I think I have heard something of the kind.

KROGSTAD   The matter never came into court; but every way seemed to be closed to me after that. So I took to the business that you know of. I had to do something; and, honestly, I don't think I've been one of the worst. But now I must cut myself free from all that. My sons are growing up; for their sake I must try and win back as much respect as I can in the town. This post in the Bank was like the first step up for me—and now your husband is going to kick me downstairs again into the mud.

NORA   But you must believe me, Mr. Krogstad; it is not in my power to help you at all.

KROGSTAD   Then it is because you haven't the will; but I have means to compel you.

NORA   You don't mean that you will tell my husband that I owe you money?

KROGSTAD   Hm!—suppose I were to tell him?

NORA   It would be perfectly infamous of you. [Sobbing.] To think of his learning my secret, which has been my joy and pride, in such an ugly, clumsy way—that he should learn it from you! And it would put me in a horribly disagreeable position—

KROGSTAD   Only disagreeable?

NORA   [impetuously]. Well, do it, then!—and it will be the worse for you. My husband will see for himself what a blackguard[15] you are, and you certainly won't keep your post then.

KROGSTAD   I asked you if it was only a disagreeable scene at home that you were afraid of?

NORA   If my husband does get to know of it, of course he will at once pay you what is still owing, and we shall have nothing more to do with you.

KROGSTAD   [coming a step nearer]. Listen to me, Mrs. Helmer. Either you have a very bad memory or you know very little of business. I shall be obliged to remind you of a few details.

NORA   What do you mean?

---

[15] blackguard: a person, particularly a man, who behaves in a dishonorable or contemptible way.

KROGSTAD   When your husband was ill, you came to me to borrow two hundred and fifty pounds.[16]

NORA   I didn't know anyone else to go to.

KROGSTAD   I promised to get you that amount—

NORA   Yes, and you did so.

KROGSTAD   I promised to get you that amount, on certain conditions. Your mind was so taken up with your husband's illness, and you were so anxious to get the money for your journey, that you seem to have paid no attention to the conditions of our bargain. Therefore it will not be amiss if I remind you of them. Now, I promised to get the money on the security of a bond which I drew up.

NORA   Yes, and which I signed.

KROGSTAD   Good. But below your signature there were a few lines constituting your father a surety for the money; those lines your father should have signed.

NORA   Should? He did sign them.

KROGSTAD   I had left the date blank; that is to say, your father should himself have inserted the date on which he signed the paper. Do you remember that?

NORA   Yes, I think I remember—

KROGSTAD   Then I gave you the bond to send by post to your father. Is that not so?

NORA   Yes.

KROGSTAD   And you naturally did so at once, because five or six days afterwards you brought me the bond with your father's signature. And then I gave you the money.

NORA   Well, haven't I been paying it off regularly?

KROGSTAD   Fairly so, yes. But—to come back to the matter in hand—that must have been a very trying time for you, Mrs Helmer?

NORA   It was, indeed.

KROGSTAD   Your father was very ill, wasn't he?

NORA   He was very near his end.

KROGSTAD   And died soon afterwards?

NORA   Yes.

KROGSTAD   Tell me, Mrs Helmer, can you by any chance remember what day your father died?—on what day of the month, I mean.

NORA   Papa died on the 29th of September.

KROGSTAD   That is correct; I have ascertained it for myself. And, as that is so, there is a discrepancy *[taking a paper from his pocket]* which I cannot account for.

NORA   What discrepancy? I don't know—

KROGSTAD   The discrepancy consists, Mrs. Helmer, in the fact that your father signed this bond three days after his death.

NORA   What do you mean? I don't understand—

KROGSTAD   Your father died on the 29th of September. But, look here; your father has dated his signature the 2nd of October. It is a discrepancy, isn't it? *[NORA is silent.]* Can you explain it to me? *[NORA is still silent.]* It is a remarkable thing, too, that the words "2nd of October," as well as the year, are not written in your father's handwriting but in one that I think I know. Well, of course it can be explained; your father may have forgotten to date his signature, and someone else may have dated it haphazard before they knew of his death. There is no harm in that. It all depends on the signature of the name; and that is

---

[16] two hundred and fifty pounds: approximately $10,432.74 in 2012. As a general reference, a $100,000 home today would have cost about $4,500 in 1890 (from How Much Stuff Cost Long Ago).

genuine, I suppose, Mrs. Helmer? It was your father himself who signed his name here?

NORA   *[after a short pause, throws her head up and looks defiantly at him]*. No, it was not. It was I that wrote papa's name.

KROGSTAD   Are you aware that is a dangerous confession?

NORA   In what way? You shall have your money soon.

KROGSTAD   Let me ask you a question; why did you not send the paper to your father?

NORA   It was impossible; papa was so ill. If I had asked him for his signature, I should have had to tell him what the money was to be used for; and when he was so ill himself I couldn't tell him that my husband's life was in danger—it was impossible.

KROGSTAD   It would have been better for you if you had given up your trip abroad.

NORA   No, that was impossible. That trip was to save my husband's life; I couldn't give that up.

KROGSTAD   But did it never occur to you that you were committing a fraud on me?

NORA   I couldn't take that into account; I didn't trouble myself about you at all. I couldn't bear you, because you put so many heartless difficulties in my way, although you knew what a dangerous condition my husband was in.

KROGSTAD   Mrs Helmer, you evidently do not realise clearly what it is that you have been guilty of. But I can assure you that my one false step, which lost me all my reputation, was nothing more or nothing worse than what you have done.

NORA   You? Do you ask me to believe that you were brave enough to run a risk to save your wife's life?

KROGSTAD   The law cares nothing about motives.

NORA   Then it must be a very foolish law.

KROGSTAD   Foolish or not, it is the law by which you will be judged, if I produce this paper in court.

NORA   I don't believe it. Is a daughter not to be allowed to spare her dying father anxiety and care? Is a wife not to be allowed to save her husband's life? I don't know much about law; but I am certain that there must be laws permitting such things as that. Have you no knowledge of such laws—you who are a lawyer? You must be a very poor lawyer, Mr. Krogstad.

KROGSTAD   Maybe. But matters of business—such business as you and I have had together—do you think I don't understand that? Very well. Do as you please. But let me tell you this—if I lose my position a second time, you shall lose yours with me. *[He bows, and goes out through the hall.]*

NORA   *[appears buried in thought for a short time, then tosses her head].* Nonsense! Trying to frighten me like that!—I am not so silly as he thinks. *[Begins to busy herself putting the children's things in order.]* And yet—? No, it's impossible! I did it for love's sake.

Scene 5. The Children

CHILDREN   *[in the doorway on the left].* Mother, the stranger man has gone out through the gate.

NORA   Yes, dears, I know. But, don't tell anyone about the stranger man. Do you hear? Not even papa.

CHILDREN   No, mother; but will you come and play again?

NORA   No, no,—not now.

CHILDREN   But, mother, you promised us.

NORA   Yes, but I can't now. Run away in; I have such a lot to do. Run away in, my sweet little darlings. *[She gets them into the room by degrees and shuts the door on them; then sits down on the sofa, takes up a piece of needlework and sews a few stitches, but soon stops.]* No! *[Throws down the work, gets up, goes to the hall door and calls out.]* Helen! bring the Tree in. *[Goes to the table on the left, opens a drawer, and stops again.]* No, no! it is quite impossible!

MAID   *[coming in with the Tree].* Where shall I put it, ma'am?

NORA   Here, in the middle of the floor.

MAID   Shall I get you anything else?

NORA   No, thank you. I have all I want. *[Exit MAID.]*

NORA   *[begins dressing the tree].* A candle here-and flowers here—The horrible man! It's all nonsense—there's nothing wrong. The tree shall be splendid! I will do everything I can think of to please you, Torvald!—I will sing for you, dance for you—*[HELMER comes in with some papers under his arm.]* Oh! are you back already?

Scene 6. Nora's Costume

HELMER   Yes. Has anyone been here?

NORA   Here? No.

HELMER   That is strange. I saw Krogstad going out of the gate.

NORA   Did you? Oh yes, I forgot, Krogstad was here for a moment.

HELMER   Nora, I can see from your manner that he has been here begging you to say a good word for him.

NORA   Yes.

HELMER   And you were to appear to do it of your own accord; you were to conceal from me the fact of his having been here; didn't he beg that of you too?

NORA   Yes, Torvald, but—

HELMER   Nora, Nora, and you would be a party to that sort of thing? To have any talk with a man like that, and give him any sort of promise? And to tell me a lie into the bargain?

NORA   A lie—?

HELMER   Didn't you tell me no one had been here? *[Shakes his finger at her.]* My little songbird must never do that again. A songbird must have a clean beak to chirp with—no false notes! *[Puts his arm round her waist.]* That is so, isn't it? Yes, I am sure it is. *[Lets her go.]* We will say no more about it. *[Sits down by the stove.]* How warm and snug it is here! *[Turns over his papers.]*

NORA   *[after a short pause, during which she busies herself with the Christmas Tree.]* Torvald!

HELMER   Yes.

NORA   I am looking forward tremendously to the fancy-dress ball[17] at the Stenborgs' the day after tomorrow.

HELMER   And I am tremendously curious to see what you are going to surprise me with.

NORA   It was very silly of me to want to do that.

HELMER   What do you mean?

NORA   I can't hit upon anything that will do; everything I think of seems so silly and insignificant.

HELMER   Does my little Nora acknowledge that at last?

NORA   *[standing behind his chair with her arms on the back of it].* Are you very busy, Torvald?

HELMER   Well—

NORA   What are all those papers?

---

[17] fancy-dress ball: masked ball; a ball at which guests wear costumes and masks

HELMER   Bank business.

NORA   Already?

HELMER   I have got authority from the retiring manager to undertake the necessary changes in the staff and in the rearrangement of the work; and I must make use of the Christmas week for that, so as to have everything in order for the new year.

NORA   Then that was why this poor Krogstad—

HELMER   Hm!

NORA   [leans against the back of his chair and strokes his hair]. If you hadn't been so busy I should have asked you a tremendously big favour, Torvald.

HELMER   What is that? Tell me.

NORA   There is no one has such good taste as you. And I do so want to look nice at the fancy-dress ball. Torvald, couldn't you take me in hand and decide what I shall go as, and what sort of a dress I shall wear?

HELMER   Aha! so my obstinate[18] little woman is obliged to get someone to come to her rescue?

NORA   Yes, Torvald, I can't get along a bit without your help.

HELMER   Very well, I will think it over, we shall manage to hit upon something.

NORA   That is nice of you. [Goes to the Christmas Tree. A short pause.] How pretty the red flowers look—. But, tell me, was it really something very bad that this Krogstad was guilty of?

HELMER   He forged someone's name. Have you any idea what that means?

NORA   Isn't it possible that he was driven to do it by necessity?

HELMER   Yes; or, as in so many cases, by imprudence. I am not so heartless as to condemn a man altogether because of a single false step of that kind.

NORA   No, you wouldn't, would you, Torvald?

HELMER   Many a man has been able to retrieve his character, if he has openly confessed his fault and taken his punishment.

NORA   Punishment—?

HELMER   But Krogstad did nothing of that sort; he got himself out of it by a cunning trick, and that is why he has gone under altogether.

NORA   But do you think it would—?

HELMER   Just think how a guilty man like that has to lie and play the hypocrite with every one, how he has to wear a mask in the presence of those near and dear to him, even before his own wife and children. And about the children—that is the most terrible part of it all, Nora.

NORA   How?

HELMER   Because such an atmosphere of lies infects and poisons the whole life of a home. Each breath the children take in such a house is full of the germs of evil.

NORA   [coming nearer him]. Are you sure of that?

HELMER   My dear, I have often seen it in the course of my life as a lawyer. Almost everyone who has gone to the bad early in life has had a deceitful mother.

NORA   Why do you only say—mother?

HELMER   It seems most commonly to be the mother's influence, though naturally a bad father's would have the same result. Every lawyer is familiar with the fact. This Krogstad, now, has been persistently poisoning his own children with lies and dissimulation; that is why I say he has lost all moral character. [Holds out his hands to her.] That is why my sweet little Nora must promise me not to plead his cause. Give me your hand on it. Come, come, what is this? Give me your hand.

---

[18] obstinate: stubbornly refusing to change one's opinion or chosen course of action, despite attempts to persuade one to do so.

There now, that's settled. I assure you it would be quite impossible for me to work with him; I literally feel physically ill when I am in the company of such people.

NORA   *[takes her hand out of his and goes to the opposite side of the Christmas Tree]* How hot it is in here; and I have such a lot to do.

HELMER   *[getting up and putting his papers in order]*. Yes, and I must try and read through some of these before dinner; and I must think about your costume, too. And it is just possible I may have something ready in gold paper to hang up on the Tree. *[Puts his hand on her head.]* My precious little singing-bird! *[He goes into his room and shuts the door after him.]*

NORA   *[after a pause, whispers]*. No, no—it isn't true. It's impossible; it must be impossible.

[The NURSE opens the door on the left.]

NURSE   The little ones are begging so hard to be allowed to come in to mamma.

NORA   No, no, no! Don't let them come in to me! You stay with them, Anne.

NURSE   Very well, ma'am. *[Shuts the door.]*

NORA   *[pale with terror]*. Deprave my little children? Poison my home? *[A short pause. Then she tosses her head.]* It's not true. It can't possibly be true.

ACT II

Scene 1. The Children's Well-being

[THE SAME SCENE.—THE Christmas Tree is in the corner by the piano, stripped of its ornaments and with burnt-down candle-ends on its dishevelled branches. NORA'S cloak and hat are lying on the sofa. She is alone in the room, walking about uneasily. She stops by the sofa and takes up her cloak.]

NORA   *[drops her cloak]*. Someone is coming now! *[Goes to the door and listens.]* No—it is no one. Of course, no one will come today, Christmas Day—nor tomorrow either. But, perhaps—*[opens the door and looks out]*. No, nothing in the letterbox; it is quite empty. *[Comes forward.]* What rubbish! of course he can't be in earnest about it. Such a thing couldn't happen; it is impossible—I have three little children.

[Enter the NURSE from the room on the left, carrying a big cardboard box.]

NURSE   At last I have found the box with the fancy dress.

NORA   Thanks; put it on the table.

NURSE   *[doing so]*. But it is very much in want of mending.

NORA   I should like to tear it into a hundred thousand pieces.

NURSE   What an idea! It can easily be put in order—just a little patience.

NORA   Yes, I will go and get Mrs Linde to come and help me with it.

NURSE   What, out again? In this horrible weather? You will catch cold, ma'am, and make yourself ill.

NORA   Well, worse than that might happen. How are the children?

NURSE   The poor little souls are playing with their Christmas presents, but—

NORA   Do they ask much for me?

NURSE   You see, they are so accustomed to have their mamma with them.

NORA   Yes, but, nurse, I shall not be able to be so much with them now as I was before.

NURSE   Oh well, young children easily get accustomed to anything.

NORA   Do you think so? Do you think they would forget their mother if she went away altogether?

NURSE   Good heavens!—went away altogether?

NORA   Nurse, I want you to tell me something I have often wondered about—how could you have the heart to put your own child out among strangers?

NURSE   I was obliged to, if I wanted to be little Nora's nurse.

NORA   Yes, but how could you be willing to do it?

NURSE   What, when I was going to get such a good place by it? A poor girl who has got into trouble should be glad to. Besides, that wicked man didn't do a single thing for me.

NORA   But I suppose your daughter has quite forgotten you.

NURSE   No, indeed she hasn't. She wrote to me when she was confirmed, and when she was married.

NORA   [putting her arms round her neck]. Dear old Anne, you were a good mother to me when I was little.

NURSE   Little Nora, poor dear, had no other mother but me.

NORA   And if my little ones had no other mother, I am sure you would—What nonsense I am talking! [Opens the box.] Go in to them. Now I must—. You will see tomorrow how charming I shall look.

NURSE   I am sure there will be no one at the ball so charming as you, ma'am. [Goes into the room on the left.]

NORA   [begins to unpack the box, but soon pushes it away from her]. If only I dared go out. If only no one would come. If only I could be sure nothing would happen here in the meantime. Stuff and nonsense! No one will come. Only I mustn't think about it. I will brush my muff.[1] What lovely, lovely gloves! Out of my thoughts, out of my thoughts! One, two, three, four, five, six— [Screams.] Ah! there is someone coming—. [Makes a movement towards the door, but stands irresolute.]

Scene 2. Nora and Christine

[Enter Mrs Linde from the hall, where she has taken off her cloak and hat.]

NORA   Oh, it's you, Christine. There is no one else out there, is there? How good of you to come!

MRS. LINDE   I heard you were up asking for me.

NORA   Yes, I was passing by. As a matter of fact, it is something you could help me with. Let us sit down here on the sofa. Look here. Tomorrow evening there is to be a fancy-dress ball at the Stenborgs', who live above us; and Torvald wants me to go as a Neapolitan fisher-girl, and dance the Tarantella[2] that I learned at Capri.

MRS. LINDE   I see; you are going to keep up the character.

NORA   Yes, Torvald wants me to. Look, here is the dress; Torvald had it made for me there, but now it is all so torn, and I haven't any idea—

MRS. LINDE   We will easily put that right. It is only some of the trimming come unsewn here and there. Needle and thread? Now then, that's all we want.

NORA   It is nice of you.

MRS. LINDE   [sewing]. So you are going to be dressed up tomorrow Nora. I will tell you what—I shall come in for a moment and see you in your fine feathers. But I have completely forgotten to thank you for a delightful evening yesterday.

NORA   [gets up, and crosses the stage]. Well, I don't think yesterday was as pleasant as usual. You ought to have come to town a little earlier, Christine. Certainly Torvald does understand how to make a house dainty and attractive.

---

[1] muff: a tube made of fur or other warm material into which the hands are placed for warmth.

[2] Tarantella: a rapid whirling dance originating in southern Italy.

MRS. LINDE   And so do you, it seems to me; you are not your father's daughter for nothing. But tell me, is Doctor Rank always as depressed as he was yesterday?

NORA   No; yesterday it was very noticeable. I must tell you that he suffers from a very dangerous disease. He has consumption of the spine,[3] poor creature. His father was a horrible man who committed all sorts of excesses; and that is why his son was sickly from childhood, do you understand?

MRS. LINDE   [dropping her sewing]. But, my dearest Nora, how do you know anything about such things?

NORA   [walking about]. Pooh! When you have three children, you get visits now and then from—from married women, who know something of medical matters, and they talk about one thing and another.

MRS. LINDE   [goes on sewing. A short silence]. Does Doctor Rank come here everyday?

NORA   Everyday regularly. He is Torvald's most intimate friend, and a great friend of mine too. He is just like one of the family.

MRS. LINDE   But tell me this—is he perfectly sincere? I mean, isn't he the kind of man that is very anxious to make himself agreeable?

NORA   Not in the least. What makes you think that?

MRS. LINDE   When you introduced him to me yesterday, he declared he had often heard my name mentioned in this house; but afterwards I noticed that your husband hadn't the slightest idea who I was. So how could Doctor Rank—?

NORA   That is quite right, Christine. Torvald is so absurdly fond of me that he wants me absolutely to himself, as he says. At first he used to seem almost jealous if I mentioned any of the dear folk at home, so naturally I gave up doing so. But I often talk about such things with Doctor Rank, because he likes hearing about them.

MRS. LINDE   Listen to me, Nora. You are still very like a child in many things, and I am older than you in many ways and have a little more experience. Let me tell you this—you ought to make an end of it with Doctor Rank.

NORA   What ought I to make an end of?

MRS. LINDE   Of two things, I think. Yesterday you talked some nonsense about a rich admirer who was to leave you money—

NORA   An admirer who doesn't exist, unfortunately! But what then?

MRS. LINDE   Is Doctor Rank a man of means?

NORA   Yes, he is.

MRS. LINDE   And has no one to provide for?

NORA   No, no one; but—

MRS. LINDE   And comes here everyday?

NORA   Yes, I told you so.

MRS. LINDE   But how can this well-bred man be so tactless?

NORA   I don't understand you at all.

MRS. LINDE   Don't prevaricate, Nora. Do you suppose I don't guess who lent you the two hundred and fifty pounds?

NORA   Are you out of your senses? How can you think of such a thing! A friend of ours, who comes here everyday! Do you realise what a horribly painful position that would be?

MRS. LINDE   Then it really isn't he?

NORA   No, certainly not. It would never have entered into my head for a moment. Besides, he had no money to lend then; he came into his money afterwards.

---

[3] consumption of the spine: a wasting disease, esp. pulmonary tuberculosis.

MRS. LINDE   Well, I think that was lucky for you, my dear Nora.

NORA   No, it would never have come into my head to ask Doctor Rank. Although I am quite sure that if I had asked him—

MRS. LINDE   But of course you won't.

NORA   Of course not. I have no reason to think it could possibly be necessary. But I am quite sure that if I told Doctor Rank—

MRS. LINDE   Behind your husband's back?

NORA   I must make an end of it with the other one, and that will be behind his back too. I must make an end of it with him.

MRS. LINDE   Yes, that is what I told you yesterday, but—

NORA   [walking up and down]. A man can put a thing like that straight much easier than a woman—

MRS. LINDE   One's husband, yes.

NORA   Nonsense! [Standing still.] When you pay off a debt you get your bond back, don't you?

MRS. LINDE   Yes, as a matter of course.

NORA   And can tear it into a hundred thousand pieces, and burn it up—the nasty dirty paper!

MRS. LINDE   [looks hard at her, lays down her sewing and gets up slowly]. Nora, you are concealing something from me.

NORA   Do I look as if I were?

MRS. LINDE   Something has happened to you since yesterday morning. Nora, what is it?

NORA   [going nearer to her]. Christine! [Listens.] Hush! there's Torvald come home. Do you mind going in to the children for the present? Torvald can't bear to see dressmaking going on. Let Anne help you.

MRS. LINDE   [gathering some of the things together]. Certainly—but I am not going away from here until we have had it out with one another. [She goes into the room on the left, as HELMER comes in from the hall.]

Scene 3. Hire Krogstad

NORA   [going up to HELMER]. I have wanted you so much, Torvald dear.

HELMER   Was that the dressmaker?

NORA   No, it was Christine; she is helping me to put my dress in order. You will see I shall look quite smart.

HELMER   Wasn't that a happy thought of mine, now?

NORA   Splendid! But don't you think it is nice of me, too, to do as you wish?

HELMER   Nice?—because you do as your husband wishes? Well, well, you little rogue, I am sure you did not mean it in that way. But I am not going to disturb you; you will want to be trying on your dress, I expect.

NORA   I suppose you are going to work.

HELMER   Yes. [Shows her a bundle of papers.] Look at that. I have just been into the bank. [Turns to go into his room.]

NORA   Torvald.

HELMER   Yes.

NORA   If your little squirrel were to ask you for something very, very prettily—

HELMER   What then?

NORA   Would you do it?

HELMER   I should like to hear what it is, first.

NORA   Your squirrel would run about and do all her tricks if you would be nice, and do what she wants.

HELMER   Speak plainly.

NORA   Your skylark would chirp about in every room, with her song rising and falling—

HELMER   Well, my skylark does that anyhow.

NORA   I would play the fairy and dance for you in the moonlight, Torvald.

HELMER   Nora—you surely don't mean that request you made to me this morning?

NORA   *[going near him]*. Yes, Torvald, I beg you so earnestly—

HELMER   Have you really the courage to open up that question again?

NORA   Yes, dear, you must do as I ask; you must let Krogstad keep his post in the bank.

HELMER   My dear Nora, it is his post that I have arranged Mrs Linde shall have.

NORA   Yes, you have been awfully kind about that; but you could just as well dismiss some other clerk instead of Krogstad.

HELMER   This is simply incredible obstinacy! Because you chose to give him a thoughtless promise that you would speak for him, I am expected to—

NORA   That isn't the reason, Torvald. It is for your own sake. This fellow writes in the most scurrilous[4] newspapers; you have told me so yourself. He can do you an unspeakable amount of harm. I am frightened to death of him—

HELMER   Ah, I understand; it is recollections of the past that scare you.

NORA   What do you mean?

HELMER   Naturally you are thinking of your father.

NORA   Yes—yes, of course. Just recall to your mind what these malicious[5] creatures wrote in the papers about papa, and how horribly they slandered him. I believe they would have procured his dismissal if the Department had not sent you over to inquire into it, and if you had not been so kindly disposed and helpful to him.

HELMER   My little Nora, there is an important difference between your father and me. Your father's reputation as a public official was not above suspicion. Mine is, and I hope it will continue to be so, as long as I hold my office.

NORA   You never can tell what mischief these men may contrive. We ought to be so well off, so snug and happy here in our peaceful home, and have no cares—you and I and the children, Torvald! That is why I beg you so earnestly—

HELMER   And it is just by interceding for him that you make it impossible for me to keep him. It is already known at the Bank that I mean to dismiss Krogstad. Is it to get about now that the new manager has changed his mind at his wife's bidding—

NORA   And what if it did?

HELMER   Of course!—if only this obstinate little person can get her way! Do you suppose I am going to make myself ridiculous before my whole staff, to let people think that I am a man to be swayed by all sorts of outside influence? I should very soon feel the consequences of it, I can tell you! And besides, there is one thing that makes it quite impossible for me to have Krogstad in the Bank as long as I am manager.

NORA   Whatever is that?

HELMER   His moral failings I might perhaps have overlooked, if necessary—

NORA   Yes, you could—couldn't you?

HELMER   And I hear he is a good worker, too. But I knew him when we were boys. It was one of those rash friendships that so often prove an incubus[6] in afterlife. I may as well tell you plainly, we were once on very intimate terms with one

---

[4] scurrilous: making or spreading scandalous claims about someone with the intention of damaging their reputation.

[5] malicious: characterized by malice; intending or intended to do harm.

[6] incubus: in this case, a cause of distress or anxiety.

another. But this tactless fellow lays no restraint on himself when other people are present. On the contrary, he thinks it gives him the right to adopt a familiar tone with me, and every minute it is "I say, Helmer, old fellow!" and that sort of thing. I assure you it is extremely painful for me. He would make my position in the Bank intolerable.

NORA   Torvald, I don't believe you mean that.

HELMER   Don't you? Why not?

NORA   Because it is such a narrow-minded way of looking at things.

HELMER   What are you saying? Narrow-minded? Do you think I am narrow-minded?

NORA   No, just the opposite, dear—and it is exactly for that reason.

HELMER   It's the same thing. You say my point of view is narrow-minded, so I must be so too. Narrow-minded! Very well—I must put an end to this. *[Goes to the hall door and calls.]* Helen!

NORA   What are you going to do?

HELMER   *[looking among his papers]*. Settle it. *[Enter MAID.]* Look here; take this letter and go downstairs with it at once. Find a messenger and tell him to deliver it, and be quick. The address is on it, and here is the money.

MAID   Very well, sir. *[Exit with the letter.]*

HELMER   *[putting his papers together]*. Now then, little Miss Obstinate.

NORA   *[breathlessly]*. Torvald—what was that letter?

HELMER   Krogstad's dismissal.

NORA   Call her back, Torvald! There is still time. Oh Torvald, call her back! Do it for my sake—for your own sake—for the children's sake! Do you hear me, Torvald? Call her back! You don't know what that letter can bring upon us.

HELMER   It's too late.

NORA   Yes, it's too late.

HELMER   My dear Nora, I can forgive the anxiety you are in, although really it is an insult to me. It is, indeed. Isn't it an insult to think that I should be afraid of a starving quill-driver's vengeance?[7] But I forgive you nevertheless, because it is such eloquent witness to your great love for me. *[Takes her in his arms.]* And that is as it should be, my own darling Nora. Come what will, you may be sure I shall have both courage and strength if they be needed. You will see I am man enough to take everything upon myself.

NORA   *[in a horror-stricken voice]*. What do you mean by that?

HELMER   Everything, I say—

NORA   *[recovering herself]*. You will never have to do that.

HELMER   That's right. Well, we will share it, Nora, as man and wife should. That is how it shall be. *[Caressing her.]* Are you content now? There! There!—not these frightened dove's eyes! The whole thing is only the wildest fancy!—Now, you must go and play through the Tarantella and practise with your tambourine. I shall go into the inner office and shut the door, and I shall hear nothing; you can make as much noise as you please. *[Turns back at the door.]* And when Rank comes, tell him where he will find me. *[Nods to her, takes his papers and goes into his room, and shuts the door after him.]*

Scene 4. Doctor Rank's Love

NORA   *[bewildered with anxiety, stands as if rooted to the spot, and whispers]*. He was capable of doing it. He will do it. He will do it in spite of everything.—No, not that! Never, never! Anything rather than that! Oh, for some help, some way out of it! *[The door-bell rings.]* Doctor Rank! Anything rather than that—anything,

---

[7] quill-driver's vengeance: Intended as a derogatory statement toward Krogstad. Helmer basically describes him as with "pencil-pushing" vengeance.

whatever it is! [*She puts her hands over her face, pulls herself together, goes to the door and opens it. RANK is standing without, hanging up his coat. During the following dialogue it begins to grow dark.*]

NORA   Good day, Doctor Rank. I knew your ring. But you mustn't go in to Torvald now; I think he is busy with something.

RANK   And you?

NORA   [*brings him in and shuts the door after him*]. Oh, you know very well I always have time for you.

RANK   Thank you. I shall make use of as much of it as I can.

NORA   What do you mean by that? As much of it as you can?

RANK   Well, does that alarm you?

NORA   It was such a strange way of putting it. Is anything likely to happen?

RANK   Nothing but what I have long been prepared for. But I certainly didn't expect it to happen so soon.

NORA   [*gripping him by the arm*]. What have you found out? Doctor Rank, you must tell me.

RANK   [*sitting down by the stove*]. It is all up with me. And it can't be helped.

NORA   [*with a sigh of relief*]. Is it about yourself?

RANK   Who else? It is no use lying to one's self. I am the most wretched of all my patients, Mrs. Helmer. Lately I have been taking stock of my internal economy. Bankrupt! Probably within a month I shall lie rotting in the churchyard.

NORA   What an ugly thing to say!

RANK   The thing itself is cursedly ugly, and the worst of it is that I shall have to face so much more that is ugly before that. I shall only make one more examination of myself; when I have done that, I shall know pretty certainly when it will be that the horrors of dissolution[8] will begin. There is something I want to tell you. Helmer's refined nature gives him an unconquerable disgust at everything that is ugly; I won't have him in my sick-room.

NORA   Oh, but, Doctor Rank—

RANK   I won't have him there. Not on any account. I bar my door to him. As soon as I am quite certain that the worst has come, I shall send you my card with a black cross on it, and then you will know that the loathsome end has begun.

NORA   You are quite absurd today. And I wanted you so much to be in a really good humour.

RANK   With death stalking beside me?—To have to pay this penalty for another man's sin? Is there any justice in that? And in every single family, in one way or another, some such inexorable retribution is being exacted—

NORA   [*putting her hands over her ears*]. Rubbish! Do talk of something cheerful.

RANK   Oh, it's a mere laughing matter, the whole thing. My poor innocent spine has to suffer for my father's youthful amusements.

NORA   [*sitting at the table on the left*]. I suppose you mean that he was too partial to asparagus and pate de foie gras,[9] don't you?

RANK   Yes, and to truffles.[10]

NORA   Truffles, yes. And oysters too, I suppose?

RANK   Oysters, of course, that goes without saying.

---

[8] dissolution: in this case, disintegration; decomposition.

[9] pate de foie gras: a food product made of the liver of a duck or goose that has been specially fattened; a popular and well-known delicacy in French cuisine.

[10] truffles: a soft candy made of a chocolate mixture, typically flavored with rum and covered with cocoa.

NORA   And heaps of port[11] and champagne. It is sad that all these nice things should take their revenge on our bones.

RANK   Especially that they should revenge themselves on the unlucky bones of those who have not had the satisfaction of enjoying them.

NORA   Yes, that's the saddest part of it all.

RANK   *[with a searching look at her]*. Hm!—

NORA   *[after a short pause]*. Why did you smile?

RANK   No, it was you that laughed.

NORA   No, it was you that smiled, Doctor Rank!

RANK   *[rising]*. You are a greater rascal than I thought.

NORA   I am in a silly mood today.

RANK   So it seems.

NORA   *[putting her hands on his shoulders]*. Dear, dear Doctor Rank, death mustn't take you away from Torvald and me.

RANK   It is a loss you would easily recover from. Those who are gone are soon forgotten.

NORA   *[looking at him anxiously]*. Do you believe that?

RANK   People form new ties, and then—

NORA   Who will form new ties?

RANK   Both you and Helmer, when I am gone. You yourself are already on the high road to it, I think. What did that Mrs Linde want here last night?

NORA   Oho!—you don't mean to say you are jealous of poor Christine?

RANK   Yes, I am. She will be my successor in this house. When I am done for, this woman will—

NORA   Hush! don't speak so loud. She is in that room.

RANK   Today again. There, you see.

NORA   She has only come to sew my dress for me. Bless my soul, how unreasonable you are! *[Sits down on the sofa.]* Be nice now, Doctor Rank, and tomorrow you will see how beautifully I shall dance, and you can imagine I am doing it all for you—and for Torvald too, of course. *[Takes various things out of the box.]* Doctor Rank, come and sit down here, and I will show you something.

RANK   *[sitting down]*. What is it?

NORA   Just look at those!

RANK   Silk stockings.

NORA   Flesh-coloured. Aren't they lovely? It is so dark here now, but tomorrow—. No, no, no! you must only look at the feet. Oh well, you may have leave to look at the legs too.

RANK   Hm!—

NORA   Why are you looking so critical? Don't you think they will fit me?

RANK   I have no means of forming an opinion about that.

NORA   *[looks at him for a moment]*. For shame! *[Hits him lightly on the ear with the stockings.]* That's to punish you. *[Folds them up again.]*

RANK   And what other nice things am I to be allowed to see?

NORA   Not a single thing more, for being so naughty. *[She looks among the things, humming to herself.]*

RANK   *[after a short silence]*. When I am sitting here, talking to you as intimately as this, I cannot imagine for a moment what would have become of me if I had never come into this house.

---

[11] port: a strong, sweet, typically dark red fortified wine, originally from Portugal, typically drunk as a dessert wine.

NORA   *[smiling]*. I believe you do feel thoroughly at home with us.

RANK   *[in a lower voice, looking straight in front of him]*. And to be obliged to leave it all—

NORA   Nonsense, you are not going to leave it.

RANK   *[as before]*. And not be able to leave behind one the slightest token of one's gratitude, scarcely even a fleeting regret—nothing but an empty place which the first comer can fill as well as any other.

NORA   And if I asked you now for a—? No!

RANK   For what?

NORA   For a big proof of your friendship—

RANK   Yes, yes!

NORA   I mean a tremendously big favour—

RANK   Would you really make me so happy for once?

NORA   Ah, but you don't know what it is yet.

RANK   No—but tell me.

NORA   I really can't, Doctor Rank. It is something out of all reason; it means advice, and help, and a favour—

RANK   The bigger a thing it is the better. I can't conceive what it is you mean. Do tell me. Haven't I your confidence?

NORA   More than anyone else. I know you are my truest and best friend, and so I will tell you what it is. Well, Doctor Rank, it is something you must help me to prevent. You know how devotedly, how inexpressibly deeply Torvald loves me; he would never for a moment hesitate to give his life for me.

RANK   *[leaning towards her]*. Nora—do you think he is the only one—?

NORA   *[with a slight start]*. The only one—?

RANK   The only one who would gladly give his life for your sake.

NORA   *[sadly]*. Is that it?

RANK   I was determined you should know it before I went away, and there will never be a better opportunity than this. Now you know it, Nora. And now you know, too, that you can trust me as you would trust no one else.

NORA   *[rises, deliberately and quietly]*. Let me pass.

RANK   *[makes room for her to pass him, but sits still]*. Nora!

NORA   *[at the hall door]*. Helen, bring in the lamp. *[Goes over to the stove.]* Dear Doctor Rank, that was really horrid of you.

RANK   To have loved you as much as anyone else does? Was that horrid?

NORA   No, but to go and tell me so. There was really no need—

RANK   What do you mean? Did you know—? *[MAID enters with lamp, puts it down on the table, and goes out.]* Nora—Mrs Helmer—tell me, had you any idea of this?

NORA   Oh, how do I know whether I had or whether I hadn't? I really can't tell you—To think you could be so clumsy, Doctor Rank! We were getting on so nicely.

RANK   Well, at all events you know now that you can command me, body and soul. So won't you speak out?

NORA   *[looking at him]*. After what happened?

RANK   I beg you to let me know what it is.

NORA   I can't tell you anything now.

RANK   Yes, yes. You mustn't punish me in that way. Let me have permission to do for you whatever a man may do.

NORA   You can do nothing for me now. Besides, I really don't need any help at all. You will find that the whole thing is merely fancy on my part. It really is so—of course it is! *[Sits down in the rocking-chair, and looks at him with a smile.]* You are a nice sort of man, Doctor Rank!—don't you feel ashamed of yourself, now the lamp has come?

RANK   Not a bit. But perhaps I had better go—for ever?

NORA   No, indeed, you shall not. Of course you must come here just as before. You know very well Torvald can't do without you.

RANK   Yes, but you?

NORA   Oh, I am always tremendously pleased when you come.

RANK   It is just that, that put me on the wrong track. You are a riddle to me. I have often thought that you would almost as soon be in my company as in Helmer's.

NORA   Yes—you see there are some people one loves best, and others whom one would almost always rather have as companions.

RANK   Yes, there is something in that.

NORA   When I was at home, of course I loved papa best. But I always thought it tremendous fun if I could steal down into the maids' room, because they never moralised at all, and talked to each other about such entertaining things.

RANK   I see—it is their place I have taken.

NORA   [jumping up and going to him]. Oh, dear, nice Doctor Rank, I never meant that at all. But surely you can understand that being with Torvald is a little like being with papa—[Enter MAID from the hall.]

MAID   If you please, ma'am. [Whispers and hands her a card.]

NORA   [glancing at the card]. Oh! [Puts it in her pocket.]

RANK   Is there anything wrong?

NORA   No, no, not in the least. It is only something—it is my new dress—

RANK   What? Your dress is lying there.

NORA   Oh, yes, that one; but this is another. I ordered it. Torvald mustn't know about it—

RANK   Oho! Then that was the great secret.

NORA   Of course. Just go in to him; he is sitting in the inner room. Keep him as long as—

RANK   Make your mind easy; I won't let him escape.

[Goes into HELMER'S room.]

Scene 5. Krogstad's Threat

NORA   [to the MAID]. And he is standing waiting in the kitchen?

MAID   Yes; he came up the back stairs.

NORA   But didn't you tell him no one was in?

MAID   Yes, but it was no good.

NORA   He won't go away?

MAID   No; he says he won't until he has seen you, ma'am.

NORA   Well, let him come in—but quietly. Helen, you mustn't say anything about it to anyone. It is a surprise for my husband.

MAID   Yes, ma'am, I quite understand. [Exit.]

NORA   This dreadful thing is going to happen! It will happen in spite of me! No, no, no, it can't happen—it shan't happen!

[NORA bolts the door of HELMER'S room. The MAID opens the hall door for KROGSTAD and shuts it after him. He is wearing a fur coat, high boots and a fur cap.]

NORA   [advancing towards him]. Speak low—my husband is at home.

KROGSTAD   No matter about that.

NORA   What do you want of me?

KROGSTAD   An explanation of something.

NORA   Make haste then. What is it?

KROGSTAD   You know, I suppose, that I have got my dismissal.

NORA   I couldn't prevent it, Mr. Krogstad. I fought as hard as I could on your side, but it was no good.

KROGSTAD   Does your husband love you so little, then? He knows what I can expose you to, and yet he ventures—

NORA   How can you suppose that he has any knowledge of the sort?

KROGSTAD   I didn't suppose so at all. It would not be the least like our dear Torvald Helmer to show so much courage—

NORA   Mr. Krogstad, a little respect for my husband, please.

KROGSTAD   Certainly—all the respect he deserves. But since you have kept the matter so carefully to yourself, I make bold to suppose that you have a little clearer idea, than you had yesterday, of what it actually is that you have done?

NORA   More than you could ever teach me.

KROGSTAD   Yes, such a bad lawyer as I am.

NORA   What is it you want of me?

KROGSTAD   Only to see how you were, Mrs Helmer, I have been thinking about you all day long. A mere cashier, a quill-driver, a—well, a man like me—even he has a little of what is called feeling, you know.

NORA   Show it, then; think of my little children.

KROGSTAD   Have you and your husband thought of mine? But never mind about that. I only wanted to tell you that you need not take this matter too seriously. In the first place there will be no accusation made on my part.

NORA   No, of course not; I was sure of that.

KROGSTAD   The whole thing can be arranged amicably;[12] there is no reason why anyone should know anything about it. It will remain a secret between us three.

NORA   My husband must never get to know anything about it.

KROGSTAD   How will you be able to prevent it? Am I to understand that you can pay the balance that is owing?

NORA   No, not just at present.

KROGSTAD   Or perhaps that you have some expedient[13] for raising the money soon?

NORA   No expedient that I mean to make use of.

KROGSTAD   Well, in any case, it would have been of no use to you now. If you stood there with ever so much money in your hand, I would never part with your bond.

NORA   Tell me what purpose you mean to put it to.

KROGSTAD   I shall only preserve it—keep it in my possession. No one who is not concerned in the matter shall have the slightest hint of it. So that if the thought of it has driven you to any desperate resolution—

NORA   It has.

KROGSTAD   If you had it in your mind to run away from your home—

NORA   I had.

KROGSTAD   Or even something worse—

NORA   How could you know that?

KROGSTAD   Give up the idea.

---

[12] amicably: (of relations between people) having a spirit of friendliness; without serious disagreement or rancor.

[13] expedient: as a noun, a means of attaining an end, esp. one that is convenient but considered improper or immoral.

NORA   How did you know I had thought of that?

KROGSTAD   Most of us think of that at first. I did, too—but I hadn't the courage.

NORA   *[faintly]*. No more had I.

KROGSTAD   *[in a tone of relief]*. No, that's it, isn't it—you hadn't the courage either?

NORA   No, I haven't—I haven't.

KROGSTAD   Besides, it would have been a great piece of folly. Once the first storm at home is over—. I have a letter for your husband in my pocket.

NORA   Telling him everything?

KROGSTAD   In as lenient a manner as I possibly could.

NORA   *[quickly]*. He mustn't get the letter. Tear it up. I will find some means of getting money.

KROGSTAD   Excuse me, Mrs Helmer, but I think I told you just now—

NORA   I am not speaking of what I owe you. Tell me what sum you are asking my husband for, and I will get the money.

KROGSTAD   I am not asking your husband for a penny.

NORA   What do you want, then?

KROGSTAD   I will tell you. I want to rehabilitate myself, Mrs Helmer; I want to get on; and in that your husband must help me. For the last year and a half I have not had a hand in anything dishonourable, amid all that time I have been struggling in most restricted circumstances. I was content to work my way up step by step. Now I am turned out, and I am not going to be satisfied with merely being taken into favour again. I want to get on, I tell you. I want to get into the Bank again, in a higher position. Your husband must make a place for me—

NORA   That he will never do!

KROGSTAD   He will; I know him; he dare not protest. And as soon as I am in there again with him, then you will see! Within a year I shall be the manager's right hand. It will be Nils Krogstad and not Torvald Helmer who manages the Bank.

NORA   That's a thing you will never see!

KROGSTAD   Do you mean that you will—?

NORA   I have courage enough for it now.

KROGSTAD   Oh, you can't frighten me. A fine, spoilt lady like you—

NORA   You will see, you will see.

KROGSTAD   Under the ice, perhaps? Down into the cold, coal-black water? And then, in the spring, to float up to the surface, all horrible and unrecognisable, with your hair fallen out—

NORA   You can't frighten me.

KROGSTAD   Nor you me. People don't do such things, Mrs HELMER
Besides, what use would it be? I should have him completely in my power all the same.

NORA   Afterwards? When I am no longer—

KROGSTAD   Have you forgotten that it is I who have the keeping of your reputation? *[NORA stands speechlessly looking at him.]* Well, now, I have warned you. Do not do anything foolish. When Helmer has had my letter, I shall expect a message from him. And be sure you remember that it is your husband himself who has forced me into such ways as this again. I will never forgive him for that. Goodbye, Mrs. Helmer. *[Exit through the hall.]*

NORA   *[goes to the hall door, opens it slightly and listens.]* He is going. He is not putting the letter in the box. Oh no, no! that's impossible! *[Opens the door by degrees.]* What is that? He is standing outside. He is not going downstairs. Is he hesitating? Can he—?

[A letter drops into the box; then KROGSTAD'S footsteps are heard, until they die away as he goes downstairs. NORA utters a stifled cry, and runs across the room to the table by the sofa. A short pause.]

NORA   In the letter-box. *[Steals across to the hall door.]* There it lies—Torvald, Torvald, there is no hope for us now!

Scene 6. Nora's Revelation

[Mrs Linde comes in from the room on the left, carrying the dress.]

MRS. LINDE   There, I can't see anything more to mend now. Would you like to try it on—?

NORA   *[in a hoarse whisper]*. Christine, come here.

MRS. LINDE   *[throwing the dress down on the sofa]*. What is the matter with you? You look so agitated!

NORA   Come here. Do you see that letter? There, look—you can see it through the glass in the letter-box.

MRS. LINDE   Yes, I see it.

NORA   That letter is from Krogstad.

MRS. LINDE   Nora—it was Krogstad who lent you the money!

NORA   Yes, and now Torvald will know all about it.

MRS. LINDE   Believe me, Nora, that's the best thing for both of you.

NORA   You don't know all. I forged a name.

MRS. LINDE   Good heavens—!

NORA   I only want to say this to you, Christine—you must be my witness.

MRS. LINDE   Your witness? What do you mean? What am I to—?

NORA   If I should go out of my mind—and it might easily happen—

MRS. LINDE   Nora!

NORA   Or if anything else should happen to me—anything, for instance, that might prevent my being here—

MRS. LINDE   Nora! Nora! you are quite out of your mind.

NORA   And if it should happen that there were some one who wanted to take all the responsibility, all the blame, you understand—

MRS. LINDE   Yes, yes—but how can you suppose—?

NORA   Then you must be my witness, that it is not true, Christine. I am not out of my mind at all; I am in my right senses now, and I tell you no one else has known anything about it; I, and I alone, did the whole thing. Remember that.

MRS. LINDE   I will, indeed. But I don't understand all this.

NORA   How should you understand it? A wonderful thing is going to happen!

MRS. LINDE   A wonderful thing?

NORA   Yes, a wonderful thing!—But it is so terrible, Christine; it mustn't happen, not for all the world.

MRS. LINDE   I will go at once and see Krogstad.

NORA   Don't go to him; he will do you some harm.

MRS. LINDE   There was a time when he would gladly do anything for my sake.

NORA   He?

MRS. LINDE   Where does he live?

NORA   How should I know—? Yes *[feeling in her pocket]*, here is his card. But the letter, the letter—!

HELMER   *[calls from his room, knocking at the door]*. Nora! Nora *[cries out anxiously]*. Oh, what's that? What do you want?

HELMER   Don't be so frightened. We are not coming in; you have locked the door. Are you trying on your dress?

NORA   Yes, that's it. I look so nice, Torvald.

MRS. LINDE   *[who has read the card]*. I see he lives at the corner here.

NORA   Yes, but it's no use. It is hopeless. The letter is lying there in the box.

MRS. LINDE   And your husband keeps the key?

NORA   Yes, always.

MRS. LINDE   Krogstad must ask for his letter back unread, he must find some pretence—

NORA   But it is just at this time that Torvald generally—

MRS. LINDE   You must delay him. Go in to him in the meantime. I will come back as soon as I can. *[She goes out hurriedly through the hall door.]*

Scene 7. Dancing Practice

NORA   *[goes to HELMER'S door, opens it and peeps in]*. Torvald!

HELMER   *[from the inner room]*. Well? May I venture at last to come into my own room again? Come along, Rank, now you will see— *[Halting in the doorway.]* But what is this?

NORA   What is what, dear?

HELMER   Rank led me to expect a splendid transformation.

RANK   *[in the doorway]*. I understood so, but evidently I was mistaken.

NORA   Yes, nobody is to have the chance of admiring me in my dress until tomorrow.

HELMER   But, my dear Nora, you look so worn out. Have you been practising too much?

NORA   No, I have not practised at all.

HELMER   But you will need to—

NORA   Yes, indeed I shall, Torvald. But I can't get on a bit without you to help me; I have absolutely forgotten the whole thing.

HELMER   Oh, we will soon work it up again.

NORA   Yes, help me, Torvald. Promise that you will! I am so nervous about it—all the people—. You must give yourself up to me entirely this evening. Not the tiniest bit of business—you mustn't even take a pen in your hand. Will you promise, Torvald dear?

HELMER   I promise. This evening I will be wholly and absolutely at your service, you helpless little mortal. Ah, by the way, first of all I will just— *[Goes towards the hall door.]*

NORA   What are you going to do there?

HELMER   Only see if any letters have come.

NORA   No, no! don't do that, Torvald!

HELMER   Why not?

NORA   Torvald, please don't. There is nothing there.

HELMER   Well, let me look. *[Turns to go to the letter-box. NORA, at the piano, plays the first bars of the Tarantella. HELMER stops in the doorway.]* Aha!

NORA   I can't dance tomorrow if I don't practise with you.

HELMER   *[going up to her]*. Are you really so afraid of it, dear?

NORA   Yes, so dreadfully afraid of it. Let me practise at once; there is time now, before we go to dinner. Sit down and play for me, Torvald dear; criticise me, and correct me as you play.

HELMER   With great pleasure, if you wish me to. *[Sits down at the piano.]*

NORA   *[takes out of the box a tambourine and a long variegated shawl. She hastily drapes the shawl round her. Then she springs to the front of the stage and calls out].* Now play for me! I am going to dance!

[HELMER plays and NORA dances. RANK stands by the piano behind HELMER, and looks on.]

HELMER   *[as he plays].* Slower, slower!

NORA   I can't do it any other way.

HELMER   Not so violently, Nora!

NORA   This is the way.

HELMER   *[stops playing].* No, no—that is not a bit right.

NORA   *[laughing and swinging the tambourine].* Didn't I tell you so?

RANK   Let me play for her.

HELMER   *[getting up].* Yes, do. I can correct her better then.

[RANK sits down at the piano and plays. NORA dances more and more wildly. HELMER has taken up a position beside the stove, and during her dance gives her frequent instructions. She does not seem to hear him; her hair comes down and falls over her shoulders; she pays no attention to it, but goes on dancing. Enter Mrs Linde.]

MRS. LINDE   *[standing as if spell-bound in the doorway].* Oh!—

NORA   *[as she dances].* Such fun, Christine!

HELMER   My dear darling Nora, you are dancing as if your life depended on it.

NORA   So it does.

HELMER   Stop, Rank; this is sheer madness. Stop, I tell you! *[RANK stops playing, and NORA suddenly stands still. HELMER goes up to her.]* I could never have believed it. You have forgotten everything I taught you.

NORA   *[throwing away the tambourine].* There, you see.

HELMER   You will want a lot of coaching.

NORA   Yes, you see how much I need it. You must coach me up to the last minute. Promise me that, Torvald!

HELMER   You can depend on me.

NORA   You must not think of anything but me, either today or tomorrow; you mustn't open a single letter—not even open the letter-box—

HELMER   Ah, you are still afraid of that fellow—

NORA   Yes, indeed I am.

HELMER   Nora, I can tell from your looks that there is a letter from him lying there.

NORA   I don't know; I think there is; but you must not read anything of that kind now. Nothing horrid must come between us until this is all over.

RANK   *[whispers to HELMER].* You mustn't contradict her.

HELMER   *[taking her in his arms].* The child shall have her way. But tomorrow night, after you have danced—

NORA   Then you will be free. *[The MAID appears in the doorway to the right.]*

MAID   Dinner is served, ma'am.

NORA   We will have champagne, Helen.

MAID   Very good, ma'am. *[Exit.]*

HELMER   Hullo!—are we going to have a banquet?

NORA   Yes, a champagne banquet until the small hours. *[Calls out.]* And a few macaroons, Helen—lots, just for once!

HELMER   Come, come, don't be so wild and nervous. Be my own little skylark, as you used.

NORA   Yes, dear, I will. But go in now and you too, Doctor Rank. Christine, you must help me to do up my hair.

RANK   [whispers to HELMER as they go out]. I suppose there is nothing—she is not expecting anything?

HELMER   Far from it, my dear fellow; it is simply nothing more than this childish nervousness I was telling you of. [They go into the right-hand room.]

Scene 8. Waiting for a Wonderful Thing

NORA   Well!

MRS. LINDE   Gone out of town.

NORA   I could tell from your face.

MRS. LINDE   He is coming home tomorrow evening. I wrote a note for him.

NORA   You should have let it alone; you must prevent nothing. After all, it is splendid to be waiting for a wonderful thing to happen.

MRS. LINDE   What is it that you are waiting for?

NORA   Oh, you wouldn't understand. Go in to them, I will come in a moment. [Mrs Linde goes into the dining-room. NORA stands still for a little while, as if to compose herself. Then she looks at her watch.] Five o'clock. Seven hours until midnight; and then four-and-twenty hours until the next midnight. Then the Tarantella will be over. Twenty-four and seven? Thirty-one hours to live.

HELMER   [from the doorway on the right]. Where's my little skylark?

NORA   [going to him with her arms outstretched]. Here she is!

ACT III

Scene 1. Krogstad's Letter

[THE SAME SCENE.—The table has been placed in the middle of the stage, with chairs around it. A lamp is burning on the table. The door into the hall stands open. Dance music is heard in the room above. Mrs Linde is sitting at the table idly turning over the leaves of a book; she tries to read, but does not seem able to collect her thoughts. Every now and then she listens intently for a sound at the outer door.]

MRS. LINDE   [looking at her watch]. Not yet—and the time is nearly up. If only he does not—. [Listens again.] Ah, there he is. [Goes into the hall and opens the outer door carefully. Light footsteps are heard on the stairs. She whispers.] Come in. There is no one here.

KROGSTAD   [in the doorway]. I found a note from you at home. What does this mean?

MRS. LINDE   It is absolutely necessary that I should have a talk with you.

KROGSTAD   Really? And is it absolutely necessary that it should be here?

MRS. LINDE   It is impossible where I live; there is no private entrance to my rooms. Come in; we are quite alone. The maid is asleep, and the Helmers are at the dance upstairs.

KROGSTAD   [coming into the room]. Are the Helmers really at a dance tonight?

MRS. LINDE   Yes, why not?

KROGSTAD   Certainly—why not?

MRS. LINDE   Now, Nils, let us have a talk.

KROGSTAD   Can we two have anything to talk about?

MRS. LINDE   We have a great deal to talk about.

KROGSTAD   I shouldn't have thought so.

MRS. LINDE   No, you have never properly understood me.

KROGSTAD   Was there anything else to understand except what was obvious to all the world—a heartless woman jilts a man when a more lucrative chance turns up?

MRS. LINDE   Do you believe I am as absolutely heartless as all that? And do you believe that I did it with a light heart?

KROGSTAD   Didn't you?

MRS. LINDE   Nils, did you really think that?

KROGSTAD   If it were as you say, why did you write to me as you did at the time?

MRS. LINDE   I could do nothing else. As I had to break with you, it was my duty also to put an end to all that you felt for me.

KROGSTAD

[wringing his hands]. So that was it. And all this—only for the sake of money!

MRS. LINDE   You must not forget that I had a helpless mother and two little brothers. We couldn't wait for you, Nils; your prospects seemed hopeless then.

KROGSTAD   That may be so, but you had no right to throw me over for anyone else's sake.

MRS. LINDE   Indeed I don't know. Many a time did I ask myself if I had the right to do it.

KROGSTAD   *[more gently]*. When I lost you, it was as if all the solid ground went from under my feet. Look at me now—I am a shipwrecked man clinging to a bit of wreckage.

MRS. LINDE   But help may be near.

KROGSTAD   It was near; but then you came and stood in my way.

MRS. LINDE   Unintentionally, Nils. It was only today that I learned it was your place I was going to take in the Bank.

KROGSTAD   I believe you, if you say so. But now that you know it, are you not going to give it up to me?

MRS. LINDE   No, because that would not benefit you in the least.

KROGSTAD   Oh, benefit, benefit—I would have done it whether or no.

MRS. LINDE   I have learned to act prudently. Life, and hard, bitter necessity have taught me that.

KROGSTAD   And life has taught me not to believe in fine speeches.

MRS. LINDE   Then life has taught you something very reasonable. But deeds you must believe in?

KROGSTAD   What do you mean by that?

MRS. LINDE   You said you were like a shipwrecked man clinging to some wreckage.

KROGSTAD   I had good reason to say so.

MRS. LINDE   Well, I am like a shipwrecked woman clinging to some wreckage—no one to mourn for, no one to care for.

KROGSTAD   It was your own choice.

MRS. LINDE   There was no other choice—then.

KROGSTAD   Well, what now?

MRS. LINDE   Nils, how would it be if we two shipwrecked people could join forces?

KROGSTAD   What are you saying?

MRS. LINDE   Two on the same piece of wreckage would stand a better chance than each on their own.

KROGSTAD   Christine I . . .

MRS. LINDE   What do you suppose brought me to town?

KROGSTAD   Do you mean that you gave me a thought?

MRS. LINDE   I could not endure life without work. All my life, as long as I can remember, I have worked, and it has been my greatest and only pleasure. But now I am quite alone in the world—my life is so dreadfully empty and I feel so forsaken. There is not the least pleasure in working for one's self. Nils, give me someone and something to work for.

KROGSTAD   I don't trust that. It is nothing but a woman's overstrained sense of generosity that prompts you to make such an offer of yourself.

MRS. LINDE   Have you ever noticed anything of the sort in me?

KROGSTAD   Could you really do it? Tell me—do you know all about my past life?

MRS. LINDE   Yes.

KROGSTAD   And do you know what they think of me here?

MRS. LINDE   You seemed to me to imply that with me you might have been quite another man.

KROGSTAD   I am certain of it.

MRS. LINDE   Is it too late now?

KROGSTAD   Christine, are you saying this deliberately? Yes, I am sure you are. I see it in your face. Have you really the courage, then—?

MRS. LINDE   I want to be a mother to someone, and your children need a mother. We two need each other. Nils, I have faith in your real character—I can dare anything together with you.

KROGSTAD   [grasps her hands]. Thanks, thanks, Christine! Now I shall find a way to clear myself in the eyes of the world. Ah, but I forgot—

MRS. LINDE   [listening]. Hush! The Tarantella! Go, go!

KROGSTAD   Why? What is it?

MRS. LINDE   Do you hear them up there? When that is over, we may expect them back.

KROGSTAD   Yes, yes—I will go. But it is all no use. Of course you are not aware what steps I have taken in the matter of the Helmers.

MRS. LINDE   Yes, I know all about that.

KROGSTAD   And in spite of that have you the courage to—?

MRS. LINDE   I understand very well to what lengths a man like you might be driven by despair.

KROGSTAD   If I could only undo what I have done!

MRS. LINDE   You cannot. Your letter is lying in the letter-box now.

KROGSTAD   Are you sure of that?

MRS. LINDE   Quite sure, but—

KROGSTAD   [with a searching look at her]. Is that what it all means?—that you want to save your friend at any cost? Tell me frankly. Is that it?

MRS. LINDE   Nils, a woman who has once sold herself for another's sake, doesn't do it a second time.

KROGSTAD   I will ask for my letter back.

MRS. LINDE   No, no.

KROGSTAD   Yes, of course I will. I will wait here until Helmer comes; I will tell him he must give me my letter back—that it only concerns my dismissal—that he is not to read it—

MRS. LINDE   No, Nils, you must not recall your letter.

KROGSTAD   But, tell me, wasn't it for that very purpose that you asked me to meet you here?

MRS. LINDE   In my first moment of fright, it was. But twenty-four hours have elapsed since then, and in that time I have witnessed incredible things in this house. Helmer must know all about it. This unhappy secret must be disclosed; they must have a complete understanding between them, which is impossible with all this concealment and falsehood going on.

KROGSTAD   Very well, if you will take the responsibility. But there is one thing I can do in any case, and I shall do it at once.

MRS. LINDE   *[listening]*. You must be quick and go! The dance is over; we are not safe a moment longer.

KROGSTAD   I will wait for you below.

MRS. LINDE   Yes, do. You must see me back to my door . . .

KROGSTAD   I have never had such an amazing piece of good fortune in my life! *[Goes out through the outer door. The door between the room and the hall remains open.]*

MRS. LINDE   *[tidying up the room and laying her hat and cloak ready]*. What a difference! what a difference! Someone to work for and live for—a home to bring comfort into. That I will do, indeed. I wish they would be quick and come— *[Listens.]* Ah, there they are now. I must put on my things. *[Takes up her hat and cloak.]*

Scene 2. Christine Advises Nora

[HELMER'S and NORA'S voices are heard outside; a key is turned, and HELMER brings NORA almost by force into the hall. She is in an Italian costume with a large black shawl around her; he is in evening dress, and a black domino which is flying open.]

NORA   *[hanging back in the doorway, and struggling with him]*. No, no, no!—don't take me in. I want to go upstairs again; I don't want to leave so early.

HELMER   But, my dearest Nora—

NORA   Please, Torvald dear—please, please—only an hour more.

HELMER   Not a single minute, my sweet Nora. You know that was our agreement. Come along into the room; you are catching cold standing there. *[He brings her gently into the room, in spite of her resistance.]*

MRS. LINDE   Good evening.

NORA   Christine!

HELMER   You here, so late, Mrs Linde?

MRS. LINDE   Yes, you must excuse me; I was so anxious to see Nora in her dress.

NORA   Have you been sitting here waiting for me?

MRS. LINDE   Yes, unfortunately I came too late, you had already gone upstairs; and I thought I couldn't go away again without having seen you.

HELMER   *[taking off NORA'S shawl.]* Yes, take a good look at her. I think she is worth looking at. Isn't she charming, Mrs Linde?

MRS. LINDE   Yes, indeed she is.

HELMER   Doesn't she look remarkably pretty? Everyone thought so at the dance. But she is terribly self-willed, this sweet little person. What are we to do with her? You will hardly believe that I had almost to bring her away by force.

NORA   Torvald, you will repent not having let me stay, even if it were only for half an hour.

HELMER   Listen to her, Mrs Linde! She had danced her Tarantella, and it had been a tremendous success, as it deserved—although possibly the performance was a trifle too realistic—a little more so, I mean, than was strictly compatible with the limitations of art. But never mind about that! The chief thing is, she had made a success—she had made a tremendous success. Do you think I was going to let her remain there after that, and spoil the effect? No, indeed! I took my charming little Capri[1] maiden—my capricious little Capri maiden, I should say—on my arm; took one quick turn round the room; a curtsey[2] on either side, and, as they say in novels, the beautiful apparition disappeared. An exit ought always to be effective,

---

[1] Capri: an island (part of Campania) in the Bay of Naples in southern Italy; a tourist attraction noted for beautiful scenery; a popular resort since Roman times, it is famous for its Blue Grotto, a picturesque cave indenting the island's high, precipitous coast.

[2] curtsey: a woman's or girl's formal greeting made by bending the knees with one foot in front of the other.

Mrs Linde; but that is what I cannot make Nora understand. Pooh! this room is hot. *[Throws his domino on a chair, and opens the door of his room.]* Hullo! it's all dark in here. Oh, of course—excuse me—. *[He goes in, and lights some candles.]*

NORA *[in a hurried and breathless whisper]*. Well?

MRS. LINDE *[in a low voice]*. I have had a talk with him.

NORA Yes, and—

MRS. LINDE Nora, you must tell your husband all about it.

NORA *[in an expressionless voice]*. I knew it.

MRS. LINDE You have nothing to be afraid of as far as Krogstad is concerned; but you must tell him.

NORA I won't tell him.

MRS. LINDE Then the letter will.

NORA Thank you, Christine. Now I know what I must do. Hush—!

HELMER *[coming in again]*. Well, Mrs Linde, have you admired her?

MRS. LINDE Yes, and now I will say goodnight.

HELMER What, already? Is this yours, this knitting?

MRS. LINDE *[taking it]*. Yes, thank you, I had very nearly forgotten it.

HELMER So you knit?

MRS. LINDE Of course.

HELMER Do you know, you ought to embroider.

MRS. LINDE Really? Why?

HELMER Yes, it's far more becoming. Let me show you. You hold the embroidery thus in your left hand, and use the needle with the right—like this—with a long, easy sweep. Do you see?

MRS. LINDE Yes, perhaps—

HELMER But in the case of knitting—that can never be anything but ungraceful; look here—the arms close together, the knitting-needles going up and down—it has a sort of Chinese effect—. That was really excellent champagne they gave us.

MRS. LINDE Well,—goodnight, Nora, and don't be self-willed any more.

HELMER That's right, Mrs Linde.

MRS. LINDE Goodnight, Mr. Helmer.

HELMER *[accompanying her to the door]*. Goodnight, goodnight. I hope you will get home all right. I should be very happy to—but you haven't any great distance to go. Goodnight, goodnight. *[She goes out; he shuts the door after her, and comes in again.]*

Scene 3. Torvald's Fantasy

[Helmer comes in again.]

HELMER Ah!—at last we have got rid of her. She is a frightful bore, that woman.

NORA Aren't you very tired, Torvald?

HELMER No, not in the least.

NORA Nor sleepy?

HELMER Not a bit. On the contrary, I feel extraordinarily lively. And you?—you really look both tired and sleepy.

NORA Yes, I am very tired. I want to go to sleep at once.

HELMER There, you see it was quite right of me not to let you stay there any longer.

NORA Everything you do is quite right, Torvald.

HELMER *[kissing her on the forehead]*. Now my little skylark is speaking reasonably. Did you notice what good spirits Rank was in this evening?

NORA   Really? Was he? I didn't speak to him at all.

HELMER   And I very little, but I have not for a long time seen him in such good form. *[Looks for a while at her and then goes nearer to her.]* It is delightful to be at home by ourselves again, to be all alone with you—you fascinating, charming little darling!

NORA   Don't look at me like that, Torvald.

HELMER   Why shouldn't I look at my dearest treasure?—at all the beauty that is mine, all my very own?

NORA   *[going to the other side of the table]*. You mustn't say things like that to me tonight.

HELMER   *[following her]*. You have still got the Tarantella in your blood, I see. And it makes you more captivating than ever. Listen—the guests are beginning to go now. *[In a lower voice.]* Nora—soon the whole house will be quiet.

NORA   Yes, I hope so.

HELMER   Yes, my own darling Nora. Do you know, when I am out at a party with you like this, why I speak so little to you, keep away from you, and only send a stolen glance in your direction now and then?—do you know why I do that? It is because I make believe to myself that we are secretly in love, and you are my secretly promised bride, and that no one suspects there is anything between us.

NORA   Yes, yes—I know very well your thoughts are with me all the time.

HELMER   And when we are leaving, and I am putting the shawl over your beautiful young shoulders—on your lovely neck—then I imagine that you are my young bride and that we have just come from the wedding, and I am bringing you for the first time into our home—to be alone with you for the first time—quite alone with my shy little darling! All this evening I have longed for nothing but you. When I watched the seductive figures of the Tarantella, my blood was on fire; I could endure it no longer, and that was why I brought you down so early—

NORA   Go away, Torvald! You must let me go. I won't—

HELMER   What's that? You're joking, my little Nora! You won't—you won't? Am I not your husband—?

Scene 4. Doctor Rank's Evening

[A knock is heard at the outer door.]

NORA   *[starting]*. Did you hear—?

HELMER   *[going into the hall]*. Who is it?

RANK   *[outside]*. It is I. May I come in for a moment?

HELMER   *[in a fretful whisper]*. Oh, what does he want now? *[Aloud.]* Wait a minute! *[Unlocks the door.]* Come, that's kind of you not to pass by our door.

RANK   I thought I heard your voice, and felt as if I should like to look in. *[With a swift glance round.]* Ah, yes!—these dear familiar rooms. You are very happy and cosy in here, you two.

HELMER   It seems to me that you looked after yourself pretty well upstairs too.

RANK   Excellently. Why shouldn't I? Why shouldn't one enjoy everything in this world?—at any rate as much as one can, and as long as one can. The wine was capital—

HELMER   Especially the champagne.

RANK   So you noticed that too? It is almost incredible how much I managed to put away!

NORA   Torvald drank a great deal of champagne tonight too.

RANK   Did he?

NORA   Yes, and he is always in such good spirits afterwards.

RANK   Well, why should one not enjoy a merry evening after a well-spent day?

HELMER   Well spent? I am afraid I can't take credit for that.

RANK   *[clapping him on the back]*. But I can, you know!

NORA   Doctor Rank, you must have been occupied with some scientific investigation today.

RANK   Exactly.

HELMER   Just listen!—little Nora talking about scientific investigations!

NORA   And may I congratulate you on the result?

RANK   Indeed you may.

NORA   Was it favourable, then?

RANK   The best possible, for both doctor and patient—certainty.

NORA   *[quickly and searchingly]*. Certainty?

RANK   Absolute certainty. So wasn't I entitled to make a merry evening of it after that?

NORA   Yes, you certainly were, Doctor Rank.

HELMER   I think so too, so long as you don't have to pay for it in the morning.

RANK   Oh well, one can't have anything in this life without paying for it.

NORA   Doctor Rank—are you fond of fancy-dress balls?

RANK   Yes, if there is a fine lot of pretty costumes.

NORA   Tell me—what shall we two wear at the next?

HELMER   Little featherbrain!—are you thinking of the next already?

RANK   We two? Yes, I can tell you. You shall go as a good fairy—

HELMER   Yes, but what do you suggest as an appropriate costume for that?

RANK   Let your wife go dressed just as she is in everyday life.

HELMER   That was really very prettily turned. But can't you tell us what you will be?

RANK   Yes, my dear friend, I have quite made up my mind about that.

HELMER   Well?

RANK   At the next fancy-dress ball I shall be invisible.

HELMER   That's a good joke!

RANK   There is a big black hat—have you never heard of hats that make you invisible? If you put one on, no one can see you.

HELMER   *[suppressing a smile]*. Yes, you are quite right.

RANK   But I am clean forgetting what I came for. Helmer, give me a cigar—one of the dark Havanas.[3]

HELMER   With the greatest pleasure. *[Offers him his case.]*

RANK   *[takes a cigar and cuts off the end]*. Thanks.

NORA   *[striking a match]*. Let me give you a light.

RANK   Thank you. *[She holds the match for him to light his cigar.]* And now goodbye!

HELMER   Goodbye, goodbye, dear old man!

NORA   Sleep well, Doctor Rank.

RANK   Thank you for that wish.

NORA   Wish me the same.

RANK   You? Well, if you want me to sleep well! And thanks for the light. *[He nods to them both and goes out.]*

HELMER   *[in a subdued voice]*. He has drunk more than he ought.

NORA   *[absently]*. Maybe.

---

[3] Havanas: from Havana, Cuba, generally considered the best cigars in the world

Scene 5. Doctor Rank's Card

NORA   [HELMER takes a bunch of keys out of his pocket and goes into the hall.] Torvald! what are you going to do there?

HELMER   Emptying the letter-box; it is quite full; there will be no room to put the newspaper in tomorrow morning.

NORA   Are you going to work tonight?

HELMER   You know quite well I'm not. What is this? Someone has been at the lock.

NORA   At the lock—?

HELMER   Yes, someone has. What can it mean? I should never have thought the maid—. Here is a broken hairpin. Nora, it is one of yours.

NORA   [quickly]. Then it must have been the children—

HELMER   Then you must get them out of those ways. There, at last I have got it open. [Takes out the contents of the letter-box, and calls to the kitchen.] Helen!—Helen, put out the light over the front door. [Goes back into the room and shuts the door into the hall. He holds out his hand full of letters.] Look at that—look what a heap of them there are. [Turning them over.] What on earth is that?

NORA   [at the window]. The letter—No! Torvald, no!

HELMER   Two cards—of Rank's.

NORA   Of Doctor Rank's?

HELMER   [looking at them]. Doctor Rank. They were on the top. He must have put them in when he went out.

NORA   Is there anything written on them?

HELMER   There is a black cross over the name. Look there—what an uncomfortable idea! It looks as if he were announcing his own death.

NORA   It is just what he is doing.

HELMER   What? Do you know anything about it? Has he said anything to you?

NORA   Yes. He told me that when the cards came it would be his leave-taking from us. He means to shut himself up and die.

HELMER   My poor old friend! Certainly I knew we should not have him very long with us. But so soon! And so he hides himself away like a wounded animal.

NORA   If it has to happen, it is best it should be without a word—don't you think so, Torvald?

HELMER   [walking up and down]. He had so grown into our lives. I can't think of him as having gone out of them. He, with his sufferings and his loneliness, was like a cloudy background to our sunlit happiness. Well, perhaps it is best so. For him, anyway. [Standing still.] And perhaps for us too, Nora. We two are thrown quite upon each other now. [Puts his arms round her.] My darling wife, I don't feel as if I could hold you tight enough. Do you know, Nora, I have often wished that you might be threatened by some great danger, so that I might risk my life's blood, and everything, for your sake.

NORA   [disengages herself, and says firmly and decidedly]. Now you must read your letters, Torvald.

HELMER   No, no; not tonight. I want to be with you, my darling wife.

NORA   With the thought of your friend's death—

HELMER   You are right, it has affected us both. Something ugly has come between us—the thought of the horrors of death. We must try and rid our minds of that. Until then—we will each go to our own room.

NORA   [hanging on his neck]. Goodnight, Torvald—Goodnight!

HELMER [kissing her on the forehead]. Goodnight, my little singing-bird. Sleep sound, Nora. Now I will read my letters through. [He takes his letters and goes into his room, shutting the door after him.]

NORA [gropes distractedly about, seizes HELMER'S domino, throws it round her, while she says in quick, hoarse, spasmodic whispers]. Never to see him again. Never! Never! [Puts her shawl over her head.] Never to see my children again either—never again. Never! Never!—Ah! the icy, black water—the unfathomable depths—If only it were over! He has got it now—now he is reading it. Goodbye, Torvald and my children! [She is about to rush out through the hall, when HELMER opens his door hurriedly and stands with an open letter in his hand.]

Scene 6. Helmer Reads Krogstad's Letter

HELMER Nora!

NORA Ah!—

HELMER What is this? Do you know what is in this letter?

NORA Yes, I know. Let me go! Let me get out!

HELMER [holding her back]. Where are you going?

NORA [trying to get free]. You shan't save me, Torvald!

HELMER [reeling]. True? Is this true, that I read here? Horrible! No, no—it is impossible that it can be true.

NORA It is true. I have loved you above everything else in the world.

HELMER Oh, don't let us have any silly excuses.

NORA [taking a step towards him]. Torvald—!

HELMER Miserable creature—what have you done?

NORA Let me go. You shall not suffer for my sake. You shall not take it upon yourself.

HELMER No tragic airs, please. [Locks the hall door.] Here you shall stay and give me an explanation. Do you understand what you have done? Answer me! Do you understand what you have done?

NORA [looks steadily at him and says with a growing look of coldness in her face]. Yes, now I am beginning to understand thoroughly.

HELMER [walking about the room.] What a horrible awakening! All these eight years—she who was my joy and pride—a hypocrite, a liar—worse, worse—a criminal! The unutterable ugliness of it all!—For shame! For shame! [NORA is silent and looks steadily at him. He stops in front of her.] I ought to have suspected that something of the sort would happen. I ought to have foreseen it. All your father's want of principle—be silent!—all your father's want of principle has come out in you. No religion, no morality, no sense of duty—. How I am punished for having winked at what he did! I did it for your sake, and this is how you repay me.

NORA Yes, that's just it.

HELMER Now you have destroyed all my happiness. You have ruined all my future. It is horrible to think of! I am in the power of an unscrupulous man; he can do what he likes with me, ask anything he likes of me, give me any orders he pleases—I dare not refuse. And I must sink to such miserable depths because of a thoughtless woman!

NORA When I am out of the way, you will be free.

HELMER No fine speeches, please. Your father had always plenty of those ready, too. What good would it be to me if you were out of the way, as you say? Not the slightest. He can make the affair known everywhere; and if he does, I may be falsely suspected of having been a party to your criminal action. Very likely people will think I was behind it all—that it was I who prompted you! And I have to thank you for all this—you whom I have cherished during the whole of our married life. Do you understand now what it is you have done for me?

NORA [coldly and quietly]. Yes.

HELMER   It is so incredible that I can't take it in. But we must come to some understanding. Take off that shawl. Take it off, I tell you. I must try and appease him some way or another. The matter must be hushed up at any cost. And as for you and me, it must appear as if everything between us were just as before—but naturally only in the eyes of the world. You will still remain in my house, that is a matter of course. But I shall not allow you to bring up the children; I dare not trust them to you. To think that I should be obliged to say so to one whom I have loved so dearly, and whom I still—. No, that is all over. From this moment happiness is not the question; all that concerns us is to save the remains, the fragments, the appearance—

Scene 7. Krogstad Repents

[A ring is heard at the front-door bell.]

HELMER   [with a start]. What is that? So late! Can the worst—? Can he—? Hide yourself, Nora. Say you are ill.

[NORA stands motionless. HELMER goes and unlocks the hall door.]

MAID   [half-dressed, comes to the door]. A letter for the mistress.

HELMER   Give it to me. [Takes the letter, and shuts the door.] Yes, it is from him. You shall not have it; I will read it myself.

NORA   Yes, read it.

HELMER   [standing by the lamp]. I scarcely have the courage to do it. It may mean ruin for both of us. No, I must know. [Tears open the letter, runs his eye over a few lines, looks at a paper enclosed, and gives a shout of joy.] Nora! [She looks at him questioningly.] Nora!—No, I must read it once again—. Yes, it is true! I am saved! Nora, I am saved!

NORA   And I?

HELMER   You too, of course; we are both saved, both you and I. Look, he sends you your bond back. He says he regrets and repents—that a happy change in his life—never mind what he says! We are saved, Nora! No one can do anything to you. Oh, Nora, Nora!—no, first I must destroy these hateful things. Let me see—. [Takes a look at the bond.] No, no, I won't look at it. The whole thing shall be nothing but a bad dream to me. [Tears up the bond and both letters, throws them all into the stove, and watches them burn.] There—now it doesn't exist any longer. He says that since Christmas Eve you—. These must have been three dreadful days for you, Nora.

NORA   I have fought a hard fight these three days.

HELMER   And suffered agonies, and seen no way out but—. No, we won't call any of the horrors to mind. We will only shout with joy, and keep saying, "It's all over! It's all over!" Listen to me, Nora. You don't seem to realise that it is all over. What is this?—such a cold, set face! My poor little Nora, I quite understand; you don't feel as if you could believe that I have forgiven you. But it is true, Nora, I swear it; I have forgiven you everything. I know that what you did, you did out of love for me.

NORA   That is true.

HELMER   You have loved me as a wife ought to love her husband. Only you had not sufficient knowledge to judge of the means you used. But do you suppose you are any the less dear to me, because you don't understand how to act on your own responsibility? No, no; only lean on me; I will advise you and direct you. I should not be a man if this womanly helplessness did not just give you a double attractiveness in my eyes. You must not think anymore about the hard things I said in my first moment of consternation, when I thought everything was going to overwhelm me. I have forgiven you, Nora; I swear to you I have forgiven you.

NORA   Thank you for your forgiveness. [She goes out through the door to the right.]

HELMER   No, don't go—. [Looks in.] What are you doing in there?

NORA   [from within]. Taking off my fancy dress.

HELMER [standing at the open door]. Yes, do. Try and calm yourself, and make your mind easy again, my frightened little singing-bird. Be at rest, and feel secure; I have broad wings to shelter you under. [Walks up and down by the door.] How warm and cosy our home is, Nora. Here is shelter for you; here I will protect you like a hunted dove that I have saved from a hawk's claws; I will bring peace to your poor beating heart. It will come, little by little, Nora, believe me. Tomorrow morning you will look upon it all quite differently; soon everything will be just as it was before. Very soon you won't need me to assure you that I have forgiven you; you will yourself feel the certainty that I have done so. Can you suppose I should ever think of such a thing as repudiating you, or even reproaching you? You have no idea what a true man's heart is like, Nora. There is something so indescribably sweet and satisfying, to a man, in the knowledge that he has forgiven his wife—forgiven her freely, and with all his heart. It seems as if that had made her, as it were, doubly his own; he has given her a new life, so to speak; and she has in a way become both wife and child to him. So you shall be for me after this, my little scared, helpless darling. Have no anxiety about anything, Nora; only be frank and open with me, and I will serve as will and conscience both to you—. What is this? Not gone to bed? Have you changed your things?

NORA [in everyday dress]. Yes, Torvald, I have changed my things now.

HELMER But what for?—so late as this.

NORA I shall not sleep tonight.

HELMER But, my dear Nora—

Scene 8. The First Serious Talk

NORA [looking at her watch]. It is not so very late. Sit down here, Torvald. You and I have much to say to one another. [She sits down at one side of the table.]

HELMER Nora—what is this?—this cold, set face?

NORA Sit down. It will take some time; I have a lot to talk over with you.

HELMER [sits down at the opposite side of the table]. You alarm me, Nora!—and I don't understand you.

NORA No, that is just it. You don't understand me, and I have never understood you either—before tonight. No, you mustn't interrupt me. You must simply listen to what I say. Torvald, this is a settling of accounts.

HELMER What do you mean by that?

NORA [after a short silence]. Isn't there one thing that strikes you as strange in our sitting here like this?

HELMER What is that?

NORA We have been married now eight years. Does it not occur to you that this is the first time we two, you and I, husband and wife, have had a serious conversation?

HELMER What do you mean by serious?

NORA In all these eight years—longer than that—from the very beginning of our acquaintance, we have never exchanged a word on any serious subject.

HELMER Was it likely that I would be continually and forever telling you about worries that you could not help me to bear?

NORA I am not speaking about business matters. I say that we have never sat down in earnest together to try and get at the bottom of anything.

HELMER But, dearest Nora, would it have been any good to you?

NORA That is just it; you have never understood me. I have been greatly wronged, Torvald—first by papa and then by you.

HELMER What! By us two—by us two, who have loved you better than anyone else in the world?

NORA [shaking her head]. You have never loved me. You have only thought it pleasant to be in love with me.

HELMER   Nora, what do I hear you saying?

NORA   It is perfectly true, Torvald. When I was at home with papa, he told me his opinion about everything, and so I had the same opinions; and if I differed from him I concealed the fact, because he would not have liked it. He called me his doll-child, and he played with me just as I used to play with my dolls. And when I came to live with you—

HELMER   What sort of an expression is that to use about our marriage?

NORA   [undisturbed]. I mean that I was simply transferred from papa's hands into yours. You arranged everything according to your own taste, and so I got the same tastes as your else I pretended to, I am really not quite sure which—I think sometimes the one and sometimes the other. When I look back on it, it seems to me as if I had been living here like a poor woman—just from hand to mouth. I have existed merely to perform tricks for you, Torvald. But you would have it so. You and papa have committed a great sin against me. It is your fault that I have made nothing of my life.

HELMER   How unreasonable and how ungrateful you are, Nora! Have you not been happy here?

NORA   No, I have never been happy. I thought I was, but it has never really been so.

HELMER   Not—not happy!

NORA   No, only merry. And you have always been so kind to me. But our home has been nothing but a playroom. I have been your doll-wife, just as at home I was papa's doll-child; and here the children have been my dolls. I thought it great fun when you played with me, just as they thought it great fun when I played with them. That is what our marriage has been, Torvald.

HELMER   There is some truth in what you say—exaggerated and strained as your view of it is. But for the future it shall be different. Playtime shall be over, and lesson-time shall begin.

NORA   Whose lessons? Mine, or the children's?

HELMER   Both yours and the children's, my darling Nora.

NORA   Alas, Torvald, you are not the man to educate me into being a proper wife for you.

HELMER   And you can say that!

NORA   And I—how am I fitted to bring up the children?

HELMER   Nora!

NORA   Didn't you say so yourself a little while ago—that you dare not trust me to bring them up?

HELMER   In a moment of anger! Why do you pay any heed to that?

NORA   Indeed, you were perfectly right. I am not fit for the task. There is another task I must undertake first. I must try and educate myself—you are not the man to help me in that. I must do that for myself. And that is why I am going to leave you now.

HELMER   [springing up]. What do you say?

NORA   I must stand quite alone, if I am to understand myself and everything about me. It is for that reason that I cannot remain with you any longer.

HELMER   Nora, Nora!

NORA   I am going away from here now, at once. I am sure Christine will take me in for the night—

HELMER   You are out of your mind! I won't allow it! I forbid you!

NORA   It is no use forbidding me anything any longer. I will take with me what belongs to myself. I will take nothing from you, either now or later.

HELMER   What sort of madness is this!

NORA   Tomorrow I shall go home—I mean, to my old home. It will be easiest for me to find something to do there.

HELMER   You blind, foolish woman!

NORA   I must try and get some sense, Torvald.

HELMER   To desert your home, your husband and your children! And you don't consider what people will say!

NORA   I cannot consider that at all. I only know that it is necessary for me.

HELMER   It's shocking. This is how you would neglect your most sacred duties.

NORA   What do you consider my most sacred duties?

HELMER   Do I need to tell you that? Are they not your duties to your husband and your children?

NORA   I have other duties just as sacred.

HELMER   That you have not. What duties could those be?

NORA   Duties to myself.

HELMER   Before all else, you are a wife and a mother.

NORA   I don't believe that any longer. I believe that before all else I am a reasonable human being, just as you are—or, at all events, that I must try and become one. I know quite well, Torvald, that most people would think you right, and that views of that kind are to be found in books; but I can no longer content myself with what most people say, or with what is found in books. I must think over things for myself and get to understand them.

HELMER   Can you not understand your place in your own home? Have you not a reliable guide in such matters as that?—have you no religion?

NORA   I am afraid, Torvald, I do not exactly know what religion is.

HELMER   What are you saying?

NORA   I know nothing but what the clergyman[4] said, when I went to be confirmed. He told us that religion was this, and that, and the other. When I am away from all this, and am alone, I will look into that matter too. I will see if what the clergyman said is true, or at all events if it is true for me.

HELMER   This is unheard of in a girl of your age! But if religion cannot lead you aright, let me try and awaken your conscience. I suppose you have some moral sense? Or—answer me—am I to think you have none?

NORA   I assure you, Torvald, that is not an easy question to answer. I really don't know. The thing perplexes me altogether. I only know that you and I look at it in quite a different light. I am learning, too, that the law is quite another thing from what I supposed; but I find it impossible to convince myself that the law is right. According to it a woman has no right to spare her old dying father, or to save her husband's life. I can't believe that.

HELMER   You talk like a child. You don't understand the conditions of the world in which you live.

NORA   No, I don't. But now I am going to try. I am going to see if I can make out who is right, the world or I.

HELMER   You are ill, Nora; you are delirious; I almost think you are out of your mind.

NORA   I have never felt my mind so clear and certain as tonight.

HELMER   And is it with a clear and certain mind that you forsake your husband and your children?

NORA   Yes, it is.

HELMER   Then there is only one possible explanation.

---

4 clergyman: a male priest or minister of a Christian church.

NORA   What is that?

HELMER   You do not love me anymore.

NORA   No, that is just it.

HELMER   Nora!—and you can say that?

NORA   It gives me great pain, Torvald, for you have always been so kind to me, but I cannot help it. I do not love you any more.

HELMER   [regaining his composure]. Is that a clear and certain conviction too?

NORA   Yes, absolutely clear and certain. That is the reason why I will not stay here any longer.

HELMER   And can you tell me what I have done to forfeit your love?

NORA   Yes, indeed I can. It was tonight, when the wonderful thing did not happen; then I saw you were not the man I had thought you were.

HELMER   Explain yourself better. I don't understand you.

NORA   I have waited so patiently for eight years; for, goodness knows, I knew very well that wonderful things don't happen every day. Then this horrible misfortune came upon me; and then I felt quite certain that the wonderful thing was going to happen at last. When Krogstad's letter was lying out there, never for a moment did I imagine that you would consent to accept this man's conditions. I was so absolutely certain that you would say to him: Publish the thing to the whole world. And when that was done—

HELMER   Yes, what then?—when I had exposed my wife to shame and disgrace?

NORA   When that was done, I was so absolutely certain, you would come forward and take everything upon yourself, and say: I am the guilty one.

HELMER   Nora—!

NORA   You mean that I would never have accepted such a sacrifice on your part? No, of course not. But what would my assurances have been worth against yours? That was the wonderful thing which I hoped for and feared; and it was to prevent that, that I wanted to kill myself.

HELMER   I would gladly work night and day for you, Nora—bear sorrow and want for your sake. But no man would sacrifice his honour for the one he loves.

NORA   It is a thing hundreds of thousands of women have done.

HELMER   Oh, you think and talk like a heedless child.

NORA   Maybe. But you neither think nor talk like the man I could bind myself to. As soon as your fear was over—and it was not fear for what threatened me, but for what might happen to you—when the whole thing was past, as far as you were concerned it was exactly as if nothing at all had happened. Exactly as before, I was your little skylark, your doll, which you would in future treat with doubly gentle care, because it was so brittle and fragile. [Getting up.] Torvald—it was then it dawned upon me that for eight years I had been living here with a strange man, and had borne him three children—. Oh, I can't bear to think of it! I could tear myself into little bits!

HELMER   [sadly]. I see, I see. An abyss has opened between us—there is no denying it. But, Nora, would it not be possible to fill it up?

NORA   As I am now, I am no wife for you.

HELMER   I have it in me to become a different man.

NORA   Perhaps—if your doll is taken away from you.

HELMER   But to part!—to part from you! No, no, Nora, I can't understand that idea.

NORA   [going out to the right]. That makes it all the more certain that it must be done. [She comes back with her cloak and hat and a small bag which she puts on a chair by the table.]

HELMER   Nora, Nora, not now! Wait until tomorrow.

NORA   *[putting on her cloak].* I cannot spend the night in a strange man's room.

HELMER   But can't we live here like brother and sister—?

NORA   *[putting on her hat].* You know very well that would not last long. *[Puts the shawl round her.]* Goodbye, Torvald. I won't see the little ones. I know they are in better hands than mine. As I am now, I can be of no use to them.

HELMER   But some day, Nora—some day?

NORA   How can I tell? I have no idea what is going to become of me.

HELMER   But you are my wife, whatever becomes of you.

NORA   Listen, Torvald. I have heard that when a wife deserts her husband's house, as I am doing now, he is legally freed from all obligations towards her. In any case, I set you free from all your obligations. You are not to feel yourself bound in the slightest way, any more than I shall. There must be perfect freedom on both sides. See, here is your ring back. Give me mine.

HELMER   That too?

NORA   That too.

HELMER   Here it is.

NORA   That's right. Now it is all over. I have put the keys here. The maids know all about everything in the house—better than I do. Tomorrow, after I have left her, Christine will come here and pack up my own things that I brought with me from home. I will have them sent after me.

HELMER   All over! All over!—Nora, shall you never think of me again?

NORA   I know I shall often think of you, the children, and this house.

HELMER   May I write to you, Nora?

NORA   No—never. You must not do that.

HELMER   But at least let me send you—

NORA   Nothing—nothing—

HELMER   Let me help you if you are in want.

NORA   No. I can receive nothing from a stranger.

HELMER   Nora—can I never be anything more than a stranger to you?

NORA   *[taking her bag].* Ah, Torvald, the most wonderful thing of all would have to happen.

HELMER   Tell me what that would be!

NORA   Both you and I would have to be so changed that—. Oh, Torvald, I don't believe any longer in wonderful things happening.

HELMER   But I will believe in it. Tell me! So changed that—?

NORA   That our life together would be a real wedlock. Goodbye. *[She goes out through the hall.]*

HELMER   *[sinks down on a chair at the door and buries his face in his hands].* Nora! Nora! *[Looks round, and rises.]* Empty. She is gone. *[A hope flashes across his mind.]* The most wonderful thing of all—?

[The sound of a door shutting is heard from below.]

The Stronger

August Strindberg
1889

Reprinted from *Plays by August Strindberg*. Trans. Edith and Warner Oland. Boston: John W. Luce and Co., 1912.

In this one-act play, only one character speaks, making this similar to a monologue. However, a monologue is a long speech in a play. Here, Strindberg has one character physically reacting throughout the play.

Characters

MME. X   an actress, married
MLLE. Y   an actress, unmarried, real name is Amelia
A WAITRESS

Character References

Bob   He does not appear in the play, but he is the husband of MME. X.
Eskil   son of MME. X. In Scandinavian the meaning of the name Eskil is: Holy cauldron. Norse Meaning: The name Eskil is a Norse baby name. In Norse the meaning of the name Eskil is: Vessel of the gods.
Maja   daughter of MME. X, a variation of Mary—Christianity's mother of Jesus

The Past

[SCENE—The corner of a ladies' cafe. Two little iron tables, a red velvet sofa, several chairs. Enter Mme. X., dressed in winter clothes, carrying a Japanese basket on her arm. MLLE. Y. sits with a half empty beer bottle before her, reading an illustrated paper, which she changes later for another.]

MME. X   Good afternoon, Amelie. You're sitting here alone on Christmas eve like a poor bachelor!

MLLE. Y   *[Looks up, nods, and resumes her reading.]*

MME. X   Do you know it really hurts me to see you like this, alone, in a cafe, and on Christmas eve, too. It makes me feel as I did one time when I saw a bridal party in a Paris restaurant, and the bride sat reading a comic paper, while the groom played billiards[1] with the witnesses. Huh, thought I, with such a beginning, what will follow, and what will be the end? He played billiards on his wedding eve! *[Mlle. Y. starts to speak]*. And she read a comic paper, you mean? Well, they are not altogether the same thing.

Family

[A waitress enters, places a cup of chocolate before Mme. X. and goes out.]

MME. X   You know what, Amelie! I believe you would have done better to have kept him! Do you remember, I was the first to say "Forgive him?" Do you remember that? You would be married now and have a home. Remember that Christmas when you went out to visit your fiance's parents in the country? How you gloried in the happiness of home life and really longed to quit the theatre forever?[2] Yes, Amelie dear, home is the best of all, the theatre next and children—well, you don't understand that.

MLLE. Y   *[Looks up scornfully. [Mme. X. sips a few spoonfuls out of the cup, then opens her basket and shows Christmas presents.]*

---

[1] billiards: a game usually for two people, played on a billiard table, in which three balls are struck with cues into pockets around the edge of the table. Pool, on the other hand, uses a cue to strike one ball at a time into pockets.

[2] theatre: Mr. X and Mlle. Y (Amelia) both worked at the theatre, presumably Mr. X as manager and Mlle. Y as an actress.

MME. X   Now you shall see what I bought for my piggywigs.[3] *[Takes up a doll.]* Look at this! This is for Lisa, ha! Do you see how she can roll her eyes and turn her head, eh? And here is Maja's popgun. *[Loads it and shoots at Mlle. Y.]*

MLLE. Y   *[Makes a startled gesture.]*

MME. X   Did I frighten you? Do you think I would like to shoot you, eh? On my soul, if I don't think you did! If you wanted to shoot me it wouldn't be so surprising, because I stood in your way—and I know you can never forget that— although I was absolutely innocent. You still believe I intrigued and got you out of the Stora theatre, but I didn't. I didn't do that, although you think so. Well, it doesn't make any difference what I say to you. You still believe I did it. *[Takes up a pair of embroidered slippers.]* And these are for my better half. I embroidered them myself—I can't bear tulips, but he wants tulips[4] on everything.

MLLE. Y   *[Looks up ironically and curiously.]*

MME. X   *[Putting a hand in each slipper.]* What little feet Bob has! What? And you should see what a splendid stride he has! You've never seen him in slippers! *[Mlle. Y. laughs aloud.]* Look! *[She makes the slippers walk on the table. Mlle. Y. laughs loudly.]* And when he is grumpy he stamps like this with his foot. "What! damn those servants who can never learn to make coffee. Oh, now those creatures haven't trimmed the lamp wick properly!" And then there are draughts on the floor and his feet are cold. "Ugh, how cold it is; the stupid idiots can never keep the fire going." *[She rubs the slippers together, one sole over the other.]*

MLLE. Y   *[Shrieks with laughter.]*

MME. X   And then he comes home and has to hunt for his slippers which Marie has stuck under the chiffonier[5]—oh, but it's sinful to sit here and make fun of one's husband this way when he is kind and a good little man. You ought to have had such a husband, Amelie. What are you laughing at? What? What? And you see he's true to me. Yes, I'm sure of that, because he told me himself—what are you laughing at?—that when I was touring in Norway that that brazen Frêdêrique came and wanted to seduce him! Can you fancy anything so infamous? *[Pause.]* I'd have torn her eyes out if she had come to see him when I was at home. *[Pause.]* It was lucky that Bob told me about it himself and that it didn't reach me through gossip. *[Pause.]* But would you believe it, Frêdêrique wasn't the only one! I don't know why, but the women are crazy about my husband. They must think he has influence about getting them theatrical engagements, because he is connected with the government. Perhaps you were after him yourself. I didn't use to trust you any too much. But now I know he never bothered his head about you, and you always seemed to have a grudge against him someway.

[Pause. They look at each other in a puzzled way.]

MME. X   Come and see us this evening, Amelie, and show us that you're not put out with us,—not put out with me at any rate. I don't know, but I think it would be uncomfortable to have you for an enemy. Perhaps it's because I stood in your way or—I really—don't know why—In particular.

The Affair

[Pause. Mlle. Y. stares at Mme. X curiously.]

MME. X   *[Thoughtfully].* Our acquaintance has been so queer. When I saw you for the first time I was afraid of you, so afraid that I didn't dare let you out of my sight; no matter when or where, I always found myself near you—I didn't dare have you for an enemy, so I became your friend. But there was always discord when you came to our house, because I saw that my husband couldn't endure

---

[3] piggywigs: a pet name for her children

[4] tulips: a bulbous spring-flowering plant of the lily family, with boldly colored cup-shaped flowers. As a perennial, the flower persists for many growing seasons. Generally the top portion of the plant dies back each winter and regrows the following spring from the same root system

[5] chiffonier: a tall chest of drawers, often with a mirror on top

you, and the whole thing seemed as awry to me as an ill-fitting gown—and I did all I could to make him friendly toward you, but with no success until you became engaged. Then came a violent friendship between you, so that it looked all at once as though you both dared show your real feelings only when you were secure—and then—how was it later? I didn't get jealous—strange to say! And I remember at the christening, when you acted as godmother,[6] I made him kiss you—he did so, and you became so confused—as it were; I didn't notice it then—didn't think about it later, either—have never thought about it until—now! *[Rises suddenly.]* Why are you silent? You haven't said a word this whole time, but you have let me go on talking! You have sat there, and your eyes have reeled out of me all these thoughts which lay like raw silk in its cocoon—thoughts—suspicious thoughts, perhaps. Let me see—why did you break your engagement? Why do you never come to our house any more? Why won't you come to see us tonight?

[Mlle. Y. appears as if about to speak.]

MME. X   Hush, you needn't speak—I understand it all! It was because—and because—and because! Yes, yes! Now all the accounts balance. That's it. Fie, I won't sit at the same table with you.[7] *[Moves her things to another table.]* That's the reason I had to embroider tulips—which I hate—on his slippers, because you are fond of tulips; that's why *[Throws slippers on the floor]* we go to Lake Mälarn in the summer, because you don't like salt water; that's why my boy is named Eskil—because it's your father's name; that's why I wear your colors, read your authors, eat your favorite dishes, drink your drinks—chocolate, for instance; that's why—oh—my God—It's terrible, when I think about it; it's terrible. Everything, everything came from you to me, even your passions. Your soul crept into mine, like a worm into an apple, ate and ate, bored and bored, until nothing was left but the rind and a little black dust within. I wanted to get away from you, but I couldn't; you lay like a snake and charmed me with your black eyes; I felt that when I lifted my wings they only dragged me down; I lay in the water with bound feet, and the stronger I strove to keep up the deeper I worked myself down, down, until I sank to the bottom, where you lay like a giant crab to clutch me in your claws—and there I am lying now.

I hate you, hate you, hate you! And you only sit there silent—silent and indifferent; indifferent whether it's new moon or waning moon, Christmas or New Year's, whether others are happy or unhappy; without power to hate or to love; as quiet as a stork by a rat hole—you couldn't scent your prey and capture it, but you could lie in wait for it! You sit here in your corner of the café—did you know it's called "The Rat Trap" for you?—and read the papers to see if misfortune hasn't befallen some one, to see if some one hasn't been given notice at the theatre, perhaps; you sit here and calculate about your next victim and reckon on your chances of recompense[8] like a pilot in a shipwreck. Poor Amelie, I pity you, nevertheless, because I know you are unhappy, unhappy like one who has been wounded, and angry because you are wounded. I can't be angry with you, no matter how much I want to be—because you come out the weaker one. Yes, all that with Bob doesn't trouble me. What is that to me, after all? And what difference does it make whether I learned to drink chocolate from you or some one else. *[Sips a spoonful from her cup.]*

Besides, chocolate is very healthful. And if you taught me how to dress—*tant mieux!*[9]—that has only made me more attractive to my husband; so you lost and I won there. Well, judging by certain signs, I believe you have already lost him; and you certainly intended that I should leave him—do as you did with your fiancé and regret as you now regret;

---

[6] godmother: a female who presents a child at baptism and responds on the child's behalf, promising to take responsibility for the child's religious education.

[7] Fie: used to express disgust or outrage.

[8] recompense: To make amends to (someone) for loss or harm suffered; compensate.

[9] *tant mieux*: so much the better

but, you see, I don't do that—we mustn't be too exacting. And why should I take only what no one else wants?

Perhaps, take it all in all, I am at this moment the stronger one. You received nothing from me, but you gave me much. And now I seem like a thief since you have awakened and find I possess what is your loss. How could it be otherwise when everything is worthless and sterile in your hands? You can never keep a man's love with your tulips and your passions—but I can keep it. You can't learn how to live from your authors, as I have learned. You have no little Eskil to cherish, even if your father's name was Eskil. And why are you always silent, silent, silent? I thought that was strength, but perhaps it is because you have nothing to say! Because you never think about anything! *[Rises and picks up slippers.]*

Now I'm going home—and take the tulips with me—your tulips! You are unable to learn from another; you can't bend—therefore, you broke like a dry stalk. But I won't break! Thank you, Amelie, for all your good lessons. Thanks for teaching my husband how to love. Now I'm going home to love him. *[Goes.]*

The Bear

Anton Chekhov
1890

First performed in Moscow on October 28, 1888. From *Plays by Anton Chekhov, Second Series*. Translated, with an Introduction, by Julius West. London: Duckworth, 1915.

Characters

ELENA IVANOVNA POPOVA. A widow whose deceased husband owes a debt to Mr. Smirnov.

GRIGORY STEPANOVITCH SMIRNOV. A middle-aged landowner

LUKA. Popova's aged footman

DASHA. Gardener, Footman, or Coachman

Character References

Nicolai Mihailovitch   deceased husband of Mrs. Popova

The Widow, Mrs. Popova

[A drawing-room in POPOVA'S house. Mrs. POPOVA is in deep mourning and has her eyes fixed on a photograph. LUKA is haranguing her.]

LUKA   It isn't right, madam . . . You're just destroying yourself. The maid and the cook have gone off fruit picking, every living being is rejoicing, even the cat understands how to enjoy herself and walks about in the yard, catching midges; only you sit in this room all day, as if this was a convent, and don't take any pleasure. Yes, really! I reckon it's a whole year that you haven't left the house!

POPOVA   I shall never go out . . . Why should I? My life is already at an end. He is in his grave, and I have buried myself between four walls . . . We are both dead.

LUKA   Well, there you are! Nicolai Mihailovitch is dead, well, it's the will of God, and may his soul rest in peace . . . You've mourned him—and quite right. But you can't go on weeping and wearing mourning for ever. My old woman died too, when her time came. Well? I grieved over her, I wept for a month, and that's enough for her, but if I've got to weep for a whole age, well, the old woman isn't worth it. *[Sighs]* You've forgotten all your neighbours. You don't go anywhere, and you see nobody. We live, so to speak, like spiders, and never see the light. The mice have eaten my livery. It isn't as if there were no good people around, for the district's full of them. There's a regiment quartered at Riblov,[1] and the officers are such beauties—you can never gaze your fill at them. And, every

---

[1] Riblov: Old spelling of the rural town of Kamen-Rybolov, Russia. It is located on the shores of Lake Khanka, near the Pacific Ocean, Inner Mongolia and South Korea. One of the farthest points of Russia.

Friday, there's a ball at the camp, and every day the soldier's band plays . . . Eh, my lady! You're young and beautiful, with roses in your cheek—if you only took a little pleasure. Beauty won't last long, you know. In ten years' time you'll want to be a peahen yourself among the officers, but they won't look at you, it will be too late.

POPOVA   [With determination] I must ask you never to talk to me about it! You know that when Nicolai Mihailovitch died, life lost all its meaning for me. I vowed never to the end of my days to cease to wear mourning, or to see the light . . . You hear? Let his ghost see how well I love him . . . Yes, I know it's no secret to you that he was often unfair to me, cruel, and . . . and even unfaithful, but I shall be true till death, and show him how I can love. There, beyond the grave, he will see me as I was before his death . . .

LUKA   Instead of talking like that you ought to go and have a walk in the garden, or else order Toby or Giant to be harnessed, and then drive out to see some of the neighbours.[2]

POPOVA   Oh! [Weeps.]

LUKA   Madam! Dear madam! What is it? Bless you!

POPOVA   He was so fond of Toby! He always used to ride on him to the Korchagins and Vlasovs.[3] How well he could ride! What grace there was in his figure when he pulled at the reins with all his strength! Do you remember? Toby, Toby! Tell them to give him an extra feed of oats.

LUKA   Yes, madam. [A bell rings noisily.]

POPOVA   [Shaking] Who's that? Tell them that I receive nobody.

LUKA   Yes, madam. [Exit.]

POPOVA   [Looks at the photograph] You will see, Nicolas, how I can love and forgive[4] . . . My love will die out with me, only when this poor heart will cease to beat. [Laughs through her tears] And aren't you ashamed? I am a good and virtuous little wife. I've locked myself in, and will be true to you till the grave, and you . . . aren't you ashamed, you bad child? You deceived me, had rows with me, left me alone for weeks on end . . .

Mr. Smirnov Arrives

[LUKA enters in consternation.]

LUKA   Madam, somebody is asking for you. He wants to see you . . .

POPOVA   But didn't you tell him that since the death of my husband I've stopped receiving?[5]

LUKA   I did, but he wouldn't even listen; says that it's a very pressing affair.

POPOVA   I do not receive!

LUKA   I told him so, but the . . . the devil . . . curses and pushes himself right in . . . He's in the dining room now.

POPOVA   [Annoyed] Very well, ask him in . . . What manners! [Exit LUKA] How these people annoy me! What does he want of me? Why should he disturb my peace? [Sighs] No, I see that I shall have to go into a convent after all. [Thoughtfully] Yes, into a convent[6] . . . [Enter LUKA with SMIRNOV.]

SMIRNOV   [To LUKA] You fool, you're too fond of talking . . . Ass! [Sees POPOVA and speaks with respect] Madam, I have the honour to present myself, I am Grigory Stepanovitch Smirnov, landowner and retired lieutenant of artillery! I am compelled to disturb you on a very pressing affair.

---

[2] Toby or Giant: horses

[3] Korchagins and Vlasovs: Families living nearby.

[4] Nicholas: Mrs. Popova is speaking to her dead husband.

[5] receiving: an old term used to describe accepting visitors or guests at a house

[6] convent: a Christian community under monastic vows, especially one of nuns.

POPOVA *[Not giving him her hand]* What do you want?

SMIRNOV Your late husband, with whom I had the honour of being acquainted, died in my debt for one thousand two hundred roubles,[7] on two bills of exchange. As I've got to pay the interest on a mortgage tomorrow, I've come to ask you, madam, to pay me the money today.

POPOVA One thousand two hundred . . . And what was my husband in debt to you for?

SMIRNOV He used to buy oats from me.

POPOVA *[Sighing, to LUKA]* So don't you forget, Luka, to give Toby an extra feed of oats. *[Exit LUKA]* If Nicolai Mihailovitch died in debt to you, then I shall certainly pay you, but you must excuse me today, as I haven't any spare cash. The day after tomorrow my steward[8] will be back from town, and I'll give him instructions to settle your account, but at the moment I cannot do as you wish . . . Moreover, it's exactly seven months today since the death of my husband, and I'm in a state of mind which absolutely prevents me from giving money matters my attention.

SMIRNOV And I'm in a state of mind which, if I don't pay the interest due tomorrow, will force me to make a graceful exit from this life feet first. They'll take my estate!

POPOVA You'll have your money the day after tomorrow.

SMIRNOV I don't want the money the day after tomorrow, I want it today.

POPOVA You must excuse me, I can't pay you.

SMIRNOV And I can't wait till after tomorrow.

POPOVA Well, what can I do, if I haven't the money now!

SMIRNOV You mean to say, you can't pay me?

POPOVA I can't.

SMIRNOV Hm! Is that the last word you've got to say?

POPOVA Yes, the last word.

SMIRNOV The last word? Absolutely your last?

POPOVA Absolutely.

SMIRNOV Thank you so much. I'll make a note of it. *[Shrugs his shoulders]* And then people want me to keep calm! I meet a man on the road, and he asks me "Why are you always so angry, Grigory Stepanovitch?" But how on earth am I not to get angry? I want the money desperately. I rode out yesterday, early in the morning, and called on all my debtors, and not a single one of them paid up! I was just about deadbeat after it all, slept, goodness knows where, in some inn, kept by a Jew,[9] with a vodka-barrel by my head. At last I get here, seventy versts from home,[10] and hope to get something, and I am received by you with a "state of mind"! How shouldn't I get angry.

POPOVA I thought I distinctly said my steward will pay you when he returns from town.

SMIRNOV I didn't come to your steward, but to you! What the devil, excuse my saying so, what have I to do with your steward!

POPOVA Excuse me, sir, I am not accustomed to listen to such expressions or to such a tone of voice. I want to hear no more. *[Makes a rapid exit.]*

---

[7] roubles: variant spelling of rubles, the Russian currency; 1,200 rubles in 1890 equals about $869 dollars in 2012 (from <u>The Inflation Calculator</u>).

[8] steward: Mrs. Popova's property manager

[9] kept by a Jew: a derogatory statement

[10] versts: a Russian measure of length, about 0.66 mile (1.1 km). Mr. Smirnov is approximately 46.2 miles from home. On a horse, travelling 3 mph, it would take about 15.4 hours to make the trip.

Mr. Smirnov's Anger

SMIRNOV   Well, there! "A state of mind." . . . "Husband died seven months ago!" Must I pay the interest, or mustn't I? I ask you: Must I pay, or must I not? Suppose your husband is dead, and you've got a state of mind, and nonsense of that sort . . . And your steward's gone away somewhere, devil take him, what do you want me to do? Do you think I can fly away from my creditors in a balloon, or what? Or do you expect me to go and run my head into a brick wall? I go to Grusdev and he isn't at home, Yaroshevitch has hidden himself, I had a violent row with Kuritsin and nearly threw him out of the window, Mazugo has something the matter with his bowels, and this woman has "a state of mind." Not one of the swine wants to pay me! Just because I'm too gentle with them, because I'm a rag, just weak wax in their hands! I'm much too gentle with them! Well, just you wait! You'll find out what I'm like! I shan't let you play about with me, confound it! I shall jolly well stay here until she pays! Brr! . . . How angry I am today, how angry I am! All my inside is quivering with anger, and I can't even breathe . . . Foo, my word, I even feel sick! *[Yells]* Waiter!

[Enter LUKA.]

LUKA   What is it?

SMIRNOV   Get me some kvass[11] or water! *[Exit LUKA]* What a way to reason! A man is in desperate need of his money, and she won't pay it because, you see, she is not disposed to attend to money matters! . . . That's real silly feminine logic. That's why I never did like, and don't like now, to have to talk to women. I'd rather sit on a barrel of gunpowder than talk to a woman. Brr! . . . I feel quite chilly—and it's all on account of that little bit of fluff! I can't even see one of these poetic creatures from a distance without breaking out into a cold sweat out of sheer anger. I can't look at them. *[Enter LUKA with water.]*

LUKA   Madam is ill and will see nobody.

SMIRNOV   Get out! *[Exit LUKA]* I will see nobody! No, it's all right, you don't see me . . . I'm going to stay and will sit here till you give me the money. You can be ill for a week, if you like, and I'll stay here for a week . . . If you're ill for a year— I'll stay for a year. I'm going to get my own, my dear! You don't get at me with your widow's weeds and your dimpled cheeks! I know those dimples! *[Shouts through the window]* Simeon, take them out! We aren't going away at once! I'm staying here! Tell them in the stable to give the horses some oats! You fool, you've let the near horse's leg get tied up in the reins again*! [Teasingly]* "Never mind . . . " I'll give it you. "Never mind." *[Goes away from the window]* Oh, it's bad . . . The heat's frightful, nobody pays up. I slept badly, and on top of everything else here's a bit of fluff in mourning with "a state of mind." . . . My head's aching . . . Shall I have some vodka, what? Yes, I think I will. *[Yells]* Waiter!

[Enter LUKA.]

LUKA   What is it?

SMIRNOV   A glass of vodka! *[Exit LUKA]* Ouf! *[Sits and inspects himself]* I must say I look well! Dust all over, boots dirty, unwashed, unkempt, straw on my waistcoat . . . The dear lady may well have taken me for a brigand. *[Yawns]* It's rather impolite to come into a drawing-room in this state, but it can't be helped . . . I am not here as a visitor, but as a creditor, and there's no dress specially prescribed for creditors . . .

[Enter LUKA with the vodka.]

LUKA   You allow yourself to go very far, sir . . .

SMIRNOV   *[Angrily]* What?

LUKA   I . . . er . . . nothing . . . I really . . .

SMIRNOV   Whom are you talking to? Shut up!

---

[11] kvass: (esp. in Russia) a fermented drink, low in alcohol, made from rye flour or bread with malt.

LUKA   *[Aside]* The devil's come to stay . . . Bad luck that brought him . . . *[Exit.]*

SMIRNOV   Oh, how angry I am! So angry that I think I could grind the whole world to dust . . . I even feel sick . . . *[Yells]* Waiter!

Past Experiences

[Enter POPOVA.]

POPOVA   *[Her eyes downcast]* Sir, in my solitude I have grown unaccustomed to the masculine voice, and I can't stand shouting. I must ask you not to disturb my peace.

SMIRNOV   Pay me the money, and I'll go.

POPOVA   I told you perfectly plainly; I haven't any money to spare; wait until the day after tomorrow.

SMIRNOV   And I told you perfectly plainly I don't want the money the day after tomorrow, but today. If you don't pay me today, I'll have to hang myself tomorrow.

POPOVA   But what can I do if I haven't got the money? You're so strange!

SMIRNOV   Then you won't pay me now? Eh?

POPOVA   I can't.

SMIRNOV   In that case I stay here and shall wait until I get it. *[Sits down]* You're going to pay me the day after tomorrow? Very well! I'll stay here until the day after tomorrow. I'll sit here all the time . . . *[Jumps up]* I ask you: Have I got to pay the interest tomorrow, or haven't I? Or do you think I'm doing this for a joke?

POPOVA   Please don't shout! This isn't a stable!

SMIRNOV   I wasn't asking you about a stable, but whether I'd got my interest to pay tomorrow or not?

POPOVA   You don't know how to behave before women!

SMIRNOV   No, I do know how to behave before women!

POPOVA   No, you don't! You're a rude, ill-bred man! Decent people don't talk to a woman like that!

SMIRNOV   What a business! How do you want me to talk to you? In French, or what?[12] *[Loses his temper and lisps]* Madame, je vous prie . . . How happy I am that you don't pay me . . . Ah, pardon. I have disturbed you! Such lovely weather today! And how well you look in mourning! *[Bows.]*

POPOVA   That's silly and rude.

SMIRNOV   *[Teasing her]* Silly and rude! I don't know how to behave before women! Madam, in my time I've seen more women than you've seen sparrows! Three times I've fought duels on account of women. I've refused twelve women, and nine have refused me! Yes! There was a time when I played the fool, scented myself, used honeyed words, wore jewellery, made beautiful bows. I used to love, to suffer, to sigh at the moon, to get sour, to thaw, to freeze . . . I used to love passionately, madly, every blessed way, devil take me; I used to chatter like a magpie[13] about emancipation,[14] and wasted half my wealth on tender feelings, but now—you must excuse me! You won't get round me like that now! I've had enough! Black eyes, passionate eyes, ruby lips, dimpled cheeks, the moon, whispers, timid breathing—I wouldn't give a brass farthing for the lot, madam!

---

[12] In French, or what?: French was generally considered the language of romance.

[13] magpie: a long-tailed crow with boldly marked (or green) plumage and a raucous voice.

[14] emancipation: In Russia, the women's movement was entwined with the labor movement against Tsarist oppression. "The women's movement was to develop together with that of the wider labour movement in the many spontaneous strikes, especially in the textile industries, that took place in the period from 1870 to 1880, where women workers were employed on a massive scale. The outcome of this movement was a law that banned children and women from working the night shift" (from In Defense of Maxism).

Present company always excepted, all women, great or little, are insincere, crooked, backbiters, envious, liars to the marrow of their bones, vain, trivial, merciless, unreasonable, and, as far as this is concerned [taps his forehead] excuse my outspokenness, a sparrow can give ten points to any philosopher in petticoats you like to name! You look at one of these poetic creatures: all muslin, an ethereal demi-goddess, you have a million transports of joy, and you look into her soul—and see a common crocodile![15] [He grips the back of a chair; the chair creaks and breaks] But the most disgusting thing of all is that this crocodile for some reason or other imagines that its chef d'oeuvre, its privilege and monopoly, is its tender feelings. Why, confound it, hang me on that nail feet upwards, if you like, but have you met a woman who can love anybody except a lapdog? When she's in love, can she do anything but snivel and slobber? While a man is suffering and making sacrifices all her love expresses itself in her playing about with her scarf, and trying to hook him more firmly by the nose. You have the misfortune to be a woman, you know from yourself what is the nature of woman. Tell me truthfully, have you ever seen a woman who was sincere, faithful, and constant? You haven't! Only freaks and old women are faithful and constant! You'll meet a cat with a horn or a white woodcock sooner than a constant woman!

POPOVA   Then, according to you, who is faithful and constant in love? Is it the man?

SMIRNOV   Yes, the man!

POPOVA   The man! [Laughs bitterly] Men are faithful and constant in love! What an idea! [With heat] What right have you to talk like that? Men are faithful and constant! Since we are talking about it, I'll tell you that of all the men I knew and know, the best was my late husband . . . I loved him passionately with all my being, as only a young and imaginative woman can love, I gave him my youth, my happiness, my life, my fortune, I breathed in him, I worshipped him as if I were a heathen, and . . . and what then? This best of men shamelessly deceived me at every step! After his death I found in his desk a whole drawerful of love-letters, and when he was alive—it's an awful thing to remember!—he used to leave me alone for weeks at a time, and make love to other women and betray me before my very eyes; he wasted my money, and made fun of my feelings . . . And, in spite of all that, I loved him and was true to him. And not only that, but, now that he is dead, I am still true and constant to his memory. I have shut myself for ever within these four walls, and will wear these weeds to the very end . . .

SMIRNOV   [Laughs contemptuously] Weeds![16] . . . I don't understand what you take me for. As if I don't know why you wear that black domino and bury yourself between four walls! I should say I did! It's so mysterious, so poetic! When some junker or some tame poet goes past your windows he'll think: "There lives the mysterious Tamara who, for the love of her husband, buried herself between four walls."[17] We know these games!

POPOVA   [Exploding] What? How dare you say all that to me?

SMIRNOV   You may have buried yourself alive, but you haven't forgotten to powder your face!

POPOVA   How dare you speak to me like that?

SMIRNOV   Please don't shout, I'm not your steward! You must allow me to call things by their real names. I'm not a woman, and I'm used to saying what I think straight out! Don't you shout, either!

---

[15] crocodile: Probably a reference to "crocodile tears," meaning a person with superficial sympathy; a false or insincere display of emotion such as a hypocrite crying fake tears of grief.

[16] Weeds: having low value

[17] Tamara: Probably a combination of Biblical and Georgian mythic origin. Tamar was a name used for two Biblical characters who are depicted as involved in controversial sexual affairs. In Georgian, Tamar is a reference to an ancient sky goddess of great beauty. She was an eternal virgin who rode through the air on a serpent saddled and bridled with gold.

POPOVA   I'm not shouting, it's you! Please leave me alone!

SMIRNOV   Pay me my money and I'll go.

POPOVA   I shan't give you any money!

SMIRNOV   Oh, no, you will.

POPOVA   I shan't give you a farthing,[18] just to spite you. You leave me alone!

SMIRNOV   I have not the pleasure of being either your husband or your fiancé, so please don't make scenes. *[Sits]* I don't like it.

POPOVA   *[Choking with rage]* So you sit down?

SMIRNOV   I do.

POPOVA   I ask you to go away!

SMIRNOV   Give me my money . . . *[Aside]* Oh, how angry I am! How angry I am!

POPOVA   I don't want to talk to impudent scoundrels![19] Get out of this! *[Pause]* Aren't you going? No?

SMIRNOV   No.

POPOVA   No?

SMIRNOV   No!

POPOVA   Very well then! *[Rings, enter LUKA]* Luka, show this gentleman out!

LUKA   *[Approaches SMIRNOV]* Would you mind going out, sir, as you're asked to! You needn't . . .

SMIRNOV   *[Jumps up]* Shut up! Who are you talking to? I'll chop you into pieces!

LUKA   *[Clutches at his heart]* Little fathers![20] . . . What people! . . . *[Falls into a chair]* Oh, I'm ill, I'm ill! I can't breathe!

POPOVA   Where's Dasha? Dasha*! [Shouts]* Dasha! Pelageya! Dasha! *[Rings.]*

LUKA   Oh! They've all gone out to pick fruit . . . There's nobody at home! I'm ill! Water!

The Duel

POPOVA   Get out, now.

SMIRNOV   Can't you be more polite?

POPOVA   *[Clenches her fists and stamps her foot]* You're a boor! A coarse bear! A Bourbon![21] A monster!

SMIRNOV   What? What did you say?

POPOVA   I said you are a bear, a monster!

SMIRNOV   *[Approaching her]* May I ask what right you have to insult me?

POPOVA   And suppose I am insulting you? Do you think I'm afraid of you?

SMIRNOV   And do you think that just because you're a poetic creature you can insult me with impunity? Eh? We'll fight it out!

LUKA   Little fathers! . . . What people! . . . Water!

SMIRNOV   Pistols!

POPOVA   Do you think I'm afraid of you just because you have large fists and a bull's throat? Eh? You Bourbon!

SMIRNOV   We'll fight it out! I'm not going to be insulted by anybody, and I don't care if you are a woman, one of the "softer sex," indeed!

POPOVA   *[Trying to interrupt him]* Bear! Bear! Bear!

---

[18] farthing: an old British coin valued one quarter of a penny

[19] impudent: not showing due respect for another person; impertinent.

[20] Little fathers: In Russia, tsar was the same as Caesar, as the supreme ruler of Russia. The Tsar was also head of the Christian Orthodox Church; subsequently, he was also referred to as "little father"—under the Pope (from BBC History).

[21] Bourbon: a reactionary.

SMIRNOV   It's about time we got rid of the prejudice that only men need pay for their insults. Devil take it, if you want equality of rights you can have it. We're going to fight it out!

POPOVA   With pistols? Very well!

SMIRNOV   This very minute.

POPOVA   This very minute! My husband had some pistols . . . I'll bring them here. *[Is going, but turns back]* What pleasure it will give me to put a bullet into your thick head! Devil take you! *[Exit.]*

SMIRNOV   I'll bring her down like a chicken! I'm not a little boy or a sentimental puppy; I don't care about this "softer sex."

LUKA   Gracious little fathers! . . . *[Kneels]* Have pity on a poor old man, and go away from here! You've frightened her to death, and now you want to shoot her!

SMIRNOV   *[Not hearing him]* If she fights, well that's equality of rights, emancipation, and all that! Here the sexes are equal! I'll shoot her on principle! But what a woman! *[Parodying her]* "Devil take you! I'll put a bullet into your thick head." Eh? How she reddened, how her cheeks shone! . . . She accepted my challenge! My word, it's the first time in my life that I've seen . . .

LUKA   Go away, sir, and I'll always pray to God for you!

SMIRNOV   She is a woman! That's the sort I can understand! A real woman! Not a sour-faced jellybag, but fire, gunpowder, a rocket! I'm even sorry to have to kill her!

LUKA   *[Weeps]* Dear . . . dear sir, do go away!

SMIRNOV   I absolutely like her! Absolutely! Even though her cheeks are dimpled, I like her! I'm almost ready to let the debt go . . . and I'm not angry any longer . . . Wonderful woman!

[Enter POPOVA with pistols.]

POPOVA   Here are the pistols . . . But before we fight you must show me how to fire. I've never held a pistol in my hands before.

LUKA   Oh, Lord, have mercy and save her . . . I'll go and find the coachman and the gardener . . . Why has this infliction come on us . . . *[Exit.]*

SMIRNOV   *[Examining the pistols]* You see, there are several sorts of pistols . . . There are Mortimer pistols, specially made for duels, they fire a percussion-cap. These are Smith and Wesson revolvers, triple action, with extractors . . . These are excellent pistols. They can't cost less than ninety roubles the pair . . . You must hold the revolver like this . . . *[Aside]* Her eyes, her eyes! What an inspiring woman!

POPOVA   Like this?

SMIRNOV   Yes, like this . . . Then you cock the trigger, and take aim like this . . . Put your head back a little! Hold your arm out properly . . . Like that . . . Then you press this thing with your finger—and that's all. The great thing is to keep cool and aim steadily . . . Try not to jerk your arm.

POPOVA   Very well . . . It's inconvenient to shoot in a room, let's go into the garden.

SMIRNOV   Come along then. But I warn you, I'm going to fire in the air.

POPOVA   That's the last straw! Why?

SMIRNOV   Because . . . because . . . it's my affair.

POPOVA   Are you afraid? Yes? Ah! No, sir, you don't get out of it! You come with me! I shan't have any peace until I've made a hole in your forehead . . . that forehead which I hate so much! Are you afraid?

SMIRNOV   Yes, I am afraid.

POPOVA   You lie! Why won't you fight?

SMIRNOV   Because . . . because you . . . because I like you.

POPOVA   *[Laughs]* He likes me! He dares to say that he likes me! *[Points to the door]* That's the way.

Feelings Change

SMIRNOV   *[Loads the revolver in silence, takes his cap and goes to the door. There he stops for half a minute, while they look at each other in silence, then he hesitatingly approaches POPOVA]* Listen . . . Are you still angry? I'm devilishly annoyed, too . . . but, do you understand . . . how can I express myself? . . . The fact is, you see, it's like this, so to speak . . . *[Shouts]* Well, is it my fault that I like you? *[He snatches at the back of a chair; the chair creaks and breaks]* Devil take it, how I'm smashing up your furniture! I like you! Do you understand? I . . . I almost love you!

POPOVA   Get away from me—I hate you!

SMIRNOV   God, what a woman! I've never in my life seen one like her! I'm lost! Done for! Fallen into a mousetrap, like a mouse!

POPOVA   Stand back, or I'll fire!

SMIRNOV   Fire, then! You can't understand what happiness it would be to die before those beautiful eyes, to be shot by a revolver held in that little, velvet hand . . . I'm out of my senses! Think, and make up your mind at once, because if I go out we shall never see each other again! Decide now . . . I am a landowner, of respectable character, have an income of ten thousand a year. I can put a bullet through a coin tossed into the air as it comes down . . . I own some fine horses . . . Will you be my wife?

POPOVA   *[Indignantly shakes her revolver]* Let's fight! Let's go out!

SMIRNOV   I'm mad . . . I understand nothing. *[Yells]* Waiter, water!

POPOVA   *[Yells]* Let's go out and fight!

SMIRNOV   I'm off my head, I'm in love like a boy, like a fool! *[Snatches her hand, she screams with pain]* I love you! *[Kneels]* I love you as I've never loved before! I've refused twelve women, nine have refused me, but I never loved one of them as I love you . . . I'm weak, I'm wax, I've melted . . . I'm on my knees like a fool, offering you my hand . . . Shame, shame! I haven't been in love for five years, I'd taken a vow, and now all of a sudden I'm in love, like a fish out of water! I offer you my hand. Yes or no? You don't want me? Very well! *[Gets up and quickly goes to the door.]*

POPOVA   Stop.

SMIRNOV   *[Stops]* Well?

POPOVA   Nothing, go away . . . No, stop . . . No, go away, go away! I hate you! Or no . . . Don't go away! Oh, if you knew how angry I am, how angry I am! *[Throws her revolver on the table]* My fingers have swollen because of all this . . . *[Tears her handkerchief in temper]* What are you waiting for? Get out!

SMIRNOV   Goodbye.

POPOVA   Yes, yes, go away! . . . *[Yells]* Where are you going? Stop . . . No, go away. Oh, how angry I am! Don't come near me, don't come near me!

SMIRNOV   *[Approaching her]* How angry I am with myself! I'm in love like a student, I've been on my knees . . . *[Rudely]* I love you! What do I want to fall in love with you for? Tomorrow I've got to pay the interest, and begin mowing, and here you . . . *[Puts his arms around her]* I shall never forgive myself for this . . .

POPOVA   Get away from me! Take your hands away! I hate you! Let's go and fight!

[A prolonged kiss. Enter LUKA with an axe, the GARDENER with a rake, the COACHMAN with a pitchfork, and WORKMEN with poles.]

LUKA   *[Catches sight of the pair kissing]* Little fathers! *[Pause.]*

POPOVA   *[Lowering her eyes]* Luka, tell them in the stables that Toby isn't to have any oats at all today.

Curtain.

The Importance of Being Ernest

A Trivial Comedy for Serious People

Oscar Wilde
1895

First performed on 14 February 1895 at the St James's Theatre in London.

The Persons in the Play

John Worthing, J.P.	Lady Bracknell
Algernon Moncrieff	Hon. Gwendolen Fairfax
Rev. Canon Chasuble, D.D.	Cecily Cardew
Merriman, Butler	Miss Prism, Governess
Lane, Manservant	

The Scenes of the Play

ACT I   Algernon Moncrieff's Flat in Half-Moon Street, W.
ACT II   The Garden at the Manor House, Woolton.
ACT III Drawing-Room at the Manor House, Woolton.
TIME   The Present.

First Act

SCENE. Morning-room in Algernon's flat in Half-Moon Street. The room is luxuriously and artistically furnished. The sound of a piano is heard in the adjoining room.

[Lane is arranging afternoon tea on the table, and after the music has ceased, Algernon enters.]

ALGERNON   Did you hear what I was playing, Lane?

LANE   I didn't think it polite to listen, sir.

ALGERNON   I'm sorry for that, for your sake. I don't play accurately—any one can play accurately—but I play with wonderful expression. As far as the piano is concerned, sentiment is my forte. I keep science for Life.

LANE   Yes, sir.

ALGERNON   And, speaking of the science of Life, have you got the cucumber sandwiches cut for Lady Bracknell?

LANE   Yes, sir. *[Hands them on a salver.]*

ALGERNON   *[Inspects them, takes two, and sits down on the sofa.]* Oh! . . . by the way, Lane, I see from your book that on Thursday night, when Lord Shoreman and Mr. Worthing were dining with me, eight bottles of champagne are entered as having been consumed.

LANE   Yes, sir; eight bottles and a pint.

ALGERNON   Why is it that at a bachelor's establishment the servants invariably drink the champagne? I ask merely for information.

LANE   I attribute it to the superior quality of the wine, sir. I have often observed that in married households the champagne is rarely of a first-rate brand.

ALGERNON   Good heavens! Is marriage so demoralising as that?

LANE   I believe it is a very pleasant state, sir. I have had very little experience of it myself up to the present. I have only been married once. That was in consequence of a misunderstanding between myself and a young person.

ALGERNON   *[Languidly.]* I don't know that I am much interested in your family life, Lane.

LANE   No, sir; it is not a very interesting subject. I never think of it myself.

ALGERNON   Very natural, I am sure. That will do, Lane, thank you.

LANE   Thank you, sir. *[Lane goes out.]*

ALGERNON   Lane's views on marriage seem somewhat lax. Really, if the lower orders don't set us a good example, what on earth is the use of them? They seem, as a class, to have absolutely no sense of moral responsibility.

[Enter Lane.]

LANE   Mr. Ernest Worthing.

[Enter Jack. [Lane goes out.]

ALGERNON   How are you, my dear Ernest? What brings you up to town?

JACK   Oh, pleasure, pleasure! What else should bring one anywhere? Eating as usual, I see, Algy!

ALGERNON   [Stiffly.] I believe it is customary in good society to take some slight refreshment at five o'clock. Where have you been since last Thursday?

JACK   [Sitting down on the sofa.] In the country.

ALGERNON   What on earth do you do there?

JACK   [Pulling off his gloves.] When one is in town one amuses oneself. When one is in the country one amuses other people. It is excessively boring.

ALGERNON   And who are the people you amuse?

JACK   [Airily.] Oh, neighbours, neighbours.

ALGERNON   Got nice neighbours in your part of Shropshire?

JACK   Perfectly horrid! Never speak to one of them.

ALGERNON   How immensely you must amuse them! [Goes over and takes sandwich.] By the way, Shropshire is your county, is it not?

JACK   Eh? Shropshire? Yes, of course. Hallo! Why all these cups? Why cucumber sandwiches? Why such reckless extravagance in one so young? Who is coming to tea?

ALGERNON   Oh! merely Aunt Augusta and Gwendolen.

JACK   How perfectly delightful!

ALGERNON   Yes, that is all very well; but I am afraid Aunt Augusta won't quite approve of your being here.

JACK   May I ask why?

ALGERNON   My dear fellow, the way you flirt with Gwendolen is perfectly disgraceful. It is almost as bad as the way Gwendolen flirts with you.

JACK   I am in love with Gwendolen. I have come up to town expressly to propose to her.

ALGERNON   I thought you had come up for pleasure? . . . I call that business.

JACK   How utterly unromantic you are!

ALGERNON   I really don't see anything romantic in proposing. It is very romantic to be in love. But there is nothing romantic about a definite proposal. Why, one may be accepted. One usually is, I believe. Then the excitement is all over. The very essence of romance is uncertainty. If ever I get married, I'll certainly try to forget the fact.

JACK   I have no doubt about that, dear Algy. The Divorce Court was specially invented for people whose memories are so curiously constituted.

ALGERNON   Oh! there is no use speculating on that subject. Divorces are made in Heaven—[Jack puts out his hand to take a sandwich. Algernon at once interferes.] Please don't touch the cucumber sandwiches. They are ordered specially for Aunt Augusta. [Takes one and eats it.]

JACK   Well, you have been eating them all the time.

ALGERNON   That is quite a different matter. She is my aunt. [Takes plate from below.] Have some bread and butter. The bread and butter is for Gwendolen. Gwendolen is devoted to bread and butter.

JACK   [Advancing to table and helping himself.] And very good bread and butter it is too.

ALGERNON   Well, my dear fellow, you need not eat as if you were going to eat it all. You behave as if you were married to her already. You are not married to her already, and I don't think you ever will be.

JACK   Why on earth do you say that?

ALGERNON   Well, in the first place girls never marry the men they flirt with. Girls don't think it right.

JACK   Oh, that is nonsense!

ALGERNON   It isn't. It is a great truth. It accounts for the extraordinary number of bachelors that one sees all over the place. In the second place, I don't give my consent.

JACK   Your consent!

ALGERNON   My dear fellow, Gwendolen is my first cousin. And before I allow you to marry her, you will have to clear up the whole question of Cecily. *[Rings bell.]*

JACK   Cecily! What on earth do you mean? What do you mean, Algy, by Cecily! I don't know any one of the name of Cecily.

[Enter Lane.]

ALGERNON   Bring me that cigarette case Mr. Worthing left in the smoking-room the last time he dined here.

LANE   Yes, sir. *[Lane goes out.]*

JACK   Do you mean to say you have had my cigarette case all this time? I wish to goodness you had let me know. I have been writing frantic letters to Scotland Yard about it. I was very nearly offering a large reward.

ALGERNON   Well, I wish you would offer one. I happen to be more than usually hard up.

JACK   There is no good offering a large reward now that the thing is found.

[Enter Lane with the cigarette case on a salver. Algernon takes it at once. Lane goes out.]

ALGERNON   I think that is rather mean of you, Ernest, I must say. *[Opens case and examines it.]* However, it makes no matter, for, now that I look at the inscription inside, I find that the thing isn't yours after all.

JACK   Of course it's mine. *[Moving to him.]* You have seen me with it a hundred times, and you have no right whatsoever to read what is written inside. It is a very ungentlemanly thing to read a private cigarette case.

ALGERNON   Oh! it is absurd to have a hard and fast rule about what one should read and what one shouldn't. More than half of modern culture depends on what one shouldn't read.

JACK   I am quite aware of the fact, and I don't propose to discuss modern culture. It isn't the sort of thing one should talk of in private. I simply want my cigarette case back.

ALGERNON   Yes; but this isn't your cigarette case. This cigarette case is a present from some one of the name of Cecily, and you said you didn't know any one of that name.

JACK   Well, if you want to know, Cecily happens to be my aunt.

ALGERNON   Your aunt!

JACK   Yes. Charming old lady she is, too. Lives at Tunbridge Wells. Just give it back to me, Algy.

ALGERNON   *[Retreating to back of sofa.]* But why does she call herself little Cecily if she is your aunt and lives at Tunbridge Wells? *[Reading.]* 'From little Cecily with her fondest love.'

JACK   *[Moving to sofa and kneeling upon it.]* My dear fellow, what on earth is there in that? Some aunts are tall, some aunts are not tall. That is a matter that surely an aunt may be allowed to decide for herself. You seem to think that every aunt should be exactly like your aunt! That is absurd! For Heaven's sake give me back my cigarette case. *[Follows Algernon round the room.]*

ALGERNON   Yes. But why does your aunt call you her uncle? 'From little Cecily, with her fondest love to her dear Uncle Jack.' There is no objection, I admit, to an aunt being a small aunt, but why an aunt, no matter what her size may be, should call her own nephew her uncle, I can't quite make out. Besides, your name isn't Jack at all; it is Ernest.

JACK   It isn't Ernest; it's Jack.

ALGERNON   You have always told me it was Ernest. I have introduced you to every one as Ernest. You answer to the name of Ernest. You look as if your name was Ernest. You are the most earnest-looking person I ever saw in my life. It is perfectly absurd your saying that your name isn't Ernest. It's on your cards. Here is one of them. *[Taking it from case.]* 'Mr. Ernest Worthing, B. 4, The Albany.' I'll keep this as a proof that your name is Ernest if ever you attempt to deny it to me, or to Gwendolen, or to any one else. *[Puts the card in his pocket.]*

JACK   Well, my name is Ernest in town and Jack in the country, and the cigarette case was given to me in the country.

ALGERNON   Yes, but that does not account for the fact that your small Aunt Cecily, who lives at Tunbridge Wells, calls you her dear uncle. Come, old boy, you had much better have the thing out at once.

JACK   My dear Algy, you talk exactly as if you were a dentist. It is very vulgar to talk like a dentist when one isn't a dentist. It produces a false impression.

ALGERNON   Well, that is exactly what dentists always do. Now, go on! Tell me the whole thing. I may mention that I have always suspected you of being a confirmed and secret Bunburyist; and I am quite sure of it now.

JACK   Bunburyist? What on earth do you mean by a Bunburyist?

ALGERNON   I'll reveal to you the meaning of that incomparable expression as soon as you are kind enough to inform me why you are Ernest in town and Jack in the country.

JACK   Well, produce my cigarette case first.

ALGERNON   Here it is. *[Hands cigarette case.]* Now produce your explanation, and pray make it improbable. *[Sits on sofa.]*

JACK   My dear fellow, there is nothing improbable about my explanation at all. In fact it's perfectly ordinary. Old Mr. Thomas Cardew, who adopted me when I was a little boy, made me in his will guardian to his grand-daughter, Miss Cecily Cardew. Cecily, who addresses me as her uncle from motives of respect that you could not possibly appreciate, lives at my place in the country under the charge of her admirable governess, Miss Prism.

ALGERNON   Where is that place in the country, by the way?

JACK   That is nothing to you, dear boy. You are not going to be invited . . . I may tell you candidly that the place is not in Shropshire.

ALGERNON   I suspected that, my dear fellow! I have Bunburyed all over Shropshire on two separate occasions. Now, go on. Why are you Ernest in town and Jack in the country?

JACK   My dear Algy, I don't know whether you will be able to understand my real motives. You are hardly serious enough. When one is placed in the position of guardian, one has to adopt a very high moral tone on all subjects. It's one's duty to do so. And as a high moral tone can hardly be said to conduce very much to either one's health or one's happiness, in order to get up to town I have always pretended to have a younger brother of the name of Ernest, who lives in the Albany, and gets into the most dreadful scrapes. That, my dear Algy, is the whole truth pure and simple.

ALGERNON   The truth is rarely pure and never simple. Modern life would be very tedious if it were either, and modern literature a complete impossibility!

JACK   That wouldn't be at all a bad thing.

ALGERNON   Literary criticism is not your forte, my dear fellow. Don't try it. You should leave that to people who haven't been at a University. They do it so well in the daily papers. What you really are is a Bunburyist. I was quite right in saying you were a Bunburyist. You are one of the most advanced Bunburyists I know.

JACK   What on earth do you mean?

ALGERNON   You have invented a very useful younger brother called Ernest, in order that you may be able to come up to town as often as you like. I have invented an invaluable permanent invalid called Bunbury, in order that I may be able to go down into the country whenever I choose. Bunbury is perfectly invaluable. If it wasn't for Bunbury's extraordinary bad health, for instance, I wouldn't be able to dine with you at Willis's to-night, for I have been really engaged to Aunt Augusta for more than a week.

JACK   I haven't asked you to dine with me anywhere to-night.

ALGERNON   I know. You are absurdly careless about sending out invitations. It is very foolish of you. Nothing annoys people so much as not receiving invitations.

JACK   You had much better dine with your Aunt Augusta.

ALGERNON   I haven't the smallest intention of doing anything of the kind. To begin with, I dined there on Monday, and once a week is quite enough to dine with one's own relations. In the second place, whenever I do dine there I am always treated as a member of the family, and sent down with either no woman at all, or two. In the third place, I know perfectly well whom she will place me next to, to-night. She will place me next Mary Farquhar, who always flirts with her own husband across the dinner-table. That is not very pleasant. Indeed, it is not even decent . . . and that sort of thing is enormously on the increase. The amount of women in London who flirt with their own husbands is perfectly scandalous. It looks so bad. It is simply washing one's clean linen in public. Besides, now that I know you to be a confirmed Bunburyist I naturally want to talk to you about Bunburying. I want to tell you the rules.

JACK   I'm not a Bunburyist at all. If Gwendolen accepts me, I am going to kill my brother, indeed I think I'll kill him in any case. Cecily is a little too much interested in him. It is rather a bore. So I am going to get rid of Ernest. And I strongly advise you to do the same with Mr. . . . with your invalid friend who has the absurd name.

ALGERNON   Nothing will induce me to part with Bunbury, and if you ever get married, which seems to me extremely problematic, you will be very glad to know Bunbury. A man who marries without knowing Bunbury has a very tedious time of it.

JACK   That is nonsense. If I marry a charming girl like Gwendolen, and she is the only girl I ever saw in my life that I would marry, I certainly won't want to know Bunbury.

ALGERNON   Then your wife will. You don't seem to realise, that in married life three is company and two is none.

JACK   [Sententiously.][1] That, my dear young friend, is the theory that the corrupt French Drama has been propounding for the last fifty years.

ALGERNON   Yes; and that the happy English home has proved in half the time.

JACK   For heaven's sake, don't try to be cynical. It's perfectly easy to be cynical.

ALGERNON   My dear fellow, it isn't easy to be anything nowadays. There's such a lot of beastly competition about. [The sound of an electric bell is heard.] Ah! that must be Aunt Augusta. Only relatives, or creditors, ever ring in that Wagnerian manner. Now, if I get her out of the way for ten minutes, so that you can have an opportunity for proposing to Gwendolen, may I dine with you to-night at Willis's?

JACK   I suppose so, if you want to.

---

[1] Sententiously: (of language or style) concise and forcefully expressive

ALGERNON   Yes, but you must be serious about it. I hate people who are not serious about meals. It is so shallow of them.

[Enter Lane.]

LANE   Lady Bracknell and Miss Fairfax.

[Algernon goes forward to meet them. Enter Lady Bracknell and Gwendolen.]

LADY BRACKNELL   Good afternoon, dear Algernon, I hope you are behaving very well.

ALGERNON   I'm feeling very well, Aunt Augusta.

LADY BRACKNELL   That's not quite the same thing. In fact the two things rarely go together. [Sees Jack and bows to him with icy coldness.]

ALGERNON   [To Gwendolen.] Dear me, you are smart!

GWENDOLEN   I am always smart! Am I not, Mr. Worthing?

JACK   You're quite perfect, Miss Fairfax.

GWENDOLEN   Oh! I hope I am not that. It would leave no room for developments, and I intend to develop in many directions. [Gwendolen and Jack sit down together in the corner.]

LADY BRACKNELL   I'm sorry if we are a little late, Algernon, but I was obliged to call on dear Lady Harbury. I hadn't been there since her poor husband's death. I never saw a woman so altered; she looks quite twenty years younger. And now I'll have a cup of tea, and one of those nice cucumber sandwiches you promised me.

ALGERNON   Certainly, Aunt Augusta. [Goes over to tea-table.]

LADY BRACKNELL   Won't you come and sit here, Gwendolen?

GWENDOLEN   Thanks, mamma, I'm quite comfortable where I am.

ALGERNON   [Picking up empty plate in horror.] Good heavens! Lane! Why are there no cucumber sandwiches? I ordered them specially.

LANE   [Gravely.] There were no cucumbers in the market this morning, sir. I went down twice.

ALGERNON   No cucumbers!

LANE   No, sir. Not even for ready money.

ALGERNON   That will do, Lane, thank you.

LANE   Thank you, sir. [Goes out.]

ALGERNON   I am greatly distressed, Aunt Augusta, about there being no cucumbers, not even for ready money.

LADY BRACKNELL   It really makes no matter, Algernon. I had some crumpets with Lady Harbury, who seems to me to be living entirely for pleasure now.

ALGERNON   I hear her hair has turned quite gold from grief.

LADY BRACKNELL   It certainly has changed its colour. From what cause I, of course, cannot say. [Algernon crosses and hands tea.] Thank you. I've quite a treat for you to-night, Algernon. I am going to send you down with Mary Farquhar. She is such a nice woman, and so attentive to her husband. It's delightful to watch them.

ALGERNON   I am afraid, Aunt Augusta, I shall have to give up the pleasure of dining with you to-night after all.

LADY BRACKNELL   [Frowning.] I hope not, Algernon. It would put my table completely out. Your uncle would have to dine upstairs. Fortunately he is accustomed to that.

ALGERNON   It is a great bore, and, I need hardly say, a terrible disappointment to me, but the fact is I have just had a telegram to say that my poor friend Bunbury is very ill again. [Exchanges glances with Jack.] They seem to think I should be with him.

LADY BRACKNELL   It is very strange. This Mr. Bunbury seems to suffer from curiously bad health.

ALGERNON   Yes; poor Bunbury is a dreadful invalid.

LADY BRACKNELL   Well, I must say, Algernon, that I think it is high time that Mr. Bunbury made up his mind whether he was going to live or to die. This shilly-shallying with the question is absurd. Nor do I in any way approve of the modern sympathy with invalids. I consider it morbid. Illness of any kind is hardly a thing to be encouraged in others. Health is the primary duty of life. I am always telling that to your poor uncle, but he never seems to take much notice . . . as far as any improvement in his ailment goes. I should be much obliged if you would ask Mr. Bunbury, from me, to be kind enough not to have a relapse on Saturday, for I rely on you to arrange my music for me. It is my last reception, and one wants something that will encourage conversation, particularly at the end of the season when every one has practically said whatever they had to say, which, in most cases, was probably not much.

ALGERNON   I'll speak to Bunbury, Aunt Augusta, if he is still conscious, and I think I can promise you he'll be all right by Saturday. Of course the music is a great difficulty. You see, if one plays good music, people don't listen, and if one plays bad music people don't talk. But I'll run over the programme I've drawn out, if you will kindly come into the next room for a moment.

LADY BRACKNELL   Thank you, Algernon. It is very thoughtful of you. *[Rising, and following Algernon.]* I'm sure the programme will be delightful, after a few expurgations. French songs I cannot possibly allow. People always seem to think that they are improper, and either look shocked, which is vulgar, or laugh, which is worse. But German sounds a thoroughly respectable language, and indeed, I believe is so. Gwendolen, you will accompany me.

GWENDOLEN   Certainly, mamma.

[Lady Bracknell and Algernon go into the music-room, Gwendolen remains behind.]

JACK   Charming day it has been, Miss Fairfax.

GWENDOLEN   Pray don't talk to me about the weather, Mr. Worthing. Whenever people talk to me about the weather, I always feel quite certain that they mean something else. And that makes me so nervous.

JACK   I do mean something else.

GWENDOLEN   I thought so. In fact, I am never wrong.

JACK   And I would like to be allowed to take advantage of Lady Bracknell's temporary absence . . .

GWENDOLEN   I would certainly advise you to do so. Mamma has a way of coming back suddenly into a room that I have often had to speak to her about.

JACK   *[Nervously.]* Miss Fairfax, ever since I met you I have admired you more than any girl . . . I have ever met since . . . I met you.

GWENDOLEN   Yes, I am quite well aware of the fact. And I often wish that in public, at any rate, you had been more demonstrative. For me you have always had an irresistible fascination. Even before I met you I was far from indifferent to you. *[Jack looks at her in amazement.]* We live, as I hope you know, Mr. Worthing, in an age of ideals. The fact is constantly mentioned in the more expensive monthly magazines, and has reached the provincial pulpits, I am told; and my ideal has always been to love some one of the name of Ernest. There is something in that name that inspires absolute confidence. The moment Algernon first mentioned to me that he had a friend called Ernest, I knew I was destined to love you.

JACK   You really love me, Gwendolen?

GWENDOLEN   Passionately!

JACK   Darling! You don't know how happy you've made me.

GWENDOLEN   My own Ernest!

JACK   But you don't really mean to say that you couldn't love me if my name wasn't Ernest?

GWENDOLEN   But your name is Ernest.

JACK   Yes, I know it is. But supposing it was something else? Do you mean to say you couldn't love me then?

GWENDOLEN   [Glibly.] Ah! that is clearly a metaphysical speculation, and like most metaphysical speculations has very little reference at all to the actual facts of real life, as we know them.

JACK   Personally, darling, to speak quite candidly, I don't much care about the name of Ernest . . . I don't think the name suits me at all.

GWENDOLEN   It suits you perfectly. It is a divine name. It has a music of its own. It produces vibrations.

JACK   Well, really, Gwendolen, I must say that I think there are lots of other much nicer names. I think Jack, for instance, a charming name.

GWENDOLEN   Jack? . . . No, there is very little music in the name Jack, if any at all, indeed. It does not thrill. It produces absolutely no vibrations . . . I have known several Jacks, and they all, without exception, were more than usually plain. Besides, Jack is a notorious domesticity for John! And I pity any woman who is married to a man called John. She would probably never be allowed to know the entrancing pleasure of a single moment's solitude. The only really safe name is Ernest.

JACK   Gwendolen, I must get christened at once—I mean we must get married at once. There is no time to be lost.

GWENDOLEN   Married, Mr. Worthing?

JACK   [Astounded.] Well . . . surely. You know that I love you, and you led me to believe, Miss Fairfax, that you were not absolutely indifferent to me.

GWENDOLEN   I adore you. But you haven't proposed to me yet. Nothing has been said at all about marriage. The subject has not even been touched on.

JACK   Well . . . may I propose to you now?

GWENDOLEN   I think it would be an admirable opportunity. And to spare you any possible disappointment, Mr. Worthing, I think it only fair to tell you quite frankly before-hand that I am fully determined to accept you.

JACK   Gwendolen!

GWENDOLEN   Yes, Mr. Worthing, what have you got to say to me?

JACK   You know what I have got to say to you.

GWENDOLEN   Yes, but you don't say it.

JACK   Gwendolen, will you marry me? [Goes on his knees.]

GWENDOLEN   Of course I will, darling. How long you have been about it! I am afraid you have had very little experience in how to propose.

JACK   My own one, I have never loved any one in the world but you.

GWENDOLEN   Yes, but men often propose for practice. I know my brother Gerald does. All my girl-friends tell me so. What wonderfully blue eyes you have, Ernest! They are quite, quite, blue. I hope you will always look at me just like that, especially when there are other people present. [Enter Lady Bracknell.]

LADY BRACKNELL   Mr. Worthing! Rise, sir, from this semi-recumbent posture. It is most indecorous.

GWENDOLEN   Mamma! [He tries to rise; she restrains him.] I must beg you to retire. This is no place for you. Besides, Mr. Worthing has not quite finished yet.

LADY BRACKNELL   Finished what, may I ask?

GWENDOLEN   I am engaged to Mr. Worthing, mamma. [They rise together.]

LADY BRACKNELL   Pardon me, you are not engaged to any one. When you do become engaged to some one, I, or your father, should his health permit him, will inform you of the fact. An engagement should come on a young girl as a surprise, pleasant or unpleasant, as the case may be. It is hardly a matter that she could be allowed to arrange for herself . . . And now I have a few questions to put to you, Mr. Worthing. While I am making these inquiries, you, Gwendolen, will wait for me below in the carriage.

GWENDOLEN   *[Reproachfully.]* Mamma!

LADY BRACKNELL   In the carriage, Gwendolen! *[Gwendolen goes to the door. She and Jack blow kisses to each other behind Lady Bracknell's back. Lady Bracknell looks vaguely about as if she could not understand what the noise was. Finally turns round.]* Gwendolen, the carriage!

GWENDOLEN   Yes, mamma. *[Goes out, looking back at Jack.]*

LADY BRACKNELL   *[Sitting down.]* You can take a seat, Mr. Worthing. *[Looks in her pocket for note-book and pencil.]*

JACK   Thank you, Lady Bracknell, I prefer standing.

LADY BRACKNELL   *[Pencil and note-book in hand.]* I feel bound to tell you that you are not down on my list of eligible young men, although I have the same list as the dear Duchess of Bolton has. We work together, in fact. However, I am quite ready to enter your name, should your answers be what a really affectionate mother requires. Do you smoke?

JACK   Well, yes, I must admit I smoke.

LADY BRACKNELL   I am glad to hear it. A man should always have an occupation of some kind. There are far too many idle men in London as it is. How old are you?

JACK   Twenty-nine.

LADY BRACKNELL   A very good age to be married at. I have always been of opinion that a man who desires to get married should know either everything or nothing. Which do you know?

JACK   *[After some hesitation.]* I know nothing, Lady Bracknell.

LADY BRACKNELL   I am pleased to hear it. I do not approve of anything that tampers with natural ignorance. Ignorance is like a delicate exotic fruit; touch it and the bloom is gone. The whole theory of modern education is radically unsound. Fortunately in England, at any rate, education produces no effect whatsoever. If it did, it would prove a serious danger to the upper classes, and probably lead to acts of violence in Grosvenor Square. What is your income?

JACK   Between seven and eight thousand a year.

LADY BRACKNELL   *[Makes a note in her book.]* In land, or in investments?

JACK   In investments, chiefly.

LADY BRACKNELL   That is satisfactory. What between the duties expected of one during one's lifetime, and the duties exacted from one after one's death, land has ceased to be either a profit or a pleasure. It gives one position, and prevents one from keeping it up. That's all that can be said about land.

JACK   I have a country house with some land, of course, attached to it, about fifteen hundred acres, I believe; but I don't depend on that for my real income. In fact, as far as I can make out, the poachers are the only people who make anything out of it.

LADY BRACKNELL   A country house! How many bedrooms? Well, that point can be cleared up afterwards. You have a town house, I hope? A girl with a simple, unspoiled nature, like Gwendolen, could hardly be expected to reside in the country.

JACK   Well, I own a house in Belgrave Square, but it is let by the year to Lady Bloxham. Of course, I can get it back whenever I like, at six months' notice.

LADY BRACKNELL   Lady Bloxham? I don't know her.

JACK   Oh, she goes about very little. She is a lady considerably advanced in years.

LADY BRACKNELL   Ah, nowadays that is no guarantee of respectability of character. What number in Belgrave Square?

JACK   149.

LADY BRACKNELL   *[Shaking her head.]* The unfashionable side. I thought there was something. However, that could easily be altered.

JACK   Do you mean the fashion, or the side?

LADY BRACKNELL   *[Sternly.]* Both, if necessary, I presume. What are your politics?

JACK   Well, I am afraid I really have none. I am a Liberal Unionist.

LADY BRACKNELL   Oh, they count as Tories. They dine with us. Or come in the evening, at any rate. Now to minor matters. Are your parents living?

JACK   I have lost both my parents.

LADY BRACKNELL   To lose one parent, Mr. Worthing, may be regarded as a misfortune; to lose both looks like carelessness. Who was your father? He was evidently a man of some wealth. Was he born in what the Radical papers call the purple of commerce, or did he rise from the ranks of the aristocracy?

JACK   I am afraid I really don't know. The fact is, Lady Bracknell, I said I had lost my parents. It would be nearer the truth to say that my parents seem to have lost me . . . I don't actually know who I am by birth. I was . . . well, I was found.

LADY BRACKNELL   Found!

JACK   The late Mr. Thomas Cardew, an old gentleman of a very charitable and kindly disposition, found me, and gave me the name of Worthing, because he happened to have a first-class ticket for Worthing in his pocket at the time. Worthing is a place in Sussex. It is a seaside resort.

LADY BRACKNELL   Where did the charitable gentleman who had a first-class ticket for this seaside resort find you?

JACK   *[Gravely.]* In a hand-bag.

LADY BRACKNELL   A hand-bag?

JACK   *[Very seriously.]* Yes, Lady Bracknell. I was in a hand-bag—a somewhat large, black leather hand-bag, with handles to it—an ordinary hand-bag in fact.

LADY BRACKNELL   In what locality did this Mr. James, or Thomas, Cardew come across this ordinary hand-bag?

JACK   In the cloak-room at Victoria Station. It was given to him in mistake for his own.

LADY BRACKNELL   The cloak-room at Victoria Station?

JACK   Yes. The Brighton line.

LADY BRACKNELL   The line is immaterial. Mr. Worthing, I confess I feel somewhat bewildered by what you have just told me. To be born, or at any rate bred, in a hand-bag, whether it had handles or not, seems to me to display a contempt for the ordinary decencies of family life that reminds one of the worst excesses of the French Revolution. And I presume you know what that unfortunate movement led to? As for the particular locality in which the hand-bag was found, a cloak-room at a railway station might serve to conceal a social indiscretion—has probably, indeed, been used for that purpose before now—but it could hardly be regarded as an assured basis for a recognised position in good society.

JACK   May I ask you then what you would advise me to do? I need hardly say I would do anything in the world to ensure Gwendolen's happiness.

LADY BRACKNELL   I would strongly advise you, Mr. Worthing, to try and acquire some relations as soon as possible, and to make a definite effort to produce at any rate one parent, of either sex, before the season is quite over.

JACK   Well, I don't see how I could possibly manage to do that. I can produce the hand-bag at any moment. It is in my dressing-room at home. I really think that should satisfy you, Lady Bracknell.

LADY BRACKNELL   Me, sir! What has it to do with me? You can hardly imagine that I and Lord Bracknell would dream of allowing our only daughter—a girl brought up with the utmost care—to marry into a cloak-room, and form an alliance with a parcel? Good morning, Mr. Worthing!

[Lady Bracknell sweeps out in majestic indignation.]

JACK   Good morning! *[Algernon, from the other room, strikes up the Wedding March. Jack looks perfectly furious, and goes to the door.]* For goodness' sake don't play that ghastly tune, Algy. How idiotic you are!

[The music stops and Algernon enters cheerily.]

ALGERNON   Didn't it go off all right, old boy? You don't mean to say Gwendolen refused you? I know it is a way she has. She is always refusing people. I think it is most ill-natured of her.

JACK   Oh, Gwendolen is as right as a trivet. As far as she is concerned, we are engaged. Her mother is perfectly unbearable. Never met such a Gorgon . . . I don't really know what a Gorgon is like, but I am quite sure that Lady Bracknell is one. In any case, she is a monster, without being a myth, which is rather unfair . . . I beg your pardon, Algy, I suppose I shouldn't talk about your own aunt in that way before you.

ALGERNON
My dear boy, I love hearing my relations abused. It is the only thing that makes me put up with them at all. Relations are simply a tedious pack of people, who haven't got the remotest knowledge of how to live, nor the smallest instinct about when to die.

JACK   Oh, that is nonsense!

ALGERNON   It isn't!

JACK   Well, I won't argue about the matter. You always want to argue about things.

ALGERNON   That is exactly what things were originally made for.

JACK   Upon my word, if I thought that, I'd shoot myself . . . *[A pause.]* You don't think there is any chance of Gwendolen becoming like her mother in about a hundred and fifty years, do you, Algy?

ALGERNON   All women become like their mothers. That is their tragedy. No man does. That's his.

JACK   Is that clever?

ALGERNON   It is perfectly phrased! and quite as true as any observation in civilised life should be.

JACK   I am sick to death of cleverness. Everybody is clever nowadays. You can't go anywhere without meeting clever people. The thing has become an absolute public nuisance. I wish to goodness we had a few fools left.

ALGERNON   We have.

JACK   I should extremely like to meet them. What do they talk about?

ALGERNON   The fools? Oh! about the clever people, of course.

JACK   What fools!

ALGERNON   By the way, did you tell Gwendolen the truth about your being Ernest in town, and Jack in the country?

JACK   *[In a very patronising manner.]* My dear fellow, the truth isn't quite the sort of thing one tells to a nice, sweet, refined girl. What extraordinary ideas you have about the way to behave to a woman!

ALGERNON   The only way to behave to a woman is to make love to her, if she is pretty, and to some one else, if she is plain.

JACK   Oh, that is nonsense.

ALGERNON   What about your brother? What about the profligate Ernest?

JACK   Oh, before the end of the week I shall have got rid of him. I'll say he died in Paris of apoplexy. Lots of people die of apoplexy, quite suddenly, don't they?

ALGERNON   Yes, but it's hereditary, my dear fellow. It's a sort of thing that runs in families. You had much better say a severe chill.

JACK   You are sure a severe chill isn't hereditary, or anything of that kind?

ALGERNON   Of course it isn't!

JACK   Very well, then. My poor brother Ernest to carried off suddenly, in Paris, by a severe chill. That gets rid of him.

ALGERNON   But I thought you said that . . . Miss Cardew was a little too much interested in your poor brother Ernest? Won't she feel his loss a good deal?

JACK   Oh, that is all right. Cecily is not a silly romantic girl, I am glad to say. She has got a capital appetite, goes long walks, and pays no attention at all to her lessons.

ALGERNON   I would rather like to see Cecily.

JACK   I will take very good care you never do. She is excessively pretty, and she is only just eighteen.

ALGERNON   Have you told Gwendolen yet that you have an excessively pretty ward who is only just eighteen?

JACK   Oh! one doesn't blurt these things out to people. Cecily and Gwendolen are perfectly certain to be extremely great friends. I'll bet you anything you like that half an hour after they have met, they will be calling each other sister.

ALGERNON   Women only do that when they have called each other a lot of other things first. Now, my dear boy, if we want to get a good table at Willis's, we really must go and dress. Do you know it is nearly seven?

JACK   [Irritably.] Oh! It always is nearly seven.

ALGERNON   Well, I'm hungry.

JACK   I never knew you when you weren't . . .

ALGERNON   What shall we do after dinner? Go to a theatre?

JACK   Oh no! I loathe listening.

ALGERNON   Well, let us go to the Club?

JACK   Oh, no! I hate talking.

ALGERNON   Well, we might trot round to the Empire at ten?

JACK   Oh, no! I can't bear looking at things. It is so silly.

ALGERNON   Well, what shall we do?

JACK   Nothing!

ALGERNON   It is awfully hard work doing nothing. However, I don't mind hard work where there is no definite object of any kind.

[Enter Lane.]

LANE   Miss Fairfax.

[Enter GWENDOLEN Lane goes out.]

ALGERNON   Gwendolen, upon my word!

GWENDOLEN   Algy, kindly turn your back. I have something very particular to say to Mr. Worthing.

ALGERNON   Really, Gwendolen, I don't think I can allow this at all.

GWENDOLEN   Algy, you always adopt a strictly immoral attitude towards life. You are not quite old enough to do that. [Algernon retires to the fireplace.]

JACK   My own darling!

GWENDOLEN   Ernest, we may never be married. From the expression on mamma's face I fear we never shall. Few parents nowadays pay any regard to what their children say to them. The old-fashioned respect for the young is fast dying out. Whatever influence I ever had over mamma, I lost at the age of three. But although she may prevent us from becoming man and wife, and I may marry some one else, and marry often, nothing that she can possibly do can alter my eternal devotion to you.

JACK   Dear Gwendolen!

GWENDOLEN   The story of your romantic origin, as related to me by mamma, with unpleasing comments, has naturally stirred the deeper fibres of my nature. Your Christian name has an irresistible fascination. The simplicity of your character makes you exquisitely incomprehensible to me. Your town address at the Albany I have. What is your address in the country?

JACK   The Manor House, Woolton, Hertfordshire.

[Algernon, who has been carefully listening, smiles to himself, and writes the address on his shirt-cuff. Then picks up the Railway Guide.]

GWENDOLEN   There is a good postal service, I suppose? It may be necessary to do something desperate. That of course will require serious consideration. I will communicate with you daily.

JACK   My own one!

GWENDOLEN   How long do you remain in town?

JACK   Till Monday.

GWENDOLEN   Good! Algy, you may turn round now.

ALGERNON   Thanks, I've turned round already.

GWENDOLEN   You may also ring the bell.

JACK   You will let me see you to your carriage, my own darling?

GWENDOLEN   Certainly.

JACK   [To Lane, who now enters.] I will see Miss Fairfax out.

LANE   Yes, sir. [Jack and Gwendolen go off.]

[Lane presents several letters on a salver to Algernon. It is to be surmised that they are bills, as Algernon, after looking at the envelopes, tears them up.]

ALGERNON   A glass of sherry, Lane.

LANE   Yes, sir.

ALGERNON   To-morrow, Lane, I'm going Bunburying.

LANE   Yes, sir.

ALGERNON   I shall probably not be back till Monday. You can put up my dress clothes, my smoking jacket, and all the Bunbury suits . . .

LANE   Yes, sir. [Handing sherry.]

ALGERNON   I hope to-morrow will be a fine day, Lane.

LANE   It never is, sir.

ALGERNON   Lane, you're a perfect pessimist.

LANE   I do my best to give satisfaction, sir.

[Enter Jack. Lane goes off.]

JACK   There's a sensible, intellectual girl! the only girl I ever cared for in my life. [Algernon is laughing immoderately.] What on earth are you so amused at?

ALGERNON   Oh, I'm a little anxious about poor Bunbury, that is all.

JACK   If you don't take care, your friend Bunbury will get you into a serious scrape some day.

ALGERNON   I love scrapes. They are the only things that are never serious.

JACK   Oh, that's nonsense, Algy. You never talk anything but nonsense.

ALGERNON   Nobody ever does.

[Jack looks indignantly at him, and leaves the room. Algernon lights a cigarette, reads his shirt-cuff, and smiles.]

ACT DROP

Second Act

SCENE. Garden at the Manor House. A flight of grey stone steps leads up to the house. The garden, an old-fashioned one, full of roses. Time of year, July. Basket chairs, and a table covered with books, are set under a large yew-tree.

[Miss Prism discovered seated at the table. Cecily is at the back watering flowers.]

MISS PRISM   *[Calling.]* Cecily, Cecily! Surely such a utilitarian occupation as the watering of flowers is rather Moulton's duty than yours? Especially at a moment when intellectual pleasures await you. Your German grammar is on the table. Pray open it at page fifteen. We will repeat yesterday's lesson.

CECILY   *[Coming over very slowly.]* But I don't like German. It isn't at all a becoming language. I know perfectly well that I look quite plain after my German lesson.

MISS PRISM   Child, you know how anxious your guardian is that you should improve yourself in every way. He laid particular stress on your German, as he was leaving for town yesterday. Indeed, he always lays stress on your German when he is leaving for town.

CECILY   Dear Uncle Jack is so very serious! Sometimes he is so serious that I think he cannot be quite well.

MISS PRISM   *[Drawing herself up.]* Your guardian enjoys the best of health, and his gravity of demeanour is especially to be commended in one so comparatively young as he is. I know no one who has a higher sense of duty and responsibility.

CECILY   I suppose that is why he often looks a little bored when we three are together.

MISS PRISM   Cecily! I am surprised at you. Mr. Worthing has many troubles in his life. Idle merriment and triviality would be out of place in his conversation. You must remember his constant anxiety about that unfortunate young man his brother.

CECILY   I wish Uncle Jack would allow that unfortunate young man, his brother, to come down here sometimes. We might have a good influence over him, Miss Prism. I am sure you certainly would. You know German, and geology, and things of that kind influence a man very much. *[Cecily begins to write in her diary.]*

MISS PRISM   *[Shaking her head.]* I do not think that even I could produce any effect on a character that according to his own brother's admission is irretrievably weak and vacillating. Indeed I am not sure that I would desire to reclaim him. I am not in favour of this modern mania for turning bad people into good people at a moment's notice. As a man sows so let him reap. You must put away your diary, Cecily. I really don't see why you should keep a diary at all.

CECILY   I keep a diary in order to enter the wonderful secrets of my life. If I didn't write them down, I should probably forget all about them.

MISS PRISM   Memory, my dear Cecily, is the diary that we all carry about with us.

CECILY   Yes, but it usually chronicles the things that have never happened, and couldn't possibly have happened. I believe that Memory is responsible for nearly all the three-volume novels that Mudie sends us.

MISS PRISM   Do not speak slightingly of the three-volume novel, Cecily. I wrote one myself in earlier days.

CECILY   Did you really, Miss Prism? How wonderfully clever you are! I hope it did not end happily? I don't like novels that end happily. They depress me so much.

MISS PRISM   The good ended happily, and the bad unhappily. That is what Fiction means.

CECILY   I suppose so. But it seems very unfair. And was your novel ever published?

MISS PRISM   Alas! no. The manuscript unfortunately was abandoned. *[Cecily starts.]* I use the word in the sense of lost or mislaid. To your work, child, these speculations are profitless.

CECILY   *[Smiling.]* But I see dear Dr. Chasuble coming up through the garden.

MISS PRISM   *[Rising and advancing.]* Dr. Chasuble! This is indeed a pleasure.

[Enter Canon Chasuble.]

CHASUBLE   And how are we this morning? Miss Prism, you are, I trust, well?

CECILY   Miss Prism has just been complaining of a slight headache. I think it would do her so much good to have a short stroll with you in the Park, Dr. Chasuble.

MISS PRISM   Cecily, I have not mentioned anything about a headache.

CECILY   No, dear Miss Prism, I know that, but I felt instinctively that you had a headache. Indeed I was thinking about that, and not about my German lesson, when the Rector came in.

CHASUBLE   I hope, Cecily, you are not inattentive.

CECILY   Oh, I am afraid I am.

CHASUBLE   That is strange. Were I fortunate enough to be Miss Prism's pupil, I would hang upon her lips. *[Miss Prism glares.]* I spoke metaphorically.—My metaphor was drawn from bees. Ahem! Mr. Worthing, I suppose, has not returned from town yet?

MISS PRISM   We do not expect him till Monday afternoon.

CHASUBLE   Ah yes, he usually likes to spend his Sunday in London. He is not one of those whose sole aim is enjoyment, as, by all accounts, that unfortunate young man his brother seems to be. But I must not disturb Egeria and her pupil any longer.

MISS PRISM   Egeria? My name is Lætitia, Doctor.

CHASUBLE   *[Bowing.]* A classical allusion merely, drawn from the Pagan authors. I shall see you both no doubt at Evensong?

MISS PRISM   I think, dear Doctor, I will have a stroll with you. I find I have a headache after all, and a walk might do it good.

CHASUBLE   With pleasure, Miss Prism, with pleasure. We might go as far as the schools and back.

MISS PRISM   That would be delightful. Cecily, you will read your Political Economy in my absence. The chapter on the Fall of the Rupee you may omit. It is somewhat too sensational. Even these metallic problems have their melodramatic side.

[Goes down the garden with Dr. Chasuble.]

CECILY   *[Picks up books and throws them back on table.]* Horrid Political Economy! Horrid Geography! Horrid, horrid German!

[Enter Merriman with a card on a salver.]

MERRIMAN   Mr. Ernest Worthing has just driven over from the station. He has brought his luggage with him.

CECILY   *[Takes the card and reads it.]* 'Mr. Ernest Worthing, B. 4, The Albany, W.' Uncle Jack's brother! Did you tell him Mr. Worthing was in town?

MERRIMAN   Yes, Miss. He seemed very much disappointed. I mentioned that you and Miss Prism were in the garden. He said he was anxious to speak to you privately for a moment.

CECILY   Ask Mr. Ernest Worthing to come here. I suppose you had better talk to the housekeeper about a room for him.

MERRIMAN   Yes, Miss.

[Merriman goes off.]

CECILY   I have never met any really wicked person before. I feel rather frightened. I am so afraid he will look just like every one else.

[*Enter Algernon, very gay and debonnair.*] He does!

ALGERNON   [*Raising his hat.*] You are my little cousin Cecily, I'm sure.

CECILY   You are under some strange mistake. I am not little. In fact, I believe I am more than usually tall for my age. [*Algernon is rather taken aback.*] But I am your cousin Cecily. You, I see from your card, are Uncle Jack's brother, my cousin Ernest, my wicked cousin Ernest.

ALGERNON   Oh! I am not really wicked at all, cousin Cecily. You mustn't think that I am wicked.

CECILY   If you are not, then you have certainly been deceiving us all in a very inexcusable manner. I hope you have not been leading a double life, pretending to be wicked and being really good all the time. That would be hypocrisy.

ALGERNON   [*Looks at her in amazement.*] Oh! Of course I have been rather reckless.

CECILY   I am glad to hear it.

ALGERNON   In fact, now you mention the subject, I have been very bad in my own small way.

CECILY   I don't think you should be so proud of that, though I am sure it must have been very pleasant.

ALGERNON   It is much pleasanter being here with you.

CECILY   I can't understand how you are here at all. Uncle Jack won't be back till Monday afternoon.

ALGERNON   That is a great disappointment. I am obliged to go up by the first train on Monday morning. I have a business appointment that I am anxious . . . to miss?

CECILY   Couldn't you miss it anywhere but in London?

ALGERNON   No: the appointment is in London.

CECILY   Well, I know, of course, how important it is not to keep a business engagement, if one wants to retain any sense of the beauty of life, but still I think you had better wait till Uncle Jack arrives. I know he wants to speak to you about your emigrating.

ALGERNON   About my what?

CECILY   Your emigrating. He has gone up to buy your outfit.

ALGERNON   I certainly wouldn't let Jack buy my outfit. He has no taste in neckties at all.

CECILY   I don't think you will require neckties. Uncle Jack is sending you to Australia.

ALGERNON   Australia! I'd sooner die.

CECILY   Well, he said at dinner on Wednesday night, that you would have to choose between this world, the next world, and Australia.

ALGERNON   Oh, well! The accounts I have received of Australia and the next world, are not particularly encouraging. This world is good enough for me, cousin Cecily.

CECILY   Yes, but are you good enough for it?

ALGERNON   I'm afraid I'm not that. That is why I want you to reform me. You might make that your mission, if you don't mind, cousin Cecily.

CECILY   I'm afraid I've no time, this afternoon.

ALGERNON   Well, would you mind my reforming myself this afternoon?

CECILY   It is rather Quixotic of you. But I think you should try.

ALGERNON   I will. I feel better already.

CECILY   You are looking a little worse.

ALGERNON   That is because I am hungry.

CECILY   How thoughtless of me. I should have remembered that when one is going to lead an entirely new life, one requires regular and wholesome meals. Won't you come in?

ALGERNON   Thank you. Might I have a buttonhole first? I never have any appetite unless I have a buttonhole first.

CECILY   A Marechal Niel? [Picks up scissors.]

ALGERNON   No, I'd sooner have a pink rose.

CECILY   Why? [Cuts a flower.]

ALGERNON   Because you are like a pink rose, Cousin Cecily.

CECILY   I don't think it can be right for you to talk to me like that. Miss Prism never says such things to me.

ALGERNON   Then Miss Prism is a short-sighted old lady. [Cecily puts the rose in his buttonhole.] You are the prettiest girl I ever saw.

CECILY   Miss Prism says that all good looks are a snare.

ALGERNON   They are a snare that every sensible man would like to be caught in.

CECILY   Oh, I don't think I would care to catch a sensible man. I shouldn't know what to talk to him about.

[They pass into the house. Miss Prism and Dr. Chasuble return.]

MISS PRISM   You are too much alone, dear Dr. Chasuble. You should get married. A misanthrope I can understand—a womanthrope, never!

CHASUBLE   [With a scholar's shudder.] Believe me, I do not deserve so neologistic a phrase. The precept as well as the practice of the Primitive Church was distinctly against matrimony.

MISS PRISM   [Sententiously.] That is obviously the reason why the Primitive Church has not lasted up to the present day. And you do not seem to realise, dear Doctor, that by persistently remaining single, a man converts himself into a permanent public temptation. Men should be more careful; this very celibacy leads weaker vessels astray.

CHASUBLE   But is a man not equally attractive when married?

MISS PRISM   No married man is ever attractive except to his wife.

CHASUBLE   And often, I've been told, not even to her.

MISS PRISM   That depends on the intellectual sympathies of the woman. Maturity can always be depended on. Ripeness can be trusted. Young women are green. [Dr. Chasuble starts.] I spoke horticulturally. My metaphor was drawn from fruits. But where is Cecily?

CHASUBLE   Perhaps she followed us to the schools.

[Enter Jack slowly from the back of the garden. He is dressed in the deepest mourning, with crape hatband and black gloves.]

MISS PRISM   Mr. Worthing!

CHASUBLE   Mr. Worthing?

MISS PRISM   This is indeed a surprise. We did not look for you till Monday afternoon.

JACK   [Shakes Miss Prism's hand in a tragic manner.] I have returned sooner than I expected. Dr. Chasuble, I hope you are well?

CHASUBLE   Dear Mr. Worthing, I trust this garb of woe does not betoken some terrible calamity?

JACK   My brother.

MISS PRISM   More shameful debts and extravagance?

CHASUBLE   Still leading his life of pleasure?

JACK   [Shaking his head.] Dead!

CHASUBLE   Your brother Ernest dead?

JACK   Quite dead.

MISS PRISM   What a lesson for him! I trust he will profit by it.

CHASUBLE   Mr. Worthing, I offer you my sincere condolence. You have at least the consolation of knowing that you were always the most generous and forgiving of brothers.

JACK   Poor Ernest! He had many faults, but it is a sad, sad blow.

CHASUBLE   Very sad indeed. Were you with him at the end?

JACK   No. He died abroad; in Paris, in fact. I had a telegram last night from the manager of the Grand Hotel.

CHASUBLE   Was the cause of death mentioned?

JACK   A severe chill, it seems.

MISS PRISM   As a man sows, so shall he reap.

CHASUBLE   *[Raising his hand.]* Charity, dear Miss Prism, charity! None of us are perfect. I myself am peculiarly susceptible to draughts. Will the interment take place here?

JACK   No. He seems to have expressed a desire to be buried in Paris.

CHASUBLE   In Paris! *[Shakes his head.]* I fear that hardly points to any very serious state of mind at the last. You would no doubt wish me to make some slight allusion to this tragic domestic affliction next Sunday. *[Jack presses his hand convulsively.]* My sermon on the meaning of the manna in the wilderness can be adapted to almost any occasion, joyful, or, as in the present case, distressing. *[All sigh.]* I have preached it at harvest celebrations, christenings, confirmations, on days of humiliation and festal days. The last time I delivered it was in the Cathedral, as a charity sermon on behalf of the Society for the Prevention of Discontent among the Upper Orders. The Bishop, who was present, was much struck by some of the analogies I drew.

JACK   Ah! that reminds me, you mentioned christenings I think, Dr. Chasuble? I suppose you know how to christen all right? *[Dr. Chasuble looks astounded.]* I mean, of course, you are continually christening, aren't you?

MISS PRISM   It is, I regret to say, one of the Rector's most constant duties in this parish. I have often spoken to the poorer classes on the subject. But they don't seem to know what thrift is.

CHASUBLE   But is there any particular infant in whom you are interested, Mr. Worthing? Your brother was, I believe, unmarried, was he not?

JACK   Oh yes.

MISS PRISM   *[Bitterly.]* People who live entirely for pleasure usually are.

JACK   But it is not for any child, dear Doctor. I am very fond of children. No! the fact is, I would like to be christened myself, this afternoon, if you have nothing better to do.

CHASUBLE   But surely, Mr. Worthing, you have been christened already?

JACK   I don't remember anything about it.

CHASUBLE   But have you any grave doubts on the subject?

JACK   I certainly intend to have. Of course I don't know if the thing would bother you in any way, or if you think I am a little too old now.

CHASUBLE   Not at all. The sprinkling, and, indeed, the immersion of adults is a perfectly canonical practice.

JACK   Immersion!

CHASUBLE   You need have no apprehensions. Sprinkling is all that is necessary, or indeed I think advisable. Our weather is so changeable. At what hour would you wish the ceremony performed?

JACK   Oh, I might trot round about five if that would suit you.

CHASUBLE   Perfectly, perfectly! In fact I have two similar ceremonies to perform at that time. A case of twins that occurred recently in one of the outlying cottages on your own estate. Poor Jenkins the carter, a most hard-working man.

JACK   Oh! I don't see much fun in being christened along with other babies. It would be childish. Would half-past five do?

CHASUBLE   Admirably! Admirably! *[Takes out watch.]* And now, dear Mr. Worthing, I will not intrude any longer into a house of sorrow. I would merely beg you not to be too much bowed down by grief. What seem to us bitter trials are often blessings in disguise.

MISS PRISM   This seems to me a blessing of an extremely obvious kind.

[Enter Cecily from the house.]

CECILY   Uncle Jack! Oh, I am pleased to see you back. But what horrid clothes you have got on! Do go and change them.

MISS PRISM   Cecily!

CHASUBLE   My child! my child! *[Cecily goes towards Jack; he kisses her brow in a melancholy manner.]*

CECILY   What is the matter, Uncle Jack? Do look happy! You look as if you had toothache, and I have got such a surprise for you. Who do you think is in the dining-room? Your brother!

JACK   Who?

CECILY   Your brother Ernest. He arrived about half an hour ago.

JACK   What nonsense! I haven't got a brother.

CECILY   Oh, don't say that. However badly he may have behaved to you in the past he is still your brother. You couldn't be so heartless as to disown him. I'll tell him to come out. And you will shake hands with him, won't you, Uncle Jack? *[Runs back into the house.]*

CHASUBLE   These are very joyful tidings.

MISS PRISM   After we had all been resigned to his loss, his sudden return seems to me peculiarly distressing.

JACK   My brother is in the dining-room? I don't know what it all means. I think it is perfectly absurd.

[Enter Algernon and Cecily hand in hand. They come slowly up to Jack.]

JACK   Good heavens! *[Motions Algernon away.]*

ALGERNON   Brother John, I have come down from town to tell you that I am very sorry for all the trouble I have given you, and that I intend to lead a better life in the future. *[Jack glares at him and does not take his hand.]*

CECILY   Uncle Jack, you are not going to refuse your own brother's hand?

JACK   Nothing will induce me to take his hand. I think his coming down here disgraceful. He knows perfectly well why.

CECILY   Uncle Jack, do be nice. There is some good in every one. Ernest has just been telling me about his poor invalid friend Mr. Bunbury whom he goes to visit so often. And surely there must be much good in one who is kind to an invalid, and leaves the pleasures of London to sit by a bed of pain.

JACK   Oh! he has been talking about Bunbury, has he?

CECILY   Yes, he has told me all about poor Mr. Bunbury, and his terrible state of health.

JACK   Bunbury! Well, I won't have him talk to you about Bunbury or about anything else. It is enough to drive one perfectly frantic.

ALGERNON   Of course I admit that the faults were all on my side. But I must say that I think that Brother John's coldness to me is peculiarly painful. I expected a more enthusiastic welcome, especially considering it is the first time I have come here.

CECILY   Uncle Jack, if you don't shake hands with Ernest I will never forgive you.

JACK   Never forgive me?

CECILY   Never, never, never!

JACK   Well, this is the last time I shall ever do it. [Shakes with Algernon and glares.]

CHASUBLE   It's pleasant, is it not, to see so perfect a reconciliation? I think we might leave the two brothers together.

MISS PRISM   Cecily, you will come with us.

CECILY   Certainly, Miss Prism. My little task of reconciliation is over.

CHASUBLE   You have done a beautiful action to-day, dear child.

MISS PRISM   We must not be premature in our judgments.

CECILY   I feel very happy. [They all go off except Jack and Algernon.]

JACK   You young scoundrel, Algy, you must get out of this place as soon as possible. I don't allow any Bunburying here.

[Enter Merriman.]

MERRIMAN   I have put Mr. Ernest's things in the room next to yours, sir. I suppose that is all right?

JACK   What?

MERRIMAN   Mr. Ernest's luggage, sir. I have unpacked it and put it in the room next to your own.

JACK   His luggage?

MERRIMAN   Yes, sir. Three portmanteaus, a dressing-case, two hat-boxes, and a large luncheon-basket.

ALGERNON   I am afraid I can't stay more than a week this time.

JACK   Merriman, order the dog-cart at once. Mr. Ernest has been suddenly called back to town.

MERRIMAN   Yes, sir. [Goes back into the house.]

ALGERNON   What a fearful liar you are, Jack. I have not been called back to town at all.

JACK   Yes, you have.

ALGERNON   I haven't heard any one call me.

JACK   Your duty as a gentleman calls you back.

ALGERNON   My duty as a gentleman has never interfered with my pleasures in the smallest degree.

JACK   I can quite understand that.

ALGERNON   Well, Cecily is a darling.

JACK   You are not to talk of Miss Cardew like that. I don't like it.

ALGERNON   Well, I don't like your clothes. You look perfectly ridiculous in them. Why on earth don't you go up and change? It is perfectly childish to be in deep mourning for a man who is actually staying for a whole week with you in your house as a guest. I call it grotesque.

JACK   You are certainly not staying with me for a whole week as a guest or anything else. You have got to leave . . . by the four-five train.

ALGERNON   I certainly won't leave you so long as you are in mourning. It would be most unfriendly. If I were in mourning you would stay with me, I suppose. I should think it very unkind if you didn't.

JACK   Well, will you go if I change my clothes?

ALGERNON   Yes, if you are not too long. I never saw anybody take so long to dress, and with such little result.

JACK   Well, at any rate, that is better than being always over-dressed as you are.

ALGERNON   If I am occasionally a little over-dressed, I make up for it by being always immensely over-educated.

JACK   Your vanity is ridiculous, your conduct an outrage, and your presence in my garden utterly absurd. However, you have got to catch the four-five, and I hope you will have a pleasant journey back to town. This Bunburying, as you call it, has not been a great success for you.

[Goes into the house.]

ALGERNON   I think it has been a great success. I'm in love with Cecily, and that is everything.

[Enter Cecily at the back of the garden. She picks up the can and begins to water the flowers.] But I must see her before I go, and make arrangements for another Bunbury. Ah, there she is.

CECILY   Oh, I merely came back to water the roses. I thought you were with Uncle Jack.

ALGERNON   He's gone to order the dog-cart for me.

CECILY   Oh, is he going to take you for a nice drive?

ALGERNON   He's going to send me away.

CECILY   Then have we got to part?

ALGERNON   I am afraid so. It's a very painful parting.

CECILY   It is always painful to part from people whom one has known for a very brief space of time. The absence of old friends one can endure with equanimity. But even a momentary separation from anyone to whom one has just been introduced is almost unbearable.

ALGERNON   Thank you.

[Enter Merriman.]

MERRIMAN   The dog-cart is at the door, sir. *[Algernon looks appealingly at Cecily.]*

CECILY   It can wait, Merriman for . . . five minutes.

MERRIMAN   Yes, Miss. *[Exit Merriman.]*

ALGERNON   I hope, Cecily, I shall not offend you if I state quite frankly and openly that you seem to me to be in every way the visible personification of absolute perfection.

CECILY   I think your frankness does you great credit, Ernest. If you will allow me, I will copy your remarks into my diary. *[Goes over to table and begins writing in diary.]*

ALGERNON   Do you really keep a diary? I'd give anything to look at it. May I?

CECILY   Oh no. *[Puts her hand over it.]* You see, it is simply a very young girl's record of her own thoughts and impressions, and consequently meant for publication. When it appears in volume form I hope you will order a copy. But pray, Ernest, don't stop. I delight in taking down from dictation. I have reached 'absolute perfection'. You can go on. I am quite ready for more.

ALGERNON   *[Somewhat taken aback.]* Ahem! Ahem!

CECILY   Oh, don't cough, Ernest. When one is dictating one should speak fluently and not cough. Besides, I don't know how to spell a cough. *[Writes as Algernon speaks.]*

ALGERNON   *[Speaking very rapidly.]* Cecily, ever since I first looked upon your wonderful and incomparable beauty, I have dared to love you wildly, passionately, devotedly, hopelessly.

CECILY   I don't think that you should tell me that you love me wildly, passionately, devotedly, hopelessly. Hopelessly doesn't seem to make much sense, does it?

ALGERNON   Cecily!

[Enter Merriman.]

MERRIMAN   The dog-cart is waiting, sir.

ALGERNON   Tell it to come round next week, at the same hour.

MERRIMAN   *[Looks at Cecily, who makes no sign.]* Yes, sir.

THE IMPORTANCE OF BEING ERNEST – SECOND ACT

[Merriman retires.]

CECILY   Uncle Jack would be very much annoyed if he knew you were staying on till next week, at the same hour.

ALGERNON   Oh, I don't care about Jack. I don't care for anybody in the whole world but you. I love you, Cecily. You will marry me, won't you?

CECILY   You silly boy! Of course. Why, we have been engaged for the last three months.

ALGERNON   For the last three months?

CECILY   Yes, it will be exactly three months on Thursday.

ALGERNON   But how did we become engaged?

CECILY   Well, ever since dear Uncle Jack first confessed to us that he had a younger brother who was very wicked and bad, you of course have formed the chief topic of conversation between myself and Miss Prism. And of course a man who is much talked about is always very attractive. One feels there must be something in him, after all. I daresay it was foolish of me, but I fell in love with you, Ernest.

ALGERNON   Darling! And when was the engagement actually settled?

CECILY   On the 14th of February last. Worn out by your entire ignorance of my existence, I determined to end the matter one way or the other, and after a long struggle with myself I accepted you under this dear old tree here. The next day I bought this little ring in your name, and this is the little bangle with the true lover's knot I promised you always to wear.

ALGERNON   Did I give you this? It's very pretty, isn't it?

CECILY   Yes, you've wonderfully good taste, Ernest. It's the excuse I've always given for your leading such a bad life. And this is the box in which I keep all your dear letters. *[Kneels at table, opens box, and produces letters tied up with blue ribbon.]*

ALGERNON   My letters! But, my own sweet Cecily, I have never written you any letters.

CECILY   You need hardly remind me of that, Ernest. I remember only too well that I was forced to write your letters for you. I wrote always three times a week, and sometimes oftener.

ALGERNON   Oh, do let me read them, Cecily?

CECILY   Oh, I couldn't possibly. They would make you far too conceited. *[Replaces box.]* The three you wrote me after I had broken off the engagement are so beautiful, and so badly spelled, that even now I can hardly read them without crying a little.

ALGERNON   But was our engagement ever broken off?

CECILY   Of course it was. On the 22nd of last March. You can see the entry if you like. *[Shows diary.]* 'To-day I broke off my engagement with Ernest. I feel it is better to do so. The weather still continues charming.'

ALGERNON   But why on earth did you break it off? What had I done? I had done nothing at all. Cecily, I am very much hurt indeed to hear you broke it off. Particularly when the weather was so charming.

CECILY   It would hardly have been a really serious engagement if it hadn't been broken off at least once. But I forgave you before the week was out.

ALGERNON   *[Crossing to her, and kneeling.]* What a perfect angel you are, Cecily.

CECILY   You dear romantic boy. *[He kisses her, she puts her fingers through his hair.]* I hope your hair curls naturally, does it?

ALGERNON   Yes, darling, with a little help from others.

CECILY   I am so glad.

ALGERNON   You'll never break off our engagement again, Cecily?

CECILY   I don't think I could break it off now that I have actually met you. Besides, of course, there is the question of your name.

ALGERNON   Yes, of course. [Nervously.]

CECILY   You must not laugh at me, darling, but it had always been a girlish dream of mine to love some one whose name was Ernest. [Algernon rises, Cecily also.] There is something in that name that seems to inspire absolute confidence. I pity any poor married woman whose husband is not called Ernest.

ALGERNON   But, my dear child, do you mean to say you could not love me if I had some other name?

CECILY   But what name?

ALGERNON   Oh, any name you like—Algernon—for instance . . .

CECILY   But I don't like the name of Algernon.

ALGERNON   Well, my own dear, sweet, loving little darling, I really can't see why you should object to the name of Algernon. It is not at all a bad name. In fact, it is rather an aristocratic name. Half of the chaps who get into the Bankruptcy Court are called Algernon. But seriously, Cecily . . . [Moving to her] . . . if my name was Algy, couldn't you love me?

CECILY   [Rising.] I might respect you, Ernest, I might admire your character, but I fear that I should not be able to give you my undivided attention.

ALGERNON   Ahem! Cecily! [Picking up hat.] Your Rector here is, I suppose, thoroughly experienced in the practice of all the rites and ceremonials of the Church?

CECILY   Oh, yes. Dr. Chasuble is a most learned man. He has never written a single book, so you can imagine how much he knows.

ALGERNON   I must see him at once on a most important christening—I mean on most important business.

CECILY   Oh!

ALGERNON   I shan't be away more than half an hour.

CECILY   Considering that we have been engaged since February the 14th, and that I only met you to-day for the first time, I think it is rather hard that you should leave me for so long a period as half an hour. Couldn't you make it twenty minutes?

ALGERNON   I'll be back in no time.

[Kisses her and rushes down the garden.]

CECILY   What an impetuous boy he is! I like his hair so much. I must enter his proposal in my diary.

[Enter Merriman.]

MERRIMAN   A Miss Fairfax has just called to see Mr. Worthing. On very important business, Miss Fairfax states.

CECILY   Isn't Mr. Worthing in his library?

MERRIMAN   Mr. Worthing went over in the direction of the Rectory some time ago.

CECILY   Pray ask the lady to come out here; Mr. Worthing is sure to be back soon. And you can bring tea.

MERRIMAN   Yes, Miss. [Goes out.]

CECILY   Miss Fairfax! I suppose one of the many good elderly women who are associated with Uncle Jack in some of his philanthropic work in London. I don't quite like women who are interested in philanthropic work. I think it is so forward of them.

[Enter Merriman.]

MERRIMAN   Miss Fairfax.

[Enter Gwendolen. [Exit Merriman.]

CECILY *[Advancing to meet her.]* Pray let me introduce myself to you. My name is Cecily Cardew.

GWENDOLEN Cecily Cardew? *[Moving to her and shaking hands.]* What a very sweet name! Something tells me that we are going to be great friends. I like you already more than I can say. My first impressions of people are never wrong.

CECILY How nice of you to like me so much after we have known each other such a comparatively short time. Pray sit down.

GWENDOLEN *[Still standing up.]* I may call you Cecily, may I not?

CECILY With pleasure!

GWENDOLEN And you will always call me Gwendolen, won't you?

CECILY If you wish.

GWENDOLEN Then that is all quite settled, is it not?

CECILY I hope so. *[A pause. They both sit down together.]*

GWENDOLEN Perhaps this might be a favourable opportunity for my mentioning who I am. My father is Lord Bracknell. You have never heard of papa, I suppose?

CECILY I don't think so.

GWENDOLEN Outside the family circle, papa, I am glad to say, is entirely unknown. I think that is quite as it should be. The home seems to me to be the proper sphere for the man. And certainly once a man begins to neglect his domestic duties he becomes painfully effeminate, does he not? And I don't like that. It makes men so very attractive. Cecily, mamma, whose views on education are remarkably strict, has brought me up to be extremely short-sighted; it is part of her system; so do you mind my looking at you through my glasses?

CECILY Oh! not at all, Gwendolen. I am very fond of being looked at.

GWENDOLEN *[After examining Cecily carefully through a lorgnette.]* You are here on a short visit, I suppose.

CECILY Oh no! I live here.

GWENDOLEN *[Severely.]* Really? Your mother, no doubt, or some female relative of advanced years, resides here also?

CECILY Oh no! I have no mother, nor, in fact, any relations.

GWENDOLEN Indeed?

CECILY My dear guardian, with the assistance of Miss Prism, has the arduous task of looking after me.

GWENDOLEN Your guardian?

CECILY Yes, I am Mr. Worthing's ward.

GWENDOLEN Oh! It is strange he never mentioned to me that he had a ward. How secretive of him! He grows more interesting hourly. I am not sure, however, that the news inspires me with feelings of unmixed delight. *[Rising and going to her.]* I am very fond of you, Cecily; I have liked you ever since I met you! But I am bound to state that now that I know that you are Mr. Worthing's ward, I cannot help expressing a wish you were—well, just a little older than you seem to be—and not quite so very alluring in appearance. In fact, if I may speak candidly—

CECILY Pray do! I think that whenever one has anything unpleasant to say, one should always be quite candid.

GWENDOLEN Well, to speak with perfect candour, Cecily, I wish that you were fully forty-two, and more than usually plain for your age. Ernest has a strong upright nature. He is the very soul of truth and honour. Disloyalty would be as impossible to him as deception. But even men of the noblest possible moral character are extremely susceptible to the influence of the physical charms of others. Modern, no less than Ancient History, supplies us with many most painful examples of what I refer to. If it were not so, indeed, History would be quite unreadable.

CECILY   I beg your pardon, Gwendolen, did you say Ernest?

GWENDOLEN   Yes.

CECILY   Oh, but it is not Mr. Ernest Worthing who is my guardian. It is his brother—his elder brother.

GWENDOLEN   [Sitting down again.] Ernest never mentioned to me that he had a brother.

CECILY   I am sorry to say they have not been on good terms for a long time.

GWENDOLEN   Ah! that accounts for it. And now that I think of it I have never heard any man mention his brother. The subject seems distasteful to most men. Cecily, you have lifted a load from my mind. I was growing almost anxious. It would have been terrible if any cloud had come across a friendship like ours, would it not? Of course you are quite, quite sure that it is not Mr. Ernest Worthing who is your guardian?

CECILY   Quite sure. [A pause.] In fact, I am going to be his.

GWENDOLEN   [Inquiringly.] I beg your pardon?

CECILY   [Rather shy and confidingly.] Dearest Gwendolen, there is no reason why I should make a secret of it to you. Our little county newspaper is sure to chronicle the fact next week. Mr. Ernest Worthing and I are engaged to be married.

GWENDOLEN   [Quite politely, rising.] My darling Cecily, I think there must be some slight error. Mr. Ernest Worthing is engaged to me. The announcement will appear in the Morning Post on Saturday at the latest.

CECILY   [Very politely, rising.] I am afraid you must be under some misconception. Ernest proposed to me exactly ten minutes ago. [Shows diary.]

GWENDOLEN   [Examines diary through her lorgnettte carefully.] It is certainly very curious, for he asked me to be his wife yesterday afternoon at 5.30. If you would care to verify the incident, pray do so. [Produces diary of her own.] I never travel without my diary. One should always have something sensational to read in the train. I am so sorry, dear Cecily, if it is any disappointment to you, but I am afraid I have the prior claim.

CECILY   It would distress me more than I can tell you, dear Gwendolen, if it caused you any mental or physical anguish, but I feel bound to point out that since Ernest proposed to you he clearly has changed his mind.

GWENDOLEN   [Meditatively.] If the poor fellow has been entrapped into any foolish promise I shall consider it my duty to rescue him at once, and with a firm hand.

CECILY   [Thoughtfully and sadly.] Whatever unfortunate entanglement my dear boy may have got into, I will never reproach him with it after we are married.

GWENDOLEN   Do you allude to me, Miss Cardew, as an entanglement? You are presumptuous. On an occasion of this kind it becomes more than a moral duty to speak one's mind. It becomes a pleasure.

CECILY   Do you suggest, Miss Fairfax, that I entrapped Ernest into an engagement? How dare you? This is no time for wearing the shallow mask of manners. When I see a spade I call it a spade.

GWENDOLEN   [Satirically.] I am glad to say that I have never seen a spade. It is obvious that our social spheres have been widely different.

[Enter Merriman, followed by the footman. He carries a salver, table cloth, and plate stand. Cecily is about to retort. The presence of the servants exercises a restraining influence, under which both girls chafe.]

MERRIMAN   Shall I lay tea here as usual, Miss?

CECILY   [Sternly, in a calm voice.] Yes, as usual. [Merriman begins to clear table and lay cloth. A long pause. Cecily and Gwendolen glare at each other.]

GWENDOLEN   Are there many interesting walks in the vicinity, Miss Cardew?

CECILY   Oh! yes! a great many. From the top of one of the hills quite close one can see five counties.

GWENDOLEN   Five counties! I don't think I should like that; I hate crowds.

CECILY   *[Sweetly.]* I suppose that is why you live in town?

[Gwendolen bites her lip, and beats her foot nervously with her parasol.]

GWENDOLEN   *[Looking round.]* Quite a well-kept garden this is, Miss Cardew.

CECILY   So glad you like it, Miss Fairfax.

GWENDOLEN   I had no idea there were any flowers in the country.

CECILY   Oh, flowers are as common here, Miss Fairfax, as people are in London.

GWENDOLEN   Personally I cannot understand how anybody manages to exist in the country, if anybody who is anybody does. The country always bores me to death.

CECILY   Ah! This is what the newspapers call agricultural depression, is it not? I believe the aristocracy are suffering very much from it just at present. It is almost an epidemic amongst them, I have been told. May I offer you some tea, Miss Fairfax?

GWENDOLEN   *[With elaborate politeness.]* Thank you. *[Aside.]* Detestable girl! But I require tea!

CECILY   *[Sweetly.]* Sugar?

GWENDOLEN   *[Superciliously.[1]]* No, thank you. Sugar is not fashionable any more. *[Cecily looks angrily at her, takes up the tongs and puts four lumps of sugar into the cup.]*

CECILY   *[Severely.]* Cake or bread and butter?

GWENDOLEN   *[In a bored manner.]* Bread and butter, please. Cake is rarely seen at the best houses nowadays.

CECILY   *[Cuts a very large slice of cake, and puts it on the tray.]* Hand that to Miss Fairfax.

[Merriman does so, and goes out with footman. Gwendolen drinks the tea and makes a grimace. Puts down cup at once, reaches out her hand to the bread and butter, looks at it, and finds it is cake. Rises in indignation.]

GWENDOLEN   You have filled my tea with lumps of sugar, and though I asked most distinctly for bread and butter, you have given me cake. I am known for the gentleness of my disposition, and the extraordinary sweetness of my nature, but I warn you, Miss Cardew, you may go too far.

CECILY   *[Rising.]* To save my poor, innocent, trusting boy from the machinations of any other girl there are no lengths to which I would not go.

GWENDOLEN   From the moment I saw you I distrusted you. I felt that you were false and deceitful. I am never deceived in such matters. My first impressions of people are invariably right.

CECILY   It seems to me, Miss Fairfax, that I am trespassing on your valuable time. No doubt you have many other calls of a similar character to make in the neighbourhood.

[Enter Jack.]

GWENDOLEN   *[Catching sight of him.]* Ernest! My own Ernest!

JACK   Gwendolen! Darling! *[Offers to kiss her.]*

GWENDOLEN   *[Draws back.]* A moment! May I ask if you are engaged to be married to this young lady? *[Points to Cecily.]*

JACK   *[Laughing.]* To dear little Cecily! Of course not! What could have put such an idea into your pretty little head?

GWENDOLEN   Thank you. You may! *[Offers her cheek.]*

---

[1] patronizing or haughty

CECILY   *[Very sweetly.]* I knew there must be some misunderstanding, Miss Fairfax. The gentleman whose arm is at present round your waist is my guardian, Mr. John Worthing.

GWENDOLEN   I beg your pardon?

CECILY   This is Uncle Jack.

GWENDOLEN   *[Receding.]* Jack! Oh!

[Enter Algernon.]

CECILY   Here is Ernest.

ALGERNON   *[Goes straight over to Cecily without noticing any one else.]* My own love! *[Offers to kiss her.]*

CECILY   *[Drawing back.]* A moment, Ernest! May I ask you—are you engaged to be married to this young lady?

ALGERNON   *[Looking round.]* To what young lady? Good heavens! Gwendolen!

CECILY   Yes! to good heavens, Gwendolen, I mean to Gwendolen.

ALGERNON   *[Laughing.]* Of course not! What could have put such an idea into your pretty little head?

CECILY   Thank you. *[Presenting her cheek to be kissed.]* You may. *[Algernon kisses her.]*

GWENDOLEN   I felt there was some slight error, Miss Cardew. The gentleman who is now embracing you is my cousin, Mr. Algernon Moncrieff.

CECILY   *[Breaking away from Algernon.]* Algernon Moncrieff! Oh! *[The two girls move towards each other and put their arms round each other's waists as if for protection.]*

CECILY   Are you called Algernon?

ALGERNON   I cannot deny it.

CECILY   Oh!

GWENDOLEN   Is your name really John?

JACK   *[Standing rather proudly.]* I could deny it if I liked. I could deny anything if I liked. But my name certainly is John. It has been John for years.

CECILY   *[To Gwendolen.]* A gross deception has been practised on both of us.

GWENDOLEN   My poor wounded Cecily!

CECILY   My sweet wronged Gwendolen!

GWENDOLEN   *[Slowly and seriously.]* You will call me sister, will you not? *[They embrace. Jack and Algernon groan and walk up and down.]*

CECILY   *[Rather brightly.]* There is just one question I would like to be allowed to ask my guardian.

GWENDOLEN   An admirable idea! Mr. Worthing, there is just one question I would like to be permitted to put to you. Where is your brother Ernest? We are both engaged to be married to your brother Ernest, so it is a matter of some importance to us to know where your brother Ernest is at present.

JACK   *[Slowly and hesitatingly.]* Gwendolen—Cecily—it is very painful for me to be forced to speak the truth. It is the first time in my life that I have ever been reduced to such a painful position, and I am really quite inexperienced in doing anything of the kind. However, I will tell you quite frankly that I have no brother Ernest. I have no brother at all. I never had a brother in my life, and I certainly have not the smallest intention of ever having one in the future.

CECILY   *[Surprised.]* No brother at all?

JACK   *[Cheerily.]* None!

GWENDOLEN   *[Severely.]* Had you never a brother of any kind?

JACK   *[Pleasantly.]* Never. Not even of an kind.

GWENDOLEN   I am afraid it is quite clear, Cecily, that neither of us is engaged to be married to any one.

CECILY   It is not a very pleasant position for a young girl suddenly to find herself in. Is it?

GWENDOLEN   Let us go into the house. They will hardly venture to come after us there.

CECILY   No, men are so cowardly, aren't they?

[They retire into the house with scornful looks.]

JACK   This ghastly state of things is what you call Bunburying, I suppose?

ALGERNON   Yes, and a perfectly wonderful Bunbury it is. The most wonderful Bunbury I have ever had in my life.

JACK   Well, you've no right whatsoever to Bunbury here.

ALGERNON   That is absurd. One has a right to Bunbury anywhere one chooses. Every serious Bunburyist knows that.

JACK   Serious Bunburyist! Good heavens!

ALGERNON   Well, one must be serious about something, if one wants to have any amusement in life. I happen to be serious about Bunburying. What on earth you are serious about I haven't got the remotest idea. About everything, I should fancy. You have such an absolutely trivial nature.

JACK   Well, the only small satisfaction I have in the whole of this wretched business is that your friend Bunbury is quite exploded. You won't be able to run down to the country quite so often as you used to do, dear Algy. And a very good thing too.

ALGERNON   Your brother is a little off colour, isn't he, dear Jack? You won't be able to disappear to London quite so frequently as your wicked custom was. And not a bad thing either.

JACK   As for your conduct towards Miss Cardew, I must say that your taking in a sweet, simple, innocent girl like that is quite inexcusable. To say nothing of the fact that she is my ward.

ALGERNON   I can see no possible defence at all for your deceiving a brilliant, clever, thoroughly experienced young lady like Miss Fairfax. To say nothing of the fact that she is my cousin.

JACK   I wanted to be engaged to Gwendolen, that is all. I love her.

ALGERNON   Well, I simply wanted to be engaged to Cecily. I adore her.

JACK   There is certainly no chance of your marrying Miss Cardew.

ALGERNON   I don't think there is much likelihood, Jack, of you and Miss Fairfax being united.

JACK   Well, that is no business of yours.

ALGERNON   If it was my business, I wouldn't talk about it. [Begins to eat muffins.] It is very vulgar to talk about one's business. Only people like stock-brokers do that, and then merely at dinner parties.

JACK   How can you sit there, calmly eating muffins when we are in this horrible trouble, I can't make out. You seem to me to be perfectly heartless.

ALGERNON   Well, I can't eat muffins in an agitated manner. The butter would probably get on my cuffs. One should always eat muffins quite calmly. It is the only way to eat them.

JACK   I say it's perfectly heartless your eating muffins at all, under the circumstances.

ALGERNON   When I am in trouble, eating is the only thing that consoles me. Indeed, when I am in really great trouble, as any one who knows me intimately will tell you, I refuse everything except food and drink. At the present moment I am eating muffins because I am unhappy. Besides, I am particularly fond of muffins. [Rising.]

JACK   [Rising.] Well, that is no reason why you should eat them all in that greedy way. [Takes muffins from Algernon.]

ALGERNON   *[Offering tea-cake.]* I wish you would have tea-cake instead. I don't like tea-cake.

JACK   Good heavens! I suppose a man may eat his own muffins in his own garden.

ALGERNON   But you have just said it was perfectly heartless to eat muffins.

JACK   I said it was perfectly heartless of you, under the circumstances. That is a very different thing.

ALGERNON   That may be. But the muffins are the same. *[He seizes the muffin-dish from Jack.]*

JACK   Algy, I wish to goodness you would go.

ALGERNON   You can't possibly ask me to go without having some dinner. It's absurd. I never go without my dinner. No one ever does, except vegetarians and people like that. Besides I have just made arrangements with Dr. Chasuble to be christened at a quarter to six under the name of Ernest.

JACK   My dear fellow, the sooner you give up that nonsense the better. I made arrangements this morning with Dr. Chasuble to be christened myself at 5.30, and I naturally will take the name of Ernest. Gwendolen would wish it. We can't both be christened Ernest. It's absurd. Besides, I have a perfect right to be christened if I like. There is no evidence at all that I have ever been christened by anybody. I should think it extremely probable I never was, and so does Dr. Chasuble. It is entirely different in your case. You have been christened already.

ALGERNON   Yes, but I have not been christened for years.

JACK   Yes, but you have been christened. That is the important thing.

ALGERNON   Quite so. So I know my constitution can stand it. If you are not quite sure about your ever having been christened, I must say I think it rather dangerous your venturing on it now. It might make you very unwell. You can hardly have forgotten that some one very closely connected with you was very nearly carried off this week in Paris by a severe chill.

JACK   Yes, but you said yourself that a severe chill was not hereditary.

ALGERNON   It usen't to be, I know—but I daresay it is now. Science is always making wonderful improvements in things.

JACK   *[Picking up the muffin-dish.]* Oh, that is nonsense; you are always talking nonsense.

ALGERNON   Jack, you are at the muffins again! I wish you wouldn't. There are only two left. *[Takes them.]* I told you I was particularly fond of muffins.

JACK   But I hate tea-cake.

ALGERNON   Why on earth then do you allow tea-cake to be served up for your guests? What ideas you have of hospitality!

JACK   Algernon! I have already told you to go. I don't want you here. Why don't you go!

ALGERNON   I haven't quite finished my tea yet! and there is still one muffin left.

[Jack groans, and sinks into a chair. Algernon still continues eating.]

ACT DROP

Third Act

SCENE. Morning-room at the Manor House.

[Gwendolen and Cecily are at the window, looking out into the garden.]

GWENDOLEN   The fact that they did not follow us at once into the house, as any one else would have done, seems to me to show that they have some sense of shame left.

CECILY   They have been eating muffins. That looks like repentance.

GWENDOLEN   *[After a pause.]* They don't seem to notice us at all. Couldn't you cough?

CECILY   But I haven't got a cough.

GWENDOLEN   They're looking at us. What effrontery!

CECILY   They're approaching. That's very forward of them.

GWENDOLEN   Let us preserve a dignified silence.

CECILY   Certainly. It's the only thing to do now.

[Enter Jack followed by Algernon. They whistle some dreadful popular air from a British Opera.]

GWENDOLEN   This dignified silence seems to produce an unpleasant effect.

CECILY   A most distasteful one.

GWENDOLEN   But we will not be the first to speak.

CECILY   Certainly not.

GWENDOLEN   Mr. Worthing, I have something very particular to ask you. Much depends on your reply.

CECILY   Gwendolen, your common sense is invaluable. Mr. Moncrieff, kindly answer me the following question. Why did you pretend to be my guardian's brother?

ALGERNON   In order that I might have an opportunity of meeting you.

CECILY   [To Gwendolen.] That certainly seems a satisfactory explanation, does it not?

GWENDOLEN   Yes, dear, if you can believe him.

CECILY   I don't. But that does not affect the wonderful beauty of his answer.

GWENDOLEN   True. In matters of grave importance, style, not sincerity is the vital thing. Mr. Worthing, what explanation can you offer to me for pretending to have a brother? Was it in order that you might have an opportunity of coming up to town to see me as often as possible?

JACK   Can you doubt it, Miss Fairfax?

GWENDOLEN   I have the gravest doubts upon the subject. But I intend to crush them. This is not the moment for German scepticism. [Moving to Cecily.] Their explanations appear to be quite satisfactory, especially Mr. Worthing's. That seems to me to have the stamp of truth upon it.

CECILY   I am more than content with what Mr. Moncrieff said. His voice alone inspires one with absolute credulity.

GWENDOLEN   Then you think we should forgive them?

CECILY   Yes. I mean no.

GWENDOLEN   True! I had forgotten. There are principles at stake that one cannot surrender. Which of us should tell them? The task is not a pleasant one.

CECILY   Could we not both speak at the same time?

GWENDOLEN   An excellent idea! I nearly always speak at the same time as other people. Will you take the time from me?

CECILY   Certainly. [Gwendolen beats time with uplifted finger.]

GWENDOLEN & CECILY   [Speaking together.] Your Christian names are still an insuperable barrier. That is all!

JACK & ALGERNON   [Speaking together.] Our Christian names! Is that all? But we are going to be christened this afternoon.

GWENDOLEN   [To Jack.] For my sake you are prepared to do this terrible thing?

JACK   I am.

CECILY   [To Algernon.] To please me you are ready to face this fearful ordeal?

ALGERNON   I am!

GWENDOLEN   How absurd to talk of the equality of the sexes! Where questions of self-sacrifice are concerned, men are infinitely beyond us.

JACK   We are. [Clasps hands with Algernon.]

CECILY   They have moments of physical courage of which we women know absolutely nothing.

GWENDOLEN   *[To Jack.]* Darling!

ALGERNON   *[To Cecily.]* Darling! *[They fall into each other's arms.]*

[Enter Merriman. When he enters he coughs loudly, seeing the situation.]

MERRIMAN   Ahem! Ahem! Lady Bracknell!

JACK   Good heavens!

[Enter Lady Bracknell. The couples separate in alarm. Exit Merriman.]

LADY BRACKNELL   Gwendolen! What does this mean?

GWENDOLEN   Merely that I am engaged to be married to Mr. Worthing, mamma.

LADY BRACKNELL   Come here. Sit down. Sit down immediately. Hesitation of any kind is a sign of mental decay in the young, of physical weakness in the old. *[Turns to Jack.]* Apprised, sir, of my daughter's sudden flight by her trusty maid, whose confidence I purchased by means of a small coin, I followed her at once by a luggage train. Her unhappy father is, I am glad to say, under the impression that she is attending a more than usually lengthy lecture by the University Extension Scheme on the Influence of a permanent income on Thought. I do not propose to undeceive him. Indeed I have never undeceived him on any question. I would consider it wrong. But of course, you will clearly understand that all communication between yourself and my daughter must cease immediately from this moment. On this point, as indeed on all points, I am firm.

JACK   I am engaged to be married to Gwendolen Lady Bracknell!

LADY BRACKNELL   You are nothing of the kind, sir. And now, as regards Algernon! . . . Algernon!

ALGERNON   Yes, Aunt Augusta.

LADY BRACKNELL   May I ask if it is in this house that your invalid friend Mr. Bunbury resides?

ALGERNON   *[Stammering.]* Oh! No! Bunbury doesn't live here. Bunbury is somewhere else at present. In fact, Bunbury is dead.

LADY BRACKNELL   Dead! When did Mr. Bunbury die? His death must have been extremely sudden.

ALGERNON   *[Airily.]* Oh! I killed Bunbury this afternoon. I mean poor Bunbury died this afternoon.

LADY BRACKNELL   What did he die of?

ALGERNON   Bunbury? Oh, he was quite exploded.

LADY BRACKNELL   Exploded! Was he the victim of a revolutionary outrage? I was not aware that Mr. Bunbury was interested in social legislation. If so, he is well punished for his morbidity.

ALGERNON   My dear Aunt Augusta, I mean he was found out! The doctors found out that Bunbury could not live, that is what I mean—so Bunbury died.

LADY BRACKNELL   He seems to have had great confidence in the opinion of his physicians. I am glad, however, that he made up his mind at the last to some definite course of action, and acted under proper medical advice. And now that we have finally got rid of this Mr. Bunbury, may I ask, Mr. Worthing, who is that young person whose hand my nephew Algernon is now holding in what seems to me a peculiarly unnecessary manner?

JACK   That lady is Miss Cecily Cardew, my ward. *[Lady Bracknell bows coldly to Cecily.]*

ALGERNON   I am engaged to be married to Cecily, Aunt Augusta.

LADY BRACKNELL   I beg your pardon?

CECILY   Mr. Moncrieff and I are engaged to be married, Lady Bracknell.

LADY BRACKNELL   *[With a shiver, crossing to the sofa and sitting down.]* I do not know whether there is anything peculiarly exciting in the air of this particular part

THE IMPORTANCE OF BEING ERNEST – THIRD ACT

of Hertfordshire, but the number of engagements that go on seems to me considerably above the proper average that statistics have laid down for our guidance. I think some preliminary inquiry on my part would not be out of place. Mr. Worthing, is Miss Cardew at all connected with any of the larger railway stations in London? I merely desire information. Until yesterday I had no idea that there were any families or persons whose origin was a Terminus. [Jack looks perfectly furious, but restrains himself.]

JACK   [In a clear, cold voice.] Miss Cardew is the grand-daughter of the late Mr. Thomas Cardew of 149 Belgrave Square, S.W.; Gervase Park, Dorking, Surrey; and the Sporran, Fifeshire, N.B.

LADY BRACKNELL   That sounds not unsatisfactory. Three addresses always inspire confidence, even in tradesmen. But what proof have I of their authenticity?

JACK   I have carefully preserved the Court Guides of the period. They are open to your inspection, Lady Bracknell.

LADY BRACKNELL   [Grimly.] I have known strange errors in that publication.

JACK   Miss Cardew's family solicitors are Messrs. Markby, Markby, and Markby.

LADY BRACKNELL   Markby, Markby, and Markby? A firm of the very highest position in their profession. Indeed I am told that one of the Mr. Markby's is occasionally to be seen at dinner parties. So far I am satisfied.

JACK   [Very irritably.] How extremely kind of you, Lady Bracknell! I have also in my possession, you will be pleased to hear, certificates of Miss Cardew's birth, baptism, whooping cough, registration, vaccination, confirmation, and the measles; both the German and the English variety.

LADY BRACKNELL   Ah! A life crowded with incident, I see; though perhaps somewhat too exciting for a young girl. I am not myself in favour of premature experiences. [Rises, looks at her watch.] Gwendolen! the time approaches for our departure. We have not a moment to lose. As a matter of form, Mr. Worthing, I had better ask you if Miss Cardew has any little fortune?

JACK   Oh! about a hundred and thirty thousand pounds in the Funds. That is all. Goodbye, Lady Bracknell. So pleased to have seen you.

LADY BRACKNELL   [Sitting down again.] A moment, Mr. Worthing. A hundred and thirty thousand pounds! And in the Funds! Miss Cardew seems to me a most attractive young lady, now that I look at her. Few girls of the present day have any really solid qualities, any of the qualities that last, and improve with time. We live, I regret to say, in an age of surfaces. [To Cecily.] Come over here, dear. [Cecily goes across.] Pretty child! your dress is sadly simple, and your hair seems almost as Nature might have left it. But we can soon alter all that. A thoroughly experienced French maid produces a really marvellous result in a very brief space of time. I remember recommending one to young Lady Lancing, and after three months her own husband did not know her.

JACK   And after six months nobody knew her.

LADY BRACKNELL   [Glares at Jack for a few moments. Then bends, with a practised smile, to Cecily.] Kindly turn round, sweet child. [Cecily turns completely round.] No, the side view is what I want. [Cecily presents her profile.] Yes, quite as I expected. There are distinct social possibilities in your profile. The two weak points in our age are its want of principle and its want of profile. The chin a little higher, dear. Style largely depends on the way the chin is worn. They are worn very high, just at present. Algernon!

ALGERNON   Yes, Aunt Augusta!

LADY BRACKNELL   There are distinct social possibilities in Miss Cardew's profile.

ALGERNON   Cecily is the sweetest, dearest, prettiest girl in the whole world. And I don't care twopence about social possibilities.

LADY BRACKNELL   Never speak disrespectfully of Society, Algernon. Only people who can't get into it do that. [To Cecily.] Dear child, of course you know that Algernon has nothing but his debts to depend upon. But I do not approve of mercenary marriages. When I married Lord Bracknell I had no fortune of any kind. But I never dreamed for a moment of allowing that to stand in my way. Well, I suppose I must give my consent.

ALGERNON   Thank you, Aunt Augusta.

LADY BRACKNELL   Cecily, you may kiss me!

CECILY   *[Kisses her.]* Thank you, Lady Bracknell.

LADY BRACKNELL   You may also address me as Aunt Augusta for the future.

CECILY   Thank you, Aunt Augusta.

LADY BRACKNELL   The marriage, I think, had better take place quite soon.

ALGERNON   Thank you, Aunt Augusta.

CECILY   Thank you, Aunt Augusta.

LADY BRACKNELL   To speak frankly, I am not in favour of long engagements. They give people the opportunity of finding out each other's character before marriage, which I think is never advisable.

JACK   I beg your pardon for interrupting you, Lady Bracknell, but this engagement is quite out of the question. I am Miss Cardew's guardian, and she cannot marry without my consent until she comes of age. That consent I absolutely decline to give.

LADY BRACKNELL   Upon what grounds may I ask? Algernon is an extremely, I may almost say an ostentatiously, eligible young man. He has nothing, but he looks everything. What more can one desire?

JACK   It pains me very much to have to speak frankly to you, Lady Bracknell, about your nephew, but the fact is that I do not approve at all of his moral character. I suspect him of being untruthful. *[Algernon and Cecily look at him in indignant amazement.]*

LADY BRACKNELL   Untruthful! My nephew Algernon? Impossible! He is an Oxonian.[1]

JACK   I fear there can be no possible doubt about the matter. This afternoon during my temporary absence in London on an important question of romance, he obtained admission to my house by means of the false pretence of being my brother. Under an assumed name he drank, I've just been informed by my butler, an entire pint bottle of my Perrier-Jouet, Brut, '89; wine I was specially reserving for myself. Continuing his disgraceful deception, he succeeded in the course of the afternoon in alienating the affections of my only ward. He subsequently stayed to tea, and devoured every single muffin. And what makes his conduct all the more heartless is, that he was perfectly well aware from the first that I have no brother, that I never had a brother, and that I don't intend to have a brother, not even of any kind. I distinctly told him so myself yesterday afternoon.

LADY BRACKNELL   Ahem! Mr. Worthing, after careful consideration I have decided entirely to overlook my nephew's conduct to you.

JACK   That is very generous of you, Lady Bracknell. My own decision, however, is unalterable. I decline to give my consent.

LADY BRACKNELL   *[To Cecily.]* Come here, sweet child. *[Cecily goes over.]* How old are you, dear?

CECILY   Well, I am really only eighteen, but I always admit to twenty when I go to evening parties.

LADY BRACKNELL   You are perfectly right in making some slight alteration. Indeed, no woman should ever be quite accurate about her age. It looks so calculating . . . *[In a meditative manner.]* Eighteen, but admitting to twenty at evening parties. Well, it will not be very long before you are of age and free from the restraints of tutelage. So I don't think your guardian's consent is, after all, a matter of any importance.

---

[1] a native or inhabitant of Oxford, England.

JACK   Pray excuse me, Lady Bracknell, for interrupting you again, but it is only fair to tell you that according to the terms of her grandfather's will Miss Cardew does not come legally of age till she is thirty-five.

LADY BRACKNELL   That does not seem to me to be a grave objection. Thirty-five is a very attractive age. London society is full of women of the very highest birth who have, of their own free choice, remained thirty-five for years. Lady Dumbleton is an instance in point. To my own knowledge she has been thirty-five ever since she arrived at the age of forty, which was many years ago now. I see no reason why our dear Cecily should not be even still more attractive at the age you mention than she is at present. There will be a large accumulation of property.

CECILY   Algy, could you wait for me till I was thirty-five?

ALGERNON   Of course I could, Cecily. You know I could.

CECILY   Yes, I felt it instinctively, but I couldn't wait all that time. I hate waiting even five minutes for anybody. It always makes me rather cross. I am not punctual myself, I know, but I do like punctuality in others, and waiting, even to be married, is quite out of the question.

ALGERNON   Then what is to be done, Cecily?

CECILY   I don't know, Mr. Moncrieff.

LADY BRACKNELL   My dear Mr. Worthing, as Miss Cardew states positively that she cannot wait till she is thirty-five—a remark which I am bound to say seems to me to show a somewhat impatient nature—I would beg of you to reconsider your decision.

JACK   But my dear Lady Bracknell, the matter is entirely in your own hands. The moment you consent to my marriage with Gwendolen, I will most gladly allow your nephew to form an alliance with my ward.

LADY BRACKNELL   [Rising and drawing herself up.] You must be quite aware that what you propose is out of the question.

JACK   Then a passionate celibacy is all that any of us can look forward to.

LADY BRACKNELL   That is not the destiny I propose for Gwendolen. Algernon, of course, can choose for himself. [Pulls out her watch.] Come, dear, [Gwendolen rises] we have already missed five, if not six, trains. To miss any more might expose us to comment on the platform.

[Enter Dr. Chasuble.]

CHASUBLE   Everything is quite ready for the christenings.

LADY BRACKNELL   The christenings, sir! Is not that somewhat premature?

CHASUBLE   [Looking rather puzzled, and pointing to Jack and Algernon.] Both these gentlemen have expressed a desire for immediate baptism.

LADY BRACKNELL   At their age? The idea is grotesque and irreligious! Algernon, I forbid you to be baptized. I will not hear of such excesses. Lord Bracknell would be highly displeased if he learned that that was the way in which you wasted your time and money.

CHASUBLE   Am I to understand then that there are to be no christenings at all this afternoon?

JACK   I don't think that, as things are now, it would be of much practical value to either of us, Dr. Chasuble.

CHASUBLE   I am grieved to hear such sentiments from you, Mr. Worthing. They savour of the heretical views of the Anabaptists, views that I have completely refuted in four of my unpublished sermons. However, as your present mood seems to be one peculiarly secular, I will return to the church at once. Indeed, I have just been informed by the pew-opener that for the last hour and a half Miss Prism has been waiting for me in the vestry.

LADY BRACKNELL   [Starting.] Miss Prism! Did I hear you mention a Miss Prism?

CHASUBLE   Yes, Lady Bracknell. I am on my way to join her.

LADY BRACKNELL   Pray allow me to detain you for a moment. This matter may prove to be one of vital importance to Lord Bracknell and myself. Is this Miss Prism a female of repellent aspect, remotely connected with education?

CHASUBLE   *[Somewhat indignantly.]* She is the most cultivated of ladies, and the very picture of respectability.

LADY BRACKNELL   It is obviously the same person. May I ask what position she holds in your household?

CHASUBLE   *[Severely.]* I am a celibate, madam.

JACK   *[Interposing.]* Miss Prism, Lady Bracknell, has been for the last three years Miss Cardew's esteemed governess and valued companion.

LADY BRACKNELL   In spite of what I hear of her, I must see her at once. Let her be sent for.

CHASUBLE   *[Looking off.]* She approaches; she is nigh.

[Enter Miss Prism hurriedly.]

MISS PRISM   I was told you expected me in the vestry, dear Canon. I have been waiting for you there for an hour and three-quarters. *[Catches sight of Lady Bracknell, who has fixed her with a stony glare. Miss Prism grows pale and quails. She looks anxiously round as if desirous to escape.]*

LADY BRACKNELL   *[In a severe, judicial voice.]* Prism! *[Miss Prism bows her head in shame.]* Come here, Prism! *[Miss Prism approaches in a humble manner.]* Prism! Where is that baby? *[General consternation. The Canon starts back in horror. Algernon and Jack pretend to be anxious to shield Cecily and Gwendolen from hearing the details of a terrible public scandal.]* Twenty-eight years ago, Prism, you left Lord Bracknell's house, Number 104, Upper Grosvenor Street, in charge of a perambulator that contained a baby of the male sex. You never returned. A few weeks later, through the elaborate investigations of the Metropolitan police, the perambulator was discovered at midnight, standing by itself in a remote corner of Bayswater. It contained the manuscript of a three-volume novel of more than usually revolting sentimentality. *[Miss Prism starts in involuntary indignation.]* But the baby was not there! *[Every one looks at Miss Prism.]* Prism! Where is that baby? *[A pause.]*

MISS PRISM   Lady Bracknell, I admit with shame that I do not know. I only wish I did. The plain facts of the case are these. On the morning of the day you mention, a day that is for ever branded on my memory, I prepared as usual to take the baby out in its perambulator. I had also with me a somewhat old, but capacious hand-bag in which I had intended to place the manuscript of a work of fiction that I had written during my few unoccupied hours. In a moment of mental abstraction, for which I never can forgive myself, I deposited the manuscript in the basinette, and placed the baby in the hand-bag.

JACK   *[Who has been listening attentively.]* But where did you deposit the hand-bag?

MISS PRISM   Do not ask me, Mr. Worthing.

JACK   Miss Prism, this is a matter of no small importance to me. I insist on knowing where you deposited the hand-bag that contained that infant.

MISS PRISM   I left it in the cloak-room of one of the larger railway stations in London.

JACK   What railway station?

MISS PRISM   *[Quite crushed.]* Victoria. The Brighton line. *[Sinks into a chair.]*

JACK   I must retire to my room for a moment. Gwendolen, wait here for me.

GWENDOLEN   If you are not too long, I will wait here for you all my life. *[Exit Jack in great excitement.]*

CHASUBLE   What do you think this means, Lady Bracknell?

LADY BRACKNELL   I dare not even suspect, Dr. Chasuble. I need hardly tell you that in families of high position strange coincidences are not supposed to occur. They are hardly considered the thing.

[Noises heard overhead as if some one was throwing trunks about. Every one looks up.]

CECILY   Uncle Jack seems strangely agitated.

CHASUBLE   Your guardian has a very emotional nature.

LADY BRACKNELL   This noise is extremely unpleasant. It sounds as if he was having an argument. I dislike arguments of any kind. They are always vulgar, and often convincing.

CHASUBLE   *[Looking up.]* It has stopped now. *[The noise is redoubled.]*

LADY BRACKNELL   I wish he would arrive at some conclusion.

GWENDOLEN   This suspense is terrible. I hope it will last. *[Enter Jack with a hand-bag of black leather in his hand.]*

JACK   *[Rushing over to Miss Prism.]* Is this the hand-bag, Miss Prism? Examine it carefully before you speak. The happiness of more than one life depends on your answer.

MISS PRISM   *[Calmly.]* It seems to be mine. Yes, here is the injury it received through the upsetting of a Gower Street omnibus in younger and happier days. Here is the stain on the lining caused by the explosion of a temperance beverage, an incident that occurred at Leamington. And here, on the lock, are my initials. I had forgotten that in an extravagant mood I had had them placed there. The bag is undoubtedly mine. I am delighted to have it so unexpectedly restored to me. It has been a great inconvenience being without it all these years.

JACK   *[In a pathetic voice.]* Miss Prism, more is restored to you than this hand-bag. I was the baby you placed in it.

MISS PRISM   *[Amazed.]* You?

JACK   *[Embracing her.]* Yes . . . mother!

MISS PRISM   *[Recoiling in indignant astonishment.]* Mr. Worthing! I am unmarried!

JACK   Unmarried! I do not deny that is a serious blow. But after all, who has the right to cast a stone against one who has suffered? Cannot repentance wipe out an act of folly? Why should there be one law for men, and another for women? Mother, I forgive you. *[Tries to embrace her again.]*

MISS PRISM   *[Still more indignant.]* Mr. Worthing, there is some error. *[Pointing to Lady Bracknell.]* There is the lady who can tell you who you really are.

JACK   *[After a pause.]* Lady Bracknell, I hate to seem inquisitive, but would you kindly inform me who I am?

LADY BRACKNELL   I am afraid that the news I have to give you will not altogether please you. You are the son of my poor sister, Mrs. Moncrieff, and consequently Algernon's elder brother.

JACK   Algy's elder brother! Then I have a brother after all. I knew I had a brother! I always said I had a brother! Cecily,—how could you have ever doubted that I had a brother? *[Seizes hold of Algernon.]* Dr. Chasuble, my unfortunate brother. Miss Prism, my unfortunate brother. Gwendolen, my unfortunate brother. Algy, you young scoundrel, you will have to treat me with more respect in the future. You have never behaved to me like a brother in all your life.

ALGERNON   Well, not till to-day, old boy, I admit. I did my best, however, though I was out of practice.

[Shakes hands.]

GWENDOLEN   *[To Jack.]* My own! But what own are you? What is your Christian name, now that you have become some one else?

JACK   Good heavens! . . . I had quite forgotten that point. Your decision on the subject of my name is irrevocable, I suppose?

GWENDOLEN   I never change, except in my affections.

CECILY   What a noble nature you have, Gwendolen!

JACK   Then the question had better be cleared up at once. Aunt Augusta, a moment. At the time when Miss Prism left me in the hand-bag, had I been christened already?

LADY BRACKNELL   Every luxury that money could buy, including christening, had been lavished on you by your fond and doting parents.

JACK   Then I was christened! That is settled. Now, what name was I given? Let me know the worst.

LADY BRACKNELL   Being the eldest son you were naturally christened after your father.

JACK   [Irritably.] Yes, but what was my father's Christian name?

LADY BRACKNELL   [Meditatively.] I cannot at the present moment recall what the General's Christian name was. But I have no doubt he had one. He was eccentric, I admit. But only in later years. And that was the result of the Indian climate, and marriage, and indigestion, and other things of that kind.

JACK   Algy! Can't you recollect what our father's Christian name was?

ALGERNON   My dear boy, we were never even on speaking terms. He died before I was a year old.

JACK   His name would appear in the Army Lists of the period, I suppose, Aunt Augusta?

LADY BRACKNELL   The General was essentially a man of peace, except in his domestic life. But I have no doubt his name would appear in any military directory.

JACK   The Army Lists of the last forty years are here. These delightful records should have been my constant study. [Rushes to bookcase and tears the books out.] M. Generals . . . Mallam, Maxbohm, Magley, what ghastly names they have—Markby, Migsby, Mobbs, Moncrieff! Lieutenant 1840, Captain, Lieutenant-Colonel, Colonel, General 1869, Christian names, Ernest John. [Puts book very quietly down and speaks quite calmly.] I always told you, Gwendolen, my name was Ernest, didn't I? Well, it is Ernest after all. I mean it naturally is Ernest.

LADY BRACKNELL   Yes, I remember now that the General was called Ernest, I knew I had some particular reason for disliking the name.

GWENDOLEN   Ernest! My own Ernest! I felt from the first that you could have no other name!

JACK   Gwendolen, it is a terrible thing for a man to find out suddenly that all his life he has been speaking nothing but the truth. Can you forgive me?

GWENDOLEN   I can. For I feel that you are sure to change.

JACK   My own one!

CHASUBLE   [To Miss Prism.] Lætitia! [Embraces her]

MISS PRISM   [Enthusiastically.] Frederick! At last!

ALGERNON   Cecily! [Embraces her.] At last!

JACK   Gwendolen! [Embraces her.] At last!

LADY BRACKNELL   My nephew, you seem to be displaying signs of triviality.

JACK   On the contrary, Aunt Augusta, I've now realised for the first time in my life the vital Importance of Being Earnest.

TABLEAU

Trifles

Susan Glaspell
1916

First performed by the Provincetown Players at the Wharf Theatre in Provincetown, Massachusetts on August 8, 1916.

Characters

GEORGE HENDERSON	County Attorney
HENRY PETERS	Sheriff
LEWIS HALE	A neighboring farmer
MRS. PETERS	wife of Mr. Peters, the Sheriff
MRS. HALE	wife of Mr. Hale, the witness

Mr. Hale's Testimony

SCENE: The kitchen is the now abandoned farmhouse of JOHN WRIGHT, a gloomy kitchen, and left without having been put in order—unwashed pans under the sink, a loaf of bread outside the bread-box, a dish-towel on the table—other signs of incompleted work.

At the rear the outer door opens and the Sheriff comes in followed by the County Attorney and Mr. Hale. The Sheriff and Mr. Hale are men in middle life, the County Attorney is a young man; all are much bundled up and go at once to the stove.

They are followed by the two women—the Sheriff's wife first; she is a slight wiry woman, a thin nervous face. Mrs. Hale is larger and would ordinarily be called more comfortable looking, but she is disturbed now and looks fearfully about as she enters. The women have come in slowly, and stand close together near the door.

COUNTY ATTORNEY *(rubbing his hands)* This feels good. Come up to the fire, ladies.

MRS. PETERS (after taking a step forward) I'm not—cold.

SHERIFF *(unbuttoning his overcoat and stepping away from the stove as if to mark the beginning of official business)* Now, Mr. Hale, before we move things about, you explain to Mr. Henderson just what you saw when you came here yesterday morning.

COUNTY ATTORNEY By the way, has anything been moved? Are things just as you left them yesterday?

SHERIFF *(looking about)* It's just the same. When it dropped below zero last night I thought I'd better send Frank out this morning to make a fire for us—no use getting pneumonia with a big case on, but I told him not to touch anything except the stove—and you know Frank.

COUNTY ATTORNEY Somebody should have been left here yesterday.

SHERIFF Oh—yesterday. When I had to send Frank to Morris Center[1] for that man who went crazy—I want you to know I had my hands full yesterday. I knew you could get back from Omaha by today and as long as I went over everything here myself—

COUNTY ATTORNEY Well, Mr. Hale, tell just what happened when you came here yesterday morning.

MR. HALE Harry and I had started to town with a load of potatoes. We came along the road from my place and as I got here I said, I'm going to see if I can't get John Wright to go in with me on a party telephone.'[2] I spoke to Wright about it once before and he put me off, saying folks talked too much anyway, and all he

---

[1] Morris Center: a reference to either an insane asylum, jail, or psychiatric hospital

[2] party telephone: This was the original phone system in the U.S., especially in rural areas. Many people on a street or road shared the same phone line.

asked was peace and quiet—I guess you know about how much he talked himself; but I thought maybe if I went to the house and talked about it before his wife, though I said to Harry that I didn't know as what his wife wanted made much difference to John—

COUNTY ATTORNEY   Let's talk about that later, Mr. Hale. I do want to talk about that, but tell now just what happened when you got to the house.

MR. HALE   I didn't hear or see anything; I knocked at the door, and still it was all quiet inside. I knew they must be up, it was past eight o'clock. So I knocked again, and I thought I heard somebody say, 'Come in.' I wasn't sure, I'm not sure yet, but I opened the door—this door *(indicating the door by which the two women are still standing)* and there in that rocker—*(pointing to it)* sat Mrs. Wright.

(They all look at the rocker.)

COUNTY ATTORNEY   What—was she doing?

MR. HALE   She was rockin' back and forth. She had her apron in her hand and was kind of—pleating it.

COUNTY ATTORNEY   And how did she—look?

MR. HALE   Well, she looked queer.[3]

COUNTY ATTORNEY   How do you mean—queer?

MR. HALE   Well, as if she didn't know what she was going to do next. And kind of done up.

COUNTY ATTORNEY   How did she seem to feel about your coming?

MR. HALE   Why, I don't think she minded—one way or other. She didn't pay much attention. I said, 'How do, Mrs. Wright it's cold, ain't it?' And she said, 'Is it?'—and went on kind of pleating at her apron. Well, I was surprised; she didn't ask me to come up to the stove, or to set down, but just sat there, not even looking at me, so I said, 'I want to see John.' And then she—laughed. I guess you would call it a laugh. I thought of Harry and the team outside, so I said a little sharp: 'Can't I see John?' 'No', she says, kind o' dull like. 'Ain't he home?' says I. 'Yes', says she, 'he's home'. 'Then why can't I see him?' I asked her, out of patience. ''Cause he's dead', says she. 'Dead?' says I. She just nodded her head, not getting a bit excited, but rockin' back and forth. 'Why—where is he?' says I, not knowing what to say. She just pointed upstairs—like that *(himself pointing to the room above)* I got up, with the idea of going up there. I walked from there to here—then I says, 'Why, what did he die of?' 'He died of a rope round his neck', says she, and just went on pleatin' at her apron. Well, I went out and called Harry. I thought I might—need help. We went upstairs and there he was lyin'—

COUNTY ATTORNEY   I think I'd rather have you go into that upstairs, where you can point it all out. Just go on now with the rest of the story.

MR. HALE   Well, my first thought was to get that rope off. It looked . . . *(stops, his face twitches)* . . . but Harry, he went up to him, and he said, 'No, he's dead all right, and we'd better not touch anything.' So we went back down stairs. She was still sitting that same way. 'Has anybody been notified?' I asked. 'No', says she unconcerned. 'Who did this, Mrs. Wright?' said Harry. He said it business-like—and she stopped pleatin' of her apron. 'I don't know', she says. 'You don't know?' says Harry. 'No', says she. 'Weren't you sleepin' in the bed with him?' says Harry. 'Yes', says she, 'but I was on the inside'. 'Somebody slipped a rope round his neck and strangled him and you didn't wake up?' says Harry. 'I didn't wake up', she said after him. We must 'a looked as if we didn't see how that could be, for after a minute she said, 'I sleep sound'. Harry was going to ask her more questions but I said maybe we ought to let her tell her story first to the

---

[3] queer: unusual behavior

coroner, or the sheriff, so Harry went fast as he could to Rivers' place,[4] where there's a telephone.

COUNTY ATTORNEY And what did Mrs. Wright do when she knew that you had gone for the coroner?[5]

MR. HALE She moved from that chair to this one over here *(pointing to a small chair in the corner)* and just sat there with her hands held together and looking down. I got a feeling that I ought to make some conversation, so I said I had come in to see if John wanted to put in a telephone, and at that she started to laugh, and then she stopped and looked at me—scared, *(the COUNTY ATTORNEY, who has had his notebook out, makes a note)* I dunno, maybe it wasn't scared. I wouldn't like to say it was. Soon Harry got back, and then Dr Lloyd came, and you, Mr. Peters, and so I guess that's all I know that you don't.

The Kitchen

COUNTY ATTORNEY *(looking around)* I guess we'll go upstairs first—and then out to the barn and around there, *(to the SHERIFF)* You're convinced that there was nothing important here—nothing that would point to any motive.

SHERIFF Nothing here but kitchen things.

(The County Attorney, after again looking around the kitchen, opens the door of a cupboard closet. He gets up on a chair and looks on a shelf. Pulls his hand away, sticky.)

COUNTY ATTORNEY Here's a nice mess.

(The women draw nearer.)

MRS. PETERS *(to the other woman)* Oh, her fruit; it did freeze, *(to the County Attorney)* She worried about that when it turned so cold. She said the fire'd go out and her jars would break.[6]

SHERIFF Well, can you beat the women! Held for murder and worryin' about her preserves.

COUNTY ATTORNEY I guess before we're through she may have something more serious than preserves to worry about.

MR. HALE Well, women are used to worrying over trifles.[7]

(The two women move a little closer together.)

COUNTY ATTORNEY *(with the gallantry of a young politician)* And yet, for all their worries, what would we do without the ladies? (the women do not unbend. He goes to the sink, takes a dipperful of water from the pail and pouring it into a basin, washes his hands. Starts to wipe them on the roller-towel, turns it for a cleaner place) Dirty towels! (kicks his foot against the pans under the sink) Not much of a housekeeper, would you say, ladies?

MRS. HALE *(stiffly)* There's a great deal of work to be done on a farm.

COUNTY ATTORNEY To be sure. And yet *(with a little bow to her)* I know there are some Dickson county farmhouses which do not have such roller towels.[8] *(He gives it a pull to expose its length again.)*

---

[4] Rivers' place: a neighbor's house

[5] coroner: an official who investigates violent, sudden, or suspicious deaths

[6] The extreme cold simply retards growth of microorganisms and slows down changes that affect quality or cause spoilage in food. Properly frozen fruits will retain much of their fresh flavor and nutritive value. Their texture, however, may be somewhat softer than that of fresh fruit (from University of Florida IFAS Extension). If fruits are frozen slowly large ice crystals form and rupture cell walls causing a soft mushy product (from National Center for Home Food Preservation).

[7] Trifles: 1) a thing of little value or importance, 2) a cold dessert of sponge cake and fruit covered with layers of custard, jelly, and cream

[8] roller towels: a long towel with the ends joined and hung on a roller, or one fed through a device from one roller holding the clean part to another holding the used part.

MRS. HALE   Those towels get dirty awful quick. Men's hands aren't always as clean as they might be.

COUNTY ATTORNEY   Ah, loyal to your sex, I see. But you and Mrs. Wright were neighbors. I suppose you were friends, too.

MRS. HALE   *(shaking her head)* I've not seen much of her of late years. I've not been in this house—it's more than a year.

COUNTY ATTORNEY   And why was that? You didn't like her?

MRS. HALE   I liked her all well enough. Farmers' wives have their hands full, Mr. Henderson. And then—

COUNTY ATTORNEY   Yes—?

MRS. HALE   *(looking about)* It never seemed a very cheerful place.

COUNTY ATTORNEY   No—it's not cheerful. I shouldn't say she had the homemaking instinct.

MRS. HALE   Well, I don't know as Wright had, either.

COUNTY ATTORNEY   You mean that they didn't get on very well?

MRS. HALE   No, I don't mean anything. But I don't think a place'd be any cheerfuller for John Wright's being in it.

COUNTY ATTORNEY   I'd like to talk more of that a little later. I want to get the lay of things upstairs now. *(He goes to the left, where three steps lead to a stair door.)*

SHERIFF   I suppose anything Mrs. Peters does'll be all right. She was to take in some clothes for her, you know, and a few little things. We left in such a hurry yesterday.

COUNTY ATTORNEY   Yes, but I would like to see what you take, Mrs. Peters, and keep an eye out for anything that might be of use to us.

MRS. PETERS   Yes, Mr. Henderson.

(The women listen to the men's steps on the stairs, then look about the kitchen.)

MRS. HALE   I'd hate to have men coming into my kitchen, snooping around and criticising.

(She arranges the pans under sink which the LAWYER had shoved out of place.)

MRS. PETERS   Of course it's no more than their duty.

MRS. HALE   Duty's all right, but I guess that deputy sheriff that came out to make the fire might have got a little of this on. *(gives the roller towel a pull)* Wish I'd thought of that sooner. Seems mean to talk about her for not having things slicked up when she had to come away in such a hurry.

MRS. PETERS   *(who has gone to a small table in the left rear corner of the room, and lifted one end of a towel that covers a pan)* She had bread set.[9] *(Stands still.)*

MRS. HALE   *(eyes fixed on a loaf of bread beside the bread-box, which is on a low shelf at the other side of the room. Moves slowly toward it)* She was going to put this in there, *(picks up loaf, then abruptly drops it. In a manner of returning to familiar things)* It's a shame about her fruit. I wonder if it's all gone. *(gets up on the chair and looks)* I think there's some here that's all right, Mrs. Peters. Yes— here; *(holding it toward the window)* this is cherries, too. *(looking again)* I declare I believe that's the only one. *(gets down, bottle in her hand. Goes to the sink and wipes it off on the outside)* She'll feel awful bad after all her hard work in the hot weather. I remember the afternoon I put up my cherries last summer.

(She puts the bottle on the big kitchen table, center of the room. With a sigh, is about to sit down in the rocking-chair. Before she is seated realizes what chair it is; with a slow look at it, steps back. The chair which she has touched rocks back and forth.)

---

[9] bread set: Because bread contains yeast, the dough is set aside overnight for the bread to "rise." The dough is normally placed in a cool, dry place where it will not be disturbed.

MRS. PETERS   Well, I must get those things from the front room closet, *(she goes to the door at the right, but after looking into the other room, steps back)* You coming with me, Mrs. Hale? You could help me carry them.

The Living Room

(They go in the other room; reappear, MRS. PETERS carrying a dress and skirt, MRS. HALE following with a pair of shoes.)

MRS. PETERS   My, it's cold in there.

(She puts the clothes on the big table, and hurries to the stove.)

MRS. HALE   *(examining the skirt)* Wright was close.[10] I think maybe that's why she kept so much to herself. She didn't even belong to the Ladies Aid. I suppose she felt she couldn't do her part, and then you don't enjoy things when you feel shabby. She used to wear pretty clothes and be lively, when she was Minnie Foster, one of the town girls singing in the choir. But that—oh, that was thirty years ago. This all you was to take in?

MRS. PETERS   She said she wanted an apron. Funny thing to want, for there isn't much to get you dirty in jail, goodness knows. But I suppose just to make her feel more natural. She said they was in the top drawer in this cupboard. Yes, here. And then her little shawl that always hung behind the door. *(opens stair door and looks)* Yes, here it is.

(Quickly shuts door leading upstairs.)

MRS. HALE   *(abruptly moving toward her)* Mrs. Peters?

MRS. PETERS   Yes, Mrs. Hale?

MRS. HALE   Do you think she did it?

MRS. PETERS   *(in a frightened voice)* Oh, I don't know.

MRS. HALE   Well, I don't think she did. Asking for an apron and her little shawl. Worrying about her fruit.

MRS. PETERS   *(starts to speak, glances up, where footsteps are heard in the room above. In a low voice)* Mr. Peters says it looks bad for her. Mr. Henderson is awful sarcastic in a speech and he'll make fun of her sayin' she didn't wake up.

MRS. HALE   Well, I guess John Wright didn't wake when they was slipping that rope under his neck.

MRS. PETERS   No, it's strange. It must have been done awful crafty and still. They say it was such a—funny way to kill a man, rigging it all up like that.

MRS. HALE   That's just what Mr. Hale said. There was a gun in the house. He says that's what he can't understand.

MRS. PETERS   Mr. Henderson said coming out that what was needed for the case was a motive; something to show anger, or—sudden feeling.

MRS. HALE   *(who is standing by the table)* Well, I don't see any signs of anger around here, *(she puts her hand on the dish towel which lies on the table, stands looking down at table, one half of which is clean, the other half messy)* It's wiped to here, *(makes a move as if to finish work, then turns and looks at loaf of bread outside the breadbox. Drops towel. In that voice of coming back to familiar things.)* Wonder how they are finding things upstairs. I hope she had it a little more red-up up there. You know, it seems kind of sneaking. Locking her up in town and then coming out here and trying to get her own house to turn against her!

MRS. PETERS   But Mrs. Hale, the law is the law.

MRS. HALE   I s'pose 'tis, *(unbuttoning her coat)* Better loosen up your things, Mrs. Peters. You won't feel them when you go out.

---

[10] close: An unusual word choice since the contemporary meaning is to use it as a verb (i.e., to end after a period of time or to shut something). Additional definitions also relate to relationships, such knowing someone on affectionate or intimate terms.

(MRS. PETERS takes off her fur tippet, goes to hang it on hook at back of room, stands looking at the under part of the small corner table.)

> MRS. PETERS   She was piecing a quilt. *(She brings the large sewing basket and they look at the bright pieces.)*

> MRS. HALE   It's log cabin pattern. Pretty, isn't it? I wonder if she was goin' to quilt it or just knot it?

The Bird Cage

(Footsteps have been heard coming down the stairs. The SHERIFF enters followed by HALE and the COUNTY ATTORNEY.)

> SHERIFF   They wonder if she was going to quilt it or just knot it![11] *(The men laugh, the women look abashed.)*

> COUNTY ATTORNEY   *(rubbing his hands over the stove)* Frank's fire didn't do much up there, did it? Well, let's go out to the barn and get that cleared up. *(The men go outside.)*

> MRS. HALE   *(resentfully)* I don't know as there's anything so strange, our takin' up our time with little things while we're waiting for them to get the evidence. *(she sits down at the big table smoothing out a block with decision)* I don't see as it's anything to laugh about.

> MRS. PETERS   *(apologetically)* Of course they've got awful important things on their minds.

(Pulls up a chair and joins MRS. HALE at the table.)

> MRS. HALE   *(examining another block)* Mrs. Peters, look at this one. Here, this is the one she was working on, and look at the sewing! All the rest of it has been so nice and even. And look at this! It's all over the place! Why, it looks as if she didn't know what she was about!

(After she has said this they look at each other, then start to glance back at the door. After an instant MRS. HALE has pulled at a knot and ripped the sewing.)

> MRS. PETERS   Oh, what are you doing, Mrs. Hale?

> MRS. HALE   *(mildly)* Just pulling out a stitch or two that's not sewed very good. *(threading a needle)* Bad sewing always made me fidgety.

> MRS. PETERS   *(nervously)* I don't think we ought to touch things.

> MRS. HALE   I'll just finish up this end. *(suddenly stopping and leaning forward)* Mrs. Peters?

> MRS. PETERS   Yes, Mrs. Hale?

> MRS. HALE   What do you suppose she was so nervous about?

> MRS. PETERS   Oh—I don't know. I don't know as she was nervous. I sometimes sew awful queer when I'm just tired. *(MRS. HALE starts to say something, looks at MRS. PETERS, then goes on sewing)* Well I must get these things wrapped up. They may be through sooner than we think, *(putting apron and other things together)* I wonder where I can find a piece of paper, and string.

> MRS. HALE   In that cupboard, maybe.

> MRS. PETERS   *(looking in cupboard)* Why, here's a bird-cage, *(holds it up)* Did she have a bird, Mrs. Hale?

> MRS. HALE   Why, I don't know whether she did or not—I've not been here for so long. There was a man around last year selling canaries cheap, but I don't know as she took one; maybe she did. She used to sing real pretty herself.

---

[11] quilt it or just knot it: We define a quilt as a top, a batting and a backing, joined together in some way to make the layers hold together without wearing. To quilt, the fabric squares are sewn or stitched together. Adding knots is done for decoration by tying in knots of yarn inside the fabric squares (from Connectingthreads.com).

MRS. PETERS *(glancing around)* Seems funny to think of a bird here. But she must have had one, or why would she have a cage? I wonder what happened to it.

MRS. HALE I s'pose maybe the cat got it.

MRS. PETERS No, she didn't have a cat. She's got that feeling some people have about cats—being afraid of them. My cat got in her room and she was real upset and asked me to take it out.

MRS. HALE My sister Bessie was like that. Queer, ain't it?

MRS. PETERS *(examining the cage)* Why, look at this door. It's broke. One hinge is pulled apart.

MRS. HALE *(looking too)* Looks as if someone must have been rough with it.

MRS. PETERS Why, yes.

(She brings the cage forward and puts it on the table.)

MRS. HALE I wish if they're going to find any evidence they'd be about it. I don't like this place.

MRS. PETERS But I'm awful glad you came with me, Mrs. Hale. It would be lonesome for me sitting here alone.

MRS. HALE It would, wouldn't it? *(dropping her sewing)* But I tell you what I do wish, Mrs. Peters. I wish I had come over sometimes when she was here. I—*(looking around the room)*—wish I had.

MRS. PETERS But of course you were awful busy, Mrs. Hale—your house and your children.

MRS. HALE I could've come. I stayed away because it weren't cheerful—and that's why I ought to have come. I—I've never liked this place. Maybe because it's down in a hollow[12] and you don't see the road. I dunno what it is, but it's a lonesome place and always was. I wish I had come over to see Minnie Foster sometimes. I can see now—*(shakes her head)*

MRS. PETERS Well, you mustn't reproach[13] yourself, Mrs. Hale. Somehow we just don't see how it is with other folks until—something comes up.

MRS. HALE Not having children makes less work—but it makes a quiet house, and Wright out to work all day, and no company when he did come in. Did you know John Wright, Mrs. Peters?

MRS. PETERS Not to know him; I've seen him in town. They say he was a good man.

MRS. HALE Yes—good; he didn't drink, and kept his word as well as most, I guess, and paid his debts. But he was a hard man, Mrs. Peters. Just to pass the time of day with him—*(shivers)* Like a raw wind that gets to the bone, *(pauses, her eye falling on the cage)* I should think she would 'a wanted a bird. But what do you suppose went with it?

The Bird

MRS. PETERS I don't know, unless it got sick and died.

(She reaches over and swings the broken door, swings it again, both women watch it.)

MRS. HALE You weren't raised round here, were you? *(MRS. PETERS shakes her head)* You didn't know—her?

MRS. PETERS Not till they brought her yesterday.

MRS. HALE She—come to think of it, she was kind of like a bird herself—real sweet and pretty, but kind of timid and—fluttery. How—she—did—change. *(silence; then as if struck by a happy thought and relieved to get back to everyday things)* Tell you what, Mrs. Peters, why don't you take the quilt in with you? It might take up her mind.

---

[12] hollow: 1) a small valley, 2) a hole or depression in something, 3) without significance

[13] reproach: an expression of disapproval or disappointment

MRS. PETERS   Why, I think that's a real nice idea, Mrs. Hale. There couldn't possibly be any objection to it, could there? Now, just what would I take? I wonder if her patches are in here—and her things.

(They look in the sewing basket.)

MRS. HALE   Here's some red. I expect this has got sewing things in it. *(brings out a fancy box)* What a pretty box. Looks like something somebody would give you. Maybe her scissors are in here. *(Opens box. Suddenly puts her hand to her nose)* Why—*(MRS. PETERS bends nearer, then turns her face away)* There's something wrapped up in this piece of silk.

MRS. PETERS   Why, this isn't her scissors.

MRS. HALE   *(lifting the silk)* Oh, Mrs. Peters—it's—

(MRS. PETERS bends closer.)

MRS. PETERS   It's the bird.

MRS. HALE   *(jumping up)* But, Mrs. Peters—look at it! It's neck! Look at its neck! It's all—other side to.

MRS. PETERS   Somebody—wrung—its—neck.

(Their eyes meet. A look of growing comprehension, of horror. Steps are heard outside. MRS. HALE slips box under quilt pieces, and sinks into her chair. Enter SHERIFF and COUNTY ATTORNEY. MRS. PETERS rises.)

COUNTY ATTORNEY   *(as one turning from serious things to little pleasantries)* Well ladies, have you decided whether she was going to quilt it or knot it?

MRS. PETERS   We think she was going to—knot it.

COUNTY ATTORNEY   Well, that's interesting, I'm sure. *(seeing the birdcage)* Has the bird flown?

MRS. HALE   *(putting more quilt pieces over the box)* We think the—cat got it.

COUNTY ATTORNEY   *(preoccupied)* Is there a cat?

(MRS. HALE glances in a quick covert way at MRS. PETERS.)

MRS. PETERS   Well, not now. They're superstitious, you know. They leave.

COUNTY ATTORNEY   *(to SHERIFF PETERS, continuing an interrupted conversation)* No sign at all of anyone having come from the outside. Their own rope. Now let's go up again and go over it piece by piece. *(they start upstairs)* It would have to have been someone who knew just the—

(MRS. PETERS sits down. The two women sit there not looking at one another, but as if peering into something and at the same time holding back. When they talk now it is in the manner of feeling their way over strange ground, as if afraid of what they are saying, but as if they can not help saying it.)

MRS. HALE   She liked the bird. She was going to bury it in that pretty box.

MRS. PETERS   *(in a whisper)* When I was a girl—my kitten—there was a boy took a hatchet, and before my eyes—and before I could get there—*(covers her face an instant)* If they hadn't held me back I would have—*(catches herself, looks upstairs where steps are heard, falters weakly)*—hurt him.

MRS. HALE   *(with a slow look around her)* I wonder how it would seem never to have had any children around, *(pause)* No, Wright wouldn't like the bird—a thing that sang. She used to sing. He killed that, too.

MRS. PETERS   *(moving uneasily)* We don't know who killed the bird.

MRS. HALE   I knew John Wright.

MRS. PETERS   It was an awful thing was done in this house that night, Mrs. Hale. Killing a man while he slept, slipping a rope around his neck that choked the life out of him.

MRS. HALE   His neck. Choked the life out of him.

(Her hand goes out and rests on the bird-cage.)

The Evidence

MRS. PETERS   *(with rising voice)* We don't know who killed him. We don't know.

MRS. HALE   *(her own feeling not interrupted)* If there'd been years and years of nothing, then a bird to sing to you, it would be awful—still, after the bird was still.

MRS. PETERS   *(something within her speaking)* I know what stillness is. When we homesteaded in Dakota, and my first baby died—after he was two years old, and me with no other then—

MRS. HALE   *(moving)* How soon do you suppose they'll be through, looking for the evidence?

MRS. PETERS   I know what stillness is. *(pulling herself back)* The law has got to punish crime, Mrs. Hale.

MRS. HALE   *(not as if answering that)* I wish you'd seen Minnie Foster when she wore a white dress with blue ribbons and stood up there in the choir and sang. *(a look around the room)* Oh, I wish I'd come over here once in a while! That was a crime! That was a crime! Who's going to punish that?

MRS. PETERS   *(looking upstairs)* We mustn't—take on.

MRS. HALE   I might have known she needed help! I know how things can be—for women. I tell you, it's queer, Mrs. Peters. We live close together and we live far apart. We all go through the same things—it's all just a different kind of the same thing, *(brushes her eyes, noticing the bottle of fruit, reaches out for it)* If I was you, I wouldn't tell her her fruit was gone. Tell her it ain't. Tell her it's all right. Take this in to prove it to her. She—she may never know whether it was broke or not.

MRS. PETERS   (takes the bottle, looks about for something to wrap it in; takes petticoat[14] from the clothes brought from the other room, very nervously begins winding this around the bottle. In a false voice) My, it's a good thing the men couldn't hear us. Wouldn't they just laugh! Getting all stirred up over a little thing like a—dead canary. As if that could have anything to do with—with—wouldn't they laugh!

(The men are heard coming down stairs.)

MRS. HALE   *(under her breath)* Maybe they would—maybe they wouldn't.

COUNTY ATTORNEY   No, Peters, it's all perfectly clear except a reason for doing it. But you know juries when it comes to women. If there was some definite thing. Something to show—something to make a story about—a thing that would connect up with this strange way of doing it—

(The women's eyes meet for an instant. Enter HALE from outer door.)

MR. HALE   Well, I've got the team around.[15] Pretty cold out there.

COUNTY ATTORNEY   I'm going to stay here a while by myself, *(to the SHERIFF)* You can send Frank out for me, can't you? I want to go over everything. I'm not satisfied that we can't do better.

SHERIFF   Do you want to see what Mrs. Peters is going to take in?

(The LAWYER goes to the table, picks up the apron, laughs.)

COUNTY ATTORNEY   Oh, I guess they're not very dangerous things the ladies have picked out. *(Moves a few things about, disturbing the quilt pieces which cover the box. Steps back)* No, Mrs. Peters doesn't need supervising. For that matter, a sheriff's wife is married to the law. Ever think of it that way, Mrs. Peters?

MRS. PETERS   Not—just that way.

---

[14] petticoat: Today, a petticoat is often a woman's light, loose undergarment hanging from the shoulders or the waist, worn under a skirt or dress. However, at the turn of the century, petticoats were often used as clothing for small children.

[15] got the team around: a reference to a team of horses for a wagon for transportation. Steam-based cars were popular in the late 1800's, but the first U.S. factory production cars first appeared in 1896 in Rhode Island ("What Was the First Car").

SHERIFF   *(chuckling)* Married to the law. *(moves toward the other room)* I just want you to come in here a minute, George. We ought to take a look at these windows.

COUNTY ATTORNEY   *(scoffingly)* Oh, windows!

SHERIFF   We'll be right out, Mr. Hale.

(HALE goes outside. The SHERIFF follows the COUNTY ATTORNEY into the other room. Then MRS. HALE rises, hands tight together, looking intensely at MRS. PETERS, whose eyes make a slow turn, finally meeting MRS. HALE's. A moment MRS. HALE holds her, then her own eyes point the way to where the box is concealed. Suddenly MRS. PETERS throws back quilt pieces and tries to put the box in the bag she is wearing. It is too big. She opens box, starts to take bird out, cannot touch it, goes to pieces, stands there helpless. Sound of a knob turning in the other room. MRS. HALE snatches the box and puts it in the pocket of her big coat. Enter COUNTY ATTORNEY and SHERIFF.)

COUNTY ATTORNEY   *(facetiously[16])* Well, Henry, at least we found out that she was not going to quilt it. She was going to—what is it you call it, ladies?

MRS. HALE   *(her hand against her pocket)* We call it—knot it, Mr. Henderson.

(CURTAIN)

---

[16] facetiously: not seriously

LITERARY TERMS

Fiction

PLOT

in medias res: Latin for "in the midst of things"

Flashback: A movement out of sequence to examine an event or situation that occurred before the story takes place

Plot: The way in which a story's event's are arranged

Exposition: Presents the basic information readers need to understand the events that follow

Rising Action: The build up of events until the climax

Crisis: Peak in the story's action or a moment of tension or importance

Climax: The point of greatest tension that presents a story's decisive action or event

Falling Action: The events in the story that lead to usually a resolution

Resolution, or Denouement: The resolution draws the action to a close; the *denouement* is French for "untying of the knot"

Deus ex machine: Latin for "a god from a machine"; a device used to

Conflict: The struggle between opposing forces that emerges as the action develops

Foreshadowing: Can occur early in the story and hint of things to come

IRONY

Dramatic: When a narrator or character perceives less than readers do

Situational: When what happens is at odds with what readers are led to expect

Verbal: When the narrator says one thing but actually means another

CHARACTER

Protagonist: The story's principal character, sometimes an object or abstraction

Antagonist: Someone or something presented in opposition to the principal character

Foil: Highlights another character by contrasting with him or her

Dynamic Character: Grows and changes

Static Character: Remain essentially the same

Motivation: A psychological driving force that compels or reinforces an action toward a desired goal

Flat Character: Barely developed

Stock Character: Easily identifiable types who behave predictably as readers would expect

Round Character: Well developed, closely involved in and responsive to the action

SETTING

Historical: Establishes a social, cultural, economic, and political environment

Geographical: Explains language and customs in characters that are different from us

Physical: Time of day, inside or out-of-doors, and the weather

POINT OF VIEW, NARRATORS

Point of View: Vantage point from which events are presented

First Person: A narrator who uses "I" or "we"

Unreliable: A narrator who can knowingly or unknowingly misrepresent events and misdirect readers; their perspective is flawed and not reflecting actuality

Omniscient: All-knowing; moves from one character's mind to another

Limited Omniscient: Focuses on only what a single character experiences

Objective: Remains entirely outside the characters' minds

SYMBOLISM

Archetypes: Certain images or ideas reside in the subconscious of all people

Allegory: A form of narrative that conveys a message or doctrine by using people, places, or things to stand for abstract ideas

Conventional: Common symbols recognized by people who share certain cultural and social assumptions
Universal: Symbols recognized by people regardless of their culture
Theme: The primary idea expressed in the story

Poetry

DICTION

Formal Diction: Elevated, impersonal language

Informal Diction: Conversational, slang

Denotation: The literal meaning of a word

Connotation: What a word suggests

SPEAKER

Apostrophe: A poetic device in which the speaker addresses someone or something which cannot reply (i.e. an absent person or an inanimate object).

Persona: (Greek: *mask*) A character or identity created by the poet to be the speaker.

Personification: A figure of speech in which a non-human thing is given human characteristics.

Speaker: The voice or persona telling the poem.

Tone: The speaker's attitude toward the subject of a poem.

Voice: Refers to the voice of the speaker in a poem

TYPES OF POEMS

Ballad: A poem or song narrating a story in short stanzas

Carpe Diem Theme: "Seize the Day." Live life now.

Didactic Poetry: Seeks to use poetry to teach lessons of value, ethics and/or beliefs

Pastoral: A poem set in an idealized rural setting

Narrative Poetry: Poetry that tells a story.

Lyric poetry: Poetry of a brief and usually intense nature, normally metrical.

Dramatic monologue: A poem with a speaker who speaks to an implied listener who never answers, but whose reactions may be commented on by the speaker.

Confessional Poetry: Poetry, typically written in first person about personal issues.

IMAGERY

Concrete imagery: Language that creates physical, tangible mental images using the five senses.

Imagery: Poetic descriptions using the five senses to recreate concrete sensations in the mind of the reader.

Synesthesia: The mixing of senses in description, such as *a smoky voice dripping thick honey notes into the microphone* (which in this example evokes the senses of smell, sound, taste, touch, and sight)

FIGURES OF SPEECH

Cliché: A worn out phrase

Conceit: An extended metaphor in a poem

Extended Metaphor: A metaphor that is sustained throughout a work, as opposed to an isolated use of it in one line

Figures of speech: Non-literal use of language that creatively heightens expression beyond literal meaning

Hyperbole: A figure of speech that uses intentional and often extreme exaggeration

Litotes: A type of understatement in which something is described by understating its opposite (describing an extremely sharp sword as "not dull")

Metaphor: A figure of speech in which something being described is compared to something with known characteristics in order to attribute those characteristics to the thing described

Metonymy: A figure of speech in which a one name for something replaces another (when a girl is called a "chick")

Onomatopoeia: the formation of a word from a sound associated with what is named (e.g., *cuckoo, sizzle*)

Oxymoron: Two contradictory words put together

Paradox: An apparently self-contradictory statement (sometimes makes sense)

Pun: A play on words

Simile: A figure of speech in which something being described is compared to something with known characteristics in order to attribute those characteristics to the thing described. In a simile, the comparison is made using "like" or "as."

Synecdoche: A figure of speech (and subtype of metonymy) in which a part of something is used as a name for the whole (a hired hand refers to the whole employee)

Understatement: An often ironic figure of speech in which a subject is intentionally treated in more slight terms than it would be expected to be described. See Litotes

SYMBOL

Conventional: Common symbols recognized by people who share certain cultural and social assumptions

Myth: Any belief that relies on faith as its basis, without empirical proof.

Symbol: Anything that can be seen as having at least one figurative meaning beyond its literal one (the American flag is *literally* a three-colored piece of cloth, but *symbolically* represents the country)

Universal: Symbols recognized by people regardless of their culture

ALLEGORY

Allegorical Symbol: A symbol with only one intended figurative meaning, usually used to teach a specific point

Allegory: A story or poem with a single symbolic meaning, usually used to teach a specific point

IRONY

Irony: Occurs when something is counter to what the reader expects. (see Dramatic, Situational, and Verbal Irony)

Dramatic Irony: When the meaning of the situation is understood by the audience but not by the characters in the play

Situational Irony: When what happens is different than what is expected

Verbal Irony: When what is said is different from what is meant; sarcasm is a form of verbal irony; when one says one thing but means the opposite (saying "nice hat" to someone with a particularly ugly hat)

SOUNDS

Alliteration: Repetition of consonant sounds in lines of poetry

Anaphora: Repetition of initial words or groups of words in lines of poetry

Assonance: Repetition of vowel sounds in lines of poetry

Cacophony: Discordant or jarring arrangements of sounds in poetry

Euphony: A pleasing arrangement of sounds in poetry. (as opposed to cacophony)

Onomatopoeia: When a word sounds like the thing it describes (pop, whoosh, crack)

RHYTHM

Anapest: A metrical foot with two unstressed syllables followed by a stressed syllable

Ballad Stanza: Quatrains of alternating iambic tetrameter and iambic trimeter, rhymed abcb

Blank verse: Unrhymed lines of iambic pentameter

Caesura: A break or pause in the middle of a line of poetry.

Common Measure: Quatrains of iambic tetrameter lines rhymed abab

Couplets: Rhymed pairs of lines in poetry

Dactyl: A metrical foot with a stressed syllable followed by two unstressed syllables

End stopped lines: Lines with punctuation at the end of each one

Enjambment: The continuation of one line of poetry into another line without the use of punctuation at the end of the first line

Eye Rhyme: Words that look like they should rhyme, but don't (rough/through)

Feminine Rhyme: (falling rhyme, double rhyme). When the last two syllables of two words sound alike (motion/ocean)

Foot: In meter, a group of syllables to be repeated for rhythmical effect

Heptameter: A line consisting of seven metrical feet

Hexameter: A line consisting of six metrical feet

Iamb: A metrical foot consisting of an unstressed syllable followed by a stressed syllable. It is the most commonly occurring metrical foot in English language poetry

Iambic pentameter: A line of five iambs. A very common meter, used in sonnets, villanelles and blank verse

Imperfect Rhyme: (Slant Rhyme, Near Rhyme) Occurs when two words have endings that almost sound alike, but not exactly. (barn/yearn, whereas barn/yarn is a perfect rhyme)

Masculine Rhyme: When only the last syllables of two words sound alike (surprise/denies)

Meter: The arrangement of stressed and unstressed syllables in repeating patterns to create rhythm in poetry

Near Rhyme: See Imperfect Rhyme

Octameter: A line consisting of eight metrical feet

Ottava Rima: An eight line stanza (abababcc) in iambic pentameter

Pentameter: A line with five metrical feet

Perfect Rhyme: When two words have endings that sound exactly alike (bat/cat/splat)

Quatrain: A four lined stanza

Rhyme: When endings of words have similar or identical sounds

Rhyme Royal: A seven lined stanza rhymed ababbcc

Scansion: The analysis of the meter of a line of poetry

Sestet: A six line stanza

Spondee: A metrical foot consisting of two stressed syllables

Terza Rima: Tercets with an interlocking rhyme scheme in which lines 1 and 3 rhyme, and line 2 rhymes with lines 1 and 3 of the next tercet: aba/bcb/cdc/efe/fgf . . .

Tetrameter: A line with four metrical feet

Trimeter: A line with three metrical feet

FORM

Closed Form: Poetry with a set format or structure, like a sonnet or villanelle

Concrete Poetry: Poetry with lines arranged to create a picture on the page

English Sonnet: See Shakespearean Sonnet

Epigram: A short, usually witty poem

Fixed Form: See Closed Form

Form: Overall structure of a poem

Free Verse (Open Form): Poetry without a set format or structure in terms of line lengths, meters, numbers of lines, rhymes, syllables, stanzas, etc.

Haiku: A Japanese form consisting usually of 17 syllables arranged in 3 lines of 5,7,5 syllables. Usually depicts a vivid natural image that evokes an emotional state

Italian Sonnet: See Petrarchan Sonnet

Ode: A long lyric poem usually with a serious tone and subject

Open Form: See Free Verse

Petrarchan Sonnet (Italian Sonnet): A sonnet consiting of an octave rhymed abbaabba and a sestet usually rhymed cdecde. A problem or question is raised in the octave and solved or answered in the sestet

Prose Poetry: Poetry that does not utilize line breaks, but continues from margin to margin just as prose does

Sestina: A complex form of six sestets and a three line envoi. It does not rhyme per say, but the last word in each line of the first stanza must be used as the last word of a line in all the following sestets, but in different orders. In the envoi, two of those words are used in each line. The typical pattern of repetition is 123456, 615243, 364125, 532614, 451362, 246531, and in the envoi line one 1&4, line two is 2&5, and line three is 3&6

Shakespearean Sonnet (English Sonnet): A sonnet consisting of three quatrains and a couplet (usually without stanza breaks) rhymed abab/cdcd/efef/gg

Sonnets: Lyric poems typically consisting of 14 lines of iambic pentameter in various stanza and rhyme schemes (See Petrarchan, Shakespearean, and Spenserian Sonnet). Usually they are love or beauty related, and pose a question or problem in the first eight lines which is answered or solved in the last six lines. The break between the question and the answer is called the Volta.

Spenserian Sonnet: A sonnet consisting of three quatrains and a couplet (with or without stanza breaks) rhymed abab/bcbc/cdcd/ee

Stanza: A group of a specific number of lines in poetry

Villanelle: A form consisting of five tercets and a quatrain, rhymed aba/aba/aba/aba/aba/abaa, in which lines one and three of the first tercet are repeated in their entirety as the last lines of subsequent tercets in an alternating pattern and as the last two lines of the closing quatrain: $a^1ba^2/aba^1/aba^2/aba^1/aba^2/aba^1a^2$, where a^1 is the first entire line and a^2 is the third entire line.

Drama

TECHNICAL

Playwrights: Authors of plays

Play: Performed by actors

Drama: From the Greek *dran*, meaning "to do" or "to perform"

One-act Play: Typically performed in one location

Acts: Divisions within a play

Scenes: Typically change when the location changes

Dialogue: Verbal exchanges between characters

Stage Directions: Typically italics, brief instructions for a character's actions or description of a location

Asides: When a character speaks to him or herself but the other characters cannot hear

Setting: The location where the play takes place

Theme: Central idea of the play

PLOT

Exposition: Background information at the beginning of play

Rising Action: Action and complications that build in intensity

Climax: The most intense moment in the play (usually involving the protagonist)

Falling Action: The intensity begins to diminish

Resolution, or Denouement: The tying up of loose ends or "unknotting"

IRONY

Irony: The expression of one's meaning by using language that normally signifies the opposite, typically for humorous or emphatic effect.

Situational Irony: What happens is different than what is expected

Verbal Irony: When what is said is different from what is meant

Dramatic Irony: Irony that occurs when the meaning of the situation is understood by the audience but not by the characters in the play

CHARACTER

Protagonist: The primary character, place or thing

Antagonist: The primary character, place or thing in opposition to the protagonist

Foil: A character whose behavior and values contrast with the protagonist

Conflict: 1) Person against Person, 2) Person against Nature, 3) Person against Him or Herself

INDEX

Made in the USA
Lexington, KY
29 December 2016